The Sage Dictionary of Policing

The Sage Dictionary of Policing

Compiled and edited
by
Alison Wakefield and Jenny Fleming

Los Angeles • London • New Delhi • Singapore • Washington DC

First published 2009

Apart from any fair dealing for the purposes of research or private study, or criticism or review, as permitted under the Copyright, Designs and Patents Act, 1988, this publication may be reproduced, stored or transmitted in any form, or by any means, only with the prior permission in writing of the publishers, or in the case of reprographic reproduction, in accordance with the terms of licences issued by the Copyright Licensing Agency. Enquiries concerning reproduction outside those terms should be sent to the publishers.

SAGE Publications Ltd
1 Oliver's Yard
55 City Road
London EC1Y 1SP

SAGE Publications Inc.
2455 Teller Road
Thousand Oaks, California 91320

SAGE Publications India Pvt Ltd
B 1/I 1 Mohan Cooperative Industrial Area
Mathura Road
New Delhi 110 044

SAGE Publications Asia-Pacific Pte Ltd
33 Pekin Street #02-01
Far East Square
Singapore 048763

Library of Congress Control Number: 2008935473

British Library Cataloguing in Publication data

A catalogue record for this book is available from the British Library

ISBN 978-1-4129-3098-7
ISBN 978-1-4129-3099-4 (pbk)

Typeset by C&M Digitals Pvt Ltd., Chennai, India
Printed in Great Britain by The Cromwell Press Ltd, Trowbridge, Wiltshire
Printed on paper from sustainable resources

Contents

List of Entries

List of Contributors

Editors

Dr Alison Wakefield, University of New South Wales, Australia
Professor Jenny Fleming, University of Tasmania, Australia

International Advisory Board

Professor David H. Bayley, University at Albany, State University of New York, USA
Professor Janet Chan, University of New South Wales, Australia
Professor Clive Emsley, The Open University, UK
René Lévy, Centre for Sociological Research into Law and Penal Institutions (CESDIP), France
Professor Eugene McLaughlin, City University, UK
Professor Peter Manning, Northeastern University, USA
Professor John Muncie, The Open University, UK
Chief Commissioner Christine Nixon, Victoria Police, Australia.
Professor Clifford Shearing, University of Cape Town, South Africa
Commissioner Simone Steendijk, Rotterdam-Rijnmond Police, The Netherlands
Professor P.A.J. Waddington, University of Wolverhampton, UK

Authors

Julie Ayling, The Australian National University, Australia
Professor David Bayley, University at Albany, State University of New York, USA
Adrian Beck, University of Leicester, UK
Professor Trevor Bennett, University of Glamorgan, UK
Dr Christopher Birkbeck, University of Salford, UK
David Bradley, Victoria Police, Australia
Professor Anthony A. Braga, Harvard University, USA
Professor Marcos Luiz Bretas, Universidade Federal do Rio de Janeiro, Brazil

Professor Jean-Paul Brodeur, Université de Montréal, Canada
Dr Fiona Brookman, University of Glamorgan, UK
Tom Bucke, Independent Police Complaints Commission, UK
Dr Karen Bullock, University of Surrey, UK
Spencer Chainey, University College London, UK
Professor Janet Chan, University of New South Wales, Australia
Dr Adrian Cherney, University of Queensland, Australia
Dr Phil Clements, University of Portsmouth, UK
Dr Bankole A. Cole, University of Hull, UK
Professor Adam Crawford, University of Leeds, UK
Professor Chris Cunneen, University of New South Wales, Australia
Associate Professor Mathieu Deflem, University of South Carolina, USA
Dr Rebekah Delsol, Open Society Justice Initiative, UK
Professor John Deukmedjian, University of Windsor, Canada
Associate Professor Benoît Dupont, Université de Montréal, Canada
Adam Edwards, Cardiff University, UK
Charlie Edwards, Demos, UK
Dr Graham Ellison, Queen's University Belfast, Northern Ireland
Professor Clive Emsley, The Open University, UK
Dr Stephen Farrell, Keele University, UK
Dr Jeremy Farrell, The Australian National University, Australia
Professor Cyrille Fijnaut, Tilburg University, The Netherlands
Professor Mark Finnane, Griffith University, Australia
Professor Jenny Fleming, University of Tasmania, Australia
Dr Gary Fooks, Bath University, UK
Professor Peter Gill, Liverpool John Moores University, UK
Detective Chief Inspector Stan Gilmour, Thames Valley Police, UK
Professor Andrew Goldsmith, Flinders University, Australia
Dr Ben Goold, University of Oxford, UK
Professor Peter Grabosky, The Australian National University, Australia
Professor Frank Gregory, University of Southampton, UK
Silvia Guglielmi, Demos, UK
Professor Steve Herbert, University of Washington, USA
Associate Professor Vincent E. Henry, Long Island University, USA
Professor Alice Hills, University of Leeds, UK
Dr Katy Holloway, University of Glamorgan, UK
Professor Ross Homel, Griffith University, Australia
Professor Gordon Hughes, Cardiff University, UK
Du Jinfeng, Chinese People's Public Security University, China
Professor Les Johnston, University of Portsmouth, UK
Trevor Jones, Cardiff University, UK
Dr Jan Jordan, Victoria University of Wellington, New Zealand
Professor Susanne Karstedt, Keele University, UK
Professor John Kleinig, City University of New York, USA and The Australian
National University, Australia
Ian Lanyon, Victoria Police, Australia

Dr Maggy Lee, University of Essex, UK
Dr Murray Lee, University of Sydney, Australia
Professor Frank Leishman, University of Gloucestershire, UK
Associate Professor Colleen Lewis, Monash University, Australia
Professor Chris Lewis, University of Portsmouth, UK
René Lévy, Centre for Sociological Research into Law and Penal Institutions (CESDIP), France
Professor Ian Loader, University of Oxford, UK
Professor Toni Makkai, The Australian National University, Australia
Professor Peter Manning, Northeastern University, USA
Dr Monique Marks, University of KwaZulu-Natal, South Africa
Professor Lorraine Mazerolle, Griffith University, Australia
Dr Abby McLeod, Australian Federal Police, Australia
Professor Eugene McLaughlin, City University, UK
Professor John Muncie, The Open University, UK
Dr Kristina Murphy, Deakin University, Australia
Andy Myhill, Home Office, UK
Chief Constable Peter Neyroud, National Policing Improvement Agency, UK
Professor Pat O'Malley, University of Sydney, Australia
Juani O'Reilly, Australian Federal Police, Australia
Professor Ken Pease O.B.E., Loughborough University, UK
Professor Martine Powell, Deakin University, Australia
Professor Tim Prenzler, Griffith University, Australia
Professor Maurice Punch, London School of Economics, UK
Dr Janet Ransley, Griffith University, Australia
Professor Jerry H. Ratcliffe, Temple University, USA
Professor Robert Reiner, London School of Economics, UK
Dr Herbert Reinke, University of Wuppertal, Germany
Dr Annette Robertson, Glasgow Caledonian University, UK
Associate Professor Mike Rowe, Victoria University of Wellington, New Zealand
Professor Rick Sarre, University of South Australia, Australia
Professor Clifford D. Shearing, University of Cape Town, South Africa
Professor James Sheptycki, York University, Canada
Professor Lawrence W. Sherman, University of Pennsylvania, USA and University of Cambridge, UK
Professor Wesley Skogan, Northwestern University, USA
Professor Nigel South, University of Essex, UK
Professor Peter Squires, University of Brighton, UK
Dr Peter Stelfox, National Policing Improvement Agency, UK
Commissioner Simone Steendijk, Rotterdam-Rijnmond Police, The Netherlands
Professor Philip C. Stenning, Keele University, UK
Dr Heather Strang, The Australian National University, Australia
Associate Professor David Thacher, University of Michigan, USA
Professor Robyn Thomas, Cardiff University, UK
Professor Nick Tilley, Nottingham Trent University, UK
Professor Sirpa Virta, University of Tampere, Finland

Professor P.A.J. Waddington, University of Wolverhampton, UK
John Wadham, Equality and Human Rights Commission, UK
Dr Alison Wakefield, University of New South Wales, Australia
Professor Sandra Walklate, University of Liverpool, UK
Professor David S. Wall, University of Leeds, UK
Dr Don Weatherburn, NSW Bureau of Crime Statistics and Research, Australia
Professor Rob White, University of Tasmania, Australia
Dr Chris A. Williams, The Open University, UK
Dr Dean Wilson, Monash University, Australia
Romy Winter, University of Tasmania, Australia
Associate Professor Jennifer Wood, Temple University, USA
Professor Kam C. Wong, Xavier University, USA
Professor Lucia Zedner, University of Oxford, UK

Preface

The origins of this book lie in the success of *The Sage Dictionary of Criminology*, thoughtfully conceived and skilfully edited by Eugene McLaughlin and John Muncie. It was the idea of Eugene and Caroline Porter at Sage that the same successful model could be applied to police studies, and we are very grateful to them both for trusting us to take it forward, and for the support and guidance they have continuously provided.

We have also benefited greatly from the support of our International Advisory Board of policing scholars and practitioners, who have provided advice on the list of terms, reviewed entries and themselves authored contributions. The Board comprises professors David H. Bayley (US), Janet Chan (Australia), Clive Emsley (UK), Eugene McLaughlin (UK), Peter K. Manning (US), John Muncie (UK), René Lévy (France), Clifford D. Shearing (South Africa) and P.A.J. Waddington (UK), and Commissioner Simone Steendijk of Rotterdam-Rijnmond Police (Netherlands) and Chief Commissioner Christine Nixon of Victoria Police (Australia).

Special thanks are owed to our 110 contributors, many of them the leading international experts in their fields, on whose scholarship the book is founded. We are proud to include academics and practitioners from 14 countries, and receiving their well thought out and authoritative contributions has been the most enjoyable aspect of this project as we have seen the book take shape.

Finally, thanks are due to all who have helped with the organization of this project. We have greatly appreciated the patience, enthusiasm and sheer hard work of Caroline's team at Sage, including Sarah-Jayne Boyd, Ian Antcliff and Louise Skelding and the efficiency of Gita Raman and her team at Keyword in preparing the manuscript. Special thanks to Laura Bevir for the comprehensive index. Richard Wild made an important contribution to the book's early development, and we are grateful to the administrative staff at the Tasmanian Institute of Law Enforcement Studies for their assistance. Finally, particular thanks are due to family, friends and colleagues, particularly Rod Rhodes and Carrie-Anne Myers, for their help and encouragement along the way.

Editors' Introduction

The development of *The Sage Dictionary of Policing* owes much to the success of its sister publication *The Sage Dictionary of Criminology*, a book that combines the accessibility of a reference book with the depth and rigour of peer-reviewed original scholarship. This is by virtue of the expert, international contributors on whose work the latter is founded, and the skill of Eugene McLaughlin and John Muncie in conceiving an invaluable framework as useful to established scholars as to the criminology undergraduates who so routinely quote from their book. Such a successful formula we were all too willing to appropriate, and apply to one of criminology's most prominent sub-disciplines, academic police studies.

In speaking to a discipline that is pragmatic as well as academic in orientation, however, our project presented its own challenges. How to blend the theoretical and practical? How to balance attention to the organization, tasks and challenges of state policing agencies with those of other players in the corporate and voluntary sectors? How to discuss practices that are usually nationally or locally organized in ways that serve readers around the world? Would it be possible to speak equally well to both our academic and practitioner audiences? In seeking to address these dilemmas we have found ourselves embarking on a journey that is still in progress.

The difficulties in defining and capturing the activity of policing in such a way are conveyed in the *Encyclopædia Britannica* entry for 'police', authored by Michael Banton, William Walsh and Jean-Paul Brodeur (2006). They emphasize how no uniform, universal system of policing has ever emerged, and point to the host of factors that help to explain the diversity of policing systems, agencies and activities worldwide. History, particularly colonialism, has shaped the early development of policing systems internationally. Demographic trends are relevant, since police forces initially emerged in urban areas, with rural areas – in countries where the continental European model of policing has applied – often being policed according to different centralized and often military systems. Political cultures, characterized for example by the degree of a society's democratic advancement, present differing conceptions and systems of police accountability. The types of crime – and methods of committing them – that are most common in a given society determine the way policing resources are directed and the nature of the policing activities carried out (as, we would argue, do public expectations in that society). Such varying policing needs and expectations around the world are addressed by a host of different bodies, with police forces, private security companies, intelligence agencies, armed services and voluntary organizations prominent among the many types of contributor.

The framework we have developed in this Dictionary is grounded in an international, pluralist view of policing as both a substantial area of scholarship and a fast-changing field of practice. The editors' respective personal missions in challenging state-centred conceptions of policing, and working collaboratively with police agencies in an effort to bind research to practice, are embedded in its structure. As an academic discipline, police studies is an established and fast changing, multidisciplinary field, bringing together robust historical inquiry, well developed sociology, theoretical diversity, and applied, evidence-based knowledge. In this book, these diverse perspectives come together – and sometimes collide – in the first mass market policing textbook tailored to an international readership. Its contributors are drawn from both the academic and practitioner communities, selected on the basis of their international standing in relation to the topic areas. Their authoritative and incisive contributions provide instructive overviews of core and emerging areas of police studies from a variety of perspectives.

The Dictionary entries might be thought of as dividing into three thematic areas concerned with *analyzing* policing, *managing* policing and *doing* policing. As regards the former, one of the book's highlights is a detailed history entry, comprising subsections from an international selection of contributors reflecting the development of policing across and within nine areas of the world, from Africa to the United States. Such analysis of policing extends also to theoretical interpretations, with a particular emphasis placed on examining the impact of globalization and pluralization processes on policing; and research, with a detailed overview provided of the evolution of policing research and the methodologies that are most prominent within police studies.

The management of policing has become almost as important in the policing literature as analysis of policing itself. Public administration trends and a preoccupation with police reform, professionalism and accountability have come to inform to a significant degree police work and its management. New public management theory continues to shape and determine the management of police organizations in many countries. Notions of professionalism and leadership are now important concepts that a manager has to promote and apply. The measurement of performance and the need to work with other agencies and actors in pursuit of partnership are all skills the manager is expected to develop. Many of the entries here reflect these imperatives and hint at the difficult and complex task of police management. Despite the differences across countries that we might expect, what is also perhaps somewhat surprising is just how many management strategies have been adopted and adapted for local consumption.

Perhaps the most representative of the thematic areas in this volume is that of *doing policing*. Various contributors, both practitioners and academics, have provided accounts of ways in which specific crime problems are actively policed, such as homicide, property crime, sexual assault and drugs. Broader functions are also identified. So crime prevention, public order policing and order maintenance are all represented as distinctive ways of policing in today's world. The sometimes controversial issues of police discretion and independence are discussed here and may be considered, for example, in the context of police powers of arrest and search and their use of force. A number of entries canvass the challenges of policing in the twenty-first century, particularly those challenges on the international stage such as cross-border policing, terrorism and organized crime. Broader and more complex challenges for police practitioners are also strongly represented in the Dictionary. How do police develop strategies to ensure that public expectations can be met? How to ensure police legitimacy? How to deal with the wicked issues of institutional racism and consent? What indeed have been the main drivers of police activity in trying to develop strategies to address these thorny dilemmas?

Any understanding of how police do business has to include the various ways in which police engage with other actors to address crime and community problems generally. Community policing has become a 'catch-all' phrase for police and their organizations. Is it rhetoric or reality? This wide-ranging concept has been developed as one of the Dictionary's more detailed entries whereby short contributions from academics and practitioners from around the world discuss the concept from their particular perspective. Multi-agency policing, private policing, third party policing and security networks all reflect the process of pluralization that has come to characterize the 'governance of security' across the world. In compiling this Dictionary, the editors have been mindful of these issues and have sought to guide and develop the various contributions in order that a specific issue may be informed by a variety of entries.

Each entry in the Dictionary should be read as a discrete essay, clarifying the parameters of the topic, making observations about important and topical themes, and reflecting tensions and debates surrounding the matter at hand, be it a theoretical concept or an established area of practice. The entries share a common format, beginning with a *definition*: a short statement about the concept that specifies its meaning and the boundaries of the author's interpretation. As with *The Sage Dictionary of Criminology*, this is where the similarity to a standard dictionary ends. A *distinctive features* section follows, in which our authors identify what they consider to be the important characteristics of their concept. This has led to a rich variety of perspectives incorporating histories, theoretical perspectives, research studies and practical considerations. Not wishing to be too prescriptive, the editors provided contributors with the freedom to establish and develop their topics from their own scholarly perspectives. The views and opinions expressed in the individual entries are therefore those of the authors. The final substantive section in each entry is an *evaluation*, in which the authors provide critical and reflective appraisals of their concept, highlighting key debates and drawing attention to perceived contradictions in research, topical issues and possible future developments. Styles of course vary. While some contributors have concentrated on the distinctive features of a particular concept others have put more emphasis on evaluation. Contributors have also provided recommendations of related entries in a list of *associated concepts*, and these can be used in conjunction with the index to direct readers to linked topics. Finally, suggested *key readings* allow readers to pursue further points that the authors have raised, and to gain a broader understanding of each concept. The entries in effect provide the building blocks for future exploration.

The development of this book was not only inspired by the authors of *The Sage Dictionary of Criminology*, which we recommend readers to adopt as a companion text to this book as it elaborates on many of the core criminological concepts that are mentioned. It was the idea of Eugene McLaughlin, and Caroline Porter at Sage Publications, and we are privileged to have been entrusted with this important project.

We have stated that this book reflects a journey that is still continuing. It does not (yet) claim to be a comprehensive overview of police studies. There are still themes to develop, theoretical and ideological perspectives to incorporate, and international dimensions to reflect. Between now and the publication of the second edition, we will be listening to feedback, identifying new avenues of inquiry and updating existing contributions. We welcome comments, ideas and expressions of interest in being part of this ongoing project.

Alison Wakefield
Jenny Fleming
May 2008

References

Banton, M.P., Walsh, W.F. and Brodeur, J.P. (2006) 'Police', in *Encyclopaedia Britannica*. Chicago: Encyclopaedia Britannica, Inc.

A

ACCOUNTABILITY

Definition

Police accountability requires police officers and the institutions to which they belong to explain, justify and answer for their conduct. Individual police officers are obliged to account internally to their superiors and to an internal investigation unit and, in established and emerging democracies, to external, independent accountability institutions. At the political level, police organizations commonly answer to a senior member of government (such as a police minister, attorney-general or general directorate of public security).

Distinctive Features

Police accountability structures and processes are determined by the nature of a sovereign state and its particular political system. For example, in totalitarian regimes the police are the tool of government and are used by those in power to exercise authoritarian control over citizens in general and to suppress any opposition to the ruling elite in particular. There is no sense of 'policing by consent' and hence no requirement that police organizations or individual officers account to the people for the way in which they exercise their coercive powers, or of police using them according to the rule of law, a doctrine which holds that all citizens are equal before the law and will be treated equally by it. In totalitarian regimes the relationship between the police and government is so intertwined that they are often referred to as 'police states'.

In contrast, in democratic societies, police are required to adhere to the rule of law, abide by due process when enforcing the law and protect citizens' human, civil and political rights. This protection encompasses any illegal action by the state and extends to all members of legislatures regardless of the position they hold. The parameters of police power and the way in which police are held to account for the exercise of those powers is laid down in legislation enacted by freely elected and representative legislatures. Regardless of how circuitous the route, ultimate accountability is to the people through their elected representatives.

External, independent civilian oversight bodies are slowly becoming an accepted feature of police accountability in established and emerging democracies. These bodies are independent of the police organizations they oversee and in some, but not all cases, are independent of government in that they report to the legislature or a committee of the legislature rather than directly to a government minister. The former reporting structure helps to depoliticize the police accountability process.

The role of civilian oversight bodies is to monitor, review and/or investigate alleged corruption and misconduct. The more advanced civilian oversight bodies have 'own motion powers' which allow them to adopt a proactive approach to police accountability. It means that they do not have to first receive a formal complaint from a member of the community or another police officer before they can act, but rather can initiate their own investigations into suspected misconduct and corruption.

The level of government that has jurisdiction over general duties police determines to whom the police are accountable in a political sense. In some countries, including the US and the UK, policing is largely a matter for local government. In other countries it is the responsibility of state/provincial/regional governments (for example Canada and Australia). Under this arrangement accountability is to a designated minister of the state, province or region. Various countries organize their police on a national level (such as New Zealand) and where this occurs, accountability is through a minister of the national government. But distinctions are not clear cut. In many countries policing takes place at each level (local, state and national) with each jurisdiction having its own distinct accountability structure.

Community consultative committees are used in many countries to enhance police accountability and to involve non-police in the accountability process. They are used widely in the UK.

To be effective, the 'policing by consent' model requires the community to trust its police and that trust is contingent on police behaving according to constitutional and legal processes established by the people through a freely elected, representative parliament. Police are expected and required to act in a responsible and ethical manner and, most importantly, to be held accountable for their behaviour if they do not.

Over the past 50 years there has been a marked increase in the level of police accountability in democratic societies. The adoption of 'new public sector management' principles in the 1980s has resulted in improved accountability in relation to budgetary, financial and administrative matters.

The media, through its reporting of police related scandals over many years, has played a key role in keeping police accountable for their actions and for placing police accountability on the political agenda. Media-exposed scandals have often resulted in the establishment of commissions of inquiry. The subsequent reports from these powerful, *ad hoc* forms of accountability have overwhelmingly criticized internal, police controlled accountability processes and recommended the establishment of independent, external civilian oversight bodies.

Police accountability in democratic societies is complicated by the doctrine of constabulary independence. In liberal democracies such as Australia, Canada, the UK and New Zealand, which adopt the Anglo-Saxon 'kin' style of policing, it is the independent discretion that attaches to the office of constable that draws a distinction between a government's democratic right to formulate policing policy and the widely held convention that the state is not to interfere in operational policing decisions, including the decision to detain, arrest and charge a person with a criminal offence. Such decisions are said to rest solely with the police and they are held accountable for the exercise of their powers and conduct more generally.

In contrast to the Anglo-Saxon model, many European and South American countries have what is referred to as a 'gendarmerie' form of policing in which military police have responsibility for policing the civilian population. Accountability is often to the ministry of defence.

Some accountability reforms introduced to improve the degree to which police in democratic societies are held accountable include better resourced and more effective police internal investigation units, also known as ethical or professional standards departments. They are staffed by police officers whose role is to investigate misconduct allegations against other police within their own organization.

Criticism that internal and external complaints processes concentrate almost exclusively on the investigative process to resolve complaints led to the introduction of informal resolution processes. This form of accountability involves the complainant and the police officer who is the subject of the complaint meeting to resolve the issue. It is increasingly used (with the consent of the complainant and police officer) to address less serious complaints. It has the advantage of being a less punitive and resource intensive form of accountability than the full-blown investigative process.

Complaints profiling is a more recent accountability management tool used by police internal investigation units and external oversight bodies to determine if a police officer who is the subject of a complaint has a history of inappropriate behaviour. Complaints profiling can act as an early warning system and as such incorporates a preventive element to the police accountability process.

Integrity testing, which can be targeted to specific officers or applied randomly across a police organization, is another more recent form of police accountability. It is designed to covertly test an officer's capacity to resist the temptation to engage in misconduct. Officers who are the subject of the test are sometimes identified and targeted through complaints profiling. Random testing has a preventive element in that police officers are never sure if the temptation they are being subjected to is the result of random integrity testing or not.

Miscarriages of justice cases and findings from commissions of inquiry into police conduct in a number of jurisdictions revealed incompetent and corrupt police interview practices, including forced confessions. The audio and visual recordings of police interviews has become a commonly used accountability tool designed to reduce misconduct and improve accountability at the crucially important interview stage of the investigative process.

Evaluation

The stressful and often confrontational nature of 'general', 'everyday' police work coupled with the many temptations and opportunities it provides for misconduct makes effective accountability an essential part of police legitimacy. Despite the many layers of accountability that police are subjected to, police corruption and abuse of police powers still occurs in police services around the world. However the chance of having that type of conduct exposed has increased dramatically through improved internal and external accountability processes.

But not all police work involves what is termed 'general', 'everyday' policing duties. Brodeur has drawn a distinction between what he defines as 'low' and 'high' policing. The accountability structures and processes outlined above relate to 'low' policing, the 'everyday' policing function performed by public police officers who, with the exception of members of criminal investigation units (detectives), normally wear identifying uniforms. 'High' policing primarily involves the gathering of intelligence by state intelligence agencies such as Britain's Security Service ('MI5') and Secret Intelligence Service ('MI6'), America's Criminal Intelligence Agency (CIA), the French *Direction de la Surveillance du Territoire* (DST), the Australian Security Intelligence Organization (ASIO) and the Canadian Security Intelligence Services (CSIS). These organizations are not subject to open, transparent accountability processes; indeed, in many instances 'high' policing personnel are protected by legislation from having to account to the people for their actions.

The introduction of a raft of counter-terrorism legislation post 11 September 2001 has significantly strengthened the powers and resources of those involved in 'high' policing. It has also resulted in the introduction of increased covert powers for police undertaking 'low' policing functions. The enacting of legislation that grants secret powers to police undertaking 'low' policing has been accompanied by diminished forms of accountability. This trend has the potential to undermine the foundations of democratic policing, which over the past 40 to 50 years have been strengthened by improved accountability, in particular by enhanced forms of external, independent oversight.

Colleen Lewis

Associated Concepts: civilian oversight, consent, discretion, independence of the constable, misconduct

Key Readings

Brodeur, J.P. (2007) 'High and low policing in post-9/11 times', *Policing*, 1 (1): 25–37.

Chan, J. (1999) 'Governing police practice: limits of the new accountability', *British Journal of Sociology*, 50 (2): 251–70.

Hocking, J. and Lewis, C. (eds) (2007) *Counter-Terrorism and the Post-Democratic State*. UK: Edward Elgar.

Lewis, C. (2005) 'Police, civilians and democratic accountability', *Democratic Audit Discussion Paper Series*, Australian National University: Canberra, http://democratic. audit.anu.edu.au.

Mawby, R.I. (ed.) (1999) *Policing Across the World: Issues for the Twenty-First Century*. London: Routledge.

ANTI-SOCIAL BEHAVIOUR

Definition

'Anti-social behaviour' has become a major political concern and policy preoccupation in recent years, most notably in the UK. In the politics of behaviour, diverse activities and risks have been conflated in the amorphous concept of the 'anti-social'. With its genesis in the management of public housing, a range of policies and interventions formulated under the rubric of 'tackling anti-social behaviour' now inform diverse aspects of social life from schooling through to urban planning. Primarily, these strategies have been focused on the question of governing youth. Anti-social behaviour (ASB) has come to categorize and demarcate a distinct policy field that blurs and transcends traditional distinctions between crime and disorder, as well as the appropriate use of civil/criminal and formal/informal regulatory responses. It constitutes a policy domain in which diverse organizational interests, working assumptions, priorities and multi-disciplinary approaches coalesce, often in awkward combinations. At the same time, it introduces the now important dimension of 'public perceptions' into issues of local safety, as a result of which fear of crime, public anxieties and community well-being have become prominent concerns in their own right.

Distinctive Features

To some degree, ASB is a misnomer, as all behaviour is 'social'. The allied concept of 'acceptable behaviour' is perhaps more accurate, as it prompts the question: 'acceptable to whom?' Nevertheless, the term ASB is now widely used to cover a range of activities, misdemeanours and crimes (sometimes quite serious). It is recognized that people's understanding of what constitutes ASB is 'determined by a series of factors including context, location, community tolerance and quality of life expectations ... what may be considered anti-social behaviour to one person can be seen as acceptable behaviour to another' (Home Office, 2004: 3). For this reason, the policy definition of ASB has been left deliberately opaque. In British legislation, ASB is defined as behaviour that 'causes or is likely to cause harassment, alarm or distress' to others. This capacious definition is both subjective and context specific as it rests on the perceptions of others. This generates difficulties of measurement and meaning, notably between agencies and across localities. ASB, by its nature, does not lie within the remit of any single agency and cuts across traditional legal, organizational and social categories.

Nevertheless, forms of nuisance behaviour do have a considerable impact on the lives of many people, with adverse implications for community life and the degradation of public spaces and where serious and persistent ASB can foster a sense of despair and mistrust which fractures informal relations, encourages those who are able to leave certain areas to move out and erodes the willingness of residents to intervene in support of communal values. Significantly, ASB, like crime, affects the poorest communities most severely. Hence, it has a compounding effect upon other forms of disadvantage.

As a policy domain in the UK, ASB arose out of the work of the inter-departmental Social Exclusion Unit (SEU) which had been set up to 'narrow the gap' between the country's worst estates and the rest of society. One report, published in 2000, focused specifically on ASB. Subsequently, in 2002, the Government launched its ASB Strategy and enacted the Anti-Social Behaviour Act 2003, introducing a swathe of new powers. In 2006, the Government outlined its intention to 'go broader, deeper and further' than before with the establishment of the Respect programme and Taskforce. The Government's aim now is to 'ensure that the culture of respect extends to everyone – young and old alike'. Some of the novel measures include: fixed penalty notices for disorder (PNDs), acceptable behaviour contracts (ABCs), parenting contracts and parenting orders, anti-social behaviour orders (ASBOs) and injunctions (ASBIs), tenancy demotion orders, child curfews, dispersal orders, as well as preventive programmes, such as youth inclusion projects and a focus on family intervention. Paradoxically, at the moment in history when the 'myth' of the monopolistic sovereign state had become increasingly exposed, in the UK at least, the state appears to have embarked upon nothing less than the attempted transformation of contemporary manners. Imposing 'civility through coercion' has become the ambitious (and ambiguous) aim of much policy. Hence, ASB is more an incitement to develop new technologies for regulating (youthful) behaviour than a description of particular types of activities (Crawford, 2008).

Evaluation

The attractiveness of ASB for policy makers is that it serves a number of strategic purposes in its tense relationship with crime and criminal justice as more established policy vehicles. First, ASB is seen as a *precursor to crime*. In line with Wilson and Kelling's (1982) 'broken windows' thesis, ASB is understood as an initial stage in both individual and community-level 'cycles of decline', which if not addressed lead to more serious offending. The presence of ASB flags the need to target interventions in order to 'nip it in the bud'. As such, it fits well with more general preoccupations with risk

prediction, crime prevention, community safety and early intervention that abound. Like the 'broken windows' thesis, ASB posits a narrative of decline in which a golden age of orderly community relations is increasingly being eroded by bad behaviour and incivilities.

Second, ASB *transcends crime*. It relates to a more extensive catalogue of problems than crime narrowly defined, linking housing, urban policy, education, employment and citizenship, with crime and security. The inter-departmental nature of the SEU work underlines this broader conception. It also points up the importance of informal social control in managing behaviour, as well as the manner in which informal mechanisms relate to, and connect with, formal systems of control.

Third, ASB is believed to necessitate *circumventing criminal justice*. By introducing new hybrid interventions that combine civil and criminal procedures with informal and non-legal strategies, ASB interventions seek to avoid the perceived ineffectiveness of traditional criminal processes. With regard to the genesis of the ASBOs, Burney notes: 'it was the perceived inefficiency of the criminal justice system that led to demands for something that would give the authorities a freer hand' (2005: p. 4). More fundamentally, these new tools not only blur criminal and civil responses, but also relegate traditional preoccupations with due process, proportionality and privacy. ASB has heralded a drift to discretionary and summary justice. While the same acts may be defined as either ASB or crime, the ways of responding to them are essentially different. While premised upon an overt critique of the ineffectiveness of criminal processes and sanctions, ASB interventions rely upon criminal coercion for their efficacy. In this sense, they supplement rather than undermine criminal justice.

Fourth, responding to ASB affords governments (both national and local) *a chance to be seen to be 'doing something'*. It provides symbolic representations of governmental activity. Many ASB interventions (ASBOs and dispersal orders in particular) have significant communicative properties. These emotive and affective dimensions to the ASB agenda have been central to its momentum, appeal and prospects. It evokes a sense of tradition, nostalgia and togetherness, which appear so absent in contemporary social life (it is not by accident that the ASB agenda also carries the moniker 'Together'). In the face of governments' limited capacity to control the global flows of capital, people, technologies and communications that infuse contemporary insecurities, the tasks associated with 'quality of life' policing have assumed a greater salience. Doing something tangible about issues that intimately affect people's lives and about which authorities might be able to effect change, however small, provide a new *raison d'être* for governments.

However, the take-up and use of ASB interventions remains highly variable in different localities, where divergences in the operational balance between prevention and enforcement prevail. Research found variation in the use of ASBOs which 'could not be explained by examining the type of behaviour leading to the application, but appeared rather to be due to the development of local preferences for a particular route' (YJB, 2006: 9). Critical academic enquiry has centred largely on the problems of definition, the potential for criminalization of non-criminal conduct and the stigmatizing of large numbers of young and disadvantaged people. However, much of the critical commentary has been 'directed at the rhetoric rather than on evidence of what the impacts of the new policies have actually been' (Smith, 2003: 233).

Against a background of decreasing aggregate crime, the 26 per cent increase in the number of children and young people criminalized in the period 2002–6 is a worrying indication that the ASB agenda may be unwittingly drawing a generation of young people into the criminal justice system. Furthermore, in the contemporary ASB policy discourse, troublesome and disturbing behaviour appears no longer to serve as a reminder of the need for a politics of social solidarity and care, but is largely seen as an outcome of personal choice in which individuals appear as the authors of their own predicament. Containing the social threat they pose and

excluding those unwilling or unable to meet the conditional pre-requisites of citizenship have become the order of the day.

Adam Crawford

Associated Concepts: broken windows, community safety, law and order politics, order maintenance, public order, youth.

Key Readings

Burney, E. (2005) *Making People Behave: Anti-Social Behaviour, Politics and Policy.* Devon: Willan.

Crawford, A. (2008) *Governing the Future: The Contractual Governance of Anti-Social Behaviour.* Cambridge: Cambridge University Press.

Home Office (2004) *Defining and Measuring Anti-Social Behaviour.* London: Home Office.

Smith, D. (2003) 'New labour and youth justice', *Children and Society*, 17 (3): 226–35.

Wilson, J.Q. and Kelling, G. (1982) 'The police and neighborhood safety', *Atlantic Monthly*, March: 29–37.

Youth Justice Board (2006) *Anti-Social Behaviour Orders.* London: Youth Justice Board.

ARREST

Definition

Arrest has a logical and etymological basis that precedes its role in the justice system. Arrest as an intransitive noun describes being at rest or at attention; as a transitive noun, it refers to stopping anything in its course; a stay in proceedings; seizing, 'The apprehending or restraining of one's person ... to answer an alleged or suspected crime' (*Blackstone*), the condition resulting from being arrested; custody, imprisonment, durance; under an arrest; the act of arresting (the attention), and a judgement, decree or order.

As a verb, to arrest, it refers to: 1) to stop, stay or remain; 2) to cause to stop, detain; 3) to stop and lay hold of. This latter meaning in a legal sense refers to, 'capture seize, lay hold of or apprehend by legal authority' and 'to restrain a man of his liberty, obliging him to be obedient to the law.' This last usage was first recorded by the *Oxford English Dictionary* (OED) from 1375. A related meaning is 'To seize (property) by legal warrant (now only Scotch and Admiralty Law).'

The meanings captured in the intransitive case denote action that is impeded, delayed or stopped resulting in 'a rest' and in the transitive case (acting upon something), to actively put a stop to something. The addition of the force of law (meanings 6–13 of the intransitive usage) includes stopping a verdict because of an error and when combined with laying hold of by law, the additional aspect of restraining in order to bring the person forward to answer for a crime. *Black's Law Dictionary* (1996: 44), a compendium of American legal usage, states that an arrest as a noun is 1) 'a seizure or forcible restraint' and as a verb is 2) 'The taking or keeping a person in custody by legal authority especially in response to a criminal charge.' 'Under arrest' (9b in the OED) refers to being under legal restraint, in the hands of the law, arrested.

Distinctive Features

Several further etymological points can be made. Delaying or stopping another citizen can be done by any other citizen in a common law country, indeed citizens are obligated to respond to crimes of which they know. This is not law enforcement, but carrying out citizens' duties. Whether one is continuously restrained is not implied by an arrest as trusted citizens may only be expected to appear in court given bail. The arrest may be for a brief period of time, until charge and indictment, or for some length prior to or including trial since many persons are retained in jail until trial and may or may not be given credit for time served while awaiting trial. The underlying notion of an arrest, going back to the fourteenth century at least, was to stop some potentially harmful

activity. In theory, arrest is not used to encourage or sustain an activity. The connection of arrest with law enforcement grew in importance as the nation state obtained sufficient authority and a network of agents who could act on command to ensure compliance by force if necessary. *Black's* point about forcible restraint suggests that arrest takes place when and in so far as coercion may be needed, and also suggests the central role of a criminal charge in association with the arrest.

In the American context, several clarifications of the legal meanings of the term are necessary. The definitions at law vary by state within the US and these state definitions contrast with definitions under federal law. This variation across the states is perhaps uniquely a US feature, as other Anglo-American societies usually have one set of laws pertaining to all states within the nation. It should at least be noted that there are 49 state police organizations, and some 50,000 local police units enforcing state and local laws. In some states, the power of officers to arrest is extremely limited and does not extend beyond the locality that employs them. American law stipulates that a citizen can make an arrest if a public offence was committed or the arrester has reasonable cause to believe that the arrestee has committed a felony (*Black's,* 1996: 44).

Evaluation

These are formal dictionary definitions of arrest and they can be contrasted with the domain of common sense usage which includes as the most salient denotation a stop of a citizen by a police officer. In the broadest sense, any constraint upon movement is an arrest, even when state statutes only consider a formal arraignment or 'booking' an arrest. In common law countries the implications of an arrest vary. In England, suspects can be held without indictment for some 72 or more hours, and even longer if they are connected to terrorism of some kind. In the US, the constitutional 'right to a speedy trial' has been extended to include booking and indictment within 48 hours.

Remedies are available in civil law for false arrest.

In the US, practices associated with arrest vary from locality to locality and from state to state in part because of local traditions and conventions, the election of judges and magistrates, and the habitus of given officers and units. The series of sub points under the term arrest in Black's (p. 44) suggest the potential for the abuse of arrest powers. Black's lists 'lawful arrest', clearly a contrast with unlawful arrest; 'false arrest,' one conducted without proper legal authority; 'malicious arrest,' or one made without probable cause or for malicious purpose, and 'pretextual arrest' which is defined as (p. 45) 'An arrest. ... for a minor offence to create the opportunity to investigate the person's involvement in a more serious offence for which there is no lawful ground to make an arrest.' Legal language is a sensitive indicator of human cunning. A field study of arrest practices (LaFave, 1965) in the US in the mid sixties found that police officers avoid arrests when a felony has been committed as well as make arrests for reasons other than the offence at issue. Since the latter tend to be consequential and indeed fateful, they are worth considering. LaFave listed: coercing respect for an officer; maintaining public belief in 'full enforcement of the law'; aiding in the investigation of other, more serious offences; punishing a chronic offender; and reducing cases which place a continued strain on insufficient police resources (e.g. domestic violence). The changed character of domestic violence is revealing insofar as now the officer can make an arrest and in some states *must* make an arrest, if there is an allegation of domestic violence. This list, even with the constraints on arrests in cases of domestic violence, makes the point starkly: arrest as applied on the street is a tool used to produce police-defined order and utility, no more, no less. The courts review those decisions that reach their purview, but most police decisions do not. As law has penetrated more deeply into arrest practices in Anglo-American societies, process based protections have become more visible. Nevertheless, police discretion produces non-reviewed and non-reviewable decisions (Reiss, 1974).

Peter K. Manning

Associated Concepts: accountability, citizen's arrest, discretion, independence of the constable

Key Readings

Black's Law Dictionary (2006) (3rd edn) Bryan A. Garner, Editor in Chief. St. Paul, Mn: Thomson West.

Blackstone, W. (1979) *Commentaries on the Laws of England: A Facsimile of the First Edition of 1765–1769.* Chicago: University of Chicago Press.

LaFave, W. (1965) *Arrest.* Boston: Little, Brown and Company.

Oxford Dictionary of Law (2006) (6th edn) edited by E. A. Martin and J. Law. Oxford: Oxford University Press.

Reiss, Albert J. Jr. (1974) 'Discretionary Justice', in. D. Glaser. (ed.) *Handbook of Criminology* Chicago: Rand McNally.

AUXILIARY POLICE

Definition

'Auxiliary police' refers to uniformed personnel – employed, sometimes in an unpaid volunteer capacity, by police forces or local government – who provide assistance to regular police officers, undertaking a range of tasks including preventive patrol, the policing of major events, public reassurance and the enforcement of parking regulations.

Distinctive Features

The term 'auxiliary police' denotes various types of uniformed staff who, while not being fully trained and attested police officers, are engaged in the delivery of a range of order maintenance, law enforcement and public reassurance tasks. Three distinct kinds of auxiliary police can be distinguished within the literature. First, there are 'volunteer' police officers who work on an unpaid basis within police forces. In some countries (for example, the US) such personnel are called 'auxiliary police'. In other countries such as the UK and Australia, the term 'special constables' is used to describe such staff. In England and Wales, special constables must work for a minimum of 16 hours per month (or 200 hours per year), although many do substantially more than this. Special constables can be paid some expenses by the police service, but their work is otherwise voluntary and unpaid. At 31 March 2007 there were about 14,000 special constables working in the police service in England and Wales. This represents a considerable decline since the early 1990s when there were about 20,000 such staff working within English and Welsh police forces, and a very significant decline in numbers since the mid-part of the twentieth century. Nevertheless, governments continue to emphasize the important role played by special constables in the delivery of policing services.

Second, in some countries there have been salaried posts created within public police forces to provide some policing tasks which arguably do not require the full powers and training of a regular police officer, but are more 'operational' than those tasks provided by civilian support staff. Examples of this type of police auxiliary include the Dutch *politiesurveillanten* or 'police assistants' and police community support officers (PCSOs) in England and Wales. In both cases, these auxiliaries are primarily patrol ranks that require a more limited amount of training and police powers, and also attract lower rates of pay. By 31 March 2007 there were nearly 14,000 PCSOs working in the police service in England and Wales, and the government plans to expand this number to 28,000 within the next few years.

A third distinct kind of auxiliary policing is delivered by staff employed by bodies other than the police. Local municipalities may employ uniformed staff to undertake patrol and other functions in their area. These go under various names: *stadtswachten* (city guards) in the Netherlands, neighbourhood and street 'wardens' in the UK. In France, local authorities have established their own local policing bodies, *polices municipales*. Although these locally organized patrolling bodies are not usually under the primary direction and control of police forces, they often work in close partnership with local forces and in general their role is to support the police rather than offer an alternative service.

There is a long history of the employment of volunteer auxiliaries in police forces, for example, the New York City Auxiliary Police dates back to 1916. The Special Constabulary in England and Wales can trace its history back even further to the Special Constabulary Act 1831 which gave Justices of the Peace the power to swear in men as special constables in order to combat riots and social unrest. With the growth of paid police forces during the latter half of the nineteenth century, the special constabulary declined in numbers, but during the early part of the twentieth century underwent a revival following the outbreak of the First World War. Another Special Constables Act was passed in 1914, creating a volunteer corps to address police staffing shortages for the duration of the war. The perceived success of this led to a further Act in 1923 continuing the Special Constabulary in peacetime. The current legal basis for the Special Constabulary in England and Wales is the Police Act 1964.

The other forms of police auxiliary outlined above emerged much more recently. The Dutch police assistants previously described were introduced in the 1990s, and the rank of PCSO in England and Wales was established by the Police Reform Act 2002. The Dutch 'city guards' first emerged during the 1980s and 1990s. In the UK, local authority areas established their own uniformed 'community safety' patrols from the 1990s onwards. In 2000, the government launched a national Neighbourhood and Street Wardens' Programme, which funded the growth of warden schemes throughout England and Wales.

While the role of police auxiliaries varies between national and local contexts, in general they conduct local patrols, deliver public reassurance, and partake in crime prevention initiatives. The most extensive operational policing roles are undertaken by those police auxiliaries working within police forces such as the PCSOs or Dutch police assistants. For example, such personnel undertake foot patrols, provide assistance at the scene of accidents, fights or fires, enforce road safety initiatives, conduct house-to-house enquiries, help to police major events, present evidence in court, tackle anti-social behaviour or conduct school visits. By contrast, auxiliaries employed outside of police organizations have had a more limited role. In most countries, such personnel have been primarily focused on delivering visible patrol to reassure local people, and acted as the 'eyes and ears' of the local police. In the UK, the more recent neighbourhood warden schemes have offered a wider range of roles and functions, including the delivery of security related services but also more general caretaking and housing management functions in local housing estates.

In terms of legal powers and equipment, there is much international variation. In some countries, auxiliary police are only given special powers in times of emergency. In others, such personnel operate with similar powers and uniforms to their regular officer colleagues. English and Welsh special constables operate with the full powers of a police constable, and since 1 April 2007 they have had jurisdiction throughout England and Wales, whether on or off duty (prior to this their powers were restricted to 'on duty' times and to their own or adjacent forces). Specials wear similar uniforms to regular police officers, and carry the same routine equipment in terms of handcuffs and batons. By contrast, the Dutch equivalents of special constables do not carry firearms and have more limited powers than full police officers. In parts of the US, volunteer auxiliaries not only have full police powers when under the supervision of a regular officer, but are also equipped with firearms. The more recently created form of police auxiliaries – such as PCSOs in the UK and police assistants in the Netherlands – operate with more limited legal capacities than regular officers, but in both countries these personnel have the power to detain members of the public in certain circumstances and also to issue fixed penalty fines. In most jurisdictions, forms of municipal policing employed by organizations other than the police operate with the same legal powers than those held by ordinary citizens, although it might be argued that their uniforms provide them with a degree of 'symbolic power' over and above that of other citizens.

Evaluation

Until relatively recently, the role of police auxiliaries has received little attention in the academic literature. The research literature on the Special Constabulary is particularly sparse, but that which does exist has highlighted the problem of marginalization of such personnel from their regular police colleagues, who have sometimes shown a tendency to dismiss them as 'hobby bobbies' (Leon, 1989). Recent research has highlighted some of the organizational problems arising from the rapid implementation of the PCSO programme in England and Wales (Johnston, 2006).

More broadly, the past decade has seen a growing focus upon the 'fragmentation' or 'pluralization' of policing (Jones and Newburn, 2006). This reflects the now widespread recognition that law enforcement, crime prevention and order maintenance activities are undertaken by a range of individuals and organizations in addition to traditional police forces. While much of this discussion has focused upon the rapid expansion of the commercial security sector across many countries, this literature has also highlighted the contribution of auxiliary policing forms organized and delivered by municipalities and police forces. These developments have given rise to important conceptual debates about what constitutes 'policing' and also, normative discussions of the forms of governance that are best placed to deliver equitable and effective forms of security provision (Jones, 2007). The emergence of auxiliary policing forms that are organized and delivered by bodies other than the public police has raised concerns about effectiveness and accountability. For example, there is a need for coordination in an increasingly crowded policing market, with the danger of duplication and overlap, or even open hostility and competition between the various policing bodies.

Developments in England and Wales are of particular interest because of the central place of police auxiliaries within the government's police reform programme. What has been termed the 'police extended family' is an important part of government attempts to meet growing public demands for a greater patrol presence on the streets. The government's response to concerns about accountability and regulation has been to give the public police central responsibility for control and monitoring of these increasingly complex policing networks. The Police Reform Act 2002 gives the police the power of accreditation of warden schemes, and other community safety bodies, and allows them to compete with the commercial security sector via the expansion of employment of PCSOs. However, this has been criticized as creating a situation in which the police are given the power to regulate the groups with whom they are in competition (Crawford et al., 2005). Some authors have argued for the establishment of new institutional forms, outside of the police service, that can bring 'security networks' under the direction of democratic governance. For example, Loader (2000) has proposed the establishment of local, regional and national 'Policing Commissions' with a statutory responsibility to monitor and direct policing policy as exercised by a wide range of policing agencies.

Trevor Jones

Associated Concepts: patrol, policing, pluralization, security networks.

Key Readings

Crawford, A., Lister, S., Blackburn, S. and Burnett, J. (2005) *Plural Policing: The Mixed Economy of Visible Patrols in England and Wales*. Bristol: The Policy Press.

Johnston, L. (2006) 'Diversifying police recruitment? The deployment of police community support officers in London', *Howard Journal*, 45 (4): 388–402.

Jones, T. (2007) 'The governance of security' in M. Maguire, R. Morgan and R. Reiner (eds) *The Oxford Handbook of Criminology* (4th edn). Oxford: Oxford University Press.

Jones, T. and Newburn, T. (eds) (2006) *Plural Policing: A Comparative Perspective*. London: Routledge.

Leon, C. (1989) 'The mythical history of the "specials": sorting out the fact from the fiction', *Liverpool Law Review*, 11 (2): 187–97.

Loader, I. (2000) 'Plural policing and democratic governance', *Social and Legal Studies*, 9 (3): 323–45.

B

BROKEN WINDOWS THEORY

Definition

The broken windows theory asserts the existence of an important connection between incivility and crime. According to the theory, if symbols of 'disorder' are left unaddressed in a neighbourhood, then more crime problems will intensify there. A corollary of the theory holds that the police should focus on misdemeanour offences to reduce disorder, because this will work to prevent more serious crime.

The broken windows theory is arguably the most popular theory of crime in recent history, and one with significant consequences for policing. The theory emerged in the early 1980s, with the publication of a short article by James Q. Wilson and George L. Kelling, 'The police and neighbourhood safety,' in *Atlantic Monthly*, an American public interest magazine (Wilson and Kelling, 1982). The authors outline a sequence that they suggest can lead to localized crime problems. It begins with an unrepaired broken window or some other instance of unaddressed disorder. For Wilson and Kelling, broken windows symbolize a neighbourhood that does not care about itself. In places where symbols of disorder accumulate, residents become more fearful. They then withdraw from public space, and become increasingly unable to exercise informal social control. This serves as a cue for those interested in criminal acts; they lack fear of detection in places where disorder is evident. As

crime becomes more common, residents withdraw even further, and a cycle of deterioration is set in motion. It is therefore considered necessary to fix broken windows quickly to prevent this cycle from ever commencing.

Distinctive Features

To understand the significance and implications of the theory requires recognizing what Wilson and Kelling mean by broken windows. Although their use of the term might suggest an emphasis on aspects of the built environment, their discussion centres on people. The symbols of disorder upon which they concentrate are 'disreputable or obstreperous or unpredictable people: panhandlers, drunks, addicts, rowdy teenagers, prostitutes, loiterers, the mentally disturbed' (Wilson and Kelling, 1982: 29). These are the symbols of 'disorder' whose prolonged presence, they believe, starts the chain of events leading to rampant crime. To fix broken windows, in other words, means the removal of these people from visibility. Tactics designed to accomplish this are thereby often referred to as 'broken windows policing', or 'order maintenance policing'.

This reorientation of policing means that officers should address the actions of those considered disorderly rather than wait for serious crime to emerge. Through the threat or use of the power to arrest, the police can pressure urban undesirables to relocate. Although police officers might prefer to make high profile arrests of suspected felony offenders, the broken windows theory suggests that they better serve communities by concentrating on low level misdemeanour offences. It is for this reason that broken windows has often morphed into 'zero tolerance' policing, where the police tolerate no misdemeanour offences associated with street level behaviour, such as public drinking or aggressive panhandling.

To assist the police in cracking down on those considered disorderly, many cities passed new laws criminalizing a wider range of behaviours. These so-called 'civility codes' give the police greater licence to arrest individuals for such acts as sitting or lying on sidewalks, camping in parks, engaging in public elimination, and storing belongings in public space. One of the architects of the broken windows theory, George Kelling, frequently works as a consultant to municipalities seeking to grant the police greater legal tools to address unwanted behaviour in public space.

Evaluation

Although its beginnings in a short magazine article were modest, the broken windows theory's prominence means that it now underwrites significant expansions of criminal law and robust uses of the power of the police to monitor and arrest. The simplicity of the theory, as well as its alleged success in helping reduce crime in places like New York City, helps to explain its increased popularity worldwide. From London to Mexico City to Johannesburg, both broken windows and its associated concept of zero tolerance are avidly embraced, if not in its exact Americanized form (Newburn and Jones, 2007). Its influence on popular thinking about crime, and on policy formulation, is not easily underestimated.

Yet critics abound. One strand of criticism centres on whether the theory's causal chain – disorder today leading to crime tomorrow – is sound. Wilson and Kelling's initial formulation is notable for a lack of evidence to support this claim. More robust subsequent tests of the disorder-crime connection suggest that there is minimal or no relation between them (see Sampson and Raudenbush, 1999). The alleged 'success' of broken windows policing

in New York City is also fiercely contested by critics, who note that similar reductions occurred in other American cities, most of which adopted different policing tactics.

A second strand of criticism concerns the over-criminalization that the theory condones. As more street level behaviours become crimes, the police possess ever more power to monitor and arrest those considered undesirable. People who spend excessive time on the streets thereby lose constitutional and other measures designed to protect them from state intrusion into their daily lives. Various civil liberties are compromised in the process (Beckett and Herbert, 2008). Further, to focus excessively on police responses to crime means a too-frequent neglect of the underlying causes of crime, such as poverty (Herbert and Brown, 2006).

Despite the power of these academic critiques, the popularity of the broken windows theory shows no signs of abating. Part of this is due to its common invocation in cities that are undergoing such significant changes as gentrification. As economic pressures increase the need to 'clean up' urban spaces for redevelopment, the broken windows theory helps legitimate attempts to relocate undesirables. The association between disorder and crime that is at the heart of the theory makes hard-edged tactics on the poor politically defensible; what might be seen as brutish harassment of the downtrodden is recast as a sensible prophylactic against robbery.

Because of its simplicity and political saliency, the broken windows theory rocketed to popularity across the globe, and influenced the practices of policing in the process. The duration and tenacity of its widespread acceptance is an open question, but few theories of crime currently shape police departments with any greater power.

Steve Herbert

Associated Concepts: Compstat, hot spots, law and order politics, order maintenance, zero tolerance

Key Readings

Beckett, K. and Herbert, S. (2008) 'Dealing with disorder: social control in the post-industrial city', *Theoretical Criminology*, 12 (1): 5–30.

Herbert, S. and Brown, S. (2006) 'Conceptions of space and crime in the punitive neo-liberal city', *Antipode*, 38 (4): 755–77.

Newburn, T. and Jones, T. (2007) 'Symbolizing crime control: reflections on zero tolerance', *Theoretical Criminology*, 11 (2): 221–43.

Sampson, R.J. and Raudenbush, S. (1999) 'Systematic social observation of public spaces: a new look at disorder in urban neighbourhoods', *American Journal of Sociology*, 105 (3): 603–51.

Wilson, J.Q. and Kelling, G.F. (1982) 'The police and neighbourhood safety', *Atlantic Monthly*, March: 28–38.

BUREAUCRATIZATION

Definition

Bureaucracies are in general terms conceived as organizations charged with the implementation of policies decided upon by government or business authorities, and adhering to a specific organizational design that is hierarchical in structure. Bureaucratic activities are formally based on general rules and are standardized and impersonal. The concept of 'bureaucratization' refers to the organization of political and economic administrative institutions on the basis of the principles of a bureaucracy. The work of the German sociologist Max Weber (1922) has been most influential in introducing this concept and the theories that are derived from it in the area of state and market institutions, including police organizations.

Processes of bureaucratization are relevant to the study of policing because the modernization of the police institution has fundamentally involved an increasing development of police organizations along bureaucratic lines. Historically, bureaucratization processes have been observed across a wide range of organizations in many societies. Despite national variations in bureaucratic organization and activities, most modern societies that are highly industrialized have historically undergone bureaucratization tendencies. Bureaucratic modes of organization have been imported in other countries as well, so that bureaucratization is a global phenomenon. The consequences of bureaucratization have extended far beyond the organizations themselves and have also affected the nature of governance and of social life in general.

In the context of policing, bureaucratization refers to the organization of police institutions as bureaucracies that are hierarchically ordered, have formalized and standardized procedures of operation, and are impersonal by reliance on general rules of conduct. The bureaucratization of policing has important consequences for the functions and organization of police.

Distinctive Features

Derived from the French term *'bureau'*, meaning desk or office, and the Greek word *'kratos'*, meaning power or rule, bureaucracy in general refers to the power of administrative offices. The term was originally introduced in eighteenth century France with a distinctly negative connotation to refer to the rigid manner in which administrative units could make decisions irrespective of their original objectives. A certain negative quality often remains associated with bureaucratization, but the concept is currently also used in a strict analytical meaning to refer to a particular mode of organization.

Weber identified seven central characteristics of bureaucracies:

(1) bureaucratic offices are subject to a principle of fixed jurisdictional areas;
(2) they are firmly and hierarchically ordered;
(3) their activities are based upon written documents or files;
(4) the executive offices of the officials are separated from their private households;
(5) specialized training is required to obtain an office;

(6) the official activity is a full-time occupation; and

(7) the management of the bureaucratic office is guided by general rules.

Among the principles that guide bureaucratic activity, Weber specified most centrally that the modern bureaucracy operates on the basis of a formal rationality to use the most efficient means given certain specified objectives. Weber conceived of formal or purposive rationalization as the most fundamental process characterizing modern societies. Analyzing the consequences of bureaucratization, Weber devoted most attention to the trend among bureaucratic organizations to achieve a position of autonomy so that the bureaucracy can operate independently from political oversight and popular control.

In the study of policing, the bureaucracy concept has been applied in the context of the agencies of internal coercion that are monopolized by the modern nation state. Sanctioned by nation states with the tasks of order maintenance and crime control, police organizations are arguably the most visible and concrete expression of the state's monopoly over the means of coercion. Organized as bureaucracies, police institutions are hierarchically ordered with a vertical structure of a rigid chain of command. Police agencies handle cases on the basis of general rules of evidence collecting and processing without regard to the person and in sole view of the stated objectives of crime control and order maintenance. Thus modern police work tends to become highly systematic, whereby police officers handle cases on the basis of files (for information) and scientific methods of investigation and evidence collecting and analysis.

Bureaucratized police work also applies considerations of efficiency in getting the work done, at the exclusion of other concerns such as questions of morality. Police work is routinized on the basis of standardized methods of investigation, often strongly influenced by scientific principles of police technique, such as technically advanced methods of criminal identification and computerized databases.

Historically, the greater need for a specialized organization of crime control and order maintenance with the growth of modern societies has been among the most central conditions favourable to police bureaucratization. As societies grew in population size and density and experienced processes of rapid urbanization, industrialization and technological progress, modern nation states began to concentrate even more policy tasks in a centralized administration. Thus, specialized police institutions were established and, in the course of their development began to operate as specialized bureaucratic apparatus in both functional and organizational respects. Functionally, police institutions became responsible for order maintenance and crime control on the basis of a formal system of laws. Organizationally, police bureaucratization is reflected in the hierarchical structure of police organizations, the formal training of police personnel, the professionalization of the police occupation, and the emphasis on technically efficient means in police work.

Evaluation

Essentially two lines of inquiry on police bureaucratization have been pursued within police studies. First, normatively oriented studies have investigated the origins and consequences of an increasing reliance on bureaucratic principles in police organizations relative to principles of due process and the protection of citizen rights. In this view, the perceived negative impact of police discretion and accountability limitations can be attributed to an excessive bureaucratization of the police. Thus, bureaucratization is seen to take on the negative connotation it originally carried to become virtually synonymous with injustice and oppression resulting from an overly rigid organization of administrative activity. Police bureaucratization can then be criticized in light of principles of democratic control and accountability, and new post-bureaucratic models of policing are proposed that rely on insights from restorative justice and community policing initiatives to bring about closer cooperation among the police and the public.

Second, from a strictly analytical perspective, police bureaucratization has been studied in terms of the factual course and observable consequences of the increasing organization of police organizations along bureaucratic lines. A central concern in this respect has been the autonomy of police institutions as a result of bureaucratization in formal and operational respects. Formally, police bureaucratization implies a growing independence of police institutions from the governments of their respective national states. Whereas police institutions were originally set up to further the political goals of governments, especially in the context of autocratic states, they gradually developed a professional ethos to focus on distinctly criminal enforcement tasks. In operational respects, police bureaucratization involves police institutions gaining independence to determine the means, as well as specifying objectives, of their tasks.

Among the consequences of bureaucratization, police professionals can insulate themselves from popular demands in favour of adherence to an occupational culture that stands apart from the community and operates on the basis of principles of command, obedience and honour (although the emphasis on community policing makes this a little less likely nowadays). Furthermore, increasing trends towards bureaucratization across the world have promoted collaboration between police organizations of different nations. Such international cooperation allows for limited collaboration between national police forces surrounding specific cases, such as the international rendition of fugitives from justice, and has been organized on a permanent basis in formally structured international police organizations such as Interpol. Though justified in terms of the rise in international crime, international police practices that result from bureaucratization may lack formal legal regulations and operate beyond democratic control (Deflem, 2002).

The autonomy of highly bureaucratized police institutions is not stable, but dependent on socio-historical circumstances, notably the degree of a society's pacification. During periods of momentous societal change, such as international warfare, police organizations are typically pressured to reconcile their activities with the political goals of their respective governments. However, as police institutions have presently attained an unprecedented level of bureaucratization, they can also better resist any political pressures to remain organized on the basis of bureaucratic principles of professional expertise. Current conditions surrounding the spread of international terrorism have revealed the relevance of police bureaucratization as an important force determining the shape and future of counter-terrorism efforts and other dimensions of police power.

Mathieu Deflem

Associated Concepts: accountability, discretion, independence of the constable, leadership, transnational policing

Key Readings

Albrow, M. (1970) *Bureaucracy*. New York: Praeger Publishers.

Bordua, D.J. and Reiss, A.J., Jr (1966) 'Command, control, and charisma: reflections on police bureaucracy', *American Journal of Sociology*, 72 (1): 68–76.

Deflem, M. (2002) *Policing World Society: Historical Foundations of International Police Cooperation*. Oxford: Oxford University Press.

Deflem, M. (2004) 'Social control and the policing of terrorism: foundations for a sociology of counter-terrorism', *The American Sociologist*, 35 (2): 75–92.

Lipsky, M. (1980) *Street Level Bureaucracy: Dilemmas of the Individual in Public Services*. New York: Russell Sage Foundation.

McLeod, C. (2003) 'Toward a restorative organization: transforming police bureaucracies', *Police Practice and Research*, 4 (4): 361–77.

Skolnick, J.H. (1966) *Justice Without Trial: Law Enforcement in Democratic Society*. New York: John Wiley and Sons.

Weber, M. [1922] (1978) *Economy and Society: An Outline of Interpretive Sociology*. G. Roth and C. Wittich (eds). Berkeley, CA: University of California Press.

C

CALLS FOR SERVICE

Definition

'Calling the cops' or calls for service are calls to the police by the public using an emergency call system, usually a (toll-free) three-digit number. In the UK this emergency call system operates nationwide, and is designed to handle emergency medical and ambulance, fire and police calls, with the majority of callers asking for police services. The emergency call system defines police activities and workloads as it comprises highly developed technologies to locate callers and analyze calls, to channel the respective request, and to dispatch police officers, firefighters and ambulances to the site of the crime or other problems. Calls for service are the main type and source of communication with the public; they constitute one of the major management problems of the police, and they are a decisive factor in the satisfaction of the public with the police. More recently the emergency call system has been complemented by non-emergency call systems and numbers in order to relieve the police from the burden of emergency call saturation.

Distinctive Features

Emergency call systems are the single most important technological innovation that have shaped police practices over the last three decades. The combination of the ubiquitousness of phones in homes and later the spread of mobile phones across the population, the use of radio communication, and ever more sophisticated computer systems to locate and analyze calls have made it the defining feature of police practice today, and the huge success that it was hailed to be at the start. Bayley (1998) describes calls for service as the cornerstone of policing in modern democracies, and the fact that every private citizen can call, expect and receive police services by dialling an emergency number is a democratic privilege. Calls for service therefore are the most frequent and arguably the most important encounters with the police for the majority of citizens, and the way in which most citizens communicate with the police. Their amount, types and outcomes are indicative of the relations between the public and the police. While most citizens' attitudes towards the police are shaped by what the public sees as the foremost task of the police – crime fighting – only a fraction of calls for service actually concern crimes. Calls for service as communication provides a rich source of useful data for the police, about the location of problems and crimes, what citizens care about, and what they expect from the police. In combination with new IT tools like geographical systems, police forces can integrate a range of information about crime and other problems.

The majority of calls concern incidents or 'troubles' in which the public turns to the police for help, including minor nuisances, conflicts, accidents, emergencies, threats by others, domestic disputes, and often information on incidents with which citizens feel unable to cope. These calls address the other two aspects of the police role: order maintenance and service, and according to the number of calls these can be deemed the two most important functions of policing. Order maintenance includes all requests by the public for dealing with any disturbance of the social and moral order. Services include a wide array of demands for assistance and advice, and calls for these presumably amount to larger numbers where social services are either nonexistent or less visible. The police are perceived as the first 'port of call' in a variety of unusual and unexpected events that citizens feel they cannot cope with, even if there is no indication that a crime might be involved.

While the emergency call system was deemed a huge success in its early days, the growing problems of call saturation and managing them soon became obvious. Calls for service take up a considerable amount of police resources, and intelligent response mechanisms are vital in dealing with calls. Though the public became increasingly critical of what was perceived as slow responses to calls, it turned out that the time it took crime victims to call was decisive. In contrast to other forms of policing (such as problem-oriented and community policing) the emergency call system seemed to be less useful in providing public safety (Mazerolle et al., 2002).

In 1988, Manning estimated the ratio of calls per person per year in the US and the UK to be between 0.29 and 0.77 (1988: 7). In 2006, with 67 million calls to the police in the UK alone, the ratio has about doubled at 1.2, and 70 per cent of these are graded as nonemergency calls. An analysis based on one police constabulary in the UK (Lancashire) showed the following distribution of calls for service for 2000 (see also Mazerolle et al., (2002) for the US):

- General problems, nuisances and conflicts: 23 per cent;
- Violent conflicts: 9 per cent;
- Burglary, theft and other property crime: 14 per cent;
- Other incidents and emergencies: 52 per cent (Hope et al., 2001).

Seventy five per cent of all calls do not concern incidents that are generally defined as crime and as the focus of police work. Hope et al. (2001) were able to relate the calls to the actual crime rates of the same year, and thus calculate absolute and relative excess rates (the proportions of calls that are *not* turned into crimes) for calls over crimes (see Waddington, 1993). The absolute excess rate for all calls over all crimes was 6.19; for nuisances and conflicts 4.9, for incidents involving violence 6.0, and for property offences 1.5. This translates into the following relative excess rates: 84 per cent for all calls, 80 per cent for nuisances and conflicts, 83 per cent for violence, but only 37 per cent for all property offences. With the exception of property offences, the majority of calls concerning nuisances, conflicts and low level violence are not likely to be defined as crimes. These figures testify to the amount of police work that is done in restoring order by warning, advising, or threatening those who cause the nuisance and by calming down those who have called and complained, often in a situation of distress.

Calls to the police are therefore indicative of public demand for police services, and in particular of how this demand is communicated to the police. In late modern society, calls to the police are communications about risk, and as such often symbolic, though highly fraught, communication. They are expressions of risks and needs that are perceived by and arise among different groups of citizens, and are addressed to the agency that is tasked to provide safety. As such they also create a 'communication problem for the police: how to anticipate, respond to, mediate and filter the communication from the public', and respond with 'controlled and calculated strategy' (Manning, 1988: 3). The equal and measured response by the police is a major factor in determining the legitimacy of the police among citizens, in particular among minority groups. Perceptions of police fairness in responding to such demands equally for all groups and social classes enhance the legitimacy of the police, and presumably the inclination of social groups to turn to the police in situations of risk and need. Consequently, improvements of police practice in responding to calls may increase the amount of calls they have to deal with.

However, such communication needs are not independent of more severe incidents like crimes, and calls to the police are indicators of a concentration of crime such as 'hot spots' of crime. They also give voice to other minor nuisances and incidents or a range of incivilities and often the threshold between a minor incident and a serious crime is easily passed in violent conflicts, thus blurring the distinction between crimes and non-crimes in calls to the police. Whether a minor incident or a crime is reported might actually change between the call and the arrival of the police. Even if their calls are finally not turned into crimes, many callers assume that they are reporting a crime.

The overload of the emergency call system with minor incidents and troubles finally led to the establishment of non-emergency call systems in order to route these away from the emergency numbers. Citizens were advised to use these numbers to report anti-social behaviour (the UK system was abolished in 2007) or more generally all non-urgent incidents and troubles (US). Their objectives were typically to free up officer time to provide problem-oriented and community policing activities, to improve response times, and to enhance citizens' satisfaction with police. As Mazerolle et al. (2002) found in a US study, the introduction of a non-emergency call system reduced the number of emergency calls roughly by one third, and the overall numbers by 8 per cent; it seems that citizens also started to call directly to other agencies, and that police officers gave direct advice over the phone. However, a reduction in non-emergency calls also reduces the information about general and 'quality-of-life problems', as well as accurate information about the location of ongoing problems.

Evaluation

Which factors determine the mobilization of the police through calls from the public? Three major theoretical accounts focusing on the communication and needs aspects have been offered during the last decades. Black's theory of the invocation of authority states that mobilization of the police is more frequent where informal social controls are less developed: informal and formal social control (as presented by the police) are inversely related. In his 'stratification hypothesis' he relates the mobilization of police to community as well as individual wealth: richer communities have higher levels of mobilization than poorer ones.

The second theoretical account is based on conceptual frameworks that focus on the capacity of communities to provide informal control. The better developed such capacities are, the more mechanisms of self-help in addressing conflicts and needs exist, the lower the amount of calls to the police will be. 'Collective efficacy' as defined by Sampson and his colleagues will decrease the demand from the public, while 'disinvestment' in social networks, or gaps in citizens' networks will cause an increase of risk communication to the police, as will conflicts between different groups (Warner, 1989; see also Hope et al., 2001). Finally, Elijah Anderson's ethnographic study suggests that alienation from mainstream society and its institutions in poverty-stricken neighbourhoods causes a profound lack of faith in, and legitimacy of, the police. Members of the public do not call the police because they do not expect them to come, or to settle the conflict in a fair and appropriate manner, and finally they fear that enlisting the support of the police might have a negative impact on their standing within the community ('code of the street') (for all perspectives/authors see Baumer, 2002; Hope et al., 2001).

Research suggests an integrated model. Hope et al. (2001) found for calls that concerned conflicts, nuisances and violence that communities which were better off and had higher levels of 'institutional integration' called more in excess of actual crime incidents, while communities with higher levels of needs had significantly lower rates of excess calls, that is, compared to the level of crime in their neighbourhoods they mobilized the police less often. Ethnic heterogeneity emerged as a strong predictor of excess calls, lending support to a conflict perspective. Baumer's (2002) study on victims' notification of simple assaults to the police shows a curvilinear relationship between socio-economic disadvantage and police notification: notification is low in better-off neighbourhoods and increases with higher levels of disadvantages; however, the most disadvantaged neighbourhoods have the lowest levels of notification, indicating that alienation and a lack of trust might prohibit them. Nevertheless, even in disadvantaged neighbourhoods, new hybrids of informal control, self-help and communication to, and engagement with, the police are emerging that are indicative of new patterns of interaction between the parochial and public arena (Carr, 2003), and consequently of different patterns of communication between the police and the public that merge and encompass a range of different types of contacts.

Susanne Karstedt and Stephen Farrall

Associated Concepts: community engagement, legitimacy, order maintenance, police property, technology

Key Readings

Baumer, E.P. (2002) 'Neighbourhood disadvantage and police notification by victims of violence', *Criminology*, 40 (3): 579–616.

Bayley, D.H. (1998) *What Works in Policing*. New York: Oxford University Press.

Carr, P.J. (2003) 'The new parochialism: the implications of the beltway case for arguments concerning informal social control', *American Journal of Sociology*, 108 (6): 1249–91.

Hope, T., Karstedt, S. and Farrall, S. (2001) *The Relationship between Calls and Crimes*. Keele: Department of Criminology, Keele University.

Manning, P.K. (1988) *Symbolic Communication: Signifying Calls and the Police Response*. Cambridge, MA: MIT Press.

Mazerolle, L., Rogan, D., Frank, J., Famega, C. N. and Eck, J.E. (2002) 'Managing citizen calls to the police: the impact of Baltimore's 311 call system', *Criminology and Public Policy*, 2 (1): 97–124.

CITIZEN'S ARREST

Definition

Under common law, citizens can take whatever steps are deemed reasonable and necessary to prevent or suppress a breach of the peace. These reasonable steps may include detaining (arresting) persons against their will. Arrest involves depriving persons of their liberty. Therefore, in any democratic society, the rules relating to citizen's arrest are strictly observed and enforced by the courts.

Distinctive Features

Public police officers can detain any person upon suspicion of that person committing an offence by virtue of specific criminal codes or the common law. If their suspicions turn out later to be incorrect, they are generally immune from civil suit. In addition, all police officers in the UK have the right to arrest any person without a warrant on suspicion that an offence is about to be committed. By virtue of their discretionary powers, public police officers, generally speaking, are permitted a general defence of reasonable suspicion or honest exercise of power.

Private citizens (including security officers acting on instructions from their principals, and civilian police auxiliaries), on the other hand, have no power to detain or arrest any persons without their consent unless they are given authority to do so either by some specific legislative power or in circumstances where their actions are justifiable by virtue of the common law (*Albert v Lavin* [1982] AC 546 at 565). Even then, the 'arrest' is limited to detaining the suspect until the public police arrive. That is, private citizens do not enjoy the immunities that public police officers have, and do not have a defence of reasonable suspicion or honest exercise of power if they make an incorrect judgement. Moreover, they cannot arrest any persons on suspicion of their being *about* to commit an offence.

Both at common law and by virtue of legislation, a person exercising a lawful power of arrest (such as a police officer) is entitled to use whatever reasonable force is necessary in order to effect that arrest. What is 'reasonable' depends upon the circumstances. The courts may determine whether the force used was reasonable by reference to, for example, the amount of resistance that was offered by the accused suspect. Persons who have been detained wrongly (or against whom excessive and unreasonable force has been used in a legitimate arrest) may sue the person who 'arrested' them for assault and false imprisonment via the civil courts.

The rules, however, are confusing. The arrest powers of citizens change from jurisdiction to jurisdiction. In some jurisdictions, the right of private citizens, security guards and police auxiliaries to make an arrest is limited to 'felonies' and not 'misdemeanours'. In other jurisdictions, it is limited to 'indictable' matters as opposed to 'summary' offences. In each pairing, the former term refers to more serious offences carrying more severe penalties, with the option of a jury trial. It is highly unlikely that a citizen or security guard or police auxiliary will know precisely which definitions apply in any given jurisdiction.

In the UK, citizen's arrest powers have been clarified somewhat by legislation. By virtue of a new Section 24A added in 2005 to the *Police and Criminal Evidence Act 1984* (UK), a citizen is permitted to arrest, without a warrant, 'anyone whom he has reasonable grounds for suspecting to be committing [an arrestable] offence'. Importantly, the new legislation demands not only reasonableness in the mind of the person making the arrest, but it must also appear to them 'that it is not reasonably practicable for a constable to make [the arrest] instead' (Section 24A (3) (b)).

In Australia, the legal rules concerning a citizen's arrest differ markedly from jurisdiction to jurisdiction. This lack of consistency is confusing and therefore unsatisfactory. In South Australia, for example, the power is outlined in section 271 of the *Criminal Law Consolidation Act 1935*. Under this section, persons can arrest and detain any person

whom they find in the act of committing (or having just committed) an indictable offence, larceny, offence against the person, or offences against property. In Victoria, section 462A of the *Crimes Act 1958* allows any person the right to use force 'not disproportionate to the objective as he believes on reasonable grounds to be necessary to prevent the commission, continuance or completion of an indictable offence or to effect or assist in effecting the lawful arrest of a person committing or suspected of committing any offence'. So, in both jurisdictions, private citizens would need to know the difference between indictable and non-indictable offences, and, in Victoria, would need to be able to establish whether the circumstances of the arrest could legitimately support their use of force.

It was only in 2004 that the Western Australian parliament repealed the ludicrous provisions of section 47 of the *Police Act 1892* which allowed any person to arrest without a warrant 'any reputed common prostitute, thief, loose, idle or disorderly person, who, within view of such person apprehending, shall offend against this Act, and shall forthwith deliver him to any constable or police officer of the place where he shall have been apprehended, to be taken and conveyed before a Justice, to be dealt with according to law ...' A private citizen would have found it rather difficult to interpret the terms 'loose' or 'idle' with any degree of legal certainty. That jurisdiction has now located its citizen's arrest powers in section 25 of the new *Criminal Investigation Act (WA) 2006*.

In the US, the extent of a citizen's arrest powers also varies depending upon the type of crime and the jurisdiction in which the crime was committed. Moreover, it may depend upon whether the crime was committed in the presence of the person making the arrest, and their status. Indeed, in *Cervantez v J.C. Penney Company* (1978) 156 Cal Rptr. 198, the Californian Supreme Court ruled that the person who made the arrest (in this case an off-duty police officer 'moonlighting' as a store detective), was operating as a private citizen at the time when he detained a person whom he believed had stolen merchandise. In that event, 'probable cause' (a defence available to police) was not available as a defence to him and the store. The store was therefore liable to the accused person for damages for wrongful arrest and false imprisonment. A significant number of US States have since legislated to circumvent the application of the *Cervantez* decision by extending a 'probable cause' defence to those who may be inclined to undertake a citizen's arrest.

In Canada, section 494 of the Canadian Criminal Code contains provisions that mirror the common law position but require the felon to be 'in flight'. According to the Code, a citizen may arrest without warrant 'a person whom he finds committing an indictable offence; or a person who, on reasonable grounds, he believes has committed a criminal offence, and is escaping from and freshly pursued by persons who have lawful authority to arrest that person.' These same powers apply in relation to property offences.

Evaluation

The contradictions, anomalies and difficulties in this area stem from parliaments and judges endeavouring to balance the citizen's right to enforce the law on the one hand, against the danger that, if such powers go unchecked, officious meddlers might abuse others' legitimate rights. The result is an unsatisfactory state of affairs for the average citizen, let alone a private security officer or police auxiliary who may work across jurisdictions and in a variety of settings.

How will courts deal with these matters? Generally speaking we can safely conclude as follows: where it is clear on the evidence that a private citizen, or security officer, in detaining a suspect, acted reasonably and the suspect unreasonably, then it is likely that the court will find in favour of the citizen or security officer and against the suspect if that suspect chooses, later, to sue the citizen for assault or false imprisonment. In other circumstances where, for example, a property owner (or an agent) arrests a thief in a manner, and in circumstances, disproportionate to the likely harm to the victim, and in clear defiance of the rights of the suspect (for example, to be taken forthwith to a police station), then the court is very likely to find in favour of the suspect (guilty or otherwise). The courts may order compensation for such suspects in appropriate circumstances.

In the following cases, judges have articulated the balancing act required. Both cases involved police officers, but the principles espoused could apply equally to cases involving citizen's arrest:

The policy of the law seems to be that, in modern times, we are to rely upon the police, who are trained to effect an arrest except in those circumstances where [citizens are empowered] to assist in keeping the peace. This does not mean that force cannot be used to protect life or property' ... provided that it is not unnecessary force and is not intended and not likely to cause death or grievous harm. (*Hulley v Hill* (1993) 91 NTR 41 at 50 per Mildren J.)

Consider also the view of the Australian High Court:

The jealousy with which the common law protects the personal liberty of the subject does nothing to assist the police in the investigation of criminal offences' ... The competing policy considerations are of great importance to the freedom of our society and it is not for the courts to erode the common law's protection of personal liberty in order to enhance the armoury of law enforcement. (*Williams v The Queen* (1986) 161 CLR 278 at 296 per Mason and Brennan JJ.)

The courts are thus looking for a middle path. They are required to weigh the perceived harm to victims and the means available to them to defend themselves and their property, against the scourge of vigilante 'justice' that affronts human dignity.

Rick Sarre

Associated Concepts: arrest, auxiliary police, force, private security

Key Readings

Button, M. (2003) 'Private security industry law in Europe: the case of Great Britain' in S. Outer and R. Stober (eds) *Recht des Sicherheitsgewerbes*. Cologne: Heymanns.

Findlay, M., Odgers, S. and Yeo, S. (2005) *Australian Criminal Justice* (3rd edn). Melbourne: Oxford University Press.

Fischer, R.J. and Green, G. (1998) *Introduction to Security* (6th edn). Boston: Butterworth-Heinemann.

Gerden, R. (1998) *Private Security: A Canadian Perspective*. Scarborough, Ontario: Prentice Hall.

Sarre, R. and Prenzler, T. (2005) *The Law of Private Security in Australia*. Pyrmont, New South Wales: Thomson LBC.

CIVILIAN OVERSIGHT

Definitions

Civilian oversight is a generic term used to imply a form of civilian (non-police) superintendence of the police. It is most commonly used in relation to police accountability and more specifically the complaints against police process. Increasingly and overwhelmingly it involves the establishment of an agency that sits physically and organizationally outside of the police and is independent, in a reporting and accountability sense, of the police organization it oversees. Civilian oversight bodies are referred to by a variety of names: Citizen Review Board (Las Vegas and Syracuse, US), Independent Police Complaints Council (Hong Kong), Police Ombudsman (Northern Ireland), Independent Complaints Directorate (South Africa), Crime and Misconduct Commission (Queensland, Australia), Independent Police Complaints Commission (England and Wales), Independent Police Complaints Authority (New Zealand), Police Integrity Commission (New South Wales, Australia), Police Complaints Authority (Bermuda, Trinidad and Tobago, Lesotho, Guyana) and Citizens Police Review Board (Pittsburgh, US), to name but a few. In some jurisdictions, oversight of police forms part of the broader public sector accountability role of the Ombudsman (for example, Namibia). In other jurisdictions, an independent, police specific agency shares the oversight function with the Ombudsman (New South Wales, Australia). Where there is a dual arrangement, the specialist agency's role is confined to more serious misconduct and corruption matters.

Distinctive Features

Until the late twentieth century, repeated allegations by civil liberty and minority groups of police brutality, racism, misuse of police powers and the failure of internal, police controlled systems to keep police accountable for their actions were largely ignored by senior police and governments. This occurred despite evidence that some police covered up the misconduct of other police, turned a wilful, blind eye to misbehaviour, abuse of power and corruption and inappropriately exonerated fellow officers who were the subject of a complaint.

An upsurge in the civil rights' movement and the peace marches of the 1960s and 1970s in many liberal democratic societies focused public attention on police behaviour, but it was television that allowed police actions to be beamed into people's living rooms. Many 'law abiding' citizens were deeply disturbed by the police response to the democratic right to peaceful protest, especially as the recipients of excessive police force were often seen as 'respectable, middle class' people and their sons and daughters. Police began to be viewed as the willing tool of governments and the oppressors of citizens' civil liberties, rather than the people's police. They were also seen as being incapable of impartially investigating their own, and as a result, their long standing monopoly over the complaints against police process was brought into question (Lewis, 1999; Maor, 2004).

The media kept a spotlight on the inability of police-controlled complaints systems to deliver effective accountability and eventually governments were forced to act. They often did so by establishing Royal Commissions or commissions of inquiry into police. In the ensuing decades, reports from numerous inquiries in various democratic societies recommended the establishment of independent, civilian oversight bodies.

The vast majority of police departments and/or police unions strongly resisted the idea of non-police involvement in the police complaints process and, in the early years of civilian oversight, this often led to the closing down of the oversight body or the watering down of its investigative powers. Functions were often restricted to a paper review of a police-controlled complaints process which involves the oversight agency reviewing the police department's files on the police investigation (Goldsmith, 1991).

While governments were reluctant to oppose the wishes of powerful police pressure groups, continued scandals and the weight of public opinion forced them to act. Gradually over the past thirty years, independent civilian oversight in its various forms has become part of police accountability processes in democratic societies around the world (Goldsmith and Lewis, 2000).

The functions of civilian oversight bodies vary. They can include monitoring, supervising, reviewing and/or investigating police conduct. Monitoring indicates an investigation undertaken by police that is watched over (often in a physical sense) by the oversight agency. Supervising implies that the oversight agency is directing the police investigation by instructing investigating police what to do. Review involves the oversight agency retrospectively conducting a paper review of a police investigation. The more powerful oversight agencies have the ability to monitor, supervise, review and/or investigate complaints against police, while less powerful and arguably less effective bodies are restricted to a *post hoc* paper review of a police investigation. Some civilian oversight bodies have a dedicated research and corruption prevention division and their staff work with police to identify processes and systems that impede effective, efficient and accountable policing. Occasionally oversight agencies have a broader remit. For example, in the Australian

state of Queensland, the Crime and Misconduct Commission (previously the Criminal Justice Commission) was given responsibility for overseeing the police reform programme introduced as a result of recommendations from a Commission of Inquiry into Possible Illegal Activities and Associated Police Misconduct (Fitzgerald Inquiry, 1987–1989). The Crime and Misconduct Commission also plays a role in the appointment of Queensland's Police Commissioner (see Lewis, 1999).

Some of the most advanced forms of civilian oversight are found in Australia (Queensland's Crime and Misconduct Commission, New South Wales' Police Integrity Commission and Western Australia's Crime and Corruption Commission), England and Wales (the Independent Police Complaints Commission) and Northern Ireland (the Police Ombudsman for Northern Ireland). They are, in effect, standing royal commissions and combine a reactive and proactive approach to police accountability matters. These agencies were established following a series of public inquiries into police corruption and abuse of power. The political fall-out which ensued placed the effectiveness of existing accountability models, which included legislatively weak, reactive and/or under-resourced civilian oversight agencies, firmly on the political agenda and led to their replacement by the more powerful and appropriately resourced civilian oversight organizations mentioned above.

But powerful and well resourced oversight bodies are not the norm. There are many examples of legislatively weak, under-funded oversight agencies that reflect little more than symbolic politics by democratic governments (Fleming, 2001). In these circumstances, citizens are under the misapprehension that the civilian oversight process is holding the police accountable for their actions when, in reality, it cannot.

Evaluation

As civilian oversight has become a more accepted part of the police accountability landscape, questions have been raised about the effectiveness of these accountability instruments. Researchers and practitioners are now examining what indicators should be used to evaluate their performance. The number of complaints received, the time taken to investigate a complaint and substantiation rates have been dismissed as crude or flawed performance measures. Other suggested indicators include case file audits, stakeholder surveys and the degree to which police act on the policy recommendations of the oversight agency. The more enlightened agencies are using all of these indicators to publicly assess their performance (Prenzler and Lewis, 2005).

The long-term legitimacy of the civilian oversight process depends on oversight bodies subjecting themselves to similar levels of accountability to that demanded of those they oversee. However, oversight agencies that fall into the symbolic politics category should not have their effectiveness evaluated on what is best described as bad policy. Under these circumstances it is government policy and not the efforts of the civilian oversight body which should be publicly evaluated.

Civilian oversight agencies are only one part of the police accountability framework. Police departments also have their own internal investigation sections and the more enlightened organizations conduct randomised integrity and drug testing, have legislated to make the reporting of suspected misconduct mandatory, regularly rotate officers in corruption-prone units such as drug and armed offender squads, include comprehensive ethics training in their recruit and middle and senior management education and training programmes and analyze complaints data to identify police who have a history of being involved in inappropriate conduct.

Even though civilian oversight is a vital part of the police accountability process, to be effective oversight agencies must work with police. A challenge they still face is to convince police departments and in particular police unions, that independent civilian oversight is a necessary part of the police accountability framework and a fundamental element of democratic policing.

Colleen Lewis

Associated Concepts: accountability, democratic policing, legitimacy, misconduct

Key Readings

Fleming, J. (2001) 'Conduct unbecoming: independent commissions and ministerial adversaries', in J. Fleming and I. Holland (eds) *Motivating Ministers to Morality*. London: Ashgate.

Goldsmith, A. (ed) (1991) *Complaints Against the Police: The Trend to External Review*. Oxford: OUP.

Goldsmith, A., Lewis, C. (eds) (2000) *Civilian Oversight of Policing: Governance, Democracy and Human Rights*. Oxford: Hart.

Lewis, C. (1999) *Complaints Against Police: The Politics of Reform*. Sydney: Hawkins.

Maor, M. (2004) 'Feeling the heat? Anti-corruption mechanisms in comparative perspective', *Governance*, 17 (1): 1–28.

Prenzler, T. and Lewis C. (2005) 'Performance indicators for police oversight agencies', *Australian and New Zealand Journal of Public Administration*, 64 (2): June, 77–83.

CIVILIANIZATION

Definition

Civilianization is a process involving the replacement of fully attested, sworn police officers with 'civilian' staff who have either no police powers or limited police powers and who provide either administrative or specialist support to policing.

Distinctive Features

Civilianization is not a new process in policing, but it is one that has gathered pace since the 1980s as managerialist approaches have been applied to policing and as policing has required more specialist skills. The development of 'civilianization' has been particularly pronounced in England and Wales, where the civilian workforce grew substantially through the 1980s and has expanded significantly since 2000 with the growth of the concept of the 'extended police family'. Less pronounced, but significant movement in the direction of civilianization has also taken place in northern Europe, Australia and New Zealand. In the case of the latter, reform of the police in 2007 has been consciously developed from the UK's model.

The UK experience is instructive and began as a response to the pressure on frontline resources in the Second World War. At the end of the War, there were some 1300 civilians working for the police. After the war, despite the return of officers from the services, there was still pressure to 'release policemen for police duty, wherever possible by the employment of civilians' (Oaksey Committee Report, 1949). By the 1960s, numbers had grown to 8500 but they had been very much in administrative positions, a supplement to police officers rather than a replacement for them. The Taverne Report in 1966 pushed this boundary further by encouraging the deployment of civilians in posts not requiring 'police training, the exercise of police powers or the special qualifications or personal qualities of a police officer'. This test of the boundaries between the sworn and attested police officer and the civilian member of staff was to remain the yardstick until the late 1990s.

While the first phases of civilianization had been driven by encouragement, in the late 1980s a Home Office circular (an official statement of Home Office policy) 105/1988 made a clear link between support for any future applications for enhanced police officer numbers and the level of 'civilianization' in the police force concerned. This circular was part of a growing trend towards the application of value for money approaches to the police, which had been given considerable impetus by the relatively higher costs of employing police officers following the Edmund Davies pay award in 1979. As a result of the circular, by 1994 some 30 per cent of the police workforce in England and Wales was made up of civilians, with control

rooms, professional support in IT, finance and human resources being particularly targeted. This also brought change at the top of the organization with the appointment of civilian assistant chief officers, who gradually won recognition as members of the Association of Chief Police Officers.

In the Police and Magistrates Court Act 1994, chief officers of police in England and Wales were given much greater freedom to manage their budgets and their staff, but were also gradually held far more to account for their use of resources and performance. The combined pressure to meet efficiency and productivity targets drove greater innovation in civilianization. This was combined with a growing impetus to consider outsourced or private provision of services. For a number of critics, particularly within the staff associations, this was characterized as a centrally driven move towards the privatization of policing. A Home Office Review of Core and Ancillary Tasks in 1995 tended to confirm this view, by its approach of dividing police tasks into 'core' and 'ancillary', with the latter being proposed for private or alternative provision.

However, instead of privatization, the next and most recent phase of civilianization in British policing has been dominated by the idea of creating a new class of auxiliary support to policing with part police powers – the 'extended police family'. This started with the provision of limited powers to civilian detention officers, which were then extended to allow them to take fingerprints and DNA samples from detainees. Powers to search and seize evidence were extended to forensic staff and then a role of civilian investigator was created, initially for those investigating serious fraud cases and then for 'volume crime investigators'. A number of these initiatives were encouraged by specific funding linked to major government drives against priority crimes, notably robbery and burglary.

The final, most dramatic shift in England and Wales experimentation with civilianization has been the creation of 'community support officers' as part of the national programme on neighbourhood policing. The ideas for a partially empowered patrol officer came from senior police officers who had visited the Dutch *'politiesurveillant'* and *'stadswacht'* schemes in the early 1990s. Supported by an independent report from the Police Foundation and Police Studies Institute, the idea took shape at a time that the government was also experimenting with 'neighbourhood wardens'. The latter were primarily employed by local government. There was also a move towards the regulation of private security patrols through the Security Industry Authority (set up in 2003).

In parallel with these developments and, not always joined up with them (Crawford et al., 2005), the government supported the piloting and then national implementation of the 'National Reassurance Policing Programme'. As part of this programme, police forces were initially invited to bid for additional funds for the piloting of 'community support officers' (CSOs) and then, following the initial evaluation of the pilots (Cooper et al., 2006), the government committed itself in its 2005 manifesto to providing 24,000 CSOs. Although this target was subsequently reduced, by spring 2007 some 16,000 CSOs, with a new range of street powers (essentially a smaller subset of the constable's powers) were recruited and in place. For many police forces in England and Wales, this meant that the composition of the force was now close to 50-50, civilian and sworn officer.

England and Wales has seen the most dramatic shift in workforce, but as has been mentioned above, a number of European police forces have also developed civilian patrol support and civilian support to the frontline. Progress towards civilianization has tended to be strongest where the police unions are less prominent. For example, the replacement of sworn officers with non-sworn has been strenuously resisted in many US police departments. In Australia as well, civilianization has been rigorously opposed by strong police unions and associations.

Evaluation

Civilianization is not an uncontentious approach to developing policing and the most recent developments in the UK, the employment of 16,000 CSOs, was strenuously resisted by the Police Federation, who represent junior officers. CSOs have been denounced as 'plastic policemen' by some media critics and politicians. However, evaluations of the CSO pilots (Cooper et al., 2006) found generally strong support from communities as had the earlier experiments in Holland. In particular, the public surveyed appreciated the fact that CSOs were less likely to be withdrawn from their core role of patrolling. Criticisms of the approach have focused on the immense confusion to the public of the different roles and types of 'police staff' and other patrolling officers. The same studies have been doubtful of the value of extending additional powers to the CSOs and other police civilian staff (Crawford et al., 2005).

The other downsides of the CSO implementation have been familiar themes from the story of civilianization. Right from the start there have been problems for the police in creating an effective career structure for civilians and for their status in the organization (Loveday, 1993). Highmore's study (1993) identified significant morale problems and a sense of inferior standing in the organization. Police forces responded by striving for a 'one force culture', seeking to bring together the terms and conditions of police officers and police staff as far as possible. However, this combined with the expansion of the CSOs with their part police powers, brought accusations from the Police Federation that the 'office of constable' – the core status of a fully attested police officer – was being eroded. These boundary and status issues seem likely to continue to be troublesome, particularly as the government in the UK has signalled an intention to continue to 'modernize' the police workforce, using parallels from the developments in the medical professions where, increasingly, the role of the medical practitioner has been encroached on by a growing number of paraprofessionals.

The England and Wales tale of CSOs stands in interesting contrast to some other jurisdictions where the proliferation of patrol and other law enforcement staff in charge of public space have tended to come from the private sector or in semi-private, institutionally-based police organizations. This approach has been more typical in North America. In the UK, the public police, through the professional commitment to the neighbourhood policing programme, seem to have managed to expand the public sector's reach into public space.

Peter Neyroud

Associated Concepts: auxiliary police, contractualism, managerialism, patrol, pluralization, private security, privatization

Key Readings

Cooper, C., Anscombe, J., Avenell, J., McLean, F. and Morris, J. (2006) *A National Evaluation of Community Support Officers.* London: Home Office.

Crawford, A., Lister, S., Blackburn, S. and Burnett, J. (2005) *Plural Policing: The Mixed Economy of Visible Patrols in England and Wales.* Bristol: Policy Press.

Highmore, S. (1993) *The Integration of Police Officers and Civilian Staff,* London: Home Office.

Jones, T., Newburn, T. and Smith, D. (1994) *Democracy in Policing.* London: PSI.

Loveday, B. (1993) *Civilian Staff in the Police Force.* Leicester: Centre for the Study of Public Order.

CLOSED CIRCUIT TELEVISION (CCTV)

Definition

Closed circuit television (CCTV) is a system whereby video cameras are linked in a loop with images transmitted to a central television monitor or recorder. The term 'CCTV' is now widely used to describe any camera-based surveillance system. CCTV is used in a wide range of settings and, while it has varied uses, the most common purpose is policing and security generally. To date, most criminological attention has focused upon public area surveillance, its effectiveness and the privacy issues associated with the increasing pervasiveness of such measures.

Distinctive Features

The two settings where CCTV has most impacted upon policing have been in public areas and within police facilities. Public area CCTV systems generally consist of a series of cameras connected via cable or microwave to a central control room. Footage is fed through to monitors observed by operators, commonly private security personnel. However, this varies, and systems may also be monitored by police personnel or even in some cases volunteers. Most public area CCTV systems have the capacity to record images. Public police are frequently key stakeholders in CCTV systems, usually through advising on camera locations and through regular interactions with control room operators.

In the UK and the US the use of CCTV in police operations can be dated back to the 1960s. However, aside from limited early experiments in public areas, the use of CCTV at that time remained largely confined to the retail sector. Nevertheless there was limited expansion of visual surveillance to other locations. In 1975, cameras were installed on the London Underground and in the same year 145 cameras were introduced to monitor London streets. During the 1970s and early 1980s police use of CCTV was primarily restricted to public order situations such as monitoring football crowds and political demonstrations (Norris et al., 2004).

The first large scale public area surveillance system in the UK was installed in Bournemouth in 1985. Over the following decade there was a gradual dissemination of CCTV to other towns and cities, although by 1991 there were still no more than ten public area systems. However, with generous government funding, public area CCTV in the UK has rapidly expanded. One estimate suggests there may be as many as 4.2 million cameras in the UK, or one camera for every 14 persons (Norris et al., 2004).

The spread of CCTV in other jurisdictions has been less dramatic than in the UK. Local political contexts may influence the extent of diffusion. In Australia, for example, where CCTV systems have largely resulted from local initiatives, there are far fewer public area cameras than in the UK (Wilson and Sutton, 2004). Nevertheless, the diffusion of public area surveillance is a global phenomenon, with the expansion of CCTV surveillance systems in public areas documented in the European Union, Canada, the US, South Africa, Australasia, the Middle East, South Asia, Eastern Europe, China and Japan (Norris et al., 2004). Post 9/11, the expansion of CCTV in public areas has gathered momentum globally, propelled by arguments for the counter-terrorist capacities of the technology. In addition to public areas, Newburn and Hayman (2002) note the increased installation of CCTV in police custody suites in the UK, a trend also replicated in other countries such as Australia.

Evaluation

Although initially heralded as a solution to spiralling crime statistics, research findings on the effectiveness of CCTV in reducing recorded crime have been ambiguous. Studies in clearly delimited spaces such as shops, buses, car parks and sports grounds have suggested CCTV might be effective in preventing specific offences. However, results of research on the impacts of CCTV in more diffuse urban locations have to date been mixed. Welsh and Farrington's (2002) meta-analysis compared thirteen evaluations in city centres and in public housing. Five found a positive effect (decrease in offences) and three an undesirable effect (increase in crime), while in the remaining five evaluations there was no effect or evidence was unclear (Welsh and Farrington, 2002). There is also considerable debate over whether crime is prevented or merely displaced (Wilson and Sutton, 2004).

Critical scholars have drawn attention to the potentially profound impact CCTV surveillance may have upon policing practice, urban space and ultimately social relations. It can be argued that the deployment of visual surveillance is implicated in broader processes of social and spatial exclusion and results in the criminalization of particular populations (Wilson and Sutton, 2004). The research of Norris and Armstrong (1999), for example, noted the discriminatory potential of CCTV surveillance, revealing CCTV operators focused disproportionately on young males, a pattern intensified if the subjects were black or had visible signs of subcultural affiliation. Nevertheless, the impact of these patterns upon actual police deployments is less clear. Both Norris and Armstrong (1999) and Goold (2004) reported that police interventions followed only a small percentage of operator-initiated calls.

This might suggest that the impact of CCTV upon police practice is more modest than has sometimes been claimed. Goold's (2004) detailed ethnographic study of policing and CCTV in an area of the UK concluded it had a negligible impact upon police practice, largely because police were unwilling to alter existing practices to take advantage of the new technology. It is probable, however, that the impact of CCTV on police practice varies across locations, depending upon the level of integration between control room operators, police dispatchers and police on the street. It is this 'system integration' which largely dictates the level of police response to incidents observed on camera.

While the level of police deployment varies, police frequently maintain CCTV is useful in coordinating police responses to (and at) incidents and that it facilitates the targeting of police resources. Officers interviewed in Goold's (2004) study also believed CCTV enhanced officer safety and resulted in reduced assaults on police. The utility of CCTV footage as evidence, in identifying suspects after an incident and in encouraging suspects to plead guilty has also been claimed.

The practices of the police themselves are also subject to the watch of public area cameras. CCTV can therefore reduce the autonomy traditionally experienced in street level policing by facilitating greater managerial supervision of officers on patrol. Thus CCTV may provide a measure of accountability, as police conduct is subject to the scrutiny of surveillance. Consequently, as Newburn and Hayman (2002) note in a study of CCTV in police custody suites, it is unhelpful to conceive of CCTV simply in terms of the extension of social control. CCTV might be a means of protecting the public from police misconduct. However it is also apparent that strategies can be (and have been) developed that shield officers from the camera's gaze.

The impact of CCTV upon policing is complex and contradictory. On the one hand CCTV potentially facilitates greater accountability and checks on abuses of police power. On the other hand it may exacerbate discriminatory practices leading to the over-policing of already marginalized groups. It is part of the Janus-faced quality of surveillance that both outcomes can occur simultaneously.

Dean Wilson

Associated Concepts: accountability, commodification of security, fear of crime, crime prevention, misconduct, technology

Key Readings

Goold, B. (2004) *CCTV and Policing: Public Area Surveillance and Police Practices in Britain*. Oxford: Oxford University Press.

Newburn, T. and Hayman, S. (2002) *Policing, Surveillance and Social Control: CCTV and Police Monitoring of Suspects*. Cullompton, Devon: Willan Publishing.

Norris, C., McCahill, M. and Wood, D. (2004) 'The growth of CCTV: a global perspective on the international diffusion of video surveillance in publicly accessible space', *Surveillance and Society*, 2 (2/3): 110–35.

Norris, C. and Armstrong, G. (1999) *The Maximum Surveillance Society: The Rise of CCTV.* Oxford: Berg.

Welsh, B. and Farrington, D. (2002) *Crime Prevention Effects of Closed Circuit Television: A Systematic Review*. Home Office Research Study 252, London: Home Office.

Wilson, D. and Sutton, A. (2004) 'Watched over or over-watched? Open street CCTV in Australia', *Australian and New Zealand Journal of Criminology*, 37 (2): 211–30.

COMMODIFICATION OF SECURITY

Definition

The commodification of security refers to the increasing tendency for security to be viewed as a 'private good'. Security is now concerned with a variety of technologies and practices provided not just by police but by commercial concerns competing in the marketplace.

Distinctive Features

In many countries, the state is no longer expected to be the sole provider of security or the only agent responsible for protecting individuals and organizations. Instead, private companies now provide a diverse range of security products and services, aimed at filling actual or perceived gaps in the provision of security by the state. As a consequence, the traditional view of security as a public good is increasingly being abandoned in countries like the UK and the US, in favour of a new account that explicitly acknowledges security as a good capable of being sold and consumed like any other.

This change in the nature and experience of security is evidenced by the recent growth in both the private security industry and in general levels of security consumption. Taking the UK as an example, according to recent British Security Industry Association (BSIA) figures, there are now over 600,000 people working in Britain's security industry, an industry with an estimated annual turnover in excess of five billion pounds. In the last decade alone, spending on manned security systems has increased from £530 to £1570 million, while spending on closed circuit television (CCTV) has leapt from £84 million in 1993 to £495 million in 2004 (Zedner, 2006). As a result, the private security industry is one of the largest and fastest growing sectors in the British economy.

As the security industry has grown, so too has the consumption of security products. Whereas thirty years ago few citizens bothered with burglar alarms, home CCTV, or car immobilizers, such products are now seen as commonplace in many countries and can be purchased without difficulty. Similarly, despite being almost unknown in the UK and the US before the 1980s, the number of gated communities continues to rise, with individuals preferring to buy security rather than rely solely on the police or local government for their protection.

Evaluation

The emergence of security as a consumable good can be explained by reference to a number of changes that have transformed the social and cultural landscape of many modern democracies over the past twenty years, changes that have fundamentally altered the relationship between the individual and state and have led to an increased emphasis on individual responses to the problem of insecurity. These transformations include the following.

The growth of markets in security services and hardware, and the expansion in the size and scale of the private security sector. In many modern states, the past decade has been marked by a sharp rise in both the use of private security services in semi-public spaces (such as shopping centres), and in the number of gated communities and privately secured homes across the country. Although the extent and implications of this shift remain the subject of dispute (Bayley and Shearing, 1996; Jones and Newburn, 1998), it is widely accepted that policing and security now involves interplay between a plurality of purchasers and suppliers. As the provision of security has become more market-driven and the belief that individuals should contribute to the costs of security has begun to take hold, however, the state's monopoly on policing has come under increasing threat (for example, Goold, 2004; Loader, 1997). In response, many criminal justice agencies – and the police in particular – have now become more market-oriented in their outlook.

The growing importance of processes of responsibilization and individual responses to risk. In light of prevailing discourses and practices of government-sponsored prudentialism and responsibilization, individuals and organizations are now being encouraged to take steps to protect their own person, property, workplace or neighbourhood, and not to rely solely on the uniformed police for protection. In particular, this shift has been accompanied by a burgeoning expectation that people should expect to pay for some services, such as visible patrolling, or responding to building alarms. This trend must also be situated against a backdrop in which anxieties about crime, order and security have moved to the forefront of everyday social relations and political life – to the extent that some commentators have claimed that Western societies are today 'governed through crime'.

The erosion of barriers to physical, economic and social mobility. The apparent 'freeing' of individuals from the constraints of class, gender, kinship and locality has led to a dramatic individualization of people's life chances and dispositions. This process of 'detraditionalization' has also seen the withering of deference towards social and political authority and a sharpening of public expectations towards government – a process that has had profound effects on modern approaches to policing. The motifs of individual freedom and choice, and the attendant idea that public services can and should be tailored to the demands of individual citizen-consumers, have come to dominate the public policy agenda both in policing and elsewhere. Consumption more generally has moved to the centre of everyday experience, becoming a key marker of social identity and belonging. In short, market logics appear to be structuring ever more domains of social relations and public life.

As a result of these various shifts, individuals and organizations have come to understand themselves – or are encouraged to understand themselves – as being responsible for their own safety and security. Furthermore, they have also begun to view the market as the place where security solutions can be found, not least as a way of asserting greater control over their lives and freeing them from dependence on state pro-vision. Security and consumption have thus become entangled in various novel ways. When we speak of security, we now tend not only to think of the police, but also of pri-vate guards or devices such as alarms and security cameras. In addition, security has come to permeate consumption decisions that ostensibly have little to do with it – such as where to buy a house and what sort of house to buy. As a result, a range of non-security goods – such as mobile phones, membership of motoring organizations, and the ownership of a sports utility vehicle (Lauer, 2005) – have gradually come to be culturally rebranded and understood as 'security products'.

Finally, it is important to recognize that the commodification of security has also been accompanied by a blurring of the boundaries between the provision of domestic and national security, and between civilian and military security organizations. As large secu-rity companies have expanded their reach and become genuinely multi-national, secu-rity staff, products, and techniques are now able to move across borders with increasing ease, interacting with and frequently replac-ing their state-run counterparts. The emer-gence of transnational security operations raises serious questions not only about the quality and effectiveness of the services being provided, but also about the appropri-ateness of the state contracting out aspects of national security and military services. In other words, the commodification of security needs to be factored in when attending to the costs and benefits of globalization, and has brought with it the challenge of thinking about, and fostering, institutions of security governance at the international – as well as the national – level.

Benjamin Goold and Ian Loader

Associated Concepts: closed circuit televi-sion, fear of crime, pluralization, private security, responsibilization, transnational policing

Key Readings

Bayley, D. and C. Shearing (1996) 'The future of policing', *Law and Society Review*, 30 (3): 585–606.

Goold, B. (2004) *CCTV and Policing*. Oxford: Oxford University Press.

Jones, T. and Newburn, T. (1998) *Public Policing and Private Security*. Oxford: Oxford University Press.

Lauer, J. (2005) 'Driven to extremes: fear of crime and the rise of the sport utility vehi-cle in the United States', *Crime, Media, Culture*, 1 (2): 149–68.

Loader, I. (1997) 'Private security and the demand for protection in contemporary Britain', *Policing and Society*, 7 (3): 143–62.

Zedner, L. (2006) 'Liquid security: managing the market for crime control', *Criminology and Criminal Justice*, 6 (2): 267–88.

COMMUNITARIANISM

Definition

Communitarianism represents the body of ideas associated with the broad philosophical, political and sociological tradition in which there is a central and defining emphasis of the inherent sociality of humans. As a conse-quence of this key emphasis and domain assumption, the embedded individuals and groups that make up a society or community are viewed first and foremost as products of that determining culture. Both normatively and sociologically, communitarianism is criti-cal of individualistic, liberal, rational choice theories of social behaviour. In terms of its ideological and political freight, it may be characterized by both neo-conservative and to a lesser degree, radical socialist and social democratic variants. Communitarian ideas feed into much of the policy discourse around local policing and community safety.

Distinct features

This body of philosophical ideas has a het-erodox pedigree and in its contemporary manifestations is most associated with theories and policy recommendations which claim to break with the traditional ideas of both the political Right and Left. Thus within much contemporary communitarian thought, especially as crystalized and popularized in the policy recommendations of its leading North American proponents, both the market and the (welfare) state are seen as being dangers to the potentially vibrant 'third way' of bottom-up community processes. Crucially for criminological and policing research and commentary, the decline of vibrant and supportive communities in the increasingly atomized and individualistic 'me, me, me' culture of contemporary consumerist societies like the US is viewed by both conservative and radical communitarian thinkers as a major cause of heightened crime and disorder. Equally important to the contemporary politics of law and order, communitarians also see the 'reinvention' of cohesive local communities with all their informal means of social control as the key means of reinvigorating the fight against crime and disorder and for justice and security.

The most influential proponents of communitarianism and what is often termed 'social capital' theory are the US policy entrepreneurs and public intellectuals, Amitai Etzioni (1994) and Robert Putnam (2000). The work of these two figures captures the dominant appropriation of communitarian ideas in contemporary policy making, including policing, across the world, in which the 'loss of community' and 'decline in social capital' are interpreted as being a crucial source of a wide range of social problems, including of course, crime, disorder and violence. Etzioni has been the most prominent proponent of the moral conservative communitarian project aiming to undertake a whole-scale 'remoralization' of society in which a culture of rights and entitlements is to be replaced by, or at least rebalanced in favour of, the restoration of a culture of responsibility. In this project there is some harking back to a vision of a more stable, orderly and thus lawful past, best exemplified in the nostalgic imagery of small-town America.

Putnam's social capital arguments have stronger sociological foundations in empirical social science research but the logic of the idea of social capital is very close to Etzioni's call for remoralization via a reawakening of the 'spirit of community'. In broad terms 'social capital' relates to the ways in which values and mundane practices of individuals, families and communities can generate particular types of relationships and bonds. Accordingly, social capital is a concept which attempts to capture the social networks, norms of reciprocity, processes of bonding, trust relations and so on which may characterize different groups and communities. In criminological terms it suggests that the loss of bonding processes (as in ten-pin 'bowling alone' rather than 'bowling together' as a form of collective association) tends to produce adverse criminogenic consequences and heightened fear and distrust of such key public agencies as the public police. Again, the solution to this cultural decline and crime conundrum, symbolized by a loss of sense of community, is the reassertion of local networks and their norms of local and thus shared trustworthiness and reciprocity.

The best and most successful policing then, according to communitarian thinking, is by communities for communities through the largely informal mechanisms of social control. In these neo-Durkheimian terms, social capital or 'community capacity' (Sampson, 2001) is the glue that can bind society together and promote the flourishing of social solidarity and the prevention of anomie and disorder. Apart from support for vigilant 'self-policing' in the community, such as neighbourhood patrols and watch schemes, the conservative communitarian agenda appears to lend support to public shaming processes for deviants.

It should be noted that there is also an admittedly less influential radical, social democratic variant of communitarianism in which the principles of bottom-up solidarity, often forged out of struggles for economic equality and social justice, rules of reciprocity and the valorization of local democracy are to the fore, alongside the necessary 'repair' and 'healing' work of the state and public bodies like the police. Put succinctly, this is a left or radical communitarianism (Hughes, 2000) in which the vision of the good society is defiantly both a public (rather than private or club) good and pluralistic in nature. Such radical forms of communitarianism may be seen in the work of left and critical realists and civic republicans such as Braithwaite (Hughes, 2007). According to this body of work, recent decades across neo-liberal and neo-conservative societies of the affluent West have seen deterioration in social relations and in turn the virtual collapse of whole communities. Most perniciously, and with clear criminogenic consequences, radical communitarianism suggests that the poor have been denied access to majority goods and many have experienced majority power as unjust. Such processes of growing inequality and social exclusion do not destroy communities *per se*, but are likely to forge in some of the most ravaged localities, new forms of particularistic and 'lawless' communities in the absence of any notion of a shared public good. According to radical communitarian arguments, collective processes of marginalization, inequality and social and political exclusion lie at the root (as 'upstream' causes) of much crime, disorder and anti-social behaviour. As a consequence, this radical, social democratic criminology gives political and normative priority to decisions over both redistribution and reintegration. In turn, a politics of community safety and social crime prevention, alongside arguments for democratically accountable local policing, is prioritized over the dominant politics of enforcement and custodial exclusion.

Evaluation

The foregoing exposition of the key ideas and policy implications of the two major variants of communitarianism illustrates the polyvalence and ideological volatility of the idea of community writ large and, in turn, of social capital and community capacity building more specifically. Community – just like communitarianism in its various guises – remains a deeply problematic notion which is often derided for its capaciousness and dangerous seductions by sociologists and critical criminologists in particular. That said, it appears hard to live without community and the notions of bonding, trust, networks, and informal mechanisms associated with communitarian normative theories in both conservative and radical guises. Community may be a necessary fiction; not least for its capacity to evoke the fundamentally social and thus communal, shared and thus interdependent, quality of human existence and the fateful pull of the local on people's lives. Perhaps especially, the immobilized working class of the affluent West and the often traumatically mobilized populations of the world's poor. The processes associated with community breakdown and communal reordering, which communitarians of various ideological hues prioritize, remain central to policing debates across the world today and into the foreseeable future.

Gordon Hughes

Associated Concepts: accountability, community engagement, community safety, crime prevention, democratic policing, localism

Key Readings

Carson, W.G. (2007) 'Catastrophe or catalyst? Futures for community in twenty-first century crime prevention', *British Journal of Criminology* 47 (5): 711–27.

Etzioni, A. (1994) *The Spirit of Community: The Reinvention of American Society.* New York: Touchstone.

Hughes, G. (2006) *The Politics of Crime and Community.* Basingstoke: Palgrave.

Hughes, G. (2000) 'Communitarianism and law and order' in T. Hope (ed.) *Perspectives on Crime Reduction,* Aldershot: Ashgate.

Putnam, R. (2000) *Bowling Alone: The Collapse and Revival of American Community.* New York: Simon and Schuster.

Sampson, R. (2001) 'Crime and public safety: insights from community level perspectives on social capital' in S. Saegert, J.P. Thompson and M.R. Warren (eds) *Social Capital and Poor Communities: Building and Using Assets to Combat Poverty.* New York: Russell Sage Foundation.

COMMUNITY ENGAGEMENT

Definition

Community engagement is the process of enabling citizens to participate in policing by providing them with information, empowering and supporting them to help identify and implement solutions to local problems, and allowing them to influence strategic priorities and planning.

Community engagement is a difficult concept to define and operationalize. This is due in part to the difficulties associated with defining 'community', and some commentators prefer to use 'citizen' or 'public' engagement. The two concepts most often used in the literature to describe citizens' interaction with the police are 'participation' and 'involvement'.

Community engagement can comprise several forms of public participation and involvement. It can be relatively passive, whereby agencies provide citizens with information and reassurance. Agencies may also consult citizens and communities on specific issues and longer term policies and planning. More active involvement occurs when citizens become involved in working in partnership with agencies and service providers to make policy or implement projects and programmes. Active engagement can ultimately see agencies relinquishing a degree of decision-making power to communities.

Several typologies for community engagement exist. Arnstein (1969, cited in Myhill, 2006) proposed an eight-step 'ladder of participation', with 'manipulation' at the bottom and 'citizen control' at the top. Others, such as the International Association for Public Participation (see Myhill, 2006), have suggested a 'spectrum', with information at one end and empowerment at the other. Myhill (2006) proposed a pyramid-shaped typology for engagement specifically in the area of policing. The pyramid acknowledges the notion that a majority of citizens may wish to be involved only at the more passive end of a spectrum, receiving information and reassurance. Fewer may wish to participate in monitoring or consultation exercises, and fewer still may wish to be involved in joint problem-solving, or in influencing longer-term priorities and planning.

Distinctive Features

Community engagement can perhaps best be seen as a delivery mechanism. Community policing became the dominant model for policing in many countries towards the end of the twentieth century – including the US, Australia, New Zealand and the Netherlands – and is premised on greater interaction between the police and citizens. The rise of community policing approaches was in part due to the recognition that the 'professional' model of policing, dominant in many countries from the 1950s, had not been effective in tackling crime, and had resulted in disengagement between the police and communities – especially minority communities.

Direct citizen participation is also recognized as being important in relation to effective public accountability of the police. Accountability has two key aspects. First, in relation to officers' conduct, some police organizations, especially in the US and Australia, have sought to effect some degree of citizen oversight of the police complaints process. Second, engaging with communities can ensure public accountability for delivery of local policing services. Open public meetings have been the most popular mechanism for affecting this, though they have often been perceived as ineffective in fulfilling this role. Attendees of such meetings have rarely been representative of their wider communities, and discussions have often been easily controlled by the police and their government agency partners (see Myhill, 2006). In the UK and Australia in particular, surveys of public opinion are also widely used to gauge public opinion of police service delivery.

In the UK, in the new millennium, the term community engagement has been used increasingly by policy makers, police managers and practitioners. Neighbourhood policing – a form of community policing premised on tangible local areas and involving a significant emphasis on community engagement – was launched in

2004. The perceived importance of community involvement in local priority setting and problem-solving, and in ensuring accountability for service delivery, is such that most UK police forces and police authorities (the key accountability bodies in the UK system) now have documented community engagement strategies.

In the US, the term community engagement appears relatively infrequently in the literature. It appears most often in relation to securing citizens' participation in local problem-solving initiatives. Skogan et al. (2000) use 'public involvement' to describe citizens' participation in the well-known Chicago Alternative Policing Strategy (CAPS), both at local action and strategic monitoring levels.

Evaluation

There are relatively few large scale, robust evaluations specifically of community engagement. More often, aspects of engagement have been considered as part of wider evaluations, for example, appraisals of community policing programmes. Lack of empirical evaluation may also be partly because the concept is difficult to quantify. While it is relatively straightforward to assess the amount and coverage of engagement (typically numbers of and attendance at public meetings, and a range of other mechanisms used), assessing the quality and impact of engagement is far more difficult. It is comparatively easier to evaluate the implementation of engagement and there is consequently more available evidence on processes, barriers, and success factors. However, due to the difficulties associated with measurement, many community engagement projects and programmes are likely to remain unevaluated, or be subject only to impressionistic practitioner assessment.

Myhill (2006) conducted a review of international literature on community engagement. A large proportion of the empirical research came from evaluations of community policing programmes in the US. There is consistent evidence to support the theory and suggested benefits of engagement as a delivery mechanism for involving citizens in policing. Commentators claim effective community engagement will impact on a range of crime, safety and public satisfaction measures, by creating a police service that is responsive to community needs and concerns. Citizens are most likely to be aware of the underlying problems in their communities and neighbourhoods and their causes, and may be able to suggest effective solutions outside the scope of a traditional police response. Increased accessibility to, and familiarity with, police should provide public reassurance, promote trust and confidence, and lead to increased levels of community intelligence and cooperation. It is also suggested that the process of implementing engagement may in itself increase community capacity and communities' ability to become more self-policing.

Empirical evaluation evidence suggests that, where implemented well, community engagement has helped to deliver some of these benefits. The collated findings of several reviews of outcome studies on community policing (Myhill, 2006) reveal weak positive evidence of impact on crime; fairly strong positive evidence of impact on disorder, anti-social behaviour, feelings of safety and police officers' attitudes; and strong positive evidence of impact on police-community relations and community perceptions of the police. There was no robust evidence of impact on community capacity.

The largest and most sustained evaluation of community policing has taken place in Chicago during and since the 1990s (Skogan et al., 2004). By 2004, the Chicago Alternative Policing Strategy (CAPS) had been subject to ten years' evaluation. Though the programme has delivered some positive outcomes, the evidence relating to community engagement has been mixed. A high proportion of Chicago's residents (80 per cent in 2003) have heard of CAPS, and attendances at 'beat meetings' (the principal engagement mechanism) have risen slightly since the programme's inception. However, attendees are not usually representative of the wider community, and public satisfaction with the meetings declined between 1998 and 2003, with fewer people feeling that they are useful for promoting action to help tackle local problems. CAPS has had limited success in relation to engagement at a strategic level. Citizen involvement in its 'district advisory committees', intended partly to set priorities for policing, has also been unrepresentative and largely passive (Skogan et al., 2004).

Several key implementation issues for community engagement recur across evaluation literature from a range of countries (see Myhill, 2006). Key among these is a lack of organizational commitment from police agencies. Effective community engagement requires culture change – it must be mainstreamed as a way of working, not regarded as a specialism. Officers must receive training in the philosophy of engagement, as well as in specific methods. They must be given the operational freedom to engage in problem-solving. Community engagement and its associated activity must also be recognized in models of performance management. Many programmes of community policing have had limited success due to police organizations being unable, or unwilling, to adopt an engagement focus.

There is mixed evidence relating to communities themselves and the process of engagement. Many project and programme evaluations have reported difficulties in stimulating active community participation (Grinc, 1994). Some commentators suggest this can be as much a result of the police and their partner agencies not enabling or facilitating community involvement, as it is with public apathy (Long et al., cited in Myhill, 2006). Common problems are lack of internal capacity in organizations and lack of initial capacity building work with communities; failure both to let communities 'own' the process, and to tailor engagement to local circumstances; and an underestimation of the effects of historical relations and trust in the police in some – particularly minority – communities. Other commentators, however, perceive a lack of interest and inclination on the part of citizens to participate in initiatives to improve their local area and, in particular, disinclination to be involved in strategic level decisions relating to local policing (see Myhill, 2006). There is a key gap in the evaluation literature around citizens' and communities' own views of the engagement process.

Community engagement is likely to remain a prominent concept and mechanism for delivery in contemporary policing as long as community policing remains in favour, and as long as politicians and police managers perceive a need for public accountability in the way officers treat citizens and deliver policing services.

Andy Myhill

Associated Concepts: community policing, legitimacy, localism, problem-orientated policing

Key Readings

Grinc, R. (1994) '"Angels in marble": problems in stimulating community involvement in community policing', *Crime and Delinquency*, 40 (3): 437–68.

Myhill, A. (2006) *Community Engagement in Policing – Lessons from the Literature.* London: Home Office.

Skogan, W.G., Hartnett, S.M., Dubois, J., Comey, J.T., Twedt-Ball, K.T. and Gudell, J.T. (2000) *Public Involvement: Community Policing in Chicago.* Washington D.C.: U.S. Department of Justice.

Skogan, W. G., Steiner, L., Benitez, C., Bennis, J., DuBois, J., Gondocs, R., Hartnett, S.M., Young, K.S. and Rosenbaum, S. (2004) *CAPS at Ten: Community Policing in Chicago.* Chicago: Illinois Criminal Justice Information Authority, http://www.northwestern.edu/ipr/publications/policing.html.

National Practitioner Panel for Community Engagement in Policing (2005) *Guide to Community Engagement.* London: Home Office/Association of Police Authorities.

COMMUNITY POLICING

Community policing has been hailed by police organizations and academics alike as a major paradigm shift from the 'professional' model of policing – with its emphasis on expertise and a centralized, bureaucratic command structure – to an inclusive philosophy that promotes community-based problem-solving strategies and encourages partnerships between the police and communities in a collaborative effort to solve crime and disorder. Defining community policing has generated much conceptual confusion, however, despite its elusiveness, most commentators agree that community policing is about partnerships, consultation and building trust in communities. It is generally regarded as representing a major philosophy of organizational change, accompanied by a range of programmes and activities designed to reduce and prevent crime by increasing interaction and cooperation between local law enforcement agencies and the public, with a view to identifying and implementing strategies aimed at ameliorating community distress, crime and disorder and providing reassurance. It generally involves decentralization and proactive localized initiatives. It is not necessarily a one-to-one link between the police and the public, but often involves a web of linkages between the police, various organizations and the public.

While some countries have gone beyond the rhetoric and symbolism that has come to be associated with some forms of community policing, not all police organizations have been successful in making community policing part of their organizational structure and philosophy. In these organizations, while features of community policing are incorporated piecemeal into police activities, the reactive traditional modes of policing are predominant. This is particularly true in high performance cultures where individuals and the organization itself are part of a performance management ethos that emphasizes results and what can be measured. In other countries and jurisdictions, community policing has become part of the organizational fabric. In some countries such as the UK and the US, legislation and policy provide the parameters for such police activity; in other countries police organizations work within existing budgets to fund community policing initiatives. Other jurisdictions insist that they have always had a community policing tradition.

Community policing processes vary considerably and are driven by a variety of concerns – in some countries it has become the dominant philosophy and in others it is a secondary consideration. What we do know is, there is no 'one size fits all' model. In the following sections, experiences of community policing are discussed with reference to Australia, Canada, China, the Netherlands, the Nordic countries, New Zealand, South Africa, the UK and the US. The entries provide some understanding of the similarities and variants of community policing and point to some of the constraints around the implementation and efficacy of such a paradigm. Specific references are provided for further reading.

Jenny Fleming

Brogden, M and Nijhar, P (2005) *Community Policing: National and International Models and Approaches.* Cullompton, Devon: Willan Publishing.

Australia

Australia, like many Western democratic countries, has embraced the concept of community policing. Through their individual annual reports and strategic plans, Australia's eight police jurisdictions pledge their commitment to the process. Police commissioners emphasize the importance of 'being in partnership with the community' and publicly commit themselves to 'actively involving the community in preventing and reducing crime'. Police ministers talk about 'engaging the community and establishing partnerships to achieve a safer, more secure community'. Despite these various commitments to community policing, unlike in the UK and the US there are no formal policy parameters or legislation that compel Australian police organizations to undertake full scale community policing initiatives.

Policing in Australia is distinctive. A single jurisdiction will police the diverse needs of capital cities, towns, rural communities and remote bush communities. In addition, some jurisdictions have indigenous communities and vast geographical areas. Community policing initiatives take a variety of forms and reflect differences in organizational structures, leadership styles, existing governance structures, resource availability and geographical scope. As each jurisdiction has its own priorities and local context, the initiatives, and indeed the general activities, defy comparison on any level. Many of these programmes have won awards and many have been sustained over several years. Few such programmes or initiatives, however, are evaluated formally. Significant among the strategic approaches commonly adopted is a commitment to close community involvement and participation. The ability of police to form networks across professional groups, other public sector agencies and a variety of communities to address common issues, the obvious expansion of servicing, particularly in rural and indigenous areas, along with the creation of mechanisms to ensure feedback opportunities from communities and other interested parties, suggests that community policing, regardless of its flaws, has led to a more proactive understanding of the role of communities in police practice.

However, what Australian police organizations cannot boast is a commitment to a philosophy of policing that would imply a full scale approach to community policing. No jurisdiction has sought to restructure its organization with a view to institutionalizing community policing as the dominant policing paradigm. In 1990, community policing in Australia was described as a secondary policing activity rather than part of core police business. This is still substantially true today. Australian police organizations, while committed to community engagement, are also committed to corporate governance. Managing by objectives, performance management, accountability mechanisms and productivity are the key drivers of police business. Such preoccupations serve to mitigate against community policing as core business. Community satisfaction levels feature heavily in an organization's performance mandate, and a community's expectations of its police will shape and determine the way that organization conducts its business. While communities are still wedded to arrival times, the arrest of offenders and their own sense of safety and security as the determinants as to whether police are doing 'the job', Australian police organizations have no choice but to allocate their resources accordingly.

Jenny Fleming and Juani O'Reilly

Fleming, J. and O'Reilly, J. (2008) 'In search of a process: community policing in Australia', in T. Williamson (ed.) *The Handbook of Knowledge Based Policing: Current Conceptions and Future Directions*. Sussex: John Wiley.

Canada

The origins of the community policing movement in Canada can be traced to a broad recognition among academics and police reformers of the inefficacy of the utilitarian and professional policing model, which sought to prevent crime uniformly through random motorized patrol, rapid response to calls for service, and reactive investigation. Another part of this was public criticism relating to the social distance, and indeed tension, that this approach had generated between police and multicultural communities.

The first wave in community policing was thus concerned with improving community relations and enhancing an image of the police as a 'service' to all that is sensitive to multiple needs and interests. In the late 1980s, police endeavoured to be community-based through various public relations and cooperation enhancing initiatives like mini storefront stations, neighbourhood watch programmes, and public education campaigns such as 'Police Week', campaigns in shopping malls, and grade school visits by 'Elmer the Elephant'.

While this first wave was largely symbolic and devoted to 'community relations policing', it sparked a second wave of 'problem-oriented' policing (POP) (conceptually inspired by the Chicago School) centred on engendering greater community efficacy through active partnerships with communities in identifying and addressing local social problems that create the conditions for crime. Based on Goldstein's original 1979 formulation of POP, organizations like the Ontario Provincial Police and the Royal Canadian Mounted Police (RCMP) developed comprehensive community policing guides for their members, such as the RCMP's CAPRA Problem-Solving Model to help police officers engage the community in finding ways to reduce and prevent crime.

Police-led restorative justice (or 'restorative policing') has perhaps been the latest wave in Canadian community policing. In this case, the police facilitate a partnership-based approach to problem resolution after a criminal act occurs. The RCMP has been a leader in the promotion of Community Justice Forums, having designed and implemented training for its own rank-and-file as well as members from other police organizations.

These waves in community relations policing, problem-solving and restorative justice now coexist across Canadian police organizations in different combinations. They also coexist with standard practices of law enforcement that continue to be essential to the public police mission. Beginning in the late 1990s, Canadian police organizations have faced new security challenges at intra-jurisdictional, national and transnational levels, especially in the areas of Internet crime, organized crime and terrorism. Like other countries, Canadian police now advocate an 'intelligence-led' policing approach, and recognize that maintaining trusting relationships with communities is now more important than ever.

Jennifer Wood and John Deukmedjian

Wood, J. and Shearing, C. (2007) *Imagining Security*. Cullompton, Devon: Willan Publishing.

China

Although community policing in China was formally implemented in 2002, its practice was established in the early 1950s. With the establishment of police organizations in the People's Republic of China in 1950, Chinese police defined the community as the core of police work and placed a significant emphasis on community work and crime prevention. As a result, some Western policing experts have suggested that modern community policing began in China.

The reform and opening up of China in 1978 brought tremendous change and development to China, both politically and economically. At the same time, reported crime statistics increased rapidly from 890,281 in 1980 to 2,216,997 in 1990 and to 3,637,307 in 2000. Facing a severe social security situation and community uncertainty, Chinese police shifted the emphasis from crime prevention and reassurance policing to a focus on crime fighting. Unfortunately this effort did not decrease the crime rate as expected.

In its attempts to curb and prevent crime, and strongly influenced by the new rhetoric of community policing in the West, the Chinese police moved to restore the community policing model in 2002. In March of that year, the Work Conference of National Police Stations was held in Hangzhou, Zhejiang Province. At this conference, the Ministry of Public Security made the decision to implement community policing in cities throughout the country. Four years later rural areas also became part of this national initiative.

Under this scheme, both cities and rural areas were divided into different policing districts. Each district, involving about 3,000 residents, was generally managed by a community police officer who worked in the official Community Policing Office. Where districts had higher crime rates, two or more police officers were designated.

Community police officers are considered as professionals in their field and are experienced in community policing work. Their main duties are as follows: collection of information, household registration, social security and public order, crime prevention and public service duties generally. In order to perform these duties, community police officers also have to do such routine work as publicizing laws and knowledge about crime prevention, issuing security warnings, talking and listening to the community, mediating domestic disputes, helping and educating juvenile delinquents and assisting released offenders to adapt to civilian life.

Crime prevention is considered the most important task in Chinese policing. In China, there are strong foundations for implementing community policing. Grassroots community security organizations with distinctive Chinese characteristics, such as the Neighbourhood Security Committees, Community Security Teams (CST), Volunteer Patrol Teams and Community Security Guards are dispersed across the country. In order to prevent crimes effectively, community police officers are usually aided by several full-time CST members. They also organize and mobilize all community forces mentioned above to patrol neighbourhoods, especially in high crime areas, to enhance community security. In addition, community police officers have responsibilities to guide and supervise the security of businesses and cultural institutions situated in their policing district. By urging these organizations to install surveillance cameras, to enhance their regular security inspections and by disseminating security and preventive education, community police officers realize their goals to prevent crime and alert directors and staff of the importance of crime prevention and security measures.

Up to now community policing in China has had many achievements. There is now a much closer relationship between police and the public and a stronger sense of security in the community. However, problems and disadvantages still exist. For example, there is an imbalance in the development of community policing between the cities and the countryside and a shortage of trained professional community police officers generally.

Du Jinfeng

Jinfeng, D. (1997) 'Police-public relations – a Chinese view', *The Australian and New Zealand Journal of Criminology,* 30 (1): 87–94.

Netherlands

In this discussion of community policing in the Netherlands it is necessary to avoid any confusion of concepts. A distinction is made between a joint safety strategy (the broad field in which the various organizations and institutions work together) and local community policing (the role of the police within this vast area).

The joint safety strategy model consists of two basic elements: citizens and businesses, and three open rings:

(1) the social fabric;
(2) professionals and corporations; and
(3) the safety partnership, which includes the police.

Only a joint effort by all parties in the model can lead to long-term safety and security.

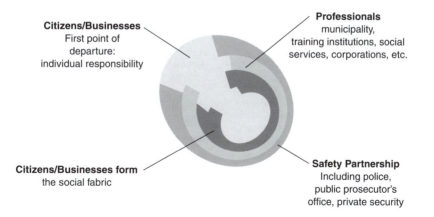

Citizens/Businesses
First point of departure:
individual responsibility

Professionals
municipality,
training institutions, social
services, corporations, etc.

Citizens/Businesses form
the social fabric

Safety Partnership
Including police,
public prosecutor's
office, private security

Figure 1

The joint safety strategy model as summarized above requires a specific interpretation of the social function of local community policing, one that stimulates the police to carry out core tasks, such as observation, surveillance, enforcement and (emergency) aid. This is combined with, for example, identifying problems and giving advice in order to contribute to the preservation of safety in the best possible way.

The leading view in the Netherlands is that the police should be close to the citizen, and that effectiveness should take precedence over efficiency. The added value of the police depends here on their continuous presence (24/7) in the frontline, helping resolve conflicts and safety problems. This objective requires a high degree of expertise on the part of individual officers on the beat. On the basis of their professional experience, they have to be able to employ discretion, assessing the situation and deciding which of the various forms of action available is the most suitable.

Police in a residential environment are often thought of as a 'best friend', the supervisor, who acts as a referee in the public domain, who knows and is known and uses relatively few formal powers. To be able to display different forms of conduct (friendly if possible, strict if necessary) weighs more heavily here than in other areas. In order to promote general safety, the local community police force should be able to organize the public to undertake action and, if necessary, mobilize other parties. That is why the police have to integrate socially within the boundaries of police policies; they must operate at the local level with a large degree of autonomy.

The definition of local community policing in the Netherlands is understood as:

> Within the context of the joint safety strategy, and on the basis of information collected systematically, a police force, which is organized intricately, offers – in collaboration with partners – clear-cut and tailor-made services to which the local community can relate. The core tasks are in this respect: to observe, to enforce, to provide emergency aid, to identify problems and to give advice.

Traditionally, the Dutch police focus on locations (areas, territories). Social processes, however, are more and more defined by flows of people, goods, money and especially information. The explicit attention the police pay to flows, where the nodes in the infrastructure serve as the point of intervention, is a new approach that calls for an appropriate new term: 'nodal orientation'.

Steendijk, Simone MPA

Punch, M., Van der Vijver, K. and Zoomer, O. (2002) 'Dutch "cop": developing community policing in the Netherlands', *Policing: An International Journal of Police Strategies and Management*, 25 (1): 60–79.

New Zealand

The centrality of community policing to contemporary discourses of governance in New Zealand, as in many other liberal democratic societies, is evident from the most recent police Statement of Intent, the introduction to which states that a safe, confident and fair community is one in which families, young and old, can participate fully in society, and individuals can realize their personal potential. Similarly, the activities of legitimate business are fostered in an environment where crime is effectively reduced and prevented. The safety of communities makes a vital contribution to achieving the government's goal of building a sustainable nation.

Rhetorical claims of community policing have featured in police policy documents for decades. In the 1970s, specialist agencies were established to foster police community relations, but these had a largely educational and advisory remit. During the 1980s, community policing developed as a crime prevention strategy that included, among other initiatives, the establishment of several thousand community crime prevention groups (Dance, 1985). In the 1990s, against a context of apparently inexorable rises in crime and in concert with international trends, the adoption of the ethos of community policing was most obviously manifest in the devolution of services to Community Police Centres in suburban neighbourhoods and the requirement for public consultation. Some commentators argue that the merger of road safety services with the police enhanced community policing because it more closely engaged the police with established networks of local relationships. Furthermore, techniques of risk analysis associated with road safety were spread to crime problems more generally and led to the targeted deployment of patrol officers. Providing public reassurance through the greater deployment of officers on patrol has been a political priority in recent years, although the extent to which the recruitment of more officers will actually provide for enhanced safety and security remains largely unresearched.

Community policing programmes in New Zealand face similar challenges to those cited in many other jurisdictions. Police culture and populist politics of law and order militate against a sustained move towards community policing. Demographic change is identified, by the police, as a significant future challenge for community policing. Ethnic diversity will accelerate in the decades leading up the middle of the twenty-first century which, for reasons of legitimacy and efficacy, is seen to require the recruitment of a more diverse workforce. Relatedly, traditional policing models based around small rural communities will become less appropriate to the increasingly urbanised metropolitan society of contemporary New Zealand.

Michael Rowe

Dance, O. (1986) 'The police and the community', in N. Cameron and W. Young (eds) *Policing at the Crossroads*. Wellington: Allen and Unwin.

Nordic Countries

Policing in Finland, Sweden and Norway could be called the Nordic way of policing. It is usually described as democratic, smooth and civilian in outlook and style. The Nordic countries are welfare states and policing reflects the egalitarian values of the societies and people. Community policing has been an important component in reducing crime and increasing public safety in the Nordic countries. In Sweden and Norway problem-oriented policing (POP) is the main strategy of implementing community policing. In Sweden, key concepts in community policing are high visibility policing and crime prevention initiatives in close cooperation with people who live or work in the community police area. POP in Sweden is focused on identifying the direct causes of crimes and public disorder. In Norway, the Norwegian Police Directorate initiated POP in 2002 as the principal method for crime prevention.

Finland, however, provides the best example of community policing in the Nordic countries. There has been a much longer tradition of community policing in Finland beginning in the 1960s when it was referred to as 'village policing'. The development and functioning of the police was peaceful and the police enjoyed a great deal of public confidence. There was a shift in thinking around community policing in 1999 with the introduction of the first national community policing strategy where the focus was on local safety planning and community safety partnerships, and where police were actively involved with municipal authorities, associations and residents with an emphasis being placed on community and customer orientation. There were changes also in police operational strategies and tactics, and a strong emphasis on the development of crime analysis, problem-solving and crime prevention. Changes in organizational structures have been less effective.

From 2000, the main ways of implementing community policing in Finland have been 'basic police work' according to community policing principles and local safety planning within community safety partnerships. The main aim of cooperation between governmental agencies, municipalities, voluntary organizations and private businesses is to set objectives and establish a local or regional safety plan. The purpose of the planning process is to build a continuing system of local security management, to share responsibility for security and crime prevention and to gain synergy advantages (that is, save resources).

The National Community Policing Strategy was launched by the Police Department of Finland's Ministry of Interior in 2007. According to the Ministry, 'community policing is managing the basic task of the police with quality and efficiency, in a citizen-focused manner'. The strategy includes sustainable local safety planning and community safety partnerships and a model of intelligence-led community policing. For the police the implementation of the community policing strategy will be an important part of the integrative security approach and the new Internal Security Programme (2008). It is also a part of implementing the European Union's Hague Programme (2005), which puts pressure on police organizations to implement community policing as a vital tool to counter local terrorism activity.

Sirpa Virta

Virta, S. (2002) 'Local security management: policing through networks', *Policing: An International Journal of Police Strategies and Management*, 25 (1): 190–200.

South Africa

The term 'community policing' in South Africa (SA) was first used in government policy in 1997 when the Department of Safety and Security published its formal policy document *Community Policing Policy Framework and Guidelines*. In this document, community policing is presented as a collaborative, partnership-based approach to (local level) problem-solving. Its logic was based on an acknowledgement that the objectives of the police can only be achieved through the collaborative efforts of the police with other government organizations and structures of civil society and the private sector. The organizing principle was that all available resources were to be mobilized to resolve safety problems and promote security. Many of these notions of community policing were 'imported' from other parts of the more 'developed' world.

The community policing narrative remains central to South Africa Police Service policy documents and is an integral part of the police basic training programmes. But 'community policing' in SA has now become focused on ways of mobilizing non-state actors to legitimize and increase the effectiveness of the police. Contrary to early conceptualizations of community policing in post-apartheid SA, talk about collaboration and partnerships is limited to conventional notions of the community assisting the police through providing information and supporting public policing initiatives.

Over the past ten years, new police narratives have come to overshadow talk of community-oriented policing. As crime, and fear of crime reached crisis levels in the 1990s, the language and strategies of police ministers and commissioners 'became more aggressive ... the new thinking emphasized cordon-and-search operations in which whole city blocks were closed down, doors were kicked in and anyone suspicious was taken in for questioning'. What we have witnessed is a remilitarization of police discourse (see Dixon, 2000). This trend is reflected in the commitments to increases in police numbers, and an almost exclusive focus on traditional indicators of police performance such as numbers of arrests and weapons seized.

Police leaders continuously make statements about mobilizing community members in the fight against crime. Community Police Forums exist as formal structures/mechanisms for police and community to come together to share problems and strategize, but in reality these forums are poorly attended, unrepresentative and police driven. This is not surprising as even in the early years of democratic government, there were signs that commitments to public empowerment were shaky.

What we find in SA is that public police bodies with serious fiscal and resource constraints are trying to reassert their authority in a manner that is incoherent and ineffective. At the same time, the state is determined to retain its monopoly over the authorization and provision of policing services. Public police are caught between two currents. On the one hand they are expected to expand their knowledge and capacities to meet the challenges of twenty-first century policing by forging deeper partnerships and by letting go of established notions of public policing. On the other hand, they are under pressure internally, and from the public to retain and demonstrate that they have the 'unique' skills, knowledge and capacity to 'own' the delivery of policing services.

This role confusion, combined with strong directives and close monitoring from the centre has had very worrying consequences. It has resulted in limited possibilities (and support) for local innovation and responsiveness. It has created the space for private companies with a very narrow set of interests to take over a range of traditionally public police roles. But, more positively, it also generates gaps or spaces for thinking more carefully about what the police should be doing, who they are, and what the 'community policing' project now means.

Monique Marks

Dixon, B. (2000). The Globalization of Democratic Policing: Sector Policing and Zero Tolerance in the New South Africa. Cape Town: Institute of Criminology, University of Cape Town, http://web.uct.ac.za/depts/sjrp/publicat/global1.htm.

United Kingdom

Though community beat officers have patrolled British streets since the 1960s, controversy about the definition, implementation and efficacy of community policing continues. In the 1970s, John Alderson, Chief Constable of Devon and Cornwall Police, a largely rural force, was the lone police advocate of community policing. However, following riots precipitated by the heavy-handed policing of young black Londoners in Brixton, the Scarman Report (1981) proposed the adoption of community policing as a means of enhancing police legitimacy and reducing urban disorder. After this, significant political investment was put

into the development of police consultative committees and the expansion of neighbourhood watch schemes. Around the same time, partnership (then called 'inter-agency cooperation') was first advocated by the Home Office. However, further urban disorder, combined with massive police deployment during the year-long Miners' Strike (1984–5), added to the politicization of policing and encouraged 'forceful', rather than community-based police solutions.

During the next decade, the introduction of New Public Management into public services caused the police to be preoccupied with 'value for money' rather than 'community'. Nevertheless, the partnership idea was consolidated in the Crime and Disorder Act 1998. The Act established Crime and Disorder Reduction Partnerships (CDRPs) (to include organizations from the public, private and voluntary sectors) and gave police and local authorities joint statutory responsibility in this area of activity. Under the legislation, CDRPs are required to audit crime and disorder problems in their areas, consult with members of the community and formulate three-year action plans for meeting specified targets.

Latterly, community policing has been reinvented in the guise of 'reassurance' and 'neighbourhood' policing. The former has arisen from growing disparity between recorded crime levels (going down) and people's fear of crime (going up). Reassurance policing involves police and other partners working together to identify, diagnose and deal with the 'signals' (for example, graffiti, poor street lighting) that cause concern within particular communities. Neighbourhood policing (called such because of growing awareness that 'community' overrides the diversity contained in neighbourhoods) will be implemented throughout England and Wales by 2008. Based upon the principle that local problems require local solutions that draw upon local knowledge, it is compatible with intelligence-led policing models. It is also part of a wider programme of police reform involving an enhanced policing role for accredited commercial and local authority security staff, police auxiliaries and volunteers (the so-called 'police extended family'). A national auxiliarization programme has led to the recruitment of Police Community Support Officers (PCSOs) (uniformed police civilians, in possession of limited powers, largely dedicated to patrol). Operationally, neighbourhood policing teams usually consist of one sergeant, two constables and four PCSOs.

Whether this 'extended family' model of neighbourhood-based policing will fare better than previous community policing experiments remains to be seen. Three immediate questions arise: whether neighbourhood policing is compatible with the wider centralizing tendencies of Home Office police policy; how well the 'brothers' and 'sisters' who make up the police extended family can be integrated; and whether a nationally-driven model can meet the particular needs of Britain's increasingly diverse local neighbourhoods.

Les Johnston

Johnston, L (2003) 'From "pluralization" to "the police extended family": discourses on the governance of community policing in Britain', *International Journal of the Sociology of Law,* 31 (3): 185–204.

United States

Community policing in the US is shaped by features of its policing system, which is decentralized, locally funded, localistic in leadership and culture, and highly responsive to politicians. There is no formula for how it should look, and no national performance standards to be met. However, so popular is the concept with politicians, city managers (who run most American cities) and the general public, that few police chiefs are without something they can point to as *their* programme. By 2003, a national survey found that more than 85 per cent of departments in cities of over 100,000 people reported having full-time, trained community policing officers.

But as a result of their diversity, cities claiming community policing point to a varied list of activities. Under the rubric, departments train civilians in police policies, open neighbourhood offices, survey community satisfaction, canvass door-to-door to identify local problems, publish newsletters, give crime prevention advice, patrol on foot, and help enforce health and safety regulations. In some areas residents participate in neighbourhood patrols as part of their city's programme, while in others they are just asked to call police promptly when crime occurs.

At root, however, community policing is an organizational strategy rather than any specific programme. It involves three central strategic commitments – to citizen involvement, problem-solving, and organizational decentralization. Effective community policing requires responsiveness to citizen input concerning the needs of the community, and it takes seriously the public's definition of its own problems. Adopting a community orientation requires that departments reorganize in order to provide opportunities for citizens to make their voices heard. Problem-oriented policing highlights the importance of identifying the causes which lie behind calls for police assistance, and designing tactics to deal with these causes. This is linked to community policing where the public is engaged in identifying and prioritizing neighbourhood problems. However, they often press for a focus on issues such as graffiti and building abandonment. These are 'non-police' in character, and traditionally this would be cause for ignoring the public's concerns. Community policing pushes police instead to form alliances with other service agencies in order to address such issues. Decentralization involves devolving authority and responsibility further down the organizational hierarchy, away from police headquarters and closer to where the work is actually being done and where solutions can be crafted to address specific problems.

Community policing in the US faces significant challenges. One is whether it can survive the withdrawal of federal financial support and attention that began in early 2001. A second is whether it can survive the 'Compstat' style of accountability management, in which top managers decide what is a success and hold mid-level managers to their standards. There is a risk that the focus of departments will shift away from community policing, back to the activities that better fit a centralized structure driven by data on recorded crime. The final question is whether community policing can live up to its promises; a recent review of research concluded that there was not enough evidence either way to assess its effectiveness.

Wesley Skogan

Skogan, W.G. (2006) *Police and Community in Chicago*. New York: Oxford University Press.

Associated Concepts: community engagement, crime prevention, localism, policing, problem-oriented policing, public reassurance

COMMUNITY SAFETY

Definition

A term used increasingly in both policy and academic circles to describe a local, multi-agency partnership approach to the reduction of crime and disorder alongside the fear of crime and disorder, and, more expansively, the promotion and achievement of public safety both for and by communities. By its very nature it defies neat compartmentalization either linguistically or organizationally and is thus marked by differing policy translations. Internationally community safety increasingly occupies the epicentre of the entanglements between policies of crime control and social welfare.

Distinctive Features

Community safety, like related notions and institutional practices of 'community' or 'neighbourhood policing', 'community justice' and 'community crime prevention', has achieved a growing policy salience in recent decades across many late modern societies. However, as a formal mode of local 'community governance' of crime, disorder and

safety it has to date been most pronounced institutionally in the UK (for an overview of this institutional context, the new expertise and policy outcomes, see Hughes, 2007).

Community safety emerged first in the UK in the 1980s among several metropolitan local authorities as a *local* governmental strategy, which sought to move beyond the traditionally public police-driven agenda of formal crime prevention. It gained nationwide institutional recognition in the so-called Morgan Report *Safer Communities: The Delivery of Crime Prevention Through the Partnership Approach* emanating from a standing committee of the UK Home Office in 1991. Community safety as a policy field is now institutionalized across the UK as a key component of local policing understood as multi-agency crime control and order maintenance, best exemplified legally in the Crime and Disorder Act 1998 in England and Wales (Hughes and Rowe, 2007).

Internationally the term community safety and its institutional embodiment as the practice of multi-agency partnership working is an increasingly salient feature of the 'preventive shift' and the new local policing across many contemporary late modern societies (Hughes, 2007). The acid test of progressive community safety policy and practice transnationally is arguably associated with attempts to govern what may be termed 'problem populations'. The term 'the governance of problem populations' captures the processes by which communities or populations get targeted in policies as people and places for intervention, due to their being perceived as both dangerous/'a risk' and simultaneously vulnerable/'at risk'. A striking and often tragic illustration of these processes is the recent history of community safety policies and practices targeted in Australia at its indigenous peoples, often termed collectively 'Aboriginal communities'. This population has been the object – as both victims and perpetrators of harms – of both national and local community safety priorities to reduce violent crime, anti-social behaviour, alcohol and substance abuse, family and child abuse and hate crimes (Blagg, 2008). There are lessons to be drawn more broadly about 'minority' issues from this most stark and disturbing example (see Hughes, 2008).

Evaluation

The policy and practice of community safety seeks to involve multiple 'social' agencies (for example, from health, fire, probation, youth, education, housing services) as well as the public police in both crime prevention and public safety promotion. According to critics, this new policy field is associated with the generation of the so-called 'criminalization of social policy' and allied process of 'governing through crime' whereby social problems (linked causally to poverty, educational and housing inequalities, etc.) only receive public attention on the basis of their criminogenic consequences rather than as a result of welfare needs and entitlements (Hughes, 1998). The example of the governance of indigenous peoples as well as other 'minority' populations often appears to illustrate this tendency. However, contemporary community safety policy and practice has also been associated with, and 'translated' in terms of, more ambitious claims both to generate greater participation and possibly leadership from all sections of the community (largely geographically defined), and to target social harms from all sources in the locality and not just those classifiable as 'crimes'. As a result of this mode of policy translation, community safety practices may possibly result in the reverse process of the criminalization of social policy, namely a 'socialization of crime control' (Edwards and Hughes, 2008). Again, examples of such trends are evident in some of the local, bottom-up community safety initiatives in Aboriginal communities in Australia (Blagg, 2008). Logically, crime and disorder reduction and crime prevention, and thus public policing itself, are subsets of community safety rather than its defining features.

Definitions of community safety – like that of 'crime prevention' and 'crime and disorder reduction' – will always remain the subject of intense debate and volatile and often contradictory translations, not least given that crime is a socially and historically contingent category.

Few academic commentators would dissent from the starting point that there is no universally accepted definition of either community safety or crime prevention (Crawford, 2007; Hughes, 1998). However, for the purposes of government and governance, it tends to be associated in the first decades of the twenty-first century with public actions aimed at a broad range of 'volume' crimes and increasingly, expressions of public 'disorder', particularly acts of 'anti-social behaviour' or 'incivilities' in specific 'problem' localities and communities. Such public actions in turn have often been focused on crime and disorder associated with young working class people, both as offenders and to lesser extent victims. Across both the routine day-to-day work of community safety partnerships and embedded in their longer term strategies it is striking that the problem of young people 'hanging around' and causing 'trouble' has been a persistent area of concern generally. Indeed it is rare to find a local partnership that does not prioritize the reduction of anti-social behaviour by young people as one of its key strategic objectives (Hughes, 2007).

At the more rhetorical level, community safety is a form of *both* crime prevention and public safety promotion *and* policing in the broadest sense that aspires to involve the participation of community members alongside formal agencies of the local state and quasi-formal voluntary and private agencies (Johnston and Shearing, 2003). In reality, research to date indicates that community safety 'work' is both 'owned' and driven by local government- and public police-dominated crime and disorder reduction partnerships (CDRPs) or community safety partnerships (CSPs), for example those often 'virtual' institutions set up under the terms of the Crime and Disorder Act 1998 in England and Wales. As the institutional manifestations of community safety, CDRPs and CSPs appear in reality to sit closer to the ambition of the new public management discourse than that of the politics, ideology and practice of community activism and communitarian crime control.

There remain striking tensions – perhaps contradictions – between the social inclusionary rhetoric and aspirations of community safety and the social exclusionary potential of crime and disorder reduction and repressive criminality prevention. According to a growing number of criminologists (Hughes, 1998, 2007; Johnston and Shearing, 2003; Edwards and Hughes, 2008), governmental logics such as community safety, crime prevention and security all necessarily involve political and normative and not just technological and administrative questions, despite the pretensions of the new so-called 'crime sciences', 'what works' experimentalists and more broadly managerialist ideology and practice. In accord with the famous distinction of the sociologist Charles Wright Mills, the concerns over prevention, fear and safety, and increasingly terror and 'homeland' security are both 'private troubles' for many individuals and 'public issues' related to the very structure and dominant processes at work in specific social formations. The potency – both instrumental and symbolic – of debates about crime and community safety, and policies designed respectively to reduce and increase their prevalence, is difficult to ignore. Perhaps the greatest challenge for community safety in the future for liberal and social democracies is getting the balance right, between local democratic control and ownership of both the problems and solutions to fear of crime and perceived lack of public safety and order, and the contribution of the expert, quasi-scientific administration to the management and solution of these pressing public issues in this digital age. In this context it is crucial to emphasize by way of conclusion that community safety, like that of 'public security', often becomes a metaphor for much wider moral and political questions about justice, social order and the 'good society'. Herein lies its centrality to the contemporary criminological imagination (Edwards and Hughes, 2008)

Gordon Hughes

Associated Concepts: communitarianism, community policing, crime prevention, problem-oriented policing, multi-agency policing

Key Readings

Blagg, H. (2008) *Crime, Aboriginality, and the Decolonisation of Justice.* Cullompton, Devon: Willan Publishing.

Crawford, A. (2007) 'Crime prevention and community safety' in M. Maguire, R. Morgan and R. Reiner. (eds) *Oxford Handbook of Criminology* (4th edn). Oxford: Oxford University Press.

Edwards, A. and Hughes, G. (2008) 'Inventing community safety' in P. Carlen (ed) *Imaginary Penalties.* Cullompton, Devon: Willan Publishing.

Hughes, G. (2008) 'Community safety and the governance of problem populations, in G. Mooney and S. Neal (eds) *Community: Crime, Welfare and Justice.* London: Sage.

Hughes, G. (2006) *The Politics of Crime and Community.* Basingstoke: Palgrave.

Hughes, G. (1998) *Understanding Crime Prevention: Social Control, Risk and Late Modernity.* Buckingham: Open University Press.

Johnston, L. and Shearing, C. (2003) *Governing Security: Explorations in Policing and Justice.* London: Routledge.

COMPSTAT

Definition

Compstat (alternative spellings COMPSTAT, ComStat, CompStat) refers to the policies, practices, systems and organizational structures subsumed by a revolutionary police management paradigm first developed and implemented by the New York Police Department (NYPD, US) in 1994 during the administration of Police Commissioner William J. Bratton. Although numerous authors have stated that Compstat stands for 'Computer Statistics', 'Compare Statistics' or other terms, they are incorrect. 'COMPSTAT' was simply the name of a computer directory where COMPSTAT's original programmer stored documents, rudimentary databases and computer files related to the process.

Distinctive Features

A key element of Compstat's operation is its operationalization of the 'broken windows theory' articulated by James Q. Wilson and George Kelling (1982). The theory holds that the minor crimes and 'quality of life' offences police often overlook or fail to enforce are in themselves criminogenic, and the incidence of 'serious' crimes including murder, robbery, rape, burglary, felony assault and vehicle theft can be dramatically reduced through the vigorous enforcement of 'quality of life' offence statutes. As in other jurisdictions where Compstat management systems are utilized, police enforcement activities in New York City focus on such 'minor' crimes as public intoxication, loitering, panhandling, prostitution, noise violations and other quality of life offences as well as on 'serious' felony crimes.

Compstat's utility as a crime control and accountability process is built around four primary 'Principles of Crime Reduction':

(1) timely and accurate crime intelligence;
(2) effective crime control strategies and tactics;
(3) rapid deployment of personnel and other resources; and
(4) relentless follow-up and assessment of results.

In the US context, these principles are operationalized at regularly scheduled Crime Control Strategy Meetings (CCSM) where headquarters executives meet with field commanders to identify emerging crime patterns and trends, develop and apply effective crime reduction strategies and tactics, organize and deploy resources to support those strategies and tactics, and assess the impact of their crime reduction efforts. These intensive strategy sessions focus the attention of the agency and its personnel on crime control issues, ensure field commanders' accountability for the enhanced discretion and control of resources they are afforded, and are intended to enhance the quantity and quality of communication and interaction between executives and operational commanders.

Compstat's CCSMs are the centrepiece of the management system. Compstat makes use of technology (including computerized statistical analysis, crime mapping and Geographical Information Systems) to quickly capture and analyze current crime statistics and to use these crime intelligence data to rapidly detect emerging crime patterns and trends. Once these trends and patterns are identified, police personnel and other resources are marshalled and deployed to make use of highly-specific strategies and tactics that are worked out at the CCSM and specifically tailored to the unique patterns they are designed to address. The efficacy of these strategies and tactics is scrutinized and rigorously assessed at subsequent CCSM where, if necessary, they can be adapted or modified to enhance their effectiveness. Importantly, these crime trends and patterns are continually monitored to ensure they are successfully eliminated and do not reemerge.

The basic processes of Compstat and the CCSM also permit executives to assess the capabilities as well as the management strengths and weaknesses of field commanders, to allocate resources where they are most needed and to become conversant with the unique crime conditions and the specific needs of individual neighbourhoods and communities. Compstat processes have also been adapted and put to practice in various forms and formats throughout the agency in order to address crime and other police management functions. Compstat principles have been applied, for example, to the management of police corruption and the internal investigative function (Henry and Campisi, 2004). Additionally, Compstat has been proposed as an effective model for the intra- and inter-agency collection and dissemination of intelligence necessary to combat terrorism (Henry, 2002).

A feature of the US Compstat process has been the emphasis on altering the department's structures, policies and practices to support a crime fighting mission, and the development of a body of strategic doctrine to harmonize the plans and approaches taken agency-wide to address crime and quality of life issues. As Henry has noted (2002),

Compstat's full effectiveness in achieving organizational goals and objectives demands that it be implemented as an overarching management paradigm or model for management practice rather than as a programme or overlay to traditional police practice.

These features of Compstat have been discussed in the US context, however, the basic principles outlined here are the key elements of Compstat programmes elsewhere. These programmes are variously called operational performance reviews, performance outcome reviews and Corporate Management Group Performance Reviews. It should be noted that while officials from many Western democratic countries have travelled to New York to review the Compstat approach, the operations of variants of Compstat are not simply exports or transplants from the US version. Such programmes need to be adapted to local circumstances. Even in the US, as Bratton and Malinowski point out (2008: 261), 'one size does not fit all ... the process as it is played out in New York City was very different from the way it now works in Los Angeles'.

Evaluation

In New York, the Compstat management system had an immediate and dramatic impact on the NYPD's capacity to reduce crime and improve quality of life. According to Bratton and Malinowski (2008), between 1993 and 1998 New York saw a 53 per cent drop in the burglary rate, a 54 per cent drop in reported robberies and a 67 per cent drop in homicide. The Compstat paradigm has been hailed as a 'revolution'. However not all observers have been as laudatory about its potential and its role in reducing crime. While many argue that Compstat can be credited with impressive reductions in crime and improvements in neighbourhood quality of life, others are not so positive about the 'New York miracle' (see, for example, Chilvers and Weatherburn, 2004). Others have suggested that despite its positive aspects, the process has the potential to distort performance because it fails to acknowledge the less tangible aspects of performance (Fleming and Scott, 2008). In Australia, the

NSW model has been criticized by senior police as 'management by fear' and by an external consultant as being too specifically focused on crime statistics as performance indicators.

Police Commissioner Bill Bratton, who was New York's Police Commissioner in 1994 and presided over the introduction of Compstat, now works in Los Angeles. He and Malinowski have argued recently that the confrontational process of Compstat operations is not conducive to assisting 'the most under-performing commands suffering from the most complex problems'. Compstat Plus has been developed with a view to incorporating Compstat principles of inspection and accountability as well as 'the use of more in-depth auditing methods, mentorship and close collaboration' with a view to 'measuring success, inspiring success [and] turning under-performance into achievement'. As Bratton and Malinowski (2008: 263) argue:

> Compstat inspections are most effective when conducted in a collaborative atmosphere that encourages discourse and respect for participants while avoiding pre-judgement and heavy-handed questioning.

As more Western democratic countries take up the potential and challenge of Compstat, we would expect to see this paradigm of the 1990s evolve positively to assist in management accountability in policing, business and the public sector.

Vincent E. Henry

Associated Concepts: accountability, broken windows theory, crime mapping, intelligence-led policing, managerialism, performance management

Key Readings

Bratton, B. and Malinowski, S. (2008) 'Police performance management in practice: taking Compstat to the next level', in Special Issue: Performance Management, *Policing: A Journal of Policy and Practice*, 2(3): 259–265.

Chilvers, M. and Weatherburn, D. (2004) 'The New South Wales 'Compstat' process: its impact on crime', *Australian and New Zealand Journal of Criminology*, 37 (1): 22–48.

Fleming, J. and Scott, A. (2008) 'Performance management in Australian police organizations', in Special Issue: Performance Management, *Policing: A Journal of Policy and Practice*, 2(3): 322–330.

Henry, V.E. (2002) *The COMPSTAT Paradigm: Management Accountability in Policing, Business, and the Public Sector*. Flushing, NY: Looseleaf Law.

Henry, V.E. and C.V. Campisi (2004) 'Current and future strategies for managing police corruption and integrity' in R. Muraskin and A.R. Roberts (eds) *Visions for Change: Crime and Justice in the twenty-first Century* (4th ed). Upper Saddle River, NJ: Prentice-Hall.

Wilson, J.Q. and G.L. Kelling (1982) 'Broken windows: The police and neighbourhood safety',*The Atlantic Monthly*, March.

CONSENT

Definition

'Policing by consent' refers to the ideal that police should operate with the support of the public, an ideal that was widely supposed to have been achieved in Britain in the first half of the twentieth century. In all democratic societies, police forces rely on the cooperation and support of the public to be effective and to gain political backing for greater power and resources. Consequently they have generally endeavoured to cultivate consent and legitimacy, with the worldwide fashion for 'community policing' in the last two decades being the most obvious example (Brogden and Nijhar, 2005).

The precise strategies pursued for achieving consent, and the degree to which they have been successful, vary according to particular forms of political economy and culture. Wilbur Miller's comparative history of the London and New York police, for example, shows that the Metropolitan Police adopted a variety of tactics to gain public support in the face of widespread opposition, especially from the politically and socially excluded working class, above all the cultivation of the appearance of strict legality, non-partisanship and identification with the communities policed. The New York police by contrast, established in a more egalitarian and less conflict-ridden social context, relied on the institutions of democracy to gain majority support, with consequent problems of apparently greater corruption, discrimination, and violence, especially against minorities (Miller, 1999). So successful was the London Metropolitan Police in its legitimating strategy that the notion of a peculiarly British style of policing, supposedly enjoying a unique degree of public consent, became an animating ideal of official discourse about British policing. It would be hard to find any major speech by a Home Secretary or a police chief, or any official inquiry into policing since the pioneering days of Sir Robert Peel, that does not invoke the legendary ideal of 'policing by consent'.

Despite its iconic status, however, the phrase 'policing by consent' is oxymoronic. Policing is an inherently conflict-ridden, potentially coercive mode of governance, concerned with the maintenance of dominant conceptions of order and the regulation of deviance, ultimately using legitimate force if deemed necessary. The establishment of modern, state-organized police forces in the early nineteenth century was a fiercely contested enterprise in Britain and the US, widely regarded as antithetical to the ideals of democracy and liberty that these societies espoused at least in principle. The founders of the modern British and American police were thus constrained to embark on a fraught project of legitimating the new institution in the eyes of the broad mass of the population.

Distinctive Features

At a fundamental level, the historical emergence of the police was related to a gradual limitation of violence in modern society. It involved the progressive concentration of the legitimate use of force, first in the sovereign power of the state, but then in the modern police as the specialist agency for maintaining order, which was mandated to deploy violence, in principle only as a last resort. In Bittner's seminal analysis, policing is thus 'a tainted occupation ... ambivalently feared and admired, and no amount of public relations work can entirely abolish the sense that there is something of the dragon in the dragon-slayer' (Bittner, 1970: 6–7).

The legitimacy of the police is bound to be tenuous and constantly subject to negotiation and redefinition, given the intimate relationship between policing, conflict and, ultimately, violence. 'Policing by consent', when the police enjoy a very high degree of legitimacy, is thus an ideal that may be aspired to, and perhaps approached asymptotically. It can never be achieved fully and always remains fragile. The legitimacy of policing is based only in part on what the police actually do, or even what they are perceived as doing. The fundamental sources of legitimacy lie in much broader social, economic and cultural processes, which the police themselves have little if any influence over. It is these that constitute the conditions of existence for success in police efforts to achieve legitimacy, structuring public expectations, perceptions, and how policing policies play out in practice.

The modern British police were established in the first half of the nineteenth century against a ferocious and complex opposition to their existence. While this lack of legitimacy survived among those socially marginal or excluded powerless groups that were the targets of police power and have been aptly labelled 'police property', the majority of the population had come by the middle decades of the twentieth century to regard the police as heroic symbols of national pride and security. 'Policing by consent' was in part achieved through the success of various strategies adopted by the founders of British policing intended to neutralize and win over opposition. These consisted of modes of recruitment, discipline and deployment that were designed to represent the police officer as honest, professional, impartial, efficient, bound by the rule of law, and embodying social consensus – 'citizens in uniform' in the phrase hallowed by successive Royal Commissions (Reiner, 2000: Chapter 2).

There is a tension within this set of police policies that sought the legitimation of the police. Some were directed at representing the police as bound by principles of justice and legality, others as effective and efficient law enforcers. The police are also vulnerable to *de*-legitimation, because they are perceived as either oppressive or as ineffective – with different sections of the population having varying priorities. This all reflects a fundamental tension in the police function: the police are responsible simultaneously for the reproduction of the conditions of any possible social order at all – 'general' order, and also of the patterns of power and privilege found within a specific society – 'particular' order. Their mandate encompasses both 'parking tickets and class repression' (Marenin, 1983).

Policing by consent involves walking a tightrope between these pressures, putting peacekeeping above law enforcement when necessary, as Peel, Rowan and Mayne (the first Commissioners of the Metropolitan Police) recognized, and Lord Scarman reemphasized in his 1981 Report on the Brixton riots. It is also vital to remember that the success of these policies depended upon wider social processes: the gradual and always tenuous incorporation of the mass of the population into political and economic citizenship, the decline of extreme inequality, and the pacification of social relations (Reiner, 2000: 50, 58–9).

Evaluation

In the last four decades there has been an increasing challenge to the tradition of policing by consent. There is evidence of declining police legitimacy throughout the Western world. In Britain this was associated with at least some reversal of the elements of policing that underlay the initial successful achievement of policing by consent in the nineteenth century. But the problems of legitimacy experienced by police around the world in recent decades are due primarily to wider developments in political economy and culture around the world. These have been described by such labels as 'post' or 'late' modernity, globalization and neo-liberalism, and have generated major transformations in the politics and practices of 'law and order' (Reiner, 2007). The preconditions of the construction of policing by consent, of the representation of the police as professional embodiments of the rule of law impartially and effectively providing security to all sections of society, have been undermined in particular by two major social changes. The first was the democratization of liberty and erosion of deference that is often characterized pejoratively as 'permissiveness'. Even more crucially the advent and eventual triumph of neo-liberal economics in the early 1970s fatally reversed the long march of social inclusion and produced a culture of egoism and anomie. This can be summed up as 'the calculus of consent': 'deepening social divisions + desubordination = declining consent' (Reiner, 1992: 683–86).

In the last three decades there has been a succession of reform attempts seeking to restore the lost legitimacy of the police, symbolized above all by the idea of 'community policing' (Brogden and Nijhar, 2005), indicating an agenda of a return to a supposedly lost mythic 'golden age'. But just as the preconditions of the successful construction of policing by consent lay in wider social inclusion, current projects of relegitimation will achieve their objectives only if the calculus of consent is addressed by reversing the growth of social inequality and division. Police reform in the absence of wider social surgery is a prescription for failure.

Robert Reiner

Associated Concepts: democratic policing, legitimacy, police property, postmodern policing

Key Readings

Bittner, E. (1970) *The Functions of the Police in Modern Society*. Chevy Chase, MD: National Institute of Mental Health.

Brogden, M. and Nijhar, P. (2005) *Community Policing: National and International Models and Approaches*. Cullompton, Devon: Willan.

Marenin. O. (1983) 'Parking tickets and class repression: the concept of policing in critical theories of criminal justice', *Contemporary Crises*, 6 (2): 241–66.

Miller, W. (1999) *Cops and Bobbies* (2nd ed). Columbus, OH: Ohio State University Press.

Reiner, R. (1992), 'Policing a postmodern society', *Modern Law Review*, 55 (6): 761–81.

Reiner, R. (2000) *The Politics of the Police* (3rd ed), Oxford: Oxford University Press.

Reiner, R. (2007) *Law and Order: An Honest Citizen's Guide to Crime and Control*. Cambridge: Polity Press.

CONTRACTUALISM

Definition

Contractualism in policing is the practice of police entering into agreements (often contracts) with third parties for the purpose of providing goods or services to them or obtaining goods or services from them. Third parties include other public sector agencies, businesses, community organizations and individuals. Where once police largely depended on their status as the embodiment of the state's monopoly on coercive force to obtain the assistance they needed to do their job, they are now increasingly reliant on such formalized arrangements of reciprocity. Examples of contractualism abound in policing's core areas of law enforcement and crime prevention. In some jurisdictions, private contracting of police personnel to provide general security or specialized patrol services is becoming increasingly widespread (Crawford and Lister, 2006; Ayling and Shearing, 2008). Contractualism is also evident in relation to the infrastructure that supports policing's core business, where goods and services are acquired from private suppliers through complex procurement processes.

Distinctive Features

Contractualism is not new to policing. Since Sir Robert Peel first introduced his 'bobbies' to London's streets, police around the globe have entered into contracts to purchase some goods and services from outside their ranks – such as stationery, uniforms and weapons and the services of janitors, caterers, publishers and builders. Likewise, some policing services, such as those involving the provision of information or licences, have generally been made available under contract for a price.

New forms of contractualism are now developing, however. Various services that were previously provided from within police ranks are increasingly being outsourced. Examples include aspects of forensic investigations such as fingerprint and DNA analyses, prisoner custody and transportation, financial management and information technology development. Some police organizations (such as the Australian Federal Police (AFP)) purchase the services of private security officers to guard their buildings. In 2005 Boston Police Department disbanded its fingerprint analysis unit and employed a private firm to undertake that function.

Police continue to charge fees to recover the costs of providing certain information, such as incident and accident reports or criminal histories, or of minor services, such as traffic escorts for long or wide loads. But more innovative forms of 'user-pays' policing services are now becoming available. In many jurisdictions, such as the Australian states of New South Wales and Victoria, police charge fees to provide security at public events. These may be community events (for example, festivals), or 'private' events, being held on private property for the profit of the organizer (such as rock concerts and sporting events). Some police organizations, particularly in the UK and the US, are being contracted by private interests to conduct patrols of privately owned

or controlled spaces, such as shopping malls and hospitals, often supplementing the services of private security officers employed there. Sometimes police services are contracted out on a large scale over a long term. In Nigeria, oil companies pay and control a public police entity, the Supernumerary Police, to provide unarmed security at their facilities. The Gold Stealing Detection Unit of the Western Australia Police is wholly funded by the mining industry under an agreement between the Western Australia Police and the Western Australia Council for Mines and Energy. The British Transport Police are 95 per cent funded by the rail industry. In Canada, city and town services in all provinces and territories, except Ontario and Quebec, contract with the Royal Canadian Mounted Police for policing services. The government of the Australian Capital Territory (ACT) purchases policing services from the AFP under an agreement between the responsible ACT Minister, the AFP Commissioner and the ACT Chief Police Officer.

Contractualism can also be observed in other areas of policing. Formal arrangements exist in many police organizations for assistance to police by citizens in both paid and voluntary capacities (for example, police reservists and auxiliaries, volunteers-in-policing programmes, informants, community patrols, etc.). Standardized arrangements are often adopted to govern donations to police organizations and sponsorship of policing activities by businesses and other groups in return for acknowledgement or other benefit. Contracts also regulate police merchandizing and intellectual property rights licensing. Northumbria Police in the UK, for instance, charge fees to writers, broadcasters and film makers for whom they provide police expertise in the form of advice, premises, chaperoning, labour and equipment.

All in all, police are becoming involved in the commercial marketplace on a hitherto unseen scale as both vendors and purchasers of goods and services, including security services. These developments stem from the adoption, over the last three decades or so, of private sector management approaches (managerialism) across the public sector, not only in the Western industrialized world but also more recently in some developing countries, such as South Africa. Public sector agencies, including police, have experienced pressures to be more efficient in the allocation of resources. As a result, these agencies have turned to outsourcing, sponsorship and commercialization as ways to save costs and bring in extra resources.

Much of the scholarly debate over contractualism in policing has focused on the risks involved in such activities (Hancock, 1998; Ayling and Grabosky, 2006). Evidence has shown, for instance, that the assumption that outsourcing cuts costs and maintains or raises quality is not always borne out. Moreover, costs and quality are not the only contentious issues. Police themselves debate which activities are appropriate for outsourcing and where the line between 'core' and 'non-core' tasks should be drawn for that purpose. Some spectacular instances where police contractual relations with private providers have led to legal proceedings and/or resulted in huge cost blow-outs (such as the New Zealand Police's agreement with IBM in the 1990s to develop an Integrated National Computerized Information System) have raised doubts over whether police are trained and equipped to properly negotiate and manage often expensive and complex contractual arrangements with third parties, and whether the risk management strategies and oversight mechanisms in place are adequate and effective. Other risks of outsourcing arrangements include the potential for corruption of involved police; possible impairment of a police organization's skills base, a loss of training opportunities for officers and damage to officers' morale; an overdependency on particular suppliers and the possibility of regulatory 'capture'; difficulties in identifying the locus of liability where injury or loss occurs as a result of an outsourced activity; and the potential for a dilution of accountability. When contractualism involves police participating in the marketplace either as service providers (Ayling and Shearing, 2008) or through sponsorship arrangements (Grabosky, 2007), the debate

has focused on the appropriate extent of this participation and its implications for policing as a public good. For example, whether police should seek to compete with providers of private security or other commercial services. If so, under what conditions, and what are the ramifications for the provision of general policing services if they do?

Evaluation

The commodification of policing, whereby policing is packaged and promoted as a thing that can be traded, is sometimes regarded as jeopardizing the equitable distribution of police services (Loader, 1999; Crawford and Lister, 2006). When some can afford to pay police for services or to purchase outsourced or privatized policing services, and others cannot, there is a risk that inequitable or 'tiered' policing will develop, with taxpayer funded public policing targeted at coercive policing of the less fortunate. Inequities in the delivery of services inevitably endanger the legitimacy of public policing itself. Commodification also raises the prospect that private interests might exercise more influence than is appropriate on police priorities and manner of service provision, and that more affluent citizens might come to resent subsidizing through their taxes the provision of services to the less fortunate.

Some scholars, however, have suggested that commodified policing need not be antithetical to the public interest. Outsourcing can provide benefits such as efficiency gains and the availability to police of a wider skills base and more resources. Transparency and accountability may be assured through the adoption of safeguards to mitigate risk, including training, monitoring, reporting and audit systems (Ayling and Grabosky, 2006). User-pays policing may be conducted in such a way as to be compatible with public interests and the provision of public goods. Fees can be charged for selected services in a manner sensitive to public needs, such as through a graduated waiver scheme. Police may also use a fee/waiver scheme as a market regulator, steering private interests towards reducing their consumption of police resources over time by encouraging them to minimize the risks their activities pose to public safety and order (Ayling and Shearing, 2008). Carefully managed contractualism may in fact improve police productive efficiency and further the public interest.

The debates over the value of contractualism and the place of police in the commercial marketplace are likely to continue both within police organizations and among scholars. It seems certain, however, that a complete withdrawal of police from the market environment is now unlikely and that new forms of contractualism will develop, further blurring the distinction between public and private spheres in security governance.

Julie Ayling

Associated Concepts: commodification of security, managerialism, privatization, private security, third party policing

Key Readings

Ayling, J. and Grabosky, P. (2006) 'When police go shopping', *Policing: An International Journal of Police Strategies and Management*, 29 (4): 665–90.

Ayling, J. and Shearing, C. (2008) 'Taking care of business: police as commercial security vendors', *Criminology and Criminal Justice*, 8 (1): 27–50.

Crawford, A. and Lister, S. (2006) 'Additional security patrols in residential areas: notes from the marketplace', *Policing and Society*, 16 (2): 164–88.

Grabosky, P. N. (2007) 'Private sponsorship of public policing', *Police Practice and Research: An International Journal*, 8 (1): 5–16.

Hancock, L. (1998) 'Contractualism, privatization and justice: citizenship, the state and managing risk', *Australian Journal of Public Administration*, 57 (4): 118–27.

Loader, I. (1999) 'Consumer culture and the commodification of policing and security', *Sociology*, 33 (2): 373–92.

CORRUPTION

See Civilian Oversight; Misconduct

COVERT POLICING

See Criminal Investigation; High Policing; Intelligence Agency

CRIME ANALYSIS

Definition

Crime analysis involves a set of systematic processes that aim to identify patterns and correlations between crime data and other relevant information sources, for the purpose of supporting decision-making that informs the design, allocation and prioritizing of police activity and crime prevention responses. Its benefits also extend to supporting the maximum use of the limited resources available for tackling crime, providing an objective means for identifying, understanding and explaining crime problems, initiating proactive actions in detecting and preventing crime, and taking advantage of the volumes of information that are collected by the police and other agencies (Osborne and Wernicke, 2003).

Crime analysis endeavours to provide the 'right information ... to the right people at the right time' (Fletcher, 2000: 114). It should not just support the monitoring of performance, nor offer only descriptive interpretations of crime issues, but should effectively understand the nature of the problem, contain explanatory content (that is, explain why the crime problem exists) and help identify specific means of how the problem can be effectively tackled.

Distinctive Features

Crime analysis has developed alongside the paradigm of intelligence-led policing, and supports the increasing requirement for measuring outcomes and the integration of research into operational strategies. It also has foundations in problem-oriented policing. This is an approach whereby formal criminology theory and scientific research methods are applied to the analysis of crime issues to conduct an in-depth examination of the crime problem, develop informed responses, and assess their impact (Boba, 2003). The developments in information technologies used in policing and the requirement to monitor police performance have also contributed to its growth. Crime analysis has therefore evolved to respect the need for an intelligence-led, problem-oriented and evidence-based approach to tackling crime.

The 3i model (Ratcliffe, 2004) offers a useful mechanism for illustrating the role of crime analysis in policing (see Figure 1). It contains three structures (criminal environment, intelligence/analysis unit and decision-makers) and three processes (interpret, influence and impact). In this model the criminal environment is assumed as being a permanent feature, though the boundaries are fluid and dynamic, requiring continual analysis and observation. This environment needs to be understood for any policing action to be effective. The first stage requires this criminal environment to be interpreted to create a pool of intelligence that understands and explains the problem – that is, the criminal environment must be analyzed. The second stage requires outputs of this analysis to form intelligence that influences decision-makers. These decision-makers must possess the skills to be able to interpret the results from crime analysis, understand why crime occurs, know how to intervene and reduce crime, and have a positive impact on the criminal environment.

Viewing the structures and processes that are involved in policing and crime reduction in this manner helps to identify where analysis plays its role and how it contributes to the other parts of an organization. Analysis should be in a position to interpret the criminal environment and its outputs should form a major part of the intelligence that is used to influence the actions of the decision-maker who then brings about a positive impact on the criminal environment.

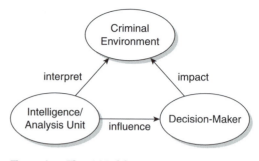

Figure 1 *The 3i Model*
(Source: Ratcliffe, 2004)

Evaluation

Contemporary crime analysis is increasingly recognizing that an effective approach to analyzing crime problems requires an understanding of the specifics of the issues (Clarke and Eck, 2003). The nature of being crime specific most typically requires the analysis to be local, exploring particular neighbourhood and situational features that identify the probable cause to the crime problem. For example, in a study of vehicle thefts in Central London, the Metropolitan Police overcame an organizational perception that the problem was related to residents' cars being stolen outside their properties at night by identifying that each area where vehicle theft was a problem had different unique and specific qualities. In one area, for example, vehicle thefts were predominantly of motorbikes, scooters and mopeds, from non-residents of the area, most usually from motorbike parking bays during daylight hours.

Crime analysis is also developing to recognize that police information systems may offer only a narrow view of the criminal environment, and that by working with local partners the understanding of the problem can be improved, including considering how a multi-agency response (rather than a single operational police response) can address the problem. These developments are occurring at a time when many other public services are becoming increasingly neighbourhood oriented in their delivery. For example, the language of local service delivery in the UK places emphasis on neighbourhood wardens, regeneration programmes that focus on neighbourhood renewal, local community engagement through neighbourhood forums, and more recently in policing, via neighbourhood policing.

As the pressures to adopt a neighbourhood focus have increased, so too has the demand for ever richer, more accurate data. Over time, accuracy has improved with crime data content being better recorded, but the inadequate use of applying standards still remains (for example, standards for entering the make and model of a vehicle, the type of building that is targeted, the name of a person, or an address) which in turn can constrain the production and the content of crime analysis. Future developments will require the better application of standards to data recording if an intelligence-led approach that is being adopted in many areas of the world is to be fully realized.

Data that can be extracted from recording systems provide only 'hard' data materials, that is, data that are recorded in response to reported incidents or calls for service. Hard data may help reveal many qualities of a crime problem but may miss many other issues and characteristics. The intelligence gaps arising from using hard data alone are increasingly recognized with many police agencies now seeking to draw on softer data sources. This includes data that are gathered by proactive interaction and engagement with the community (such as neighbourhood surveys or visual audits), and identification of issues that either go unreported or are difficult to capture in formal incident reporting. An example of this is the signal crimes perspective, developed by Innes and Fielding (2002), where an incident (that may not necessarily be a crime, but can be an event that prompts the public to react and behave differently to protect their safety) may act as a form of 'warning signal' that is disproportionately influential in causing a person or persons to perceive themselves as being at

some degree of risk. This type of community intelligence is acutely situational, and can depend on a range of factors, not least the person's life experience. The incorporation of hard data alongside more qualitative considerations in crime analysis poses several unique challenges, but these must nevertheless be addressed as part of an intelligence-led approach that tackles neighbourhood issues through improved performance (reflected in reductions in crime) and effective reassurance of and engagement with the public.

Spencer Chainey

Associated Concepts: crime mapping, evidence-based policing, intelligence-led policing, problem-oriented policing, technology

Key Readings

Boba, R. (2003) *Problem Analysis in Policing.* Washington DC: United States Police Foundation.

Clarke, R. V. and Eck, J. (2003) *Become a Problem Solving Crime Analyst in 55 Small Steps.* Jill Dando Institute of Crime Science: London.

Fletcher, R. (2000) 'An intelligent use of intelligence: developing locally responsive information systems in the post-Macpherson era', in A. Marlow and B. Loveday (eds) *After Macpherson: Policing After the Stephen Lawrence Inquiry.* Dorset: Russell House Publishing.

Innes, M. and Fielding, N. (2002) 'From community to communicative policing: signal crimes and the problem of public reassurance', *Sociological Research Online,* 7 (2).

Osborne, D. A. and Wernicke, S. C. (2003) *Introduction to Crime Analysis: Basic Resources for Criminal Justice Practice.* New York: The Haworth Press.

Ratcliffe, J. H. (2004) *Strategic Thinking in Criminal Intelligence.* Sydney: Federation Press.

CRIME MAPPING

Definition

Crime has an inherent geographical quality. For a crime to occur it involves an offender and a suitable target coming together at a location. It also involves the offender originating from a location and travelling along a particular route (if the location of the crime is different to the offender's origin), illustrating that other elements that result in a crime occurring also display geographical qualities. Understanding the role that these geographical qualities play in the act of committing a crime can offer vital clues that contribute to improving how policing agencies can respond to crime problems and detect offenders.

Crime mapping is the direct application that comes from considering this inherent geography in crime. Crime mapping draws from geographical and environmental criminology theory to help explain why crime occurs, and most usually makes use of geographical information systems (GIS) to capture, analyze and visually interpret these geographical qualities.

Distinctive Features

The study of crime has traditionally been the preserve of other disciplines such as sociology and psychology and it was not until the late 1970s that the geographical dimension to crime began to be more fully explored. This subset of mainstream criminology, known as environmental criminology, is the study of criminal activity and victimization and how factors of space influence offenders and victims (Bottoms and Wiles, 2002). Developed alongside these theoretical considerations were new techniques for identifying geographical concentrations of crime, the exploration of relationships between crime and environmental characteristics, and techniques to assess the effectiveness of geographically targeted policing programmes (Chainey and Ratcliffe, 2005). These techniques did though require a suitable computing environment to help them to be effectively applied.

At a similar time to developments in environmental criminology, GIS began to emerge as a discipline. Beginning in land use applications in Canada, it then grew through applications that included supporting the automation of cartographic drafting, and acting as a platform into which imagery could be displayed and analyzed for the purpose of military intelligence gathering. Developments in GIS use in policing took until the 1980s to emerge, in large part due to computer hardware prices being too prohibitively expensive before this time, and because of new developments in computer software. GIS use in policing also had to wait for the computerization of police records to begin for the realization that this material could be used in crime mapping.

The early use of GIS for mapping crime was often held back by organizational and management problems, issues with sharing information, technical problems, and geocoding issues. These problems were shared with many of the other industries and disciplines trying to implement GIS, and it took several innovators to resolve these problems and show how they could be overcome. In reality several of these problems still persist, but many have also been overcome through the developments in the practical use of GIS technology (Chainey and Ratcliffe, 2005).

Innovators in crime mapping include the US National Institute of Justice's Mapping and Analysis for Public Safety (MAPS) programme. The MAPS programme has raised awareness of crime mapping, not just in the US but also internationally, through seminars, conferences and publications, and by developing crime mapping software tools. Other leading innovators include academics at Temple University (Philadelphia, US), Simon Fraser University (Vancouver, Canada), and the Jill Dando Institute of Crime Science at University College London (England), who all apply a close sense of operationalizing new techniques and theories by working directly with policing agencies (for an example, see Johnson, 2008).

Crime mapping contributes to policing by helping to generate a real understanding of criminal activity and providing direction in tackling it. Examples of its use include:

- Responding and directing police calls for service;
- Collecting data at the scene of a crime;
- Supporting the briefing of operational police officers;
- Identifying and interpreting crime hot spots for targeting, deploying and allocating suitable policing and crime reduction responses;
- Through pattern analysis with other local data, helping to effectively understand the crime distribution and explore the mechanisms, dynamics and generators to criminal activity;
- Catching serial crime offenders (geographic profiling);
- Supporting reassurance policing; and
- Monitoring the impact and performance of targeted policing and crime reduction initiatives.

Evaluation

Examples of crime mapping applications and their successes are beginning to be published. These publications also identify pitfalls and challenges that may hold back its application, and offer ways in which these can be addressed (see Chainey and Tompson, 2008, and Home Office, 2005 for a comprehensive range of examples). Examples of its practical and effective use include supporting intelligence development and investigations.

As regards intelligence development, Hampshire Constabulary in England set a target to reduce vehicle crime by 17 per cent in the town of Portsmouth between 2001 and 2004. In the first year they had little success with increases of 16 per cent and further increases being projected. They decided that whatever they were doing was not working and that they needed to consider the application of new techniques that would help them tackle this crime problem. One of the main techniques they applied was to explore the geographic patterns of crime. This helped them identify that 10 per cent of vehicle

crime occurred in just 12 of Portsmouth's 1600 streets – something they had not previously realized. Their new crime reduction strategy focused problem-solving responses to these worst affected areas. Its impact – 33 per cent reduction in thefts of vehicles across Portsmouth, and a 37 per cent – 58 per cent reduction in vehicle crime in areas that had been determined as 'hot-streets'. These reductions were not dependent on large additional resource inputs (existing resources were used in a much more focused way) and, as described by Chief Inspector Julie Earle who led the work, 'during parts of the Operation, due to competing resource priorities offender based activity had to be completely suspended, yet reductions in crime continued to be sustained from just focusing on victim and location work alone.'

In its contribution to the investigative process, geographic profiling has become a proven technique to aid serial crime investigations. It has been fundamental in supporting many serious serial crime cases in several countries around the world. One example includes Operation Lynx in West Yorkshire, England. Between December 1982 and July 1995 a series of rapes in and around the city of Leeds led to the biggest police manhunt in the UK since the Yorkshire Ripper case. All the police had to go on was a partial fingerprint of the offender, and knowledge that he was between the ages of 35 and 52 and likely to have a criminal history for minor offences. The geographic profile identified that he was likely to live in a particular area in Leeds. This helped turn the investigation to records held within police stations in this area. The investigation identified the offender within a matter of days from fingerprint records that were held at the second police station where records were searched.

In terms of future developments, advances in computing technology have brought opportunities to apply more sophisticated analysis of geographical patterns and implement technology such as global positioning systems into operational policing (such as through the use of in-car or handheld computing technology – see Home Office, 2005 for an example).

Greater use of Internet-based crime mapping tools is also beginning to emerge to support the publication of neighbourhood-level crime statistics to the public.

To date, geographical analysis of crime patterns in policing has generated descriptive material that helps identify geographical patterns of crime (such as crime hot spots) but has yet to fully embrace more sophisticated forms of analysis that have emerged from geographical information science. New developments that are expected in crime mapping include:

- Analysis of the significance of geographical patterns – spatial significance testing identifies geographical patterns that are statistically considered to be unusual or significant;
- A harmonization of the geographical and temporal exploration of crime patterns, so that each are explored together and as a continuum rather than in isolation, and as a snapshot of the past;
- The development of local spatial regression techniques to help answer why crime occurs at certain places;
- Spatial modelling that tests 'what if' scenarios such as predicting what impact additional police patrols in an area may have on crime levels; and
- The development of techniques that predict where and when crime will occur in the future (see Johnson, 2008 for an example).

Spencer Chainey

Associated Concepts: crime analysis, criminal investigation, hot spots, technology

Key Readings

Bottoms, A.E. and Wiles, P. (2002) 'Environmental criminology', in M. Maguire, R. Morgan and R. Reiner (eds) *The Oxford Handbook of Criminology*. London: Oxford University Press.
Chainey, S.P. and Ratcliffe J.H. (2005) *GIS and Crime Mapping*. London: Wiley.

Chainey, S.P. and Tompson, L. (2008) *Crime Mapping Case Studies: Practice and Research*. London: Wiley.
Hirschfield, A., Brown, P. and Todd, P. (1995) 'GIS and the analysis of spatially-referenced crime data: experiences in Merseyside, UK', *International Journal of Geographical Information Systems*, 9 (2): 191–210.
Home Office (2005) *Crime Mapping: Improving Performance*. London: Home Office Police Standards Unit: http://www.jdi.ucl.ac.uk/ crime_mapping/crime_mapping_guide/ind ex.php.
Johnson, D. (2008) 'The near repeat burglary phenomenon', in S.P. Chainey and L. Tompson (eds) *Crime Mapping Case Studies: Practice and Research*. London: Wiley.

CRIME PREVENTION

Definition

Crime prevention seeks to intervene in the processes and conditions that cause criminal events. It can be targeted at the general population, vulnerable locations or people and known offenders. Many core police activities are defined as having a preventive impact such as patrolling or the targeting of prolific offenders. Crime prevention is not limited to police related activities. It encompasses a range of practices (for example, youth mentoring, nurse home visitation, parental training, improved street lighting and property marking) and can occur in a variety of settings (such as communities, car parks, shopping centres, housing estates and pubs). The activities of different social institutions are related to crime prevention such as those occurring in the contexts of schools and families. Crime prevention is practised by both corporations and individuals who adopt routine precautions to protect sensitive information and property. Crime prevention techniques address proximate causes of crime by reducing criminal opportunities, such as situational crime prevention or crime prevention through environmental design, or focus on modifying distal, remote causes, within the family, neighbourhood or community context that render some people far more likely to commit offences than others. This includes developmental crime prevention.

Distinctive Features

The General Instructions of the London Metropolitan Police 1829 emphasized that the principal objective of the police should be the prevention of crime. To this effort, resources were directed towards uniformed patrols and regular visible police beats. Today many taken for granted features of modern policing are presumed to prevent crime such as motorized patrolling, rapid response to police calls for service, criminal investigation and apprehension. However, the preventive capacity of these modern customary police practices can be called into question. Many are largely reactive and fail to address the causes of problems coming to the attention of police (Sherman and Eck, 2006). Many police tactics may not necessarily prevent crime or improve community safety. For example, results from the famous Kansas City patrol experiment conducted in the 1970s, raised doubts about the capacity of motorized patrols to reduce levels of crime or fear of crime (Kelling et al., 1974).

Crime prevention continues, however, to be regarded as a key police function, with police organizations moving to endorse crime prevention as a core policy through the implementation of initiatives concerned with community policing and problem-oriented policing. Many police organizations have been instrumental in promoting the adoption of crime prevention through environmental design (CPTED). In both the UK and the Netherlands Police, architectural liaison officers provide advice to private sector bodies about how to incorporate crime prevention design principles into building developments. Such efforts have required that police forge cooperative relationships with external agencies and groups. This partnership approach is a distinctive feature of crime

prevention policy and practice worldwide. It underpins many national and local strategies and is based on the premise that crime is by nature complex and beyond the capacity of any one agency to address – particularly the police. Hence, crime prevention partnerships allow for the coordination of effort, expertize, information and the pooling of resources which affords a multi-level, comprehensive response to crime.

Police crime prevention partnerships have occurred at a number of levels and have been initiated through formal and informal mechanisms. The most well known police community partnership aimed at crime prevention is neighbourhood watch. In the UK police and local authorities are mandated to work together in 'crime and disorder reduction partnerships' to develop local crime prevention plans. Formalized community partnerships have been facilitated through police policy such as has occurred in the Australian jurisdiction of Victoria under Local Priority Policing (Palmer and Cherney, 2001). Police have initiated collaborations with the private sector to identify and address practices that provide opportunities for crime, for example in relation to the irresponsible serving of alcohol or the sale of precursor chemicals required for the production of illicit drugs. In UK and US jurisdictions, police have forged partnerships with particular groups to facilitate the collection of intelligence that can help prevent terrorism. Research indicates however, that developing crime prevention partnerships can be a challenging task, particularly in achieving cooperation between different groups with often conflicting demands and priorities. Such conflict can be particularly pronounced in community crime prevention programmes as illustrated in evaluation of the U.S. community based strategy Weed and Seed. This involved police action to 'weed out' prolific and known offenders through arrest and prosecution, coupled with 'seeding' initiatives that included the provision of social programmes. However some communities resented and resisted the weeding phase, demanding more social welfare support (Miller, 2001).

Evaluation

In relation to the crime prevention function of the police, the key issue for police and policy makers is not 'do the police prevent crime?', but 'how can the police prevent crime?' Police have a key role in crime prevention; the central question raised by police scholarship is where best should police resources be focused to maximize crime prevention outcomes?

This question is particularly pertinent given that many institutions and individuals outside of the police have a 'policing' function in a broad sense and thereby contribute to crime prevention (for example, place managers such as private security personnel, property managers, bar staff, concierges, store assistants or capable guardians such as parents, peers, employers or teachers). Also, much that passes for police crime prevention relies on pre-emptive surveillance and information gathering which is predicated on the willingness of individuals, agencies and communities to share information with the police. Hence in order to improve their crime prevention capability, a critical issue for the police is to identify ways they can best act as brokers of public safety, engaging external agencies to take on greater responsibility in the prevention of crime.

Work to maximize the police crime prevention function has also led to greater scrutiny of police policies and tactics through evaluation methodologies that empirically measure crime reduction outcomes. This has led to a rethink of traditional police practices such as random patrolling. For example, evaluation evidence indicates that patrolling is far more effective when it is directed and focused on high crime areas (Sherman and Eck, 2006). Evaluating police crime prevention practices is also important because they can, in some circumstances, produce counter productive outcomes such as displacement of crime to another location, or even to a more serious type of crime. Crime prevention research has noted how interventions can produce differential impacts (preventing crime in some locations but not others, or reducing offending among a particular target group but not another) and should be kept in mind when designing and implementing prevention schemes (Cherney, 2006).

Enhancing the crime prevention function of the police has also required the adoption of new technologies that help the police more systematically analyze crime problems. In this regard, the use of geographical information systems has become an important tool in improving the analytical capacity of the police to identify crime hot spots (locations where crime is concentrated) which assists police to formulate place-based prevention strategies. There are jurisdictional variations though in the extent to which police organizations engage in crime prevention activities with community policing and problem-oriented policing largely remaining the purview of specialist areas or left to the initiative of individual officers (Tilley, 2003).

The key future challenge facing police leaders is ensuring that processes are in place to encourage and assist police in developing and implementing crime prevention approaches. Commitment to a more evidence-based approach in which evaluation becomes an ingrained part of police policies and practices is critical to such an objective. An evidence-based approach also requires an understanding of theory, because crime prevention techniques are underpinned by explicit theories about how they achieve their preventive effects (Cherney, 2006). Understanding these underlying mechanisms is essential to ensuring that crime prevention strategies are tailored to the nature of the crime problem in question. Enhancing the police crime prevention function requires commitment to theory, evidence and evaluation.

Adrian Cherney

Associated Concepts: community engagement, community policing, multi-agency policing, policing, problem-oriented policing, situational crime prevention

Key Readings

Cherney, A. (2006) *Problem Solving for Crime Prevention*, Trends and Issues in Crime and Criminal Justice No. 314. Canberra: Australian Institute of Criminology, http://www.aic.gov.au/publications/tandi2/tandi314.html.

Kelling, G., Pate, T., Dieckman, D. and Brown, C. E. (1974) *The Kansas City Preventative Patrol Experiment*. Washington: Police Foundation.

Miller, L. L. (2001) *The Politics of Community Crime Prevention: Implementing Operation Weed and Seed in Seattle*. Ashgate: Dartmouth.

Palmer, D and Cherney, A. (2001) "'Bending granite?' Recent attempts at changing police organizational structures in Australia: the case of Victoria Police", *Current Issues in Criminal Justice*, 13 (1): 47–59.

Sherman, L. and Eck, J. (2006) 'Policing for crime prevention', in L. W. Sherman, D. P. Farrington, B. C. Welsh and D. L. MacKenzie (eds) *Evidence Based Crime Prevention* (revised edition). New York: Routledge.

Tilley, N. (2003) 'Community policing, problem oriented policing and intelligence-led policing' in T. Newburn (ed.) *Handbook of Policing*. Cullompton, Devon: Willan Publishing.

CRIMINAL INVESTIGATION

In its traditional form, criminal investigation involves the application of standard techniques and practices to establish the circumstances of an act or event which appears at first sight likely to involve a breach of the criminal law, to identify and (where appropriate) apprehend and question possible suspects, and to gather sufficient information and evidence to bring one or more of them to justice. In this form, it is normally a precursor activity to a criminal trial involving a common set of activities and methods. While these are elements that apply across jurisdictions, international differences apply in terms of the judicial framework in which criminal investigations are carried out, and the governance arrangements applying to the investigative process as part of the wider structures of police accountability and the parameters of police powers.

In adversarial justice systems, typically located in Anglophone, common law jurisdictions, the police 'own' the investigative process. In such systems, the court sits in arbitration between the prosecution and the defence, and having made an allegation it is the role of the prosecution to prove their case beyond reasonable doubt. Inquisitorial criminal justice systems, in which the process is controlled by the judiciary, are present in most other European, civil law jurisdictions as well as Scotland's 'mixed' legal system. The court's role in inquisitorial systems is one of a tribunal, establishing the facts of a case and striving to identify the 'truth', so that the judge has a much more active role in directing the proceedings and calling and questioning the witnesses. In practice in such systems the police fulfil the greater part of the investigative role, with minimal supervision from prosecutors and magistrates except in the most serious or sensitive cases, but they are expected to conduct their work in a detached and impartial way.

There are structural limitations in both adversarial and inquisitorial systems as regards the maintenance of acceptable standards for the prosecution of cases. For example, in the adversarial system the prosecution has far greater resources than the defence, including the services of the police. Campaigners against serious miscarriages of justice, one of the gravest outcomes of police misconduct in the investigative process, have led calls in the UK to replace existing structures of justice with inquisitorial processes. Yet the inquisitorial system's inherent trust in the integrity of government – including its police – to do right may also be open to challenge, particularly as societies become more diverse. Its approach may be questionable if there is mistrust between the state and the community. Moreover, in both systems, investigators and criminal justice personnel are involved in constructing an account of the criminal event that inevitably involves translating 'social reality' into 'legal reality'. This requires interpretative activity, even of what might be considered the most scientific of 'evidence', such as DNA. More generally, the integrity of both types of system may be threatened by the political and media pressures generated by the law and order politics that now prevail in many Western countries. The particular fascination with major criminal cases is reflected in the extensive press coverage often devoted to these.

There are two approaches to criminal investigation: reactive and proactive, although these are not mutually exclusive. The former begins with the discovery and reporting of a potential crime, and its goal is to bring the perpetrators to justice by identifying the suspects and uncovering the evidence required for the court to determine their guilt. The investigative process involves interviewing victims, witnesses and suspects, examining crime scenes and linking the suspect to the offence through forensic, and other, procedures. The latter, alternatively described as 'intelligence-led' investigation, is oriented less to securing immediate convictions and more towards managing and controlling criminal groups and individuals. Proactive investigations are usually instigated as a result of intelligence analysis that an individual or group is involved in criminal enterprise, often organized crime.

The growing emphasis on proactive methods acknowledges the problem of low reporting by the public of serious crime, and the need for alternative information sources; and reflects the growing status of new analysis disciplines, often staffed by civilians, in the investigative infrastructure. Ratcliffe ('intelligence-led policing', this volume) notes how the concept of 'intelligence-led policing', which emphasizes proactive approaches and has its foundations in UK policy reports from the 1990s, has gained currency internationally, extending to continental Europe, Australasia and, post 9/11, the US.

The following sections examine four major areas of investigative practice in more detail, under the headings of forensic strategies,

interviewing strategies, profiling strategies and surveillance strategies.

Stelfox, P. (2008) *Criminal Investigation*. Cullompton, Devon: Willan Publishing.
Maguire, M. (2008) 'Criminal investigation and crime control' in T. Newburn (ed.) *Handbook of Policing* (2nd edn). Cullompton, Devon: Willan Publishing.

Forensic Strategies

Forensic science is the application of the natural sciences to the analysis and interpretation of evidence relating to criminal activity. It can involve any of the scientific disciplines but the main fields include chemistry, biology, pathology, entomology, psychology, dentistry/odontology, engineering, geology and anthropology. 'Criminalistics' is a term often used interchangeably with forensic science, although in practice it refers to the work of forensic investigation scientists employed in forensic laboratories in police departments or other public agencies, including dedicated organizations such as the UK's Forensic Science Service, as well as private companies. The label 'forensic' derives from the Latin word *'forensis'* meaning 'of the forum', the forum being the central public square of an ancient Roman city in which business and public affairs – including legal procedures – were conducted.

The collection of forensic evidence can occur at a crime scene, in other locations relating to the crime, or directly from victims, suspects or witnesses. It needs to be processed with absolute care to avoid contamination, misinterpretation or loss of evidence. Crime scenes should be rapidly secured to preserve the integrity of recovered material, and materials recovered by trained personnel. Forensic examination of such material can support a number of investigative objectives including helping to clarify the circumstances of the offence, eliminate or incriminate suspects and corroborate the accounts of victims, witnesses and suspects.

Forensic science evidence is also known as 'trace' evidence, reflecting the words of the pioneering French police inspector Edmond Locard in 1910, 'every contact leaves a trace', and can take a great many forms. Bodily samples, the most commonly used forms of physical evidence, along with fingerprints (McCartney, 2006) include blood, hair, semen, saliva, sweat, faecal matter, stomach contents and organs. These can be analyzed for DNA, which is used to associate a victim or offender with a crime scene; or in order to establish their properties and effects (a branch of science known as serology), including testing for drugs or poisons, or blood pattern analysis to reconstruct a crime scene. Fingerprints, DNA and other anatomical, physiological or behavioural human characteristics (ranging from iris pattern to the sound of a person's voice) are forms of biometric evidence that can be used for identification or verification of identity ('biometric' being a combination of the words 'biological' and 'measurement'). Other examples include:

- Documents, which may be handwritten, typed or printed materials examined for the purpose of determining their authenticity or source;
- Drugs and controlled substances seized in an investigation and subject to testing for drug presence, identity and quantity;
- Materials such as fibres, glass, paint, plastic and wood which may, for example, show cross-transfer between persons and/or objects;
- Impressions such as tyre markings, footprints, bite marks, fabric impressions or tool marks;
- Fire debris and explosives residue; and
- Firearms and ammunition.

The expansion of forensic science in the investigative process brings with it a number of benefits and concerns. It can speed up the investigative process, improving the efficiency of the criminal justice process and supporting the prosecution of the guilty. It can be and has been, used to exonerate the wrongly convicted. On the other hand, forensic science processes and practices require close supervision, adequate resourcing and

regulation to ensure the integrity of evidence and avoid errors and abuse, and they are not infallible. Human rights concerns may legitimately be raised by such practices as the non-consensual collection of bodily samples, and retention of information in large forensic identification databases such as the UK's National DNA database. We may even ask whether the pace of scientific development is promoting hasty law making: as McCartney notes, 'Police powers have been extended to keep up with science and technology, raising the question of whether the technology itself is dictating the development of the law and police powers' (2006: 64).

McCartney, C. (2006) *Forensic Identification and Criminal Justice: Forensic Science, Justice and Risk*. Cullompton, Devon: Willan Publishing.

Interviewing Strategies

The management of victims, witnesses and suspects is a fundamental aspect of all investigations, and successful investigations are dependent on quality material being obtained from them. The manner in which this process is handled by investigators has an important bearing on the supply of evidence to assist the investigator, as well as interviewees' perceptions of the criminal justice system. Investigators therefore need to take account of the anxieties that interviewees may feel, including trauma from the events that have taken place or fear of the consequences of giving information; their diverse social, cultural and religious needs; and possibly the need for medical treatment or security.

In the case of witnesses, including victims, investigators need to assess prior to the interview whether they are vulnerable (for example, in terms of age, intelligence or disability/disorder) or intimidated (such as by reason of age, culture or other personal circumstances, or the behaviour of the accused or their associates). Specialist interviewing skills may be required for the interviewing of vulnerable, intimidated and/or 'significant' or 'key' witnesses whose evidence is seen to have significant evidential value, including eye witnesses and those with important relationships to central parties in an investigation.

When a suspect in a case is identified, an investigator has to decide whether they can or should be arrested. If there is no power of arrest, the consent of the suspect is required for some investigative strategies such as an 'interview under caution' or a 'noncustodial interview'. Where grounds to arrest are present, investigators need to consider the planning of the arrest, such as resourcing, logistics, whether to conduct simultaneous searches to recover evidence, and timing. Relevant factors in the latter case may relate to whether the suspect poses a risk to the victim, witnesses or public; will commit further offences or will remove or falsify evidence; or whether further surveillance is needed.

Interviews of victims, witnesses and suspects should be planned in accordance with guidance on investigative interviewing (see also 'investigative interviewing', this volume). In the UK, the Home Office developed seven principles of investigative interviewing in 1992, and these continue to underpin UK practice as well as having been adopted by other Western jurisdictions. Schollum (2005: 26) argues, 'Any policing jurisdiction needs a similar list of principles, which in turn must be understood by all officers. They provide the foundation for ethical interviewing, and can make a striking contribution to public confidence in police'. Her literature review for the New Zealand Police also includes an examination of how the seven principles have stood up to evaluation, and describes some of the internationally recognized interview models.

The PEACE model for interviewing victims, witnesses and suspects was launched in the UK alongside the seven principles, and has been implemented to varying degrees in other jurisdictions such as Australia, New Zealand, Canada and Europe. The model requires of investigators a core set of skills relating to the preparation for, and execution of, the interview, with the acronym standing for 'Planning and Preparation', 'Engage and Explain', 'Account Clarification and Challenge', 'Closure' and 'Evaluation'.

The interview process presents potential for police misconduct ranging from duress and threat to torture, examples of which are well documented in the misconduct literature. A shift can be noted in police terminology from 'interrogation' to 'investigative interviewing', reflective of a strategic movement away from questioning for the purpose of obtaining a confession, towards questioning for the purpose of gathering information. This is intended to escape the negative connotations associated with the term 'interrogation', and to improve confidence in evidence gathered from police interviews. Past miscarriages of justice, such as those in the UK involving suspected Irish Republican Army terrorists, have hinged on convictions mainly based on confessions, despite allegations of coercion. Relatedly, a movement towards 'ethical interviewing' which advocates a less dominant and more respectful and positive approach to the suspect has, in recent years, gained significant international currency.

Schollum, M. (2005) *Investigative Interviewing: The Literature*. Wellington, New Zealand: Office of the Commissioner of Police, http://www.police.govt.nz/resources/2005/investigative-interviewing/.

Profiling Strategies

Profiling, in relation to policing, is the practice of discerning crime patterns. It may be applied to *people*, for the purpose of identifying suspect groups or individuals, or of predicting individual behaviour; or to *crimes*, identifying patterns in order to inform strategic decision-making and the allocation of policing resources. Whether used independently or in combination, such techniques may be employed in criminal investigations for the purpose of identifying suspects and avenues of inquiry, and their expansion in policing is a further reflection of the growing status of proactive methods.

'Offender profiling' is a source of public and media fascination, often misrepresented in fictional depictions of the expert detective with the ability to get inside the 'mind of the killer'. Alison et al. (2007) review its origins, in the work of the US Federal Bureau of Investigation's Behavioural Science Unit in the 1970s to develop techniques to assist investigations into serial killings, noting that the practice of profiling suspects developed as a way of narrowing down large suspect populations or identifying new directions of inquiry.

Aspects of an offender profile may include the perpetrator's gender, age, ethnicity, marital status, employment, educational level, criminal career and temperament, personality and behavioural characteristics. The profiling of victims, in terms of their behavioural and personal characteristics, may also help illuminate the victim-offender relationship. Profiling strategies, including Criminal Investigative Analysis, Investigative Psychology and Crime Action Profiling, can be used to assist a criminal investigation in a number of ways: investigator decision making, intelligence-led policing, investigative interviewing, informant handling and prioritization of suspects (Alison et al., 2007: 501).

A more prevalent form of profiling is 'geographic profiling': the collection and analysis of data to identify locational concentrations of crime ('hot spots') and relationships between environmental characteristics and crime, and to evaluate subsequent policing responses. Its foundations are in environmental criminology and particularly the research and theory of Brantingham and Brantingham, whose work draws attention to criminogenic conditions in the built environment. Analysis of the criminal environment provides a starting point for contemporary strategic policing models such as problem-oriented policing, Compstat and intelligence-led policing.

In the course of their work, the police collect huge volumes of calls for service data and crime data, much of which is recorded in computerized databases. Geographic profiling provides a way of managing such large volumes of data. Analysis of such data, by trained analysts using software products such as Rigel, Dragnet and CrimeStat, may reveal geographical or temporal skews in the locations in which crimes occur. Such patterns are illustrated by crime mapping, which historically has been illustrated by 'pin maps' (revealing offence clusters by means of pins on a map), and is today (in well resourced jurisdictions) supported by specialist Geographical Informations Systems (GIS) software packages. The proliferation of computerized databases to support police work means there is increasing scope for the linking of data on crime incidents and other data sources such as suspect and motor vehicle databases, and technological advancement is certain to render such methods a major area of future growth.

Alison, L., McLean, C. and Almond, L. (2007) 'Profiling suspects' in T. Newburn, T. Williamson and A. Wright (eds) *Handbook of Criminal Investigation.* Cullompton, Devon: Willan Publishing.

Ashby, D. and Craglia, M. (2007) 'Profiling places: geodemographics and GIS' in T. Newburn, T. Williamson and A. Wright (eds) *Handbook of Criminal Investigation.* Cullompton, Devon: Willan Publishing.

Surveillance Strategies

Another aspect of proactive investigation is the gathering of intelligence using covert methods. As well as being common to police work, such methods constitute the primary strategies of national security agencies, whose activities are secretive by definition and have become increasingly targeted against terrorism and organized crime since the end of the Cold War. Intelligence generated by covert or other means may be strategic, for the purpose of identifying patterns and trends of criminal activity, or tactical, for immediate operational use to further an investigation. Much of the information collected through covert strategies remains as intelligence rather than becoming evidence used to support prosecutions, often due to agencies' reluctance to require informants to testify or reveal their surveillance methods.

Technological surveillance methods available to police, intelligence agencies and other public authorities include interception of telephone and electronic communication, listening devices, access to mobile phone records and financial trails and, in the case of high policing agencies, photography and communications interception via satellite. Covert human intelligence sources consist of undercover police and informants. Undercover policing strategies include the following of suspects and recording of their movements, sting operations whereby covert officers entice likely offenders to commit crimes and then make arrests (for example, disruption of drug markets through 'buy-busts'/ 'test purchase operations' against drug sellers or 'reverse stings' against buyers, or the establishment of false storefronts directed at penetrating illegal fencing operations) and the infiltration of criminal networks. Confidential 'informers'/'informants', usually known or former offenders, typically trade information in exchange for indemnity from prosecution or discounted sentences, or financial gain. Their use involves a reliance on individuals of dubious integrity, emphasizing the need for well defined authorization, handling and supervision procedures.

Covert methods are becoming more prevalent in police work, due in part to the heightened threat of terrorism internationally. The need to balance public safety and human rights' objectives places a particular importance on the presence of effective systems of governance and accountability. The use of covert methods should be proportionate to the seriousness of the crimes being investigated. Appropriate authorization procedures and accountability structures must govern access to communications data in order to preserve public trust and confidence. Effective police supervision is of particular importance where undercover work is concerned since, as noted by Lee and South (see 'drugs', this volume) low levels of supervision and the potential for high financial reward offer incentive and opportunity for corruption. The secrecy associated with such policing activities, however, routinely places them beyond the radar of such mechanisms.

Alison Wakefield and Fiona Brookman

Marx, G. (1988) *Undercover: Police Surveillance in America*. Berkeley, CA: University of California Press.

Associated Concepts: accountability, crime analysis, crime mapping, intelligence agency, intelligence-led policing, investigative interviewing, misconduct, search

CROSS-BORDER POLICING

Definition

A term that refers to forms of social control involving the deployment of surveillance, backed up by the potential to threaten or use coercion that transgresses formally demarcated geographical boundaries. Modern policing has primarily been understood to concern the internal social order of states, but there is ample historical evidence to suggest that policing power has been deployed internationally, albeit on a relatively small scale, throughout the modern period. Theories that concern policing in its fully transnational aspect have framed it in terms of high and low policing, taking place under public, private or hybrid auspices and, further, have incorporated aspects of globalization theory, network theory, and theories about the impact of information technologies on social organization. Some authors argue that the technological underpinnings of globalization are leading in the direction of a globalizing surveillance apparatus with distinctly totalitarian tendencies, albeit under a variety of simulations whereby the liberal democratic legacy can be made to substitute for liberal democratic practices. Other scholars focus on border enforcement and migration control in the reproduction of nation state sovereignty.

Distinctive Features

Controlling populations and territory is an essential aspect of policing. Early ethnographies of beat policing revealed the importance of craft knowledge concerning the significance of formal boundaries for police patrol units. For example, the displacement of trouble from one beat to the next was an often observed feature of territorially based policing, whether or not such displacement took effect as the result of formal or informal (subcultural) policy choices. Boundaries are both a tactical and strategic resource for policing. By the 1990s advances in communications and transportation technologies led some theorists of globalization to suggest that the modern state (which had been built with the more limited technologies of an earlier age) might be practically transcended as governance became transnational and, eventually, global in scope. Since the police were understood to be the keystone of modern executive government it was hypothesized that, like the proverbial canary in the mine, transformations in policing would be indicative of the character of this newly emerging social and political form.

Historical studies of international policing reveal that, in order to better guarantee the internal order of nationally bounded societies, it has sometimes been thought necessary for policing agents to undertake international police missions. For example, in the nineteenth century, a variety of European policing agencies undertook cross-border surveillance because of concerns about anarchist agitators and other political radicals. A notable example of this was the occasional surveillance by Prussian police of Karl Marx during the years he remained resident in London. The interests of public police agencies in cross-border cooperation in the control of political radicalism and ordinary law crime, initially primarily in Europe, eventually led to the establishment of Interpol in the period just prior to the Second World War, not by treaty or other similar international legal instrument, but rather by the multi-lateral efforts of police administrators themselves. This demonstrates the relative autonomy of police agents *vis-à-vis* the state, especially in the space between sovereignties that exists in the cross-border situation. There are also many interesting examples of cross-border policing under private auspices and by municipal police forces that date back to the nineteenth century, which again suggests that policing power is only loosely coupled to national-state sovereignty. While it has been established that modern policing has transgressed national boundaries

from time to time almost from its inception, it is also generally agreed that in the post-Cold War era this type of practice became more significant and frequent.

The literature on the topic reveals cross-border policing to be a matter of considerable theoretical complexity. Not only must theory take account of the policing of politics (high policing) and or ordinary law crime (low policing), it must also aid in the task of mapping the networks of policing agents that operate across national borders. This latter task is made more complicated due to the existence of networks of public police agents and networks of private police actors, and sometimes the existence of networks that are hybrids of the two. Additionally, such theories must stretch to explain the relationship between policing agents and agencies with their 'external environment', that is, such theories must account for police *in* society. This issue is particularly difficult because notions of society and its boundaries have been considerably challenged as a result of the various dimensions of globalization: political, economic, and cultural (all of which impinge on policing).

In recent years, cross-border police cooperation came under intense scrutiny from academics and civil liberties groups, when it was revealed that a number of policing agencies were engaging in extra-legal practices of intelligence exchange and even the clandestine international movement of supposed terrorists and the facilitation of torture in interrogation, all under the rubric of the worldwide 'War on Terror'.

Evaluation

The longstanding tactical and strategic usefulness of territorial borders for the management of populations, coupled with the mobility of individuals and populations under conditions of global neo-liberal capitalism probably means that the variety of observable cross-border policing phenomena will not recede in the near future. Empirical studies reveal that this type of ordering and control suffers from lack of democratic accountability and control and raise profound questions about the rule of law under conditions of globalization. Worryingly, the contemporary practices of cross-border policing indicate that the character of the emerging global society has been founded on feelings of great fear and insecurity and has decidedly illiberal tendencies.

James Sheptycki

Associated Concepts: globalization, high policing, history, intelligence agency, Interpol, technology, transnational policing

Key Readings

Andreas, P. and Nadelmann, E. (2006) *Policing the Globe*. Oxford: Oxford University Press.

Bajc, U. and Torpey, J. (eds) (2007) *American Behavioural Scientist*, Special Issue on *Surveillance in an Age of Security*, 50 (12).

Bigo, D. (1996), *Polices en Réseau: L'Expérience Européenne*. Paris: Presses de Science Po.

Pratt, A. (2005) *Securing Borders: Detention and Deportation in Canada*. Vancouver: UBC Press.

Sheptycki, J. (2000) *Issues in Transnational Policing*. London: Routledge.

Sheptycki, J. (2002) *In Search of Transnational Policing*. Aldershot: Avebury.

CULTURE

Definition

Police culture refers to the values and assumptions shared by police officers as a group or as an occupation. These shared values and assumptions underpin how officers see the role of the police, their judgement about people, how they relate to each other and how they interact with the public. Police culture also includes special knowledge and skills, ways of thinking and working, rituals and rules of thumb, language and vocabulary, sensibilities and even body language that police have developed in their work.

Distinctive Features

Researchers have identified a number of key features of mainly street level police culture. Police traditionally see their work in terms of waging a 'war against crime', maintaining order and protecting people's lives and property. Officers often regard their work with a sense of mission: they see themselves as the 'thin blue line' between order and chaos. As a result, police tend to make a distinction between 'real' police work and the work they routinely perform. 'Real' police work involves potentially dangerous situations, catching criminals, saving a life, and so on, while day-to-day police work is generally mundane, repetitive, trivial and frustrating. Most officers are attracted to the varied and action-oriented nature of their job.

After being in the job for some time, police often develop a cynical view of their social environment, a constantly suspicious attitude, and an isolated social life with a strong sense of solidarity with other police officers. They tend to categorize the public into stereotypes and are often prejudiced against ethnic minorities.

Another well-known aspect of police culture is the 'code of silence' and solidarity among police officers when faced with allegations of misconduct. Police who complain against another police are ostracized and live in fear that colleagues may not assist them in emergencies.

The masculine culture of police forces was taken for granted by researchers in the 1960s and 1970s, since most officers at that time were male. The gradual increase in the proportion of female officers in recent decades has not, on the whole, made much difference to this masculine culture. Even with the passage of anti-discrimination laws and the introduction of equal employment opportunity policies in many jurisdictions, policing is still generally regarded by officers as 'a man's job'.

There is a well-recognized distinction between the 'street cop culture' and the 'management cop culture'. 'Street cops', or operational officers at the street level, often see management as being out of touch with the reality of policing, while 'management cops' are concerned with making the police more professional, efficient and responsive. Police officers felt the need to protect each other against the police organization, a need that grew out of the fear of getting into trouble for minor mistakes and a sense of cynicism against management. One consequence of the fear of mistakes and lack of trust in management is the development of a 'cover your arse' approach to work.

Police culture is often regarded as the product of the demands of police work. For example, officers' sense of solidarity with each other comes from their need to be able to rely on the support of their workmates in dangerous or difficult situations. Similarly, police cynicism results from arbitrating numerous disputes among citizens who regularly try to shift blame on others. The hard 'shell' police develop is to protect themselves from the bad treatment they regularly experience while doing society's dirty work.

Police culture has often been linked with police misconduct. The 'brotherhood' and the 'code of silence' help to protect corrupt police and condone illegal behaviours. Racism and discriminatory treatment of ethnic minorities are also seen as part of this culture. Police brutality – the use of excessive force against citizens – is another area that can be protected by a culture that supports 'noble cause' corruption.

Evaluation

A focus on police culture has the distinct advantage of not limiting our understanding of police conduct by resorting simply to psychological and individualistic explanations. For example, a cultural explanation of police corruption would steer away from the 'bad apple' theory and look for tell-tale signs in the working habits, values and ethos of police officers that may breed or condone corruption. Similarly, a cultural explanation of police racism would not simply rely on identifying individual officers who are racially prejudiced. Rather, it would broaden the search for explanations to discriminatory language, values and behaviour that are routinely used and accepted by police officers as a group. Thus, police

culture provides a broader perspective for understanding police practice and malpractice.

However, like other cultural explanations, police culture can be of limited utility for a number of reasons. First of all, police culture is not uniform or monolithic. Even within one police organization, there can be a diversity of cultures. Most discussions of police culture have been based on street level officers in Western democracies. There can be enormous variations in police culture between countries and between jurisdictions within the same country.

Second, cultural explanations are usually flawed because they tend to downplay the agency of members of the group, even though individual officers often exercise judgement in deciding what they want to do. Of course, there are group dynamics involved and police do often strive to be accepted and respected by others in the group. But police culture is a defence mechanism and a support system that officers themselves develop so that they can carry out their work; it is not something imposed from above or externally. Police officers are not passive agents in the construction of their culture.

Third, police culture does not develop in isolation from wider social and political conditions. For example, police corruption is often a consequence of 'bad laws' that are impossible to enforce. Similarly, police racism is more likely to thrive in a xenophobic social climate in the wider society. Thus, police culture itself is shaped by these external factors.

Finally, the term 'culture' is often used in a static and functionalist sense: culture is something that has been developed over a long period of time; it serves a particular function and is taught to the next generation of workers, therefore it is likely to remain stable over time. But policing is an occupation that has been experiencing a great deal of social, cultural and technological change. With the globalization of security threats, advances in communications and biotechnology and the phenomenal growth of private policing, the stability of police culture can no longer be taken for granted. Even the transmission of police culture from one generation to the next is not a straightforward or predictable task, especially when the police organization and its environment are undergoing major changes.

Police are not unique in having a distinct culture; all occupational groups have shared values and assumptions and develop ways of dealing with the constraints and stresses of the job. Police culture is seen by police themselves as functional to their survival and sense of security while working under dangerous, unpredictable and alienating conditions. Yet it is the negative, rather than the positive, influence that has become prominent in discussions about police culture.

Recent research on police culture recognizes the positive functions of police culture and examines mechanisms to bring about a professional police culture. Researchers increasingly recognize the limitations of cultural explanations and have begun to conceptualize police practice in a dynamic way – as an interaction between the structural conditions of policing and the cultural knowledge developed by groups of officers with shared experience. The active role played by officers in maintaining or changing police culture is explicitly investigated.

Future research could benefit from comparative and multiple-site case studies to examine how different police cultures interact with different structural conditions of policing. More work is needed on how police culture is affected by the changing mix of gender, ethnicity and educational level among police officers. The impact of terrorism, technological change, and the pluralization of policing on police culture is another important area for future research. Finally, comparative studies of private security and public police cultures and how they influence each other would open up a whole new area for police culture research.

Janet Chan

Associated Concepts: reform, identity, institutional racism, professionalization, research, socialization

Key Readings

Chan, J. with Devery C. and Doran S. (2003) *Fair Cop: Learning the Art of Policing.* Toronto: University of Toronto Press.

Foster, J. (2003) 'Police cultures', in T. Newburn (ed.) *Handbook of Policing.* Cullompton, Devon: Willan Publishing.

Manning, P.K. and Van Maanen J. (eds) (1978) *Policing: A View From The Street.* Santa Monica: Goodyear.

O'Neill, M., Marks M. and Singh A-M., CA (eds) (2007) *Police Occupational Culture: New Debates and Directions.* Amsterdam: Elsevier

Shearing, C.D. and Ericson R.V. (1991) 'Culture as figurative action', *British Journal of Sociology,* 42 (4): 481–506.

CYBERCRIME

Definition

Cybercrimes are criminal acts that have been transformed by networked technologies. Hacking, identity theft, Internet fraud, hate crime, cyber-terrorism – not to mention the criminal exploitation of a new generation of pornographic vices – each expose Internet users to a range of risks that degrade the quality of life online. If the hallmark of cyberspace is that it is informational, networked and global, then these qualities must also be characteristic of cybercrimes. Therefore, if we think about what happens to cybercrimes if the Internet is removed, then we can understand more about them. Three distinctive types or generations can be discerned. The first are *traditional* or ordinary crimes that use computers – usually to communicate or gather precursor information that assists in the organization of a crime. Remove the Internet and the behaviour continues because offenders simply revert to using other forms of available communication or information gathering. The second are the *hybrid cybercrimes,* or 'traditional' crimes for which network technology has created entirely new global opportunities. Take away the Internet and the behaviour continues by other means, but not upon such a global scale. In contrast to the earlier generations, the third generation are *true cybercrimes* and solely the product of the Internet – remove it and they vanish. This third generation is defined by the use of malicious software (viruses and worms) to automate victimization and includes spamming, identity theft, intellectual property piracy and others. It is a new world of low-impact multiple-victim crimes that creates new challenges for law enforcement and for the policing of offenders.

Distinctive Features

Although there seems to be a common agreement that cybercrimes exist, confusion thrives in the absence of consensus as to what they actually are. Not only does this confusion prevent the formation of good criminal justice policy, but it also perpetuates misunderstandings. Particularly confusing, for example, is the common tendency to call just about any offence involving the Internet a 'cybercrime'. As a consequence, public opinion is easily swayed by contradictory messages which, on the one hand, depict the Internet as a wonderland of personal, commercial and governmental opportunity while, on the other hand, simultaneously demonize it as a place where youngsters are groomed by paedophiles and upstanding citizens are robbed of their identity (and savings). Although they are a topical and newsworthy subject, we know little in fact about cybercrime other than from press and television reportage. As a consequence, rising public concern creates even greater demands for effective police action, particularly in light of the apparent disparity between the seemingly thousands, even hundreds of thousands, of alleged cybercrimes and the very low prosecution rates – a common trend across most jurisdictions.

Is this shortfall *prima facie* evidence that localized police forces working within tightly prescribed budgetary constraints simply cannot cope with crimes arising from globalized electronic networks? Network technologies that disadvantage the police by enabling criminals to reach their victims across infinite spans of time and space? Or should we be looking more critically at what is being understood as cybercrime, before reexamining our expectations of the police role in this field? Else, is it the case that cybercrimes are being policed by others? The answer is a combination of each of the factors.

Despite the existence of applicable bodies of law backed up by international harmonization and police coordination treaties, cybercrimes pose a number of challenges for the traditional investigative process. Simply put, their informational, networked and globalized qualities cause them to fall outside the traditional localized operational purview of police. They clearly differ from the regular police crime diet, which is one reason that they can evade the criminal justice radar. Cybercrimes, for example, tend to be individually *de minimis,* too small in impact to warrant the expenditure of finite police resources in the public interest. They also tend to fall outside routine police activity and also police culture which means that the police have little general experience in dealing with them as a mainstream crime. Furthermore, there also exist disparities in legal coding across jurisdictions which can frustrate international law enforcement initiatives.

A further reason that cybercrimes may fall outside the criminal justice arena is that they are under-reported. Individual losses may either be too small to warrant reporting or simply not regarded as serious by victims. Alternatively, corporate victims may be reluctant to expose their commercial weaknesses, raising clear conflicts between the private versus public justice interest with regard to cybercrimes. Very often the consequences of victimization may not be apparent to victims. *Computer integrity cybercrimes* such as hacking or identity theft are often precursors for more serious offending. Information gathered may later be used against the owner, or hackers may use 'Trojans' to control the computers of others. *Computer-related* cybercrimes, such as Internet scams, tend to be individually minor in impact, but serious by nature of their sheer volume. *Computer content crimes*, on the other hand (such as pornography) mainly tend to be informational, yet extremely personal and/or politically offensive or could subsequently contribute to the incitement of violence or prejudicial actions against others.

Clearly, cybercrimes are characteristically not compatible with traditional routine police practice, which begs the question as to what, then, is the role of the public police in policing cybercrime? Despite being in the twenty-first century information age, the police still continue to work mainly along the lines of their 170 year old public mandate to regulate the 'dangerous classes'. Hence, the (understandable) focus upon policing paedophiles, child pornographers, fraudsters and, those (for example, terrorists) who threaten the infrastructure. However, this is not to say that cyberspace goes un-policed, nor is it necessarily the case that police activity is either inefficient or ineffective. Rather, the public police role has to be understood within a broader and largely informal architecture of networked Internet policing, which not only enforces laws, but also maintains order in very different ways.

Internet users and user groups, for example, maintain online behaviour through moral censure. *Network infrastructure providers* draw upon the terms and conditions of their contracts with clients. They, themselves, are also subject to the terms and conditions laid down in their contracts with the telecommunications providers who host their services. *Corporate security organizations* preserve their corporate interests through contractual terms and conditions; but also use the threat of removal of privileges or the threat of private (or criminal) prosecution. *Non-governmental, non-police organizations*, such as the Internet Watch Foundation, act as gatekeepers by accepting and processing reports of offending then passing them on (mostly related to obscenities), as well as contributing to cybercrime prevention and public awareness. *Governmental non-police organizations* use a combination of rules, charges, fines and the threat of prosecution. Not

normally perceived as 'police', they include agencies such as Customs, the Postal Service, and Trading Standards, etc. A higher tier of these agencies also oversees and enforces national Internet infrastructure protection policies. *Public police organizations*, as stated earlier, therefore play only a relatively small, but nevertheless significant, role in imposing criminal sanctions upon wrongdoers. Although located within nation states, the public police are joined together in principle by a tier of transnational policing organizations, such as Europol and Interpol.

Evaluation

We are gradually learning more about the impact of networked technologies on criminal behaviour and in the years to come will be in a better position to challenge some of the misinformation about cybercrime. Independent research findings are yielding useful data. Within the police services, the maturation of the various hi-tech crime units at national and regional levels is establishing a corpus of policing experience in the field. In the field of legislation, computer misuse laws have been revised to assist the policing of cybercrime. But when formulating responsive strategies to cybercrime we need to have realistic expectations of what the police can and cannot do. We need to accept that not all policing lies in the purview of public police but also in other structures of order. The governance of online behaviour should therefore be designed to assist and strengthen the Internet's natural inclination to police itself, keeping levels of intervention relevant while installing appropriate structures of accountability. This latter point is important because the same networked technologies that empower criminals also provide the police with a highly effective investigative tool that enable police to investigate at a distance by capturing the data trails created by each network transaction. Indeed, much of the debate in past years about equipping a beleaguered and under-equipped police service is rapidly being replaced by increased concerns about over-surveillance through the gradual 'hard-wiring of society'. We need to be clear about where we set the balance between the need to maintain order online and the need to enforce law.

David S. Wall

Associated Concepts: Europol, intelligence agency, Interpol, security networks, technology, transnational policing

Key Readings

Grabosky, P. (2007) *Electronic Crime*. Upper Saddle River, NJ: Prentice Hall.

Jewkes, Y. (ed.) (2007) *Crime Online*. Cullompton, Devon: Willan Publishing.

McQuade, S. (2006) *Understanding and Managing Cybercrime*. Boston: Allyn and Bacon.

Wall, D.S. (2007) *Cybercrimes: The Transformation of Crime in the Information Age*. Cambridge: Polity Press.

Yar, M. (2006) *Cybercrime and Society*. London: Sage.

D

DEATHS IN CUSTODY

Definition

While there is no internationally agreed definition, the term 'deaths in police custody' tends to refer to those fatalities which occur at the point of arrest through to release from police detention. This definition includes cases where a person has been restrained by officers during an arrest, where someone dies on the way to a police station, and where a detained person is taken ill and subsequently dies in hospital.

Distinctive Features

Information on deaths in custody differs widely across countries and some of the best evidence can be found for England and Wales. This suggests that deaths in police custody are relatively rare events. Approximately 30 people die in police custody in England and Wales each year, giving a rate of three deaths per 100,000 people arrested. However, the total number of deaths is not what gives this subject area its importance. Instead, a series of high profile cases have led to a focus on the police treatment of ethnic minority men who have died in police custody. Involving long-term campaigns, such cases centre on allegations of stereotyping, ill-treatment and neglect, and have led to public protests and, on some occasions, disorder both in reaction to a death and the subsequent response of State agencies. Concerns about the deaths of ethnic minorities in police custody can also be found in a number of other Western societies and are closely linked to wider debates about racism and the police.

This debate is especially pertinent in Australia, where in 1987 a Royal Commission into Aboriginal Deaths in Custody was established in response to concerns about the number of deaths of Aboriginal and Torres Strait Islander people in custody. The Commission found that Aboriginal people in custody were no more likely to die than were non-Aborigines. The Commission found 'no common thread of abuse, neglect or racism' but confirmed that 'their Aboriginality played a significant and in most cases a dominant role in their being in custody and dying in custody'. The Commission reported in 1991 and over the following decade the deaths of Aborigines dropped in line with a decline in all deaths in custody. However, the idea that Aborigines are still unsafe in police custody lingers. A case in North Queensland in 2004 where a young Aborigine, Cameron Doomadgee, died in custody after being apprehended for being drunk in a public place led to a revival of these concerns and civil disturbances.

Arguably, the most controversial death in custody cases concern the actions of officers during arrests. In England, concerns about deaths, such as those of Shiji Lapite, Wayne Douglas, Brian Douglas and Roger Sylvester in the 1990s, centre on the use by officers of head locks, baton blows to the head and methods of restraint leading to the arrestee not being able to breathe ('known as positional asphyxia').

Another key focus of concern is the treatment received by arrestees once they have arrived at the police station. Questions here have been raised about police neglect, and more specifically failure to provide adequate care for detainees. Relevant here is the case of Christopher Alder, a black man who died on the floor of a custody suite reception area in Hull, England in 1998. The resulting investigation report stated that his care was inadequate and comments made by officers and captured on CCTV were unacceptable.

Issues of police care also encompass cases involving drugs and alcohol. These include where heavily intoxicated people are found unconscious in their cells, and on arrival at hospital have been declared dead. They also include deaths where drugs have been swallowed on arrest and have leaked from their wrappings while the detainee is in custody. Overall, concerns relating to deaths at police stations centre on the management of detainees, and especially on risk assessment, cell design and regular checking of detainees.

Official responses in Europe to deaths in custody are shaped by Article 2 of the European Convention on Human Rights which places a responsibility on the state to protect life. Associated case law views those in state detention as vulnerable to abuse, especially as it is unlikely that there will be any independent witnesses in relation to their treatment. A strong obligation is therefore placed on the state to provide an explanation about the treatment of any individual who dies in police custody or another type of custodial setting (*Salman v Turkey* (2000) 34 EHRR 102, para 99). Such an explanation needs to follow from an investigation which, when state agents have played a role in a death, must be independent from the organization concerned (*Jordan v UK* (2001) 37 EHRR 52, para 106). This means that when an apparent link exists between the actions of the police and a death in custody, officers from the same force cannot investigate the case. In England and Wales, this requirement has led to non-police investigators from the Independent Police Complaints Commission investigating all cases where Article 2 applies.

Apart from the need for an independent investigation following a death there will also be an inquest with a jury who will be asked to decide on the causes of the death and can rule on the lawfulness or otherwise of the death (although they cannot decide on the culpability of any individual). In England and Wales, the coroner can make recommendations designed to avoid such deaths in the future and this power is likely to be considerably strengthened by a proposed Coroners Bill. Subsequent proceedings may involve a criminal prosecution or disciplinary action being taken against the officers. In addition civil actions by the family of the deceased can be initiated either on the basis of an unlawful assault, negligence or a breach of the substantive provision of Article 2 of the European Convention of Human Rights, the right to life. On the latter see the English case of *Van Colle v Chief Constable of Hertfordshire*, Court of Appeal, 24th April 2007.

Evaluation

Despite allegations of police neglect and mistreatment in many high profile cases, it is rare for investigations or subsequent proceedings to make an explicit causal link between the actions of officers and a death. The absence of criminal or misconduct sanctions as a result of a death partly explains the strong feelings of injustice commonly expressed by bereaved families. Furthermore, there is no conclusive evidence on whether ethnic minorities are over represented among those who die in custody when compared to the wider custody population. While this touches on debates about disproportional numbers of ethnic minorities being held in custody, it does not address the point that it is the circumstances of specific cases which raise questions about differential treatment, not the overall number of ethnic minority deaths.

Individual police officers can be prosecuted for murder, manslaughter (either unlawful act manslaughter or gross negligence manslaughter), assault or misconduct in a public office. Such prosecutions and convictions are very rare. Individual officers can also be subject to disciplinary proceedings or dismissed. But again it is very rare for a death to lead to a serious disciplinary sanction, such as dismissal. However, in England and Wales the Corporate Manslaughter and Corporate Homicide Act 2007 will allow the prosecution and conviction of those in overall control of the custody regime and not just junior officers. Health and safety legislation also provides for criminal offences for failing to provide the necessary duty of care.

Deaths in custody vary widely in their character. High profile deaths resulting from restraint, such as those seen in England in the 1990s, along with cell suicides now appear to be fewer in number. This may be the result of changes in police restraint techniques and improvements in cell design made in response to past cases. With approximately 1.3 million people annually passing through police custody suites each year in England and Wales, it might be impossible to reduce the numbers of people who died suddenly from a heart attack or stroke. However, a greater focus on better health provision and risk assessment at point of entry into custody may help to reduce deaths linked to drugs, alcohol and self-harm. Initiatives by the Independent Police Complaints Commission and the Forum for the Prevention of Deaths in Custody seek to share lessons learnt across police forces and other custodial organizations. It remains to be seen if these will reduce the number of deaths in the future.

Tom Bucke and John Wadham

Associated Concepts: accountability, civilian oversight, force, human rights

Key Readings

Best, D. (2004) *Analysis of Ethnic Minority Deaths in Police Custody*. London: Police Leadership and Powers Unit, Home Office.

Institute of Race Relations (1991) *Deadly Silence: Black Deaths in Custody*. London: Institute of Race Relations.

Joudo, J. (2006) *Deaths in Custody in Australia 1990–2004*. Trends and Issues in Crime and Criminal Justice No. 309. Canberra: Australian Institute of Criminology.

Leigh, A., Johnson, G. and Ingram, A. (1998) *Deaths in Police Custody: Learning the Lessons*. Police Research Series Paper 26. London: Home Office.

Royal Commission into Aboriginal Deaths in Custody (1991) *National Report: Volume 1*. Canberra: Australian Government Publishing Service.

Teers, R. and Menin, S. (2006) *Deaths During or Following Police Contact: Statistics for England and Wales 2005/06*. Independent Police Complaints Commission Research and Statistics Series: Paper 4. London: Independent Police Complaints Commission.

Williams, P. (2001) *Deaths in Custody: 10 Years on from the Royal Commission*. Trends and Issues in Crime and Criminal Justice No. 203. Canberra: Australian Institute of Criminology.

DEMOCRATIC POLICING

Definition

Police are democratic when they act as authorized by law, when the laws they follow incorporate international standards of human rights, when they are accountable to authorities outside of themselves, and when they give priority to responding to the security needs of individuals. There is general agreement about the first three characteristics. Few would say that policing is democratic if police can make their own rules, if the rules they follow are arbitrary, repressive, and abusive, or if police operate without the possibility of corrective supervision. Accountability implies, of course, an appropriate measure of transparency. The uncommon element in this definition is responsiveness to individuals. I add it to distinguish policing that is preoccupied with serving the political needs of regimes, from policing that 'serves and protects' the population in its own terms. A democratic police serves its population directly. It regards them as clients to be served rather than subjects to be regulated.

Some commentators add another element to the definition of democratic policing, namely, that its own processes of internal management must be legal, fair, and participatory. Being democratic, in this view, involves not only how police treat the public but how they treat one another. This is not only a normative requirement, but may have important effects on police behavior. Police are more likely to act fairly and respectfully to the public, it is argued, if they have themselves been so treated.

Distinctive Features

The connection between democratic policing and democratic government is both conceptual and empirical. One would hesitate to call a government democratic if its police operated illegally, behaved in a consistently abusive and arbitrary way, and were a law unto themselves. At the same time, the behaviour of the police can contribute to the legitimacy of government in the eyes of its population, especially in their regulation of the processes of elective politics. Police are often the arbiters of electoral conduct and the associated freedoms of speech and assembly. The implication is, then, that democratic policing is necessary to democratic government as a crucial facilitator of public support as well as an indicator of its character.

But the converse is also true: democratic government requires democratic policing, but democratic policing requires democratic government. Policing cannot be democratic if government does not require it to be, or, at least, does not prevent it from being. Authoritarian government with a democratic police is not a contradiction in terms, but it is impossible institutionally. The police tail cannot wag the political dog.

The phrase community policing is often used synonymously with democratic policing. This is a mistake. Community policing describes a style of service delivery that emphasizes working in close cooperation with communities to achieve shared objectives of public safety. When done in genuine partnership with communities, it fulfils the responsiveness criteria for democratic policing. However, authoritarian regimes too sometimes require community participation in public safety, but wholly on terms set by government. Community policing that does not treat the community as an equal partner is not democratic policing. It is regime policing in democratic clothing.

Evaluation

Democratic policing is a relatively new concept. Governments have commonly been characterized as democratic or non-democratic, but not police. Instead, police have usually been described in narrower behavioral terms, such as approachable and fair or brutal and corrupt. This changed in the 1990s with the end of the Cold War. The great powers, rather than continuing their ideologically based competition for power, now joined in international efforts to quell civil wars, especially those founded on ethnic divisions, and avoid humanitarian catastrophes by developing effective institutions of government. Peacekeeping became an international enterprise and democracy emerged as the dominant model for political reconstruction. Furthermore, experience quickly showed that police played a crucial role both in the stabilization of conflict and the rebuilding of governments. As a result, concerted attention was given by developed countries as well as multilateral agencies (UN, OSCE, EU) to reforming and reconstructing police in countries where governments had failed, collapsed in civil wars, or were transitioning from authoritarianism to some form of more humane government. In this context, it made sense to talk about democratic policing in order to describe one element of the new international effort to improve governance worldwide.

Because the leaders in police reform and reconstruction are democracies, one finds 'democratic', and to a lesser extent 'community', policing commonly being stipulated as the goal in authorizing legislation. In the

United Nations, too, democratic policing has become the normative template for development. This was first formulated by the UN mission to Bosnia-Herzegovina in seven principles (1996). These became the basis for The Commissioner's Guidance for Democratic Policing in the Federation of Bosnia-Herzegovina, which was the first detailed plan for implementing democratic police development (1996). Democratic policing has since become synonymous with adherence to international principles of human rights as outlined in *International Human Rights Standards for Law Enforcement: A Pocket Book on Human Rights for the Police* (United Nations High Commissioner for Human Rights, 1996) and the *European Code of Police Ethics* (Council of Europe, 2001).

Because of the political space created by the end of the Cold War, the world has learned the importance of reforming police in order to create effective as well as humane governance, but it has also learned that creating and sustaining democratic policing is not easy. A substantial literature has developed assessing collective experience in this regard and making recommendations for more effective multi- and bilateral programmes of assistance. This growing body of knowledge represents the promise of the post-1990 period. But the underlying lesson is cautionary: efforts to develop democratic policing, both at home and abroad, depend upon the overarching security environment. Governments that feel threatened by violence, terrorism, or crime, especially when it seems to emanate from abroad, will be tempted to compromise democratic principles of policing. The result is that while democratic policing has become a popular concept for describing the desired mode of policing in the early twenty first century, its future is far from assured.

David H. Bayley

Associated Concepts: accountability, community policing, human rights

Key Readings

Bayley, D. (2006) *Changing the Guard: Developing Democratic Police Abroad*. New York: Oxford University Press.

Council of Europe (2001) *European Code of Police Ethics*. Strasbourg: Council of Europe, http://polis.osce.org/library/.

Diamond, L. (1995) *Promoting Democracy in the 1990s: Actors and Instruments, Issues and Imperatives*. New York: Carnegie Commission on Preventing Deadly Conflict.

Goldsmith, A. and Lewis, C. (eds) (2000) *Civilian Oversight of Policing: Governance, Democracy, and Human Rights*. Oxford: Hart Publishing.

Independent Commission for Policing in Northern Ireland (1999) *A New Beginning: Policing in Northern Ireland*. London: HMSO.

United Nations High Commissioner for Human Rights (1996) *International Human Rights Standards for Law Enforcement: A Pocket Book on Human Rights for the Police*. Geneva: Office of the United Nations High Commissioner for Human Rights.

DIFFUSION

Definition

Crime prevention initiatives are an important part of policing. In recent years, intelligence-led policing has resulted in police services focusing on specific crime prone locations in order to prevent and reduce offending. Linked with crime prevention initiatives is the concept of diffusion. Diffusion refers to benefits created from an initiative which targets a specific location, benefits that spread into nearby locations not targeted by the initiative (Bowers and Johnson, 2003; Ratcliffe and Makkai, 2004). In other words, the advantages of the crime prevention campaign unintentionally diffuse into surrounding areas. Diffusion is also sometimes referred to as the 'free rider effect', the 'halo effect' or the 'diffusion of benefits' (Bowers and Johnson, 2003). There is limited research on diffusion, with most research undertaken on the related and opposing issue of the displacement of crime. It is hypothesized that crime prevention initiatives targeting specific areas will merely displace crime to be committed in other areas (Weisburd et al., 2006). Often the two concepts are discussed in tandem, with some evidence pointing to diffusion being more likely the outcome of area-specific crime prevention initiatives rather than displacement.

Distinctive Features

The concept of diffusion is underpinned by several well-established criminological perspectives such as environmental criminology and the importance of place in offending, especially 'hot spots' (Weisburd et al., 2006; Braga, 2005). Some researchers have argued that diffusion operates under the assumption that offenders are rational people who evaluate the costs and benefits of committing an offence. Diffusion occurs because offenders perceive increased risks in committing a crime, even in areas not targeted by a crime prevention campaign (Ratcliffe and Makkai, 2004). This is most likely to be the result of an erroneous understanding of the extent of the police intervention (Weisburd et al., 2006) with offenders believing the intervention includes not only the target area, but surrounding areas as well, or not just one crime but several crimes (Eck, 1997).

Diffusion also results from increasing the effort involved in committing crime and decreasing the benefits of crime (Ratcliffe and Makkai, 2004). When a crime prevention strategy targets a particular area, offenders perceive that it requires additional time and effort to reestablish criminal activities in another area. If forced from a familiar location, the effort involved in reestablishing criminality can sometimes lead to offenders ceasing all their criminal activities (Weisburd et al., 2006). Alternatively, displacement of crime activity into other locations may not be at the same level or seriousness as the original offending. For example, linked to the offence of burglary are other offences such as the sale of stolen goods and credit card fraud. If burglary is reduced in a hot spot, this can lead to a reduction in associated and dependent crimes in surrounding areas (Felson and Clarke, 1998).

Incapacitation of offenders also has diffusion benefits, since apprehended offenders are no longer able to commit more offences in the target area, as well as in nearby areas, at least for the period they are incarcerated (Ratcliffe and Makkai, 2004). There is a growing body of evidence which suggests diffusion is a likely effect of area-specific crime prevention campaigns. An example is *Operation Anchorage,* a police operation run in the Australian Capital Territory over a four-month period in 2001. The operation focused on reducing burglary by targeting repeat offenders, monitoring hot spots and investigating offences quickly. An evaluation of the operation found no noticeable crime displacement of burglary or car offences from the target area to surrounding areas. In fact in both areas there was a reduction in burglary and car offences, suggesting a diffusion of benefits may have occurred (Ratcliffe and Makkai, 2004).

Overseas research also demonstrates evidence of diffusion. In a review of 21 crime prevention initiatives conducted in England, 15 programmes were successful in preventing and reducing crime in the designated target area (Bowers and Johnson, 2003). Of these 15 successful programmes, seven showed potential signs of diffusion of benefits compared with only five displaying a possible displacement of crime (Bowers and Johnson, 2003). Many studies demonstrate that diffusion is the more likely outcome of area specific policing programmes than crime displacement (Weisburd et al., 2006). Diffusion also makes area-specific initiatives appealing as they have the potential to create significant reductions in crime (Felson and Clarke, 1998).

Diffusion effects for violent crime have also been found with a street level policing intervention resulting in 'bubbles of relative safety' around the targeted areas (Lawton et al., 2005: 446). However, there were mixed results in relation to drug crimes, with displacement and diffusion both being found, depending on the statistical test used. This suggests diffusion does not always occur, and is somewhat dependent upon what crime is being targeted.

Evaluation

While the concept of diffusion can have a significant impact upon policing, it is rarely considered as an effect by those responsible for crime prevention. This is often the result of the concept not being well known and the benefits not always explicit. Also the dominant ideology in area-specific crime prevention initiatives is that crime displacement is inevitable (Ratcliffe and Makkai, 2004). However, failure to recognize the issue of diffusion creates the risk of evaluations reporting initiatives as being less successful than they are, as well as perpetuating misleading conclusions about controlling and understanding crime in general. This emphasizes the importance of constant and thorough evaluations of crime initiatives (Ratcliffe and Makkai, 2004).

Any discussion of diffusion, however, must address the issue of 'anticipatory benefits' as discussed by Smith et al. (2002). Smith and her colleagues argue that, 'Insofar as crime reduction tactics work at all, they work through changes in perception' (p. 72). Thus the anticipation of a specific crime prevention initiative, even before it is implemented, may induce a decline in targeted activity. The authors cite several studies demonstrating that many crime prevention initiatives exhibit positive effects too early for them to be attributed to the practical implementation of the initiative. The authors argue that traditional evaluations that focus on pre- and post-analysis inevitably disguise such anticipatory effects which, according to their research, 'seem to be very widespread' (p. 80).

The authors cite a number of reasons for these anticipatory effects. These include:

- Seasonal effects masking the absence of change, where an initiative takes effect at the same time as a seasonally predictable decline. This is possible because action is likely at a time when matters are at their worst;
- Regression effects, where a place chosen for intervention because it is extreme relative to other places is also extreme relative to itself at other times, and will thus tend to experience declines over time;
- Creeping implementation, where some elements of a programme are put in place before an official start date (p. 78).

There is also the fact that 'some studies appear to have effects driven by publicity/disinformation' (p. 82). It has been argued that the practical implications of anticipatory benefits mirror those of diffusion of benefits generally, namely:

> Recognition of diffusion ... provides an opportunity for maximizing crime control benefits. If the processes that lead to diffusion could be identified, crime prevention programmes designed to harness this phenomenon could be more clearly defined.
>
> (Clarke and Weisburd, 1994: 169)

Smith et al. argue that researchers have been too quick to 'assume that how crime prevention *should* work is the way crime prevention *does* work'. It is true 'that social processes are complex, and capable of giving rise to substantial unforeseen effects masquerading as the effects of the 'real' variables manipulated' (2002: 72). However, much more research is needed to untangle these variables before we can establish unequivocally the forces at work.

Toni Makkai and Jenny Fleming

Associated Concepts: crime prevention, crime analysis, crime mapping, displacement, hot spots

Key Readings

Bowers, J. and Johnson, S. (2003) 'Measuring the geographical displacement and diffusion of benefit effects of crime prevention activity', *Journal of Quantitative Criminology*, 19 (3): 275–301.

Braga, A. (2005) 'Hot spots policing and crime prevention: a systematic review of randomized controlled trials', *Journal of Experimental Criminology*, 1 (3): 317–42.

Clarke, R. V. and Weisburd, D. (1994) 'Diffusion of crime control benefits', in R. V. Clarke (ed.). *Crime Prevention Studies, Vol. 2.* Monsey, NY: Willow Tree Press.

Lawton, B., Taylor, R. and Luongo, A. (2005) 'Police officers on drug corners in Philadelphia, drug crime, and violent crime: intended, diffusion, and displacement impacts', *Justice Quarterly*, 22 (4): 427–51.

Ratcliffe, J. and Makkai, T. (2004) *Diffusion of benefits: Evaluating a Policing Operation* Trends and Issues in Crime and Criminal Justice No. 278, Canberra: Australian Institute of Criminology.

Smith, M. J., Clarke, R. V, and Pease, K. (2002) Anticipatory benefits in crime prevention, in N. Tilley (ed.) *Analysis for Crime Prevention*, Crime Prevention Studies vol. 13.

Weisburd D., Wyckoff L., Ready J., Eck J., Hinkle, J. and Gajewski, F. (2006) 'Does crime just move around the corner? A controlled study of spatial displacement and diffusion of crime control benefits', *Criminology*, 44 (3): 549–91.

DISCRETION

Definition

Discretion is defined as 'liberty of deciding as one thinks fit, absolutely or within limits' (*Concise Oxford Dictionary*). It is a central feature of every stage of the administration of criminal justice within common law jurisdictions (and in this respect may be contrasted with the 'principle of legality' which prevails in many European civil law systems). The legal authority of the police is a critical element of this system of discretionary justice. Most of the legislation from which police derive their most significant legal powers (of investigation, detention, arrest, surveillance, search and seizure, use of force, laying criminal charges, etc.) states that police 'may', rather than 'shall', do this or that when carrying out their duties. In exercising these powers, therefore, police are authorized to exercise discretion.

Distinctive Features

Because of the typical organizational arrangements of most police services, frontline officers in practice most frequently exercise power over citizens and spend most of their working hours either alone or in pairs. Because they are often out of direct communication with supervisors, effectively governing their exercise of discretion, and holding them effectively accountable for it, presents significant problems for police management.

Supervision is by necessity indirect and remote most of the time, and often the only witnesses to the exercise of coercive legal powers are those in relation to whom they are exercising them. The question of whether any given power has been exercised lawfully or in accordance with the service's policies, therefore, often comes down to the suspect's word against the officer's word (and commonly there will be more officers than suspect witnesses). This largely explains why such a high proportion of complaints against abuses of power by police officers are determined to be 'unfounded' or 'unsubstantiated' when investigated by police or external civilian bodies.

Both laws and police services (through policies and training), however, seek to place limits within which discretion is to be exercised by police officers in the execution of their duties. Such limits are said to 'fetter' discretion, and police officers and other criminal justice operatives are typically not (officially at least) recognized as enjoying 'unfettered' discretion. One of the common legal limits within which the discretionary power of arrest is usually required to be exercised, for instance, is that before exercising this power officers must have a 'reasonable suspicion' or belief that the suspect has committed, or is committing (or, in some circumstances, is about to commit) an offence. Court rulings have established criteria for determining what 'reasonable suspicion' entails and whether this requirement has been met in particular cases.

Of great concern in many jurisdictions in recent years have been allegations of discriminatory exercises of discretion by police officers against members of particular groups, such as racial and ethnic minorities, youth, members of particular religious groups, gays and lesbians, low-income and homeless people, etc. Sociologists of the police have long observed how police, in doing their patrolling and investigative work often seem to focus disproportionately on the activities of those whom they perceive to be the 'usual suspects', who frequently belong to such groups. In their most extreme and systematic form, these practices are known as 'profiling', whereby a person is particularly targeted for police attention solely because he or she belongs to such a group (the alleged 'offence' of 'driving while black' is a particularly controversial example of this).

While discretion may thus often be abused to the detriment of members of certain less powerful groups in society (referred to by some sociologists for this reason as 'police property'), it may also be abused to inappropriately benefit members of other, typically more powerful, groups (including other police officers who are caught breaking the law). If such abuse becomes widespread, of course, it creates a reality, as well as public perceptions, that there is in practice 'one law for the rich (or powerful) and one law for the poor (or disadvantaged)'.

Evaluation

Despite these problems with discretion, it is more or less universally accepted (and has been reflected in legal rulings) that discretion is an essential feature of the exercise of authority by police. There are two main reasons for this, one pragmatic, the other normative. The pragmatic reason arises from the reality that there would never be enough police and other criminal justice resources to enforce the law strictly against all violators at all times. This reality means that enforcement must inevitably be in some way selective, and the instrument for applying such selectivity is, of course, discretion. Discretion thus operates at two levels within police services. At the institutional level, a police service has to decide how to prioritize the deployment of its limited resources to enforce the law and perform other policing tasks. This will vary both from one police service to another and, within any one police service, from one area to another and from one time to another. This strategic discretion is exercised by police leaders and managers,

often after consultation with their governing authorities and members of the communities that they police (so-called 'community policing'). It is implemented, and communicated to frontline officers, through line management, and provides the context within which frontline officers exercise their routine operational discretion in performing their duties, discussed above.

The normative justification for recognizing discretion as an essential (and desirable) feature of the exercise of police authority reflects concerns that overly rigid enforcement of the law, without appropriate compassion in suitable cases, will lead to injustice. Society may not feel that it is just, for instance, for a police officer to arrest or charge a man for speeding who is exceeding the posted speed limit in his car because he is desperately trying to get his wife to hospital in time to deliver her baby. Police officers frequently encounter such situations, in which they are expected to exercise good judgement and would be praised, rather than criticized, for exercising their discretion not to apply the law in situations where it is technically applicable. In the training that they receive, police officers are instructed about the kinds of situations in which such benign exercise of discretion is acceptable, and the kinds of situations in which it is not.

Another, more controversial, type of situation in which the benign exercise of discretion (that is, discretion not to invoke the law) is commonly considered acceptable, is when such discretion is considered helpful to the police service itself in its efforts to enforce the law. A good example of this is when, in return for information about more serious offending or offenders which it could not otherwise easily obtain, a police service exercises its discretion not to charge an informant who may themselves have committed an offence. This kind of discretion is highly controversial because it can so easily lead to abuse and corruption, and for this reason police services typically have very detailed and strict protocols for the handling of informants.

By its very nature, the exercise of discretion by police will probably always be controversial. It is hard to imagine good police work without it, however, and the challenge for police leaders, and those responsible for governing police, is to train police officers to exercise it appropriately, effectively monitor how well they do so in the performance of their duties, hold them effectively accountable for their exercise of discretion, and take appropriate remedial or disciplinary action when it is alleged to have been abused. The appropriate exercise of discretion, however, also poses significant challenges for frontline police officers, which are well summed up by the following soliloquy of 'Officer Jim' in the 1999 American film *Magnolia*:

> A lot of people think this is just a job that you go to take a lunch hour, job's over, something like that. But it's a twenty-four hour deal, no two ways about it. And what most people don't see, just how hard it is to do the right thing. People think if I make a judgement call that that's a judgement on them. But that's not what I do, and that's not what should be done. I have to take everything and play it as it lays. Sometimes people need a little help. Sometimes people need to be forgiven. And sometimes they need to go to jail. Now, it's a very tricky thing on my part, making that call. The law is the law, and heck if I'm gonna break it. You can forgive someone. Well, that's the tough part. What can we forgive? Tough part of the job. Tough part of walking down the street.

Philip C. Stenning

Associated Concepts: accountability, arrest, independence of the constable, performance management, police property

Key Readings

Davis, K. C. (1971) *Discretionary Justice: A Preliminary Inquiry*. Baton Rouge: Louisiana State University Press.

Ericson, R. (1982) *Reproducing Order: A Study of Police Patrol Work*. Toronto: University of Toronto Press.

Fielding, N., Norris, C., Kemp C. and Fielding, J. (1992) 'Black and blue: an analysis of the influence of race on being stopped by the police', *British Journal of Sociology* 43 (2): 207–24.

Harris, D. (1999) 'The stories, the statistics, and the law: why "driving while black" matters', *Minnesota Law Review*, 84 (2): 265–326.

Kleinig, J. (ed.) (1996) *Handled with Discretion: Ethical Issues in Police Decision Making*. London: Rowman and Littlefield.

DISPLACEMENT

Definition

Displacement is the notion that prevented crimes pop up elsewhere in different guise, or committed by different people. It posits that the offender will find alternative ways of achieving criminal ends or, where crime opportunities are sufficiently compelling, new offenders will take advantage of them. Displacement is deemed to reduce or remove intended crime reduction effects.

Distinctive Features

The traditional classification of displacement types is as follows:

- *Spatial*: an offender commits the same type of crime in another place.
- *Temporal*: an offender commits the same crime against the same target but at another time.
- *Tactical*: an offender commits the same crime against the same target but by another means.
- *Crime type*: an offender commits a different type of crime against a different target in lieu of that originally intended.
- *Target*: an offender commits the same crime type against a different *type* of target (e.g., burgles schools or businesses rather than homes).
- *Perpetrator*: a target is so attractive that, even if the original intending criminal is incapacitated or desists from crime, others will take his or her place. The profitability

of many drug markets, and the poverty of many of the countries from which drugs arrive in Europe and North America, means that there will be no shortage of replacements for drug 'mules'.

The classification is crude. For example, spatial displacement must also be temporal displacement for those offenders incapable of time travel. Further, it invites interpretation of the ubiquitous fluctuation in crime rates in terms of displaced crime. If burglary declines in Town A, an increase in the rate of burglary in Town B will be interpreted as spatial displacement. An increase in vehicle theft in Town C may be interpreted as crime type displacement. An increase in identity theft in Town A can be passed off as tactical displacement. It is this slipperiness of focus which so frustrates those mounting crime reduction projects. There will always be somewhere and some crime type where prevented crime can be deemed to have migrated. Displacement is thus a useful fallback explanation for crime drops among the 'extreme case pessimists' whose implicit position is that crime reduction is a fruitless enterprise since crime will always find somewhere to go. In the frequent local manifestations of extreme case pessimism, displacement accounts are often difficult to challenge. The assertion 'Our burglars now ply their trade in Nexttown' requires a pattern of arrests and/or forensic evidence and/or human intelligence to sustain them. This is never likely to be forthcoming when there are more pressing demands on analyst time. Such assertions of displacement thus tend to be accepted, or at least not demonstrated to be false.

Of course, what we know about the heterogeneity of criminal careers makes for the plausibility of displacement accounts of crime switch, and research on the affinity of burglary and shop theft within the same criminal career (Schneider, 2005) is persuasive evidence that the balance of these offences will be responsive to presenting opportunities and circumstances. Domestic burglary is an offence of uneven but sometimes great profitability. Shop theft keeps the wolf from the door or provides enough cash for the next fix.

It makes sense that these offences are committed by many of the same people, and that there is displacement as presenting opportunities change. The denial of displacement *tout court* is as unsatisfactory as its blanket untested use to explain crime drops. Equally unsatisfactory is the neglect of the effect opposite to displacement, namely diffusion of benefits whereby crime reduction initiatives have effects beyond their immediate spatial range, and period of operation.

Perhaps the fundamental problem with the concept of displacement has two aspects. First, it has become separated from the notion of crime *placement*, that is, the general understanding of how and where crime is likely to occur. An understanding of factors leading to the observed distribution of crime will enable understanding of the likely consequences of attempts to suppress crime in particular places. The second problematic aspect is the lack of a nuanced view of crime change. Specifically, one should distinguish malign and benign displacement (Barr and Pease, 1990). Benign displacement may occur when the displaced crimes are less serious, or committed against less vulnerable people. A case can be made, for example, that attacks on the elderly are likely to have more severe, long-lasting and costly consequences than attacks on younger people. Initiatives to reduce such attacks may thus be defensible even in the unlikely worst case scenario that all such attacks are displaced to younger victims. How unlikely that worst case scenario is will be understood only by thinking about crime placement generally, rather than the sub-type of crime placement termed displacement which is the term used specifically to qualify the success of crime reduction efforts. Put generally, crime placement is the general thing to be understood. Social or physical change may lead to the deflection of criminal behaviour into other gainful efforts, which may or may not be criminal. The deflected behaviour which is criminal may be more or less socially destructive than the original behaviour. If it is less socially destructive (benign) the deflection is less troubling than it would otherwise be.

Detaching displacement from placement generally places the evaluator of displacement effects in an impossible situation, as will be seen below. Whenever displacement is shown not to occur in a particular way, in the absence of understanding the distribution of crime generally, there is always somewhere else it can be deemed to have moved. Burglary of homes in a town in Scotland can move to burglary in other Scottish towns. If it does not occur there, it could have moved to vehicle crime in Scotland, or burglary in England, or perhaps insider trading in the City of London. There is not enough evaluation funding in the world to demonstrate that the crime is not displaced, and if it is deemed to have been displaced to a poorly reported crime, the search will be futile anyway.

Evaluation

The major reviews of displacement are in accord that observed displacement is seldom total and often inconsequential, certainly never complete enough to offset the crime reductive gains of a programme (Eck, 1993; Hesseling, 1994). While persuasive, reviews cannot cover all the bases, in the sense that there is always some crime outside the scope of the comparison areas used, to which crime might have migrated. Even the most sophisticated evaluations, such as those of Weisburd et al. (2006), Bowers and Johnson (2003) and McLennan and Whitworth (2008) which sought to distinguish areas to which displacement was plausible, areas to which displacement was not plausible, and target areas, could not cover all possible routes of displacement. Their analyses were statistically the most sophisticated (and they concluded, as the earlier reviews had, that displacement did not offset crime reduction gains) but are unlikely to persuade the extreme case pessimist. The same message is communicated for white collar crime by Weisburd and Waring (2001) and by Weisburd and Green (1995) in relation to drug markets.

Ken Pease

Associated Concepts: crime prevention, diffusion, hot spots, situational crime prevention

Key Readings

Barr, R. and Pease, K. (1990) 'Crime placement, displacement and deflection,' in M. Tonry and N. Morris (eds) *Crime and Justice*: A Review of Research, vol. *12*. Chicago: University of Chicago Press.

Bowers, K.J. and Johnson, S.D. (2003) 'Measuring the geographical displacement of crime', *Journal of Quantitative Criminology,* 19 (3): 275–301.

Eck, J. (1993) 'The threat of crime displacement,' *Criminal Justice Abstracts*, 25, 527–46.

Hesseling, R. (1994) 'Displacement: A Review of the Empirical Literature,' in R.V. Clarke (ed.) *Crime Prevention Studies 3*. Monsey NY: Criminal Justice Press.

McLennan, D. and Whitworth, A. (2008) *Displacement of Crime or Diffusion of Benefit: Evidence from the New Deal for Communities Programme*. London: Department of Communities and Local Government.

Schneider, J.L. (2005) 'The link between shoplifting and burglary: The booster burglar.' *British Journal of Criminology*, 45 (3): 395–401.

Weisburd, D. and Green, L. (1995) 'Policing drug hot spots the jersey city drug market analysis experiment', *justice quarterly*, 12 (4): 711–35.

Weisburd, D. and Waring, E. (2001) *White-Collar Crime and Criminal Careers*. Cambridge: Cambridge University Press.

Weisburd D., Wyckoff L., Ready J., Eck J., Hinkle, J. and Gajewski, F. (2006) 'Does crime just move around the corner? A controlled study of spatial displacement and diffusion of crime control benefits', *Criminology*, 44 (3): 549–91.

DIVERSITY

Definition

There is no single agreed and generally accepted definition of diversity. At its simplest level the term diversity refers to the differences between people. Given that people differ in such a wide variety of ways, such a simplistic conceptualization of diversity is not necessarily helpful when considering the police policy response. Other definitions attempt to delineate the differences between people that have most significance in terms of the potential for discrimination and these include issues such as race, class, culture, educational background and disability. More recently however, the aspects of diversity (or specific differences between people) that have received close attention have been the six strands: age, disability, faith and belief, gender, race, and sexual orientation. These aspects of difference are prominent internationally and in many jurisdictions align with anti-discrimination legislation.

Distinctive Features

While thinking about diversity is not new, in many ways it has now taken prominence over the notion of equal opportunities (EO). The difference between EO and diversity lies mainly in the focus. The idea of EO has at its roots the principle that people (particularly in employment) should receive fair and equal treatment and that this fair treatment is largely defined in the relevant employment legislation. Diversity on the other hand paints a richer picture of how fairness in society generally should be manifest. It is not restricted to employment issues (although these are implicit in it) but extends to a wider conceptualization of fairness in all aspects of society including the way society is policed. Diversity is about responses not only of policing organizations but also of the individuals working in them. It is not just about legislative compliance but goes further to examine ways in which responses to difference between people may lend themselves to prejudicial or discriminatory behaviour. Diversity in its broader meaning seeks to challenge these responses.

Thinking about diversity in relation to policing needs to take two forms: how diversity should look and be managed *inside* the police service and how it should be responded to in terms of delivering a service to people on the *outside* of policing. From the inside perspective police forces have needed to address a number of key issues, for example recruitment, progression, grievance and discipline, and retention of police officers. This perspective of course in the wider sense, refers to the way in which police officers and staff from minority groups experience being on the inside of policing.

The focus on diversity outside of the police service has in many respects been driven by high profile cases that have served to bring issues of equality and fairness to the fore and have, in some cases, led to major reforms of policing policy and practice as well as legislation. In the UK for example, the Stephen Lawrence Inquiry report (Macpherson, 1999) was a fundamental driver of the police response to diversity issues. The inquiry examined events surrounding the racist murder of a young black man, Stephen Lawrence in 1993, and was a direct result of pressure by his parents. While the focus of the report was on race issues, its recommendations led directly to changes in police policy and practice which went far beyond the issue of race alone. The Race Relations (Amendment) Act 2000, for example, placed a duty on all public authorities, including the police, to be proactive in addressing issues of discrimination. Central to the Stephen Lawrence Inquiry report was the much debated idea of institutional racism which has subsequently been expanded to include the idea of institutional discrimination generally where the same principles are applied to forms of discrimination in the other diversity strands. While the Stephen Lawrence Inquiry provided an impetus for change and debate in the UK, similar events have impacted similarly elsewhere. Cases in Australia, for example, have focused on the deaths in custody of Aborigines. A Criminal Justice Commission report (1994) into the death after arrest of Daniel Yock, a young Aboriginal dancer, and the events of the Palm Island incident (2004) which surrounded the death of Cameron Doomadgee, served to intensify the debate about the treatment of minority groups by police in Australia. In Los Angeles, US, in 1991, the beating of a black taxicab driver, Rodney King by police officers, led to intense riots the following year after the officers charged with his beating were acquitted. Again major questions were raised about the relationships between the police and minority groups.

The 'outside' perspective of diversity refers to the service that is delivered to the general population. The point of departure is a recognition that diversity in society is a given and that policing by its very nature will be about policing a diverse society. This has led to a much more proactive attempt to identify communities in a given policing area, including 'hard to reach' groups. The latter refer to those groups or communities who may well be on the fringes of society or who, for whatever reason, do not want to engage with the police.

Evaluation

Implicit in the concept of diversity is the nature and significance of difference between people and the implications this has for their right to be treated fairly. The developing diversity agenda has led to the notion that treating people equally (i.e., the same) is not necessarily the same as treating people fairly. There now seems to be wide acceptance that in responding to a diverse society fair treatment is best delivered by treating people according to their differing *needs*. The needs of one group or individual are likely to be very different from those of others.

In terms of the police organizational response to diversity, there have been many changes in both policy and practice that have demonstrated a commitment to change. Examples of these changes include more robust arrangements for family liaison, changes in the way murders are investigated, greater commitment to community consultation and partnership working and the removal of discretion in deciding what constitutes a racial incident. In terms of a murder investigation for example, there now exist, in many jurisdictions, sets of guidelines on the investigation of murder and the requirement for specific training to investigate certain murders, including those that are racially motivated. Thinking about institutional racism (and other forms of discrimination) we might note that at the heart of the phenomenon lies the attitudes, thoughtlessness, and racial stereotyping of *individuals* who collectively make up an organization. An effective response to diversity and the elimination of discrimination and disadvantage lies very much in the gift of individual police officers in the awareness, understanding, attitudes and behaviour that they display. Undoubtedly such negative traits are less overtly apparent but most commentators would agree that there is still much to do (Rowe, 2007).

The so-called 'war on terror' that has been a significant feature of twenty-first century life has served to illustrate how easily a commitment to a proper response to a diverse society can be challenged. For example, there have been debates about the length of detention without charge, freedom of speech, the use of stop and search powers, particularly those under anti-terrorist legislation and the notion of over and under policing of particular communities. All of these issues have challenged thinking about policing a diverse society.

A common theme in the development of a strong positive response to diversity has been the need for good quality leadership at all levels within the police. In most cases, analysis of events that have triggered discussion and debate about the way the police respond to diversity have identified failures in leadership of one kind or another.

Responding to diversity effectively is a particularly complex endeavour for police services who have to balance the need to deliver an effective non-discriminatory police service with the imperative to take account of the needs of a diverse population. This is also set in the context of debates about whether the very concept of diversity (and the associated concept of multiculturalism) is particularly helpful. Some have argued that stressing difference as can happen with diversity makes the task of responding to it harder rather than easier. It is likely that as globalization, the need to respond to transnational crime and migration grow, these issues will become more complex rather than less.

Phil Clements

Associated Concepts: community engagement, culture, institutional racism, reform

Key Readings

Chan, J. B. L. (1997) *Changing Police Culture: Policing in a Multicultural Society.* Cambridge: Cambridge University Press.

Commission for Racial Equality (2005) *The Police Service in England and Wales: Final Report of a Formal Investigation by the Commission for Racial Equality.* London: CRE.

Her Majesty's Inspectorate of Constabulary (2003) *Diversity Matters.* London: Home Office.

Macpherson, Sir W. (1999) *The Stephen Lawrence Inquiry: Report of an Inquiry by Sir William Macpherson of Cluny*, CM 4262-1. London: Home Office.

Rowe, M. (2007) (ed.) *Policing Beyond Macpherson: Issues in Policing, Race and Society.* Cullompton, Devon: Willan.

DOMESTIC VIOLENCE

Definition

Domestic violence occurs when one partner in a current or former relationship attempts physically or psychologically to dominate and control the other. Often called intimate partner violence, domestic violence can take a number of forms of which the most commonly acknowledged are physical and sexual violence, threats and intimidation, emotional and social abuse and economic deprivation. The non-physical types of abuse usually co-occur with physical and sexual violence to create a climate of fear within which the victim is frightened into compliance.

Distinctive Features

The precise incidence of domestic or intimate partner violence in any population is difficult to assess as it often goes unreported. However, available statistics show that domestic violence occurs in all societies although national and regional variations exist, with higher rates in communities and relationships which place emphasis on conventional gender roles, male honour and female chastity. Women are the primary victims (85 per cent) and men the primary perpetrators. A United Nations survey of 24,000 women in 10 countries in 2006 found that the experience of physical and sexual violence by an intimate partner in a woman's lifetime ranged from 15 per cent in urban Japan to 71 per cent of women in rural Ethiopia (UN General Assembly, 2006).

Police represent the first response for help and protection at any time of day or night. Police officers attending a domestic violence incident are faced with investigating volatile and highly emotionally charged confrontations between intimate partners or ex-partners. Domestic violence is a most complex matter to police effectively because, while evidence of physical assault is often present, it can often be difficult to prove other kinds of abuse. Victims typically endure a history of abuse and brutality from their partner and population surveys suggest that less than one in three incidents is reported to the police (Paradine and Wilkinson, 2004). Factors that precipitate or inhibit reporting are still poorly understood although international research suggests that perhaps 20 violent incidents have occurred before the first report to the police (Walby and Myhill, 2000) with differential rates of reporting between subgroups of victims based on race or sexuality for example (Hoyle and Sanders, 2000). A progressive dynamic often operates, where brief explosive episodes of violence are followed by periods of denial or minimization and remorse. There may or may not be a peaceful phase before tension begins to build up towards another violent incident. It is important to recognize that the dynamics associated with domestic violence are complex and multifaceted, warning signs and symptoms are often ambiguous and complicated by the social, psychological, sexual, financial, and parental relationships between the parties.

The precise role of police has been a matter of debate over the years. Police powers (under statute law, common law or police standing orders) operated in an environment of reluctance to intervene in the private sphere. Research during the 1980s found that police often tried to end a domestic disturbance without arrest or downgraded domestic assaults to a less serious charging category. Police were criticized for this as well as for failure to attend, having greater concern for officer safety than safety of family members, refusal to arrest, and exhibiting unsympathetic or unhelpful stances towards victims or otherwise ineffective intervention which would lead to repeated attendances (Buzawa and Buzawa, 2003). Additional criticisms were made regarding the failure of police to provide victims with advice about safety and security or conversely, using referral to the civil jurisdiction or other agencies as a substitute for law enforcement (Hoyle and Sanders, 2000). It was suggested that the failure of police officers to record incidents as being domestic violence incidents exacerbated the hidden nature of domestic violence by adding under-recording to under-reporting by victims. Under-recording was viewed as minimizing as well as discriminatory and perceived as denying victims their rights for protection under the law. From the 1970s onwards, policies and policing practices began to incorporate research findings around the magnitude, severity and risks associated with domestic violence including risks connected with non-action (Buzawa and Buzawa, 2003).

The recognition of domestic violence as a public issue in many countries has manifested a range of law reforms since the 1970s, aimed at reshaping the police response so they could treat domestic violence as a crime, including recording and investigating cases between intimates in the same way as assaults by strangers. There are currently 89 countries with social policies that address domestic violence with 44 countries having enacted legislation to make it a criminal offence (UN General Assembly, 2006). Common reforms include new powers for law enforcement officers such as mandatory arrest and the capacity to issue police family violence intervention orders (PFVO) based on the realization that victims can be unwilling to take out orders on their own behalf for a variety of reasons, including fear of retaliation. These police orders augment the historic remedy of civil protection orders.

Contemporary police services in Australia, the US, UK, Canada and New Zealand investigate and prosecute domestic violence crimes within a broader policy framework, often including cooperative partnerships with stakeholders in other health and social service agencies, because of the recognition that there are a myriad of interconnections between the structural, interpersonal and cultural factors affecting domestic violence which require management in a comprehensive and integrated framework.

Evaluation

The criminalization of domestic violence has simplified police action to some extent but debate continues over pro arrest and related policies. Early evidence that arrest was very effective in reducing violent recidivism has not proved to be universal. Arrest appears to deter some groups of offenders, it has no effect on others and may actually increase the violence (Garner, Fagan, and Maxwell, 1995). From the victim's perspective, while discretionary arrest policies led to the belief that law enforcement officers would not help victims and led to under reporting, mandatory arrest can also deter reporting because victims may not necessarily want their partner arrested. Victims want the violence to stop, whether they have any hope that the relationship can be reformed and continued or want to end the relationship (Hoyle and Sanders, 2000).

While the role of police is primarily one of enforcement of the law in a given jurisdiction, policing incidents of domestic violence involves sifting through complex situations, often characterized by considerable ambiguity. This presents significant challenges to police regarding collection of evidence, appropriate arrests and charges, and processing cases through to prosecution. Police officers need professional training to deal with this complex area and need to remain sensitive to client needs. The role of police has shifted to one of increased intervention enhanced by criminal sanctions in cases of domestic violence and providing greater degrees of protection for victims, for example, protection orders, with a corresponding move towards coordinated responses between police, the courts and support services for victims. The aim of a coordinated policy response is to achieve a reduction of perpetrator recidivism via a mix of criminal justice and counselling/ education initiatives.

Many jurisdictions in the UK, US, Australia and New Zealand have designated specialist domestic violence support teams to fully investigate criminal offences and facilitate access to other agencies. Both the specialist and generalist approaches to policing of domestic violence have their strengths and weaknesses. In practice, specialist police domestic violence teams experience high rates of staff turnover, which impacts on the training and maintenance costs of specialist units.

The policing process needs to include a network of criminal justice and other agencies with the aim of disempowering perpetrators of violence and yet empowering victims. Victims need support and counselling and to have the choice whether the relationship continues or not (and have this choice respected). The process or system needs to include checks and balances to ensure that the violence does in fact cease. Finally, the process should include sufficient deterrence to send the message to the wider community that intimate partner violence is a serious offence. Researchers, lawyers, social workers and medical professionals around the world are working together with law enforcement agencies on multifaceted projects to develop understanding of the complexities and dynamics of domestic violence including the impacts of policies and programmes to extend best practice in policing domestic violence.

Romy Winter

Associated Concepts: arrest, criminal investigation, policing, sexual assault

Key Readings

Buzawa, E. S. and Buzawa, C. G. (2003) *Domestic Violence: The Criminal Justice Response*. Thousand Oaks, CA: Sage Publications.
Garner, J., Fagan, J., and Maxwell, C. (1995) 'Published findings from the spouse assault replication program: A critical review', *Journal of Quantitative Criminology*, 11 (1), 3–28.
Hoyle, C. and Sanders, A. (2000) 'Police response to domestic violence' British Journal of Criminology, 40 (1), 14–36.
Paradine, K. and Wilkinson, J. (2004) *Protection and Accountability: The Reporting,*

Investigation and Prosecution of Domestic Violence Cases. London: HMIC. www.hmcpsi.gov.uk/reports/DomVio0104LitRev.pdf.
United Nations General Assembly, (2006) *In-Depth Study on All Forms of Violence against Women: Report of the Secretary General.*New York: UN Division for the Advancement of Women. http://www.un.org/Womenwatch/daw/vaw/SGstudyvaw.htm
Walby, S., and Myhill, A. (2000) *Reducing Domestic Violence ... What Works? Assessing and Managing the Risk Of Domestic Violence*. London: Home Office.

DRUGS

Definition

The policing of drugs refers to the legitimate enforcement of laws and rules regulating the possession, exchange, sale and – in some though not all jurisdictions – use, of drugs as defined in relevant legislation. Policing may be directed towards both illegal drugs and also legal substances influencing behaviour, most commonly alcohol, though different laws are likely to be in place and hence govern both legal powers and actions.

Distinctive Features

Via the process of their criminalization, possession of and dealing in illegal drugs became both a target for the police and a spur to the development of various styles, techniques and organization of policing. Drugs policing is influenced by a wide variety of factors: from the priorities of public policy and fashions in political and public opinion; through changes in law; innovations in treatment methods and developments in detection and surveillance technologies; to other micro and macro matters, whether at the level of local street dealing and prices or global economics and trade policies.

Drugs policing is not new; it has been intertwined for centuries with the history of smuggling and border control, and with religion and morality. When the trade in drugs has been legal it has been a source of profit and power for commercial enterprises and taxation for states. These interests have in turn required police and occasionally military protection from competitors and organized criminals, pirates and so forth. One distinctive feature of drug trafficking and drug-related law enforcement is the significant international dimension – for example, in relation to the cultivation of plant-based drugs or production of synthetic drugs for both local consumption and export (at times legally but for the most part since the early twentieth-century illegally). As commodities that are traded illegally, drugs have been the subject of numerous domestic laws and international treaties and agreements prohibiting or restricting cultivation, preparation for use, sale, export, transportation, distribution and possession. At all these points within the global drug economy, some form of policing will be tasked and targeted. Of course, such policing is a wide-ranging concept and embraces inputs from more than any single police agency or tier of police work.

Traditional enforcement-led approaches to drug control emphasized the role the police could play in interdiction and supply reduction, in other words in enacting prohibitions and restrictions by intercepting the commodity. The underlying assumption of policy and practice is that reduced supply would control and reduce demand (that is, dealers would be deterred by loss of profit, users deterred by increased price and obstacles posed by scarcity). Evidence that supply-reduction strategies have had any notable or sustainable impacts is lacking, however. Drugs operate in a market economy and supply requires demand. Broader prevention strategies have recognized this, embracing a range of interventions aimed at reducing the number of end-users and increasing resistance to experimentation and early-onset of use. Here policing plays a part in a broader spectrum of initiatives also involving education and treatment.

As the sophistication of drug traffickers and organized criminals has increased, the police and related bodies (e.g., customs, taxation, and intelligence agencies) have sought to match this through increasing specialization of skills and functions. Obvious examples are specialist drug squads, undercover work, financial detection and forensic techniques. Policing generally, but drugs policing in particular, has seen a move away from simple reactive investigation and detection of individual crimes to a more strategic approach to crime control. The adoption of intelligence-led policing and a proactive, targeted approach were characteristic key features of drugs-related policing, initially in relation to high-level drugs-crime enterprises and markets, later applied at local levels in attempts to break-up local street level markets. In most jurisdictions legislation now permits forms of financial enquiry and asset seizure that override certain traditional assumptions about personal privacy, standard of evidence and proof of guilt. There has been some debate about the merits and dangers of extending police and intelligence agency powers within a range of settings from street searches to satellite surveillance, but given contemporary political and popular apprehension about local and global threats such as drugs, terrorism and organized crime, support for such powers is likely to continue.

Locally-based police initiatives can involve any combination of a number of elements which inhibit drug transactions or manage the drug market, for example, by increasing the risks of arrest and general inconvenience faced by buyers and sellers, disrupting the criminal business, evicting tenants or removing key individuals from the area. Policing activities may take the form of surveillance, use of intelligence, test-purchase operations, highly visible patrols and police crackdowns. Such 'problem-oriented policing' (POP) approaches to drug enforcement have often been developed in partnership with other public, commercial and voluntary bodies with a view to protecting communities from drug-related nuisance and anti-social behaviour and to reducing the fear of drug-related crime.

The rise of POP has dovetailed with the so-called harm-reduction approach to drugs in shaping contemporary drugs policing. Based on the pragmatic principle that the problems associated with drugs should be minimized (if not eradicated) for the users, families and communities affected, the harm-reduction approach has taken the form of police cautioning for drug offences, treatment-type interventions (such as referral to drug advice agencies) and police promotion of drug education in schools. In some cases, arguments have been made for greater emphasis on a public health as opposed to enforcement-led response to street level or community-based drug problems. Internationally, such arguments have been more influential in the UK, Australia, Canada and some European nations, than in the US.

Evaluation

Within the subculture of police work, drugs-related law enforcement represents much that is valued greatly (action, risk and crime targeting). In both factual and fictional representations, it can be seen as necessary 'dirty work' carried out to protect communities and young people. Past enthusiasm about problem-oriented, community-based approaches to drug enforcement has to be understood not only as part of a wider debate about the role of the police but also as a response to the pressure to deliver results and to focus on 'what works' measures. Yet, drugs work is an area where performance indicators can be crude and inappropriate and success hard to quantify. Evidence about the success or failure of community policing initiatives whether directed at drugs, burglary or public nuisance has often been mixed. Indeed, it is not necessarily the case that intensified police operations in a locality followed, almost inevitably, by a withdrawal of this exceptional level of attention leaves communities feeling safer or with a higher quality of life, especially if drug markets have simply been driven out of plain sight but continue to thrive.

Another area of concern relates to the use of stop and search powers in street level drug policing, which has a long history and equally long association with controversy and legal challenge since at least the early twentieth century. As a technique directed against those who constitute 'the usual suspects' in any society, this has been a feature of what many critics have seen as the over-policing of particular groups, most notably from black minority backgrounds, with serious implications for police-community relations and wider social cohesion. 'Zero-tolerance' style policing and the 'War on Drugs' (especially in the American context) have filled up juvenile institutions, jails and prisons with drug convicts, impacting disproportionately on young black men and minority communities.

Anti-drugs policing has often relied upon a high degree of discretion and autonomy whether exercised by local, front-line police officers, in informant handling and undercover or surveillance work, or at the level of globally coordinated, multi-agency operations. Such factors may be essential to success in many cases but also cause difficulties for the regulation of police work generally, and especially where it involves sensitive or secret elements. Drugs policing has a number of characteristics, some shared with other forms of policing, which make it particularly prone to corrupt practice, notably its low levels of visibility and managerial scrutiny and high levels of financial temptation. Research studies and official inquiries have found evidence of a range of misconduct in drugs-related police work, including opportunistic theft, the planting of drugs, illegal searches, the protection of informants in circumstances contravening rules, involvement in violence, participation by officers in drug dealing, and shielding of major drug criminals.

Maggy Lee and Nigel South

Associated Concepts: criminal investigation, misconduct, organized crime, transnational policing

Key Readings

Crowther-Dowey, C. (2007) 'The police and drugs', in M. Simpson, T. Shildrick and R. Macdonald (eds) *Drugs in Britain*. Basingstoke: Palgrave.

Jacobson, J. (1999) *Policing Drug Hot-Spots*. Home Office Police Research Series No. 109, London: Home Office.

Shiner, M. (2006) 'Drugs, law and the regulation of harm', in R. Hughes, R. Lart and P. Higate (eds) *Drugs: Policy and Politics*. Maidenhead: Open University Press.

South, N. (2007) 'Drugs, alcohol and crime', in M. Maguire, R. Morgan and R. Reiner (eds) *The Oxford Handbook of Criminology* (4th ed). Oxford: Oxford University Press.

Royal Society of Arts Commission on Illegal Drugs, Communities and Public Policy (2007) *Drugs – Facing Facts*. London: RSA.

E

ECONOMIC CRIME

Definition

Economic (or financial) corporate crime covers the vast range of business offences which underpins the legal framework governing the exchange of goods, services and financial instruments in contemporary market economies. Among other things, these offences encompass bribery and corruption, accounting and securities fraud, tax evasion and anti-competitive practices – a variation which is reflected in the highly fragmented range of public and private organizations responsible for regulating (policing) economic corporate crime. These include auditors, statutory regulatory authorities – such as the Financial Services Authority in the UK and Securities and Exchange Commission in the US – and criminal justice organizations such as the Serious Fraud Office (SFO) in the UK. As with other areas of corporate crime control, economic corporate crime is not regarded as a key priority by the police and, as a result, even where the police have jurisdiction to investigate, the matter is often left to statutory regulatory authorities.

Distinctive Features

In Anglo-Saxon economies the regulation of economic crime is typically organized around three interlinked tiers of control: a primary tier, which encompasses the professional agents of the board (such as investment banks, commercial lawyers and auditors); a secondary tier comprising statutory and other public regulatory authorities; and a tertiary tier constituted by mainstream criminal justice organizations which work through the traditional media of criminal justice.

In terms of setting the regulatory tone and coordinating the network of practices and institutions that constitute financial regulation, the primary tier of economic crime control is of secondary importance to statutory regulatory authorities which oversee the work of the primary stratum of private regulation. However, in terms of detecting crime they play a far more important role, since public authorities are rarely sufficiently resourced to systematically review, inspect and analyze business transactions and corporate accounts (Coffee, 2006).

Despite massive differences in the use of enforcement by public regulators, where the intelligence and surveillance apparatus of public regulators identify potential cases of economic crime they are rarely investigated and processed as such. This is partly because thoughts of the possibility that a crime may have been committed do not typically frame the practices of officials working for public regulatory agencies. Potential witnesses, as such, are not necessarily interviewed, or, where interviewed, are not asked the right questions to elicit evidence of dishonesty or malpractice. Likewise, unearthing documentary material which might implicate senior company officers is not prioritized and standard regulatory practices – such as advanced notice of a pending visit – work against the discovery of incriminating evidence. In addition to this, costly delays involved in gathering sufficient evidence for prosecution provide public regulators with a strong motivation to use alternatives to prosecution (such as the revocation of a firm's licence to operate) which do not require evidence that a crime has been committed. Finally, statutory regulators' commitment to encouraging growth and competitiveness within regulated industries places them under a permanent pressure to select enforcement options which cause the least reputational damage to commercially significant firms and the markets in which they operate (Fooks, 2003b).

Economic crime units within conventional policing institutions primarily constitute the tertiary tier of financial regulation. A lack of training, expertize and resources for economic crime investigation within the police has been an important factor in the establishment of specialist organizations dedicated to economic crime control, such as the SFO. Changes to the institutional framework of economic corporate crime control do not however, seem to have had a significant impact on under-criminalization, which is widely thought to be widespread (Fooks, 2003a). This is partly a question of supply. Referral of cases to criminal justice agencies is curbed by both the regulatory focus of statutory organizations and the commercial imperatives of private institutions responsible for economic crime detection, which limit their capacity and motivation to thoroughly investigate suspect transactions. A second reason is under-resourcing, which is exacerbated by the fact that effective investigation involves the collation of a vast amount of geographically and institutionally dispersed evidence. A third reason relates to the specific difficulties involved in investigating economic corporate crime. Officials involved in economic crime investigation work on building up paper trails to recreate the multitude of financial transactions which collectively constitute an offence. This highly time-consuming process is easily disrupted by the creation of false documents, which suspects use to conceal offences and make otherwise illegal transactions appear legal. A fourth reason concerns ill-designed powers of investigation

which are thought to severely limit economic crime investigators' capacity to collate evidence. Design and resource obstacles to effective policing are thought to raise a serious risk of the criminal justice agencies investigating only the simplest cases, or omitting higher level suspects from an investigation (Fooks, 2003b; Alvesalo, 2003; Coffee, 2006).

Economic crime investigators often stress the diversity and complexity of laws that effective investigation demands and the available evidence suggests that the law plays a far more prominent role in the work of public officials investigating economic crime than is the case with ordinary crime. This is partly a function of the fact that economic corporate crime takes place under conditions of low visibility, but it is also likely to be a result of the constant risk of legal action from socially powerful suspects (Alvesalo, 2003).

Notwithstanding the general consensus that non-criminalization is widespread, financial regulation is considered to be more developed and exacting than other forms of corporate crime control: partly because economic corporate crime subverts the fabric of commercial trust necessary for the effective operation of market economies; and partly because the victims of economic corporate crime are just as likely to be large commercial institutions as they are individuals and small businesses. The strength of these arguments is difficult to determine. Efforts to control economic corporate crime often remain symbolic and, at best, spikes in activity quickly decline once the focus of political debate and media interest moves on (Fooks, 2003a).

Evaluation

Recurrent financial scandals suggest that regulatory failure is common. This is commonly traced to the massive conflicts of interest that characterize the relationship between regulated businesses and private 'gatekeeper' organizations within the primary tier. The capacity of gatekeepers to detect and report fraud is dependent on their independence from regulated businesses. In practice, this is compromised by the fact that gatekeepers are hired, paid and dismissed by the organizations they are formally meant to monitor (rather than existing or potential shareholders or creditors).

Most of the research on this issue has focused on the role of auditors, whose independence and general ability to uncover fraud is said to have been compromised further by the significant downward pressure on audit fees brought about by competitive tendering. The declining value of audits (which has been compounded by an increase in audits costs, such as insurance) is said to have placed auditors under considerable pressure to meet unrealistic deadlines, which has fed directly into higher levels of dysfunctional behaviour, such as misreported errors or problematic items being rejected. At one and the same time, it has also encouraged auditors to reengineer audit processes and placed increased pressure on audit firms to focus on the sale of non-audit services. This is thought to have brought about a chronic deterioration in the quality of audits, leading to less economic crime being detected and reported. On the one hand, reengineered audit processes have placed a bigger emphasis on verifying processes and systems used to generate financial information at the expense of direct testing of underlying transactions and account balances which constitute a more effective method of monitoring the actions of senior corporate officers. The increase in provision of non audit services on the other hand, has given audit clients greater leverage over the audit process, while weakening auditors' motivation to take a robust view of the company's accounts (Sikka, 2004; Coffee, 2006).

Crises of political legitimacy, economic recession, structural change in financial markets and scandal are all associated with substantive efforts to build up the infrastructure of economic crime control. In attempting to understand why shifts towards greater use of enforcement take place, but then seem to quickly fade away, existing studies have attempted to disaggregate the respective motivations of interest groups that lobby for more exacting enforcement. Spikes in enforcement activity, including the establishment of new organizations responsible for economic crime

control, usually take place within a milieu of competing and, sometimes, contradictory interests which play an important role in politicizing economic crime control. While business organizations generally lobby for more effective enforcement of economic offences committed against larger corporations by smaller, rogue, businesses or organized criminals, the process of politicization and the relative autonomy of enforcement activity from business interests can cause the law to be enforced against a far wider range of targets. Divergence between business interests and the practice of economic crime control tends, however, to be short-lived. Politicization is rarely sustained, allowing enforcement practice to steadily converge with the interests of organized business. The process exemplifies the prevailing wisdom in political science that narrow interests inevitably triumph over the public interest (Fooks, 2003a).

Gary Fooks

Associated Concepts: criminal investigation, environmental crime, health and safety, property crime

Key Readings

Alvesalo, A. (2003) 'Economic crime investigators at work', *Policing and Society,* 13 (2): 115–38.

Coffee, J. C. (2006) *The Role of Professions in Corporate Governance.* Oxford; Oxford University Press.

Fooks, G. (2003a) 'Contrasts in tolerance: The curious politics of commercial fraud Control', *Contemporary Politics,* 9 (2): 127–42.

Fooks, G. (2003b) 'In the valley of the blind the one-eyed man is king: corporate crime and the myopia of financial regulation', in S. Tombs and D. Whyte (eds) *Unmasking the Crimes of the Powerful: Scrutinizing States and Corporations.* New York: Peter Lang.

Sikka, P. (2004) 'Some questions about the governance of auditing firms', *Journal of Disclosure and Governance,* 1.(2): 186–200.

EDUCATION AND TRAINING

Definition

Police education and training refers to the formal learning arrangements provided by police forces designed to turn novitiate recruits into expert uniformed operational practitioners. These arrangements include the way training is organized, managed and delivered; the status of recruits and trainers; the content and length of the curriculum and the nature and standards of the pedagogy used, including methods of teaching, learning and assessment. These arrangements, though, have a contingent and problematical connection to the actual learning and socialization processes that help shape the development of police practitioners, their values and their practices.

Distinctive Features

While police education and training varies across jurisdictions and countries, the relatively small amount of published literature about it reveals many common distinctive elements and features. To start with, each policing agency organizes and manages recruit education and training in police academies. The latter are specialist departments located within and accountable to the larger police bureaucracy. This contrasts strongly with other 'people service' occupations such as teaching, nursing and social work where the preparation for full practitioner standing is organized and delivered by specialist and independent learning institutions. In the latter, would-be practitioners enjoy the status of students, usually paying their educational way, while police recruits are paid organizational employees from the start of their training and hence in a very different relationship to their trainers.

The training role is not one of high status within police organizations. While they may receive some short preparation for their roles, trainers remain members of the lower ranks within a strongly hierarchical many-layered police organization. They will teach a curriculum of which the content, length, pedagogy and assessment methods are precisely dictated by headquarters. Moreover, there is evidence to indicate that foundational education and training is very much viewed as a primary method of managerial control over policing practice, performance and conduct. Within such an approach, formal education and training may come to be seen as a production process through which passive and subordinated (rather than active and resilient) recruits are turned into competent and disciplined police officers.

In contrast to some continental European police jurisdictions, for example Sweden and Norway, where police students do three years in full time police studies before being employed and deployed to the field, in most Australian, British and American jurisdictions, the initial academy-based training is of short duration, rarely exceeding six months. This briefness places severe limits on the amount and kind of formal learning that can take place.

Generally, recruits will spend between 25 per cent and 50 per cent of their time on physical activities, being drilled in defensive tactics, the use of less than lethal force, the safe handling and use of firearms, and car driving skills. Drilled marching also constitutes a major part of the curriculum. Recruits almost everywhere will spend more time being marched up and down and standing on parade grounds being shouted at by drill instructors than they will, for example, learning and practising investigative interviewing. This militaristic academy regime is justified, not so much in terms of its appropriateness as a preparation for doing police work, but as an effective form of induction into a disciplined organization.

Also during this short period of initial academy training, recruits will learn by rote the basic police administrative procedures, criminal law proofs, and core police powers, all of which are usually assessed at short intervals by multiple choice question testing.

What are regarded as the 'softer' and more theoretical dimensions of the training, such as communication skills, understanding domestic violence, understanding the nature of crime and its prevention and an understanding of vulnerable people and diverse communities, take up the remainder of the academy time.

The absence of deeper forms of learning based on reading and reflection is not usually a cause for concern for either recruits or trainers. Book-based knowledge is not highly valued in police academies where the pressure is on ensuring that recruits acquire a survival kit of necessary legal knowledge and technical skills before their all too soon immersion into police work.

The initial academy training will end with an open air, well rehearsed and elaborate attestation or graduation ceremony attended by headquarter senior officers and by recruits' parents and friends. Recruits then commence a one to two year period of learning on the job as probationary constables before becoming full constables.

Following a report by Her Majesty's Inspectorate of Constabulary (2002) the training of English and Welsh police recruits has been reorganized with a new Initial Police Learning Development Programme established in all forces from April 2006. Much of the induction training curriculum had been nationally organized and delivered at regional training centres. In the new system individual police forces have regained responsibility for providing training that better meets local community needs. They have been encouraged to enter into partnerships with local higher education service providers in doing so. For example, South Wales has entered into a partnership with Cardiff and Glamorgan universities to form a Universities Police Science Institute through which police educational reforms will be pursued.

In some police agencies the on-the-job period of recruit training is formally organized as an extension of the initial academy experience. For their first few weeks on the job probationary constables may be required to be mentored and supervised by field trainers or tutor constables at specially designated training stations. They may also be required to compile a portfolio of assessable work tasks and cases and be deployed across a range of different types of police duties. It is common too for them to return to the police academy for short periods of further classroom-based learning to allow the opportunity to reflect on their experience of police work.

In a very small number of police agencies there have been moves to acquire public accreditation for recruit training courses through the vocational part of the higher education system. Many Australian police agencies have become 'registered training organizations' which enables them to award a diploma in public safety (policing) to constables completing recruit education. One Australian police agency partners a university in delivering its recruit education through an associate degree in applied policing, a course which is taught to undergraduate generic and technical capabilities' standards using a mixture of classroom, work-based learning (practicum) and distance education learning systems.

In the US there has been an almost continuous debate about higher education and police training since the early twentieth century. Do police officers with college degrees make better police officers than those who do not, and if so why and in what ways? The 1968 Omnibus Crime Control and Safe Streets Act led to the Federal government funding large numbers of criminal justice programmes for serving police officers taught by community colleges. These courses were generally found to be extensions of academy courses and of poor quality. In Australia, recent commissions of inquiry into police corruption have recommended that foundational police training commence with recruits completing university-based degrees in policing.

Evaluation

Because of their enclosure within police bureaucracies, their relatively low status, and poor resource levels, the available research suggests that police academies generally fail to have much impact upon the competence and conduct of new police practitioners. The academy experience is more a rite of passage into the relatively closed world of public policing, rather than a process through which rich and deep learning about how to police takes place.

When they enter their field training phase, rooky cops quickly appreciate how inadequate their academy preparation had been. Through doing police work and working with experience-hardened senior colleagues, many will also come to view what the academy provided as narrow, insufficient and overly idealistic.

Many will find their experience of the job, with its heavy paper workload and its often mundane service tasks, at odds with their initial expectations. Many features of their work-based learning may fall seriously short of what had been formally designed. Posted to busy but short-staffed police stations they may see little of field tutors (mentors or 'buddies') and find those they do were not volunteers for the position and given little training for it.

However, even if their field experience meets formal expectations, research consistently shows that the formal provisions for police training will only be one relatively small influence on their development as police practitioners. Other factors include the political, social and community circumstances within which they learn their policing. Critical too will be the nature, ethos and diversity of the occupational culture they find themselves in. Generally, and in pace with the larger population, more and more police recruits will have completed tertiary education, and so at any rate be older, more mature and resilient adults, less liable to undertake radical shifts in character, more able to choose to be the kind of police officers they want to be.

With regard to college and university educated recruits, the connection between this and their qualities as police officers, the research evidence shows mixed results. For example, there is some evidence that college graduates generate fewer complaints and use less force than non-graduate officers.

What is evident in the research literature on police education is the relative lack of rich descriptions and analyses of good and effective police practices of the sort needed to provide the content of better training. That the latter is needed there is little doubt. There is a general consensus among police scholars that increasingly into the twenty-first century, policing is beset by changes that collectively and persistently have led to a demand for higher and more complex standards and expectations from those who deliver it. These changes, along with what accounts we have of the realities of police education and training, strongly suggest that the current conventional police training systems have clearly run past their used-by dates.

David Bradley

Associated Concepts: culture, socialization, professionalization, reform

Key Readings

Chan, J. with C. Devery and S. Doran (2003) *Fair Cop: Learning the Art of Policing.* Toronto: University of Toronto Press.

Fielding, N. (1988) *Joining Forces: Police Training, Socialization, and Occupational Competence.* London and New York: Routledge.

Her Majesty's Inspectorate of Constabulary (2002) *Training Matters.* London: Home Office.

Sherman, L. (1978) *The Quality of Police Education.* San Francisco: Jossey-Bass.

Skogan, W. and Frydl, K. (2004) *Fairness and Effectiveness in Policing: The Evidence.* Washington D.C.: The National Academies Press.

Smith, D. (2007) 'New challenges to police legitimacy', in A. Henry and D. J. Smith (eds) *Transformations of Policing.* Aldershot: Ashgate Publishing Ltd.

ENTRAPMENT

Definition

Characterizations of entrapment remain a matter of dispute. Almost all are agreed that entrapment refers to the actions of government agents (such as police or their informants), though English common law also recognizes the phenomenon of private entrapment (*R. v. Shannon*, [2001] 1 Cr.App.R. 12). Almost all are agreed that the actions are such as to 'induce' a target to commit a crime for the purpose of prosecution. Most of the debate revolves round the predisposition of the target and the nature of the agent's involvement. On some accounts, entrapment does not occur if the target is predisposed to commit the crime that is induced. On other views, entrapment is a function of how 'creatively' a government agent – the focus of this article – is involved in the commission of the crime. The latter view may focus on pressure brought to bear on the target, the extent to which vulnerabilities or emotions were exploited, how much the government agent contributed to the crime's realization and the availability of alternative means of criminal investigation.

Entrapment may occur if a government agent supplies a prohibited substance to a target who wishes to use it or sell it to others. It may occur when a government agent seeks to purchase a prohibited substance from a target. It may occur when government agents supply a prohibited substance to a target for sale to a government agent who has asked for it. Although many entrapment cases have focused on prohibited substances (because of the difficulties otherwise involved in prosecuting their possession, use, or sale), other criminalized activities – especially those involving willing collaborators, such as counterfeiting, the distribution of pornography, or the handling of stolen goods – may also be investigated in such a way that entrapment occurs.

Distinctive Features

In the US, entrapment is an affirmative defence. That is, if defendants can establish that the crime for which they are charged came about as a result of entrapment, then charges will be dropped. The defence is not greatly used, and when used is not often successful. It requires an admission that the crime was committed, and the onus is on the defendant to establish that entrapment occurred. The prevailing account of entrapment in U.S.

law focuses on the defendant's predisposition (variously understood), though there has always been minority support for the view that entrapment is constituted by government 'overstepping' and should be seen as a violation of due process. The respective approaches are commonly referred to as subjective and objective. There has been some debate over whether predisposition requires more than a 'readiness' to respond affirmatively to the government's approach, and also over whether the readiness to do the prohibited act must include a readiness to do it as prohibited, a critical issue in *Jacobson v. U.S.*, 112 S.Ct. 1535 (1992).

In other countries, entrapment tends to be construed more broadly, and judicial responses to it are discretionary. The focus, moreover, is not so much on predisposition as on governmental conduct. A showing of entrapment may lead to the exclusion of evidence or, in certain cases, to a stay of proceedings. Until 1998, when the UK incorporated the European Convention on Human Rights (ECHR) into English law, the prevailing view from *R. v. Sang*, [1980] A.C. 402 was that a showing of entrapment could lead at most to a mitigation of sentence. In light of the ECHR, the House of Lords has now determined – in *R. v. Looseley*, [2001] 1 W.L.R. 2060 – that in extreme cases, abuse of process grounds justify a stay of prosecution. The European Court of Human Rights had previously determined that where government agents had 'instigated' rather than merely 'investigated' an offence, the defendant had been deprived of a fair trial under Article 6 of the ECHR (*Teixeira di Castro v. Portugal*, [1999] 28 E.H.R.R. 101). Even so, the House of Lords placed as much weight on the impact of such conduct by government agents as on the abuse of process. By moving in the direction of a concern with instigation or incitement (*agents provocateurs*), the UK was bringing its position closer to that which has prevailed in Canada since 1988 (*R. v. Mack*, [1988] 2 S.C.R. 903). In that case, the court took the view that entrapment occurred when government agents went beyond providing an opportunity for the commission of a crime in cases in which they suspected a person's involvement in criminal activity. Subsequent to a determination of a person's guilt by a jury, a judge could determine that there had been an abuse of process and that proceedings be permanently stayed. The grounds for this lying in the need to maintain public confidence in the processes of criminal justice. Australia's approach to entrapment is largely governed by *Ridgeway v. The Queen*, (1995) 184 C.L.R. 19, a case in which government agents imported a prohibited substance on behalf of the defendant. In that case concern was expressed about the effect that it would have on the integrity of the courts were evidence admitted that had been gained by means that violated the law (government agents importing a prohibited substance); the focus was not so much on any abuse of process. This left open the possibility of Australian government agents being given statutory permission to do what in other circumstances would have violated the law, a permission that was given shortly thereafter.

Evaluation

Although not identical, the contrasts involved in the different characterizations of entrapment are slightly artificial. Because the kind of instigation that is often involved when government agents entrap would not serve to relieve a defendant of responsibility were the inducer just a private citizen (though this ignores the anomalous common law case of private entrapment), even those who focus on predisposition must have in mind some conception of what it is appropriate for government agents to do in the prosecution of crime.

Both subjective and objective approaches to entrapment must come to terms with a number of difficulties. In the case of the subjective approach, the question of predisposition can be quite problematic. As became apparent in *Jacobson v. U.S.*, 112 S.Ct. 1535 (1992), there may have been a predisposition to purchase child pornography without there being a predisposition to purchase it illegally. And there may be cases in which, even if there is a desire to engage in illegal activity, there is little likelihood that without the intervention of government agents, this would ever have translated into action. In the case of the objective approach, there is a real question about what constitutes going too far. A distinction sometimes made between the active and merely passive involvement of government agents is none-too-clear. If the government agents have strong reason to believe that the target is involved in criminal activity, but do not have enough evidence to proceed, does their active engagement in the criminal enterprise now entrap (when surely it would have, had there been no prior evidence of criminality)? When does an opportunity that might constitute a temptation 'incite' or 'instigate'? Is it one that would induce an ordinary person into committing a crime? At what point in the repetition of an opportunity does it become excessive? In presenting opportunities, do the government agents imply some threat if the opportunity is not taken up? In addition, the active passive distinction leaves out of account a number of additional factors that need to be considered – such as the seriousness of the crimes being investigated, the difficulty of getting access to evidence of criminality, and the vulnerabilities of the person being targeted.

At the level of justification there are also several problems that have to be addressed. Is the problem with entrapment that it is fundamentally unfair to defendants? Or does the problem lie with the impact that certain tactics used by government agents will have on the integrity or public standing of the criminal justice system? Or is the problem that governmental participation leaves us with reasonable doubt about whether the defendant would have engaged in criminal activity had it not been for governmental involvement?

John Kleinig

Associated Concepts: discretion, drugs, ethical policing, misconduct

Key Readings

Ashworth, A. (2002) 'Re-drawing the boundaries of entrapment', *Criminal Law Review*, 161–79.

Bronitt, S. (2004) 'The law in undercover policing: a comparative study of entrapment and covert interviewing in Australia, Canada and Europe', *Common Law World Review* 33 (1): 35–80.

Hofmeyr, K. (2006) 'The problem of private entrapment', *Criminal Law Review*, 319–36.

Marcus, P. (2002) *The Entrapment Defense* (3rd edn), annual supplements. Newark, N.J.; San Francisco: Michie and Co/LexisNexis.

ENVIRONMENTAL CRIME

Definition

Environmental crime is now starting to garner much greater public and political attention as a distinct category of crime, one that poses special challenges for law enforcement officials such as the police.

The categorization of environmental harm is varied in that there are different ways in which environmental crimes have been conceptualized and sorted (see for example, White, 2005; Beirne and South, 2007). For instance, Carrabine et al. (2004) discuss environmental crimes in terms of primary and secondary crimes. Primary crimes are those crimes that result directly from the destruction and degradation of the earth's resources through human actions. They include such things as air pollution, deforestation, animal abuse, etc. Secondary or symbiotic green crime is crime arising out of the flouting of rules that seek to regulate environmental disasters, and can include specific incidents such as the French government bombing of the Greenpeace boat, Rainbow Warrior, in 1985 in New Zealand, through to the dumping of toxic waste in Abidjan, the capital city of the Ivory Coast in August 2006, that led to the deaths of 15 people.

From the point of view of international law enforcement agencies such as Interpol, the major issues relating to environmental crime are the trans-border movement and dumping of waste products, the illegal traffic in real or purported radioactive or nuclear substances, and the illegal traffic in species of wild flora and fauna. Issues such as illegal logging and illegal fishing are also starting to figure more prominently in discussions of transnational environmental crime.

Distinctive Features

The nature of environmental crime poses a number of challenges for effective policing. Such crimes may have local, regional and global dimensions. They may be difficult to detect (as in the case of some forms of toxic pollution that is not detectable to human senses). They may demand intensive cross-jurisdictional negotiation, and even disagreement between nation states, in regards to specific events or crime patterns. Some crimes may be highly organized and involve criminal syndicates, such as illegal fishing. Others may include a wide range of criminal actors, ranging from the individual collector of endangered species to the systematic disposal of toxic waste via third parties.

One of the initial questions to be asked of environmental crime is who is actually going to do the policing? Many jurisdictions at both national and state level have specialist agencies – such as Environmental Protection Agencies which are given the mandate to investigate and prosecute environmental crimes. The police generally play an auxiliary role in relation to the work of these agencies.

In other countries, members of the police service receive specialist training to fulfil environmental policing roles. In Israel, for example, an environmental unit was established in 2003 within the framework of its police service. It is financed by the Ministry of the Environment and includes police officers who form the Green Police. These police carry out inspections, enforcement and investigation under a variety of laws in areas such as prevention of water source and marine pollution, industrial and vehicular pollution, hazardous substances, and prevention of cruelty to animals. Each year they carry out thousands of inspections of factories, landfills and sewerage treatment sites, in the process liaising with regional offices of the Ministry of the Environment.

Within a particular national context, there may be considerable diversity in environmental law enforcement agencies and personnel, and police will have quite different roles in environmental law enforcement depending upon the city or state within which they work (see Tomkins, 2005). In a federal system of governance for example, such as with the US, Canada and Australia, there will be great variation in environmental enforcement authorities, ranging from police operating at the local municipal level through to participation in international forums.

Specific kinds of crime may involve different agencies, depending upon the jurisdiction. For example, the policing of abalone poaching in Australia is generally undertaken by civilian authorities, except in Tasmania and the Northern Territory where it is in the hands of the marine police. The cross-border nature of illegal fishing operations – across state as well as international boundaries – means that often a local police service will necessarily have to work collaboratively with national police agencies that, in turn, will have relationships with regional police partnerships (such as Europol) and international organizations such as Interpol.

In some jurisdictions, including Canada, the task of enforcing the law against illegal fishing (for example, of lobsters) is in the hands of unarmed fishery officers. The powers and resources available to specific law enforcement officials will vary greatly from jurisdiction to jurisdiction, and from agency to agency, depending upon whether or not the police are directly involved, and whether or not agents have been granted specific powers of investigation, arrest and use of weapons for example to enforce environmental laws. Criminal enforcement of environmental law is basically shaped by specific national context, and the legislative and organizational resources dedicated to policing local environmental harms as well as those involving cross-border incidents (see for example, Faure and Heine, 2000).

Evaluation

Environmental crimes frequently demand a high level of collaboration with non-police agencies. For example, illegal fishing often involves customs officials, quarantine officials, federal and local police officers and sometimes the Navy. How best to organize law enforcement activities in regards to different environmental crimes is a perennial issue. Should specific environmental police units, within police services, be created, as in the case of Israel? Or, should 'flying squads' be created, that are comprised of personnel from different agencies and that reflect inter-agency collaboration and expertize? Or, should it be the specific crime in question that ought to shape the organizational make-up and operational activities of law enforcement? It has also been suggested that there is a need to develop systematic environmental crime policing strategies to provide broad policy guidance to police jurisdictions and to ensure consistency in the expanded police interactions with non-police environmental agencies (Blindell, 2006).

Related to organizational matters, the dynamics of environmental crime are such that new types of skills, knowledge and expertize need to be drawn upon as part of the policing effort. For example, illegal land clearance can be monitored through satellite technologies. Toxic waste and pollution spills may require the sophisticated tools and scientific know-how associated with environmental forensics. DNA testing is already being used in relation to logging, fishing and endangered species, that is, to track illegal possession and theft of animals and plants. Powers of investigation, particularly in relation to the gathering of suitable evidence for the specific environmental crime, will inevitably be shaped by state, federal and international conventions and protocols, as well as by availability of local expertise, staff and resources.

The enhancement of police capabilities in environmental law enforcement requires the raising and prioritizing of such crimes on national and international political agendas. Accompanying this, policies, principles and practices will need to be developed that are tailored specifically to the nature and dynamics of particular environmental crimes.

The place and role of civilian scientists and experts within police law enforcement agencies and the appropriate professional training of police staff are further issues that will require continuing review and assessment. Alongside a general familiarity with emergent technologies and techniques relevant to the detection, investigation, prevention and prosecution of environmental crime, police officers will need to be trained to be able to work in multi-disciplinary, multi-agency teams that also have the capacity to liaise with counterparts in other countries and jurisdictions.

Environmental law enforcement is a relatively new area of police work and is at a stage when perhaps more questions are being asked than answers can be provided. Certainly what would be useful is comparative assessment of local and nationally based 'good practice' in this area. Equally, any assessments of how successful police work translates into prosecution processes and actual sentences for environmental offenders will provide insight into how the work of the courts impacts upon the morale and activities of those working in the field.

Rob White

Associated Concepts: criminal investigation, cross-border policing, organized crime, transnational policing

Key Readings

Bierne, P. and South, N. (eds) (2007) *Issues in Green Criminology: Confronting Harms Against Environments, Humanity and Other Animals*. Cullompton, Devon: Willan Publishing.

Blindell, J. (2006) *'Twenty-First Century Policing – The Role of Police in the Detection, Investigation and Prosecution of Environmental Crime'*, ACPR Issues No. 2. Adelaide: Australasian Centre for Policing Research.

Carrabine, E., Iganski, P., Lee, M., Plummer, K. and South, N. (2004) *Criminology: A Sociological Introduction*. London: Routledge.

Faure, M. and Heine, G. (2000) *Criminal Enforcement of Environmental Law in the European Union*. Copenhagen: Danish Environmental Protection Agency.

Tomkins, K. (2005) 'Police, law enforcement and the environment', *Current Issues in Criminal Justice*, 16 (3): 294–306.

White, R. (2005) 'Environmental crime in global context: exploring the theoretical and empirical complexities', *Current Issues in Criminal Justice*, 16 (3): 271–85.

ETHICAL POLICING

Definition

Morality can be understood to refer to the basic norms of human interaction – those more or less universal expectations of attitude and conduct that govern our dealings with each other. Ethical standards explicate those expectations within the framework of various social institutions and for those acting in various social roles. Thus, ethical policing will refer not so much to the morality of police officers and their institutions but to that morality as it is refracted through various roles and institutional purposes. Ethical policing is not, for example, directly concerned with whether police officers cheat on their tax returns or spouses, or with the accounting procedures used by a police department, but with how they act – individually or institutionally – when providing police services. Broadly, moral concerns are relevant only to the extent that they derogate from the capacity or authority needed to provide such services. Nevertheless, it will normally be possible to provide a moral justification for ethical conduct, because the latter will have its rationale in a social role, and the social role will have its rationale in a broader social purpose that will itself be justified as a legitimate expression of general moral standards.

Distinctive Features

The police role is one of social peacekeeping. This is somewhat broader than – though it also encompasses – crime prevention, law enforcement, and order maintenance. It refers to a range of social tasks that police are authorized to perform – often in situations of crisis or emergency – in order that the various activities and structures of social life are able to operate with a minimum of disruption. Police work has its rationale in natural human vulnerability, frailty, and wilfulness, and the need that we have for social structures capable of securing the requisites for human flourishing (including the securing of our rights). Once a communal or private function, for much of the past two centuries, policing in liberal democratic societies has been vested in public officers. Not that police have exclusive responsibility for social peacekeeping. They are, for example, answerable to a legislature and courts. And of course they do not replace families, schools, and religious organizations as sources of social good order. But the latter are limited in their ability to secure social peace and police are given special powers to prevent or handle breakdowns of social peace when they cannot be adequately handled in other ways.

In particular, police are authorized to use force and deception in the prosecution of their tasks. For many these distinctive prerogatives of the police role constitute its defining features, though their use for the most part represents an allowable limit rather than standard operating procedure. Along with special powers, police are also granted considerable discretion in their use. Such discretion, however, though it calls for individual judgement in using the powers made available to them, is not arbitrary, but bounded by certain professional understandings.

Discretionary authority tends to be conceptualized differently in the US and Anglo-Australian policing. Although police organizations in both cases are hierarchically organized (often along quasi-military lines), Anglo-Australian police are said to possess an 'original authority' that vests in the individual constable the ultimate discretion – under the law – whether, for example, to arrest or not arrest *Enever v. R.* (1906), 3 C.L.R. 969. Within the US however, police officers are seen as employees with delegated authority who may be directed whether or not to arrest.

Such complications aside, ethical policing is at bottom an ethic of professionalism. That is, it is a collective ethic focused on the attitudes and conduct appropriate to the provision of services required by the social peacekeeping role. Such collective ethics are frequently embodied in the statements of a general professional code such as the Law Enforcement Code of Ethics promulgated by the International Association of Chiefs of Police or, sometimes, the more specialized codes that are developed to accommodate specific ranks – or specific police tasks (see Kleinig with Zhang, 1993).

Evaluation

Codes of ethics, though valuable attempts to crystallize the expectations of ethical policing, also suffer from serious defects. For one thing, there is a dynamism and vitality to ethical judgement that is easily lost in the frozen formulations of a code: their requirements become yet another regulatory demand delivered from above rather than an expression of professionalism on the part of those called to make appropriate decisions. Ideally, codes should be revisited regularly and be informed by a broad spectrum of input to ensure their ownership by those for whom they are intended.

In addition, codes lack sufficient nuance for many of the circumstances in which professional judgement needs to be exercised. Aggravating this is a tendency for the requirements of codes to stand in some tension in particular cases. Concern for victims and due process may seem to pull in different directions, and police sometimes believe themselves to be required to 'dirty their hands.' Whether this phenomenon, commonly invoked in the political realm, has a place in policing is a matter of continuing debate. It frequently underpins the controversy about 'noble cause corruption' and the extent to which ends can be appealed to in justification of problematic means.

Appropriate limits on the critical police powers of coercive force and deception figure prominently in discussions of ethical policing. Within a liberal democratic framework, we can best frame our understanding of the limits within which they are to be exercised by seeing such prerogatives as delegations exercised on behalf of a wider community. Force will thus need to be exercised with constraint – employed only as less coercive measures fail, and then proportionately to the situation. Many police departments work with a graduated scale of authoritative engagement (a continuum of force) and a range of devices and techniques to bring situations under appropriate control with as little injury as possible. One of the key ethical challenges, as coercive strategies are refined, is that a disabling but non-injurious device for applying intermediate force may, if placed in ethically insensitive hands, be used in punitive, retaliatory, or inhumane ways. The use of deadly force – more likely in societies in which police are armed as a matter of course – now tends to be heavily constrained and justified only in circumstances in which officers or others have been placed at grave risk and must act defensively.

Deception, increasingly used as an investigative technique now that reliance on confessions has declined, also requires careful calibration, lest the criminal justice system's larger goals of truth and justice – or at least a fair trial – are not subverted. Deception that may be liberally (but not indiscriminately) used as part of an initial process of investigation is to be kept out of a courtroom in which fairness should prevail – not only with respect to the outcome of a rational process, but also with respect to the monitoring of deception at other stages of the investigative process.

Although the ethical quality of police work will often be closely involved with the use of special powers such as those concerning force and deception, there is also a collective dimension to policing that will be critical to its ethical character. A great deal of policing is coordinated, cooperative, and supervised, and how ethically it is conducted will depend on the quality of its communal or associational relations. Because policing is hierarchically organized, the quality of leadership that is shown, not only by those at its administrative apex but also by those in operational supervisory positions, will be of vital significance. Leadership will contribute to the ethical quality of police work through example, expectations, and professionalism-building initiatives. Failures in leadership (at various levels) are also likely to be accompanied by the development of perverted loyalties within the ranks – a blue code of silence that covers up corruption and failure. In an occupation known for the moral hazards it encounters, this can have profound and regrettable social consequences.

John Kleinig

Associated Concepts: discretion, force, leadership, misconduct

Key Readings

Carabetta, J. (2003) 'Employment status of the police in Australia,' *Melbourne University Law Review,* 27 (April): 1–32.

Delattre, E. (2002) *Character and Cops: Ethics in Policing* (4th edn). Washington, DC: AEI.

Kleinig, J. with Zhang, Y. (ed. and comp.) (1993). *Professional Law Enforcement Codes: A Documentary Collection.* Westport. CT: Greenwood.

Kleinig, J. (1996) *The Ethics of Policing.* Cambridge: Cambridge University Press.

Miller, S., Blackler, J., and Alexandra, A., (2006) *Police Ethics* (2nd edn). NSW: Allen and Unwin.

ETHNIC MINORITY COMMUNITIES

See Diversity; Hate Crime; Institutional Racism; Police Property; Racial Profiling

EUROPOL

Definition

Europol is the criminal intelligence organization of the European Union, established with a mandate to support Member States in working together to control transnational organized crime and terrorism. Its headquarters are in The Hague, in the Netherlands, where its over 500 personnel include Europol Liaison Officers seconded from the law enforcement agencies of the Member States.

The organization was preceded by Trevi, a forum established in 1975 for police cooperation among countries of the then European Economic Community, which was dissolved following the Treaty on European Union (TEU) (1992), otherwise known as the Maastricht Treaty. A Trevi working group began the process that led to the establishment of Europol, beginning with the creation of a Europol Drugs Unit (EDU), which commenced its operations in early 1994. Gradually other forms of criminality were added to its scope, and following the Europol Convention in 1998, in 1999 Europol was officially created.

Distinctive Features

The role and character of Europol as it currently stands can be understood by looking at its origins and development. The German Federal Republic has been the most important driving force since the 1960s behind the development of police cooperation between the Member States of the EU. By the 1970s, many leading figures in Germany were of the view that the economic and political unification of the European states needed to be accompanied by a considerable reinforcement of their mutual cooperation in police work by, for instance, the establishment of a European Police Service. There were differences of opinion, however, about how such a service should be organized, and what its tasks and powers should be. Some proponents felt it should be established within the existing structure of Interpol, while others favoured its establishment within the framework of the European Economic Community (EC, or EEC prior to 1992) or in that provided by European Political Cooperation (the Community's arrangement for foreign policy cooperation pre-1992).

The second area of contention related to whether a European Police Service required executive powers so that it could independently conduct criminal investigations on the territory of the Member States, or whether the establishment of such a body – in a similar format to that of the American Federal Bureau of Investigation (FBI) – was unfeasible or even wholly undesirable. Those of the latter view argued that such a police service should only serve to promote the exchange of information between the police services of the Member States of the EC.

This discussion was taken to the European level in the second half of the 1980s in the context of the further development of the Common Market between the Member States of the EC. The then German Chancellor, Helmut Kohl, argued vigorously that the formation of such a market should be supported by joint security arrangements. At the Summit of the European Council in Luxemburg at the end of June 1991, he presented a proposal that, in the coming TEU, a European Police Service should be established. First, Kohl opted for not embedding this police service in the EC but in the intergovernmental Third Pillar ('Justice and Home Affairs') of the future EU. Second, he proposed that such an agency should not be fully established at one stroke but built up in phases. In the first phase, according to his proposal, this service would function only as a clearing house for information. In the second phase, it would obtain powers to be able to act independently on the territory of the Member States.

It was to be expected that the other governmental leaders would react cautiously to this proposal: an independent executive police service on the territory of all of the Member States not only aroused grim memories of very grim times – from the Napoleonic empire to the German SS police state and its oppressions – but was also irreconcilable with the sovereignty of the Member States as regards domestic security. In the conclusions of the Summit, therefore, it was only stated that the European Council would ask the ministers of Justice and Home Affairs to present proposals in relation to the German proposal at the next Summit in Maastricht. These proposals came down to the establishment of a European Police Office on the basis of a convention that would be allowed only to support the police services of the Member States by means of the 'exchange of information and experience'.

The TEU established the Union according to a 'Three Pillars' structure, whereby the first pillar of the EC was to operate in parallel to the Common Foreign and Security Policy pillar, and the Justice and Home Affairs pillar. In the Treaty, the above proposals were enacted in provisions for a system for the exchange of information within a European Police Office (Europol) at the level of the Union (Title VI, art. K.1.9). To bridge the period of time until the ratification of a Europol Convention, it was decided to set up immediately its predecessor, the EDU, in The Hague.

The fact that it was not until July 1995 that the Europol Convention was signed by the governments of the Member States, and that it then took until the summer of 1998 before this Convention was ratified by all of the Member States and took effect, is illustrative of the significant effort involved in establishing the European Police Office. The content of this Convention, however, also made it abundantly clear that many of the Member States had a great deal of difficulty with the implementation of the agreement that was made in Maastricht. Not only was the supporting task of Europol strictly adhered to in the exchange and the analysis of information regarding serious organized crime involving two or more Member States, but the office was also organized – with national units in the Member States and only liaison officers in The Hague with a management board consisting of representatives of the Member States and with detailed regulations to mitigate concerns such as data protection – so that the Member States have complete control over its operation. That Europol is an intergovernmental organ *par excellence* is demonstrated by the organs of the EC – the European Parliament, the Luxembourg Court of Justice, and the European Commission – formally having little or no involvement with the way in which this European Police Office is managed and actually works.

The amendment of the TEU by the Treaty of Amsterdam (1997) stipulated in Article 30 that, within five years after it took effect (i.e., from 1999), the European Council would promote police cooperation between the Member States via Europol and would enable Europol 'to facilitate and support the preparation, and to encourage the coordination and carrying out, of specific investigative actions by the competent authorities of the Member States, including operational actions of joint teams comprising representatives of Europol in a support capacity'. These and other changes enabled efforts to involve Europol more closely in the combating of cross-border organized crime to be realized. This led to the drafting of three protocols between 2000 and 2003 to modify the Europol Convention.

These protocols, after intense debate between the European Council, the European Commission, and the Member States, became operative in March and April 2007. The implementation of these protocols has had, at certain points, important consequences for the organization and operation of Europol. For example, under certain conditions, they make it possible for police services from the Member States to work directly – and thus apart from the national units – with Europol, for third party countries such as Canada and the US contribute to the analysis of data, and for members of Europol to be able to participate in joint investigation teams of the Member States. The organization's supporting role in the tracing of serious crime has been further strengthened by a decision by the European Council in July 2005, making Europol the central office for combating Euro counterfeiting in the EU in the framework of the Geneva Convention of 1929.

Evaluation

The formation and development of Europol have involved, as would be expected, significant discussion and deliberation about its organization and functioning. The central issue in this debate includes such questions as: is it acceptable that no direct judicial control over Europol has been put in place? To what extent do Europol staff members have immunity if they participate in one way or another in criminal investigations in the Member States? And to what extent does the involvement of Europol in concrete criminal investigations constitute an infringement of the rights of the suspect in the criminal proceedings? Neither in political nor academic circles have the discussions provided unequivocal answers to these questions. This has much to do with the fact that, in such discussions – in spite of the detailed stipulations in the Convention – there are widely divergent conceptions about the actual nature of Europol and about its role in the criminal justice proceedings in the Member States.

In January 2006, the Austrian Presidency placed the future of Europol on the political agenda and was able to gain support from the European Council in June 2006 to replace the Europol Convention as of 1 January 2008 by a Council Decision. The arguments for this important revision of the legal foundation of Europol were incorporated in a report entitled The Future of Europol. These related to the excessively restricted mandate of Europol in relation to the evolution of serious crime in the EU, the need to embed its activities in all kinds of new forms of police cooperation between the Member States, and the need for greater involvement of Europol in the actual operation of the national police services.

All of this led the Commission to publish a proposal on 20 December 2006 for a Council Decision Establishing the European Police Office (Europol), in which not only has the content of the protocols mentioned above been included, but also the operational role of Europol further strengthened. With this, however, Europol still does not come anywhere close to the executive police service envisaged by Helmut Kohl at the end of the 1980s. It remains politically and legally impossible for power to be granted to allow criminal investigations to be conducted independently on the territory of the EU.

Cyrille Fijnaut

Associated Concepts: cross-border policing, intelligence agency, Interpol, organized crime, terrorism, transnational policing

Key Readings

Commission of the European Communities (2006) *Proposal for a Council Decision Establishing the European Police Office (Europol)*, COM (2006) 817 Final, Brussels, 20.12.2006.

Fijnaut, C. (1993) 'The 'communitization of police cooperation in Western Europe', in H.G. Schermers, C. Flinterman, A.E. Kellermann, J. C. van Haersolte and G-W. A. van der Meent (eds) *Free Movement of Persons in Europe*. Dordrecht: Martinus Nijhoff Publishers.

Loader, I. (2002) 'Policing, securitization and democratization in Europe', *Criminology and Criminal Justice*, 2 (2): 125–53.

Rauchs, G. and Koenig, D.J. (2001) 'Europol', in D. Koenig, and D.K. Das, (eds) *International Police Cooperation: A World Perspective*. Lanham, MD: Lexington Books.

Walker, N. (ed.) (2004) *Europe's Area of Freedom, Security and Justice*. Oxford: Oxford University Press.

EVIDENCE-BASED POLICING

Definition

Evidence-based policing is the use of the best available scientific research on the outcomes of police work to implement guidelines and evaluate agencies, units, and officers. Evidence-based policing uses research to guide practice and evaluate practitioners. In terms of crime prevention practice, evidence-based policing (where it is applied) involves the police using the highest quality available research evidence on what works best to reduce a specific crime problem and implementing that research appropriately, tailoring the intervention to the local context and conditions.

Distinctive Features

Evidence-based policing is a part of a larger and increasingly expanding evidence-based movement. In general terms, this movement is dedicated to the improvement of society through the utilization of the highest quality scientific evidence on what works best. The evidence-based movement first began in medicine and has, more recently, been embraced by the social sciences. Lawrence Sherman, David Weisburd, and groups such as the Campbell Collaboration's Crime and Justice Group have been leading advocates for the adoption of an evidence-based approach to policing. In an evidence-based model, the source of scientific evidence is empirical research in the form of evaluations of programmes, practices, and policies. Not all evaluation designs are considered equal, however. Some evaluation designs, such as randomized controlled experiments, are considered more scientifically valid than others. The findings of stronger evaluation designs are privileged over the findings of weaker research designs in determining 'what works' in policing. The Maryland Scientific Methods Scale is sometimes used to indicate to scholars, practitioners and policy-makers that, for example, studies evaluating criminological interventions may differ in terms of methodological quality of evaluation techniques (see Farrington et al., in Sherman et al., 2002).

It is considered critical that the most rigorous methods be used to locate, appraise, and synthesize the available research evidence on police practices. Careful research methods, such as meta-analyses and systematic reviews, are strongly recommended by those advocating an evidence-based approach. These approaches are known for their comprehensiveness, adherence to scientific rules and conventions, and

transparency. Another important feature of the evidence-based policing model is the outcome of interest. While it is acknowledged that evidence-based policing can serve other useful purposes (for example, improving police training standards, improving police-community relations), the main outcome of interest or 'bottom line' is crime prevention.

Implementation is critical to the development of the evidence-based policing model. It is not enough to evaluate what strategies work best when implemented properly under controlled conditions. Ongoing research is necessary to determine the results particular police agencies are achieving by applying (or not) the recommended practices. Some critics of the evidence-based paradigm claim that it fails to adequately account for local context and conditions in reaching conclusions about what works (or does not work). The main thrust of this argument is that unless local context and conditions are investigated, undue weight may be ascribed to any effects of the police intervention on the outcome of interest (usually crime prevention). Taking account of local context and conditions in the implementation of new strategies is an important component of the evidence-based policing model. One key challenge then for researchers is the development of an accessible body of scientific evidence on what works best in crime prevention that can guide local police in targeting risk factors and tailoring recommended practices to local context and conditions. Proactive efforts are necessary to direct accumulated research evidence into policy and practice via national and community guidelines. These guidelines can then focus particular police agencies on in-house evaluations of what works best across agencies, units, victims, and officers. Detailed information on the local crime problem and its setting can be matched with proven practice, and modifications to recommended crime prevention strategies can then be made as needed. The combination of basic research on what works and ongoing action research that generates additional evidence on varied applications of a particular strategy creates a feedback loop. This process increases the amount of information available that documents how police agencies might obtain the best crime prevention effects. The review of this accumulated body of evidence may lead to the further development of practical strategy guidelines that take law, ethics, and community culture into account.

In his seminal 1998 paper on evidence-based policing, Sherman offers policing domestic violence as an illustration of the paradigm. The large body of available research evidence on police practices in dealing with domestic violence offers a fair and scientifically valid approach for holding police agencies, units, and officers accountable for the results of police work, as measured by repeated domestic violence against the same victims. The research has revealed that police practices vary greatly in their implementation and these variations generate differing results for repeat offending against victims. Even when varying practices are controlled for, responses to arrest vary by offender, neighbourhood, and city. For instance, a series of experiments revealed that mandatory arrest and prosecution policies reduce domestic violence in some cities but increase it in others; reduce domestic violence among employed people but increase it among unemployed people, and reduce domestic violence in the short run but can increase it in the long run. The experiments also suggested that police can predict which couples are most likely to suffer future violence. Clearly, the police need more options than simply mandatory arrest and subsequent prosecution. Rather than a one-size-fits-all policy, the evidence suggests specific guidelines should be used under different neighbourhood conditions and in the absence or presence of the offender. Structured police discretion that allows officers, after receiving training, to select from a range of approved options based on their assessment of the situation could be substituted for mandatory arrest laws. The available evidence could also support guidelines about listening to suspects' side of the story before making arrest decisions. Other policy options could include giving the police

enhanced arrest powers in misdemeanour domestic violence cases that they did not witness, issuing arrest warrants for domestic violence offenders who are not present or flee the scene and the development of special police units and policies that focus on chronically violent couples. As the police implement and evaluate these new approaches, they contribute to and continually refine the body of research evidence on best practices in dealing with the problem of policing domestic violence.

Evaluation

It is not known to what extent police departments undertake evidence-based research to aid in the development and implementation of programmes and practices to prevent crime. It seems likely that few, if any, police departments have engaged the specific approach recommended by Sherman. However, there have been a few influential reviews of research on which police practices are effective at reducing crime and which practices are not effective. Recently, the US National Academy of Sciences established a panel of social science experts to review all police research including the question of police crime prevention effectiveness. To have an effect on crime, the available evidence strongly suggests that police strategies must include two elements. First, the police must diversify their approaches to crime and disorder. That is, policing must address crime and disorder using a greater range of tools than simply enforcing the law. There is evidence that working with the public, and going beyond law enforcement, can have modest crime and disorder reduction affects, and the more personal the police-citizen contacts the more likely it is that they will have an effect on crime (Tyler, 2004). The second element necessary to highly effective policing is focus. There is solid evidence that geographically concentrated enforcement at crime or disorder hot spots can be effective, at least in the short term (see 'hot spots', in this volume). The US Department of Justice has made a concerted effort to support the development of problem-oriented policing (POP) by disseminating these ideas through the publication of guides on effects of specific policing strategies on different types of crime problems. With its emphasis on developing appropriate responses to the underlying conditions that give rise to crime problems, POP is a clear beneficiary of the evidence-based movement as it promotes the use of practices with proven effectiveness.

Some commentators on evidence-based policing are concerned that by focusing too much on the experience that can be captured in quantitative observational studies and controlled experiments, the evidence-based approach will end up, paradoxically, both reducing the amount of experience that is available to decision makers, and slowing the rate at which the field as a whole can learn about what works in policing. Mark Moore (2006), for example, suggests that the focus on *evidence-based*, rather than *experience-based* knowledge will limit important commonsense insights from detailed qualitative case studies that can be used in developing a more solid base for action.

Evidence-based policing has not been empirically tested as a holistic model of policing. However, evidence-based police departments would draw policies and practices from a solid research base of strategies that have proven to be effective in controlling crime elsewhere. Whether or not the strategy is transferable is something that needs to be evaluated in itself. While an evidence-based approach to policing may have the unintended effect of limiting the ability of police to innovate by privileging evidence over experience, there is little reason to believe that engaging an evidence-based approach would undermine the crime and disorder control effectiveness of police departments.

Anthony A. Braga

Associated Concepts: crime prevention, legitimacy, problem-oriented policing, research

Key Readings

Farrington, D.P., Gottfredson, D.C., Sherman, L.W. and Welsh, B.C. (2002) 'The Maryland Scientific Methods Scale', in L. W. Sherman, D. P. Farrington, B. C. Welsh and D. L. MacKenzie (eds) *Evidence-Based Crime Prevention*. Routledge: London.

Moore, M.H. (2006) 'Improving police through expertise, experience, and experiments', in D. Weisburd and A. Braga (eds) *Police Innovation: Contrasting Perspectives*. New York: Cambridge University Press.

Sherman, L.W. (1998) *Evidence-Based Policing*. Ideas in American Policing series, Washington, DC: Police Foundation.

Skogan, W.G. and Frydl, K. (eds) (2004) *Fairness and Effectiveness in Policing: The Evidence*. Committee to Review Research on Police Policy and Practices, Washington, DC: National Academies Press.

Tyler, T.R. (2004) 'Enhancing police legitimacy', *Annals of the American Academy of Political and Social Sciences*, 593 (1): 84–99.

Welsh, B.C. (2006) 'Evidence-based policing for crime prevention', in D. Weisburd and A. Braga (eds) *Police Innovation: Contrasting Perspectives*. New York: Cambridge University Press.

F

FEAR OF CRIME

Definition

The term fear of crime is used to describe an anxious emotional state reflecting the belief that one is in danger of criminal victimization.

Distinctive Features

Fear of crime is a concept born of the implementation in the 1960s of crime and victim surveys. Widespread disillusionment among social scientists, policy makers and criminal justice professionals about the available sources of crime data, and the wish to reveal the 'dark figure' of unrecorded crime, led to criminal justice and statistical bodies producing new survey instruments. These were partly based on the modern census and partly on opinion polling. Among other things these surveys, first conducted in the US as part of the President's Commission on Law Enforcement and Administration of Justice, attempted to reveal public perceptions about crime. Negative concerns or states of alarm and anxiety about crime came to be termed fear of crime, although respondents were rarely asked specifically if they were fearful. As a result of these surveys, and perhaps more importantly their social scientific interpretation, it was revealed that fear of crime was pervasive in the US. Similar surveys have consequently been conducted in the UK (the British Crime Survey), Australia (the Australian Bureau of Statistics household survey of crime and safety) and elsewhere echoing the US state of affairs and bringing attention to the fear of crime as a policy problem. While by the mid 1980s policy makers in the UK became fascinated with fear of crime (and its reduction) more recently it has become a policy and social scientific issue in Scandinavian and former Eastern Block countries.

An exhaustive review of the relevant literature by Hale (1996) indicated how quickly fear of crime came to have policy significance and criminological salience. It also quickly came to have political salience. By the 1980s, fear of crime came to be seen by many Western governments and criminal justice agencies as almost as much of a problem as crime itself. Interestingly, as reported crime rates dropped in much of the Western world throughout the late 1990s and into the early twenty-first century, levels of fear of crime have proven more difficult to shift. This highlights the claim made by many researchers that the link between the actuarial risk of being victimized and the fear of crime is spurious. Initially researchers and policy makers debated whether fear of crime was a rational or irrational response to the threat of victimization. Such debate was driven by the consistent finding that those less likely to be victimized often reported higher levels of fear – in particular women and the elderly. However, a concerted critique by feminists and left realists who argued that vulnerability and the everyday threat of sexual violence for some groups could account for higher fear levels rendered the 'irrational' thesis untenable. Thus fear of crime was to be taken seriously. It thus became a cultural theme of late modernity. Surveys indicate that populations believe that crime rates are getting worse regardless of actual patterns and that police and the courts are largely powerless to do anything about this.

However since its 'discovery', conceptual debate about what fear of crime is and how to measure it has proliferated. Yet conceptual development has not mirrored this proliferation, and the conservatism inherent in large scale time series survey work has led to recorded levels of fear of crime being highly misrepresentative. While surveys may over estimate levels of public fear by ignoring how infrequent fearful episodes are for respondents, Ditton et al.'s work (1999) also suggests that given the choice (and most surveys do not give such a choice) respondents were more likely to report being more *angry* than *fearful*. The conservatism of survey work – generally seeing concern about crime quantified on a Likert scale – has been criticized by Hollway and Jefferson (2000) who note that the common 'scenario question' asked in many surveys, *how safe do you (or would you) feel walking alone in this neighbourhood after dark?* 'fails to address the way in which respondents' meanings are related to circumstances. Reliance on coding isolated responses strips any remaining context from these responses' (2000: 8). Lee (2007) goes further suggesting that the very surveys which would claim to measure fear of crime have in part invented it and that its political salience and governmental instrumentality, on top of a thirst for social scientific indicators of public well-being, have kept the concept alive. In this sense, fear of crime is not a pre-discursive phenomenon but a product of knowledge and power arrangements. This does not mean that people do not fear crime, quite the contrary. Rather, fear of crime, once invented, feeds off itself in a fear of crime 'feedback loop'. While these critiques have not tempered advocates of the large scale survey it has resulted in something of a 'qualitative turn' in fear of crime research, at least in academic circles.

There is little doubt that public concerns (and/or perceived public concerns) about crime can have detrimental effects on communities. Such concerns can encourage individuals to remove themselves from the public sphere undermining the ability to collectively address social problems, including crime and disorder. It can undermine community policing strategies, create suspicion of strangers and even neighbours, and distort the empirical reality that most serious crime is committed by persons known to their victims in private, not public places. One somewhat ironic consequence of fear of crime is that public places become more dangerous as people avoid them by reducing natural surveillance and eroding the sense of well-being engendered by populated public space. Moreover, security hardware like gates, bars and grills can make streetscapes appear more dangerous, engendering the very fear they often seek to reduce. In jurisdictions with liberal gun control laws, fear of victimization added to disillusionment with criminal justice organizations has encouraged citizens to arm themselves with concealed weapons, again making the public feel less safe. Fear of crime is also a driver in the proliferation of CCTV in public places with some research suggesting that public knowledge of CCTV installation reduces concern about crime. As with the closely related fear of terrorism, the majority of the public often seems more than happy to trade off individual rights and freedoms in the name of increased security.

Evaluation

Negative public perceptions have concrete effects and have accompanied both a reorientation of crime policy and a new politics of law and order. Such shifts include new styles of policing aimed at being; tougher (zero tolerance); more proactive (quality of life policing); and more public (high visibility or reassurance policing). The politicization of law and order has also become prominent with public fears being used to justify harsher sentencing legislation such as the 'three strikes' and 'one strike' models and the removal of judicial discretion for many offence categories. In Australia and elsewhere, many political parties have engaged in law and order auctions where each party tries to outbid the other with increasingly tough crime policy and rhetoric.

The importance attached to reducing fear of crime is also borne out in the mission statements of many modern policing organizations. For example in New South Wales, Australia, the Police Commissioner is employed 'to reduce crime and the fear of crime'. Reducing fear of crime has become a performance indicator on which successful careers can hinge, hence the capacity for crime fear to drive policing practice despite its propensity to warp the reality of crime problems. While high visibility policing may do nothing to reduce rates of crime, the belief that it reduces fear and instils public confidence makes it politically attractive. Somewhat ironically, it is not uncommon for policing organizations or police unions to appeal to public anxieties about crime to legitimate arguments for extra officers or increased powers at the very same time they are charged with allaying fears.

Despite these criticisms and debates it appears that fear of crime will continue being a prominent cultural and political theme, a performance indicator for governments and some criminal justice organizations, a policy object, and a research topic for some time to come. According to scholars of the late modern condition, distrust of strangers and the need to confront difference in complex multi-cultural urbanized contexts has eroded our sense of security. Risks and dangers are perceived to be everywhere and are continually identified by a news hungry media, an insurance industry increasingly ready to insure almost any part of modern living, a security industry ready to protect us for a price, and even a real estate industry providing us with the protection of a gated community. So while policy might be aimed at reducing fear of crime, a whole fear of crime industry relies on its proliferation.

Murray Lee

Associated Concepts: closed circuit television, community safety, law and order politics, public reassurance, vigilantism, zero tolerance policing

Key Readings

Ditton, J., Bannister, J., Gilchrist, E. and Farrall, S. (1999) 'Afraid or Angry? Recalibrating the "fear" of crime', *International Review of Victimology*, 6 (2): 83–99.

Ditton, J. and Farrall, S. (eds) (2000) *The Fear of Crime*. Ashgate: Aldershot.

Hale, C. (1996) 'Fear of crime: a review of the literature', *International Review of Victimology*, 4 (2): 79–150.

Hollway, W. and Jefferson, T. (2000) *Doing Qualitative Research Differently: Free Association, Narrative and the Interview Method*. London: Sage.

Hope, T. and Sparks, R. (2000) *Crime, Risk and Insecurity*. London: Routledge.

Lee, M. (2007) *Inventing Fear of Crime: Criminology and the Politics of Anxiety*. Cullompton, Devon: Willan Publishing.

FIREARMS

Definition

Firearms are weapons that ballistically discharge projectiles designed to inflict lethal injury upon human or animal targets. They fall into two broad categories: handguns and 'long arms'. Handguns used for police purposes are of two types: revolvers, in which bullets are located in a chamber set into a rotating cylinder that, with each depression of the trigger, aligns successively each chamber with the barrel; and self–loading (or 'semi–automatic') pistols that store bullets in a magazine from which they are in turn mechanically extracted and inserted into the breech ready to fire. Handguns are normally carried in a holster worn at a convenient place on the wearer's body: commonly the hip, but for concealment it may be worn under the armpit or on the ankle. For this reason handguns are also commonly referred to as 'side arms'.

'Long arms' refers to a wide array of long–barrelled weapons including shotguns, rifles and carbines. Shotguns are smooth barrelled weapons that fire a bewildering array of munitions including: varying numbers of lead balls designed to hit the target simultaneously, sufficient to cause death and injury to a person; 'beanbags' designed to inflate upon being fired and non-lethally incapacitate an adversary; single rifled slugs sufficiently powerful to kill large livestock; CS irritant and much else besides. Shotguns for police use are normally 'pump-action': that is, cartridges are stored in a magazine and are inserted into the breech by operating a slide-mounted device parallel to the barrel. However, modern 'battle' shotguns have been developed that use a self-loading mechanism akin to that of a self-loading pistol.

Shotguns are distinguished from all other firearms (handguns and 'long arms' alike) by their smooth barrels. The barrels of other firearms are 'rifled': that is, the barrels are grooved in spiral so as to impart spin to the bullet as it passes down the barrel thus creating gyroscopic stability to the flight of the bullet thereby enhancing accuracy. 'Rifles' are (confusingly) just one type of rifle barrelled weapon that have many variants, most notably the sniper rifle equipped with a telescopic sight designed to hit distant targets and military-style 'assault rifles' that can fire automatically. Carbines are distinguished from 'rifles' by the power of the ammunition they are designed to fire. For all practical purposes, carbines fire 9mm pistol ammunition, but have greater range than pistols because their longer barrel imparts greater muzzle velocity, and also they are more accurate since they are normally gripped in both hands and secured against the shoulder. Carbines that fire automatically are normally referred to as 'sub-machine guns' and for some specialist police purposes these weapons have a shortened barrel and no shoulder stock so that they may be carried covertly.

Guns do not kill or injure, it is the ammunition they fire that does the damage and ammunition varies in calibre and power. The calibre of a bullet is measured by the diameter of the barrel along which it is fired, but even here there are subtle variations according to how this measurement is taken. For instance, a .38 inch standard revolver has the same diameter as a .357 inch. The most commonly used calibre is the .38 inch/.357 inch revolver and 9mm self-loading, but heavier calibres are becoming more popular. While a larger calibre creates a bigger entry wound, the amount of injury inflicted upon a target depends upon the muzzle-velocity of the bullet (which depends roughly on the amount of propellant), its weight and its shape. Muzzle-velocities in excess of 2000 feet per second are regarded as 'high velocity' and inflict distinctive injuries. As the bullet travels through flesh it creates a shock wave that ruptures surrounding tissue. Travelling at such a speed the bullet invariably exits the target causing a characteristically large wound. Low-velocity ammunition inflicts injury by losing momentum as it encounters the resistance of tissue; this causes kinetic energy to convert into heat, which creates a cavity with associated shock and blood loss. Low-velocity bullets are designed not to exit from target (that is to avoid 'over-penetration' that might inflict unintended injury upon others). To enhance de-acceleration and thus injury, as well as preventing over-penetration, low velocity ammunition is manufactured in various shapes. The more flattened the nose of the bullet ('wadcutter'), the greater resistance will be encountered and the more rapid the rate of de-acceleration. 'Hollow point' bullets are designed to distort into the shape of a mushroom upon impact and are among the most injurious types of ammunition.

Finally, there is an assortment of weapons for use in public order situations that discharge munitions containing smoke and irritants, and also a diverse array of projectiles intended to cause superficial injury and prompt dispersal of disorderly gatherings.

Distinctive Features

It is near universal that police officers carry firearms, although the type of firearm carried varies from one jurisdiction to another. However, in a few jurisdictions police *do not* routinely carry firearms. The most prominent members of this exclusive club are the police of mainland Britain, whose patrol officers and non-specialist detectives are not trained in the use of, and do not have access to, firearms. When an incident occurs involving the use or threat of lethal violence, specialist officers are deployed, usually in Armed Response Vehicles. Detectives specializing in duties that are likely to expose them to armed criminals and terrorism may also be trained and equipped in the use of firearms. In addition, most British police forces maintain one or more squads of officers trained and equipped for particularly challenging armed operations, such as hostage rescue and who are indistinguishable from Special Weapons and Tactics (SWAT) officers found throughout the world. The *Garda Síochána* of the Republic of Ireland are also not routinely armed. Neither are the New Zealand Police, but all officers are trained to a basic standard of firearms proficiency. In Norway, officers do not routinely carry firearms on their person, but are trained in their use and most police vehicles are equipped with firearms.

The use of firearms lays bare the role of the police as custodians of the state's monopoly of legitimate force and throughout liberal democracies the use of firearms is controversial. Policy controversies have concerned the type of weapons and the ammunition employed. Decisions about whether or not to upgrade the propellant power of ammunition and hence its muzzle-velocity thus increasing the severity of injury and likelihood of death has proven controversial. So too have decisions to replace revolvers with self-loading pistols that contain two or three times the number of bullets. In Britain the decision, in 1986, overtly to arm officers guarding Heathrow airport with the Heckler and Koch MP5 carbine attracted a storm of protest.

It is when guns are fired that most controversy arises. Often this focuses upon specific shootings, such as that of Amadou Diallo, shot 41 times by plainclothes New York City Police Department (NYPD) officers who mistakenly believed he was reaching for a concealed weapon. Indeed, the shooting of people who turn out to be unarmed is a problem that haunts police in all jurisdictions. So too do shootings of ethnic minorities that have attracted the suspicion that prejudice among the police reaches all the way down to the trigger finger.

The controversy surrounding police use of firearms has crystallized around tactics adopted to counter the growing menace of 'suicide bombers'. Because these terrorists are intent on sacrificing their lives, there is little realistic prospect of their surrender. Nor is it sufficient to aim for the torso, since the bomb they are carrying may be (and on occasion has been) detonated as the bomber dies from gunshot wounds. The only viable tactic is to aim multiple shots at the head, preferably at such close range that the muzzle blast adds to the injury inflicted by the bullets fired. This is intended to sever the brain from the peripheral central nervous system so as to prevent detonation. As the shooting of Jean Charles de Menezes in London on 22 July 2005 demonstrates, the killing of an innocent man mistaken for a terrorist suspect in such brutal circumstances severely undermines the legitimacy of the police.

Evaluation

What effect does equipping police officers with firearms have upon armed and violent crime, the safety of police officers, and public satisfaction with the police? The fact that routinely armed policing is ubiquitous against a background of wildly fluctuating levels of crime and vulnerability of officers suggests that arming the police has very limited impact on any of these variables. The unarmed police of London confront an armed crime problem that ranks alongside many comparable cities in jurisdictions where police are armed. Surprisingly, perhaps, international crime surveys suggest that unarmed police forces receive approval ratings no higher and in some cases less than many jurisdictions in which police are armed. Whether police are armed or not reveals more about the history and traditions of policing in a jurisdiction than the threats that officers currently face.

P.A.J. Waddington

Associated Concepts: force, gun crime, legitimacy, paramilitary policing, technology

Key Readings

Blumberg, M. (1993) 'Controlling police use of deadly force: assessing two decades of progress,' in R.G. Dunham and G. P. Alpert (eds) Critical Issues in Policing: Contemporary Readings. Prospect Heights, IL: Waveland.

Bunker, R.J. (2005) *Training Key # 581: Suicide (Homicide) Bombers Part I. El Segundo, California: Counter-OPFOR Program, National Law Enforcement and Corrections Technology Centre-West, National Institute of Justice: 6.

Bunker, R.J. (2005) *Training Key # 582: Suicide (Homicide) Bombers Part II. El Segundo, California: Counter-OPFOR Program, National Law Enforcement and Corrections Technology Centre-West, National Institute of Justice.

Geller, W.A. and Scott, M. S. (1991) 'Deadly force: What we know,' in C. B. Klockars and S. D. Mastrofski (eds), Thinking About Police: Contemporary Readings. p. 453.

Kraska, P.B. and Kappeler, V.E. (1997) 'Militarizing American police: the rise and normalization of paramilitary units', *Social Problems,* 44 (1): 1–18.

Mayhew, P. and White,. P. (1997) 'The 1996 International Crime Victimization Survey', in *Research Findings No 57.* London: Home Office Highstown NJ: McGraw-Hill.

Waddington, P.A. J. (1991) *The Strong Arm of the Law.* Oxford: Clarendon.

FORCE

Definition

Force is physical interference with a person's body through manipulation, restraint, or incapacitation (including injuries and death). The means for such interference are very varied and in policing include the officer's own body (for holding, hitting, punching, or kicking the other person), mechanical devices and objects (handcuffs, batons, flashlights, stun guns, water cannons, firearms, etc.), chemical weapons (such as pepper spray and tear gas), and animals (dogs for attack, horses for crowd control). Failed attempts at physical interference also count as force; for example, when shots miss the target. In addition, the concept of force includes overt threats of physical interference (for example, when an officer draws a gun), because even threats may have a powerful effect on the other person, and in some cases may be considered an assault. Apart from the threat to use force, other kinds of psychological coercion in policing (for example, the threat to press all possible charges if a suspect does not collaborate with an investigation) are not usually considered to be force. Likewise, arrest (maintaining a person in the physical presence of the police for the purposes of investigating a suspected crime) is not an instance of force, although force may be used to make the arrest (for example, when suspects are handcuffed). A distinction is often made between lethal force and non-lethal force, with firearms placed in the first category and other types of physical interference in the second. However, it should be remembered that firearms do not always cause death, while non-lethal means of force may sometimes do so.

Distinctive Features

Force is regularly used in a number of occupations, such as nursing, emergency services, prison custodial services, policing and the military. The distinctive features of the force used in policing derive from the nature of police work and the levels of permissible force that can be employed. Among the tasks particularly associated with policing are the apprehension and control of suspected offenders and crowd control. These bring the police into contact with a wider range of people than either prison officers or the military, although no wider than medical personnel and emergency service workers. Moreover, the potentially conflictive nature of suspect and crowd management, and the levels of force that citizens are sometimes prepared to use against officers or other citizens, have generally led to the police being equipped with a broader range of types of force (from martial arts through to high-powered firearms) than any other occupation. Thus, compared to other professions, the use of force in policing has either a wider social distribution or a greater potential for physical interference.

These distinctive features of the use of force in policing do not, however, mean that force is used frequently or abundantly in police work. Studies uniformly find that force is used in only a small percentage of encounters between the police and citizens, and officers rely for the most part on verbal orientation and control. In addition, on the relatively rare occasions when it is used, force is mainly drawn from the lower end of the intensity scale and involves such things as leading the suspect by the arm, applying bodily restraint, or using handcuffs. Empirical studies – conducted mainly in the US – find that the variables most strongly associated with the use of force refer to citizens' behaviour and departmental or jurisdictional characteristics, rather than officers' characteristics.

In pre-modern times, the police were authorized to use force for the purposes of punishment, for example by whipping, or placing the offender in the pillory. As corporal punishment has disappeared from penal culture, so the use of force has been confined to the task of control, and the police are no exception to this. Currently, the police may use force in self-defence or defence of another, to affect an arrest or prevent a suspect from fleeing, and to disperse groups that threaten public order.

Differences exist between jurisdictions in the types of force that are available to the police. Resource-rich departments, particularly in wealthy countries, may possess an extensive variety of firearms, including revolvers, pistols, shotguns, rifles, and machine guns, and other types of technology, such as batons, chemical sprays, emergency restraint belts, handcuffs, plastic bullets, stun guns and tasers. Resource-starved departments, particularly in poorer countries, may operate with a much narrower inventory, comprising revolvers, shotguns,

batons and handcuffs, which often must be shared by groups of officers. Differences in the deployment and use of different types of force also depend on policies governing the use of force. Most notable in this regard are the variations in the authorizations governing the carrying and use of firearms. In many countries most officers routinely carry guns, but in some (for example, the UK and New Zealand) firearms are not normally carried and may only be issued on certain occasions or deployed by specially trained units. Even in these countries, however, the deployment and use of firearms is on the increase.

Evaluation

The use of force is a sensitive issue in policing because of the prima facie rejection of physical interference as a means of conducting social business. Under ordinary circumstances, people obviously do not like to be pushed, pulled, punched, kicked, gassed, restrained, incapacitated, injured or killed by anyone (including the police), and they are usually willing to convert this dislike into a general principle mandating non-forceful social interaction for all. Nevertheless, under certain circumstances the use of force is considered acceptable (for example, in self-defence) and, similarly, police work carries an authorization to use force. The problem lies in defining the acceptable circumstances and controlling officers' behaviour.

The definition of acceptable force is a challenging task, undertaken with varying degrees of clarity in three discursive domains: policy, inquiry and commentary. Policy is mainly formulated at departmental level (although other normative texts, such as human rights charters, constitutions and criminal codes also contain provisions of relevance), and involves one or more of three conceptual approaches. The first is an instrumental perspective, focusing on the legitimate objectives for which force may be used, such as to effect an arrest, or to restore public order. The second is a type-based approach, prescribing methods and purposes for using particular means of physical interference, such as firearms or chemical weapons. The third is a behavioural approach, indicating the appropriate responses to citizens' behaviour in the encounter. The use of force 'continua', which are very popular in the US, are an example of this latter strategy.

None of these approaches is without its problems. Thus, an exclusively instrumental perspective may downplay the use of non-forceful tactics; a type-based approach is usually limited to some means of force, leaving others effectively unregulated; and a behavioural approach may lock officers into an escalating strategy of physical control that belies the initial nature of the matter in hand and produces serious harm to the citizen. Administrative or judicial inquiries into instances of force used by officers may be based on these policies, but they may also introduce other concepts, such as 'reasonable force' or 'proportionality', which are not easily interpreted. Finally, the media and the public often offer relatively simplistic commentary on the use of force, which sometimes implies its use as a form of punishment for criminals.

Controlling the use of force depends mainly on three institutional procedures: training, monitoring and investigation. Irrespective of their conceptual problems, policies on the use of force will only influence police behaviour if they are given due weight in initial training and revisited periodically during officers' careers. Monitoring allows managers and researchers to obtain individual and aggregate incident-based data on the frequency, types, circumstances and outcomes of the use of force, and to make decisions about changes in policy. Thus, in some jurisdictions, officers are required to report all uses of firearms and even the use of selected non-lethal types of force. Investigation, whether done by internal affairs, civilian review boards or the judiciary, generates authoritative statements about the use or misuse of force, and sanctions officers who have ranged into the terrain of excessive force. While enormously helpful, these procedures cannot guarantee that the use of force will always be unproblematic. Even the best trained and best intentioned officers face difficulties, such as lack of experience, the occasional need to make split-second decisions, and lack of information about one or more aspects of the encounter. And when policies regarding the use of force are vague, while training, monitoring and supervision are scarce, excesses and abuses are even more likely to occur, as witnessed in many countries where the institutional structure of policing is weak.

Christopher Birkbeck

Associated Concepts: accountability, arrest, ethics, firearms, gun crime, misconduct, public order policing

Key Readings

Alpert, G. and Dunham, R. (2004) *Understanding Police Use of Force: Officers, Suspects and Reciprocity*. Cambridge: Cambridge University Press.

Birkbeck, C. (2007) 'Police use of force and transnational review processes: the Venezuelan Police under the Inter-American System', in J. Sheptycki and A. Goldsmith (eds) *Crafting Global Policing*. Oxford: Hart.

Bittner, E. (1975) *The Functions of the Police in Modern Society*. New York: Jason Aaronsen.

Chevigny, P. (1997) *Edge of the Knife: Police Violence in the Americas*. New York: The New Press.

Geller, W. A. and Toch, H. (eds) (1996) *Police Violence: Understanding and Controlling Police Abuse of Force*. New Haven: Yale University Press.

FORENSIC SCIENCE

See Criminal Investigation

G

GEOGRAPHIC PROFILING

See Crime Mapping; Criminal Investigation

GLOBALIZATION

Definition

Globalization refers to transnational economic linkages and dependencies, as well as transnational political enmeshment and cultural flows. The term refers to a variety of social processes that, in sum, constitute the process whereby 'global society' will emerge. The idea of a global society can be traced back at least to Emanuel Kant's *Perpetual Peace* (1795) – the first book to postulate the possibility of an international system wherein 'peace' was other than an interlude between wars. The term is often criticized as ambiguous, but it does signal an important shift in thinking about international affairs, heretofore the preserve of international relations theorists and a select few others. In the late twentieth century, scholars stretched their terms of discourse in order to make sense of the broadening and deepening transnational interconnections among politics, economy and culture. Prior to that time, international relations revolved around the fears and anxieties stirred up by geo-political rivalries between states. Under conditions of globalization, a whole new catalogue of fears and anxieties emerged, notably ones having to do with ecological and environmental catastrophe, raising urgent questions about global governance capacities. In bellwether fashion, a variety of transnational crime phenomena were identified as world system woes soon after the end of the Cold War and the sociology of policing was therefore well positioned to contribute to debates about the nature of globalization.

Distinctive Features

Globalization is relevant to all of the social sciences and humanities disciplines and is no less relevant to the sociology of policing. The global system is ripe with existential anxieties that are symptoms of momentous historical change and, for good or ill, issues of crime definition and control – and other topics pertinent to the practices of policing – have become central to the transnational condition. Consequently, changes in definitions of policing and security are illuminating of much broader shifts.

A central debate among globalization theorists has concerned its effects on the nation state. Some contend that globalization signals the transcendence of the nation state system while others argue that the state form is more robust and likely to adapt to the vicissitudes of globalization. The sociology of policing contributed centrally to these debates. How could it not? Classical theories of the modern state postulated 'the police' as the keystone of executive government, the very embodiment of state sovereignty. Under the influence of neoliberal theories concerning 'governance beyond the state', early twenty-first century theories of policing were stretched to include many kinds of regulatory acts and social controls effective outwith the power of the state *qua* State. Theories regarding the pluralization and multilateralization of policing abounded and concerns emerged about the governability of policing, to wit: is it possible to conceive of transnational policing power that is not merely the exercise of rival gut reactions exercised by the leaders of seigniorial states in triumphalist demonstrations of hard power? Normative questions which ask how the idea of policing can be brought into accord with the interests of the global commonwealth were among a range of questions the attempted answers to which were productive of insights into the changing nature of state sovereignty. The conclusions can be summarized first by acknowledging that transnational influences are uneven and imperfect and are undoubtedly distorted by the *realpolitik* practised by would be seigniorial states, but that the nation state-system has indeed been superseded and become the transnational-state-system.

Several good examples of transnational influences of, on and within policing organizations can be found in the literature. One transnational influence *of* policing organizations concerns the articulation of suitable targets for policing power. Although this is difficult to measure with precision, it seems oddly true that Internet paedophilia and Internet piracy attract more public censure from policing agencies through the mass media than does the dumping of toxic waste on the high seas or gun smuggling. Debates about how to orchestrate policing power, not only with absolute regard for the general commonweal but also with balanced regard based on solid measures of social harm, are examples of transnational attempts at influences *on* policing. Many police development aid programmes take place internationally, and police technology transfer is an example of transnational influences operating *within* policing organizations. Observing the transnational influences of, on and within policing institutions is to observe, in microcosm, the operations and practices of the newly emerging transnational-state-system. The question still remains, what will be the character of global society?

Evaluation

The fruitful intersection of enquiry that stands at the crossroads between the sociology of policing and of globalization has yet to be exhausted, but it became increasingly politicized during the first decade of the twenty-first century. Theories that raised the possibility of a global cosmopolitan democracy operating under the rule of law and the aegis of universal human rights were rudely challenged as the US, and then other seigniorial states, became ever more bellicose. The declaration of the worldwide 'War on Terror', later pursued under more muted terminology, accented the hard edge of policing. In such circumstances suspect profiling, watch lists, and the whole panoply of intelligence-led policing was extremely corrosive of community policing ideas and ideals. The ideals of community policing were submerged under a tidal wave of insecurity. The result was that the discourse of police professionals lost linguistic connections to the idea and ideals of democracy and transnational policing power became more, and more evidently, merely the exercise of hard power. The sociology of global policing reveals a pattern of authoritarian drift which does not augur at all well for the future character of the world system and which stands in contrast to the hopeful prognostications of Immanuel Kant. Kant might not have been surprised believing, as he did, that '... democracy is, properly speaking, necessarily a despotism, because it establishes an executive power in which 'all' decide for or even against one who does not agree; that is, 'all', who are not quite all, decide, and this is a contradiction of the general will with itself and with freedom' (Kant, 1957: 352). Looked at globally, it seems that policing lies at the cruel heart of that contradiction.

James Sheptycki

Associated Concepts: community policing, cross-border policing, intelligence-led policing, pluralization, postmodern policing, technology, transnational policing

Key Readings

Beare, M. (ed.) (2004) *Critical Reflections on Transnational Organized Crime, Money Laundering and Corruption*. Toronto: Toronto University Press.

Deflem, M. (2002) *Policing World Society*. Oxford: Oxford University Press.

Edwards, A. and Gill, P. (eds.) (2004) *Transnational Organized Crime Perspectives on Global Security*. London: Routledge.

Goldsmith, A. and Sheptycki, J. (eds) (2007) *Crafting Transnational Policing*. Oxford: Hart.

Gray, S. (2006) *Ghost Plane: The True Story of the CIA Torture Program*. New York: St. Martin's Press.

Kant, I. (1957) *Perpetual Peace* Translated by L. White Beck. New York: Liberal Arts Press.

Sheptycki, J. and Wardak, A. (eds) (2004) *Transnational and Comparative Criminology*. London: Taylor and Francis.

GOVERNMENTALITY

Definition

Governmentality is a term invented by Michel Foucault to refer to a way of governing that began to emerge in the eighteenth century and that has as its principal characteristic the assumption that what is to be governed also governs itself – in particular this refers to individuals, populations and economies. A key corollary is that it seeks to align these self-governing properties with the aims of the government. In his analysis of this 'complex' form, Foucault deployed a type of analysis that has been developed, also under the label 'governmentality', into an influential approach in social theory and research. This 'governmental analytic' focuses on mentalities of rule – ways of imagining the nature of problems and corresponding solutions – and the techniques that are deployed in order to put these solutions into effect. With respect to criminology, it is this analytical approach that is generally referred to as 'governmentality'.

Distinctive Features

Unlike grand social theories that identify government with 'the state', and the state with the interests of powerful interests or classes, governmentality as a mode of analysis focuses on government as the 'conduct of conduct'. Government is that which seeks to align the conduct of self-governing entities in order to maximize their capacities in pursuit of the ends sought. Consequently government can be performed by individuals, corporations, police departments, voluntary associations as well as by states. Government is thus 'dispersed' – which the approach takes to be a feature of contemporary life. Linked with this, governmentality is rarely interested in power as emanating from some central source, such as capitalism or 'the state'; nor does power appear primarily as a form of securing conformity through coercion. Power instead becomes the multiple techniques deployed in pursuit of the programmatic ends sought by government. Thus governmentality analyses do not assume that police are repressive tools of class or state interests, or simply enforcers of law and order. Instead the emphasis has been on the diverse and changing assumptions held by police management, government departments and others about how police should be organized; what duties they should perform and what techniques should they use; who should be their targets; what ends they should aim to achieve; to whom they should be accountable and how.

As this indicates, governmentality is empirical in the sense that it attends to demonstrable plans and formal procedures. It does not provide 'ideal types' of policing, as some assume – in the sense of theoretically accentuated pure models which cannot be found empirically – but examines actually existing plans and programmes. Nevertheless, it is not sociology in the sense of examining whether or how these are carried out in practice, what unintended effects they have and whether they 'work'. Thus governmentality has been used to investigate the development of crime prevention, community policing, and new approaches to making police 'publicly accountable' as this appears in such 'government' programmes as departmental reports and White Papers, police publications, neighbourhood watch pamphlets and insurance industry publicity campaigns. Such work has been carried out especially in terms of the ways in which these link programmes to broader formulae or rationalities such as neo-liberalism or the 'new managerialism'. Crime prevention, for example, is understood in its current form as closely related to the rise of neo-liberalism in the 1970s and as reflecting the latter's assumptions. These include the idea that state should render 'the community' and individuals more responsible for their own government; that loss prevention is more important than the ceremonial of punishment; and that offenders are rational choice actors who can most effectively be deterred by opportunity reduction rather than by social reform. Likewise, changes in the organization and structure of policing have been linked to neo-liberal and new-managerial beliefs that markets are the optimal distributors of goods and services. This assumption is seen to have generated the rise of police audits, increased outsourcing of police functions, and competition between public and private providers of police services. Also prominent in governmentality analyses of policing has been recognition of the ways in which risk-based assumptions and techniques have been deployed. This is especially clear in relation to the rise of situational crime prevention with its focus on the use of statistical data to identify criminogenic situations and to implement risk-reducing changes.

Notable in governmentality analysis of police has been a general refusal to deploy 'grand theoretical' and 'epochal' approaches, such as regarding these shifts in policing as effects of 'postmodernity' or 'late capitalism'. This reflects governmentality's roots in Foucault's stress on genealogy: analysis that emphasizes the contingency of history. Rather than seeing what exists as the outcome of an unfolding of a logic, such as 'progress' or 'reflexive modernization', it stresses that things could have been otherwise – thus intending to destabilize the necessity of the present. However an important and influential exception to this has been the attempt by Richard Ericson and others to understand contemporary changes in policing in terms of a fusion of governmentality analysis with Ulrich Beck's risk society thesis. This work deploys governmentality as a technique for investigating the changes in the nature of police practice, but argues that these changes are effects of the emergence of a society in which risk has become central to government as a result of the unfolding destructive powers of science and technology.

Evaluation

As noted, governmentality does not pretend to be a sociology mapping out how programmes actually pan out. This is regarded by many critics as a severe limitation, tending to create an impression that government is automatically successful in its projects, and directing attention away from the unintended effects and failures of policy. Indeed, some critics interpret the approach as ignoring resistance and its effects on government. One response has been for governmentality scholars to suggest that governmentality is not a theory, and should instead be treated as a tool, useful only for limited purposes. In this view, there is nothing to stop analysts using governmentality to study the nature of government blueprints and their implications, and then turning to a more conventional sociology to track their implementation and impact. In practice, however this is rarely performed. One reason may be that governmentality invites a questioning of 'reality', tending to suspend judgements about what is real in order to focus on the reality 'imagined' in government programmes and rationalities. It is neither easy nor unproblematic to shift from one mode to another.

This is linked with a further criticism that governmentality does not offer a critique of policing (or any other object of analysis), in the sense familiar to most criminologists and sociologists. Governmentality can thus appear as accepting a *realpolitik* of rule. The response to this attack has been to agree that critique is missing, but for good reason. Critique is said to assume that the critic knows the truth – has privileged access to some concealed reality, usually by virtue of a theory. Foucaultian analysis generally is deeply suspicious of such truth claims, regarding that sort of critique as inviting a new regime of government based on the new theory (Marxism is an example). Instead, governmentality proposes to show what kinds of subjects government is trying to create, how it desires to change our lives, and what it assumes the nature of problems to be. As well, through genealogical analysis, it seeks to show how things might have been different – and thus still could be – without prescribing a new programme of rule. While it has often proven very effective in these respects, it is not clear that this necessitates an abandonment of the question 'which side are we on', which some do interpret it as requiring. As well, governmentality need not – but sometimes does – provide a convenient excuse not to resist what is repugnant or to identify what is to be done. In other words, these are dangers rather than necessary features of the approach. At a more analytical level, there are unresolved ambiguities concerning the difference between a programme of government and its implementation. The decision by a local police precinct or even patrol car crew to interpret a directive from senior police management in a certain way could be seen as 'implementation' and thus not part of the analysis. It could also be viewed as the development of a new governmental programme at a local level. Clearly the implications for this with respect to separating plans from 'what actually happens' go to the heart of points raised above, but have yet to be closely considered.

Pat O'Malley

Associated Concepts: accountability, community policing, crime prevention, managerialism, postmodern policing, responsibilization, situational crime prevention

Key Readings

Dean, M. (1999) *Governmentality*. London: Sage.

Ericson, R. and Haggerty, K. (1998) *Policing the Risk Society*. Oxford: Oxford University Press.

O'Malley, P. (1997) 'Policing, politics and postmodernity', *Social and Legal Studies*, 6 (3): 363–81.

O'Malley, P. and Palmer, D. (1996) 'Post keynesian policing', *Economy and Society*, 25 (2): 137–55.

Rose, N. (1999) *The Powers of Freedom*. Cambridge: Cambridge University Press.

GUN CRIME

Definition

The policing of gun crime raises several definitional issues, regarding the notion of 'gun crime' itself and the particular police contribution to tackling crimes involving firearms. Despite a tendency to regard gun crime as a relatively homogenous phenomenon, it needs subdividing into at least four separate 'types' – although there are important overlaps between them. There is sound research evidence to suggest an important distinction exists between *instrumental* gun crime (the use of firearms to facilitate serious 'organized' crime) and *expressive* gun crime (the use of guns by street gang members to gain power and respect among their peers) (Hale et al., 2006). This phenomenon is sometimes linked to notions of a criminal 'gun subculture' with guns reportedly carried as 'fashion accessories'. These two types of gun crime give rise to the most pressing operational policing concerns.

A third sphere of gun-related criminality (sometimes separately bracketed off as the special preserve of 'gun control' policy) has to do with the supply, distribution or 'trafficking' of firearms and the policing of (legal and illegal) gun markets. Where firearms licensing systems exist, police responsibilities often extend to the oversight of gun owners themselves. In the US, where gun ownership is widespread, the Federal Bureau of Alcohol, Tobacco and Firearms has a broad responsibility to enforce federal laws with respect to the sale, distribution and use of firearms and to cooperate with local policing agencies to reduce gun violence. In the UK, local police forces are responsible for firearm licensing and monitoring the safe storage of weapons by private owners, gun clubs and dealerships. A final area of 'gun supply' policing concerns police inter-agency collaboration with Customs and Excise, the Immigration Services and the Security Services which, since 2006 in the UK, is overseen by the Serious Organized Crime Agency.

A fourth type of gun crime has often been overlooked, even though it poses some acute dilemmas for the police. This issue involves the use of air weapons, or other lower-powered, and even non-firing, imitation firearms, in (predominantly) nuisance-related 'anti-social' behaviour. In the UK, police support for tighter controls over such weapons reflects concerns beyond the immediate problems arising from their misuse by teenagers. First, police managers have argued that around 25 per cent of armed response vehicle deployments involved imitation firearms. Second, research in the mid-1990s confirmed that replica weapons were known to be used in a substantial proportion (around 40 per cent) of opportunist armed robberies (Matthews, 2002). Finally, replica weapons are difficult to distinguish from the real thing when pointed at you – of 24 persons shot by armed police officers between 1998 and 2001, seven were carrying imitation firearms.

Distinctive Features

Notwithstanding the contribution of 'gun nuisance' offences to overall gun crime trends, most concerns regarding gun crime have involved the use of firearms in urban areas by gang affiliated offenders. Underlying these issues have been wider questions of race and social exclusion, and claims about the adoption, by marginalized youth groups, of an expressive and hyper violent gun culture. Serious gang-related armed criminality

occurs in many countries and police agencies have responded by the development of proactive anti-gang units. A range of issues have emerged regarding the types of policing strategies adopted – it seems fair to suggest that, just as the 'community reassurance' agenda has been a key influence at one end of the spectrum of activities defining the 'new policing', so the need to police violent criminal gun cultures of late modernity has had an equally significant impact upon police methods, tactics and equipment.

Aggressive, enforcement-led policing initiatives against violent gangs (perhaps best exemplified by the US Police Special Weapons and Tactics (SWAT) units) are sometimes seen (alongside counter-terrorist policing) as evidence of a new militarization of policing. Other policing cultures have their own equivalent specialist units although, in the UK, where the ethos of a largely unarmed routine policing culture still prevails (in common with New Zealand, Norway and the Republic of Ireland), the debate on arming the police has assumed a deeper significance. Of late, the UK government has committed itself to increases in the training of armed response officers and in the deployment of more vehicles. Following initiatives in a number of US cities, British police managers have also deployed regular armed patrols in gun crime hot spots to 'chill' an area down to deter an escalation of hostilities or retaliation shootings. Such tactics remain controversial; the 'heavy handed' policing they often entail can risk alienating the very communities they are intended to protect (not unlike the use of 'stop and search' tactics which have proven controversial in both London and New York).

Evaluation

More strategic responses to the policing of gun crime have generally been developed through a combination of multi-agency community crime prevention initiatives and the adoption of specialist intelligence-led operations such as Operation Trident in London and the Manchester Multi-Agency Gang Strategy. Here, American experiences have proven influential.

In the UK, following the 2003 new year shootings in Birmingham, the government launched a high profile initiative ('Connected') intended to draw the police and a range of public agencies together with community organizations in the areas worst affected by gangs and gun crime. The issues at stake were both political (racism, social exclusion and political marginalization) and tactical (the communities most affected by gun crime tended to have the worst experiences of policing and, whether through fear or mistrust, were the least likely to provide information to the police). In London, Operation Trident made strenuous efforts to include Independent Advisory Group members representing gun crime affected communities to help advise and direct their policing strategy. In Manchester, however, lessons were drawn directly from Operation Ceasefire, a successful initiative to tackle problems of firearms and youth violence in Boston, Massachusetts.

In the US, Operation Ceasefire emerged from the paradigm of 'problem-oriented policing', establishing an inter-agency working group comprising police, justice system personnel, representatives of community groups and, crucially, street outreach youth workers to address the problem of gun crime at all levels – from personal contacts with young people 'at risk' in the community to disrupting the supply of trafficked firearms into Massachusetts. Evaluated by the US National Institute of Justice, the project apparently achieved a significant reduction in levels of firearm-related violence and youth homicide. A version of Operation Ceasefire was also developed in Chicago where, adopting an intervention methodology drawing upon epidemiological principles (youth violence understood as an infectious disease), the initiative has achieved major reductions in youth-involved gun violence.

A familiar series of issues and dilemmas confronting the policing of gun crime has been encountered in many parts of the world. Whether or not a police service is routinely armed, heavy handed enforcement-led approaches raise many issues for communities; they tend to attract political censure and often prove quite counter-productive (Kraska and Kappeler, 1997). Equally, where police forces have come to develop more successful reassurance, community problem-solving and/or intelligence-led approaches, other problems have surfaced.

There has been some investment in new technologies to support police-led community gun crime prevention initiatives. In the US, partly by virtue of the country's widespread legal gun ownership, metal detection and weapon scanning systems have become familiar (scanners are employed in schools, shopping malls as well as a range of public buildings, even as some legal scholars have disputed the constitutionality of 'gun free zones'). Proposals to equip police officers with portable weapon scanning equipment have tended to run into constitutional problems concerning whether such scans constitute an illegal search. In the UK, scanning technologies have tended to be deployed only at fixed entry points to sensitive locations (such as passenger transit points or government buildings) although researchers are considering the development of police deployable weapon scanning technologies (disguised within familiar street furniture) and a UK research council has funded a project to develop enhanced digitized closed circuit television systems for recognizing 'weapon carrying behaviour'.

In respect of intelligence-led policing, a number of familiar problems relating to police culture and the self-fulfilling nature of police offender targeting arise. A recent UK survey of police officers and intelligence analysts responsible for gun crime operations indicated significant areas of ambiguity and disagreement in police perceptions of gun crime, as well as perceptions which were not supported by available research evidence (Squires, 2007). Another problem with police firearms intelligence systems concerns the balance between evidence gathering and intelligence development. Until recently in the UK, police firearms intelligence development came a poor second to evidence gathering. Forces had to pay for the forensic examination of firearms, so officers only submitted for examination those weapons directly involved in prosecutions. Consequently, more than half the illegal firearms seized by police were never subjected to proper forensic analysis and information which could have been useful for tracing, sourcing, and understanding the nature and operation of illegal firearms markets was lost. A National Firearms Forensic Intelligence Database was established in 2003 and a National Ballistics Intelligence Programme followed in 2006, intended to lead to the development of a National Ballistics Intelligence Service to support the work of the police in tackling gun crime.

Finally, whatever the broader strategic approaches adopted by police forces the world over to tackle gun crime, in the course of their duties, individual police officers will continue to encounter armed offenders. Similarly, firearm incidents of all kinds will require effective management to minimize risk and the loss of life. Hence questions of officer selection, training, tactics, support, equipment, protection, accountability and legality will continue to surface as vital issues whenever weapons are drawn, let alone fired, and whenever police officers are injured.

Consistent with international efforts to render police authorities more accountable for their use of firearms (Control Arms, 2004) the UK Association of Chief Police Officers (ACPO) published its firearms manual in 2001. However, the carefully crafted accountability surrounding this document was thrown into disarray in 2005 by the deployment of Operation Kratos against a suspected suicide bomber, shot several times in the head at point-blank range in an underground station in London. Kratos revived fears of a *de facto* police shoot-to-kill policy. The case raised issues of international significance concerning the training, stability and psychological preparedness of police officers dealing with potentially life-threatening situations. Similarly, the 41 shots fired in 1999 by New York police officers at a suspect who later turned out to be unarmed appeared to confirm allegations about a 'spray and pray' approach to shooting made possible by new, high capacity semi-automatic firearms issued to police. In the UK, research conducted by the Police Complaints Authority into cases where police officers have fired their weapons, emphasized the influence of policing methods and contextual factors on officers' decision making, rather than assessments of the risk presented by suspects (Best and Quigley, 2003). Such findings confirm the results of psychological tests designed to assess police decision-making under the stress of armed response. Taken together, the evidence appears to raise important questions regarding policing in a 'gun culture': in particular concerning notions of the minimum use of force, the availability of 'less-lethal' technologies and the application of the 'continuum of force' principle when firearms are deployed against the police.

Peter Squires

Associated Concepts: culture, force, firearms, intelligence-led policing, multi-agency policing, technology

Key Readings

Best, D. and Quigley, A. (2003) 'Shootings by the police: what predicts when a firearms officer in England and Wales will pull the trigger?', *Policing and Society,* 13 (4): 349–64.

Control Arms (2004) *Guns and Policing: Standards to Prevent Misuse*. Washington, DC: Amnesty International, IANSA and Oxfam, www.controlarms.org.

Hales, G., Lewis, C. and Silvertone, D. (2006) *Gun Crime: The Market in and Use of Illegal Firearms*. Home Office Research Study 298, London: Home Office, http://www.homeoffice.gov.uk/rds/pdfs06/hors298.pdf.

Kraska, P. and Kappeler, V. E. (1997) 'Militarizing American police: the rise and normalization of paramilitary units', *Social Problems*, 44 (1):1–18

Matthews, R. (2002) *Armed Robbery*. Cullompton, Devon: Willan Publishing.

Squires, P. (2007) *Police Perceptions of Gang and Gun Related Offending: A Key Informant Survey*. York: MAGNET project. http://www.york.ac.uk/management/magnet/.

HATE CRIME

Definition

Hate crime can be defined as a crime (commonly violence) motivated by prejudice, bias or hatred towards a particular group of which the victim is presumed to be a member. Hate crime is generally directed towards a class of people; the individual victim may not be significant to the offender except as a member of the targeted group. The victim may be a stranger to the offender.

Hate crime goes beyond simple hostility or prejudice. It is motivated by the offender's hatred of a person because of their membership of a group defined by their race, colour, ethnicity, nationality, religion, gender, sexual orientation or disability.

It is widely acknowledged that hate crime can take many forms: at the most extreme it can include murder, serious physical assault, arson and the destruction of property. It can also include a myriad of other crimes including graffiti, neighbourhood disputes, public disorder, abusive and threatening telephone calls, bullying and intimidation in school or the workplace.

Distinctive Features

The emergence of hate crime as a key concern for police dates back to the 1970s and 1980s. Numerous studies indicated that racist and homophobic violence was a serious and growing issue.

In the UK, a survey of housing authorities by the Commission for Racial Equality in 1987 found that 80 per cent stated that racist harassment was an issue in their areas and 77 per cent said that it was getting worse. In Australia, the National Inquiry into Racist Violence (1990) found that racist attacks were a serious problem among some communities. However the police had very little information on the nature or extent of hate crime. The revival of neo-Nazi racist activities in Europe, particularly in Germany and France, were also reminders that racist violence could escalate to a point of fragmenting the community and threatening the stability of the society as a whole.

As a response to evidence of the increasing incidence of hate crimes in the US, the US Congress passed the Hate Crimes Statistics Act in 1990. Under this Act, all law enforcement agencies in the US are required to report via the US Department of Justice on all crimes that manifest prejudice based on characteristics such as race, religion or sexual preference. In 1994 the scope was increased to include prejudice based on disability. The Federal Bureau of Investigation (FBI) reports on hate crime statistics under its Uniform Crime Reporting Program.

Annual FBI data provides some insight into the nature of hate crime in the US. In 2005, the FBI reported 7160 incidents of hate crime involving 8373 offences, 8795 victims and 6800 offenders. The majority of these incidents took place in public places including public buildings, schools, colleges, places of religious worship, restaurants and streets. Some 30 per cent of incidents occurred in or near a home. Data on hate crime from the UK shows that the majority of hate crimes occur near to the victim's home and while they are going about their daily business.

Of the reported incidents in the US, some 55 per cent were motivated by race, 17 per cent by religion, 14 per cent by sexual orientation, 13 per cent by ethnic or national origin and 1 per cent by disability. Some 62 per cent were crimes against persons and 38 per cent were crimes against property. Crimes against the person were nearly evenly divided between assaults and intimidation. To the extent that there is a typical 'hate crime', it is an offence against a person which is racially motivated.

In the UK, the police record much higher levels of racially and religiously motivated hate crimes than in the US. The Home Office notes the reporting of some 50,000 of these offences across the UK in 2006. In the same year the London Metropolitan Police reported 11,799 incidents of racist and religious hate crime and 1359 incidents of homophobic hate crime. Many police services have no systematic recording of hate crime. For example, in Australia there are no regular police reports on the incidence or nature of hate crime.

A defining feature of hate crime is that the individual is targeted because of their group membership. Persistent verbal abuse, threats and racist graffiti can have a devastating effect on individuals and families, although they are traditionally regarded as minor offences. It is necessary to understand that racist motivation renders any incident more serious in terms of its impact on the victim and on the victim's community. The victim of a hate crime may be an individual, a business (e.g., a shop or restaurant), or an institution (e.g., a synagogue, mosque or a school).

On the basis of FBI data, in more than two-thirds of racially motivated hate crimes, the victim was black; in more than two-thirds of the religiously motivated hate crime, the victim was Jewish. The targeting of groups will depend largely on particular local or national contexts: for example the targeting of Gypsies in the UK, or Aboriginal people in Australia, or African or Turkish immigrants in Europe.

The evidence shows that many people are unwilling to come forward to give evidence of hate crime because they fear retaliatory attacks, they are embarrassed, they do not believe the police will take them seriously, or because they do not believe that anyone can help them. Police in the UK estimate that only 10 per cent of homophobic incidents and crimes are reported (Home Office Police Standards Unit and the Association of Chief Police Officers, no date: 86).

FBI data reveals that 60 per cent of hate crime offenders were white and 20 per cent black. Some 12 per cent were of unknown racial identity and the remainder of various racial backgrounds. The UK Home Office describes the typical hate crime offender as being a young white male with most homophobic hate crime offenders being aged between 16–20 years, and race hate crime offenders under 30 years of age. Most offenders live locally to the victim.

Evaluation

Hate crime is a general concept that includes a range of substantive criminal offences. As such it can be a difficult idea to translate into everyday police work. As a general matter, the criminal law has not been concerned with either the identity of the victim of a violent crime or a crime against property or with the motive of the perpetrator. A crime aimed at the personal integrity or the property interests of a member of a minority group is no different, as a matter of principle, for the criminal justice system than any other crime. Thus, although 'hate' may well be the most important factor for both the victim and the perpetrator, it has historically been a matter of principled indifference for the official actors in the formal criminal justice system, from the police charged with the investigation to the judge or jury who must determine whether the act was committed with the requisite criminal intent.

This 'principled indifference' has been modified in recent years through changes in the substantive criminal law, changes in sentencing and developments in racial vilification and anti-discrimination laws. For example, the

UK Crime and Disorder Act 1998 (as amended) created racially aggravated and religiously aggravated assault, criminal damage, public order and harassment offences. In addition, the same legislation increased sentences for offences (other than those listed above) by requiring the courts to treat racial or religious aggravation as a serious factor in determining sentence. A similar change to sentencing law has occurred in some jurisdictions in Australia where racial motivation is also now an aggravating factor in sentencing.

Racial vilification and incitement to racial hatred may contain a range of civil and criminal penalties. For example, in Australia the New South Wales Anti-Discrimination Act contains a criminal offence of serious racial vilification with a maximum sentence of six month's imprisonment. However at the Federal level, while the Racial Discrimination Act outlaws racial hatred, there are no criminal sanctions. In the UK the Racial and Religious Hatred Act 2006 criminalizes incitement to hatred on the basis of religion.

The improvement of police responses to hate crime centres around increasing the confidence of victims to report offences, improving local responses in areas like crime prevention, improving police intelligence and the likelihood of prosecutions, and developing an effective evidence base on the nature and extent of hate crimes.

There are various methods used for identifying hate crime. In the US it is the police who make a decision as to whether an incident is a 'suspected bias incident'. Victim perceptions of the offender's motivation are one of the factors which will be taken into account. In the UK there appears to be greater reliance on victim classification. A recommended definition is:

> Any hate incident, which constitutes a criminal offence, perceived by the victim or any other person, as being motivated by prejudice or hate.
> (Home Office Police Standards Unit and the Association of Chief Police Officers, no date: 9)

Beyond monitoring the existence and nature of hate crime, the response of police services has been primarily to provide training on hate crime for police, to establish special response units among police, and to provide special support services and counselling for victims of hate crimes.

Given that there is a low reporting rate for hate crimes, a key initiative for police is to improve reporting rates. An example of such a campaign directed at homophobic violence is the 'Seen it? Heard it? Report it' campaign sponsored jointly by the New South Wales Police Force and the City of Sydney and aimed at encouraging reporting of homophobic violence and crimes. Another widely recognized campaign in the UK in relation to hate crime is the 'Hate Crime is a Menace in Society' campaign run by the Essex Police.

One of the first attempts at a special police response unit was the establishment by the Boston police of the Community Disorders Unit in 1978 (Wexler and Marx, 1986). In the 30 years since then, specialist units have become far more commonplace. For example, the London Metropolitan Police has Community Safety Units (CSUs) in most boroughs. The CSUs have a wide ambit in relation to hate crime which includes racist crime, homophobic crime and domestic violence. CSU officers specialize in investigating these crimes.

Police have also developed community policing strategies with specialist officers. In New South Wales, Gay and Lesbian Liaison Officers (GLLOs) are police officers specially trained to address gay and lesbian issues. The aim of the GLLOs is to work with gay and lesbian community groups to foster confidence in the police and to encourage reporting of homophobic violence and crimes. The GLLOs also assist in developing and implementing local and corporate initiatives to reduce and prevent anti-gay/lesbian violence.

There is recognized scope for police to improve their intelligence in relation to hate crime. The Home Office Police Standards Unit and the Association of Chief Police Officers (no date: 15–18) note that community intelligence, covert human intelligence sources, open sources (such as media, Internet, etc.) and hate material can all provide important sources of intelligence on hate crime.

Chris Cuneen

Associated Concepts: calls for service, community policing, criminal investigation, diversity, homicide, intelligence-led policing, property crime, victim

Key Readings

Bell, J. (2003) 'Policing hatred: police bias units and the construction of hate crime,' in B. Perry (ed.) *Hate and Bias Crime: A Reader*. New York: Routledge.

Hall, N. (2005) *Hate Crime*. Cullompton, Devon: Willan Publishing.

Stanko, E. (2001) 'Re-conceptualizing the policing of hatred: confessions and worrying dilemmas of a consultant', *Law and Critique*, 12 (3): 309–29.

Tomsen, S. (2002) *Hatred, Murder and Male Honour. Anti-Homosexual Homicides in New South Wales 1980–2000*. Canberra: Australia Institute of Criminology.

Wexler, C. and Marx, G. T. (1986) 'When law and order works: Boston's innovative approach to the problems of racial violence', *Crime and Delinquency*, 32 (2): 205–32.

HEALTH AND SAFETY

Definition

Occupational health and safety policing covers the combination of practices used to secure compliance with health and safety regulation and prevent death or injury resulting from work-related activities.

Distinctive Features

Despite being underpinned by the criminal law and despite the devastating physical and psychological effects of health and safety offences, conventional policing techniques and conventional policing institutions are rarely used to enforce occupational health and safety regulation. Instead, dedicated health and safety authorities, such as the British Health and Safety Executive, or, as is more typically the case in European countries, Labour Inspectorates, have primary responsibility for preventing and investigating suspected violations of work-related health and safety offences. In one sense, this stands as an historical monument to what Carson (1980) has called the institutionalization of ambiguity that characterized early factory crime – a term originally used to describe the way in which the conflicting purposes of early factory legislation (which included legitimizing the emergent class relations of the nineteenth century, disciplining the workforce and equalizing the conditions of competition) quickly manifested themselves in the routines and processes of its enforcement. However, the fact that enforcement of health and safety law and regulation still operates independently, or largely independently, of conventional law enforcement must also be understood as a signature of contemporary divisions of power and wealth (Tombs and Whyte, 2007).

In English speaking Commonwealth jurisdictions, health and safety regulation takes effect in a framework of self-regulation in which employers and employees cooperate within a range of formal and informal work-based structures, with state inspectors providing advice and overseeing compliance through a mix of inspection (used to determine the causes of occupational incidents, as well as acting as a medium for conveying best practice to industry), incident investigations, administrative enforcement action and prosecution. While this approach predominates, more recently regulatory authorities have placed a greater emphasis on securing compliance through partnerships with industry and other non-inspection based means of promoting compliance (such as influencing the supply chain and process of design) (Davis, 2004; Fooks et al. 2007; Tombs and Whyte, 2007).

Of the four basic types of inspection – targeted, complaint-based, referral and follow-ups – targeted inspections are most common. Regulatory authorities often argue that improvements in targeting limit any adverse effects that might be caused by reduced rates of inspection. In this sense, contemporary targeting practices can only really be understood with reference to the modern phenomenon of risk-based regulation – a term used to describe forms of regulation in which the tools of risk assessment and cost-benefit analysis are used to direct resources to where they are most needed. Confidence in the ability of the most common methods of targeting to offset the overall decline in the rate of inspection is probably misplaced since they rely heavily on health and safety data reported by firms which are widely regarded as fragmentary, unreliable and inconsistent (Fooks et al., 2007). In most developed countries, regulatory authorities typically adopt persuasive, rather than deterrence based styles of inspection, which emphasize the provision of advice, education, negotiation and compromise as a means of securing compliance. This has typically been rationalized on the basis that corporations are independently capable of responsible and moral decision-making (Tombs and Whyte, 2007).

The institutional framework of incident investigations varies greatly. In the Canadian province of British Columbia, for example, dedicated units have been established within regulatory agencies to undertake investigations and prepare cases for prosecution. This contrasts with the UK where the police are called in at a relatively early stage to lead investigations. In most countries criminal investigation and case preparation falls to ordinary officials working within labour inspectorates, insurance agencies (as in Germany) and health and safety agencies. Although common in some jurisdictions (such as France and Italy), the available evidence suggests that investigation with a view to prosecution under the conventional criminal code is rare even where permitted by law (Fooks et al., 2007).

Evaluation

As with other European Union countries, the UK has used a modified form of target deregulation (targeted enforcement) as a philosophical basis for scaling back inspection and reallocating scarce resources to alternative techniques for securing compliance which rely on economic incentives, partnerships and voluntarily

strategies. This approach is not consistent with the available evidence and has to be understood in the first instance as a function of declining (or unchanging) government funding (Davis, 2004; Fooks et al., 2007). The specific form this process has taken has been conditioned by a range of powerful (but as yet untested) political assumptions about how best to reconcile the competing interests of business and labour in the context of the less stable employment relations and working conditions that characterize deregulated labour markets and a more fragmented process of production. To this effect, the pressures on investment created by more open capital markets (which have themselves set the context of the gradual shift towards less stable forms of work) has clearly had an impact on the thinking of governments and regulatory authorities. Moreover, the declining social power of organized labour has reduced its influence over the policy-making process. However, although concerns over increased capital mobility and the impact of more open, competitive markets seem to set the assumptions of public policy (and, as such, are often used to explain the greater consideration now given to business interests in the policy-making process), there is little evidence to suggest that reduced inspection and enforcement either significantly lowers compliance costs, or, more importantly, influences investment decisions. In a sense, it is probably better to understand the direction this process has taken partly as a consequence of the sort of perceptions public officials have about business interests and partly also as a result of the increasing ability of business to ensure that policy reflects its thinking on improving competitiveness (Fooks et al., 2007; Pearce and Tombs, 1998).

Although criminal investigations undertaken with criminal prosecution in mind are usually reserved for serious injuries or deaths following some sort of traumatic injury, the rate of investigation and prosecution for serious injuries is extraordinarily low. Even in regulatory jurisdictions with a wide range of potential offences which might form the basis of prosecution and no system of administrative fines, non-investigation is the norm.

In the UK for example, fewer than one in five major injuries currently result in an investigation. Scalpings and amputations of digits past the first joint no longer require formal investigation (Tombs and Whyte, 2007).

Outright opposition to criminal investigation is rarely expressed by regulatory authorities, but rather reveals itself in the routines and practices of regulation and the densely layered nature of decision-making involved in determining whether a prosecution should follow on from an investigation. This acts as a bureaucratic deterrent to field officers contemplating the value of thorough investigation and middle managers contemplating diverting resources to criminal investigation. In the US, the absence of administrative incentives for officials within the Occupational Safety and Health Administration to prepare time-consuming and resource intensive prosecutions and a lack of relevant training underscore institutionalized ambivalence and concern over the value of using the criminal law as means of censuring companies and company officers responsible for serious health and safety violations. That these sorts of administrative arrangements reflect higher level policy is powerfully illustrated by the imposition of procedural obstacles to prosecution. In British Columbia, for example, approval of the Workers' Compensation Board is necessary before a prosecution can be commenced and in the US, the Solicitor of Labour (a senior presidential appointee), is responsible for making the final decision on whether a case should be referred to the Justice Department (Fooks et al., 2007).

The fact that corporate decision makers rarely have the time, capability, knowledge or information to compare and assess all possible outcomes, suggests that under-enforcement is likely to have a major impact on the level of occupational health and safety offending. Decisions within firms are typically a product of compromise, limited information, unacknowledged cultural beliefs and internal political and bureaucratic battles and are not, as such, fully rational. Corporate officers are said to operate within a 'bounded' rationality in which they weigh up the costs and benefits of particular decisions, policies and practices on the basis of imperfect and poorly understood information. By implying a combination of censure, reprobation and denunciation, and by imposing relatively high regulatory costs on employers, deterrence-based inspections and criminal investigation impose substantially greater costs on business than more cooperative forms of state intervention. These include direct costs – such as fines and the costs associated with preparing for an inspection and managing an investigation – and indirect costs – such as the damage well-publicized criminal investigations cause to a firm's reputation. Given the organizing role that generating returns plays in framing business decision-making, these higher costs are more likely to pierce the 'background noise' to decision-making within complex organizations so that the commercial disadvantages of poor occupational health and safety still appear a significant consideration through the sometimes fragmented and disorganized process of organizational decision-making (Fooks et al., 2007; Tombs and Whyte, 2007).

Gary Fooks

Associated Concepts: criminal investigation, economic crime, environmental crime, pluralization

Key Readings

Carson, W.G. (1980) 'The institutionalisation of ambiguity: early British Factory Acts', in G. Geis and E. Stotland (eds) *White-Collar Crime: Theory and Research*. London: Sage.

Davis, C. (2004) *Making Companies Safe: What Works?* London: Centre for Corporate Accountability.

Fooks, G., Bergman, D. and Rigby, B. (2007) *International Comparison of (a) Techniques used by State Bodies to Obtain Compliance with Health and Safety Law and Accountability for Administrative and Criminal Offences and (b) Sentences for Criminal Offences*. London: HSE Books.

Pearce, F. and Tombs, S. (1998) *Toxic Capitalism: Corporate Crime and the Chemical Industry*. Aldershot: Ashgate.

Tombs, S. and Whyte, D. (2007) *Safety Crimes*. Cullompton, Devon: Willan Publishing.

HIGH POLICING

Definition

Dr Johnson acknowledged in his *Dictionary of the English Language* that the word 'police' was borrowed from the French and meant 'the regulation and government of a city or country, so far as regards the inhabitants'. This definition accords with that proposed in 1779 by J.C.P. Lenoir, then the French General Lieutenant of Police: policing is 'the science of governing men and doing them good'. The word 'police' originally came from the Greek 'politeia', meaning polity, and was synonymous with the word 'governance'. The first treatise on policing was published in 1722 by Nicolas De La Mare in France. Policing therein applied to 11 fields that became traditional thereafter: religion; morals; public health; food supplies; public roads, bridges and buildings; public safety; sciences and the liberal arts; commerce, factories and the mechanical arts; servants and labourers; and finally, the poor. The primary objects of policing were determined to be religion – the policing of public beliefs, which later begot the 'thought police' – and the poor, whose collective riots threatened the regime.

Napoleon's Minister of Police, Joseph Fouché, who articulated the concept of high policing at the beginning of the nineteenth century, made an explicit distinction between protecting the emperor and preserving his rule on the one hand, and all other tasks of the police including public safety.

Police agents engaged in political governance as such – protecting national security – were performing 'high policing' tasks, as they were the executive arm of the head of the state; police dispatching the myriad of duties related to community security and public order – these duties were referred to by Fouché as 'the policing of lampposts' (close to which often stood prostitutes) – were doing 'low policing' and were accountable to the judiciary rather than the political hierarchy. High and low policing were thus also associated with a scale of prestige depending on how close to the seat of power the police were.

In our time, agencies belonging to the 'intelligence community' (for example, the counter-terrorist arms of the Federal Bureau of Investigation and the Central Intelligence Agency in the US, and the British security services MI5 and MI6) are involved in high policing. High policing aims to protect the state and its institutions against internal and external threats through the use of surveillance and coercion. The mention of external threats implies that the state is understood in the present context as either a national state or a limited federation of sovereign states.

Distinctive Features

High policing is not only defined by its function but also by its operational features, which are closely intertwined. The first of these is *prevention*: no single crime threatens by itself a political regime, not even the assassination of the head of the state. However, it takes only one successful coup to overthrow a government. Terrorism, which is a crime with almost no potential of bringing down a whole regime, can be construed as an act of war that endangers national security as such. Consequently, high policing cannot afford to be merely reactive, as most low policing is, because it may not get a second chance to bring a situation under control once a putsch has successfully taken place. This reasoning extends to other breaches of national security such as terrorism, which result in a high number of civilian casualties and have an overwhelming resonance in public opinion that may undermine the legitimacy of the state because of its failure to protect its population.

Prevention is achieved through *surveillance* paired with quick and decisive action to forestall the happening of a threatening event. Surveillance is achieved through the use of technology (signal intelligence and its various derivatives) and covert infiltration (human intelligence). Signal intelligence is germane to military operations but much less to the identification and monitoring of threatening individuals and small groups, such as a dormant terrorist cell. The means best suited for this task are of informants, who remain the preferred tool of high policing. In non democratic states such as the former East Germany, a significant part of the population was coerced into informing the high policing apparatus (the Stasi). Deeply infiltrated informants are treasured assets of high policing organizations, which go to great lengths to protect their identity. These agencies are particularly reluctant to have their informants testify in criminal proceedings, because their cover is at great risk of being blown despite all the precautions taken. This reluctance creates a gap between criminal *evidence*, which is sought to buttress prosecution in low policing operations, and national security *intelligence*, which is stored away awaiting further action, often never taken.

A third operational feature of high policing concerns the *conflation of separate powers*. The double-bind problem that must be solved by high policing is how to protect its intelligence assets, while acting upon the information that they provide. The solution that was initially provided is the most far-reaching feature of high policing. When the first police organizations were created in late seventeenth century France, the head of the police was given legislative, judicial and executive powers. He could then define new kinds of criminal offences, prosecute offenders in a parallel court system over which he presided and apply coercive measures as he saw fit. In particular, the police minister resorted to extended preventive custody and blocked the release of prisoners deemed too dangerous, after they had served their sentence. This conflation of powers remained a defining feature of high policing in non democratic countries from Metternich's Austria to the USSR. Under the umbrella of the 'global war against terrorism', high policing thus conceived as the appropriation of legislative and judicial prerogatives by the executive power is resurgent: covert executive orders that supersede the law are now issued, suspects are kept in unlimited preventive custody, potentially tried by special commissions, and their sentence is applied under the most punitive of conditions.

A final element is that of *extra-legality*: violation of the due process of law is not a contingent feature of high policing, which can be wholly remedied. By its very name, high policing implies that the *raison d'état* trumps all other considerations including human rights. Institutionally, the protection of state security falls somewhere between national defence and criminal justice and it is easily drawn into a war model in times of crisis. There are three ways to resolve this tension between high policing and the rule of law: to cloak it in impenetrable secrecy; to make it legal through rules of exception; and to make security agencies accountable to an oversight body. In democracies, all three means are used in varying degrees at the same time.

Evaluation

The notion of high policing was reintroduced in the theory of policing by Brodeur (1983) and updated in subsequent writings (Brodeur, 2007). It raises several issues for the future.

A first question is of robustness: whether the distinction between high and low policing is an enduring one. After the end of the Cold War, security intelligence agencies were looking for a new mandate and started to operate aggressively in fields devolved to low policing, such as the fight against drug trafficking and organized crime. At the same time, low policing moved closer to high policing through the development of models such as problem-oriented and intelligence-led policing which were based on the collection and processing of information. It then seemed that high and low policing were merging together and that the distinction was losing its relevancy. This relevancy was reasserted with the utmost clarity by the numerous commissions that scrutinized police performance in the wake of the September 2001 terrorist attempts against the US and of subsequent bombings in other countries. These commissions emphasized the existence of a 'wall' between traditional police organizations such as the FBI and the intelligence community, forces mainly devoted to low policing being particularly wanting in their capacity to analyze intelligence. There were even recommendations to strip the FBI of its national security functions.

A further question concerns the impact of privatization trends, with two separate issues being involved here. The first is the growing outsourcing of surveillance and data-mining to private industry. The second is that high policing does not only protect against the subversion of the state; private high policing agencies also protect against the subversion of 'the client' (O'Reilly and Ellison, 2006: 647). Both issues are real and will be examined more thoroughly in future research, as the trend towards privatization will grow and affect high policing as it did low policing. However, it must be emphasized that the privatization of high policing is limited to its surveillance and intelligence components and that it does not take into account the element of coercion implied by the creation of a shadow penal justice system. Furthermore, the analogy between protecting the state and protecting 'the client' breaks down when it is noticed that the state is one body whereas clients are many. Private high policing is a volatile mix of competing interests rather than a concerted network.

The most intractable issue is the compatibility between the extra-legal character of high policing and the democratic state, which is grounded in the rule of law. If the state apparatus is divorced from civil society and only serves the interest of a minority, then high policing is only an instrument of oppression devoid of legitimacy. When the state and its institutions serve the common good, a difficult balance may be struck where a police practice is acknowledged to be both extra-legal and legitimate under specific circumstances.

Jean-Paul Brodeur

Associated Concepts: accountability, criminal investigation, cross-border policing, intelligence-led policing, privatization, terrorism, transnational policing

Key Readings

Brodeur, J-P. (2007) 'High and low policing in post-9/11 times', *Policing: A Journal of Policy and Practice*, 1 (1): 25–37.

Brodeur, J-P. (1983) 'High and low policing: remarks about the policing of political activities', *Social Problems*, 30 (5): 507–21. (reprinted in R. Reiner (1996), (ed.) *Police Discretion and Accountability, Policing Vol. II.* Aldershot: Dartmouth Pub.)

Liang, H-H. (1992) *The Rise of the European State System from Metternich to the Second World War.* New York: Cambridge University Press.

O'Reilly, C. and Ellison, G. (2006) 'Eye spy private high: reconceptualizing high policing theory', *British Journal of Criminology*, 46 (4): 641–60.

Radzinowicz, L., Sir (1956) *A History of English Criminal Law and its Administration from 1750.* Vol. 3. London: Stevens and Sons Limited.

HISTORY

Police, and the European variants of the word (such as *politie*, *Polizei*, *polizia*), pre-date the bureaucratic institutions that emerged during the nineteenth century. The word has its origins in Classical Greek and by the mid sixteenth century, across continental Europe, it was equated with governance. In the German-speaking lands it was used particularly with reference to policies that promoted the general good. In eighteenth century France it appears to have been employed primarily with reference to the internal management of a town or city.

The first officials that might, admittedly anachronistically, be labelled as police in the post Classical world were the local men, commonly recruited for a year or so from small property owners, to enforce local norms – these were constables in England, *consuls* or *syndics* in France. The urban watches of the middle ages, usually recruited from householders on a part-time, often unpaid basis, were similar. In the process of state formation princes were content to leave the municipalities to govern themselves and to maintain their own internal security, providing there was no threat to the prince's authority. It was a rather different story, however, in areas that a prince had only recently brought under his control or that were distant from his centre of power. The Spanish monarchs organized a military brotherhood, the *Santa Hermandad*, to establish and maintain their authority after unification. In France the *Maréchaussée*, originally created in the early sixteenth century to police the royal armies, was increasingly given jurisdiction over the rural population.

As well as extending their authority to new or distant parts of their territories, princes were also conscious of a need to check conspiracies and maintain stability at the centre of their power. As capital cities developed, so princes and their ministers took an increasing interest in the maintenance of order in those cities. In 1667, Louis XIV created a police chief (*lieutenant general de police*) for Paris and during the eighteenth century other European princes looked to this French model for their own capitals. Britain, however, France's great economic and political rival, resisted French models and British hostility to centralized government and pride in what its inhabitants considered as a unique and distinctive form of liberty, meant that they kept up a vocal hostility to what they understood as policing that was both military and oppressively intrusive into people's lives.

The Revolutionary and Napoleonic Wars saw a revised French system – the *Maréchaussée* reorganized as the *Gendarmerie Nationale* and a structure of state civilian police in capitals and a few officials in other big towns – spread across continental Europe. Civilian municipal police remained the norm in urban areas. The new London Metropolitan Police established under Sir Robert Peel in 1829, which became very popular with European liberals who sought to emulate Britain's economic and political success, was a variant of the state civilian model. While in Ireland and the more remote areas of their empire the British commonly adopted a variant of the state military/gendarmerie style police.

As state bureaucracies became ever more specialized in the nineteenth and twentieth centuries, so the police role became increasingly concentrated on crime and public order. At the same time, various specialisms developed within the police institutions, not least with the advent of new technologies seen as invaluable in crime fighting, surveillance and order maintenance both of crowds and burgeoning motor traffic. By the inter-war period the days of the steady beat patrol were already numbered by vast urban expansion and different forms of mechanization.

Similar patterns of development can be detected beyond the Western world, from part-time officials enforcing norms to growing intervention by the prince. Moreover, as estern dominance began increasingly to influence those Asian states that escaped European colonization, so European ideas of policing began to be absorbed into their administrative bureaucracies.

In the following sections, the historical development of policing is elaborated further with reference to nine areas of the world: Africa, Australia, China, France, Germany, Latin America, Russia, the UK and the US, with additional readings recommended.

Clive Emsley

Emsley, C. (1999) 'A typology of nineteenth-century police', *Crime, Histoire et Sociétés/ Crime, History and Societies*, 3 (1): 19–24.

Africa

Historical evidence indicates that policing structures existed in Africa prior to the arrival of Europeans. Pre-colonial policing in Africa was local and voluntary, consisting of a variety of civilian, military and supernatural methods in which villagers, hunters, warriors and oracle priests maintained order and carried out policing functions such as arrest, detention and interrogation of offenders. Colonization meant the imposition of European policing methods as the main types whilst the indigenous types were left intact or modified to imitate European types.

Colonial policing in Africa evolved in response to changing colonial economic and political needs. The state civilian policing model was common during the early years of colonization, when the primary concern was the provision of basic security for colonial settlers and traders in an unsettled environment where opposition to European presence or authority remained a permanent threat. The need to secure inland trading routes and access mining sites meant that colonial activities had to extend into African hinterlands where conflict with the indigenes was inevitable. The logistical problems of funding colonial armies abroad led to the preference for a paramilitary or state military model of policing. African paramilitary police forces were fashioned along similar lines as the Royal Irish Constabulary and the French Gendarmerie and were used to coerce respect for colonial authority and open up the African hinterland for trade in 'legitimate' goods.

The 1885 Berlin Conference set new rules on claims to colonial territories in Africa. All claims to areas of influence had to be backed by evidence of 'effective occupation'. In the scramble for territories that ensued, the use of military force to ensure effective occupation was common, especially in areas where there were competing interests by rival colonial powers. Resistance by the indigenes to claims of colonial land ownership had to be met by force. The mid to late nineteenth century was therefore characterized by the expansion of paramilitary policing in Africa. Colonial authorities and mercantile companies operating in the continent set up paramilitary police forces and used them to coerce the indigenes into signing treaties of protection that placed their lands firmly under colonial rule.

After Africa was fully partitioned, colonial governments reverted back to state civilian policing in the form of national police forces. In addition, municipal provincial or local government policing structures were introduced in the protectorates, in the form of Native Authority police forces under the control of colonially-appointed local 'chiefs'. Native Authority police officers had a reputation for brutality and abuse of power as they were symbols of colonial authority, unaccountable to the peoples they policed.

During the period of decolonization and fight for independence, the need for state institutions to symbolize national unity was a primary political goal. Hence, after independence, the state civilian model of policing was overwhelmingly adopted in Africa whilst the municipal civil approach was invariably abolished as they were perceived to represent ethnic rather than national interests.

The greatest colonial legacy for Africa is political policing. African countries have continued in the colonial tradition of retaining the police as national institutions, in constitutional arrangements that place heads of police forces under the control of heads of governments. African police forces are not democratically accountable. Allegations of incompetence and corruption are common and have led to the growth of private security as crime in urban areas has reached unprecedented levels in recent years.

Bankole A. Cole

Cole, B. A. (1999) 'Post-colonial systems', in R. I. Mawby (ed.) *Policing Across the World*. London: UCL Press.

Australia

The history of Australian public policing is one of centralized state forces organized in jurisdictions of very large geographical scope. Within a few decades of the establishment of the convict settlement at Sydney (1788) colonial governors established small constabulary forces, usually under the control of local magistrates. Domestic threats to the security of the settler colonists led to the development in the 1830s of specialized units to combat bushrangers (many of them escaped convicts) or the widespread resistance of the Indigenous peoples. In a number of colonies from the 1840s to the 1890s the policing of conflict between settlers and Indigenous peoples was managed through 'Native Police', special forces of white officers (many of them former British military officers) and black troopers. Many such units were involved in killings and even massacres of Indigenous people. Their history remains one of the most controversial aspects of Australian policing, with long-term consequences for the legitimacy of policing among the country's Indigenous population.

The establishment of colonial self-government in the 1850s was generally accompanied by the consolidation of the police constabularies into single, centralized police forces. Only in Tasmania did the more English tradition of local constabularies under the control of municipal councils persist, only to end in conformity to the pattern in other colonies in 1898. The colonial police forces were commonly recruited in their early years from immigrants with prior military (usually British Army) or policing (very often Irish Constabulary) experience. Employment in the police was an important vehicle for social mobility. Organization and training were much influenced by the centralized Irish policing model, but in the highly urbanized colonies English beat policing was equally influential.

With the establishment of the Federation in 1901, each state police force was established under the command of a commissioner (the title varied), responsible to a minister of the Crown for the administration of policing throughout the state. Although criminal law remains typically a state responsibility, the Commonwealth government has developed an increasingly important role in recent decades, following the consolidation of Commonwealth policing functions in the Australian Federal Police in 1979. That force has developed an influential regional policing role in the South Pacific and South-East Asia, as well as working with state police in domestic law enforcement in areas of increasing priority such as organized crime and counter-terrorism.

In Australian constitutional convention, government ministers did not ordinarily intervene in operational policing, a convention much challenged in the breach as the twentieth century wore on. From the 1960s conflict around policing strength and priorities became a permanent feature of the political landscape. Governments sought advantage from demonstrating their commitment to law and order, often responding to the demands of the powerful police unions, whose influence in policing dates back to the 1910s. Critics questioned the role of police in the suppression of dissent (especially through the role of the police 'Special Branches') and the treatment of minorities. In most Australian jurisdictions in recent decades evidence of police corruption has led to official inquiries, resulting often in new institutions and mechanisms of accountability and oversight. The long-term effectiveness of these new arrangements in improving the quality and fairness of policing remains to be seen.

Mark Finnane

Finnane, M. (1994) *Police and Government: Histories of Policing in Australia*. Melbourne: Oxford University Press.

China

In classical Chinese the term 'police' consisted of two Chinese characters, *jing* and *cha*. The term *jing cha* together literally means to warn (*jing*) and be subjected to supervision (*cha*). In China since antiquity, policing functions, from political control to social ordering, have been achieved informally and provided for by way of family and with the help of the community. Western ideas of policing came to China around 1889.

The earliest record of policing activities appeared under Emperor Shun (2255–2205 B.C.), whose tribal coalition committee (*buluo lianmeng yihui*), a decision-making body of tribal elders, established nine kinds of official (*guan*). Among these, the *situ* was responsible for resolving people's disputes and maintaining social order, and the *shi* was responsible for policing the border, investigating crime, and maintaining prisons.

The *Qin* dynasty (221–207 B.C.) united China with vertical rule, legal control, central administration, and coercive governance, that is, a criminal justice bureaucracy with the emperor serving as the fountain of virtue (*de* and *ren*) under heaven (*tianzhi*). In *Qin*, the smallest and lowest political/social administrative unit was the *li*. For every *li* there were ten *ting.* The day-to-day administration of justice and the policing of the local population was delegated to the *lidian* who was responsible for keeping peace and order in the local community. The *lidian* was responsible for the accurate maintenance of a household registration system, monitoring the whereabouts and status of every person in the state. Anyone who failed to register, or without household registration, was labelled *wang ming* (anonymous) and subject to punishment.

In 375 B.C. the legalist Shang Yang established the *baojia* system. This was a community policing system performing communal security, informal surveillance and collective accountability functions.

China's first experience with foreign policing began in 1876 in the international settlement port of Shanghai. Under the Charter for Shanghai Settlement, *xunbu fang* (police stations) were established in various foreign – British, French, American – concessions. These were staffed by approximately equal numbers of Western and Chinese officers. The chief of police was appointed by the Municipal Council Board, with members elected by Western commercial leaders.

Huang Zunxian (1848–1905), the putative father of Chinese modern policing, experimented with foreign police ideas in establishing the *Hunan Baowei Ju*, public security bureaus with duties to preserve the safety of the citizen and deter, investigate and prosecute crime.

In China the police have been referred to as *gongan* (literally 'public peace') and more recently as *jingcha* (police). There are now two types of police in China; *minjing* or people's police and *renmin wuzhuang jingcha budui* (shortened to *wujing*) or People's Armed Police (PAP). The functions of *gongan* are the maintenance of social order, securing public safety, protecting public and private property, and preserving citizens' personal rights.

The first public security force was set up in Nanchang, Jiangxi province, on 1 August 1929, but it was really from 1979 onwards that professional policing began to spread and take root in the People's Republic of China. Between 1978 and 1990 the police establishment

expanded from 400,000 to 800,000 officers, complemented by 600,000 *wujing* and 870,000 special function public security officers (e.g., railway, traffic, aviation, agriculture, enterprise safety and economic security police). Altogether There were around 2.3 million public security officers of various capacities by 1990, amounting to one officer for every 500 citizens (based on the 1990 population census). The number is likely to be closer to 3 million today, organized into 30 provincial police departments and operating out of 38,648 *paichushuo* (police stations) around the nation.

Kam C. Wong

Wong, K. C. (2008) *Policing with Chinese Characteristics: Idea, History, Philosophy, and Reform.* New York: Peter Lang Publishing.

France

What is most remarkable about the history of French police institutions is the continuity, from the Revolutionary and Napoleonic era, through the subsequent, roughly nine, widely different political regimes. Until the Second World War policing, for most French citizens, was a municipal matter, with occasional encounters with the gendarmerie, a state military police.

Whereas civilian uniformed police were invented by the English with Peel's 'New Police', the French invented the state military police model with the *Maréchaussée*, which became the National Gendarmerie (NG) under Napoleon I. The Napoleonic conquests exported it to other European countries where it served as a model for many police forces, and French colonialism exported it to other parts of the world. It also inspired British colonial police forces, such as the Royal Irish Constabulary. The *Maréchaussée* was first established in the sixteenth century to control disbanded mercenaries turned bandits when war ended and to keep the highways safe. It has retained this dual military and civilian police function ever since, with the civilian duties becoming prevalent in peacetime. Organized in small brigades of six, the men were stationed in small towns and villages, living in barracks with their families. They were the only national police force of the *Ancien Régime*, but they never exceeded 4000 men. Nowadays, *gendarmes* number about 100,000, including a substantial number of specialized mobile anti-riot personnel. Most are stationed in the countryside and suburban areas, where they exercise a type of community policing. The NG constitutes a separate entity within the army, under the authority of the Ministry of Defence, with its own hierarchy and its lowest officers rank as non-commissioned officers.

The French Revolution did not break with the *Ancien Régime's* tradition of municipal policing, but established that municipal police in cities with more than 5000 inhabitants should be headed by a police commissioner. Initially elected, by 1800 the commissioner became a state appointed official, accountable both to the mayor (who paid his wages) and the *Préfet* (the regional representative of the state). In smaller municipalities, the mayor (appointed and supervised by the government) had responsibility for policing. In 1882, however, the Third Republic (1870–1940) decided that they should be elected, and this laid the foundation for potential conflict between the mayor and the police officers that he appointed, and the commissioner appointed by the government and backed by the *Préfet*.

From then on, the trend was for greater state involvement in local policing, something strongly supported by the commissioners. Until the advent of the Vichy regime, state involvement was limited by the wish to leave the financial burden of policing to the municipalities. The Vichy government, eager to improve police effectiveness to assert its authority and sovereignty while satisfying German demands and fighting the Resistance – incorporated urban forces into a national civilian police. In 1941, the police of cities with more than 10,000 inhabitants were integrated into the *Sûreté Nationale* – the National Police (NP).

Before the 1941 reform, the state police comprised the police of Paris and, gradually, the police of a few major cities; small regional criminal investigation, intelligence and border police services; and the local commissioners (paid by municipalities), under the responsibility of the Ministry of Interior. The capital had been under state police authority ever since the establishment of the *Lieutenant Général de Police* in 1667. After the fall of the monarchy, the *Préfecture de Police* of Paris, the largest and most modern police agency in the country, remained a distinct agency under direct supervision of the government. This remains the case, although the *Préfecture* was formally integrated within the National Police in 1966, and the *Préfet de Police* still ranks as highly as the NP's general director. Today, the NP has about 145,000 officers, operating in urban and suburban settings distinct from those of the NG.

What will be the future of the French police system? Since the 1980s, there have been major changes. Growing local dissatisfaction with the NP has led many cities to recreate municipal police. These currently number about 20,000 officers but they enjoy more limited powers under French law than NP or NG; it is expected that they will develop further. The customs service has been reborn as a third national police; and, finally, the private security sector has been incorporated into partnerships with police forces. However the most significant trend is towards greater integration of the NP and NG. Since 2002, the NG has been under the operational authority of the Ministry of Interior; a further distancing from the Ministry of Defence has been announced for 2009. In the meantime, communication and information systems are being integrated with those of the NP, while the respective territories of the two agencies have been better delineated. These changes make a future merger of these agencies more likely than ever.

René Lévy

Emsley, C. and Weinberger, B. (eds) (1991) *Policing Western Europe: Politics, Professionalism, and Public Order, 1850–1940*. New York: Greenwood Press.

Germany

Since the beginning of the nineteenth century, responsibility for the maintenance of law and order has, for the most part, been devolved to the *Länder*, the German federal states. The exceptions to this, when state policing has been organized centrally, occurred under the Nazi regime, and in East Germany under communism.

The origins of the existing police system are in the *Policey* (meaning 'state of an overall 'good order') of the *Ancien Régime*. At the end of the eighteenth century, the *Policey* held a number of administrative functions, among them economic and welfare activities (such as making sure that the markets functioned properly and supervising poor relief). Although crime control became an important feature of policing in Germany during the nineteenth century, 'order' in the broadest sense remained a key police function.

The collapse of the *Ancien Régime* system of German states during the wars against France around 1800 was a turning point which led to the introduction of modern policing in Germany. The German states modernized their administrative structures, including the police, adopting French models such as the Gendarmerie.

Germany was a relative latecomer in Europe in terms of industrial progress, with industrialization and urbanization – and the law and order problems associated with it – not really beginning until the latter half of the nineteenth century. There was a dual response to this emerging crime problem: urban police practice continued along the lines established by the *Policey* model, because this allowed a flexible response to urban problems. But with the establishment of professional municipal administrations and the rise of the *Kriminalpolizei*, the relevance of the old model decreased. The main purpose of the *Kriminalpolizei* was to control urban crime, although crime was not a serious urban problem before the First World War (except in Berlin).

Large scale public disorder problems became increasingly commonplace in Germany during the 1800s, culminating in major labour disputes at the end of the nineteenth century. At that time, public disorder was primarily controlled by military means. By the time of the First World War, however, many saw the use of military force as being counterproductive, fuelling rather than calming public order problems. Efforts to establish specific police units for public order policing intensified amid the threat of civil war during the early years of the Weimar Republic, leading to the establishment of paramilitary police units. These were commanded by officers almost exclusively drawn from the ranks of the army, and trained according to military methods.

During the Nazi period from 1933 to 1945, the federal system of police was abolished in favour of a national police structure with very strict hierarchies and command structures. The police were transformed into an omnipotent and deadly tool of the Nazi regime, complicit in the mass murder of European Jews and other populations. Following the overthrow of the Nazi regime, the Allied Forces sought to reinstate federal policing as part of the authority of the *Länder*, and the Americans and the British went even further by implementing local policing comparable to their own models.

When the state governments in West Germany regained responsibility for policing at the end of the 1940s, they reverted back to the policing models of the Weimar Republic. By contrast, the centralized system of policing that remained in the former German Democratic Republic (East Germany) existed not only to fulfil traditional police functions, but also to support and maintain the Communist regime and its power structure. Political policing by the *Staatssicherheit* (Ministry for State Security, popularly known as the Stasi) pervaded all aspects of life in East Germany. After the reunification of the two Germanies in 1990, East Germany not only adopted the political system of the Federal Republic, but its police system as well.

Responsibility for political policing in the Federal Republic is now shared between a relatively small section of federal states' *Kriminalpolizei* and Germany's domestic intelligence agency, the *Verfassungsschutz*

(Federal Office for the Protection of the Constitution). There also exists a federal police infrastructure, consisting of the *Bundeskriminalamt* (Federal *Kriminalpolizei* Office) and the *Bundespolizei* (Federal Police), comprised of the former border police and the railway police.

Herbert Reinke

Reinke, H. (1991) '"Armed as if for a war": the state, the military and the professionalization of the Prussian police in Imperial Germany', in C. Emsley and B. Weinberger (eds) *Policing Western Europe: Politics, Professionalism, and Public Order, 1850–1940*. New York: Greenwood Press.

Japan

During the Edo era (1600–1867), Japan entered a period of self-imposed national isolation under the centralized rule of the Tokugawa shoguns. Edo age Japan was a minutely regulated feudal society based upon strict hierarchical principles, with a sophisticated policing apparatus administered by the *samurai* (warrior) class. In addition, neighbourhood groups of five households (*gonin-gumi*) were held responsible for order maintenance in their areas.

In the mid-nineteenth century, Japan was forced to accept that its isolationist policy was no longer tenable. The shogunate collapsed and the authority of the Emperor (*Meiji*) was restored in 1868 and Japan embarked on a rapid modernization programme to catch up with the Great Powers of the day. This involved borrowing and adapting to Japanese circumstances a whole range of Western technologies and institutions.

With regard to policing, Japan was heavily influenced by continental European models of policing, notably those in France and Prussia, whose highly centralized police administration seemed a natural model for Japan to emulate. The Tokyo Metropolitan Police was founded in 1874, headed by Toshiyoshi Kawaji, a former *samurai* from Kagoshima.

Kawaji is regarded as the modern Japanese police's 'founding father'.

Like its continental counterparts, Japan's new police had a wide range of administrative and surveillance functions and was controlled by a powerful Home Ministry (*Naimusho*). However, on the recommendation of police advisers from Berlin, a nationwide network of police boxes was established throughout Japan to provide a prominent local presence. By the end of the Meiji period in 1912, there were over 15,000 rural residential police posts (*chuzaisho*) and urban neighbourhood boxes (*koban*), a combined total that has remained remarkably constant until the early twenty-first century.

Following the Second World War, the US Occupation of Japan (1945–52) launched reforms aimed at demilitarizing and democratizing the country. As part of this, the 1948 Police Act sought to decentralize and reconstruct Japanese policing by introducing municipal forces for towns with populations over 5000, and a National Rural Police Force to cover less populated areas. However, this proved unsuccessful and recentralization occurred under the 1954 Police Act. This gave each of the 47 prefectures and major metropolitan areas (*todofuken*) its own police force, while the National Police Agency of Japan (*Keisatsucho*) was established to provide central government administrative and policy direction.

The Japanese *koban* system began to attract significant worldwide attention in the 1970s. At a time when crime rates were rising in other developed countries, Japan's crime rate remained remarkably low. The neighbourhood location and service orientation of the Japanese police box system were widely seen as key elements underpinning social cohesion and crime control. Consequently, many countries then and since have adopted the *koban* concept as part of their reassurance and community policing strategies.

However, by the late 1990s, the 'celebratory' discourse surrounding policing in Japan came to be questioned as it became increasingly apparent that the country's social relations were 'thinning' and recorded crime – while still comparatively low – was rising.

Public concern in Japan over 'empty' (that is, unstaffed) *koban* (*aki koban*), was reflected in a rise in demand for private policing services among Japanese citizens.

In the early twenty-first century, Japanese policing appears to be moving in the direction of a 'partnership' footing as in many Western policing jurisdictions, and away from extensive reliance on its traditional mode of *koban* operation.

Frank Leishman

Leishman, F. (2007) 'Koban: neighbourhood Policing in contemporary Japan', *Policing*, 1 (2): 196–202.

Latin America

The history of policing in Latin America remains to be written. An important part of its development derives from the colonial experience. Domination of new territories by European states was based upon their military superiority, and a marked differentiation between colonizers and natives. The hierarchical characteristics of the *Ancien Régime* were reinforced in the colonial experience and survived the process of independence. The maintenance of order involved the State and the white elite, cooperating in patrolling tasks and repression of crime. The forces of order were mostly public but fell under private control.

During the nineteenth century the constitution of states in Latin America established diverse forms of arranging those colonial traits: the military character of policing and the influence of private power over public apparatuses of social control. State building and stability were problems, and the police could be a useful instrument but also objects of dispute between central and local forces, with some countries centralizing their institutions while others left them under the control of local elites. The success in building State police forces was only partial and the traditional militarized and oppressive character was ever present.

By the end of the nineteenth century, modernizing elites relied heavily upon European models and scientific innovation in policing, proposing that modern states ought to have modern forces with investigative models based on science. Attempts were made and international exchange favoured. A first international police conference was held in Buenos Aires in 1905 with officials from Brazil, Argentina, Chile and Uruguay, who agreed to trade information on criminals. Those countries quickly adopted photography, fingerprinting and other innovations.

The modern, scientific trend, however, had little effect over those in charge of daily policing. The low salaries attracted poorly qualified workers, many appointed by politicians in exchange for votes or other private services, and the use of force remained the basis for policing. These traits came to good use when political policing became an important basis for authoritarian regimes. Due process and accountability never became central issues in policing and violent methods were largely deployed.

Military regimes in the second half of the twentieth century consolidated the use of violence in policing. Their demise and the return to democracy from the 1980s posed a serious problem in how to deal with the police and their tasks. Poor social conditions and the lack of interest demonstrated by the military in dealing with crime motivated high increases in urban crime. The return to democracy brought many proposals of police reform, stressing respect for human rights, but saw public opinion hesitating in extending rights and democracy for 'criminals.' Some countries have been more successful in reducing crime rates – Colombia representing the best example – but most still have to deal with the difficult balance of carrying on a police reform that public opinion perceive as softening control while crime rates soar. The debate over new forms of policing and accountability thrive in these countries; police officers are more and more aware of the need to establish new patterns but resistance to change is enormous and the future of policing in Latin America is not easy to foresee.

Marcos Luiz Bretas

Chevigny, P. (1997) *Edge of the Knife: Police Violence in the Americas*. New York: The New Press.

Russia

Russian law enforcement agencies have carried out various functions during their long history, not always focused exclusively on maintaining public order and fighting crime. The police did not emerge as a key state institution in Russia until the early nineteenth century, until when policing tasks were conducted in conjunction with other legal and administrative functions by various state bodies. Although police organizations in Russia have experienced much change during their long history, key concerns about transparency and accountability have run through their evolution.

Prior to the eighteenth century there were no dedicated policing groups as such: instead various groups carried out policing and judicial functions simultaneously. The first dedicated policing units – the *'Razbojniy prikaz'* (central investigative unit within local crime fighting units) appeared during the sixteenth century. In 1802 the Ministry of Internal Affairs was created and consequently oversaw the development of a regular police force, which resulted in the merging of city and district police units and a narrowing of police functions. The Gendarmes were created in 1792, initially to police military units, before being expanded to include Moscow and St. Petersburg divisions in 1817. The Gendarmerie continued to develop throughout the nineteenth century, eventually numbering more than 15,000 in 1916, including 1,000 senior officers from the army corps. One year later the Gendarmerie was abolished following the Revolution.

The Soviet militia (1917–1991) was developed with the chief aim of suppressing political, ideological and economic opposition to the communist regime. Initially comprised of informal workers' brigades (including Red Guards), voluntary people's brigades, special guard units and public order units, these groupings were consolidated in 1917 by NKVD (the People's Commissariat of Internal Affairs) decree. In 1918, a law was passed by the NKVD and the People's Commissariat of Justice for the creation of an official state body for the maintenance of public order, based on the worker and peasant militias. This new militia was a highly militarized, centralized and bureaucratized organization, governed by decree rather than law. This placed the militia firmly under the control of the ruling elite, who operated a policy of strict political repression. A measure of change occurred in the late 1950s/early 1960s in the wake of Khrushchev's political 'thaw', when attempts were made to decentralize control of the Ministry of Internal Affairs (MVD: *Ministerstvo Vnutrennykh Del*) to the republics, but the resultant structural changes did little to curb corruption within the militia. Greater specialization was introduced to the militia during the 1970s and 1980s as police training and discipline improved. Towards the end of the 1980s some decentralization of policing took place as police control was transferred to the Soviet Union's 15 republics, but for the most part the Soviet militia remained a totalitarian force. At the same time some resources were hived off (beginning in 1991) from the regular militia to create the OMON (*Otryad militsii osobogo naznacheniya*) special forces to deal with serious unrest.

With the collapse of the Soviet Union in 1991 came the creation of 15 sovereign (ex Soviet) militia forces under the control of their own MVDs. The Russian militia comprises the Public Security Militia *(PSM: Militsiya obshestvennoi bezopasnosti)* and the Criminal Militia *(CM: Kriminal'naya militsiya)*, both under the control of the Federal and regional MVDs: additionally the Public Security Militia are subordinate to local authorities. The PSM (local police force) are responsible for police stations, temporary detention centres and road safety and transport; they also have special units that deal with juvenile delinquents, secret and classified buildings, and passports and visas. The Extra-Departmental Guard

Service (*Upravleniye vnevedomstvennoi okhrany*) is also part of the PSM: it provides commercial guard services to private individuals and businesses and thus operates as a private police service within the regular police force. The CM encompasses various divisions, including the CID and units to combat economic, drug-related and organized crime. In addition to these two main services the MVD also has a Transport Militia force, Internal Troops (part of the armed forces, but under MVD control) and the Internal Troops own Special Forces – the *Spetsnaz*. In spite of changes to the political climate, the police still face serious problems caused by the legacy of the Soviet era.

Adrian Beck and Annette Robertson

Beck, A. and Robertson A. (2005) 'Police reform in Russia', in W. Pridemore, (ed.) *Ruling Russia: Crime, Law, and Justice in a Changing Society*. New York: Rowman and Littlefield Publishers.

United Kingdom

In 1700, Britain was policed by amateur householders in the office of parish constable, who were joined in the towns by less skilled full-time night watchmen. Around 1750, Henry Fielding introduced several innovations in London: control by magistrates, uniforms, and a salary, in a small-scale effort to professionalize the system. Between 1760 and 1830, some constables increasingly made a full-time living, and many urban parishes incrementally reformed their watch forces, creating a pattern of uniformed preventive police. The 'state civil' Metropolitan Police was created in 1829 by Sir Robert Peel, then Home Secretary, in response to increasing fears that London's disparate localized policing systems were not able to cope with crime in the city: they soon found a national role as a riot control squad.

Outside London, following worry about the ability of the old system to repress crime in a fast-changing world, provincial police reform was precipitated by fear of Chartism (a working class movement for democratic rights), but forces had 'municipal civil' governance. In boroughs, from 1835, this meant watch committees elected from the corporation; in counties, from 1839, committees of the justices of the peace. Government began to subsidize police costs, and inspect now-mandatory police forces, in 1857. From 1888, the police were not controlled by the new county councils, instead by committees of councillors and magistrates.

Ireland was a testing ground for police reform, from 1836 under a 'state military' model. Yet by 1919, a generation of largely 'domestic' policing tasks had eroded the Royal Irish Constabulary's paramilitary edge.

Peel's 'New Police' were subject to strict discipline and long hours: only job security and (after 1890) pension rights made the job attractive. From the turn of the century, illegal trade union activity grew, culminating in the police strikes of 1918-1919. The outcome was that terms and conditions were set nationally (eroding local autonomy) and a statutory body, the Police Federation, was empowered to negotiate with the employers. At the same time, the 1914–1918 manpower crisis led to the grudging acceptance of some women as police officers, with (until the 1960s) curtailed roles.

Its ethos was public service, yet until the 1950s, police were generally available for hire by anyone who could pay. Twentieth century changes in British lifestyle threatened the nineteenth-century style of policing. Lower-density housing and increased use of cars (a source of tension with the middle classes), stopped the foot patrol surveilling of public life on the streets. In response, technology was used, beginning in the late 1930s with the 999 system linked to centralized control of police in cars. Its ubiquity, reached in the 1970s, marked a practical shift from prevention to reaction.

Enforced mergers of boroughs into counties stemmed from the 1964 Police Act. In the 1970s police claims of professional capacity peaked, as the issue of 'law and order' became politicized once more. By the 1980s a new political assertiveness by many chief constables drew attention to their lack of accountability. The present 'community safety' orientation marks a retreat from this point, and together with the growing 'family' of police institutions, harks back to the multi-layered system of 1800.

Chris A. Williams

Rawlings, P. (2001) *Policing: A Short History*. Cullompton, Devon: Willan Publishing.

United States

From the beginning policing in the US was about creating and sustaining boundaries between members of the valued society and the 'others'. The history of American policing therefore reflects the tensions between classes, ethnic groups, and regions mediated by the ideology of secular equality.

Unlike the English model, American policing was patterned by the ever widening frontier, ethnicity brought by waves of immigration, and was political in the sense of responding to local centres of power and authority. The history of policing in the US, however, charts primarily the rise and development of public police in north eastern cities, organizations with a bureaucratic organization, a public mandate, powers of arrest and a legitimate use of violence. This vision does not include seeing this development in contrast and competition with other forms of social control, sanctioning and regulation including quasi-public forms, state, federal and private police.

As colonial society differentiated, that is as policing and social control became distinct from local customs and the teachings of the church, the sheriff and deputies became secular agents, paid and charged with order maintenance, serving subpoenae and making tax collections. Because of common law traditions, citizens were held responsible for the hue and cry and expected to take action in the face of disturbances. America, from the colonial period until the early nineteenth century, saw a variety of non-vocational, voluntary policing forms – posses, vigilantes, bounty hunters, and *ad hoc* self-help groups that functioned at the edges of official police

authority. These competitive forces were in fact essential to the flourishing of democratic policing.

American policing is local policing and it reflects customary views of majority and minority rights. The history of American law enforcement is perhaps revealed in the efforts over some 350 years to legislate some semblance of equality while the police enforced the interests of the majority. The American constitution provides no legal basis for federal or state police, or gendarmes with responsibilities for national security. In many respects, this role has been played by the state-based National Guard(s) that are under the control of the governors of the 50 states. The 43 federally based police came into being via interpretations of the Interstate Commerce Clause.

As very large cities with high density and concentration of immigrants emerged in the nineteenth century, New York, Boston, and Philadelphia, formal policing organizations were formed. The Peel model was adopted by negotiation and compromise within the political system, rather than imposed as in other colonial territories initially under British rule. These large city departments were patterned on the Peel model of preventive patrol, reactive policing and uniformed presence. In time, they were armed. Outside these large cities the pattern was systematic policing and exclusion of minorities by law and custom. These modes include slave patrols, militias, and informal policing of minorities in both the North and South.

The period between the 1830s and the Civil War was punctuated by civil disorders and riots, largely against the weak and powerless by the more powerful. The period of antebellum slave patrols and policing of slaves-as-property was reproduced postbellum Civil War by troops who policed and acted as an occupying army in the South. This mode of targeting minorities became more public in the 1960s in America when the least powerful rebelled against repression and for greater equality. The virtual exclusion of African Americans from police employment until after the Second World War sustained this policing pattern.

The concentration of poverty and disadvantage in large American cities, especially of African Americans, that occurred through the nineteenth century was moderated after the Second World War by three factors: 1) new employment opportunities, in part due to booming war industries such as auto, ship and airplane building; 2) the benefits of unionization; and 3) efforts to expand public housing in large cities. Policing remained a white, male occupation. New forms of discrimination, especially public housing, isolated blacks in northern cities. The riots of the late 1960s symbolized a powerful combination of rising expectations, police violence and radical politics. These rebellious activities are the most important indication of American policing's new professionalism, violence and subcultural insulation (Uchida, 2005). As Uchida points out, crime doubled between 1960 and 1970, and because the police defined themselves actively as professional crime fighters, they were blamed for the riots as well as the crime which they could not control. This was a turning point that led to a reform attempt: community policing.

Policing in the US remains locked into three strategies: random patrol, investigation of crimes and response to citizens now enhanced by a 911 number and computer assisted dispatch. The core function is now carried out by a huge, more diverse, work force still patrolling the boundaries of communities, serving the worthy and arresting others.

Peter K. Manning

Uchida, C. (2005) 'The development of the American police', in R. Durham and G. Alpert (eds) *Critical Issues in Policing*. Prospect Heights, IL: Waveland Press.

Associated Concepts: community policing, misconduct, patrol, pluralization, police property, Pacific policing, paramilitary policing, policy transfer, professionalization, transnational policing

HOMELAND SECURITY

Definition

In policing, 'homeland security' refers to police activities designed to prevent and respond to terrorism. Because terrorism is itself an ambiguous and contested concept, homeland security does not admit to precise and consensual definition either. This inherent ambiguity is exacerbated by the connections and overlap between anti-terrorism work and other policing tasks (such as the response to natural disasters), which make it difficult to distinguish a hard core of homeland security activities.

Distinctive Features

The phrase 'homeland security' first came into widespread use after the September 11, 2001 terrorist attacks in the US. (A different use of the term appeared in apartheid South Africa, where security agencies for the ten Bantu homelands were sometimes called 'homeland security' forces.) The 9/11 attacks eventually led the US government to create a national 'Department of Homeland Security', which popularized the phrase as a term for anti-terrorism work. That initiative, in turn, drew from the pre-9/11 work of the US Commission on National Security/Twenty-First Century, which had already recommended a new national 'homeland security' agency in a report released several months before the 9/11 attacks. The term 'homeland security' has inspired controversy in the US, as many listeners hear echoes in it of unsavoury historical terms such as the Nazi 'fatherland' and Stalinist 'motherland'. Other nations, and some US cities, have used terms such as 'counterterrorism' in place of 'homeland security'.

Linguistics aside, the homeland security function extends far beyond policing. In the US, primary responsibility for it rests in the federal Department of Homeland Security, a cabinet-level agency that encompasses organizations ranging from the Citizenship and Immigration Services to the Coast Guard.

Most other nations lack a centralized counterterrorism agency on this scale, and even in the US a wide variety of other public and private institutions play substantial roles in homeland security, including public health agencies, national intelligence agencies, port authorities, transportation agencies, private businesses, and the military. This massively diffused responsibility of homeland security reflects the complexity of the terrorist threat, which potentially imperils a wide variety of public and private targets in a wide variety of ways – from cyber-terrorism against information systems, to chemical and biological attacks on food and water supplies, to direct attacks on people using a range of conventional and non-conventional weapons.

These central characteristics of terrorism and the fragmented responsibility for combating it have important implications for police efforts to promote homeland security. In particular, the fragmentation of authority for homeland security places a premium on inter-organizational cooperation (as illustrated by the wide variety of 'terrorist task forces' that assemble myriad institutional actors involved in counterterrorism), and the breadth of counterterrorism work implies a need for a wide range of policing duties beyond investigation and patrol.

The police role in homeland security can be divided into two broad components: Community protection (which focuses on protecting a specific *place* against terrorism) and offender search (which involves identifying and investigating particular *people* suspected of terrorism) (Thacher, 2005). Each of these components can in turn be divided into prospective and retrospective dimensions (Innes, 2006).

Community protection encompasses a variety of activities focused on the prevention of terrorism and the response to attacks. Prospective community protection includes physical security, preventative patrol, and other forms of target hardening. It may be motivated by a general concern about critical infrastructure and buildings or by a specific threat against an identified target. Retrospective community protection involves a wide variety of responses in the aftermath of a terrorist attack. Because local police are likely to be among the first responders, they typically have substantial emergency response duties – from crowd control, to emergency medical assistance, to the control and prevention of racial and ethnic conflict following a terrorist incident. Disaster planning designed to improve police readiness for all of these tasks is an important component of community protection, as are efforts to upgrade the technological resources, expertise, and inter-organizational relationships that police can rely on when they respond to emergencies.

Offender search involves surveillance and investigation of possible terrorists. Prospectively, offender search activities attempt to disrupt planned attacks. Police and other homeland security agencies attempt to do that most obviously through surveillance and investigation of suspected terrorists, but they may also attempt to undermine the support and resources that terrorists rely on (e.g., by freezing financial assets). Retrospectively, offender search generally relies on traditional techniques of criminal investigation.

Evaluation

The attention that homeland security and its synonyms have recently received throughout the world reflects a widespread sense that this policing function needs to be strengthened. That sense stems most obviously from the massive casualties suffered during the 9/11 attacks and more recent incidents orchestrated by global terrorist networks, such as the 2004 commuter train bombing in Madrid and the 2005 attacks on the public transportation system in London.

The weakness of offender search capacity results partly from the origins of policing expertise and organization, which were largely developed to address the problems of crime and disorder rather than terrorism. Terrorism differs from those problems in at least two significant ways that potentially hamper offender search.

First, in the great majority of cities worldwide, terrorism is an extremely rare event, and new and unexpected threats continually emerge. Focusing on counterterrorism work in Britain, Innes (2006) has argued that existing intelligence methods and networks are ill-suited to this problem, particularly because of their heavy reliance on 'professional' police informants as opposed to other sources of information such as community intelligence.

Second, the geographic organization of terrorism differs markedly from that of most crime and disorder. Since terrorism is a national or international problem, the benefits of offender search may not accrue to the jurisdiction where would-be terrorists reside, while the costs of surveillance, financial or otherwise, generally do. In nations like the US where policing is heavily decentralized, this fact suggests that few local police departments have much reason to pursue offender search (though visible terrorist targets like New York City and Jerusalem are important exceptions). If so, then strengthening offender search capacity may require a shift of resources towards centralized police forces. Alternatively, it may require federal-local partnership institutions (such as the joint terrorism task forces that have proliferated throughout the US since 9/11), which minimize the costs of antiterrorism work for local communities and provide them with a voice in shaping investigations in a way that meets local concerns about civil liberties. In these respects, strengthening police capacity for offender search may require deep structural changes in policing institutions.

The efforts to strengthen offender search capacity also raise a variety of important concerns – most obviously, concerns about civil liberties, but also subtler concerns about the ideal of federalism. At the national level, the US Patriot Act dramatically extended surveillance and detention capacities for federal and local police and those provisions have sparked intense political controversy. At the local level, the prospect of new surveillance and collaboration with federal law enforcement have also raised a variety of concerns about privacy, police-community relations, ethnic profiling of Arab-Americans, and threats to the traditional autonomy of local police in a federalist system. (Some of these concerns were illustrated vividly shortly after 9/11,

when several US cities rebuffed entreaties from federal officials to help interview young male immigrants from countries suspected of harbouring terrorists.) These controversies reflect the general conflict between liberty and order that lies at the heart of democratic policing. Homeland security exacerbates this dilemma because the rare and uncertain nature of terrorism heightens the demand for intrusive surveillance.

Questions about police capacity for community protection have also been raised. Many of these questions revolve around resource constraints. After 9/11, local governments throughout the US expressed concerns about their ability to provide adequate target hardening, investigations, and emergency response for homeland security without compromising their other responsibilities. More specific concerns, such as the interoperability of communications technologies between police and other response agencies, have also been raised. Since community protection tasks lie squarely within the interests and competence of traditional police agencies, for most agencies the most promising and likely contribution of police to homeland security is likely to lie in this area. The more dramatic and controversial area of offender search, by contrast, may fall more readily to national intelligence agencies such as Britain's MI5 and the FBI in the US.

David Thacher

Associated Concepts: community safety, intelligence-led policing, search, security networks, terrorism

Key Readings

Clarke, R. V. and Newman, G. R. (2007) 'Police and the prevention of terrorism', *Policing* 1 (1): 9–20.
Davis, L. M., K., Riley, J., Ridgeway, G., Pace, J., Cotton, S. K., Steinberg, P. S., Damphousse, K. and Smith, B. L.. (2004) *When Terrorism Hits Home: How Prepared are State and Local Law Enforcement?* Santa Monica: RAND Corp.

Innes, M. (2006) 'Policing uncertainty: countering terror through community intelligence and democratic policing', *Annals of the American Academy of Political and Social Sciences*, 605 (2): 222–41.

Richman, D. (2004) 'The right fight: local police and national security', *Boston Review*. December.

Thacher, D. (2005) 'The local role in homeland security', *Law and Society Review*, 39 (3): 635–76.

HOMICIDE

Definition

Homicide means the taking of a life and all jurisdictions classify it as lawful (as in the case of the death penalty or fatal war related combat) or unlawful. Unlawful homicide is often categorized to distinguish between degrees of seriousness or offender culpability. The most common categorization is between premeditated homicides (first degree murder in the US; murder in the UK and other English speaking countries), and those which are not premeditated (second degree murder in the US and manslaughter in many other English speaking countries). A third category is often found which encompasses homicide in special circumstances such as infanticide, deaths resulting from road traffic collisions, assisted suicide and unintended deaths resulting from neglect. The success with which legal frameworks classify homicide on grounds of severity is debatable because key elements such as intent, diminished responsibility or justification are often not easily established. In addition, the divide between acceptable and unacceptable killings is socially, historically and culturally constructed, which is reflected in police and judicial practice as well as legal definitions. Cultural differences also influence the types of homicides that occur within a particular society and the way individuals respond to it (Brookman, 2006).

Given these variations, caution is required when comparing international rates of homicide. However, the differences are so great in some cases that it seems probable that they reflect real differences in frequency. For example, the homicide rate per million population in Russia is 223; in Lithuania 104.4; in the US 55.4; in Finland 27.7; in Australia 17.8; in England and Wales 17.5; in Japan 10.8 and in Sweden 6.6 (Levi et al., 2007). Despite these international variations, homicide within individual countries generally makes up a small proportion of all violent crime (in England and Wales, for example, it comprises less than 0.1 per cent of all violent crime recorded by the police).

Distinctive Features

Wherever it occurs, homicide is considered to be among the most serious of crimes and generates considerable public, media and political concern. The police response to homicide is taken as an important barometer of their effectiveness more generally and so often attracts a higher priority and more resources than other types of crime. Traditionally, the police response has been confined to the investigation of homicide once it had occurred. Increasingly, however, police agencies are developing strategies aimed at reducing homicide.

Investigative practice differs between jurisdictions. However, many of the key features of homicide investigation are similar wherever they occur. These are exemplified in the British police's *Murder Investigation Manual* (ACPO, 2006). According to the manual, investigations typically have three distinct stages:

(1) instigation and initial response, which involves responding to reports of potential homicide and taking action to save life where possible, identify victims, preserve scenes, secure evidence and arrest suspects;

(2) the investigation, which involves gathering the material needed to confirm that the incident involves homicide, identifying and arresting suspects (if not done already) and gathering material for a prosecution;

(3) case management, which involves post-charge enquires, preparing the material gathered for the prosecution and the defence, and managing witnesses and exhibits throughout the trial. There is some overlap between these stages and the resources needed at each will vary between cases depending upon their complexity.

The high priority given to a successful homicide investigation means that their effective management is a key concern for the police. Cases which are solved quickly will be managed in ways similar to other serious crimes and may have a relatively modest resource allocation. Harder to solve cases have a much higher level of resourcing and often adopt organizational structures developed specifically for the investigation of homicide. In Britain this comprises specially trained Senior Investigating Officers (SIO) who manage the overall investigation using a Major Incident Room (MIR). This provides the administrative hub of the investigation by using the Home Office Large Major Enquiry System (HOLMES) to manage information and tasks. In countries where multiple police agencies have jurisdiction over the same area, which is the case in many parts of the US, such management can occur at the multi-agency level. In some jurisdictions, such as France, the investigative team will be directed by a member of the judiciary rather than a police officer.

In addition to the systems used to manage individual cases, most police agencies adopt measures designed to assure the quality of homicide investigation overall. These can involve systematic reviews of homicide enquiries by independent teams of officers and cold case review to ensure that new information or new forensic opportunities are effectively followed up. The investigation of homicide is also unique in the range of specialist support used. This can include offender and geographical profilers, forensic specialists, databases of offender behaviour, and pathologists. In addition, because of the unique impact of homicide, specific processes have been put in place by many police agencies to assist victim's families, to reassure communities and to manage the media.

Evaluation

Homicide investigation rarely involves a protracted search for an elusive suspect and many cases are solved quickly. Such homicides often involve deaths that are the unplanned outcomes of other violence, like domestic violence and child abuse, or crimes such as burglary or robbery. They also include cases where those involved react differently after the homicide than they would to other crimes. Stelfox (2006) found that 10 per cent of all suspects gave themselves up shortly after committing homicide, at least a quarter told someone what they had done, and many committed homicide in front of witnesses who knew them. This scale of self-incrimination and witness cooperation appears to exceed that found in other crime types, which partly explains why such a large proportion of homicides (around three quarters) are classed as 'self-solvers' (Innes, 2003). Difficult to solve cases often involve homicide where some degree of planning has taken place or where the choices made by witnesses are governed by mistrust of the police, fear of offenders or a belief that the level of violence used was justified.

While 'intrinsic difficulties' such as these influence how hard it will be for the police to solve a case, 'extrinsic difficulties' such as mistakes made by the police during investigations also influence outcomes (Innes, 2003). The latter include factors such as failing to properly preserve evidence or crime scenes through to identifying the wrong suspect. Cases that are not solved, or those where errors are made, can lead to significant criticism of the police. Examples of such cases are the Steven Lawrence investigation in the UK and the Dutroux case in Belgium. Such cases are rare and, compared to most other offence categories, the investigation of homicide results in a high 'clear up' rate. However, many would argue that the probability of an offender being convicted of a homicide offence is a more robust measure of police and judicial performance and this figure differs substantially between jurisdictions. For example, for every 1000 homicide offenders in England and Wales, the probability is that about 600 will be convicted in any given year (although the number per year fluctuates widely); in the US the historic average is 447 and the figure is slightly less in Australia. In contrast, the probability of an offender being convicted of homicide in Switzerland is almost 100 per cent (Farrington et al., 2004).

Aside from its reactive investigation, the police are increasingly adopting strategies aimed at reducing or preventing homicide. The diverse and relatively infrequent nature of homicide makes it more difficult to predict and prevent than some high volume offences (Brookman and Maguire, 2005). However, there are examples of successful initiatives that focus upon particular forms of homicide. These often use a multi-agency approach and work on the assumption that homicide reduction cannot be achieved in isolation because the difference between an assault and a homicide is often happenstance. Therefore, violence reduction is viewed along a continuum from simple assaults to murder. For example, it is now well established that key risk factors for domestic homicide include separation (or threats to separate), escalation in the frequency and severity of violence and stalking. This knowledge enables the police to work with practitioners in other agencies to create safety plans for high-risk victims with a view to preventing the escalation of domestic violence into homicide. Specialist units dedicated to preventing gang-related homicide adopt intelligence-based methods but also work at the community level with schools, vulnerable youth and community leaders to erode cultures that condone violence. Some initiatives, such as CeaseFire in Chicago and Operation Trident in London, start from the principle of community mobilization in tackling gun-related homicide. The success of such proactive initiatives is dependent on the relationship between the police and public at a community level.

The importance of police relationships with communities appears to be central to both the reduction and the investigation of homicide, because both rely on an effective two-way flow of information. Poor relationships impede this flow. It may be that in the final analysis it is the nature of such relationships, rather than differences in legislation and police organization, that explain differences in the police response to homicide.

Fiona Brookman and Peter Stelfox

Associated Concepts: crime analysis, culture, domestic violence, gun crime, intelligence-led policing, criminal investigation, multi-agency policing, victim

Key Readings

ACPO Centrex (2006) *The Murder Investigation Manual* (3rd edn). Bedfordshire: Centrex.

Brookman, F. (2005) *Understanding Homicide.* London: Sage.

Brookman, F. and Maguire, M. (2005) 'reducing homicide: a review of the possibilities', *Crime, Law and Social Change,* 42: 325–403.

Farrington, D. P., Langan, P. A. and Tonry, M. (2004) *Cross-national Studies in Crime and Justice.* Washington DC: US Department of Justice Bureau of Justice Statistics.

Innes, M. (2003) *Investigating Murder.* Oxford: Oxford University Press.

Stelfox, P. (2006) 'The role of confidants in homicide investigation', *Journal of Homicide and Major Incident Investigation,* 2 (1): 79–91.

HOT SPOTS

Definition

A 'hot spot' of crime is a small geographic location in which the rate of crimes per square foot, but not necessarily the rate of crimes per person, is far higher than in the areas that surround the hot spot. The ratio of crime rates between 'hot' and 'cool' locations may vary, but one threshold is that the probability of one or more types of crime occurring at a hot spot must exceed 50 per cent over the next 12 months. Operational thresholds have been set as high as 365 crimes a year: one a day, on average. The geographic size of such areas may vary for analytic and operational purposes, but the concept is more useful for allocating police patrols when it can focus on the exact location to which a patrol should be directed. One definition (Sherman et al., 1989; Sherman and Weisburd, 1995) limits the size of hot spots to places that can be seen in their entirety by the human eye at one location on the ground. Time can also be a key element in defining a hot spot, since crimes in hot spots can be disproportionately concentrated by time of day and day of week. Thus some locations may not be hot spots from 7am to 3pm on weekdays, with the 'heat' of high rates of crime limited to a period between 7pm and 3am on weekends.

Distinctive Features

Hot spots are places with a distinctive social ecology of 'routine activities.' That ecology elevates the number of opportunities for criminal events. Such opportunities are defined generically, although often ambiguously, as the situational crime 'triangle': the intersection in time and space of motivated offenders, suitable crime targets and unguarded opportunities for crime (Cohen and Felson, 1979). Patterns of routine human activity at hot spots tend to concentrate elements of one or more sides of the crime triangle: either high numbers of pedestrians (suitable targets), high numbers of persons – such as unsupervised young males – at high risk of committing crimes (motivated offenders), or low visibility of crime targets – such as women's handbags placed on the floor under a chair in a crowded bar (unguarded opportunities).

Hot spots may be crime-general or crime-specific (Weisburd et al., 1992). A crime-general hot spot is one in which a wide range of crime types occurs at an elevated rate per square foot. A crime-specific hot spot is one in which one or several crime types may be reported at an elevated rate per square foot, but not a wide range of types. Crime-general hot spots tend to have very high average hourly populations, such as train stations in Tokyo or regional shopping malls outside of Washington, DC in the US. Crime-specific hot spots tend to have smaller populations, but distinctive ecology sustaining a particular type of crime. High population sizes – for example, thousands of people in one relatively small space – create opportunities for many diverse kinds of crimes, even if the crime rate per person may make these locations safer for each individual than the surrounding cool spots – or even than their own homes, where domestic violence or burglary risks may be very high.

Low population sizes may sustain high rates of specific types of crime, per capita or even per square foot, when the crime requires a distinctive social ecology. Hot spots of gun crime (Braga, 2001), for example, require concentrations in time and space of people carrying guns.

The difference between hot spots of crime per square foot and areas of high crime per capita creates anomalies that often confuse the public and policymakers. These anomalies may concern the appearance of a location or area, relative to its crime statistics. The apparent wealth and orderly behaviour of the large number of people using a commercial hot spot does not predict a high rate of auto theft per square foot, which is simply a function of the high numbers of cars parked per square foot. Similarly, the apparent good grooming of lawns and gardens in a high homicide area does not predict the high rates of gun crime at night concentrated at hot spots within the area, at certain street corners where young pedestrians may congregate. These anomalies run directly counter to the assumption that hot spots or high crime may be predicted by 'broken windows' indicators of physical and social disorder.

These anomalies can be clarified by careful address-specific estimation of both the numerator of crimes (by specific type) and the denominator of persons at risk of committing, or of being victimized, by crimes. Estimation of numerators can be taken directly from police records, private security records, or both (when they do not have 100 per cent overlap, as they rarely do). Estimation of denominators requires a means of calculating the average number of person-hours in the hot spot: the number of people entering the hot spot each day times the number of hours they remain. Person-hours can then be translated into person-days by aggregating the minutes or hours that *different* people were present to form the equivalent of *one* person being present there over a 24-hour period. Estimating person-hours is a straightforward matter of reliable and comprehensive measurement. If a shopping mall uses car-counting devices at all of its parking lot entrances, for example, and uses observational data to estimate the average number of occupants in each car and how long they stay at the premises, the person hour estimate can be derived directly from the daily number of cars counted. By such methods the Tysons' Corner Shopping Mall in northern Virginia, US was able to show that its high volume of property crime per square foot was accompanied by a rate of violent crime per person-hour on the premises was far lower than the comparable per person-hour rate in the Washington, DC metropolitan area.

Evaluation

The concept of crime hot spots has been widely used to test the effectiveness of patrol strategies (Braga, 2001). These tests have been largely restricted to the micro-local definition of a hot spot as a place visible in one glance of the human eye. Using this definition, concentrations of directed police patrol can yield substantial reductions of crime in hot spots, without any detectible evidence of displacement of crime to adjacent areas. If anything, Weisburd reports, there is evidence of a 'diffusion of benefits' in which the deterrence of crime by police patrols in hot spots spills over into adjacent areas, sometimes

even in areas larger than the eye can see. What has not been as effective is increases in patrol concentrations in very large areas, such as police beats in low-density populations, in which the concentration of crime per square foot is too low for concentrations of patrol to make a difference.

The effectiveness of hot spot police patrols may be enhanced by reliance on the 'Koper Curve,' which shows that 10 to 15 minutes of police patrol presence is the optimal length of time to spend in a hot spot in order to deter crime. This curve, derived by Christopher Koper from over 7,500 hours of observations of crime and police patrols in 110 hot spots in Minneapolis, US in 1988–1989, focused on the length of time after a police car left the hot spot until the first crime occurred. The length of time that such 'residual deterrence' lasts rises with the length of time police remain in the hot spot (in uniform, either inside police cars or on foot), up to a peak from 10 to 15 minutes, after which there is diminishing returns. This finding suggests that a common practice of directing police to 'sit' on a hot spot for 8 to 24 hours a day is wasteful, at least in terms of the opportunity cost for deterring crime at other hot spots by a policy of rotation across hot spots every 10 to 15 minutes.

Because hot spot patrols are so effective, they create a paradox for police officers conducting such patrols: the more crime they prevent, the more boring they may find police patrol to be. This initial reaction may provoke protests that the hot spots are not really hot, or that their time would be spent better driving around looking for crime. That conventional 'random patrol' hypothesis may be testable by different research designs, but no evidence has ever been found to support it. Evidence-based policing would suggest that police focus patrols on hot spots, if only because they seem to be well located to minimize response times to crime emergency calls when they come in. There is no evidence of a conflict between directed hot spot patrol and rapid response time. Police can therefore spend time in hot spots more productively by talking to persons who work in or use the location on a regular basis, getting to know their problems and concerns. Such discussions may also have value for reassuring the public that police are responsive to their fears and concerns about crime.

Lawrence W. Sherman

Associated Concepts: broken windows, crime analysis, crime mapping, diffusion of benefits, evidence-based policing, patrol, situational crime prevention

Key Readings

Braga, A. (2001) 'The effects of hot spots policing on crime', *The Annals of the American Academy of Political and Social Science*, 578 (1): 104–25.

Cohen, L. and Felson, M. (1979) 'Social change and crime rates: a routine activities approach', *American Sociological Review*, 44 (4) 588–608.

Sherman, L.W., Gartin, P. and Buerger, M. (1989) 'Hot spots of predatory crime: routine activities and the criminology of place', *Criminology*, 27: 27–55.

Sherman, L.W. and Weisburd, D. (1995) 'General deterrent effects of police patrol in crime "hot spots": A randomized controlled trial', *Justice Quarterly*, 12 (4): 625–48.

Weisburd, D., Maher, L., and Sherman, L. (1992) 'Contrasting crime general and crime specific theory: the case of hot spots of crime', in F. Adler and W.S. Laufer (eds), *Advances in Criminological Theory, 4*. New Brunswick, NJ: Transaction Publishing.

HUMAN RIGHTS POLICING

Definition

At its most basic level, 'human rights policing' refers to policing strategies, policies and practices that are supportive of, and in compliance with, international human rights principles and standards. However, conceptual and definitional difficulties abound and it is often used synonymously with 'democratic policing' in the police studies literature.

Distinctive Features

During the past two decades the concept of 'human rights' has come to occupy an increasingly visible space as the mainstay of democratic governance, enshrined in a myriad of constitutional protections or national legislation such as the UK's Human Rights' Act, the Canadian Charter of Rights' and Freedoms and so forth. Through the 'export' of human rights discourses from democratic states in the North and West by their respective international development agencies and International Non-Governmental Organizations (INGOs), the attainment of internationally recognized human rights standards is promoted among developing and transitional societies as a requirement for global recognition. Recent years have also witnessed a proliferation of human rights consultants, again chiefly from the North and West, who operate at the transnational level and offer their expertise (for a fee) on the global market.

While a consideration of human rights policing cannot be easily divorced from the more general universalizing impact of human rights' discourse, it has found its most vociferous expression within legal and policy making circles and the NGO/INGO sector. This is because the emphasis on human rights in policing has, in the main, been conceived in a technical and practical sense (for example, monitoring adherence to human rights' legislation and enhancing police training) which lends itself more easily to the activities of non-statutory agencies, both at the national and international levels. While there have been any number of evaluation studies and 'how to' handbooks, there has been a dearth of academic research and a general undertheorizing of 'human rights policing' conceptually (for a notable exception see Sheptycki, 2000). This reflects the position in relation to human rights discourse more generally which, until relatively recently, has remained largely immune to critical and intellectual scrutiny (Douzinas, 2007).

In definitional terms, 'human rights policing' can usefully be delineated in terms of a 'thin' (legal and technical) and a 'thick' (political and structural) formulation. In its 'thin' sense, 'human rights policing' reflects a commitment by the police organization to perform its obligations according to the rights enshrined in a particular state's domestic legislation, supranational frameworks such as the EU's *acquis communautaire,* the Universal Declaration of Human Rights and various framework documents laid down by the Council of Europe. While acknowledging that there is likely to be considerable variation across and between jurisdictions, here the emphasis is on the role that the public police can play in protecting and promoting individual rights (life, liberty and property); shifting the emphasis away from crime control (a preoccupation with convictions) to due process (a broader commitment to justice and fairness); maintaining a commitment to the 'rule of law'; and, with varying degrees of enthusiasm, establishing institutional mechanisms to ensure transparency, oversight and accountability in relation to the conduct of policing.

The Council of Europe has attempted to provide a concise template for policing and human rights in the 44 countries it represents under the Police and Human Rights Programme 1997–2000. Drawing upon 14 international conventions and covenants and a further 13 international declarations, standards and guidelines, the Council has distilled the essence of what human rights should mean for policing into seven benchmark indicators:

(1) Basic Values – the emphasis placed on promoting and protecting human rights by the police organization.
(2) Staff – inculcating a normative commitment to human rights standards among serving police officers.
(3) Training – the degree to which human rights standards are mainstreamed into police education and training programmes.
(4) Management Practice – transparent and accountable managerial structures that inculcate an organizational and normative commitment to fair and impartial policing.
(5) Operational Policing – the embeddedness of human rights legislation and principles in operational policing decisions.
(6) Structure – the degree to which human rights considerations are embedded throughout the entire structure of the police organization and the ways that compliance can be assessed and monitored.
(7) Accountability – the national legal framework within which the police operate and the capacity for internal and external review of police actions, such as a robust police complaints machinery. The aim here is to generate public trust in policing structures and arrangements.

The institutional relationship between policing and human rights has been given a powerful expression in the proposals of the Independent Commission on Policing (ICP) in Northern Ireland. This went further than most national and international frameworks in arguing that the maintenance and protection of human rights was *the* point of policing: a core activity that is mainstreamed into police policy and practice. The ICP proposals are somewhat unusual in that they established a number of oversight mechanisms with wide statutory powers to ensure that the Police Service of Northern Ireland (PSNI) complies with human rights principles (for example, the existence of a fully independent complaints machinery based around a model of civilian control, and the establishment of a Policing Board with statutory powers to require senior officers to explain operational policing decisions). Nevertheless, the Northern Ireland example represents something of a unique case, and for many police agencies (even those in established democracies) the commitment to human rights principles has been somewhat rhetorical, and there has been a longstanding resistance to ceding too much power to oversight bodies by placing them on a strong independent and statutory footing, such as those dealing with police complaints.

Over the course of the past decade, 'human rights policing' has been linked in a 'thick' sense to broader processes of democratization and reconstruction in transitional and post-conflict states. Recent literature in 'law and development' theory advocates a model of democratic policing that adheres to international human rights standards and which is tied to conceptions of good governance, human security and social capital (Trubek and Santos, 2006). Stronger variants of this thesis have acknowledged the role that human rights discourses can play in creating a normative framework for governing complex global arrangements and in so doing acting as a brake on the excesses of global neo-liberalism (Sheptycki, 2000).

Evaluation

In evaluating the relationship of human rights to policing, one is confronted by a dilemma. On the one hand, inculcating human rights into policing in a normative sense is self-evidently a good and desirable outcome insofar as it has the potential to contribute to fair and effective police work, restrict the potential for abuses and contribute to police democratization. On the other hand, the ways that human rights are promoted in general, and many initiatives to promote human rights' policing in particular, are more problematic. Difficulties can be identified in four main areas:

(1) conceptual framework;
(2) implementation;
(3) the context of current global (in)security; and
(4) strategic and economic exigencies.

In terms of a conceptual framework, a problem concerns the primacy that is accorded to individual rights at the expense of economic and social rights within dominant legal formalism. Human rights discourses have tended to prioritize the former, but the police's relationship to the marginalized, the poor and the dispossessed is arguably a consequence of the latter. It is the inequalities at the macrostructural level (social and economic) that create those groups deemed by the police to be 'their property' and thus provide the space for abuses and capriciousness to occur. Conceptual issues are also manifest at the global level. Postcolonial theorists have pointed to what they perceive as the Occidentalism of human rights discourses, insofar as they are deeply rooted in Western philosophy and culture, and for non-European states are perceived as alien insofar as they prioritize individual rights over communal and group rights. While we need to be alert to the potential for moral and cultural relativism in this argument, it is nevertheless the case that many Western agencies have not been overly sensitive to the nuances of local history, politics and culture when they embark on police reform initiatives.

The second problem concerns implementation. While we should avoid the temptation to generalize, the research literature highlights two things. First, it should be noted that, with few exceptions, it is notoriously difficult to enforce human rights standards, and many treaties, frameworks and covenants remain largely aspirational with limited statutory incorporation. Similarly, while a normative commitment to human rights by the police is important and desirable, it is no substitute for the existence of robust accountability and oversight structures. Operating on the premise that the police will attempt to do what they feel they can get away with, the establishment of such structures are vital for ensuring compliance with human rights standards in operational behaviour. The limitations of human rights training by itself can be seen in early evaluations of a training programme undertaken by officers in the PSNI. These evaluations suggested that there was a perception among some officers that the point of human rights training was to keep them out of trouble by identifying 'how far they could go' rather than something that instilled human rights as a core value of modern police work (Ellison, 2007). Again, this corresponds with the view often articulated within the police occupational culture that human rights legislation and protections amount to a 'criminal's charter'.

Second, in terms of global efforts at police reform, intersectorality is key, and the most successful programmes for inculcating a workable and sustainable pattern of police democratization and adherence to human rights standards are those that are long-term, and where reforms take place across a range of sectors, to include the police, courts, prosecution and prisons (Chesterman, 2004). This needs to occur in parallel to a transformation of economic and political structures. Many of the initiatives in relation to police reform, particularly those promoted by human rights consultants, are 'flash in the pan' efforts that are often poorly conceived and will have little sustainable impact. In fact, they may make a bad situation worse, and convey a degree of unwarranted legitimacy on repressive regimes that are seen to be engaging with the international human rights community, but are in reality continuing unabated with their abusive practices. Furthermore, what many of these initiatives fail to do is connect human rights and policing to any concrete analysis of the structural conditions in many transitional and post-conflict contexts that give rise to abuses by police officers in the first place.

The third problem concerns changes to the nature of global (in)security and the effect that this will have on the relationship between policing and human rights in the longer term. The mass-casualty terrorist attacks of recent years have witnessed a number of Western states faced with what can be termed the 'democratic dilemma': how to balance the competing demands of combating fundamentalist terrorism while evading allegations of infringing civil liberties. It is in this context that the current 'war on terror' has resulted in an undeniable weakening of human rights and constitutional protections across the nations of the North and West, though primarily in the US and the UK. In the former, the Patriot Act awarded a vast range of powers to the various agencies of national security including the newly formed Department of Homeland Security; while extraordinary rendition, not to mention the spectacles of Abu Ghraib and Guantanamo Bay, have also struck a discordant note in human rights' terms. In the UK, in addition to the expansion of anti-terror legislation, police chiefs have successfully lobbied for an increase in the length of time they are allowed to detain a suspect without charge from 14 to 28 days, and at the time of writing there are proposals in place to extend this to 42 days.

Finally, the strategic and economic motives of key Western states have resulted in a somewhat ambivalent global position on human rights. In their efforts to establish regional security corridors in the context of the current threat from terrorism, both the UK and the US have tended to overlook human rights abuses in those states that are deemed to be useful allies, or somehow within their sphere of interest (examples here might include Saudi Arabia, Egypt, Pakistan and Jordan). More generally, and in something that applies equally to those Western states not currently engaged in the 'war on terror', economic and strategic exigencies have historically meant that arms and military contracts are pursued with regimes that have a questionable human rights record internationally. It is not unusual to find several government departments pursuing contradictory policies in this regard. Human rights' and police reform may be promoted as part of an overseas development assistance programme, whereas arms and other military hardware are simultaneously exported to the very police and military that the former is attempting to democratize.

Any consideration of what human rights should mean for policing needs to consider the concept in the light of each of these four areas. The essential point is that the existence of a human rights rhetoric, however well intentioned, is no substitute for substantive and meaningful mechanisms of police oversight and control.

Graham Ellison

Associated Concepts: democratic policing, ethical policing, globalization, human security, legitimacy, terrorism, transitional policing, paramilitary policing

Key Readings

Chesterman, S. (2004) *You The People: The United Nations, Transitional Administration, and State Building*. Oxford: Oxford University Press.

Douzinas, C. (2007) *Human Rights and Empire: The Political Philosophy of Cosmopolitanism.* London: Routledge.

Ellison, G. (2007) 'A blueprint for democratic policing anywhere in the world? police reform, political transition and conflict resolution in Northern Ireland', *Police Quarterly,* 3 (10): 243–69.

Sheptycki, J. W. E. (2000) 'Policing and human rights: an introduction', *Policing and Society,* Special Issue on Policing and Human Rights, 10 (1): 1–10.

Trubek, D. M. and Santos, A. (2006) *The New Law and Economic Development: A Critical Appraisal.* Cambridge: Cambridge University Press.

HUMAN SECURITY

Definition

Human security is a relatively new concept born out of the convergence of research and policy making in development economics, international relations and human rights. Rejecting the traditional focus of security upon the nation state and the protection of territory, human security makes the protection of individuals its primary referent. It seeks to protect not only against external and military threats but also against economic deprivation, starvation, disease, pollution, physical violence, sectarian and ethnic violence, and human rights abuses.

Distinctive Features

The concept of human security gained international prominence in the mid 1990s following its adoption by the United Nations Development Programme (UNDP) as a means of advancing 'freedom from fear and want'. Human security was promoted as a new paradigm focused not only on state sovereignty but also on the security of peoples. It was argued that security would better be fostered by its integration with development, humanitarian, and human rights concerns. Security between states remains a necessary condition of the security of peoples but is not regarded as sufficient to guarantee people's security in their everyday lives. In addition, security must be addressed by political, social, environmental, economic, and cultural programmes designed collectively to give people 'the building blocks of survival, livelihood and dignity' (UNDP, 1994). In crude terms it asserts that security can only be ensured where people have a basic income, access to food, health care, minimum protection from disease (such as HIV/AIDS), a decent environment and access to water, as well as protection from physical violence. Two important aspects of human security are that the range of actors responsible for security is extended beyond the state alone and that people must not simply be protected but empowered to fend for themselves, not least through the development of local capacity for self-governance. The ultimate goal of human security is the promotion of human dignity and the extension of people's capacity beyond mere survival.

Human security thus resists the tendency of threats like weapons of mass destruction and terrorism to solidify a narrower conception of security as state security. The narrow interpretation of security as pertaining only to the state is said to give insufficient attention both to the daily sources of insecurity suffered by people, particularly in developing countries, and also to the ways in which pursuit of state security can trample human rights and impede humanitarian action, not least in conflict situations and in the 'war on terror'. Another important distinction between traditional and human security is that whereas the former is principally defensive, the latter signifies a commitment to developing and implementing creative solutions to sources of insecurity.

From its origins with the UN and development agencies, human security has since become an important term for policy makers, policy analysts, and lobbyists. By appropriating the term security, it succeeds in conveying a sense of urgency and consequence that attracts public attention and governmental resources to the otherwise lower profile field of development. As a tool of political campaigning, therefore, human security has had considerable success and become a fashionable term of art. It has had less appeal as a basis for academic analysis.

Evaluation

Clearly human security greatly expands the definition of a security threat well beyond those things that have traditionally classified as threatening state security. Indeed the scope of its definition of threat is potentially vast and it is arguable that human security has deliberately been formulated without any clear definitional boundaries. The definitional elasticity of human security is justified on the grounds that it is 'all encompassing', 'holistic', and 'inclusive' but this has not prevented debate about the utility of so broadly defined a concept.

While human security analysts and proponents generally agree that the individual should be the primary referent, there is larger disagreement about the scope of the concept, what threats it should encompass, and how best it can be achieved. Proponents of a narrower concept of human security focus upon violent threats to individuals. Proponents of a broader concept argue that the agenda be widened to include hunger, disease, environmental disaster and other such threats on the grounds that these kill far more people than war, genocide, or terrorism. The broadest usage of human security extends even to threats to human dignity. There is a lively debate about which of these usages is to be preferred. Proponents of the broader concept argue that the range of threats are so interrelated, particularly in developing countries, that it cannot make sense to distinguish military threat or violence from the larger sources of insecurity. Proponents of a narrower concept argue that this broad usage is so expansive and vague as to lack analytical clarity and to be of little use either for policy analysis or as a research category. To these criticisms it is often countered that it is the very breadth of human security that provides its rhetorical force, its ability to encompass divergent interests, and to act as a 'glue' holding together diverse states, development agencies and non-governmental organizations (NGOs).

This broad coalition of interests is made possibly only by its imprecision and in this human security is said to be 'slippery by design' (Paris, 2001). The expansiveness of human security has clearly served the political interest of coalition building and this may explain much of its success on the international scene. It is less obvious that it is a useful analytical tool for academic research. Unsurprisingly, therefore, academic engagement with the term has focused upon formulating greater precision of definition and developing rigorous measures by which threats to human security can be calculated and averted, particularly through risk assessment and prevention (King and Murray, 2002). In this project lies a possible connection between human security and policing more broadly conceived in its historical continental European meaning relating to ideas of good government, the condition of order in the community, and the prerequisites to good order.

Lucia Zedner

Associated Concepts: environmental crime, human rights policing, security, terrorism, transitional policing

Key Readings

Commission on Human Security (2003) *Human Security Now*. New York: Commission on Human Security, http://www.humansecurity-chs.org/finalreport/.

King, G. and Murray, C. (2001–2) 'Rethinking human security' *Political Science Quarterly*, 116 (4): 585–610.

MacFarlane, S. N. and Khong, Y. F (2006) *Human Security and the UN: A Critical History*. Bloomington, Indiana: Indiana University Press.

Parris, R. (2001) 'Human security: paradigm shift or hot air?', *International Security*, 26 (2): 87–102.

United Nations Development Program (1994) *New Dimensions of Human Security*. New York: Oxford University Press.

IDENTITY

Definition

Identity can be understood as a reflexively organized narrative, stimulated by social interaction and ordered by institutional patterns of being and knowing. Identities are crafted through 'identity work', a concept that describes the ongoing mental activity that an individual undertakes in constructing a coherent and distinct identity. Identity work is prompted by social interaction that raises questions of 'who am I?' and 'who are we?'. In attempting to answer these questions, we craft our own self-narrative by drawing on cultural resources as well as our memories and desires to reproduce or transform our sense of self. Identity issues become salient for police officers when the routinized production of self-identity is challenged through uncertainty, anxiety, or self-doubt, for example, during organizational change initiatives.

Distinctive Features

Identity has become one of the key themes in social sciences, cutting across debates from globalization and national identities through the identity politics of gender and sexuality and to specific contemporary concerns over issues such as identity theft and regional governance. Given the diverse theoretical disciplines concerned with identity, there is a wide difference in the ways in which identity is conceptualized. The traditional understanding of identity, originating in social psychology, is to view identity as an essence: an enduring and cohesive 'given', making up the distinctive core of one's self. However, more recent understandings have conceived of an individual as having multiple, often overlapping and contradictory identities, crafted as an ongoing project when confronted with questions of who they are. In the study of identities, this has meant a shift in conceptual focus, from 'being' to becoming and from identity to identities and identification.

Identity has emerged as an important and popular area of analysis within work organizations. This popularity can, in part, be attributed to the dual role of identity as an analytical concern for both the individual and organization. Therefore, policing organizations are significant sites for various forms of 'identity work'. Officers and other members associate themselves with their organizations and define themselves as organizational members. In identifying with the organization, individuals not only create a sense of self, they also construct the organization's identity. At the collective level, studies of the *identities of organizations* have gained popularity. Here, identity is the answer to questions posed by organizational members of 'who are we?', 'what business are we in?' and 'what do we want to be?'. Statements of identity are a self-referencing aspect of organizational culture, however, in comparison with culture, organizational identity is seen to be more explicit (Hatch and Schultz, 2004).

Studies on organizational identities have examined, *inter alia*: the ability to change organizational identities and their relationship with organizational members; individual identification with organizational identities; manipulating organizational identities as a means of securing competitive advantage; and the relationship between organizational identity, culture and image (see Hatch and Schultz, 2004). Studies focusing on *identities in organizations* have traditionally been dominated by social psychology, where the concern has been on how to develop or match individuals' needs with those of the organization (for example, in recruitment and selection, team working, culture management, motivation and leadership). More contemporary studies, drawing on a fluid and multiple conceptualization of identity have focused on the extent to which organizations attempt to influence the construction and nature of individual identities, that is, 'identity control' (Alvesson and Willmott, 2002) or, conversely, on gaining a better understanding of how individuals draw on specific 'identity resources' within the organization in constructing their sense of self. Such studies have been concerned with understanding better the dynamic interrelationships between individual 'identity work' and organizations, recognizing that organizations are not only settings in which individual identities are constructed, but also that identities are materials out of which larger, more recognizably social or institutional identities are built.

Identities and identity work are therefore of increasing concern for those studying a range of issues within work and organizations. From a wider socio-economic perspective, it has been argued that increased identity work is evident in contemporary Western organizations due to increased uncertainty, instability and fragmentation over an individual's sense of self. For those working within policing organizations, large scale organizational change can also heighten questions over occupational and self-identity, especially when change is targeted at redefining employees' self-images and work orientations. Here, an understanding of identities and identity work in the implementation of change is of fundamental importance, given that individual's understanding of their self

may be a target of change initiatives as well as a source of resistance to that change.

Evaluation

Where there are also strong occupational identities involved, such as with the police, appreciating the dynamics between individual-occupational-organizational identities is important, especially in contemporary policing reform agendas. In particular, the pressure to implement radical change programmes in the police services in many countries has highlighted the importance of identity in understanding change and change resistance. Contemporary policing reforms are often concerned with the repositioning of policing organizational identity from that of a reactive crime-fighting one, to one based on community-oriented problem-solving and inter-agency partnerships. A better understanding of the processes of identity work within the policing profession can help to refine change initiatives, targeting them more at the meanings around 'real policing' and what it means to be an effective police officer (Davies and Thomas, 2003).

Contemporary policing often involves working in partnership with other public service providers and the community. The complex processes of mutual constitution between self and organization is further complicated in partnership working. Such collaborative engagements involve crossing social boundaries where distinctions between self and other are likely to be heightened. Crucially, partnership working requires individuals to draw on understandings of individual, occupational and organizational identities, as well as other identity categories, to act collectively. Furthermore, as organizational boundaries become looser, external stakeholders may also become drawn into closer relationships with organizational members (Hatch and Schultz, 2004). External views of organizational image, reputation and identity are important factors that influence collaboration, identity work and processes of identification. For the police, therefore, identity issues lie at the core of change targeted at reorienting the service to become more representative of the communities that they serve.

Studying identity in organizations is, however, far from straightforward. It is becoming apparent that identity and identity work cannot be easily appreciated through words alone. Therefore, greater in-depth ethnographic studies are needed that take a broad exploration of what people do as well as say. Further research in the study of identities in policing is needed to understand better the dynamics of the individual-organizational interface, especially where organizational boundaries are becoming increasingly ambiguous and blurred and to consider the impact this has on policing practice.

Robyn Thomas

Associated Concepts: culture, multi-agency policing, socialization

Key Readings

Alvesson, M. and Willmott, H. (2002) 'Identity regulation as organizational control: producing the appropriate individual', *Journal of Management Studies*, 39: 619–44.
Chan, J. B. L. (1997) *Changing Police Culture: Policing in a Multicultural Society.* Cambridge: Cambridge University Press.
Davies, A. and Thomas, R. (2003) 'Talking COP: discourses of change and
policing identities', *Public Administration,* 81 (4): 681–99.
Hatch, M. J. and Schultz, M. (eds) (2004) *Organizational Identity: A Reader.* Oxford: University Press.
Jenkins, R. (2004) *Social Identity* (2nd edn). London: Routledge.

INDEPENDENCE OF THE CONSTABLE

Definition

An official is said to have 'independent' authority if he or she is entitled to exercise authority free from direction, control or undue influence from anyone else. In this sense, the idea of independence bears some resemblance to the concept of discretion.

There have been many elaborations of this concept over the years, through judicial rulings, reports of commissions of inquiry, ministerial statements in Parliament, public statements of senior police leaders, and academic writings, and it is fair to say that there remains little consensus about exactly what 'independence of the constable' entails, or what the precise implications of it are for the governance, accountability and autonomy of the police. Almost all such definitions of the concept, however, share some common features. At the heart of the concept is the idea that in making decisions and taking actions in the *enforcement of the law*, the police are entitled (or have a duty) not to accept direction or control from anyone.

Distinctive Features

Ever since the establishment of the 'New Police' in the early nineteenth century in England, there has been concern that the very substantial power and authority that these modern public police are granted over the lives and liberty of citizens might be abused for partisan purposes or for personal advantage. This concern has focused in particular on the authority of the police to enforce the law, and the enormous powers they are granted for this purpose. It has led to a particular concern about the relationships between the police and their governmental 'masters', and with other particularly powerful groups within society. And it is such concerns that led to the gradual evolution, during the nineteenth century, but which did not come to be fully expressed until well into the twentieth century, of a concept of 'constabulary independence'.

Definitions of constabulary (or police) independence have varied greatly. Such variation has mainly centred on three aspects of the concept (or doctrine, as it is sometimes referred to). Precisely to which kinds of decisions and activities of the police is the concept applicable? How is the concept to be reconciled with the realities of command and management within modern police services? And what are the implications of the concept for the public accountability of police for their 'independent' decisions and actions?

Evaluation

On the first question, some formulations of the doctrine of police independence have suggested that it is applicable only to the so-called 'quasi-judicial' decisions (for example, to investigate, arrest, search, and charge suspects) made by police in enforcing the law in 'particular' or 'individual' cases. Other formulations suggest that it applies to all decisions and activities that might be thought to be included within the rubric of 'law enforcement' (e.g., crowd control, intelligence gathering, etc.). In an attempt to bring clarity to this issue, many commentators have sought to draw a distinction between 'policy' decisions on the one hand, and 'operational' decisions on the other, suggesting that the police must be recognized as enjoying independence with respect to the latter, but not with respect to the former. So, for instance, it has been argued that setting policies for policing is properly within the purview of responsible government ministers, but dictating how particular police operations are to be handled is not. While this appears at first blush to be a straightforward distinction, unfortunately attempts to secure agreement as to which kinds of decisions are properly characterized as policy decisions, and which as operational decisions, have consistently foundered. There has remained, therefore, quite a bit of disagreement about the theoretical scope of application of the doctrine of police independence, especially with respect to the *political* independence of the police.

The compatibility of the doctrine with traditional command structures within modern police services has presented further problems. Early notions of police independence (mostly by judges in judicial rulings) tended to characterize it as an emanation of the 'original authority' of the office of constable (or 'peace officer'), and emphasized that most law enforcement police powers require the individual officer who exercises them to personally believe that there is reasonable cause for their exercise in any particular situation. This suggests, of course, that every individual constable enjoys independence from direction or control with respect to the decisions and actions to which the concept applies. Reconciling this with the reality of command and disciplinary traditions within modern police services, whereby constables are required to obey the commands of their superior officers without question and may be subject to discipline if they fail to do so, is not easy, and cases have arisen in some jurisdictions in which individual constables have sought (some successfully, some not) to invoke the concept of constabulary independence to justify refusing to obey superior orders with respect to the investigation of particular offences. In some cases, judges have ruled that constables enjoy independence from direction and control by anyone outside their police services, but not from the orders of their superior officers.

Even when these difficulties over the application of the concept are set aside, however, a further question has arisen about the implications of the concept of police independence for the accountability of the police. The most well-known, and most commonly quoted, modern statement of the doctrine of police independence – that of the English judge, Lord Denning, in the case of *R. v. Metropolitan Police Commissioner, ex parte Blackburn* (1968) – illustrates this issue well:

I have no hesitation … in holding that, like every constable in the land, the Commissioner should be, and is, independent of the executive. He is not subject to the orders of the Secretary of State, save that under the Police Act 1964 the Secretary of State can call on him to give a report, or to retire in the interests of efficiency. I hold it to be the duty of the Commissioner of Police, as it is of every chief constable, to enforce the law of the land. He must take steps so to post his men that crimes may be detected; and that honest citizens may go about their affairs in peace. He must decide whether or not suspected persons are to be prosecuted; and, if need be, bring the prosecution or see that it is brought; but in all these things he is not the servant of anyone, save of the law itself. No Minister of the Crown can tell him that he must, or must not, keep observation on this place or that; or that he must, or must not, prosecute this man or that one. Nor can any police authority tell him so. The responsibility for law enforcement lies on him. He is answerable to the law and to the law alone. (at p. 769)

This statement of the doctrine, which suggests that with respect to their 'law enforcement' decisions the police enjoy immunity not only from political direction or control, but also from any political 'answerability' or accountability, has been criticized by several commentators as being a much too expansive definition of the doctrine, which is not compatible with liberal democratic principles. Nevertheless it has continued to be cited with approval as a definitive statement of the doctrine by superior courts almost everywhere in the common law world.

The doctrine of police independence, as described above, is peculiar to common law jurisdictions, but even in these jurisdictions it has not been universally accepted. In many of these jurisdictions (such as the US, Scotland and several other Commonwealth countries), for instance, direction and control of police investigations by independent prosecutors is the norm, and decisions with respect to the laying of charges in particular cases are the exclusive preserve of prosecutors, not the police. However, while such subordination of police to the authority of prosecutors may be considered acceptable and appropriate, subordination of police to direction or control by elected politicians, even by government ministers responsible for policing, in matters concerning the enforcement of the law in 'individual cases', almost never is. There is too much concern that such subordination will lead to the mobilization of the police for crude partisan advantage (harassing political opponents and critics of government policy, etc.), and such subordination is considered by many as a hallmark of a 'police state'.

There will doubtless always be controversy over the scope and applicability of the concept of constabulary independence.

Regardless of such disagreements, however, in many common law jurisdictions it has developed into an accepted constitutional or legal principle or convention. The main challenge it poses nowadays seems to be about how it can best be reconciled, in theory and in practice, with democratic expectations concerning effective public accountability of the police for their decisions and actions.

Philip C. Stenning

Associated Concepts: accountability, arrest, bureaucratization, discretion, reform

Key Readings

Fleming, J. (2004) '*Les liaisons dangereuses*: relations between police commissioners and their political masters', *Australian Journal of Public Administration*, 63 (3): 60–74.

Jones, T. (2003) 'The governance and accountability of policing', in T. Newburn (ed.) *Handbook of Policing*. Cullompton, Devon: Willan Publishing.

Hann, R., McGinnis, J., Stenning, P. and Farson, S. (1985) 'Municipal police governance and accountability in Canada: an empirical study', *Canadian Police College Journal* 9 (1): 1–85.

Lustgarten, L. (1986) *The Governance of Police*. London: Sweet and Maxwell.

Marshall, G. (1965) *Police and Government*. London: Methuen.

Stenning, P. (2006) 'The idea of the political "Independence" of the police: international interpretations and experiences', in M. Beare, and T. Murray (eds) *Police and Government Relations: Who's Calling the Shots?* Toronto: University of Toronto Press.

INFORMANT

See Criminal Investigation; Entrapment; High Policing; Intelligence-Led Policing

INSTITUTIONAL RACISM

Definition

Allegations that the police service is institutionally racist have dominated media, political, policy and academic debate in the UK during the last decade or so. The extent to which they have applied elsewhere is considered further below. In the UK, these debates can be traced back to the 1999 publication of the Macpherson Report, the findings of a public inquiry into the investigation of the murder of Stephen Lawrence, a young black man killed by a gang of white racists in south London in April 1993. The Macpherson Report detailed a catalogue of policing errors and inadequacies that had contributed to a failure to bring the five men arrested in connection with the murder to trial. The Macpherson Report suggested that the murder inquiry had been botched because of a combination of a failure of leadership, incompetence, and institutional racism. The Macpherson Report came to the stark conclusion that the police service was institutionally racist, defined in the following terms (Macpherson, 1999: 6.34):

> The collective failure of an organization to provide an appropriate and professional service to people because of their colour, culture or ethnic origin. It can be seen or detected in processes, attitudes and behaviour which amount to discrimination through unwitting prejudice, ignorance, thoughtlessness and racist stereotyping which disadvantages minority ethnic people.

While this definition has become widely accepted in the British context, and influenced the 2000 Race Relations (Amendment) Act that requires all public sector agencies to take a proactive role in confronting racism and promoting antiracism and equal opportunities, it does not, as is explained below, resolve ambiguities that have always surrounded the concept of institutional racism.

Distinctive Features

Essentially, the suggestion that the police service is institutionally racist appears to offer a new way of understanding, and responding to, over-policing of certain minority ethnic communities, through the disproportionate use of stop and search powers, for example, and the under-policing of racist violence and harassment. Similarly, it appears to provide a useful perspective on the inability of the police to attract, and retain, staff of a minority ethnic background. These disparate but related issues have bedevilled the police service in the UK – and elsewhere – for many decades. For much of this time, though, problems of police-minority ethnic relations have been understood in terms of either the problematic characteristics of black and Asian communities, or the racism of some police officers who, through ignorance at best, or racist prejudice at worst, failed to provide a proper level of service. By explaining these failings in terms of institutional racism, the Macpherson Report suggested a more fundamental problem exists in terms of the structure of the service, organizational culture, leadership, and governance. Conceiving matters in these terms leads to a broad understanding and suggests that solutions need to be wide-ranging, which was reflected in the seventy recommendations contained in the Macpherson Report.

The concept of institutional racism developed alongside the black power movement in the US in the late 1960s and the 1970s (Singh, 2000). The concept denoted a break with prevailing understandings of racism that located the problem with the pathologies of individuals who were conceived either as deviants subscribing to illiberal and outmoded pseudo-scientific notions of racial supremacy or, more commonly, as misguided people afraid of groups unknown to them and perceived as threatening. Whichever model of racism may have been applied in various circumstances, the analytical focus remained on the values, attitudes and social practices that reinforced prejudice and discrimination among individuals. In contrast, the notion of institutional racism focuses attention on broader power relations, and structural dimensions of society were included in analysis of the production and reproduction of racism, and the relation of this to other forms of marginalization.

Perhaps the key distinction between individual and institutional racism is that the latter places greater emphasis on outcomes and effects, rather than intent. Practices and procedures that result in inequality may be regarded as institutionally racist, whatever their expressed purpose. An illustration of this related to policing might be that stop and search powers have not been devised in order to encourage or allow police officers to focus undue attention on certain minority ethnic groups, but in practice there has been a over-representation, even if the individual officers concerned are not motivated by prejudice. Institutional racism, as Oakley's (Macpherson, 1999: 6–31) evidence to the Lawrence Inquiry outlined, describes the position that arises from the broader social position of the police, such that: '... if the predominantly white staff of the police organization have their experience of visible minorities largely restricted to interactions with such groups, then negative racial stereotypes will tend to develop accordingly'.

Evaluation

Although widely accepted by policy and practitioner communities, the concept of institutional racism has been critiqued by academic commentators. Clearly, there are those who do not accept that the police service discriminates or over-polices certain ethnic communities; such concerns are not addressed here since they are not directed at institutional racism, but at the extent of racism in policing more generally. However, those who do tend to accept that the police have a problem with racism, several concerns arise relating to whether this can be explained in institutional terms. First, it has been argued that the controversy surrounding Macpherson's allegation belied the fact that his analysis actually offered little that was qualitatively new. As Solomos (1999) pointed out, the definition contained in the report is broadly similar to indirect racial discrimination that was outlawed by the 1976 Race Relations Act, which – as with Macpherson's definition – refers to the unintended consequences of actions that might not have been designed to discriminate.

Other concerns about the concept of institutional racism relate to the difficulties of identifying precisely how problems derive from operational practices, or why and how some individuals seem to be part of the same institution but are not affected. If police subculture, for example, encourages cynicism and stereotyping, and is thus blamed for racist attitudes, it is difficult to understand how some officers are not influenced. Third, as Souhami (2007) noted, on a practical level, conceptualizing racism in collective terms has the unintended consequence of allowing individuals to evade their own responsibility. If the problem is of the police service in general terms then there might seem to be little that an individual, even if in a management position, can do to address the problem. Racism is everywhere and so nowhere in particular can it be challenged.

Finally, particular concerns about Macpherson's influential approach reflect more general problems with the concept of institutional racism. Chief among these is the problem of 'conceptual inflation' (Miles, 1989), such that any discrimination or disadvantage experienced by minority ethnic communities is explained in terms of racism. It might be that more complex processes of exclusion, not all of which are related simply to racism, explain the difficulties faced by minority ethnic groups. Stenson and Waddington (2007) argued that assumptions about the disproportionate representation of minority ethnic communities in police stop and search needs to be reconceptualized in the light of evidence suggesting that it is actually young white males that are over-represented in some localities. For this reason they suggested that the issues of the disproportionate exercise of police powers needs to be widened to include factors such as class, gender, age and space, as well as race and ethnicity.

Many of the problems that have surrounded police-minority ethnic relations in Britain for decades appear similar to those experienced in other countries that share similar policing arrangements. In the US, for example, the disproportionate impact of police on sections of the African American population are extensively documented. The killing by police of Sean Bell in New York City in 2006 led to considerable debates about racial profiling and aggressive police tactics in black neighbourhoods. New York Police Commissioner Kelly noted that concerns had continued despite the substantial increase in the recruitment of non-white officers in recent years. Allegations of racism arose even though three of the five officers involved in Bell's shooting were black. Clearly such analysis raises questions about management and leadership, organizational subculture and the fundamental framework of policing, but these debates were not conducted in terms of institutional racism. In Australia, former Prime Minister Howard's pledges when in power to intervene in the Northern Territory to address problems relating to crime, child abuse, and drug and alcohol addition among Aboriginal communities led to considerable opposition, some of which related to the reliance on using the police to 'enforce' discipline in ways that seem to parallel the oppressive policing directed at Aboriginal communities in colonial periods thought to have been consigned to the past. In New Zealand, the poor history of relations with Maori communities is often related to the nineteenth century role of the police in supporting the military to enforce colonial rule. As with the US, these debates in Australasia have not been conducted in terms of institutional racism, even though they appear to have much in common with the British experience.

Each of these experiences has its own distinct context that means that generalizations are inevitably simplistic. Clearly minority ethnic relations with police are spatially and temporally specific, and yet parallels persist that suggest that some features might be linked broadly to the structural relation of the police to the state, and the institutional frameworks that this gives rise to. If the police service is bound up with state sovereignty, and, in certain societies at certain times, this engages the police in difficult relations with minority ethnic communities then this might mean that the concept of institutional racism is useful to conceptualizing the disproportionate impact that policing arrangements have on marginalized groups. For that reason the concept of institutional racism will continue to be important, even though it does not provide a clear framework for understanding specific instances of malpractice or inappropriate service or conduct.

Michael Rowe

Associated Concepts: culture, diversity, hate crime, racial profiling

Key Readings

Lea, J. (2000) 'The Macpherson report and the question of institutional racism', *The Howard Journal*, 39 (3): 219–33.

Macpherson, Sir W. (1999) *The Stephen Lawrence Inquiry*, Report of an Inquiry by Sir William Macpherson of Cluny. CM 4262–1. London: HMSO.

Miles, R. (1989) *Racism*. London: Routledge.

Singh, G. (2000) 'The concept and context of institutional racism', in A. Marlow, and B. Loveday, (eds) *After Macpherson: Policing after the Stephen Lawrence Inquiry*. Lyme Regis: Russell House.

Solomos, J. (1999) 'Social research and the Stephen Lawrence Inquiry', *Sociological Research Online*, 4(1).

Souhami, A. (2007) 'Understanding "institutional racism": the Stephen Lawrence Inquiry and the police service reaction', in M. Rowe, (ed.). *Policing Beyond Macpherson*. Cullompton, Devon: Willan Publishing.

Stenson, K. and Waddington, P.A.J. (2007) 'Macpherson, police stops and institutional racism', in M. Rowe, (ed.) *Policing Beyond Macpherson – Issues in Policing, Race, and Society*. Cullompton, Devon: Willan Publishing.

INTELLIGENCE AGENCY

Definition

An intelligence agency may be defined as an organization conducting mainly secret activities – targeting, collection, analysis and dissemination – intended to enhance security and/or power by forewarning of threats in time to take preventive action.

Distinctive Features

The main types of intelligence agency (or, units within agencies) in the state sector are military, foreign, internal security, police and border guards. In addition, we see increasing numbers of people employed in intelligence roles in the corporate sector, not usually in organizations that are identified as intelligence agencies but more often as units or even just roles within private military and security companies.

Since the end of Cold War, barriers between these agencies have reduced in the face of changing threat perception. In particular, terrorism, which occurs at home and abroad, blurs the traditional division between foreign and domestic intelligence. Also, terrorism is a criminal offence so police forces are brought into greater cooperation with intelligence agencies than was the case historically.

However, the rapid growth of surveillance – both actual and virtual – begs the question of what, if anything, is distinctive about the intelligence agency? All government departments and private corporations devote significant resources to gathering information on the population in the belief that this will enable them better to implement their policies or sell their products – in other words, the relationship of knowledge and power is at the very heart of public and private governance. But intelligence agencies are distinctive: first, their objective is defined in terms of *security* and, usually, traditional notions of national, state or 'hard' security. Second, secrecy is a central defining element. Agencies may now have websites (for example, the UK's Security Service, also known as MI5) and advertize in the press for recruits but key elements of their work, especially information regarding their sources and methods, remain closely guarded secrets, backed up by laws for the punishment of those who 'leak' information. Various techniques are deployed to enhance secrecy and counter the attempts of others to penetrate the agency: extensive vetting of personnel prior to and during employment, classifying documents and 'compartmentalizing' information about specific operations so that access is limited only to those who 'need to know'.

The process by which agencies develop 'intelligence' is sometimes described as a 'cycle'. In practice it is much more complex and messier than is implied by that term but it is useful to describe and evaluate the process in terms of various stages. Resources are limited and so agencies must determine priorities for investigation. There is a misconception that, with the aid of modern information technology, they can simply scan the universe of digital information from which 'threats' will emerge. Therefore, the initial stage is to *target* particular individuals, groups or patterns of behaviour that are believed to be threatening.

Starting with what, if anything, is already known about the target, the agency will seek to gather further information. The potential sources of information are many: much is gathered from open sources including, for example, systematic surveillance of websites run by target groups. Also, agencies access databases held by other government departments, for example, employment and health. But the particular speciality of intelligence agencies is to gather information covertly. This may be done by *technical* means such as telephone interception ('taps'), electronic surveillance ('bugs'), the gathering of electronic information or photography via satellites and, of increasing importance, the interception of Internet and e-mail traffic. The development and deployment of these techniques can be very expensive and it is not always clear that the money invested in them has been very productive. For example, US Secretary of State Colin Powell presented a sophisticated and striking compilation of audio and photographic 'intelligence' to the United Nations Security Council in February 2003 in order to demonstrate the presence of weapons of mass destruction (WMD) in Iraq. The only problem was that it was wrong in most important respects.

Additionally, *human* sources are deployed. In financial terms using 'agents' or 'informers' is generally cheaper than technical means but it can be very difficult if not impossible to find them or place them close to targets. Informers pose far greater problems for law, ethics and practice just because they are so penetrative of the privacy of the target. Their recruitment normally involves coercion, deception or bribery and their handling poses significant difficulties if they are to remain under the control of the agency rather than acting as freelances who take advantage of their privileged access to police or officials to sustain their own illegal activities.

However information is gathered, its accuracy and meaning must be evaluated. Analysis is what turns information into intelligence: facts do not speak for themselves! There is something of a positivist illusion in intelligence that yet more information will solve its mysteries and puzzles, an illusion fed by a corporate sector ever anxious to sell increasingly sophisticated and expensive equipment. Yet, as far as counter-terrorist work is concerned, skills in the development of human sources and analysis are much more important when it comes to developing intelligence and translating it into policy.

Once intelligence is developed the question is what to do with it? Too often, the whole process can degenerate into the accumulation of vast stores of material on the principle that 'you never know today what you might need tomorrow...' and it is not passed to anyone who can actually use it productively. Inquiries into 9/11 showed up the perennial problem of agencies' reluctance to share intelligence with others. In some cases this is for sound security reasons – once you have passed on intelligence you lose control of it and there is a danger that your source might be exposed – but in others it derives from simple ignorance as to what other agencies need or fear that someone else might claim credit for a subsequent operation. There are now greater efforts to increase intelligence sharing both within and between countries which may increase effectiveness but it also risks serious infringements of rights. For example, the US practice of 'extraordinary rendition', in which suspects are kidnapped and 'rendered' to regimes where torture is routinely used in interrogation, is dependent in part on the sharing of information between

intelligence allies and, in some cases, this has been shown to be quite wrong (see Arar Commission, 2007).

Finally, whether disseminated to others or not, what is to be done with the intelligence? Some intelligence agencies, for example the Canadian Security Intelligence Service, are empowered only to develop intelligence and disseminate it to government departments while others, for example the UK's MI5, may also act, such as by disrupting groups planning violence by disarming their weapons. Police also deploy intelligence in this way, for example, seeking to disrupt criminal markets by confiscating drugs or using surveillance overtly in a way that 'warns off' those planning a crime. Compared with these 'tactical' or short-term operations, 'strategic' intelligence seeks to inform longer term policies with respect to foreign, military, security and crime policies. In some circumstances, agencies themselves may take action secretly. Such actions can range from planting information through maintaining contact with violent groups via 'back channels' to assassination; but in all cases the advantage for the sponsoring state is that the action is 'deniable' by the government. Thus covert action is, like war, 'politics by other means'.

Evaluation

The central question is 'does intelligence work?' Does it succeed in gathering the information and developing the intelligence necessary to prevent bad things happening? Well, sometimes it does and, at others, more spectacularly, it does not. The success of al Qaeda's attacks on the US in September 2001 and the fiasco over Iraqi WMD are often described as 'intelligence failures' whereas closer examination suggests that, while there were shortcomings in the *intelligence* process, there were perhaps even greater failings in the *political* process, that is, governments either did not listen to intelligence (or listened only to the messages they wanted to hear) and then, when selling policies to the public, cynically exaggerated intelligence.

Counter-terrorist work remains the greatest challenge – in the UK, for example, some planned attacks in recent years have been prevented and others have not, but it must be remembered that any agency that had resources and powers sufficient to *guarantee* security against political violence would itself constitute a massive threat to freedom.

Intelligence agencies exist in close proximity to political power and their relationship with governments can be fraught if not actually corrupt. There are some patterns of political abuse, for example, ministers in power may simply view the agency as responsible for guarding their political fortunes by means of surveillance and harassment of their political opponents. On the other hand, agencies may make use of their special powers to augment their own power in such a way that they are answerable to no political superior – the agency as 'rogue elephant'. In either of these cases, agencies may be responsible for serious human rights abuses.

All states (formally democratic or not) have a weak history of subjecting intelligence agencies to the same kind of control and oversight as other state sectors. Indeed, it is only within the last quarter century or so that greater efforts have been made. The circumstances of this 'democratization' of intelligence varied: in Latin America it was the demise of various military dictatorships, in Eastern Europe the collapse of the Soviet bloc and in 'older' democracies a combination of the end of the Cold War and various scandals. As a result, there has been a rapid spread of legislation, clearer procedures for ministerial control, safeguards against political abuse of agencies, increased transparency and parliamentary oversight. However, important questions remain as to whether these legal changes have been matched by changes in organizational cultures and practices, especially in countries where democracy is largely formal. Beyond this, yet larger questions loom, for example, despite their murky reputation, intelligence agencies may contribute to peacekeeping, public safety and monitoring climate change – yet their proximity to political power, pervasive security and special powers mean that they must always be subject to strenuous oversight.

Peter Gill

Associated Concepts: criminal investigation, cross-border policing, culture, high policing, human rights policing, Interpol, peacekeeping, security networks, terrorism, transnational policing

Key Readings

Arar Commission (2007) *Commission of Inquiry into the Actions of Canadian Officials in Relation to Maher Arar*. Ottowa: Arar Commission.

Born, H. and Caparini, M. (eds) (2007) *Democratic Control of Intelligence Services: Containing Rogue Elephants*. Aldershot: Ashgate.

Gill, P. and Phythian, M. (2006) *Intelligence in an Insecure World*. Cambridge: Polity.

Jophnson, L. (ed.) (2007) *Handbook of Intelligence Studies*. London: Routledge.

Kean, T. and Hamilton, L. (2004) *9/11 Commission Report: Final Report of the National Commission on Terrorist Attacks upon the United States*. New York: W.W. Norton.

Smith, M. (2002) *The Spying Game*. London: Politico's.

INTELLIGENCE-LED POLICING

Definition

Intelligence-led policing was originally articulated as a law enforcement operational strategy that sought to reduce crime through the combined use of crime analysis and criminal intelligence in order to determine crime reduction tactics that concentrate on the enforcement and prevention of criminal offender activity, with a focus on active and recidivist offenders. This approach emphasizes information gathering through the extensive use of confidential informants, offender interviews, analysis of recorded crime and calls for service, surveillance of suspects, and community sources of information. These sources are analyzed so that law enforcement managers can determine objective policing tactics in regard to enforcement targets, prevention activities and further intelligence gathering operations. In the last few years, the interpretation of 'intelligence-led policing' appears to be broadening in scope. While still retaining the central notion that police should avoid getting bogged down in reactive, individual, case investigations, intelligence-led policing is evolving into a management philosophy that places greater emphasis on information-sharing and collaborative, strategic solutions to crime problems at the local and regional level.

Distinctive Features

Originating in the UK, the intelligence-led policing paradigm has its foundations in the recognition that police were spending too much time responding to crime and too little time targeting offenders. Reports by the Audit Commission in 1993 and Her Majesty's Inspectorate of Constabulary in 1997 advocated increased use of intelligence, surveillance and informants to target recidivist offenders so that police could be more effective in fighting crime, and the call was quickly taken up by some police forces, most noticeably Kent Constabulary. Since then, the use of the term has extended to many countries, including Australia, New Zealand, continental Europe, and since 11 September, 2001, it has become increasingly common in the US.

Intelligence-led policing is philosophically closest to problem-oriented policing, and to a degree the accountability mechanism of Compstat, yet is distinct from both of these in different ways. Problem-oriented policing emphasizes the tackling of underlying problems that cause crime, problems that are identified and deciphered through effective crime analysis. Intelligence-led policing similarly defines a strong role for analysis, establishing it as the basis for decision-making that follows. However, where problem-oriented policing is a bottom-up philosophy that places street level police

officers at the forefront of problem identification and resolution, existing implementations of intelligence-led policing are more hierarchical and emphasize the top-down, rank-oriented nature of law enforcement. Criminal intelligence flows up to decision-makers at the executive level, who set priorities for enforcement and prevention and pass these down to lower levels of the organization as operational taskings.

The hierarchical nature of the intelligence flow is, organizationally at least, similar to Compstat. Compstat also has a top-down operational structure, where senior managers hold lower ranks accountable for crime levels. Intelligence-led policing however has a more holistic view of the analysis of the criminal environment, in that it aims to include information from a wider and richer range of sources in order to better understand the context of the crime patterns often seen in Compstat meetings. Intelligence-led policing also attempts to seek longer-lasting solutions to complex local and organized crime problems, and to be future oriented and strategically focused.

Intelligence-led policing also retains differences with community policing, and in its original formulation could be considered incompatible with the tenets of community policing's philosophy of community contact and empowerment. Where community policing emphasizes policing to the needs and the desires of the local community, intelligence-led policing is a process whereby strategy and priorities are determined through a more objective analysis of the criminal environment. As such, it is possible that crime reduction priorities can differ from the needs of the community as perceived by local people. For example, local community groups may indicate to community officers that they are concerned about local youths hanging out on a street corner, but may be unaware that an organized crime gang operates in the same neighbourhood. Objective analysis of the criminal environment may suggest to police managers that the organized crime group is a more pressing priority. Community input, while often sought, is therefore not necessarily a dominant information source or policy determinant for intelligence-led policing.

Evaluation

It is too early to pass judgement on the crime reduction benefits of intelligence-led policing, as long-term studies of police forces that have fully implemented and adopted intelligence-led policing have yet to be conducted. In the UK, some recent studies have identified implementation problems associated with intelligence-led policing in police forces. These problems include technical, organizational and cultural factors that are inhibiting a rapid adoption of intelligence-led policing. For example, the strategy emphasizes both horizontal and vertical information and intelligence sharing among police agencies so that executive decision-makers can establish objective crime reduction policies, but this approach is being implemented into a policing environment that has traditionally rewarded individual (not shared) knowledge of the criminal world, knowledge often used to effect arrests without thought to any longer-term crime reduction strategy. Furthermore, a clear definition of what would be evaluated appears elusive. In some parts of the world the interpretation of 'intelligence-led policing' appears to be relatively fluid as police departments experiment with different organizational philosophies, priorities and configurations, and as they attempt to integrate community-oriented concerns into the managerial decision-making of law enforcement.

There have also been concerns in regard to the adoption of a strategy that places greater emphasis on the use of confidential informants and surveillance. While policing has a long tradition of using informants, questions have been raised about their increased use both in terms of the financial benefits of using paid informants and in regard to the ethical and legitimacy issues for police services. Increased use of surveillance, while not only potentially expensive, has also been questioned because some people view this as an intrusive and excessive tactic for the government to employ against (often minor) offenders. In both these cases it can be argued that these objections stem from a misunderstanding of the difference between the tactics used to gather information, and intelligence-led

policing: a management strategy used to determine priorities and police activity.

In the US, debate continues about the use of the word 'intelligence' within the context of policing because of public concerns stemming from abuses of police intelligence activity investigating non-violent organizations in the US in the 1950s and 1960s. As a result, the term information-led policing is sometimes used. This term is however misleading. Information is simply raw data, while intelligence is analyzed information that has been synthesized to create a more holistic view of the criminal environment. Further concerns that are commonly voiced in the US are that government legislation resulting from the abuses of the 1950s and 1960s limit the right of police departments to retain information in criminal intelligence files. This sometimes results in police departments being over-cautious in their interpretation of 28 Code of Federal Regulations (CFR) Part 23 and as a result over-cautious in their handling of potentially useful criminal intelligence.

In the UK, the concept of intelligence-led policing is intertwined with the National Intelligence Model. Contrary to some views, the National Intelligence Model is not synonymous with the notion of intelligence-led policing, however it does provide a business model that creates a framework on which intelligence-led policing can be conducted. Evaluations of the National Intelligence Model have, to now, focused on the effectiveness of the model to provide for effective information sharing and clear setting of priorities rather than its ability to deliver crime reduction. The National Intelligence Model is being refined in many parts of the UK in order to better incorporate aspects of community and reassurance policing. More recently, some UK police forces have tried to use the National Intelligence Model as a way to manage and integrate the intelligence-led policing paradigm of information evaluation and decision-making with the community policing philosophy of addressing community concerns. Although this could be argued as being different from the original conceptualization of intelligence-led policing, it is likely that, in the UK at least, the future success of intelligence-led policing will be judged alongside the success of the National Intelligence Model.

Jerry H. Ratcliffe

Associated Concepts: calls for service, community policing, Compstat, crime analysis, crime prevention, criminal investigation, managerialism, problem-oriented policing

Key Readings

Cope, N. (2004) 'Intelligence-led policing or policing led intelligence?: integrating volume crime analysis into policing', *British Journal of Criminology*, 44 (2): 188–203.

Heaton, R. (2000) 'The prospects for intelligence-led policing: some historical and quantitative considerations', *Policing and Society*, 9 (4): 337–56.

Maguire, M., and John, T. (2006) 'Intelligence led policing, managerialism and community engagement: competing priorities and the role of the National Intelligence Model in the UK', *Policing and Society*, 16 (1): 67–85.

Ratcliffe, J. H. (2005) 'The effectiveness of police intelligence management: a New Zealand case study', *Police Practice and Research*, 6 (5): 435–51.

Tilley, N. (2003) 'Community policing, problem-oriented policing and intelligence-led policing' in T. Newburn (ed.), *Handbook of Policing*. Cullompton, Devon: Willan Publishing.

INTERPOL

Definition

Interpol is the acronym of the International Criminal Police Organization, an international non-governmental police organization that presently counts member agencies from 186 nations. Interpol primarily facilitates international cooperation among criminal law enforcement agencies from different parts of the world, and also cooperates with other organizations involved with combating international crime. To achieve its mission, Interpol operates a central headquarters, the General Secretariat located in Lyon, France, that is linked for information exchange with its member agencies via so-called National Central Bureaus. Since its formation in 1923, Interpol has continually expanded its membership, even in periods of international instability.

Formally, Interpol has three core functions. First, the organization oversees a system of international police communications among its members. Originally conducted by regular mail, since 2003 these communications have been electronically secured through an encrypted Internet-based system called I-24/7 connecting the General Secretariat in Lyon with the National Central Bureaus. Second, Interpol provides its member agencies with operational data and databases containing information, such as names, fingerprints and DNA profiles, on international fugitives from justice as well as information on stolen property such as passports and works of art. Third, Interpol offers operational assistance, particularly in Interpol's priority areas, which presently include public safety and terrorism, international fugitives from justice, drugs and organized crime, human trafficking, and financial and high-tech crime. In support of these operational services, Interpol organizes a Command and Coordination Centre that operates as the primary point of contact for any member agency that seeks immediate support. Other operational support can, at the request of a member agency, be provided by a Crisis Support Group, a Criminal Analysis Unit, and Incident Response Teams or Disaster Victim Identification Teams.

Distinctive Features

Interpol was established at an international meeting of police in Vienna in 1923 in order to facilitate international police cooperation in response to rising international crime following the end of the First World War. Then known as the International Criminal Police Commission, the organization was from the start not set up as a supranational police force sanctioned by an international governing body, but as a non-governmental collaborative network among the criminal law enforcement authorities of various nations, as remains the case today. To facilitate inter-agency collaboration, a central headquarters was established in Vienna, Austria, and various institutions of cooperation, such as a radio network, regular meetings, and printed publications, were organized to facilitate international police communications. By the late 1930s, police of the German Nazi regime gradually took control of the organization, and the headquarters were subsequently moved to Berlin where they were institutionally linked to the SS police structure. Absent of any meaningful form of international cooperation during the Second World War, the organization was revived in 1946 at an international police meeting in Brussels, Belgium. The headquarters were then moved to France, where they have since been located, first in Paris and, since 1989, in Lyon. The formal name change to the International Criminal Police Organization, abbreviated as ICPO-Interpol or just Interpol, came about in 1956.

The formal goals of Interpol, as specified in its constitution, are 'to ensure and promote mutual assistance [among] criminal police authorities within the limits of the laws of their respective nations and in the spirit of the Universal Declaration of Human Rights (Interpol, undated). The functions of Interpol are restricted to the prevention and suppression of ordinary law crimes or violations of criminal law, at the exclusion of 'activities of a political, military, religious or racial character' (ibid.). Membership of the organization is assigned by Interpol's Secretary General to national police agencies selected by the governmental authorities of their respective nations as their representatives. Presently, the four official languages of the organization are English, French, Spanish and Arabic.

The structure of Interpol consists of a General Assembly, an Executive Committee, a General Secretariat, and the National Central Bureaus. The General Assembly is Interpol's main governing organ, which meets annually and comprises delegates appointed by each member agency. The Assembly takes all important decisions related to Interpol's policies, resources, methods, finances, and activities. The Assembly also elects the 13-member Executive Committee, which comprises a President, three Vice-Presidents, and nine delegates covering the regions of Africa, the Americas, Asia, Europe and the Middle-East and Northern Africa. Interpol's President is elected by the General Assembly for a period of four years. The General Assembly and the Executive Committee together comprise Interpol's governance bodies.

The General Secretariat is located in the Lyon headquarters and has six regional offices, in Argentina, the Ivory Coast, El Salvador, Kenya, Thailand, and Zimbabwe, in addition to a liaison office at the United Nations in New York. Since 1996, Interpol has had a formal agreement with the United Nations, granting each organization observer status in sessions of their respective general assemblies and enabling cooperation in various matters of the fight against international crime. Interpol has reached similar cooperation agreements with Europol (the European Police Office), the International Criminal Court, and other police and legal organizations.

The National Central Bureaus are maintained in the individual nations of the member agencies. The Bureaus function as the designated contact points for the General Secretariat, the regional offices, as well as the other member agencies for all official Interpol police communications concerning international investigations and the location and apprehension of fugitives. These communications are conducted on the basis of a specialized colour-coded notification system whereby each one of six possible colours represents a specific type of request. For example, a red notice is a request for the arrest of a wanted person in view of extradition, and a blue notice is a request to collect information about a person in relation to a crime. In 2005, an Interpol-United Nations Special Notice was added for requests concerning groups or individuals that are subject to actions formally sanctioned by the United Nations against Al Qaeda and the Taliban.

Evaluation

In terms of membership, Interpol is one of the world's largest international organizations. The ability to attract a wide and in many ways diverse membership clearly counts among the organization's most notable achievements. Yet, while Interpol has secured a measure of cooperation despite the political and other differences that exist among the nations of the world, the wide scope of the organization's membership has ironically also hindered effective cooperation due to frequent mistrust between the police of different nations. As a result, police from the member countries often prefer to conduct international police work in a bilateral or otherwise limited form rather than rely on the multilateral structure of Interpol.

Interpol has been able to institute various means of communication among police that are driven by professional concerns of efficiency in police work, relatively unhindered by periods of international instability. Following the terrorist incidents of September 11, Interpol has technologically upgraded and expanded its facilities. Problematic is the fact that Interpol's ways of working may operate at the cost of considerations of accountability and formal legality. A constant concern for Interpol is finding a way to balance a quest for efficiency in police performance with due concern for democratic accountability – a dilemma shared by police organizations worldwide.

Mathieu Deflem

Associated Concepts: accountability, cross-border policing, Europol, intelligence agency, multi-agency policing, security networks, transnational policing

Key Readings

Anderson, M. (1989) *Policing the World: Interpol and the Politics of International Police Cooperation.* Oxford, UK: Clarendon Press.

Barnett, M. and L. Coleman (2005) 'Designing police: Interpol and the study of change in international organizations', *International Studies Quarterly,* 49: 593–619.

Bresler, F. (1992) *Interpol.* London: Sinclair-Stevenson.

Deflem, M. (2002) *Policing World Society: Historical Foundations of International Police Cooperation.* Oxford, New York: Oxford University Press.

Deflem, M. (2006) 'Global rule of law or global rule of law enforcement? International police cooperation and counter-terrorism', *The Annals of the American Academy of Political and Social Science,* 603: 240–51.

Interpol (undated) *ICPO-INTERPOL Constitution and General Regulations.* Interpol: Lyon, http://www.interpol.int.

INTERROGATION

See Criminal Investigation; Investigative Interviewing

INVESTIGATIVE INTERVIEWING

Definition

An 'investigative interview' is an interview conducted to elicit evidence or information from a person (i.e., witness, victim, complainant or suspect) during the process of an investigation. Investigative interviews conducted by police can vary greatly in purpose, scope and content. The common objective of all investigative interviews, however, is to elicit the most *accurate, complete* and *detailed* account of an incident in question. Although physical evidence can also be useful, interviews are usually central to police investigations. This is particularly the case for those interviews conducted in the initial phase of the investigation when people's memory is more complete, their perceptions are less likely to be tainted by later influences and the direction of the investigation is still being determined.

Distinctive Features

A wide range of interrelated factors can determine the outcome of an investigative interview. Some of these factors include the physical, mental and emotional state of the interviewee at the time of the event and the interview, the interview procedure and setting, and the nature of the incident being recalled (Milne and Bull, 1999). It is well established, however, that the interviewer's questions have the greatest impact on the accuracy, detail and completeness of information provided by respondents. For example, when interviewers adhere to best-practice questioning procedures, differences in the memory and language abilities of different respondents have a negligible impact on the accuracy of responses (Agnew and Powell, 2004; Lamb et al., 2003). In contrast, poorly conducted interviews can impede the investigation by distorting the witness' memory and contaminating the entire investigative process.

Several distinct investigative interviewing protocols have been developed for use by police for different populations and situations. For instance, the National Institute of Child Health and Human Development Protocol and the Guidance for Achieving Best Evidence in Criminal Proceedings were developed for interviewing children as well as other vulnerable or intimidated witnesses. Conversation Management was designed to provide interviewers with skills in guiding a hostile respondent (e.g., alleged offender) to be more forthcoming when volunteering information. In contrast, the Cognitive Interview was developed mainly for interviewing cooperative adults, however it does contain some provisions for interviewing children. Although the above-mentioned interview protocols contain some unique components, they all adhere to the common goal of maximizing the *quality* (that is, accuracy, coherence) as well as *quantity* of information elicited. Further, they each adhere to a similar structure. Elements common to all interview protocols include: greeting, establishing rapport with the interviewee, establishing the topic of concern and/or aims of the interview, eliciting an uninterrupted free report of the incident (or related matter), clarifying information with specific or focused questioning and closure.

Experts agree that the most critical skill of investigative interviewers (irrespective of the respondent group) is the ability to maintain the use of non-leading, open-ended questions. Non-leading questions refrain from presuming or suggesting details that were not previously mentioned by the respondent. Open-ended questions are defined as those questions that encourage elaborate (as opposed to brief or one-word) responses. In the child witness arena, open-ended questions are also defined as questions that do not dictate or suggest what information related to the event should be reported. Children are more vulnerable than adults to suggestions and social demands to provide a response. Thus it is even more critical with these interviewees that interviewers broaden the range of response options as well as encourage elaborate responses (Poole and Lamb, 1998). Open-ended questions are ideal for all respondents because they maximize the accuracy of the interviewee's account of the offence and minimize the opportunity for confusion, contamination and/or misunderstandings. An open-ended questioning style is also critical to tasks such as the development of rapport and for eliciting (where appropriate) a clear and coherent disclosure or confession.

Despite the presence of well-defined 'best-practice' guidelines in investigative interviewing, numerous concerns have been voiced regarding the underuse of non-leading, open-ended questions by investigative interviewers around the globe. This has led several researchers in recent years to focus on the content, structure and efficacy of investigative interviewer training courses. While research is still in its infancy, the research findings support those within the broader expertise literature: that ongoing practice of specific skills and expert feedback is critical in maintaining effective questions (see Powell, Fisher and Wright, 2005 for review). In other words, lack of continual and high quality professional training is the main reason for poor interview outcome.

Police organizations typically record interviews with suspects and vulnerable witnesses so as to preserve the evidence and establish the integrity of the information obtained. In some jurisdictions, recorded interviews with vulnerable witnesses who allege abuse (e.g., children or persons with an intellectual disability) may be used as evidence-in-chief. The difficulty that arises when combining investigative and evidentiary interviews is that the goals and process of the interviews are somewhat different. In investigative interviews, witnesses need to be encouraged to recall everything that comes to mind irrespective of whether it seems trivial, out of place or inconsistent (Fisher and Geiselman, 1992). This encourages an elaborate memory process which maximizes the degree of accurate detail provided. Greater detail, in turn, provides investigators with greater opportunity to follow leads and obtain additional evidence that may be used to corroborate the account. In court, however, lawyers need to be selective regarding what detail is presented, and there are usually more restrictions on the way the evidence must be elicited. Further in evidential interviews, the credibility of the account in the eyes of the jury is potentially important even though accuracy and credibility are not related concepts. Indeed, some witnesses (e.g., those who believe their account to be true) can provide coherent, detailed and highly convincing accounts of incidents that never happened.

Evaluation

As mentioned above, there is considerable overlap in approaches across different interview protocols. This is because the protocols are based on a common, public pool of knowledge derived from interviewing respondents. Some of this knowledge arises from experimental, laboratory research and reflects controlled testing of specific interview techniques. Typically, this research is conducted by cognitive and social psychologists and is directed towards testing formal theories of memory and communication. Other knowledge is more experiential and reflects the personal insights gained from having conducted many interviews or from modelling the differences between effective and ineffective interviewers. This knowledge typically emanates from interviews conducted in real-world (uncontrolled) settings and reflects a more global and retroactive analysis of interview styles.

Irrespective of the data-gathering technique, there is considerable agreement across the experimental and experiential approaches about the importance of using open-ended questions as well as the importance of other precepts. These precepts include the value of: proper preparation and evaluation of the interview, keeping an open mind, being sensitive to the individual needs of the interviewee, and conducting and closing the interview in a manner that is fair and maintains (as much as possible) a positive interviewer-interviewee relationship. Obtaining a confession from a suspect or a disclosure of abuse from a child should not be the *primary* goal of investigative interviews because these can subsequently be disputed or rejected as evidence by a court. Rather, the goal should be to obtain as much information as possible to assist in establishing which explanation, among several alternatives, is most likely to be true. In other words, the process of a good investigation (as with any scientific method) is not about gathering confirmatory evidence *per se*, but about gathering sufficient evidence to dispute alternative explanations.

Prior research in the area of investigative interviewing has focused primarily on the effect of various factors (for example, age, question type, retention interval) on the accuracy and detail of information obtained from witnesses, and of evaluating interviewers' performance in adhering to best-practice interview guidelines. Recently, however, the focus has expanded to:

(1) identifying ways to promote the use of best-practice interviewing within police organizations;

(2) identifying ways to tailor the interview to the needs and abilities of various interviewee groups; and

(3) understanding the important inter relationship between the interviewee and interviewer behaviours.

In the area of child witnesses, recent research has also focused on identifying ways to assist children to particularize offences. Particularization, a legal requirement of most jurisdictions, refers to the ability to identify each separate act of which the suspect is charged with reasonable precision in relation to time, place or some other unique contextual detail.

Martine Powell

Associated Concepts: criminal investigation, victim

Key Readings

Agnew, S. E. and Powell, M. B. (2004) 'The effect of intellectual disability on children's recall of an event across different question types', *Law and Human Behaviour*, 28 (3): 273–94.

Fisher, R. P., and Geiselman, R. E. (1992) *Memory-Enhancing Techniques in Investigative Interviewing: The Cognitive Interview.* Springfield, IL: C.C. Thomas.

Lamb, M. E., Sternberg, K. J., Orbach, Y., Esplin, P. W., Stewart, H. and Mitchell, S. (2003) 'Age differences in young children's responses to open-ended invitations in the course of forensic interviews' *Journal of Consulting and Clinical Psychology,* 71: 926–34.

Milne, R. and Bull, R. (1999) *Investigative Interviewing; Psychology and Practice.* Chichester, UK; John Wiley and Sons.

Poole, D. A., and Lamb, M. E. (1998) *Investigative Interviews of Children.* Washington: American Psychological Association.

Powell, M. B., Fisher. R. P. and Wright, R. (2005) 'Investigative interviewing', in N. Brewer and K. Williams (eds) *Psychology and Law: An Empirical Perspective.* New York: Guilford Press.

Wilson, J. C. and Powell, M. B. (2001). *A Guide to Interviewing Children.* Sydney: Allen and Unwin.

L

LAW AND ORDER POLITICS

Definition

The term 'law and order politics' describes a pattern of public discourse in which one political party or politician seeks to gain electoral advantage over another through exaggerated (or false) claims about crime and promises of (ever) tougher policies to deal with it. Practitioners of law and order politics routinely deride their opponents as 'soft on crime' and with being more concerned about the rights of offenders than the welfare of crime victims. This form of political attack appears to have become popular in many Western countries during the 1980s and 1990s.

Distinctive Features

The distinctive feature of law and order politics is the notion that crime is 'out of control' and the only way to bring it back in control is to introduce tougher law and order policies. Allied claims include the proposition that police are tied up in red tape, that crime has become much more violent, that more offenders are escaping conviction, that convicted offenders are treated too leniently by sentencing courts, that the justice system ignores the rights of victims; and that so-called 'crime experts' can't be trusted. Practitioners of law and order politics employ a variety of techniques to persuade people of the truth of these claims. These include whipping up public hysteria about particular crime problems or types of offender, treating particularly distressing crimes as if they were typical, selective or misleading use of crime statistics, encouraging disgruntled police officers to attack government law and order policy, ridiculing crime experts as 'out of touch', presenting a distorted picture of the facts surrounding individual criminal cases and parading distraught crime victims at media conferences to highlight government 'failure' to deal with crime.

The most common demand made by practitioners of law and order politics is for tougher penalties – usually longer prison terms. In the context of policing, however, practitioners of law and order politics commonly demand (or promise) increased police numbers, increased police powers and increased aggression on the part of police in dealing with offenders. Each of these demands trades on a popular and superficially plausible assumption about crime and crime control. People are drawn to the promise of more police because they believe that more offenders will be caught or deterred from offending. They are attracted by the promise of increased police powers because they are repeatedly told, by police and the media, that police are hampered in their 'fight against crime' by red tape and laws designed to protect civil liberties. Promises that police will 'crack down' on suspected offenders gain their appeal from the widespread belief that many offenders simply 'thumb their nose' at police. Tough law and order policies of any description carry considerable emotional appeal, especially for those rendered insecure by changing economic or social conditions.

Many politicians are well aware that appointing more police, increasing police powers and encouraging police to be more aggressive towards those who break the law may not help to reduce crime. Indeed, once in government some politicians embrace so-called 'soft' law and order strategies (for example, treatment for drug dependent offenders) they abjured when they were in opposition. The stigma associated with being labelled 'soft on crime' is usually so strong, however, few politicians seek to publicly challenge the assumptions on which tough law and order policies are based. As a result, public debate about crime control often descends into a competition between political parties over who is tougher on crime. These competitions often focus on issues that are of symbolic rather than practical importance, such as statutory limitations on the length of time a suspect can be held in custody without charge or trial; legal presumptions surrounding an alleged offender's 'right to silence'; legal rules requiring unanimous verdicts and legal limits on police powers in dealing with anti-social behaviour (for example, drunkenness, swearing in a public place).

The precise nature of the putative relationship between legal constraint and crime control is rarely spelt out. For the most part, the public is simply invited to believe that if the constraint in question were removed, crime rates would fall. As with promises to increase police powers, promises to crack down on crime are rarely accompanied by a detailed account of how policing has been too lenient or why more punitive policing will reduce crime. When a rationale is provided, it is often highly speculative. Advocates of zero tolerance policing, for example, argue that police should be as zealous in their pursuit of minor crime, such as incivility and vandalism, as they are in their pursuit of serious crime, such as robbery or murder. The rationale presented to support this claim is that serious offenders are sensitive to the way in which police respond to minor crime. If police fail to respond to it aggressively, the

argument runs, serious offenders will feel emboldened to commit more serious kinds of crime. Advocates of zero tolerance policing have never actually presented any evidence to support the claim that those who commit serious crime are sensitive to the way in which police respond to minor crime.

Evaluation

The influence of law and order politics on law and order policy has been profound. Even before the rise in public concern about terrorism, criminal justice responses to crime in most Western democracies had become markedly more punitive. In fact the growth of what some have called 'penal populism' has been so dramatic it has spawned an entire field of sociological enquiry. Some attribute the rise in penal populism to growing concern about crime and growing public demands for tougher law and order policies. An alternative view is that, far from responding to public concern about crime, politicians and the media have deliberately set out to stimulate it, in the former case for electoral advantage and in the latter case for commercial gain. A third view is that the rising level of public concern about crime and support for tougher policies as a response to general economic and social insecurities. A fourth blames the problem on public ignorance about crime and political ignorance about the true nature of public opinion on matters of crime and justice. It is likely that each of these explanations contains some measure of truth.

Whatever its causes, the politics of law and order usually has damaging effects on policing and other aspects of public policy. The dismissive treatment of civil liberties increases the risk that innocent people will end up harassed by police, arrested, convicted and in some cases imprisoned. The incessant demand to 'get tough' discourages police from dispassionately analyzing crime problems and selecting strategies to address them that are supported by evidence. On the other hand it encourages police to behave in ways that threaten public respect for the rule of law, thereby undermining public willingness to cooperate with police. The irony in all this is that, while some 'get tough' policing strategies have been shown to work, most appear to have either no effect or only a minor effect. Weapons confiscation, active policing of crime hot spots and proactive targeting of offenders do seem to reduce crime. Simply appointing more police and encouraging them to be more aggressive, however, seems to be of limited value. Studies of the relationship between police numbers and crime generally only find a weak relationship. The claims made on behalf of zero tolerance policing in the late 1990s by New York Mayor Rudolph Guiliani have long since been discredited. It is now clear crime in the US began falling prior to its introduction and fell in locations where zero tolerance policing had never been introduced.

The best thing that can be said about the politics of law and order is that it has had a stimulating effect on criminological research. In the 1960s most criminologists were preoccupied with the social and economic causes of crime. Now large numbers of criminologists are engaged in testing popular claims about the effect of police and the criminal justice system on crime. This is good news for law and order policy.

Don Weatherburn

Associated Concepts: anti-social behaviour, hot spots, terrorism, victim, zero tolerance policing

Key Readings

Garland, D. (2001) *The Culture of Control: Crime and Social Order in Contemporary Society.* Oxford: Oxford University Press.
Roberts, J. V., Stalans, L. J. Indermaur, D. and Hough, M. (2003) *Penal Populism and Public Opinion: Lessons from Five Countries.* Oxford: Oxford University Press.
Sherman, L. W., Farrington, D. P., Walsh, B. C. and MacKenzie, D. L. (2002) *Evidence-Based Crime Prevention.* New York: Routledge.

Tonry, M. (2004) *Punishment and Politics. Evidence and Emulation in the Making of English Crime Control Policy.* Devon: Willan Publishing.
Weatherburn, D. (2004) *Law and Order in Australia: Rhetoric and Reality.* Sydney: Federation Press.

LEADERSHIP

Definition

Police leadership refers to the varied nature of the interpersonal relationships between police managers and supervisors and the impact of these upon organizational performance. It is also used to refer to the general influence that police chiefs and commissioners may have upon the performance and organizational commitment of the police officers within their agencies. The concept has further been used in reference to the influence police officers may have upon the wider polity and communities they serve and the effect of this on police-public relationships, police effectiveness and police legitimacy. It is the first meaning that is reviewed in this entry.

Distinctive Features

Due in part perhaps because senior police officers carefully guard access to their organizations by outsiders, there is only a very small body of published research on police managers and their leadership behaviour. Most of this is not based upon empirical research and that which is, is almost wholly based on surveys and interviews rather than direct observations and institutional ethnographies.

Police autobiographies suggest that senior police themselves appear to claim that their leadership has a potent effect upon organizational performance. However, there is evidence that a new and urgent attention to leadership has recently emerged. Governments have visited 'new public management' upon police services. This, with its emphasis on stronger vertical accountability, performance outcomes, and value for money, has led to heightened attention to the relationship between police leadership and organizational performance. It has also led to significant increases in the level of resources devoted to police leadership training and development. Leadership is seen as a primary and effective tool for delivering much needed police organizational reform.

There are many psychological, social psychological and sociological conceptual approaches to the study of organizational leadership. The approach which dominates studies in the published literature on police leadership is one which compares and contrasts the incidence and impact of what are termed 'transactional leadership' and 'transformational leadership' upon the work performance of subordinates.

Transactional leadership refers to managerial behaviour which primarily focuses upon the calculative nature of the employment relationship within work organizations. It includes a management-by-exception style in which employees are left to get on with the job with discipline-based interventions made only when things go wrong, and a contingent reward style that links material rewards with acceptable organizational behaviour.

Transformational leadership in contrast to the self-interest-based approach of transactional leadership centres upon capturing the intrinsic commitment of employees to the goals and values of their work organization. Transformational leadership, through a variety of consciousness-raising behaviours, is seen as endeavouring to extend or transcend the transactional basis of employment, through its impact upon the motivation of employees. Its four 'I' categories of behaviour are: 'idealized influence'; 'inspirational motivation; 'individualized consideration'; and, 'intellectual stimulation'.

Idealized influence refers to the impact of strong role-modelling by superordinates upon subordinates, through which employees acquire a sense of mission and pride in the goals and work of their organizations.

Inspirational motivation is achieved by leaders when they successfully use powerful symbols and images within their organizations, ones designed to raise the expectations and commitment of followers to the goals of their organization. *Individualized consideration* refers to leadership practices that encourage employees to participate in organizational decision-making, that provide them with mentoring, development and support, and which treat each employee as an individual. *Intellectual stimulation* is the work-based learning and increased capability that employees can experience when their leaders allow them to challenge the status quo and to experiment, innovate and explore new and more effective ways of doing things.

Densten (1999) used this conceptual approach in his study of police leadership. He surveyed a sample of 480 senior police officers in a large Australian police force, inviting them to identify the types of leadership behaviour they experienced from their senior officers and to report on what kinds of impact they thought these had on their job satisfaction and work performance. He compared the findings with those from similar empirical research undertaken in American (non-police) work organizations. He found that the level or incidence of transformational leadership in the Australian police force was much lower than the American norm. The most frequently observed type of police eadership behaviour was management-by-exception. Densten also found there were quite high levels of satisfaction with this among police officers who generally appeared happy to be left to get on with the job. However, he concluded that if significant organizational change was required within contemporary policing, as he believed it was, then there was a critical need for the development of transformational leadership.

A later English-based study of police leadership by Dobby et al. also used the transactional/transformational leadership framework. The authors of this 2003–2004 study noted that to that date no published research had demonstrated any significant link between different styles of police leadership and police effectiveness. The researchers interviewed 150 police officers from across the rank structure of the police service and conducted a postal survey of over 1000 police officers. In contrast to Densten (1999), though, the authors of this study asked the police officers to report in their own words on what they wanted from police leadership. They also asked them to report on whether they had experienced poor leadership and if so to describe the forms it took.

The findings demonstrated that most if not all police officers wanted leaders who made them feel proud of the police services provided to the public and of their contribution to this. They favoured senior officers who walked the talk by demonstrating their commitment to high quality police service to the community and who demonstrably went out of their way to support their staff to deliver such service. They wanted leaders who actually demonstrated high personal and professional standards. They wanted their senior officers to challenge rather than tolerate poor behaviour in their subordinates. They wanted leaders who demonstrated high levels of professional and ethical competence. All reported that they had experienced negative leaders, senior officers who were lazy, moody and unethical.

The researchers found that their analysis of the detailed leadership qualities reported in the survey showed that nearly all were locatable within the transformational style. They ended by recommending that all recruitment and promotional processes should include a means through which officers unable to engage in transformational leadership, from recruits to chief constables, be weeded out of the service.

In his overview of police leadership and performance management in the UK context, Long (2003) notes that the New Labour government has identified a crisis in public service leadership generally and specifically a significantly underperforming police leadership. He too argues that the growing importance attached to the subject of police leadership stems from the growth of new public management and the government's requirement that police leaders be much more proactive and interventionist than in the past. He maintains that this will necessarily entail a shift from a transactional to a transformational leadership approach, one in which officers will have to appreciate the importance of developing their 'emotional intelligence' and move from their current attachment to a command and control style to one which empowers their subordinates. However, he fears that there is a tension between the need for these progressive forms of leadership and the current culture of performance management within the police service. The latter, he asserts, is turning police officers, from chiefs to basic command unit commanders, into bureaucrats, with the emphasis being on management, that is transactional leadership, rather than on transformational leadership.

Evaluation

The structural and cultural reality of police bureaucracies together with the top down pressure of new public management performance regimes present formidable barriers to organizational reform through attempts at transformational leadership. As Metcalf and Dick's (2001) study of organizational commitment in one large English police force discovered, most officers reported little opportunity to participate in decision-making, and did not experience strong supportive management. They argue that the strength of the rank culture and rank mentality along with the top down pressures emanating from a value for money performance regime indicates that much more than training officers in interpersonal skills will be required in order to pursue successful organizational reform.

Silvestri, too, in her (2003) study of English women police managers identified a fiercely embedded and dominant masculine gendered management within the police service. Her subjects reported that the new performance regimes have encouraged the emergence of a 'smart macho' culture of police management. She discovered too, that notwithstanding the existence of an organizational discourse claiming a movement away from a militaristic leadership model, the reality was quite different. Structurally, the police service remains dominated by hierarchy and rank, and there remains a strong cultural attachment to the rituals, signs and symbols of militarism. She discovered that while more women with feminist ideas and practices of leadership consistent with the transformational leadership style are rising up the hierarchy, they generally find themselves socially isolated and valued only as a complement to an otherwise tough, forceful and masculine leadership ethos. The failure of police reform packages is likely to continue without a better appreciation through further research of the deeply embedded range of masculine cultures within senior police management and what it will take to change them. The latter will have to include much more than attempts to change styles of leadership.

David Bradley

Associated Concepts: bureaucracy, culture, identity, managerialism, performance management

Key Readings

Densten, I. (1999) 'Senior Australian law enforcement under examination', *Policing: An International Journal of Police Strategies and Management*, 22 (1): 45–57.
Dobby, J., Anscombe, J. and Tuffin, R. (2004) *Police leadership expectations and impacts.* London: Home Office.
Long, M. (2003) 'Leadership and Performance Management', in T. Newburn, (ed.) *Handbook of Policing.* Cullompton, Devon: Willan Publishing.
Metcalf, B. and Dick, G. (2001) 'Exploring organization commitment in the police: implications for human resource strategy', *Policing: An International Journal of Police Strategies and Management*, 24 (3): 399–419.
Silvestri, M. (2003) *Women in Charge: Policing, Gender and Leadership.* Cullompton, Devon: Willan Publishing.

LEGITIMACY

Definition

Over the years social scientists have offered numerous definitions for legitimacy. Suchman defines legitimacy as the 'generalized perception or assumption that the actions of an entity are desirable, proper, or appropriate within some socially constructed system of norms, values, beliefs, and definitions' (1995: 574). Max Weber – the founding father of contemporary legitimacy research – defines legitimate authority as 'the probability that certain commands from a given source will be obeyed by a given group of persons' (1947: 324). He added that a basic criterion of legitimate power is a 'minimum of voluntary submission'. Police legitimacy, therefore, is the belief that the police are entitled to call upon the public to comply with the law.

Distinctive Features

A core function of the police is to ensure that citizens comply with the law. To be effective as maintainers of social order the police must be widely obeyed. This obedience must occur in both personal encounters with the police, as well as in people's everyday compliance with the law. Given it is difficult for police to gain compliance solely via threats or through use of force, police therefore need people to both accept their decisions and follow the law voluntarily.

The value of voluntary compliance and cooperation from the public raises the question of how such behaviour can be elicited. Skogan and Frydl (2004) identify three major factors that can help explain why people voluntarily obey the law:

(1) when it is instrumental;
(2) when they believe in the moral rightfulness of the law; and
(3) when they believe in the legitimacy of the authority enforcing the law.

The police play an important role in the first and third of these compliance processes.

Traditionally, compliance with the law has been viewed as being motivated through the creation of a credible risk that people will be caught and punished for wrongdoing. This instrumental perspective underpins notions of deterrence, sanctions (such as fines or custodial sentences) or social control models of social regulation. While there is some evidence to suggest that sanctions will be generally effective in determining people's behaviour towards the law, such effectiveness is dependent on a number of variables. As Skogan and Frydl point out:

> the problem … is that deterrent effects are apparently modest, certainty of punishment is low … and there are political constraints on resource allocation. As a consequence, deterrent strategies alone are unlikely to be a sufficient basis for an effective system of social regulation. (2004: 296)

A second view on why people comply with legal directives is what Skogan and Frydl refer to as substantive morality. That is, compliance is motivated by personal values. If these values coincide with the law, cooperation and compliance will be voluntarily extended. So, 'the degree to which people view law as consistent with their own values is clearly one factor shaping their law-related behaviour, independent of issues of legitimacy' (2004: 296). However, just as values can coincide with the law, so too, compliance with the law can be undermined by contrary values.

A third view in the literature is that police can promote public compliance and cooperation by using strategies that build the perceived legitimacy of police – 'the belief that the police are entitled to call upon the public to follow the law and help combat crime and that members of the public have an obligation to engage in cooperative behaviours' (Tyler, 2004: 87). Tyler argues that when people view the police as legitimate, they authorize them to determine what their behaviour will be within a given set of situations. In other words, people feel responsible for following the directives of legitimate authorities. Tyler argues that voluntary deference brought

about by perceptions of legitimacy is more reliable than instrumentally motivated compliance because it does not vary as a function of the circumstances or situation involved.

A significant body of research has now shown that people's views about the legitimacy of a legal authority can influence their willingness to accept decisions, can leave people feeling more satisfied with the decisions of an authority, and can shape compliance behaviour. In the policing context, Tyler and Huo (2002; cited in Tyler, 2004) found that two factors shaped people's willingness to accept decisions: (1) the degree to which decisions were regarded as favourable and fair, and (2) more importantly, the degree to which the police were generally regarded as legitimate. Tyler and Huo also explored people's motivations to comply with the law, finding that if people generally viewed the police as legitimate, they were more likely to report that they followed the law in their everyday lives. Sunshine and Tyler (2003) replicated this test of the influence of legitimacy on compliance. They found that those people who viewed the police as more legitimate were more likely to comply with their directives. Their study also examined the influence of police legitimacy on cooperation with the police. They found that those residents who viewed the police as more legitimate were more willing to cooperate with them both by reporting crimes or identifying criminals and by engaging in community activities to combat the problems of crime. Similar findings have been obtained by others in the US and internationally. Thus, increasing perceptions of police legitimacy may reduce crime both indirectly – by increasing resident cooperation with the police – and directly.

Evaluation

Given the important role that legitimacy appears to play in determining the level of voluntary compliance and cooperation with the police, it is important to understand how police legitimacy can be developed and maintained. A debate in the literature centres around whether police legitimacy can be best shaped by instrumental or normative aspects. According to the instrumental perspective, police legitimacy is linked to instrumental evaluations of three elements: police performance, risk, and judgements about distributive justice (Sunshine and Tyler, 2003). This instrumental view suggests that police can gain legitimacy when they:

(1) effectively control crime and criminal behaviour (performance);
(2) create a credible risk of detection and sanction for those who break the law (deterrence); and
(3) fairly distribute police services across people and communities (distributive justice).

In other words, the instrumental perspective of legitimacy suggests that police develop and maintain legitimacy through their effectiveness in controlling crime and disorder in the community.

The normative perspective of legitimacy, in contrast, suggests that 'the legitimacy of police is linked to public judgements about the fairness of the processes through which the police make decisions and exercise authority' (Sunshine and Tyler, 2003: 514). This procedural justice perspective suggests that if the police use fairness in their dealings with citizens then people will view the police as being more legitimate. Sunshine and Tyler (2003) argue that if the police use unfair procedures when they exercise their authority this can lead to alienation, dissatisfaction, defiance and non-cooperation from the public.

Important factors that people consider when deciding whether they have received procedural justice in an encounter with police are whether they are treated in a fair way, whether they are treated with respect and dignity, and whether concern was shown for their views and arguments about the event/incident. Tyler (2004) specifies the following key aspects of procedural justice:

(1) active participation in discussions prior to police decision-making (i.e., explaining their views/behaviour before police decide on a course of action);

(2) police decision-making that is neutral and objective (i.e., evidence that police treat everyone in a like manner); and
(3) being treated with dignity and respect.

Research in the policing context consistently indicates that evaluations of police legitimacy are based on people's views about the way police treat them, independent of people's views about how well police perform their job. For example, Sunshine and Tyler (2003) found that judgements about the legitimacy of the police were based predominantly on procedural justice concerns, and to a lesser extent on performance evaluations and distributive justice judgements. Sunshine and Tyler (2003) argue that findings such as these are very important from the perspective of policing, because the police have more control over how they treat people than they do over the crime rate. They argue that by becoming procedurally sensitive, police can have more control over the way people see their legitimacy than if they had to rely solely on deterrence or their performance to control crime.

Tyler (2004) further argues that legitimacy-based policing has clear advantages for the police and the community. He argues that when people act based upon their feelings of obligation and responsibility, they are engaging in self-regulatory behaviour. Society benefits from such behaviour because it does not depend upon the maintenance of a credible system of deterrence.

Kristina Murphy

Associated Concepts: calls for service, community policing, intelligence-led policing

Key Readings

Skogan, W.G. and Frydl, K. (2004) *Fairness and Effectiveness in Policing: The Evidence.* National Research Council, Washington, D.C.: The National Academies Press.
Suchman, M.C. (1995) 'Managing legitimacy: strategic and institutional approaches', *The Academy of Management Review,* 20 (3): 571–610.

Sunshine, J. and Tyler, T.R. (2003) 'The role of procedural justice and legitimacy in shaping public support for policing', *Law and Society Review,* 37 (3): 513–47.

Tyler, T.R. (2004) 'Enhancing police legitimacy', *The Annals of the American Academy of Political and Social Science,* 593(1): 83–99.

Weber, M. (1947). *The Theory of Social and Economic Organization.* New York: The Free Press.

LOCALISM

Definition

Localism refers to the political and professional philosophy that policing should be organized, managed and governed at the most local level possible. This philosophy is in active tension with the trends towards national, transnational and global forms of policing, particularly to combat organized crime and counter-terrorism and to the universalist, social democratic principles of fairness, equality of treatment and national standards.

Distinctive Features

Although the creation of the Metropolitan Police could be seen as an attempt by Sir Robert Peel and the modernizers to create a more universal model of policing, the local basis of policing in England and Wales and Scotland before Peel was rapidly succeeded by a local pattern of County and borough police forces through the early Victorian era.

This pattern of local forces persisted in policing in the UK right through to the early 1960s, when, despite a series of amalgamations of very small entities, there were still 156 police forces, ranging from the 18 officers of Shetland to 3000 in Lancashire. Moreover, the pattern of governance was local, with local 'watch committees' and 'county police committees having virtually complete control over the local police. The Royal Commission on the Police in 1962 described the powers of the Home Secretary as 'scanty' – a situation that would also have been recognized across the Atlantic where the US system accorded (and, indeed, still accords) primacy to the local. The 1962 Royal Commission's recommendations that created the 'tripartite system' – a shared system of governance between the Home Secretary, Police Authority and Chief Constable – was, therefore, something of a watershed, accompanied as it was by amalgamations that reduced the number of forces to 51.

Over the ensuing decades, UK policing has experienced a gradual drift of power from the local to the national, driven through funding, the need to combat organized crime and terrorism and, most recently, the push to drive up performance through national targets and intervention. This trend towards nationalization has also been felt in a number of other European countries whose systems, as in Holland and Sweden, have traditionally been fairly decentralized. However, as with all swings of the pendulum, there is a point at which the swing reverses, even if the reversal appears to be happening in different ways in the various jurisdictions.

In the UK, the push for 'neighbourhood policing' and the rediscovery of 'localism' by all three major parties has produced a dramatic reinvestment in very local policing and a vigorous debate about the merits of different forms of local governance, ranging from the 'community call to action' (a trigger mechanism that is designed to allow local people to escalate concerns about policing issues through their local council) to proposals for locally elected sheriffs. In Sweden and Holland, after a debate about the potential for much greater nationalization, a similar pressure for local reinvestment has led, in the case of Sweden, to a 30 per cent increase in police numbers to provide more 'local policing'. In the wider Europe, the Napoleonic Gendarmerie model has been adapted to provide more local ownership and, in several countries, such as Spain, a much greater emphasis on local, devolved police forces.

Where the pendulum is swinging less clearly is the US where one of world's most localist policing systems is confronting the post 9/11 challenges of tackling terrorism with over 14,000 police departments. Cases like the 'Washington sniper' (a pair of offenders killed several people in a series of apparently random sniper shootings) have exposed the frailties of a system that relies on local jurisdictions with relatively weak federal systems. In contrast to the investment in local policing in the UK and Europe, the US Government has, instead, largely shifted investment away from the 'COPS' programme of the Clinton government (which provided additional funding for local community officers) and into 'homeland security' with, from the perspective of local chiefs, some problematic consequences for levels of serious street crime (Bratton, 2007).

Evaluation

Bratton's critique of the Federal government goes to the heart of the debate about localism in policing. At its simplest, the question to be asked is 'which is most effective: local policing with local governance or national approaches with national governance?' The answer, where answers can be found, is 'it depends'. One of the few studies (Ostrom, 1973) to look at the relative size of police forces and the relationship to their effectiveness was inconclusive. She found an apparent relationship between the proportion of officers on patrol and the scale of the local force – a small force tended to have a higher level of officers nominally committed to patrol duties and a lower level on managerial and other duties. However, when Langworthy and Hindelang (1983) looked at the data relating to larger forces, they concluded that demerging larger forces into smaller ones would have no benefit because larger forces do different things, for example, a greater emphasis on dealing with serious and organized crime.

In short, neither localism nor amalgamation or nationalization provide a solution to the problems of policing, they are structural answers to choices about what the police should be doing. A police force that is required only to provide a local neighbourhood policing approach can afford to be very local in both its governance and its extent. In contrast, a police force or law enforcement agency that is expected to tackle serious crime, particularly transnational crime which has its origins 'upstream' (in another jurisdiction such as is the case with most drugs and human trafficking offences) will need a much more national organization and far greater linkages to national or supranational governance. The solution in many jurisdictions is to segment by purpose, with local policing organized at a local level and national forces taking on national and international problems.

The other major challenges for localism are the problems of consistency, equality and standards. Even in the US, Congress has recognized through the Violent Crime and Law Enforcement Act 1994 that there has to be some wider regulation which allows federal intervention in local governance. The legislation allows the Justice Department to bring a lawsuit against a department that shows a 'pattern of practice of illegal or unconstitutional police actions' and provides for a system of 'consent decrees' in which local jurisdictions can agree terms for reform under the direction of a federal monitor. In the case of Pittsburgh, the consent decree and subsequent reform programme has produced significant change, which allowed the removal of the federal monitor. Davis et al. concluded (2005: 46) 'a reform process that relies on legitimacy not from local sources, but from a federal court, could succeed'. However, the authors also admitted that the approach ran counter to the localizing trend of the other major reform – community policing – that was being promoted by the same COPS Office of the Justice Department in the US that was driving the consent decree. However, they might equally have commented on the very fact that it was the Justice Department – an arm of federal government – that was promoting a reform that was so very localist in its philosophy, a parallel to the UK Home Office and the Swedish Justice Ministry's promotion of neighbourhood policing.

In all three cases there is a clear recognition that an approach to professionalizing and improving the effectiveness of local policing that relies solely on the mechanism of a local chief working within local governance is unlikely to be sufficient. Above all, given the potential for a localist policing approach to veer off into corruption and inefficiency, a solely localist approach without regulation by a framework of national standards, a regulator (whether this be the Inspectorate in the UK or the Justice Department in the US) and a national improvement agency (the COPS Office in the US or the National Policing Improvement Agency in the UK) appears to be a sub-optimal approach to twenty-first century policing.

Peter Neyroud

Associated Concepts: community policing, neighbourhood watch, problem-orientated policing

Key Readings

Bratton, W. (2007) 'The unintended consequences of September 11th', *Policing: A Journal of Policy and Practice*, 1 (1): 21–25.

Davis, R., Henderson, N.J. and Ortiz, C.W. (2005) 'Can Federal Intervention Bring Lasting Improvement in Local Policing? The Pittsburgh Consent Decree. New York: Vera Institute of Justice', http://www.vera.org/publications.

Langworthy, R.H. and Hindelang, M.J. (1983) 'Effects of police agency size on the use of police employees: a re-examination of Ostrom, Parks and Whitaker', *Police Studies*, 5 (4): 11–19.

McLaughlin, E. (2007) *The New Policing.* London: Sage.

Ostrom, E. (1973) 'Does local community control of police make a difference? Some preliminary findings', *American Journal of Political Science*, 17 (1): 48–76.

Royal Commission on the Police (1962) London: HMSO

M

MANAGERIALISM

Definition

Managerialism has two strands. First, it refers to the introduction of private sector management methods to the public sector. It is variously referred to as 'new public management' or 'new management techniques'. It stresses outputs rather than inputs, specific standards and measures of performance, managing by results and 'doing more with less'. There is a strong emphasis on meeting 'customer' demands. Second, it refers to 'marketization', introducing incentive structures (such as market competition) into public service provision. It emphasizes the disaggregation of bureaucracies, business plans, greater competition through contracting out and quasi-markets and consumer choice.

Distinctive Features

Since the 1980s governments in the major industrialized countries have sought to achieve greater efficiencies in public sector expenditure. New management techniques derived primarily from the private sector have been introduced to restructure public sector agencies along broadly corporate lines. In the past twenty years managerialism has come to dominate public and police administration in most advanced Western nations. The move to reconstruct police services as corporate entities has seen police organizations flatten their structures (primarily through reducing their rank structures) and the introduction of such managerial practices as strategic planning, performance management, performance-based contract employment, decentralized authority for budgetary and resource allocation with an emphasis on local accountability and customer satisfaction. Budgetary considerations forced police organizations to adopt programme management schemes and to decentralize command. As responsibility for planning and budgeting was devolved to frontline managers, budgetary practices, once concerned solely with the management of police numbers, were refocused on the distribution of limited financial resources and operational outcomes. Policing by objectives, financial constraints to encourage efficiency and cost savings, a high performance culture, multi-agency policing and the externalization of non-essential responsibilities have in varying degrees become distinctive features of managerialism.

Such features emphasize 'value for money', economy and efficiency, competition and collaboration and the importance of tasking and results over routine and procedure. These distinctive features are common between advanced Western nations and have been particularly influential in Canada, Australia, New Zealand and the UK. However, there have also been important national and regional variations in the impetus to adopt such principles. While the restructuring process and the accompanying reforms have reflected the principles of managerialism, the context within which such reform has taken place has had variable influence. For example, in the UK, the raft of reforms proposed by the Home

Secretary in the 1990s must be considered against a backdrop of spiralling public expenditure, rising crime rates and perceived inefficiencies in internal management. Similarly, the reorganization of the Dutch police force in 1993 should be considered in the context of national and regional concerns about rising crime, police accountability and a series of police scandals. Kettle (2000) argues that 'New Zealand proved to be the flagship of this global movement' as a New Zealand Labour government embarked upon a quest for a 'smaller and smarter' government. The subsequent reforms and New Zealand's particular version of a free market and neoliberal economics were acclaimed internationally but were perceived at home largely as part of a broader party political agenda and a response to economic crisis. In Australia, where reforms were relatively slow to take effect (largely through the vigorous resistance of senior police officers, rank and file police and their unions), the impetus for reform came in part from revelations of entrenched corruption and police misconduct in successive police inquiries.

Despite these variations, what these and other police organizations in advanced Western countries have in common is a commitment to managerialism. That is, they have opted for a customer-focused model that emphasizes outputs rather than inputs; specific standards and measures of performance; managing by results and 'value for money' and 'doing more with less'. However, not all countries have demonstrated a similar commitment to marketization, although 'contracting out' is common.

In the context of police, outsourcing has become a distinctive feature of marketization. In the UK for example, certain activities have been removed from the control of police services. These include prisoner transport between courts and detention centres, forensic services, vehicle maintenance, police training and the administration of criminal records. Another example of marketization has been the privatization of policing services – particularly security. Thus, private security is more likely to be 'policing' shopping malls

and major sports events than police. Government agencies themselves are more likely now to use security agencies rather than police to provide security for schools, hospitals and courts. Such activity is a direct consequence of managerialism. The rationale is that trained police officers are better employed providing a police service than being involved in activities that can be done by other organizations. The same rationale governs the principles of civilianization whereby sworn police officers are replaced with 'civilian' staff who provide either administrative or specialist support to policing, thus freeing up trained officers with specific powers to focus on operational policing.

Evaluation

New managerial techniques have administratively transformed police organizations and the old ways of doing business are long gone. We can agree that asking police to be more efficient and effective is a reasonable request. Yet as with so many reform processes it is the unintended consequences of reform that become the hallmark of assessment. Managerialism has become the key organizing principle in police organizations. Budgets are tight, business cases are required for extra resources, managers compete for staff and equipment, and a high performance culture ensures that minds are concentrated on what gets measured. Inevitably proactive policing activities and those services that are not identified as core objectives are neglected to a significant degree for more tangible and measurable tasks that will lead to a 'result'. As an example, in many countries community policing as an organizing principle has been constrained by managerialism. Risk averse management strategies and corporate governance are the central drivers of police activity. Community policing is a time-consuming activity that is resource intensive and requires specialist training. Such resources are not available and specialized training is not provided. For such resources and training to be added to law enforcement duties, conflict resolution and general service would add considerably to an organization's budgetary bottom line.

There is a certain irony about the concept of managerialism and its devolution of authority to middle management for budgetary and resource allocations. True decision-making still lies at the heart of police organizations. They retain strong elements of authoritarian, hierarchical governing structures, featuring command and control management systems and are regulated through strict organizational rules and legislation. The performance management and auditing culture, whereby targets and objectives are 'to be met', may have curtailed the discretion and autonomy that senior officers once enjoyed, but it has made hierarchy more effective. Sceptics are prone to comment that the rhetoric of decentralization and devolution has done no more than create scapegoats for when things go wrong. The Compstat structure, evident in most police organizations in some form, has gone some way to confirming such observations. Academic researchers charting the advent of managerialism in Britain are agreed that the governance of policing has become increasingly centralized subject to state control through the managerial calculus of national performance indicators. Others have noted that the proliferation of directives, performance indicators, targets and audit inspections have served to stifle innovation and foster unhealthy competition within organizations. Strict accountability controls have created a risk averse culture. It is unclear whether or not managerialism or indeed marketization as explored here has resulted in increased effectiveness and efficiency. Nor do we know whether consumers are satisfied with the way in which police now do business. Certainly the area in terms of impact is under-researched. We can say with certainty, however, that while police organizations retain strong elements of bureaucracy, the mangerialist imperative is well entrenched.

Jenny Fleming

Associated Concepts: bureaucracy, contractualism, Compstat; multi-agency policing; performance management; privatization, public value

Key Readings

Fleming J. and Rhodes, R.A.W. (2005) 'Bureaucracy, contracts and networks: the unholy trinity and the police', *Australian and New Zealand Journal of Criminology*, 38 (2): August, 192–205.

Fleming, J. and Lafferty, G. (2000) 'New management techniques and restructuring in police organizations', *Policing: An International Journal of Police Strategy and Management*, 23 (2): 154–68.

Gianakis, A.G. and Davis, G.J. (1998) 'Reinventing or repackaging public services? The case of community-orientated policing', *Public Administration Review*, 58 (6): 485–98.

Kettle, D. (2000) *The Global Public Management Revolution: A Report on the Transformation of Governance*. Washington DC: Brookings Institute.

McLaughlin, E. (2007) *The New Policing*. London: Sage Publications.

Rhodes, R.A.W. (1997) *Understanding Governance*. Buckingham, Open University Press.

MASS PRIVATE PROPERTY

See Pluralization; Security

MEDIA

See Law and Order Politics; Postmodern Policing

MISCONDUCT

Definition

Police misconduct is a container concept: you can drop anything in it, competing in diffuseness with police *deviance* and *corruption*. All three are ambiguous but concern the fundamental issue: why do police officers, who are meant to abide by the rules, bend and break them? In a narrow sense misconduct can be associated with breaking internal disciplinary rules. These involve a range of offences including disrespect for the public and/or superiors, lack of punctuality, misuse of police property and unexplained absence while on duty. These non-criminal offences are dealt with in a form of private justice inside the organization. In a broader sense, misconduct overlaps with deviance, which covers almost anything where an officer deviates from a norm; with *corruption* (a sub-category of misconduct); and with other forms of police crime than conventional corruption that include *brutality*, drug-dealing and providing services for criminal gangs (see the Mollen Report [New York, 1994]).

Distinctive Features

In its broad sense misconduct can be understood as serious breaches of duty and trust that reach the media and lead to internal and external sanctioning, including prosecution in the criminal courts. One thinks of violence and brutality, fraud, theft, sexual harassment, gross incompetence, distorting and destroying evidence (sometimes by consuming it), serious negligence, drug use and dealing, perjury and discrimination. Some misconduct takes place externally when officers are off-duty, such as trashing a hotel or getting into a fight when out in a group, or individual misuse of authority as in gaining favours by waving a warrant card. These are highly serious matters which damage the trust people have in the police (or reinforce their distrust), besmirch the reputation of a particular force and can ruin the career of an officer. So why do officers engage in misconduct?

Explanations can range from the individual level, through conduct in units, to the force level and even to the macro-level. In some South American countries, for example, the police collude with politicians in illegality, cooperate with organized criminals, act as vigilantes in death squads and employ excessive violence. This is misconduct at an extreme, systemic level, rarely encountered in Western systems. Yet some murky deeds concerning police, security services and paramilitaries took place in Northern Ireland which led to innocent people being murdered. And the French government has been convicted of torture following a case where a number of police officers publicly intimidated and humiliated a suspect for several days. Serious police misconduct is, then, not confined to South America.

Evaluation

This may well be untypical of routine policing in Western Europe but such affairs suggest that the misconduct may be widespread and to assess this we are reliant on reliable information about incidents – from the media, academic research, internal reports and commissions of inquiry. These incidents do raise three crucial features of all forms of police misconduct. First, the structural nature of policing, with high autonomy and discretion, provides unique opportunities for misconduct; second, police officers have considerable advantages and skills in covering their tracks, aiding them in avoiding exposure and evading prosecution; and there is an occupational ideology justifying rule-bending. Let me turn, then, to a number of explanations along the spectrum of misconduct.

First, when policing is seen simply as 'work' there are a range of practices which make work enjoyable or easier but are against regulations or laws. Every ethnography of policing recounts numerous instances of rule-breaking: unnecessary speeding in the patrol car, drinking in out-of-bounds bars, leaving the official area, conducting private business on duty, sexual shenanigans, indulging in perks and free meals, fiddling expenses, appropriating confiscated property and just 'goofing off' (Manning, 1977). Low level policing was traditionally the preserve of young men and at times there is the boisterous, bawdy style of all-male preserves, like the army. On a night duty, when there is literally nothing to do, officers may 'play around' simply to pass the time. Operational policing has an element of 'fun' and practical jokes involving rule-breaking which can, nevertheless, have serious consequences if things go wrong (say an accident with injuries when speeding unnecessarily).

Another work-related feature is when legally regulated duties and obligations, with regard to arrests, prisoners and evidence, become commodities so that prisoners are bartered as part of informal bargaining, arrests are geared to financial rewards ('collars for dollars' in US parlance), evidence is tampered with and cases are sold for a price.

Second, related to this is the occupational code of policing which sets out guidelines for informal behaviour and justifies breaches of rules (Reuss-Ianni and Ianni, 1983). For instance, police often have a strong sense of territory and a group 'getting above itself' may encounter reprisals to restore balance in the police perception of social order by showing who is 'the boss' on their patch. When the police took a hammering in London's Brixton Riots of 1981, they retaliated through officers out of uniform beating people in a form of rough justice. The police code on rough justice may also dictate that an assailant who injures an officer will be tackled 'robustly' on arrest, or following arrest in the cells, by fellow-officers. A drug dealer who is never caught in possession of drugs may be set up simply because, under the code, he is 'due' and 'deserves' it. It can scarcely be elevated to *'noble cause'* but is just how informal business is instrumentally conducted according to some feeling of just deserts (Punch, 1985).

In its extreme form the code may well justify setting people up for long jail sentences by tampering with evidence, eliciting false confessions and lying in court; rationalize the stealing of money and drugs from dealers and excuse excessive violence against a suspect (such as the vicious attack on Louima in New York). The miscarriages of justice involving suspected Irish Republican Army (IRA) terrorists in the UK are prime examples. There may be a moral tone to this of noble cause, that the ends justify the means, but the danger is that the 'crusaders' slide down the slippery slope to venality, drug use and addiction, stealing of money and recycling of drugs, gratuitous violence against the vulnerable, riding shotgun for gang, rape and even murder. That 'slope' can start with illicit

initiation rituals, bullying, off-duty drinking and drug bouts and macho behaviour leading to manipulative gangs of 'cowboys' who intimidate supervisors, create autonomy for themselves, break the rules and start to revel in misconduct (like the hedonism of some criminals). Misconduct *in extremis* is when officers become full-time criminals (Leuci, 2004).

In short, policing provides rich and enticing opportunities for misconduct and the occupational culture justifies some of it. The practices can range from the frivolous, and the low level rule-bending to be found in most organizations, to the most grave. Police can deprive citizens of their liberty, and even of their life, and there is consequently a strong assumption that they who enforce the law should both abide by the law and be held accountable for any transgressions. It is particularly serious, then, if misconduct is in some way condoned by supervisors, colluded in by senior officers, is covered up from scrutiny and its victims have no redress. This is a perversion of the idea of policing in a modern democracy.

Of importance, then, is to place the misconduct in an institutional context where, what may be being passed off as low level incidents or 'bad apples', can be associated with informal or even formal policies from above (or outside). Are there informal quotas for arrests with a blind eye turned to due process; is there a record of excessive violence in a particular squad or force with regard to making arrests, prisoners in custody or public order situations; and is there a culture of cover-up, unwillingness to testify against fellow officers ('the blue wall of silence') and of evidence incriminating officers disappearing?

It is an illusion to think that it is possible to run a rule-bound institution like the police with total compliance. In some respects policing and misconduct go together. Officers are routinely exposed to adversarial situations that can generate aggression and violence, where they can make an error of judgement and overreact. They may face constant inducements from legal and illegal establishments to bend the rules and face powerful pressures from colleagues to break them. This is not to condone the practices but rather to state that misconduct is a permanent occupational hazard. To minimize misconduct requires a concerted effort of solid, first-line supervisors; committed senior officers who raise issues of integrity; proactive 'professional standards' units with teeth and resources; strong external oversight like the Police Ombudsman in Northern Ireland; a watchful and fearless media; and politicians who are not afraid to grasp the nettle of police misconduct. And, last but certainly not least, a strong culture of professional competence, integrity and service to the public among police officers.

Maurice Punch

Associated Concepts: accountability, civilian oversight, culture, ethical policing, legitimacy

Key Readings

Leuci, R. (2004) *All the Centurions.* New York: HarperCollins.

Manning, P. K. (1977) *Police Work.* Cambridge, MA: MIT Press.

Mollen Commission (1994) *The City of New York Commission to Investigate Allegations of Corruption and the Anti-Corruption Procedures of the Police Department.* New York: City of New York.

Punch, M. (1985) *Conduct Unbecoming.* London: Sage.

Reuss-Ianni, E. R. and Ianni, R. (1983) 'Street cops and management cops: the two cultures of policing', in M. Punch (ed.) *Control in the Police Organization.* Cambridge, MA: MIT Press.

MULTI-AGENCY POLICING

Definition

The coordinated response of public sector agencies to address crime, social disorder and community safety. Often referred to as inter-agency policing or partnership policing.

Distinctive Features

Multi-agency cooperation is a distinctive feature of managerialism and in the past decade has become the cornerstone in crime prevention activities and community safety initiatives. The managerialism discourse maintains that cost-effective and practical solutions to a wide range of economic and social problems (including crime) can be found if good management principles are followed. Such ideas have come to dominate the management and operational work of the police particularly where cooperation and collaboration are seen to be beneficial for the prevention and reduction of crime. Although some commentators perceive multi-agency policing as a 'corporatist policing exercise' aimed at policing whole communities and neighbourhoods rather than individuals, others have seen the move to partnership policing as a practical solution to multifaceted problems. It is generally agreed that police cannot tackle crime on their own – there is a recognition that most crime activity and palliative solutions are linked with other policy areas. For example, transport, education, housing and urban planning agencies are seen as all being well-placed to play a useful role in crime prevention. Collaboration is seen as a way of pooling resources and information and coordinating activities to address specific issues – in line with the 'doing more with less ethos'. Ordinarily these multi-agency initiatives are coordinated from the top-down. Responsibility for the coordination and running of the partnership is usually vested in one agency and in line with managerialist principles, such initiatives are organized around mission statements, performance indicators, objectives, outcomes and evaluation.

The multi-agency policing approach has been a feature of policing in the US where police are encouraged to promote multi-agency problem-solving agencies based on data collected from various databases across municipal departments. They then must consider how to use such data in collaboration with municipal ordinances and civil injunctions to address specific issues. For example, in a bid to address street crime and vagrancy, police used zoning restrictions and property regulations to rid neighbourhoods of 'adult' shops, pimps, prostitutes, homeless vagrants and drug dealers.

In the UK, working through partnerships and multi-agency policing is an important component of the police agenda. Managing other agencies in crime prevention work is formally encouraged through policy initiatives and legislation. In 1998, the Crime and Disorder Act made working in partnerships generally (not just with other public sector agencies) a statutory requirement for police and local authorities. Police are required to collaborate with public agencies (and others if required) to establish and promote community safety strategies. Importantly, the legislation allows police and local authorities to share information with other agencies in the interests of such collaboration. As a consequence, police managers are expected to demonstrate the success of such partnerships and their efforts are formally assessed.

New Zealand government officials based its policy on inter-agency partnerships to facilitate crime prevention initiatives on the French example of the *Conseil National de Prevention de la Delinquance*. While the New Zealand model did not emulate France's bipartisan membership approach, it was considered a major policy initiative and infrastructure, funding, objectives and pilots were all formally put in place.

In Australia, there is a strong commitment to collaboration and multi-agency policing. This commitment is not, as in the UK, enshrined in legislation and official policy but rather promoted through publicly available annual reports and strategic plans. There is no official mandate to work with other agencies and there are no formal policy parameters within which the various police organizations work. There is no extra funding for such activity and where police organizations engage in such collaboration they do so for the most part within existing funding arrangements. In some jurisdictions, senior police managers have been formally encouraged, through employment contracts, to pursue multi-agency partnership approaches to crime prevention. However, for the most part

such activity is not a strong performance measurement.

Evaluation

Multi-agency policing strategies are now commonplace across many contemporary states. In most cases these strategies are not formally evaluated and it is unclear just how successful the various initiatives are in terms of crime prevention and crime reduction. What we can say is that police organizations are much more likely nowadays to collaborate with other agencies in pursuit of their objectives.

However, as many commentators have pointed out, even where there is a collective will to engage in such partnerships there are a number of constraints that work against the success of such collaboration. Academic research has highlighted the importance of trust and reciprocity to successful partnerships. They have also demonstrated the difficulties of developing and sustaining that trust. Police officers interact with other agencies as part of their everyday work. That work is not always a positive experience. Other agencies' 9–5 schedule, lack of resources and a perceived willingness to 'pass the buck' often result in police officers feeling (rightly or wrongly) resentful of their own full time role in the community. Other researchers have commented on the difficulties of getting agencies to collaborate, arguing that departments are more likely to use crime prevention as an opportunity to illicit more funds from government for their own organizational requirements. Trust is also difficult to build when representatives are continuously moving around their organization, passing their representative role to someone else. Staff movement is often an issue for police officers who are deployed or transferred for a number of reasons. Such staff turnover undermines the development and consolidation of trust relations in potential partnerships.

Effective collaboration can also be constrained by differential power relationships between agencies. There will be a number of different reasons why agencies wish to participate in such initiatives with accompanying differences in what resources they are prepared to share and what access to data they are willing to allow. Information sharing and different understandings about what constitutes privacy are difficult issues to circumnavigate. Not all jurisdictions have enacted legislation like the UK to allow police and local authorities to share information in the interests of multi-agency work (although it should be noted that the UK legislation is not without its problems). While the various representatives may have shared goals in the context of the partnership, each participant brings with them different cultural understandings of the problem. They bring divergent views, experiences and attitudes to the forum which can often undermine capacity and sustainability in the long term.

Perhaps from a police organizational perspective the main constraint around multi-agency policing is building it into the police organizational structure successfully. In the UK policy and legislation have made the task easier. During the 1990s, in the US federal funding also made partnership work a relative priority. In other jurisdictions however, police struggle to fit such activity into a schedule that does not measure multi-agency work in the same way as it does arrests, traffic infringement notices and clear up rates. Priority is given to what is considered a priority and measurable. Command and control is still very much a feature of crisis-driven organizations like the police. There is an inherent contradiction between a bureaucratic mentality dominated by rules and process, hierarchical subordination with the emphasis on competition and performance assessment and multi-agency policing that relies on trust, resource sharing and collegial decision-making. It is difficult sometimes for officers to gauge the importance of working with other agencies against meeting targets and community expectations on the street.

Formal assessments of multi-agency policing projects are rare although formal evaluation reports and case study-based papers have provided some information about how these partnerships work and to what extent they achieve sustainable aims. There are obviously some multi-agency initiatives that have worked well and have been sustained over time. Regardless of the success rate, however, the multi-agency partnership has broad appeal to politicians and the community. After all there is a logic about such work that suggests it might just be the answer to crime and social disorder.

Jenny Fleming

Associated Concepts: bureaucracy, community safety, crime prevention, culture, managerialism, performance management, problem-oriented policing, security networks, third party policing

Key Readings

Bradley, T. and Walters, R. (2002) 'The managerialization of crime prevention and community safety', in G. Hughes, E. McLaughlin and J.Muncie (eds) *Crime Prevention and Community Safety: New Directions*. London: Sage Publications.

Crawford, A. (1997) *The Local Governance of Crime: Appeals to Community and Partnerships*. Oxford: Oxford University Press.

Fleming, J. and Rhodes, R.A.W. (2005) 'Bureaucracy, contracts and networks: the unholy trinity and the police', *Australian and New Zealand Journal of Criminology*, 38 (2): 192–205.

Fleming, J. (2006) 'Working through networks: the challenge of partnership policing', in J. fleming, and J. Wood, (eds) *Fighting Crime Together: The Challenges of Policing and Security Networks*. Sydney: University of New South Wales Press.

McLaughlin, E. (2006) *The New Policing*. London: Sage Publications.

NATIONAL SECURITY

See Criminal Investigation; Cross-Border Policing; Homeland Security; High Policing; Human Security; Intelligence Agency; Security; Security Networks; Transnational Policing

NEIGHBOURHOOD WATCH

Definition

Neighbourhood watch (also known as block watch, apartment watch, home watch, citizen alert and community watch) is a crime prevention programme that aims to reduce residential burglary by encouraging neighbours to look out for suspicious activities and report these to the police. It is intended that increased neighbourhood surveillance will deter potential offenders by altering their perceptions of the area and decision making. It might also reduce crime by enhancing informal social control and improving police detection.

Distinctive Features

There is some debate about the origins of neighbourhood watch. It is widely reported that neighbourhood watch started in the US with the Community Crime Prevention Project launched in Seattle in September, 1973. However, there are several other schemes that predate this. The Block Association of Philadelphia was formed in 1971 and was based on neighbours meeting at monthly intervals to discuss methods of watching each other's homes and exchanging information on home security. One of the earliest schemes recorded in the US was established in Oakland in 1966 under the name of Home Alert. Participants in the Home Alert schemes were expected to attend regular meetings, display window stickers, mark their property and to act as the 'eyes and ears' of the police. It is also widely believed that the first neighbourhood watch in the UK was the Home Watch programme implemented in July 1982 in Cheshire. The design of the programme was similar to the North American schemes and included neighbours looking out for suspicious people, property marking and home security surveys. However, there is evidence of earlier schemes. Elements of neighbourhood watch can also be found in the crime prevention programme, launched in 1943 by the Metropolitan Police, under the heading of 'Good Neighbours Can Prevent Crime' which encouraged neighbours to look out for and report suspicious incidents to the police. Another rival first scheme is the one launched in Hampshire in 1978 under the title of Home Watch. The programme contained several elements including improving home security, reducing signs of occupancy and involving neighbours in mutual protection (Bennett, 1990).

Since the establishment of schemes in the US and UK there has been an expansion of neighbourhood watch programmes in other countries around the world. Many of these schemes are based strongly on the programmes established in the US and in the UK. The first neighbourhood watch scheme in Australia is reported to have been launched in Victoria in 1983. Neighbourhood watch was established in Canada at about the same time. Neighbourhood watch in South Africa was first established in 1985 and in Taiwan in 1989. The first schemes in Belgium were implemented in 1994.

Neighbourhood watch can be implemented as a stand-alone programme or as part of a comprehensive package. The typical package is sometimes referred to as the 'big three' and includes neighbourhood watch, property-marking and home security surveys. Some programmes include other elements such as increased regular foot patrols, citizen patrols, educational programmes for young people, and victim support services. Neighbourhood watch schemes vary in terms of the size of the area covered. Some of the earlier schemes in the US and the UK were based on areas covering just a few households. Some of the smallest schemes were the 'cocoon' neighbourhood watch programmes in Rochdale in England covering just one dwelling and its immediate neighbours. Some recent schemes cover many thousand households. Neighbourhood watch schemes can be both public and police initiated. Schemes launched in the UK during the early period of a programme tended to be police initiated, whereas more recent schemes tend to be launched at the request of the public. In the US, block watches are usually run by a block captain who is responsible to a block coordinator or block organizer. The block coordinator acts as the liaison person to the local police department. Neighbourhood watch schemes in the UK often include street coordinators (equivalent to block captains) and area coordinators (equivalent to the block organizer).

Evaluation

One of the first published evaluations of neighbourhood watch schemes in the UK was of the Home Watch programme implemented in 1982 in Cheshire. This found that burglary in the area reduced from 19 burglaries in the pre-test period to 2 burglaries in the post-test period. The author concluded that Home Watch in Cheshire was one of the most successful crime prevention initiatives ever. One of the first evaluations of neighbourhood watch in the US was the Seattle programme implemented in Washington. The research concluded that burglary rates among participants in the scheme reduced by over one half compared with no change among non-participants. The authors concluded that the programme was successful in reducing the number of burglary victimizations among neighbourhood watch participants.

There are several reviews of evaluations of neighbourhood watch programmes. One of the earliest conducted in the US summarized the results of nearly forty community crime prevention programmes. Most of these included elements of neighbourhood watch. The majority of studies were conducted by police departments or included data from police departments. Nearly all found that neighbourhood watch areas were associated with favourable changes in crime. However, most of the evaluations were described as 'weak' in terms of their ability to guard against threats to validity.

Another study reviews the effectiveness of community watch programmes selected only evaluations with the strongest research designs (Sherman, 1997). The results of these evaluations were largely negative. The author concluded, 'The oldest and best-known community policing program, Neighbourhood Watch, is ineffective at preventing crime'.

The most recent review of the effectiveness of neighbourhood watch was a systematic review of evaluations conducted as part of the Campbell Collaboration in Crime and Justice (Bennett, Holloway and Farrington, 2007). The review included only evaluations that matched the selection criteria, which included the type of programme implemented, the outcomes measured, and the quality of the methods used. In total, 43 evaluations were included in a narrative review and 18 of these were selected for a meta-analysis. The results of the narrative review showed that the findings were mixed. About half the studies found that neighbourhood watch areas had lower levels of crime than the comparison areas and about half found that comparison areas had lower levels of crime than the neighbourhood watch areas. However, the results of the meta-analysis of all studies combined indicated that neighbourhood watch areas were associated with lower levels of crime than the comparison areas. The review concluded that, while neighbourhood watch was shown to be effective across all evaluation combined, the results of individual schemes were variable.

Trevor Bennett and Katy Holloway

Associated Concepts: community engagement, localism, public reassurance, responsibilization

Key Readings

Bennett, T.H. (1990) *Evaluating Neighbourhood Watch*. Aldershot: Gower.

Bennett, T.H., Holloway, K. and Farrington, D.P. (2007) 'Does neighbourhood watch reduce crime? A systematic review and meta-analysis', *Journal of Experimental Criminology*, 1 (4): 459–87.

Fleming, J. (2005) *'Working Together: Neighbourhood Watch, Reassurance Policing and the Potential of Partnerships'*, Trends and Issues in Crime and Criminal Justice No. 303, Canberra: Australian Institute of Criminology.

Sherman, L.W. (1997) 'Policing for crime prevention', in L.W. Sherman, D.C. Gottfredson, D.L MacKenzie, J. Eck, P. Reuter and S. Bushway (eds), *Preventing Crime: What Works, What Doesn't, What's Promising*. Washington, D.C.: US Office of Justice Programmes.

Sims L. (2001) *Neighbourhood Watch: Findings from the 2000 British Crime Survey*. Findings 150. London: Home Office.

OFFENDER PROFILING

See Criminal Investigation

ORDER MAINTENANCE

Definition

'Order maintenance' is the aspect of policing concerned with regulating the fair use of public spaces. Examples include the enforcement of rules that restrict public drinking, noise pollution, public indecency, verbal harassment, and aggressive panhandling. The term is often used in a broader sense, as a residual category that refers to most everything the police do that does not involve enforcing the core elements of the criminal law – a task that Michael Banton dubbed 'peacekeeping'. But it is useful to distinguish order maintenance as the aspect of peacekeeping concerned with the regulation of public behaviour.

Distinctive Features

Order maintenance has always been part of policing, but the phrase itself came into widespread usage after the publication of James Q. Wilson's *Varieties of Police Behavior*. Wilson defined order maintenance broadly, as the attempt to regulate behaviour 'that disturbs or threatens to disturb the public peace or that involves face-to-face conflict among two or more persons' (1968: 16), but Wilson particularly emphasized the regulation of behaviour

in public spaces. Wilson argued that this task was central to the police officer's role. In most cities, police officers encounter few clear violations of core provisions of the criminal law but many occasions for order maintenance. When they do so their task is not so much to enforce the law as to handle a disorderly situation using whatever means are available to them. In this respect, police seek to maintain a condition – public order – that the law never explicitly defines. The law serves as a constraint and a potential resource for order maintenance, but it provides little positive guidance about when and how to intervene. As Egon Bittner observed in an article that heavily influenced Wilson, 'virtually any set of norms could be used in this manner, provided that they sanction relatively common forms of behaviour' (1967:201).

This perspective raises the question of where the authority for order maintenance derives from. Bittner attributed the existence of both law enforcement and order maintenance roles in policing to what he called the 'dual patronage' of police in all democratic countries: their law enforcement role derived from the judiciary, while their order maintenance role derived from the executive branch. In practice, however, his study of peacekeeping in several skid row neighbourhoods found that informal occupational norms rather than any explicit directives from the executive defined the meaning of 'order' for police. Other scholars argue that community norms do, or should; define the legitimate scope for order maintenance, though Wilson's own research found that the influence of the political community on police behaviour was relatively limited.

Although Bittner and Wilson argue convincingly that the law does not direct order maintenance to the same extent that it directs law enforcement, the legal basis for order maintenance should not be discounted entirely. The relevant legal framework varies widely across countries, and it has changed substantially within some of them over time. British common law, for example, itemizes a wide variety of specific behaviours that qualify as disorderly, while through the 1960s most jurisdictions in the US located the legal basis for order maintenance in a few general statutes prohibiting broad offences such as 'disorderly conduct', 'public intoxication', and 'vagrancy' (Force, 1972).

Changes to the US system since that time illustrate the need to qualify Bittner and Wilson's analysis. The statutory framework for order maintenance in the US came under attack in the 1960s, as critics argued that these statutes served as exclusionary tools for driving out undesirables, that they unfairly enforced a middle class definition of virtue, and that they gave police too much discretion and thereby opened the door to discriminatory enforcement. (The latter concern was not an abstract one, as police in some cities used broad statutes for offences like breach of the peace to harass civil rights activists.) Many of these statutes were eventually struck down as unconstitutionally vague. Although many were succeeded by new, more narrowly tailored statutes (Livingston, 1998), this legal transformation had a fundamental effect on American policing. For example, while the categories of drunkenness, disorderly conduct, and vagrancy accounted for 44 per cent of all arrests reported in the 1965 Uniform Crime Reports, by 2005 that share was less than 9 per cent. Whether the nature and amount of order maintenance activity also declined is impossible to verify (since order maintenance does not necessarily end in arrest and may invoke other laws when it does), though few observers doubt that it did.

Although this episode illustrates the influence that law does exert over order maintenance,

Bittner and Wilson's basic insight – that order maintenance never amounts to a simple application of the law – remains correct. Although the law *authorizes* action against more-or-less specific kinds of disorder, and although these legal provisions have become more specific over time, police still have considerable discretion in determining whether to invoke the law when its requirements are met. Usually police maintain order without invoking the law, though the threat of arrest typically lies in the background and gives force to their informal interventions.

Evaluation

Order maintenance has been at the centre of controversies about the scope and limits of the police role since the inception of modern police forces, and the basic concerns have remained remarkably constant over time. In particular, the concerns that motivated legal challenges to the US statutes during the 1960s remain important today. Order maintenance is still shot through with discretion that may be abused, it still raises contentious questions about the standards of order that should prevail in a community, and it still implicates important concerns about civil liberties.

Recent debates have paid particular attention to the dilemmas posed by the homeless. On one hand, public concern about the behaviour of some homeless people has motivated heightened attention to order maintenance in many cities. In several cases (such as the New York City subway system during the 1980s and San Francisco's city parks in the early 1990s), the level of disorder associated with some segments of the homeless population began to undermine the viability of important public spaces. On the other hand, the demands made in the name of public order bear especially heavily on the homeless, whose condition is defined by the fact that they have no unconditional access to a private space of their own. Many norms of public order do not prohibit behaviour outright but attempt to restrict it to private spaces. (Rules against public drinking, sleeping in public, and public drinking are examples.)

Those norms implicitly assume that residents have access to private spaces they can retreat to, and as a result they place heavy and in some cases literally impossible burdens on the homeless.

Both the general problems of discrimination and civil liberties and the specific versions of those problems as they bear on the homeless make order maintenance a difficult and contentious aspect of policing. These challenges cannot, however, be avoided by attempting to abolish order maintenance, which is an unavoidable and ultimately necessary part of the police role. More promising ways of addressing these concerns attempt to advance the cause of police professionalism and to craft careful guidance and oversight for order maintenance practice. Many scholars, such as Livingston (1997), argue that this oversight task cannot be assigned solely to the courts but that political and administrative control is also essential. Kelling and Coles (1996) describe efforts to develop political and administrative guidelines in several US cities, and Thacher (2004) argues that policing scholarship should contribute to this movement through empirically-based ethical analysis.

Apart from concerns about the potential for abuse, order maintenance has also been attacked as trivial by comparison with crime control. One response to this concern has been to try to demonstrate that disorder and crime are linked (as in Wilson and Kelling's 'broken windows' theory. The debate about this empirical link between disorder and crime has in fact emerged as the major framework for debating the merits of order maintenance policing in policing scholarship today. Thacher (2004) has criticized this emphasis, arguing that it has diverted attention from the intrinsic importance of public order. Although individual incidents of disorder may appear trivial when compared with individual incidents of serious crime, it does not follow that order maintenance is unimportant. In fact much wrongdoing that clearly justifies government intervention appears trivial when individual acts are viewed in isolation: Pollution, littering, and petty vandalism

are all examples. The problem in these cases is that if many people engaged in these activities, important public interests would be threatened. As a result, society establishes fair terms of cooperation that require everyone to share the burdens of self-restraint. Many examples of disorder can be understood in this way.

David Thacher

Associated Concepts: anti-social behaviour, broken windows theory, professionalization, public order policing

Key Readings

Bittner, E. (1967) 'The police on skid-row: a Study of peace keeping', *American Sociological Review,* 32 (5): 699–715.

Kelling, G. and Coles, C. (1996) *Fixing Broken Windows: Restoring Order and Reducing Crime in Our Communities.* New York: Free Press.

Force, R. (1972). 'Decriminalization of breach of the peace statutes: a nonpenal approach to order maintenance', *Tulane Law Review,* 46, (3): 367–493.

Livingston D. (1997) 'Police discretion and the quality of life in public places: courts, communities, and the new policing', *Columbia Law Review,* 97 (3):

Thacher D. (2004) 'Order maintenance reconsidered', *Journal of Criminal Law and Criminology,* 94 (2): 381–414.

Wilson J.Q. *Varieties of Police Behavior.* Cambridge: Harvard University Press.

ORGANIZED CRIME

Definition

In 2000, 124 states signed the Palermo United Nations Convention on transnational organized crime acknowledging that such crime accounted for up to 5 per cent of the World's Gross National Product. This included the broad definitions of organized crime.

However, each country interprets these individually, defining organized crime with a mixture of its own laws and international criteria (Reichel, 2005). Typically, a crime is classified as 'organized' if certain characteristics are present, concerning collaboration between the actors involved, duration of their activity, the exercise of power and use of control methods, the seriousness of the crime and a potential or actual international context (Lewis, 2007).

Within these broad parameters, organized crime can cover a large number of specific crime types. A study of 15 countries (Savona et al., 2005) identified the following; crimes against children, people smuggling, trafficking in women, thefts of cultural property works or art, cross border vehicle crime, drugs trafficking/cultivation, financial crime, identity card and identity theft, denial of service attacks and environmental crime. This study also confirmed that measurement of organized crime is poor, involving proxy measures and rudimentary counting structures

There are very blurred boundaries to these definitions, particularly in the extent to which organized crime is associated with the activities and the funding of terrorist groups and how governments' actions against terrorism since 2001 have driven more of these groups into organized criminal activity (Sanderson, 2004.) It is also difficult to classify such actions as the corruption and election rigging seen in many developing states which have many of the characteristics of organized crime and are just as likely to limit economic growth.

Distinctive Features

The police in most countries now combat crimes by dividing them into different 'levels', for example, those dealt with by local police forces, crimes needing cross-border cooperation, and serious or organized crime needing a national, federal or international response.

Typically, countries have developed new policing structures to cope with organized crime developments. Examples are the setting up of the Australian Crime Commission, the UK's Serious Organized Crime Agency (SOCA), the US Department of Homeland Security (DHC), or the slightly different groups set up in developing countries, such as the anti-corruption commissions set up in Kenya, Mauritius and Tanzania.

An important characteristic of the activities of all these structures is that they have developed wider tools in their armoury than the traditional police collection of evidence to bring offenders to justice. Such tools vary by country but often include: the use of new technology in investigation (access to records of mobile phone use, e-mail use, bank accounts, car hire, covert actions); other surveillance activities; tough powers for seizing criminal assets, with the onus transferred to the organized criminal to show he obtained his possessions legally; tighter laws on money laundering; sharing information with other countries; and tougher use of regulatory powers (for example, registration, deportation) to disrupt potential criminal groups.

Some of these policing structures are short term, and relate to the need to police international conferences, sporting events or the Olympic Games (for example, Bali, Beijing, London). These are likely to be the focus of large numbers of protestors or the targets of terrorist attacks and international gangs and require different techniques of policing such as quarantining areas or heavy electronic surveillance.

Such organizations also support victims of organized criminal activities, often in an attempt to encourage such people to give evidence against their abusers, such as children or women trafficked for sexual or employment purposes, people supplying human body parts, or victims of Internet abuse who can now report such activity to a virtual police station.

At the International level, law enforcement bodies assist national forces with crimes that need extra-state help in investigation: examples include Interpol, which globally provides assistance on crimes against children, trafficking in women, people smuggling, thefts of cultural property works or art, vehicle crime drugs, financial and environmental crime and identity theft; Europol, which makes a significant contribution to EU law enforcement by improving cooperation of authorities to combat terrorism, unlawful drug trafficking and other serious organized crime; and the Financial Action Task Force (FATF), which globally develops policies against money laundering and terrorist funding.

A common characteristic of these and similar bodies is the way they are developing their structures and ways of working to understand and to counteract the influence of the organized crime and terrorist networks that have developed in the last 20 years. Such 'dark networks' are growing in numbers and complexity and form a greater challenge than has previously been recognized (Raab and Milward, 2005) The need for new techniques to counter these threats has already been recognized but further tools will need to be developed, for example in developing the ability to counter activities within 'failed states' which act as sources for illegal drugs, guns, terrorist activities, human trafficking, etc.

There is also a growing need for enabling arrests, the taking of evidence, and other judicial procedures in states other than where the offence was committed. And, for some offences, such as those which are Internet-based, the geographical base of the offence is not territorial. Mechanisms for coping with such judicial processes are in their infancy, although countries such as those within the European Union have developed, via agencies such as Europol and Eurojust, strong polices to enhance the effectiveness of states to deal with the investigation and prosecution of serious cross-border and organized crime.

Evaluation

Organized crime is not new. For many years some crimes have been committed through criminals working together or with the connivance of some higher authority. However, recent developments in illegal markets, technology, transport, migration and commercial structures have increased the number of such crimes, the likelihood they have been organized in another state, or that the criminal will escape to another state afterwards.

Policing of organized crime, as a consequence, has evolved as governments and organizations respond to changes in way organized crime is developing. It has become essentially a pragmatic response from the authorities, rather than driven by a more fundamental understanding of the criminological aspects of organized crime.

Individual countries have responded to the actions of organized criminals by setting up new structures but some commentators feel there is an inherent tension between the power and resources of such new national policing bodies and the more traditional police forces whose task it is to police the cities where organized criminals work. Metropolitan police forces will not turn a blind eye to organized crimes committed on their patch but national organized crime police have been slow in setting up the necessary networks with local police. It will be necessary to closely monitor this as the organized criminal will soon exploit any tensions, such as between the Spanish National Police and the Madrid Municipal Police, between SOCA and the London Metropolitan Police, or between the Anti-Corruption Commission in Kenya and the National Police Force (Lewis, 2007).

Part of this will depend on the profile maintained by the new police authorities. Forces in individual states tend to maintain a high profile, whereas organizations such as Europol, FATF and Interpol mainly keep a low public profile, tending to work in the background on essential, but non-headline grabbing initiatives such as terrorism and organized crime infrastructure.

Despite all these new structures, especially at an international level, the development of effective policing in detecting organized crime is likely to lag behind the ability of the criminal to disrupt modern societies. Both national jurisdictions and transnational bodies have proved very slow at changing their structures and moving resources to where they are best deployed, whether this is disrupting supply routes for illegal traffic in drugs, money, stolen goods or human beings; or dealing with the organized criminal when caught. Many states, especially in developing countries, still have politicized police forces, existing primarily to support their government, rather than to combat crime, whether organized or not.

Throughout the world, modern societies are vulnerable to the people trafficker, money launderer, urban terrorist or denial of service IT attacker. Policing of organized crime needs to develop faster than it has to counter the likely future threats that will emerge.

Chris Lewis

Associated Concepts: cross-border policing, drugs, economic crime, environmental crime, transnational policing, terrorism

Key Readings

Lewis, C. (2007) 'International structures and transnational crime', in T. Williamson, (ed.) *Handbook of Criminal Investigation.* Cullompton, Devon: Willan Publishing.

Raab, J. and Millward, H.B. (2003) 'Dark networks as problems', *Journal of Public Administration Research and Theory.* 13 (4): 413–39.

Reichel, P. (2005) *Handbook of Transnational Crime and Justice.* London: Sage.

Sanderson, T. (2004) *'Transnational terror and organized crime: Blurring the Lines',* SAIS Review 24:1, 49–61.

Savona, E., Lewis, C. and Vettori, B. (2005) *Developing an EU Statistical Apparatus for Measuring Organized Crime, Assessing its Risk and Evaluating Organized Crime Policies,* Trento/Milan: Transcrime, http://transcrime.cs.unitn.it/tc/419.php.

P

PACIFIC POLICING

Definition

The Pacific comprises the broad cultural areas of Polynesia (Tonga, Samoa, American Samoa, Tokelau, Niue, Tuvalu, Wallis and Futuna, Cook Islands and the islands of French Polynesia), Melanesia (Papua New Guinea, Solomon Islands, Fiji, Vanuatu and New Caledonia) and Micronesia (the Federated States of Micronesia, the Republic of the Marshall Islands, the Republic of Palau, Commonwealth of the Northern Mariana Islands, the Republic of Nauru, the Republic of Kiribati, the Territory of Guam and the Territory of Wake Island). The region encompasses independent states, sovereign states with Compacts of Free Association (e.g., Palau, the Federated States of Micronesia) and overseas territories (e.g., New Caledonia, Wallis and Futuna, which are overseas territories of France).

Each of the Pacific island nations has a formal legal system based upon a Western model (be it common law or civil), including law enforcement agencies. Throughout the region, formal legal systems operate alongside informal mechanisms of social control, commonly known as 'traditional' or 'customary' legal systems.

Distinctive Features

Distinctive features of policing in the Pacific cannot be disentangled from the broader socio-cultural context in which law enforcement occurs. As elsewhere in the world, contemporary Pacific island nations face the challenge of integrating local systems of social order with Western legal orders, which were introduced during colonization and maintained after independence. This is a challenge not only for Pacific island nations, but also for larger neighbours such as Australia and New Zealand, which view the promotion of Western policing models as a means of encouraging regional security.

Throughout the region, island nations are geographically dispersed, of comparatively small size, and distant from global markets. Consequently, the island nations have fragile economies. This impacts greatly upon government service delivery, including services provided by the law and justice sector. Many Pacific police institutions – particularly in Melanesia – are chronically under resourced, rendering them unable to offer adequate financial recompense to employees who lack basic necessities such as habitable accommodation, transport and stationery. This makes the performance of basic police tasks (such as attending to complaints) difficult and provides a potential environment for various levels of corruption. In addition, limited infrastructure and communications impede the penetration of police into rural areas, where the vast majority of Pacific populations are concentrated.

Pacific Island societies are characterized by group (e.g., clan and tribe) rather than individual sociality. In the absence of social security provided by the state, in many Pacific island countries people rely upon kin for survival. Consequently, people entertain ongoing reciprocal relationships with kin, both outside of and within the formal structures of the state. To external observers, the outcomes of expressed allegiances are often labelled corruption and nepotism, yet to many Pacific Islanders it is culturally appropriate behaviour. This poses a variety of challenges to Pacific police forces, which are attempting to enforce criminal laws based upon the impartial administration of justice to individual citizens.

The independence of Pacific states has only recently been achieved (indeed, a number of foreign territories – for example, New Caledonia – still exist). In many countries, colonizers failed to adequately prepare local people for independence, leaving public servants ill equipped to serve in introduced institutions such as police organizations. Many Pacific police forces remain poorly trained and are judged by external (Western) observers as lacking in basic police skills. Furthermore, the appropriateness of imported institutional models to Pacific Island circumstances continues to be debated throughout the region by local educated elites and foreign observers alike.

In all Pacific Island nations, formal state structures operate in tandem with non-state structures of governance. The extent to which colonial authorities and subsequently post-independence governments have sought to integrate 'customary law' with introduced legal structures (such as criminal codes) varies throughout the region. So too does the degree of 'fit' between introduced and indigenous notions of right and wrong. Most significantly, while Western notions of order are premised upon state monopoly over violence, in some Pacific countries, such as Papua New Guinea, violence perpetrated within locally determined parameters is an acceptable means of dispute resolution. This presents a significant challenge to local police, many of whose primary allegiance is to kin, rather than to the state.

The misfit between state and local perceptions of violence and social order is particularly obvious in relation to violence against women, whereby violence perpetrated by men against wives is deemed legitimate, resulting in police inaction. In some Pacific island states, those in charge of quasi-official and unofficial dispute resolution forums such as village and island courts challenge the jurisdiction of police to intervene in local wrongs. Consequently, in many circumstances police play a marginal role in law enforcement.

Evaluation

In light of the aforementioned distinctive features, the appropriateness of Western policing models in the Pacific – which are in part incompatible with local practices – is contestable. In particular, fragile economies, geographic dispersal and institutional misfit pose significant challenges, as do the blatant cleavages (in some instances) between local and imported notions of right and wrong and modalities of dispute resolution. While both internal and external attempts are being made to strengthen Pacific police organizations, serious consideration of alternative law enforcement options has not been undertaken, despite the seeming incongruence of these introduced structures.

Regional organizations have an important role to play in determining the Pacific policing agenda, which is often considered within the context of broader regional and international security concerns. Relevant key organizations include the Pacific island Forum and the Pacific island Chiefs of Police, in which both Australia and New Zealand play a key role. The Pacific island Chiefs of Police comprises 21 member countries, whose representatives meet annually to share information and promote regional strategies for policing the region. Key areas addressed by the organization include police legislation, terms and conditions of service, use of force, transnational crime, terrorism, human rights and HIV/AIDS.

External perceptions of instability – and in some instances internal perceptions – have resulted in growing international attention to matters of regional security, including the 'strengthening' of Pacific Island police forces, which have long received donor support from Australia (and to a lesser degree from countries including New Zealand, the US, France, Japan and Taiwan). In the wake of September 11 (2001) and the Bali bombings (2002), Australia has assumed an increasingly hands-on approach to its nearest Pacific neighbours, most notably Papua New Guinea and the Solomon Islands, on the basis of fears that 'weak' and 'failing' states provide potential launching points for transnational terrorist and criminal activity.

This shift in approach has not been uncontested, being accompanied by claims that Australia is behaving in a neo-colonial manner, which transgresses the sovereignty of Pacific Island nations. In particular, in Papua New Guinea, the policing component of the Australian Enhanced Cooperation Program was deemed unconstitutional (the key issue being the immunity of Australian police officers) and discontinued less than a year after commencement, and in the Solomon Islands – despite the fact that assistance was invited – there have been frequent threats to eject Australia.

The Regional Assistance Mission to Solomon Islands (RAMSI) is most emblematic of the new 'hands on approach'. Following the Solomon Islands crisis of 1998–2000, in response to a request from the government of Solomon Islands, the Australian led RAMSI was mounted in attempts to restore law and order and reestablish functioning institutions of government. Policing is a significant – and the most visible – component of the mission, involving members of contributing forces from a range of Pacific Island countries including (but not limited to) Papua New Guinea, Tonga, Samoa, Federated States of Micronesia and Vanuatu. In keeping with RAMSI's phased approach to the provision of assistance, the function of international police working in Solomon Islands has changed from one of post-conflict peace building to long-term capacity building, including the promotion of community policing. This presents a variety of challenges for practitioners posted to this mission.

Externally funded police capacity building projects in the region have struggled to find productive means of engaging with the socio-political and material realities of the countries in which they operate. International police actors tasked with strengthening Pacific police organizations (through capacity development, mentoring and training), require an understanding of the interface between the state justice system and local justice mechanisms, highlighting on a daily basis the tension between universal notions such as 'human rights' and local practices. Training initiatives for Pacific Islander police will only impact upon local policing practices if they take account of the local context (including the importance of non-state dispute resolution procedures) and if they recognize why Pacific Islanders police in the manner that they do. This requires international police actors to be skilled not only in policing, but to have the capacity to read and adapt to local circumstances, to shift their *modus operandi* from task completion to gently guiding others and to have a long-term view to sustainable reforms. Ultimately, however, it is Pacific Islanders – not external donors – who must determine the modern policing agenda in their own countries.

Abby McLeod and Juani O'Reilly

Associated Concepts: community engagement, cross-border policing, culture, peace-keeping, reform, transitional policing

Key Readings

Australian Strategic Policy Institute (2003) *Our Failing Neighbour: Australia and the Future of Solomon Islands*. Barton, ACT: Australian Strategic Policy Institute, http://www.aph.gov.au/Senate/committee/fadt_c tte/completed_inquiries/2002–04/PNG/su bmissions/sub78.pdf

McLeod, A. (2007). 'Social order in Papua New Guinea: challenges to police reform' in Brown, A. (ed.) *Security and Development in the Pacific island Region*. Boulder, CO: Lynne Rienner, in press.

McLeod, A. (ed) and Dinnen, S. (2007) 'Police building in the southwest Pacific – new directions in Australian regional policing' in

A. Goldsmith and J. Sheptycki, (eds).
Transnational Policing, Oxford: Hart.

Newton, T. (1998) 'An introduction to
policing in the South Pacific region',
Journal of South Pacific Law – Working
Papers, Working Paper 4 of Volume 2,
http://www.vanuatu.usp.ac.fj/journal_spl
aw/Working_Papers/Newton1.htm.

PARAMILITARY POLICING

Definition

Paramilitary policing is a controversial topic.
A simple or traditional definition refers to
military-style enforcement by armed state or
non-state groups. But paramilitarism is not a
self-evident concept, its meaning is historically and culturally relative, and attempts to
categorize the policing associated with it
often lead to acrimonious debate. As a result,
most definitions are based on the technology,
tactics, uniforms or organizational structures
used by the groups concerned, or on their
relationship with military forces.

Distinctive Features

The term 'paramilitary policing' is commonly
used to describe the enforcement activities of
armed groups that, while organized on military lines, possessing military-style capabilities or missions, and behaving or looking like
soldiers, are not part of a regular military.
Understanding paramilitarism matters for
two reasons: (1) it offers potential insight into
the nature of policing, and (2) paramilitary
policing is common wherever there are internal security threats.

In the English-speaking world, 'paramilitary' is commonly applied to public police
capable of armed and rapid response to terrorism. For example, it was commonly used to
describe Northern Ireland's Royal Ulster
Constabulary before it was assimilated into the
Police Service of Northern Ireland (PSNI) in
2001. It is also applied to police whose duties

and chains of command overlap with those of
their military. This category ranges from the
South African Police during Apartheid and
China's People's Armed Police to France's
Gendarmerie, many of whom are accountable
to their defence ministries, rather than interior
ministries, and act in support of militaries during war. Other paramilitary police (such as
those in Milosevic's Serbia) provide a source of
quasi-military manpower. Comparable considerations apply to some border police. For example, the operating procedures of Israel's Border
Police are similar to those of its army.

Other groups typically described as paramilitary include special volunteer units operating in civilian clothing (for example, Haiti's
Tontons Macoutes). Punishment squads used
by terrorist, criminal or sectarian groups such
as the Irish Republican Army and the Ulster
Volunteer Force in Northern Ireland are also
referred to as paramilitaries.

As this suggests, the term 'paramilitary'
lacks precision. This is partly because many
such groups are neither police nor military,
but share the characteristics of both. Others
are informal, operating beyond the control of
the state, and 'police' for essentially political,
sectarian or personal reasons. Further, in
many parts of the world (Latin America is a
case in point) distinctions between what is
military, police or civilian are imprecise, and
several organizations may share police attributes. Definitional issues are for this reason
central to understanding paramilitarism.

In practice, definitions tend to be based on
function or organization. That is, on whether a
group plays a quasi-military role, or is organized and equipped on military lines. Of the
various groups that might be studied, the public police have received most attention. Indeed,
this is where academic interest has focused.

It is only in certain countries and contexts
that paramilitarism is a value-laden – and
usually derogatory – term. Thus paramilitary
policing did not become politically and acad-
emically controversial in the English-speaking
world until the 1980s. British journalists
describing the activities of Nazi thugs may
have coined the term during the 1940s, but
debate developed primarily in response to

political prompts such as the use of the police to enforce apartheid in South Africa. Other incitements included the US assistance to brutal police in Latin America, and the use of tactics originally developed for colonial riot squads against strikers in mainland Britain in the 1980s.

There is nothing new or unusual about paramilitary policing. Military discipline cannot easily be transferred to public police, but colonial police, for example, often acted as soldiers wearing police uniforms. Police in Anglophone Africa were structured, organized and administered on military lines, and riot drill and weapons training were a priority.

Four aspects of this trend deserve note. First, police in most of the world exhibit paramilitary traits. Most recruits receive drill training, most officers wear uniforms, and all are divided into hierarchical ranks. Second, most police include well-trained rapid response units equipped with military-style technology and clothing. Such units are specifically designed for policing thought to be beyond the capacity of ordinary police but not requiring the equipment or training of the army. This applies as much to London's Metropolitan Police as to Nigeria's Mobile Police. Many such units have a reputation for robust or heavy-handed policing. Third, the need to provide security during peacekeeping operations has led to the increased use of gendarmeries, which traditionally operate at the interface between police and military. Witness the role of Argentina's *Gendarmerie Nacional* in the Balkans, or Italy's *Carabinieri* in Iraq. Meanwhile, United Nations operations may include formed police units capable of acting in support of peacekeepers.

Fourth, policing in the US has become increasingly militarized, with Special Weapons and Tactics Teams (SWAT) equipped with military-style technology proliferating. SWAT teams typically wear body armour and Twalon/Kevlar helmets; they carry semi-automatic handguns or even submachine guns when involved in hostage rescue, counter-terrorism, and serving high-risk warrants. This matters because trends in US policing are influential on police fashions and police studies.

Evaluation

The debate surrounding the nature and desirability of paramilitary policing is analytical, rather than functional, hence the centrality of definitional issues. With the exception of certain politicized incidents and controversies, the debate has been conducted within the academy.

The contested nature of paramilitarism is evident from a series of exchanges conducted between two UK academics, Tony Jefferson (1990) and P.A.J. Waddington (1993), in the 1980s and 1990s, and between Waddington and the US academic Peter Kraska (1999) in the late 1990s. Their publications offer a guide to the most influential concepts and issues. However, all three base their arguments on their experience of UK and US policing and police studies. They exclude insights from security studies, for example, and comparative policing.

The exchange began with a series of articles by Jefferson and Waddington on the subject of paramilitarism in the British police in the context of policing public order.

At the heart of the debate lies the fact that there is no agreed definition of paramilitarism. Rather, as Jefferson noted, there is 'a degree of confusion about the significance of various aspects that we regard as characteristically paramilitary' (1990: 2). Also, the exchange was shaped by the author's personal standpoints. Writing about public order policing in Britain, Jefferson adopted the perspective of those being policed while Waddington considered Jefferson's emphasis on the provocative nature of paramilitary as denying the police the means to efficiently suppress dissent (Jefferson, 1990; Waddington, 1993).

Both authors regarded paramilitary policing as a matter of quasi-military policing, and their analyses were developed in terms of function and organization. Thus Jefferson defined paramilitary policing as 'the application of (quasi-) military training, equipment, philosophy and organization' (Jefferson, 1990: 16), while Waddington identified superior (that is, military) forms of 'centralized

217

command and control' as the essence of quasi-military policing (Waddington 1993: 353). They differed primarily in the desirability of such policing.

Jefferson thought its cost unacceptable. Indeed, the theoretical heart of his argument was that although the use of military-style solutions to public order often represents a gain in terms of coordinated discipline, it always results in provocation (Jefferson, 1993: 375). In practice, he argued, the combination of military practice and police discretion results in 'provocation minus collective discipline'. This, he insisted, 'is the proper meaning of the phrase 'paramilitary policing' (1993: 376).

As this implies – and as Jefferson acknowledged – the dispute originated in a fundamental difference of standpoint, rather than an unwillingness to engage with the other's arguments. In contrast, Kraska's approach is more polemical (1999). He did not engage with definitional issues so much as emphasize the extent to which quasi-military SWAT teams have become integrated into US public policing.

Based on his ethnographic research into the policing of American cities, Kraska argued that the difference between police and military was eroding. This was facilitated by America's increased militarism, by which he meant 'the prevalence of war-like values in society' (Kraska, 1999: 123).

Kraska's theorizing was based on the three factors he considered prompted or facilitated the paramilitarization of American policing (1999: 142). These were Washington's war on drugs; the seductiveness of paramilitary subculture, and its promotion by military-industrial interests; and the desire of state organizations to manage coercion more efficiently.

The debate faltered in the aftermath of September 2001. However, the 'war on terror' has been accompanied by a marked militarization of policing in many countries. This is particularly noticeable in the European Union where internal and external security concerns converge (Lutterbeck, 2005).

In conclusion, there is as yet no universally accepted definition, theory or paradigm of paramilitary policing, and the term continues

to be used analytically and descriptively (Hills, 1995: 450). On the other hand, there is no retreat from quasi-military policing. This suggests that paramilitary policing is probably best defined in terms of function and organization.

Alice Hills

Associated Concepts: peacekeeping, public order policing, technology, terrorism

Key Readings

Cawthra, G. (1993) *Policing South Africa.* London: Zed.
Hills, A. (1995) 'Militant tendencies: para-militarism and UK policing', *British Journal of Criminology,* 35 (3): 450–58.
Jefferson, T. (1990) *The Case Against Paramilitary Policing.* Milton Keynes: Open University.
Kraska, P. (ed.) (1999) 'Special Issue: Militarizing Criminal Justice', *Journal of Political and Military Sociology,* 27 (2).
Lutterbeck, D. (2005) 'Blurring the dividing line: the convergence of internal and external security in Western Europe', *European Security,* 14 (2): 231–53.
Waddington, P.A.J. (1993) 'The case against paramilitary policing considered', *British Journal of Criminology,* 33 (3): 353–68.

PARTNERSHIPS

See Communitarianism; Community Policing; Community Safety; Multi-Agency Policing; Responsibilization; Third Party Policing

PATROL

Definition

In its simplest sense, patrol is a deployment tactic in policing. More precisely, 'Patrol is a policing tactic or technique that involves movement around an area for the purpose of observation, inspection or security. Since it is based on the allocation of officers between spatial areas, it is also a method of organizing policing resources and managing policing personnel' (Wakefield, 2006: 12). It is performed by police officers as well as other agents of policing, operating alone or in pairs, in uniform or in plain clothes. It may be undertaken on foot, on a bicycle, on horseback or in a vehicle.

In defining the concept of patrol it is instructive to look at the range of activities carried out in the course of such activity. Van Maanen notes of the range of tasks entailed in the policing of city streets, 'Some ... are mundane; many of them are routine; and a few of them are dangerous'. He argues that 'patrol work defies a general job description since it includes an almost infinite set of activities – dogcatching, first aid, assisting elderly citizens, breaking up family fights, finding lost children, pursuing a fleeing felon, directing traffic, and so forth (2005 [1978]: 283).

In police studies, the controversies associated with patrol work demonstrate that the topic itself is far from a mundane or routine matter. The strategic value of patrol to policing has been debated for decades. Demands for more officers on patrol are a continuous feature of public debates about policing. The proliferation of patrol initiatives delivered by bodies other than police represents society producing its own responses to needs unmet by the state. These themes provide continuous avenues for research and debate.

Distinctive Features

Foot patrol was a distinctive feature of Sir Robert Peel's 'New Police' model introduced in London in 1829, and exported to cities in the US. This preventative, high visibility approach was to become an entrenched feature of policing in the UK, and through the latter half of the twentieth century, the image of the friendly 'bobby on the beat' remained powerful even as officers were increasingly being diverted into new strategic areas. Yet in the UK and other jurisdictions, foot patrol came to be replaced as the main means of delivering policing, as new technologies such as the car and the telephone began to transform the social environment. Motorized patrols were considered to offer a much better use of police resources, and emergency call systems, centralized control arrangements and radio networks would allow the police to respond more efficiently to calls for service. This, it was thought, would improve police-public relations, as well the morale of police officers by allowing for a more professionalized, effective service. Yet by the late 1970s, the effectiveness of this new 'professional' police model was being called into question. Crime rates in Western jurisdictions were rising, and the public were becoming more critical of the police. The reactive, distant style of policing that had evolved was increasingly being seen to be achieving the exact opposite of what had been intended, eroding the relationship between the police and the community.

One of many subsequent policing innovations that developed in response to deteriorating police-community relations and the need to improve the 'service' orientation of the police was community policing, which grew to become an influential, international movement. In the UK, where it was originally advocated by progressive police chief John Alderson, its expansion was hastened as a result of the endorsement of Lord Scarman in 1981 following race riots in Brixton, London. At this time, a solution was urgently required to address the critically poor relations between the police and minority communities in several areas of the country. Its rising status was not limited to Britain, however: as Reiner argues, community policing came to be 'an influential movement among progressive police chiefs in the US and elsewhere' (2000: 74), supported by a number of studies in the US that were highly critical of random motorized patrol (see Ericson, 2005 [1982]). Among the innovations associated with community policing (and problem-oriented policing, with which it is often associated) are a host of foot and car patrol initiatives. Prominent among these are strategies that have revived the 'beat policing' methods characteristic of more consensual times past, where areas are divided into small 'beats' patrolled on foot by dedicated teams of personnel working closely with the community; and 'directed' patrols targeted towards crime 'hot spots'. Both are strategies associated with the well established Chicago Alternative Policing Strategy (CAPS) in the US.

In the UK, policy makers hope to mirror the success of CAPS by means of a new 'neighbourhood policing' programme recently implemented throughout England and Wales, structured according to a beat system similar to that used in Chicago. The implementation of neighbourhood policing in the UK has been a response to rising levels of public dissatisfaction concerning the police's ability to control crime, high demand for police foot patrol, and concern about the level of police resources typically devoted to the activity. Such sentiments have been a regular feature of social survey findings (see Wakefield, 2006). Policy development in the UK has seen a reemphasis of some of the key objectives underpinning community policing and problem-oriented policing, with the aim of reorganizing local policing in an integrated way, delivered primarily by means of foot patrol, that can provide citizens with more 'reassurance'. 'Neighbourhood policing' has been positioned at the forefront of police strategy, and awaits evaluation.

The popularity of preventative patrol among citizens and corporations is also evident from 'pluralization' trends whereby non-police bodies are becoming increasingly involved in the visible patrol of communal spaces. Such bodies include private security personnel, community members patrolling the streets on a voluntary basis, and uniformed 'auxiliary police'. The latter term includes volunteer police officers; local authority 'wardens' as are now commonplace in the Netherlands, Britain and France; or civilian police employees dedicated to patrol, as in the case of the *politiesurveillant* in the Netherlands or British police community support officers.

Evaluation

The UK's new strategy for local policing, based on considerable investment in foot patrol, offers no panacea for declining public confidence in the police. The limitations of the police in the UK mirror those elsewhere. Common citizen complaints relate to slow response times, not keeping people informed, lack of police interest, poor demeanour, and a serious lack of trust among many minority communities (see Wakefield, 2006). None of these concerns are directly addressed by patrol interventions, although the innovations in Chicago and across the UK are intended as among the means for engaging with, and improving the quality of service to, communities. Community engagement can, however, take many forms: Japan's *koban* (police box) system, for example, brings the police into the community by effectively taking (mini) police stations to them, rather than deploying patrollers into the community from centralized police stations. Effective community engagement is itself dependent on careful selection and training of officers, for both reactive and community roles, and it is widely documented that police officers themselves value 'real police work' – crime fighting, including the excitement of 'search, chase and capture' – over the 'rather dry, monotonous , and relatively mundane activities of a service nature' (Van Maanen, 2005 [1978]: 284). These considerations, and the findings of the American police patrol evaluations of the 1970s referred to above, reflect that patrol in itself – motorized or on foot, randomized or directed, or in expanded number – offers little to alleviate the challenges of contemporary policing. Rather, it is a mode of deployment that facilitates the delivery of policing services within a broader strategic framework.

An alternative framework which contrasts markedly with community and problem-oriented approaches in its underlying philosophy is that of 'zero tolerance', 'order maintenance' or 'quality of life' policing, in which police patrol is employed in a very different way. Policing resources are directed towards low-level misdemeanours that blight the quality of life in neighbourhoods and are thought, where not addressed, to foster a climate in which more serious offending may flourish. An assertive, visible and intelligence-led policing strategy targets signs of disorder, including vagrancy, drunkenness, prostitution and loitering, in public spaces and especially 'hot spots' of crime. Its delivery relies on 'aggressive patrol' whereby hard-line tactics such as 'field interrogations'/'stop and search' and random traffic stops are routinely employed in the course of patrols, coupled with a strict policy of arrest and prosecution. Zero tolerance policing and its strategic alternatives are not mutually exclusive: in the UK, for example, neighbourhood policing involves increased numbers of patrollers targeting low level crime and anti-social behaviour, supported by a vast array of new powers and punitive measures. However, these different approaches illustrate the relationship between patrol as a mode of deployment, and the broader strategic framework in which it is undertaken.

Alison Wakefield

Associated Concepts: auxiliary police, community policing, public reassurance, zero tolerance policing

Key Readings

Ericson, R.V. (2005) 'The police as reproducers of order', in T. Newburn (ed.) *Policing: Key Readings.* Cullompton, Devon: Willan Publishing, from R.V. Ericson (1982) *Reproducing Order: A Study of Police Patrol Work.* Toronto: University of Toronto Press, pp. 3–30.

McLaughlin, E. (2006) *The New Policing.* London: Sage.

Reiner, R. (2000) *The Politics of the Police* (3rd edn). Oxford: Oxford University Press.

Van Maanen, J. (2005) 'The asshole', in T. Newburn (ed.) *Policing: Key Readings.* Cullompton, Devon: Willan Publishing, from J. Van Maanen and P. Manning (eds) (1978) *Policing: A View from the Streets.* New York: Random House.

Wakefield, A. (2006) *The Value of Foot Patrol: A Review of Research.* London: Police Foundation.

PEACEKEEPING

Definition

Peacekeeping involves the deployment of foreign, neutral military forces in a post-conflict zone, with the consent of the parties to the conflict (Doyle, 2007). The aim of peacekeeping is to maintain peace and stability in the aftermath of conflict, in order to create space for the parties to negotiate and/or implement a peace settlement. Peacekeeping operations originally consisted almost exclusively of military personnel, who assumed limited responsibilities for monitoring and maintaining ceasefire lines. However, the evolution of complex peacekeeping operations, which undertake a diverse range of activities, from disarming ex-combatants to fulfilling on a temporary basis practically all the functions of government, has drawn in a wide array of police and civilian actors. Contemporary peacekeeping operations routinely include a civilian police component. Civilian police contribute to efforts to secure short-term law and order, but they also play a critical role in building long term, sustainable peace by supporting the development of efficient, accountable national police forces which reinforce the rule of law.

Distinctive Features

Peacekeeping is generally undertaken by a group of countries, under the auspices of an international organization such as the United Nations (UN). Regional organizations have also deployed peacekeeping operations, which sometimes cooperate with or are converted into UN operations. The European Union deployed peacekeepers to the former Yugoslavia Balkans; the Economic Community of West African States has implemented a number of peacekeeping operations in destinations such as Liberia and Sierra Leone; and the African Union has deployed peacekeepers to the Sudan. Another example of a regional peacekeeping initiative is the Regional Assistance Mission to Solomon Islands, delivered by a partnership of 15 Pacific region countries (Peake, 2005).

UN peacekeeping operations traditionally monitored and maintained ceasefire lines. During the Cold War, the deployment of peacekeeping operations was a relatively rare event: in more than four decades from 1945 until 1988, the UN deployed 13 peacekeeping operations. By contrast, since 1988 49 peacekeeping operations have been deployed by the UN Security Council. More than 60 UN peacekeeping operations have thus been deployed around the globe, from Haiti to East Timor and from the Balkans to Mozambique.

This vast expansion in peacekeeping operations has been matched by a brisk evolution in peacekeeping responsibilities. UN peacekeeping operations now tend to be much more complex and multidimensional (Doyle, 2007). UN operations can assume responsibility for practically all the tasks normally carried out by state institutions. Indeed, in Kosovo and East Timor the UN assumed transitional administrative responsibilities for the conduct of state affairs. In between the extremes of basic ceasefire monitoring and complete transitional administration, there are almost limitless permutations. Peacekeeping operations have thus been tasked with implementation of a peace agreement; maintenance of stability through military and police interventions; disarmament, demobilization and reintegration of former combatants; return of refugees and internally displaced persons to their homes; delivery of humanitarian services to those in need; restructuring and reform of local armed forces and police; strengthening of court and judicial systems and prison facilities; promotion and protection of human rights; conduct and monitoring of elections; and promotion of development and economic reconstruction (Farrall, 2007).

The importance of policing to post-conflict peace building cannot be over-emphasized. A credible, effective police force must be in place before peacekeepers can safely transfer law and order responsibilities to local authorities. Civilian police components of peacekeeping operations traditionally played an advisory, training and monitoring role in support of local, pre-existing police forces. However, the report of the Panel on United Nations Peace Operations (UN, 2000), commonly referred to as 'the Brahimi report', recommended a doctrinal shift in civilian police operations.

The Brahimi report argued that UN civilian police monitors were not peacebuilders if they simply documented or attempted to discourage by their presence abusive or other unacceptable behaviour by local police officers. Instead, Brahimi proposed that civilian police should play a role in reforming, training and restructuring local police forces according to international standards for democratic policing and human rights. Since the Brahimi report, UN peacekeeping operations in East Timor, Liberia, Côte d'Ivoire, Haiti and the Sudan have incorporated civilian police mandates not only to respond to threats to law and order, but also to support police reform, training and restructuring. There is also an awareness of the need to have a standing police capacity available for rapid deployment to support surges in civilian police needs. At the 2005 World Summit, Heads of State and Government endorsed 'the creation of a standing police capacity to provide coherent, effective and responsive start-up capability for the police component of UN peacekeeping operations and to assist existing operations through the provision of advice and expertise'.

The role of policing in peacekeeping activities, which has been referred to both as 'policekeeping' (Day, 2003) and as 'policebuilding' (Peake, 2005), is being refined through policy developments in the broader fields of security sector reform and strengthening the rule of law. Security sector reform encompasses efforts to reform and restructure the branches of the state that are traditionally responsible for providing national security and law and order, including the military, police and other security agencies. The rule of law sector encompasses initiatives designed to (re)build state institutions responsible for securing justice and adherence to the law, including the police force, the corrections system, the legal system and human rights and transitional justice institutions (Farrall, 2007).

Evaluation

In the post-Cold War era, the international community has increasingly turned to peacekeeping operations as a means of stabilizing fragile post-conflict situations. The deployment of peacekeepers generally achieves the primary purpose of bringing short-term stability to vulnerable environments. But the long-term goals of peacekeeping have proven more elusive.

There have been some notable success stories, such as Namibia, El Salvador and Mozambique. But there have also been examples where peacekeeping operations have failed to foster sustainable peace. In Somalia the UN was forced to withdraw its peacekeeping operation after warlords escalated attacks against peacekeepers. Other countries, such as Haiti and Liberia, have been host to multiple generations of peacekeeping operations. In East Timor, which was initially considered a model success story, efforts to reform and strengthen policing and governance have not succeeded in triggering meaningful, sustainable change.

The innovations to 'policekeeping' advocated by the Brahimi report and the 2005 World Summit represent a step forward. Civilian police peacekeeping components have an integral role to play in building credible, efficient and sustainable local police forces which adhere to international standards of policing and human rights and therefore strengthen the rule of law. Yet more could be done to ensure that civilian police components are as prepared as possible to meet the stringent demands of participating in peacekeeping operations. Specialist training should be provided to potential civilian police peacekeepers not only in international standards of policing and human rights, but also with respect to the specific conditions and culture of the situation into which deployment will take place (Hansen, 2002).

The field of peacekeeping continues to evolve rapidly. The international community is constantly refining its peacekeeping approach, in an attempt to improve the track record of peacekeeping operations in fostering sustainable peace in post-conflict environments. Civilian policing forms a dynamic and critical component of contemporary peacekeeping operations. As recent developments in East Timor illustrate, the failure to ensure the emergence of an effective, impartial police force which adheres to international standards of policing can dramatically undermine the best efforts of peacekeeping operations to build sustainable peace.

Jeremy Farrall

Associated Concepts: cross-border policing, democratic policing, human rights policing, human security, Pacific policing, paramilitary policing, security networks, transitional policing, transnational policing

Key Readings

Day, G. and Freeman, C. (2005) 'Operationalizing the responsibility to protect: the policekeeping approach', *Global Governance*, 11:139–46.

Doyle, M.W. and Sambanis, N. (2007) 'Peacekeeping operations', in T.G. Weiss, and S. Daws, *The Oxford Handbook on the United Nations*. Oxford, Oxford University Press.

Farrall, J. (2007) *United Nations Peacekeeping and the Rule of Law*. Canberra: ANU Centre for International Governance and Justice.

Hansen, A.S. (2002) *From Congo to Kosovo: Civilian Police in Peace Operations*. Oxford: Oxford University Press.

Peake, G. and Brown, K.S. (2005) 'Policebuilding: the International Deployment Group in the Solomon Islands', *International Peacekeeping*, 12(4): 520–532.

United Nations (2000) *Report of the Panel on United Nations Peace Operations* ('The Brahimi Report'). New York, United Nations.

PERFORMANCE MANAGEMENT

Definition

An approach to managing public sector organizations that typically emphasizes performance rather than process and outputs rather than inputs. The term performance management (PM) is used to refer to either organizational or individual performance. Individual PM is usually the province of human resource management professionals who seek to maintain and improve individual and team performance in order to achieve organizational goals. This entry, in line with most of the police literature, focuses on organizational PM. It should be noted that PM is not specific to either the public sector or the police but is part of a much broader trend across workplaces. It is most commonly found however in the public sector.

Distinctive Features

The notion of performance in police organizations is closely tied to the managerialist trends of the late twentieth century. Managerialism in most Anglophone and many European countries has provided a base for setting, measuring and benchmarking performance outcomes in police organizations. Goal setting, resource allocation and PM in police organizations have replaced the process driven practicalities of delivering policing services to the community. The era of managerialism has made it clear that police organizations are expected to deliver value through the socially and fiscally responsible allocation of resources and ensure effective service delivery. It is expected that police officers will demonstrate a responsive attitude to the communities they serve. In effect, as some commentators have noted, there is a dual agenda – one which stresses the public accountability aspect of reporting at agency level and a management agenda that is required to encourage police officers to aim for, and achieve organizational targets and priorities. In the context of either agenda, PM emphasizes performance indicators, measurement and transparency. It involves the establishment of consistent and mutually reinforcing aims and objectives, with tasks being related to specific organizational objectives. Most police organizations concerned with PM have converted their mission statements into tangible objectives they can quantify and report on. A distinctive feature of PM has been the setting of key performance indicators to enable the auditing of efficiency and effectiveness. Such indicators generally include service delivery, quality of service and efficiency measures: measures that encompass the public accountability and managerial agendas.

Service delivery indicators focus on how well a service has been delivered in line with the strategic objectives of the organization. Such indicators are concerned with, for example, motor vehicle theft, violence (public and private), road traffic infringements, recorded crime figures, arrests and administrative tasks. Quality of service is largely assessed through community satisfaction indicators gathered through, for example, surveys and number of complaints. Asking the public to comment on police services is a feature of most Anglophone countries but in France for example, the notion that the public could rate the police remains iconoclastic, even today. There is a general reluctance in that country to take citizens' opinions of policing into account. Cost and efficiency indicators seek to ensure that resources allocated are effectively being turned into positive outcomes/outputs.

The notion of 'what works', particularly in the context of reducing crime and recidivism has provided a strong focus for PM, especially in the US and the UK, and much research has been committed to identifying evidence based policy and practice in the criminal justice field. While sceptics would argue that evidence-based research is rarely translated into practice, there are examples such as 'hot spots' patrolling, the policing of domestic violence and situational crime prevention research, where research has clearly informed the development of police practice. 'Evidence-based' research is a primary mechanism in many countries to support arguments for the allocation of resources and data-based strategic management such as Compstat. Compstat is an objective-oriented process that uses computer technology, strategy and accountability mechanisms to structure the way in which a police department provides crime control data to management. Compstat is used in various forms in countries such as the UK, US, New Zealand and Australia (although not in Canada) to encourage the translation of organizational strategic goals into operational activities and regional/departmental business plans.

The issue of 'creating public value' has become an important argument for PM particularly in the UK and the US. Managers are now being asked to consider what would be valuable for their agencies to do as well as carrying out mandated services. Maintaining an effective and efficient police service is paramount but adding value is seen as a more proactive approach to promoting equity and building social capital. The emphasis is on efficiency savings and continuous improvement. In the UK, 'public value' is legislatively supported by certification, audit and inspection.

Evaluation

The notion of PM, particularly in police organizations, is a contested one. Supporters of such managerial regimes point to the role PM can play in meeting the requirements of external accountability. A PM framework that links performance to corporate planning, budgeting and resource management provides clarity and transparency. Accountability has also been used to defend 'name and shame' strategies whereby poorly performing forces are threatened with public exposure. Additionally, it has been argued that PM provides management with an opportunity to learn from both success and failure, in that it allows good strategy and practice to be identified and at the same time allows management to detect poor performance. Benchmarking, it is argued, within and between police organizations can act as an incentive and promote innovation. Management cites the importance of PM to improving the quality of policy and decision-making in an organization. They argue quantitative measures ensure that

organizations collect timely, relevant, numerical information that can be used to inform 'evidence-based' decision-making, policy development and evaluation.

Critics however point to the potentially distorting effects of PM. The debate about performance measurement in police organizations has largely focused on whether or not numerical measurement can do justice to the complexity of the activities performed by police. While numerical performance measurement in police organizations can capture critical data such as reported crime rates, overall arrests, clearance rates and response times, it is not so good at capturing the quality and effectiveness of the work involved and the many important contributions that police make to a community's quality of life. The proactive and problem-solving activities that contribute to creating legitimacy, such as reassurance policing, building relationships with communities and multi-agency policing fall into this category. Such intangibles are difficult to measure and there is a risk that they may be the first casualties when limited and diminishing resources dictate specific types of activity.

Potentially unintended consequences of this failure to acknowledge the intangibles include quality reduction (where more attention is paid to quantity), a stimulus to strategic behaviour (whereby figures are recorded imaginatively and with a view to 'meeting the targets') and unimaginative decision-making (where risk is minimized and initiative discouraged). In effect, it is argued, measurement rewards the *status quo*. What gets measured gets done, often at the expense of locally identified problems and the conditions that create them.

In policing, as part of the mangerialist agenda, there is a strong emphasis on multi-agency cooperation whereby agencies work together to address problems in the community. It is difficult to attribute performance and results to a single organization. If the measure wrongly links the outcomes to only one organization it is misleading and those involved may become frustrated and cynical about the process. In the criminal justice field specifically, police regularly interact with prosecutors, courts, prisons and probation agencies. Indeed, much police work relies on the cooperation and professionalism of these agencies and a police organization's contribution, to crime statistics for example, cannot always be isolated from the inputs of these and other agencies.

The relation between the policing input and results as measured by crime statistics can often be hard to demonstrate. Where causality is assumed or wrongly attributed, the distorted picture can lead to resources being targeted inappropriately. Conversely, true causality may be hard to establish. It can be tempting to assume cause and effect from a particular set of statistics which appear to be attributable to a particular policing input when the connection may be tenuous.

In recent years there has been some concern about how specific areas within policing can be measured. For example, how is drug law enforcement or the policing of domestic violence incorporated into an effective PM plan? In the context of drug law enforcement, agencies have consistently used drug seizure and arrest data to measure the effectiveness of their work performance but have found it difficult to develop measures that adequately capture and assess the extent and nature of their work. In the UK, US and Australia, significant developments in law enforcement performance measurement are now being incorporated into new models of PM that can be directly applied to areas such as drug law enforcement.

The trend to PM in policing has been a long and arduous process. The UK have been the front runners in developing mechanisms by which police practice can be measured in the context of national objectives. Benchmarking, target-setting and key performance indicators are widely utilized by central authorities such as the Home Office, the Audit Commission and the Inspectorate of Constabulary, to ensure the efficient and effective use of police resources addressing the dual agendas of external accountability and internal management. Legislation and formal policy parameters have institutionalized police PM in the UK and shifted the 'operational independence' of senior police officers to the notion of him/her being 'operationally responsible'. It is the Home Office now, through its National Policing Plan, which sets the national strategic priorities for policing and ensures compliance through codes, rules and regulations governing police practice. Considerable debate surrounds the nature of the targets against which success is measured and the extent to which centrally set targets are appropriate. The irony is that a distinctive feature of managerialism has been the devolvement of authority and autonomy to the regions. PM as an off shoot of managerialism has arguably centralized planning and performance requirements, reduced levels of autonomy in senior officers and constrained the ostensibly important principles of localized policing.

Centralized police PM schemes and National Policing Plans are unlikely in federal countries such as the US and Australia with multiple, autonomous police jurisdictions. However, the enthusiasm for PM in police organizations is unlikely to recede. Most democratic countries are seeking ways to demonstrate to the public that their police organizations are using taxpayers' money resourcefully to improve safety and security; reduce crime and generally add value to their services. The issue of how we measure the success of performance management in achieving these objectives remains to be researched. The pursuit of better strategies and programmes to accomplish these objectives continues.

Jenny Fleming

Associated Concepts: accountability, Compstat, evidence-based policing, managerialism, multi-agency policing, public value

Key Readings

Alpert, G.P. and Moore, M.H. (1993) 'Measuring police performance in the new paradigm of policing', in J.J. Dilulio J. (ed.) *Performance Measures for the Criminal Justice System*. US Department of Justice, Washington, DC.

Carter, N., Klein, R. and Day, P. (1992) *How Organizations Measure Success: The Use of Performance Indicators in Government.* New York: Routledge.

Ferlie, E., Lynn, L. E. and Pollittt, C. (eds) (2005) *The Oxford Handbook of Public Management.* Oxford: Oxford University Press.

Fleming, J. and O'Reilly, J. (2008), 'In search of a process: community policing in Australia', in T. Williamson (ed.) *The Handbook of Knowledge Based Policing: Current Conceptions and Future Directions.* Sussex: John Wiley.

Henry, V. E. (2003) *The Compstat Paradigm.* Flushing, NY: Looseleaf Publications.

Home Office (2004) *The Policing Performance Assessment Framework.* London: Home Office.

Fleming, J. (ed.) (2008) *Policing: A Journal of Policy and Practice*: Special Issue: *Performance Management*, August, 2 (3).

PLURALIZATION

Definition

'Pluralization' refers to a perspective within police studies observing the expanding role of non-police service providers in policing, and the variety of different public, private and voluntary bodies now engaged in the activity. The term originates in the early work of Shearing and Stenning (1981, 1983), which observed the changing composition of formal social control, focusing particularly on the expanding social role of private security within an increasingly pluralist framework of provision. Over the last two decades, Clifford Shearing has developed a thesis in association with Stenning, Bayley, Johnston, Wood and others making sense of pluralization trends. He asserts the significance of such developments in a seminal paper with David Bayley in which the authors argued: 'Modern democratic countries ... have reached a watershed in evolution of their systems of crime control and law enforcement. Future generations will look upon this era as a time when one system

of policing ended and another took its place' (1996: 585).

Distinctive Features

Private security personnel, police auxiliaries and voluntary bodies are among the multiplicity of agencies whose contribution to contemporary policing is being recognized in this thesis, as well as in the ongoing work of the host of authors now acknowledging the significance of such developments (for example, Button, Crawford and Lister, Jones and Newburn, Loader and Walker, Rigakos, Sarre and Prenzler, Sheptycki, Wakefield, Zedner). 'Plural perspectives' are now an established feature of contemporary police studies, and it is widely recognized that 'policing' does not simply equate with the work of 'the police', despite the discipline's predominant traditional focus on the public police organization and its strategies. In the context of crime prevention other policing bodies are now coming to be regarded as being as theoretically interesting as the police. Although many scholars now contribute to 'plural perspectives' in policing, the primary focus of this entry is the development of the Shearing thesis in order to elucidate a body of work that has helped stimulate so many other contributions.

The 'mass private property' thesis is an important aspect of this body of work, set out in the early papers of Shearing and Stenning (1981, 1983). They argued that the increasing prominence of the private security industry was due in large part to trends in the privatization of urban space, which have seen the rise of shopping malls, leisure parks and other large commercial facilities – privately controlled spaces that rely on public access for their commercial success. The authors observed how owners of such properties frequently drew on private security services in exercising their legal rights to maintain control of the policing of their own territories. Rather than relying on traditional policing methods based on apprehending offenders during or after the commission of offences, property owners could initiate a more proactive, pre-emptive approach to the policing of their properties by deploying private security personnel to carry out continuous surveillance and supervision. The security requirements of this sector are seen by Shearing and Stenning as having contributed to the rapid post-war expansion of the private security industry, as well as to an increased social visibility of private security personnel since they effectively function as private police in such settings. Subsequent research has illustrated how the deployment of private security officers in sites of mass private property extends beyond the fulfilment of traditional policing functions; security personnel play an important role in the broader management of the social environments of these settings, to give an impression of security and maximize visitor comfort in order to encourage custom (Wakefield, 2003).

In his later paper written with Bayley, Shearing identifies policing pluralization (also referred to as 'multilateralization') and 'the search by the public police for an appropriate role' as being the defining features of the 'watershed' to which they refer. Together these developments are seen to amount to a restructuring of policing, outside and inside the police organization, the latter reflecting a police 'identity crisis' involving a loss of confidence in the organization's effectiveness and efficiency in controlling crime (Bayley and Shearing, 1996: 585). The forces identified as driving such change include fear of crime, the limitations of social policy interventions, the shortcomings of deterrence-based policing and punishment, the growth of mass private property and the commodification of security. The effect, they argue, is that, 'Policing now belongs to everybody – in activity, in responsibility, and in overview' (p. 591). To challenge the 'distortions of equity, human rights and accountability' in policing that will be, in their view, the likely consequences in the absence of intervention, Bayley and Shearing advocate the development of mechanisms that will allow greater participation of the poor in security markets, and for community policing to be established as 'the organizing paradigm of public policing' (p. 604).

These perspectives are the foundations of Shearing's security governance thesis, developed in conjunction with Johnston, Wood and others. Johnston and Shearing (2003) prefer to conceive security initiatives not as 'policing' but as elements of the broader 'governance of security' because of the perceived narrowness of the former concept, in terms of the limited range of activities and (state) agencies to which it is seen as being conventionally associated. Their concept refers to 'programmes for promoting peace in the face of threats (either realized or anticipated) that arise from collective life' (p. 9) and their stated focus is 'the analysis of diversified networks of security' (p. 10). Its use is intended by Johnston and Shearing to challenge notions of 'professional police hegemony' (p. 11) and provide an alternative conceptualization of policing diversity than the vague and still often state-centred concept of 'social control'.

The authors argue that the governance of security in Western, and particularly Anglo-American, countries is underpinned by two security paradigms operating in parallel. The first, stated to have dominated such systems for two centuries, is based on the premise that security is the responsibility of the state, underpinned by 'a reactive and punitive mentality'. The second paradigm, they argue, 'sometimes supports, sometimes obstructs and sometimes merely works alongside' the first, and regards security as no longer the sole or even the primary preserve of the state. Companies are viewed as the most significant of the new authorities to have emerged in this pluralist framework, acting as 'guarantors of security' for particular groups of people in particular locations, such as the customers and staff of shopping malls and theme parks, where 'they actively define the order to be guaranteed, developing strategies and providing resources for securing that order' (p. 15). Empirical research illustrates how such environments operate as microcosms with their own rule structures and control mechanisms in place (Wakefield, 2003). Johnston and Shearing (2003) go on to discuss the various types of agent, underlying mentalities, strategies and forms of authority characteristic of this new security paradigm.

In their work, and Shearing's subsequent book co-authored by Wood, a 'nodal governance', network-based perspective is developed which gives no privilege to the state, but rather situates the range of governmental actors and agencies within a network of nodes also encompassing those of the corporate, NGO (non-governmental organization) and informal/voluntary sectors. It is recognized that neo-liberal societies will inherently favour the wealthy and widen the gap between the rich, protected in their gated environments, and the poor, resigned to the residual spaces in between. Shearing and his colleagues argue that the 'networking' of non-state nodes with each other as well as those of the state should allow for new forms of accountability that help maximize the strengths and minimize the dangers of private nodes. Moreover, poor communities, according to their model, can be empowered by local capacity building interventions including the provision of 'block grants' from public funds to meet their security needs.

Evaluation

McLaughlin (2006) briefly summarizes some of the main criticisms made of the security governance thesis, and discusses it alongside a number of competing plural perspectives in the literature which he terms 'residualization', 'managerialization', 'resovereignization' and globalization, grounded respectively in the work of Reiner, McLaughlin and Murji, Loader and Walker and Sheptycki. Evaluating what he terms the 'nodalization' thesis of Shearing and his colleagues, McLaughlin notes that, while these authors have held a neutral stance regarding the emergence of forms of security governance within neo-liberal societies, their refusal to give analytic priority to the state remains contentious. Also controversial, McLaughlin observes, are the implications that, through networks, marketplace accountability mechanisms such as competition and consumer demand can be applied to state nodes, particularly the police; and that communities, given the choice, might elect to employ private security in preference to the police; as well as the authors' critique of state-based systems as a means of regulating

private security when compared with the 'regulatory pluralism' implicit in their model.

Such criticisms are weakened when considered in relation to transnational policing, to which the 'watershed' argument equally applies. Transnational policing has no clear structure and comprises an infinite diversity of public, commercial and voluntary bodies, organized internationally, regionally, nationally or locally, co-operating across borders and, where such structures are even present, subject to uneven and disparate accountability mechanisms. An important contribution of the security governance thesis, therefore, is also to expose the limitations of scholarship in mapping out, and making sense of, policing as an increasingly global project.

Alison Wakefield

Associated Concepts: auxiliary police, commodification of security, contractualism, policing, private security, privatization, responsibilization, security networks, third party policing, transnational policing

Key Readings

Bayley, D.H. and Shearing, C.D. (1996) 'The future of policing', *Law and Society Review*, 30 (3): 585–606.

Johnston, L. and Shearing, C.D. (2003) *Governing Security: Explorations of Policing and Justice*. London: Routledge.

McLaughlin, E. (2006) *The New Policing*. London: Sage.

Shearing, C.D. and Stenning, P.C. (1981) 'Modern private security: its growth and implications', in M. Tonry and N. Morris (eds) *Crime and Justice: An Annual Review of Research Vol. 3*. Chicago: University of Chicago Press.

Shearing, C.D. and Stenning, P.C. (1983) 'Private security: implications for social control', *Social Problems*, 30 (5): 498–505.

Wakefield, A. (2003) *Selling Security: The Private Policing of Public Space*. Cullompton, Devon: Willan Publishing.

Wood, J. and Shearing, C. (2007) *Imagining Security*. Cullompton, Devon: Willan Publishing.

POLICE

See Culture; Policing

POLICE PROPERTY

Definition

As an analytic concept the idea of 'police property' was introduced in 1981 in a seminal article by Canadian sociologist John A. Lee. Lee himself attributed the term to a 1972 book by the radical professor of journalism Ed Cray, *The Enemy in the Streets*. Its origins thus lie in the radical critiques of police power and practice that flourished during the heyday of critical criminologies from the late 1960s to the 1980s. The idea has proved influential in analyses of police deviance and accountability, as it helps make sense of the variety of forms of police discrimination that have been found in studies throughout the world.

The idea of police property has in part the descriptive claim that some groups are much more likely to be subject to police power than others. Analyses of police statistics, as well as observational accounts of police work around the world, have repeatedly shown that the police (private as well as public) process some types of people as suspects particularly frequently. Young, poor, ethnic minority and gay men are disproportionately stopped, searched, questioned, arrested, detained, and prosecuted by the police, in all countries where research has been conducted on policing, and this pattern has been evident throughout police history. This has been the subject of political controversy and conflict at many times and places. It has also generated a substantial volume of research on its causes, in particular exploring the extent to which the imbalances result from police discrimination, or from differences in the behaviour of the groups involved. Cycles of scandal and reform about discrimination are features of police history in most liberal democracies.

Distinctive Features

Being disproportionately at the receiving end of the use or abuse of police powers is a necessary but not sufficient condition constituting a group as police property. Any category of citizens who lack power in the major institutions of their society (institutions in the economy, polity, education, media, etc.) are liable to become police property. At one time or another, such diverse categories as winos, hobos, unemployed drifters, labour union organizers, the Japanese, blacks, long-haired youth, and homosexuals have been appropriated by the police as their property; that is categories over whom the police successfully exert superior power (Lee, 1981: 53).

But discrimination in itself is not the cutting edge of the concept of police property. Cray conceived of police property as those relatively powerless social groups that were at the mercy of the police because of an at least tacit social consensus that the police should be left alone to handle them. Lee defined the concept more explicitly: 'A category becomes police property when the dominant powers of society (in the economy, polity, etc.) leave the problems of social control of that category to the police. Let the police deal with these (niggers, queers, hippies ...)' (Lee, 1981: 53–4). It is the relative impunity of the police in discriminating against certain groups that marks them out as police property. Police property signifies not only that the police disproportionately target some people in the legal or illegal exercise of their powers. It implies also that this is seen as acceptable or even desirable by the powers that be, and by the broad mass of the population. The process is mediated by 'the politics of discreditability' (Box and Russell, 1975). The acid test of a group being police property is that its accounts and complaints are routinely discredited or ignored not only by legal institutions but also by the media, popular culture, and politicians.

The concept of police property carries force particularly in liberal democracies, which are nominally based on the value of equality before the law. In societies that are characterized by open, formally legal structures of discrimination (e.g., the ante-bellum US South, Nazi Germany, and Apartheid South Africa) the police evidently have certain groups as their property, sanctioned explicitly by law. But what Lee demonstrates is that this also happens, *de facto* albeit not *de iure*, in societies that claim to accord with principles of due process of law. There too have typically been groups so low in power that they are not only subject to disproportionate use and abuse of police power against them, but this is at least implicitly accepted by a widespread social consensus.

Cray and Lee were writing about the 1960s and '70s, and primarily about North America, although their arguments had resonance in Britain and other liberal democracies too. They noted the increasing prevalence of challenges to police authority by groups that had hitherto been their 'property', with the rise of the civil rights movement, youth culture and the counterculture, and the assertion of gay rights. In response the police often reacted with particular brutality to their loss of control over these previously 'discreditable' elements. Policing was increasingly politicized around a struggle between claims for autonomy and justice by hitherto suppressed groups, and police attempts to defend their diminishing sovereignty over their erstwhile property.

Evaluation

In the quarter century since Lee's seminal article (and the thirty-five years since Cray coined the notion), the application of the concept of police property has become increasingly problematic. Not that inequality in general has diminished – far from it: overall economic disparities have widened, and ethnic, gender and other forms of discrimination remain rife and are highly contested political issues. The operation of police powers continues to be as heavily structured by class, race, age and gender as before. But in an ever less deferential and more individualistic society, in which many discriminated against groups have successfully asserted their voices against their subordination and established increasing creditability,

the police do not enjoy consensual support for differential uses of power that cannot be justified by legal criteria or at least the emergency demands of security and order. So they have faced continuous challenges over allegations of discrimination and malpractice, as for example the 1999 report of the Macpherson Inquiry into the investigation of the murder of the black teenager Stephen Lawrence illustrated most vividly in Britain. It is hard to think of groups now that occupy the position of police property in the full sense of relatively consensual support for the police to act as they will towards them. Indeed crimes against some of the traditional police property groups, if seen as motivated by prejudice against particular races or sexual preferences, are categorized as 'hate crimes' in many jurisdictions. It must be reemphasized that this does not mean that discriminatory and unequal policing is no longer a virulent problem. But any apparent differentiation requires justification in terms of legality or at least the demands of maintaining security and public protection, and is no longer a taken-for-granted 'property' right.

Robert Reiner

Associated Concepts: diversity, hate crime, institutional racism, racial profiling, youth

Key Readings

Lee, J.A. (1981) 'Some structural aspects of police deviance in relations with minority groups', in C. Shearing (ed.) *Organizational Police Deviance*. Toronto: Butterworth.

Cray, E. (1972) *The Enemy in the Streets: Police Malpractice in America*. New York: Anchor.

Box, S. and Russell, K. (1975) 'The politics of discreditability', *Sociological Review,* 23 (2): 315–46.

Reiner R. (2000) *The Politics of the Police* (3rd edn). Oxford: Oxford University Press, Chapters 2–4,

Macpherson, Sir W. (1999) *The Stephen Lawrence Inquiry*, Report of an Inquiry by Sir William Macpherson of Cluny. CM 4262–1. London: HMSO.

Phillips, C. and Bowling, B. (2007) 'Ethnicities, racism, crime and criminal justice', in M. Maguire, R. Morgan and R. Reiner (eds) *The Oxford Handbook of Criminology* (4th edn). Oxford: Oxford University Press.

POLICING

Definition

As Waddington reminds us, 'The simple answer to the question 'What is policing?' is that policing is what police officers do' (1991: 1). What makes this slightly more complex than it seems on the surface is that there is often very little agreement about what police *actually* do. To compound this dilemma moreover, police studies in the twenty-first century are no longer focused specifically on public police but are now acknowledging the plurality of non-policing actors who are providing policing services (see 'pluralization', this volume). The 'new policing' (McLaughlin, 2006) reflects this plural perspective and indeed entries throughout this volume confirm the pertinence of a rapidly expanding literature that locates police within a broader framework of governance, private security and networks. Entries in this volume on 'privatization', 'contractualism', 'third party policing' and 'pluralization' all testify to the realities of the 'new policing'.

Distinctive Features

The history of policing gives a sense of the origins and character of the many different policing cultures and organizations that exist internationally (see 'history', this volume). How then to discuss with any conviction the distinctive features of policing generally? Further, compounding our dilemma, we have noted that public police are no longer the only actors on the security stage.

The distinguishing feature of public police is that they exercise authority (in the name of the state) over the civil population. That authority is grounded in the notion of justified force or legitimate coercion. The deprivation of liberty is part of that authority. This is what makes public police distinctive and this is what accounts for the distinctive nature of their role. The relationship police have with the civil population and the compliance that police experience are effective determinants of the way in which policing takes place.

The role of police is broadly to prevent crime, maintain order and deliver the variety of services that the communities have come to expect. These roles are usually confined to a single jurisdiction. Increasingly however police officers in Western democratic countries are requested to exercise their duties in other jurisdictions, through networks of transnational cooperation and sometimes through overseas postings on peacekeeping or community capacity building exercises. Much of the work in public police organizations is mundane. It is concerned with, for example, patrol, surveillance, traffic duties, local community liaison, writing reports, responding to incidents and emergency calls and controlling crowds in public places. This is the 'stuff' of policing and on this level, as many commentators have noted, the role varies little between police jurisdictions around the world. However for those who wish to extend their policing knowledge and career, there are opportunities for police to specialize or become part of broader networks. Specialization might relate for example to homicide, drug control, community policing, firearms or fraud. Making oneself available for international deployment duty (see for example, 'Pacific policing', this volume) is a way of being part of much larger security networks and working with officers from other jurisdictions and countries.

What public officers in Western jurisdictions are not doing nowadays is the administrative and operational support work that was once part of an officer's daily grind. Civilian employees conventionally support police officers in administrative, IT, finance and human resources roles. But it is also the case that you will rarely find a trained police officer staffing the station reception desk or receiving your emergency call. It is frequently civilians who collect evidence, analyze crime data or deliver custodial functions. A process of civilianization (whereby civilians provide either administrative or specialist support to policing) has ostensibly freed many trained police officers for front line duties. In the UK this process has been extended to the employment of community support officers, 'auxiliary police' who with limited police powers patrol the streets. These partially empowered civilians are also a feature of policing in the Netherlands and other parts of Europe. In the US, Australia and New Zealand, however, these appointments have been up until now resisted by strong police unions and associations.

Other traditional police roles, particularly those that have a security dimension, have in many countries and in a variety of ways been transferred to, or absorbed by, commercial or voluntary security providers. Police custodial and prisoner escort services may be outsourced to the private sector. The police have relinquished primary responsibility for the policing of many communal spaces to private security, including that of shopping malls, transport terminals, business complexes and large public events. Citizens are actively mobilized as partners in local policing, as in the case of neighbourhood watch schemes, or may augment public policing through collective action if they feel their security needs are not being sufficiently met.

The managerialist agenda in public organizations has shaped the new policing in many ways, and enabled public police to adapt to the changes. A 'more with less' philosophy has made it much easier for public police to relinquish their traditional security, regulation and, as we have seen, patrolling roles to other bodies. Privatization and contractualism are also features of the 'new policing', a trend that has further extended the number of providers involved in delivering the traditional police services. Many commentators talk about 'the extended police family' to illustrate the growing diversity of regulation and security provision. Scholars, including Shearing, Stenning and Johnston, have however been signalling the new world of security

provision for some time. The pluralization discourse identifies and acknowledges the proliferation of private security providers in Western democratic societies and indeed elsewhere.

Evaluation

Clearly our understanding of what policing means is very different now to twenty years ago. We have noted the similarities of public police work internationally although as Mawby (1990) has cautioned it is better not to assume too much from these similarities. Different constitutions, histories and operational styles will be reflected in the rules and procedures by which public police engage with the public and approach their various duties. Strong public administrations with high performance cultures may make a difference to what will be policed and to what degree. Tendencies to centralization in some jurisdictions, coupled with a stronger political influence than is necessarily the case elsewhere, will also affect the process of policing. In some societies, the notion of coercion is understood very differently from how it is perceived elsewhere. In other words the immediate context will shape and determine the act of policing.

More broadly we can see the changing nature of policing in the social context. Globalization, neo-liberal politics, increasing prosperity, geographical and social mobility, the breakdown of the nuclear family, the decline of the welfare state, terrorism, and technology that at once enhances and diminishes our lives, have combined to change the social context in which we live. Such changes have meant changes to society in a number of ways. The act of policing has been part of that change. As the world appears more uncertain, citizens look to authorities (in whatever guise) for confirmation of their security. One of the challenges for public police now is managing these expectations. Liaising with the community, developing trust and establishing (some would say reestablishing) networks that will support intelligence-informed policing are priorities. Organizationally there are other challenges that must be met. Internationally, police organizations must ensure they are part of security networks and agencies committed to addressing terrorism, organized crime, human trafficking, international drug rings and other criminal activity that crosses international borders so much more easily than we might have imagined twenty years ago. How do police organizations address these complex and 'wicked' problems? How do they reconcile the seemingly contradictory paradigms of community policing and national security; globalization and localism? How do they ensure compliance and legitimacy in the face of rising fears of crime (which in many cases have no foundation) and media representations of irresponsible, incompetent and morally deficient police officers who have no idea how to control crime?

It is unlikely that the trend to pluralization and the expansion of security provision generally is going to diminish in the near future. Problems both global and local will continue to be a central focus for all security providers. The challenge for the state will be in developing regulatory and accountability mechanisms for members of the 'extended police family'. The challenge for all members of this family will be to develop trust and reciprocity mechanisms whereby policing can become a more effective, and indeed collective activity committed to addressing security issues at the local, national and international level.

Jenny Fleming and Alison Wakefield

Associated Concepts: auxiliary police, civilianization, contractualism, commodification of security, community policing, globalization, history, intelligence agency, managerialism, pluralization, private security, privatization, security networks, technology, transnational policing

Key Readings

Bayley, D.H. and Shearing, C.D. (1996) 'The future of policing', *Law and Society Review*, 30 (3): 585–606.
Crawford, A., Lister, S., Blackburn, S. and Burnett, J. (2005) *Plural Policing: The*

Mixed Economy of Visible Patrols in England and Wales. Bristol: Policy Press.
Mawby, R.I. (1990) *Comparative Policing Issues*. London: Unwin Hyman.
McLaughlin, E. (2006) *The New Policing*. London: Sage.
Morgan, R. and Newburn, T. (1997) *The Future of Policing*. London: IPPR.
Waddington, P.A.J. (1999) *Policing Citizens*. London: Routledge.
Wakefield, A. (2003) *Selling Security: The Private Policing of Public Space*. Cullompton, Devon: Willan Publishing.

POLICY TRANSFER

Definition

A renowned definition of policy transfer regards it as, 'a process in which knowledge about policies, administrative arrangements, institutions etc., in one time and/or place is used in the development of policies, administrative arrangements and institutions in another time and/or place' (Dolowitz and Marsh, 1996: 344). In criminology the concept has been used to question the methodological nationalism of much research into the origins and outcomes of policy responses to crime and forms part of a broader call for transnational and comparative analyses of control.

Distinctive Features

Apropos the Dolowitz and Marsh definition, the concept of policy transfer has its origins in political science research into the policy process, specifically attempts to explain this process in terms of the isomorphic import/export of ideas and practices. Here the idea of transfer can be counterposed to that of 'autopoiesis' in government; the idea that policy-makers generate their own responses to their own governing problems, this being an often implicit assumption underpinning the methodological nationalism of much research into crime control. If policy-makers cannot afford the time or expense of tailoring their own bespoke solutions, an attractive alternative is to shop around for 'off-the-peg' products; to be, in this regard, net importers of policies. Otherwise, and cognisant of this market in governing ideas, governments with substantial research and development capacities, or indeed more modestly sized but dedicated think tanks, pressure groups and other policy entrepreneurs, can export their products elsewhere, whether for economic and/or political advantage.

The import/export trade in policies is perceived, along with other marketplaces, to have become global, provoking in turn concerns over forms of intellectual imperialism that project the governing visions, priorities and methods of net-exporters more effectively around the world while traducing the complexity and priorities of control in destination states (Aas, 2007: 174ff). In the global market for criminological ideas, the key net exporter is thought to be the US whose budget for research and development dwarfs that of its nearest European states and whose 'penal common sense' is believed to have been diffused across the Atlantic even to European administrations with relatively well-resourced capacities for policy development (Wacquant, 1999).

For critics of the 'Washington consensus' the Americanization of policing and punishment is lamented for recycling policies that are at best products of, and limited in relevance to, their origins in American cities and, at worst, peripatetically damaging as they obviate indigenous cultures of control and social order. It is argued that, notwithstanding its flourishing in other disciplines of social science, a post-colonial perspective has been slow to emerge in criminology precisely because the discipline is so closely aligned with Western political and economic, as well as philosophical, interests perceived to be of limited relevance to the developing world (Agozino, 2003).

In the specific field of policing, the most notable American export has been the 'zero tolerance' or aggressive street policing of misdemeanours and incivilities, proselytized by the New York Police Department. Less

renowned but of arguably greater impact has been the export of 'problem-oriented' policing, specifically the notion that police work should be 'intelligence-led', in which police do not simply react to discrete calls for assistance but seek to ascertain any patterns to these calls, interpret the underlying causes of these patterns, undertake responses tailored to the solution of these causes and evaluate the outcomes of these responses. The 'SARA' process of problem-oriented policing ('scanning' for evidence of the patterned qualities of policing problems, such as 'hot-spots' of crime and disorder, 'analysis' of the potential causes of these problems, implementing a 'response' that is tailored to these causes, and 'assessment' of the outcomes of this response), has become a key focus of police reform in the UK, forming a key part of the £400m Home Office Crime Reduction Programme that ran from 1999 to 2002.

In addition to the American export of specific policing measures, there have been important methodological exports for evaluating these measures, most notably the 'Maryland Scale' of criteria for establishing 'what works, what doesn't and what's promising' in community policing strategies and other forms of crime prevention (Sherman et al., 1997). Again, the Maryland Scale, which prioritizes quasi-experimental methods for evaluating preventive measures using randomized control trials, has been enthusiastically adopted by the British Home Office and explicitly formed the basis of the action research element of its Crime Reduction Programme. In these terms not only are particular policing technologies such as the SARA process transferred, but also the means of assessing their efficacy. Such attempts to police even the grounds on which policing measures can be criticized are the ultimate instance of an intellectual imperialism that privileges generalizations about policing practices while obviating contextualized insight into particular policing conditions.

Evaluation

A more sceptical note has, however, been struck by findings from empirical research into the actual content of policy transfer in crime control (Newburn and Sparks, 2004). Research into the transatlantic trade in crime control polices, such as zero tolerance policing, between the US and UK suggests there is little evidence of direct lesson-drawing (Jones and Newburn, 2007). Moreover, policy differences among states within the US were striking, suggesting significant limitations in the capacity of any Washington Consensus to project its influence within the US, much less further afield.

The uneven diffusion of policy ideas within the US alerts us to the messy and contested qualities of policy transfer. Contrary to the over-rationalized imagery of policy-making found in much of the policy transfer literature, attempted exports are often filtered, subverted, resisted and adapted by importing destinations, both within as well as between sovereign nation states according to established political cultures (Stenson and Edwards, in Newburn and Sparks, 2004). The direction of policy change and learning is neither simple nor linear with problems and solutions, questions and answers, circulating around the 'political stream' with no necessary relationship to one another (Newburn and Sparks, 2004: 12). This is the *realpolitik* context in which 'evidence-based policy-making' becomes transmuted into 'policy-based evidence' and in which policy entrepreneurs search for problems to the ready-made solutions they wish to market to various political consumers seeking advantage over their opponents.

Further distinctions can be made between the trade in policy 'talk', policy 'decisions' and policy 'action'. Whereas the trade in talk about, for example 'zero tolerance', may have been extensive, certainly around the Anglophone world, the translation of this talk into control practices which bear much resemblance to one another is a moot point. The political investment that policy actors have in particular crime control policies can make them especially resilient to reform, acting as a further blockage to the fungibility of policies developed elsewhere.

Beyond arguments over the verisimilitude of policy talk, decisions and action in different jurisdictions of crime control, the very possibility of policy transfer has been questioned. It is argued that complete transfer of policies is impossible, given that the concepts which render them meaningful are embedded within specific cultural contexts that are not entirely accessible to those outwith these contexts (Melossi, in Newburn and Sparks: 2004: 82–4).

Notwithstanding the considerable barriers to policy transfer, the proposition that policy actors can learn little from those outside of their cultural milieu is as improbable as the proposition that policy-makers, even net-importers of criminology, are subservient to criminological exporters. This would be to substitute a false particularity in understanding policy change and learning for the false universalism of the more hubristic entrepreneurs of Western criminology. Rather, the distinction between 'autopoietic' and 'isomorphic' learning is better regarded as an heuristic device, identifying tendencies towards self-reliance or emulation among policy-makers with differential traditions and resources for research and development.

In these terms the debate over policy transfer remains vital for disturbing the methodological nationalism that has characterized much of criminology, specifically the presumption that any national culture of control can be understood in its own terms. Research into the practice of criminal law enforcement suggests considerable differences at the sub-national level and the importance of local context is accentuated further when the focus is shifted from the enforcement of criminal legal codes, which are constitutive of nation states, to more preventive strategies of control which permit greater local discretion in decision-making. A focus on sub-national crime control policies reveals multi-lateral networks among local actors within and across nation states, for example the transnational policing networks forged through the European Union's institutions for police and judicial cooperation, the transnational network of municipal authorities involved in the European Forum for Urban Safety or the intra-national community safety network in Britain. Such networks generate hitherto non-existent opportunities for learning about crime control policies that circumvent more established lines of communication and command between national ministries of the interior on the one hand and local agencies on the other. That such opportunities may not generate the simple replication of policies, or 'total transfer', should not detract from their importance in generating and circulating alternative ideas and technologies.

Understanding such prospective, as well as retrospective, origins of policy change and learning matters both for empirical and normative debates over criminological variants of the globalization question; whether the perceived 'imperialism' of Western, specifically American, criminology or the aspiration for a genuinely global, cosmopolitan criminology. Such questions cannot be posed, much less corroborated or falsified, within a national or even international frame of reference. They entail a more nuanced investigation of the temporal and spatial scales through which criminological knowledge can be produced. Policy transfer remains useful as a means of conceptualizing such research and an important focal point for developments in transnational and comparative criminology.

Adam Edwards

Associated Concepts: community policing, evidence-based policing, problem-oriented policing, research, zero tolerance policing

Key Readings

Aas, K. F. (2007) *Globalization and Crime.* London: Sage.

Agozino, B. (2003) *Counter-Colonial Criminology: A Critique of Imperialist Reason.* London: Pluto Press.

Dolowitz, D. and Marsh, D. (1996) 'Who learns what from whom? A review of the policy transfer literature', *Political Studies,* 44 (2): 343–57.

Jones, T. and Newburn, T. (2007) *Policy Transfer and Criminal Justice: Exploring US Influence over British Crime Control Policy.* London: McGraw-Hill.

Newburn, T. and Sparks, R. (eds) (2004) *Criminal Justice and Political Cultures: National and International Dimensions of Crime Control.* Cullompton, Devon: Willan Publishing.

Sherman, L., et al. (1997) *Crime Prevention: What Works, What Doesn't and What's Promising.* Washington DC: National Institute of Justice.

Wacquant, L. (1999) 'How penal common sense comes to Europeans: notes on the transatlantic diffusion of the neoliberal doxa', *European Societies,* 1 (3): 319–52.

POSTMODERN POLICING

Definition

A quick literature review suggests that there is no possibility of constructing uncontested definitions of the terms 'postmodern', 'postmodernity' and 'postmodernism' because of their disparate origins and interdisciplinary utilization. Consequently, prominent practitioners of postmodern thinking exhibit considerable differences in the nature and scope of their enquiries, as well as their particular emphases. It should also be noted that the terms have moved in certain academic disciplines from being intellectual buzzwords to becoming tired clichés.

Within police studies three 'postmodern' perspectives can be discerned, one analyzing what the advent of a 'postmodern society' means for policing, another concentrating on the unfolding relationship between the police and the 'postmodern state' and a third considering the police and 'postmodern culture'.

Distinctive Features

The sociological analysis of Robert Reiner illustrates the first perspective most fully (Reiner, 1992). Reiner's task is to account for the changing position of the police in British society. His key premise is that the police must be understood as a cultural category because the role of the police is symbolic as well as instrumental. A drawn out process of civilization and winning of public consent led to a golden era of the late 1940s and early 1950s, when the British police constable was the embodiment of the ideal citizen of a civilized modern society. The role of the police constable in the social democratic settlement was to protect the weak and vulnerable from the criminal and anti-social. He played a crucial role in binding communities together and establishing a common conception of citizenship and solidarity. The fictional character PC George Dixon (of Dock Green) exemplified this emergent post-war 'golden age' of public tranquillity, social consensus and police legitimacy.

However, since that time, Reiner notes an ongoing decline in public support for the police, particularly among the young, ethnic minorities, and marginal groups in British society. This has been accompanied by dramatically increasing levels of crime, disorder and anti-social behaviour, the exposure of a number of scandals and the loss of unquestioning state support. In accounting for this shift, Reiner looks to the fundamental transformations in Britain's social structure and culture which constitute the coming of a postmodern society. As this unity and consensus have fragmented, so inevitably have perceptions of the police. The once 'sacred' institution has been thoroughly profaned and is subject to constant scrutiny and reform.

For Reiner, post-Fordist 'turbo capitalism' is defined by:

- competitive consumerism which generates increasing diversity, difference and fragmentation;
- neo-liberal ideologies which prioritize the free market over public services; and
- shifting social values and attitudes which produces a less hierarchical, less deferential culture and a resultant loss of respect for and trust of public authority.

These dramatic socio-economic shifts and cultural changes form the pincer movement in which the police have been caught. He is only too well aware that the clock cannot be turned back to a mythical 'golden age' of social democratic policing.

There is a strong sense of loss and fear woven into the heart of his analysis. The loss relates to the passing of the possibility of a consensual social order. The fear relates to worries about the fall out from the unstoppable postmodernization of social relations and policing. Reiner believes that we are moving towards an anomic non-society characterized by pervasive insecurity and paranoia. Those who can afford to do so will live in 'security bubbles' shielded by space, architecture, surveillance technologies and private guards, while the underclass will be consigned to the 'dreadful enclosures' of ghettoes and 'no go areas'. In this bleak scenario, public police forces will be instrumentalized with few sources of cultural authority and legitimacy. A very real risk is 'residualization' with the public police being supplemented or even replaced by an assortment of private policing and security bodies, and a more diffuse array of policing, surveillance and control techniques: what Reiner refers to as 'pick-n-mix' policing for a postmodern age'. Police officers will have to perform a limited range of mundane, crime control and coercive order maintenance tasks in an unsupportive context.

The second postmodern perspective is articulated by Sheptycki. Writing from a political science perspective, he conceives of postmodernism as a fundamental break with modernity reflected in changes in political economy, wrought by transnationalization of goods, services and people. For him the category of the 'postmodern' indicates that we have entered into something beyond what has gone before. Like Reiner he believes that the modern police emerged as part of the governmental project of the European nation state. Nineteenth century police agencies were 'the concrete expression of the state's monopoly of coercive force *within* its territory, just as the branches of the military were the expression of that power at the borders' (1998: 488).

As the boundaries of nation state sovereignty de-territorialize, this historical correlation is inevitably called into question. The 'character of the nation state system is currently undergoing significant transformations that is both visible in changing forms of policing and constitutive of these new forms' (1998: 498). Sheptycki acknowledges that transnationalization *per se* is not necessarily new and that there are also tendencies towards the localization of certain policing functions. However, 'the local' is not his centre of attention. Amongst an array of factors that makes the various trends and shifts postmodern he sees the following as being the most significant:

• The freeing up of global markets and globalizing of criminal opportunities;
• An intensification of 'panic scenes' and corresponding 'folk devils' that contributes to increasing insecurity;
• 'Responsibilization' strategies through which the state increasingly places the emphasis on individuals and communities to protect themselves from crime and disorder; and
• The expansion of a 'security market' as reflected in the growth of private policing.

For Sheptycki, the most likely outcome will be a 'patchwork quilt' of policing, reflecting unevenness in the extent to which the shift to postmodern statehood has occurred in a given jurisdiction. In certain instances, there could be a residual public police force, dwarfed by a much larger omnicompetent private sector or a hybrid model in which there is some sort of partnership between the two sectors. Political or 'high policing' will be increasingly pulled into the global realm as reflected in the growth of international policing and criminal justice arrangements. An obvious 'watch this space' reference point for Sheptycki is the development of a European Union policing agenda which is beginning to blur domestic and foreign jurisdictional matters. Europeanization is replete with possibilities for 'spill-over' into as yet unidentified new policing domains.

McLaughlin and Murji (2000) augmented the work of Reiner and Sheptycki with an emphasis on the postmodern 'cultural turn' which is 'hyper-realizing' the police. They utilized Baudrillard's theorizing on a 'hyper-real' universe in which the boundaries between fact and fiction, information and entertainment are seen to have been ruptured. For McLaughlin

and Murji, the police are trapped within a highly unpredictable, imaginary 24/7, global 'police entertainment complex' that has the potential at any moment to trigger an uncontrollable crisis of 'hyper-real' representation. Mediatized representations 'without guarantees' may undercut, stand in for and/or replace the foundational narratives of the 'real' police. A combination of audience demands for cop shows, an over flowing of media spaces to be filled and the consequent over-production is producing unpredictable results. Popular dramas based on successful formulas continue to endlessly recycle nostalgic stereotypes regarding the capabilities of the detective.

Then there is a bricolage of media representations that make very uncomfortable watching. The commercial media recognize that changing racial, gender and age demographics and cultural shifts in public attitude must be taken into account in the construction of new cop shows. As a consequence, unconventional, counter or marginal narratives which could not be previously represented are being aired and authenticated. These range from unflattering or ambivalent fictional representations which play with layers of ambiguity and foreground images of moral disorientation and organizational lawlessness, through to the various 'hot button' docudramas on police malpractice. Police chiefs protest about alterations in viewing position and the impact of this intolerable, uncontrollable excess of reality on public opinion of the police. It also causes difficulties for relatively straight prime time cop shows that engage in multiple contortions in attempting to cope with the burden of representing the policing of contemporary London, as episodes have to inscribe and subvert, assert and deny the generic narratives, conventions and stereotypes of fictional police work.

Thus within the 'police entertainment complex' we can witness a dual shift. First, of setting: displacing monolithic images with a plurality of images, and blurring the boundaries between fiction and reality; and second, of perspective, where the police rather than the policed are the object of the problematizing televisual gaze. For

McLaugh-lin and Murji, the circulation and proliferation of hybrid, hyper-real and 'counterfeit' images of policing in various media spaces means that old distinctions between the real and the fictional are rapidly collapsing. Media representations of policing are flickering so intensely that 'real' policing is in danger of 'disappearing'. Ironically, because the police cannot evade or deny the problem of watching their own cultural de-valuation, they have to invest ever more resources in managing public relations which reinforces dependence on the media.

Evaluation

Policing scholars recognize that globalization, the advent of new information and telecommunication technologies, unfolding Europeanization, internal multi-pluralization, and the 'new individualism' means that Western societies are in the process of rapid transformation. Alongside radically different forms of risk, uncertainty and instability, and the way they are perceived, an incisive reordering of the techniques and logics of policing, security and social control is taking place. The tectonic plates of policing are undoubtedly shifting.

Although there has been acknowledgement of the urgent need to rethink the assumptions and registers on which police studies has been premised, policing scholars are extremely cautious in their engagement with broader social analysis. For the most part, they have been reluctant to engage with any form of postmodern theorizing. For some it is intellectually compromised by its denial of social scientific rationality and objectivity. For others, it represents a cynical celebration of neo-liberalism and consumer society.

As a consequence, we have a variety of what might be best defined as anti-postmodern police studies. Administrative police scholars tend not to analyze the policing implications of broader social transformations. Their primary focus remains practical in orientation, for example, assessing operational effectiveness, the quality of policing and organizational reform. Sociologists of the police still prefer to address the transformations through the general theory of late, high or reflexive modernity and/or risk society associated with theorists such as Anthony Giddens and Ulrich Beck. Consequently, the main perspectives remain wedded to an understanding of modernity as an on-going project still charged with the reformist potential of claims to universal citizenship, progress, justice and organizational rationality. More recently, debate has focused on examining the reconstitution of policing within the broader project of neo-liberal governmentality and security.

The strength of utilizing postmodern analysis lies in making both bold assertions and posing a broad spread of critical questions about privatization, pluralization and globalization of policing and security, changing forms of neo-liberal governance, the post-social society and examining the police as a cultural phenomenon. By definition, postmodern analysis sanctions scepticism about the assumptions, claims and promises of modernist inspired police reform projects.

Eugene McLaughlin

Associated Concepts: consent, globalization, governmentality, legitimacy, pluralization, reform, security, transnational policing

Key Readings

Ericson, R. and Haggerty, K. (1997) *Policing the Risk Society*. Oxford: Clarendon Press.
McLaughlin, E. and Murji, K. (1999) 'The postmodern condition of the police', *Liverpool Law Review*, 21 (2–3): 217–40.
O'Malley, P. (1997) 'Policing, politics and postmodernity', *Social and Legal Studies*, 6 (3): 363–81.
Reiner, R. (1992) 'Policing a postmodern society', *Modern Law Review*, 55 (6): 761–81.
Sheptycki, J. (1998) 'Policing, postmodernism and transnationalization', *British Journal of Criminology*, 38 (3): 485–503.

POWERS

*See Arrest; Citizen's Arrest; Discretion; Firearms;
Force; Search*

PRIVATE SECURITY

Definition

'Private security' encompasses all crime prevention, investigative and law enforcement activities carried out on a contractual commercial basis or within private firms. In other words, it concerns those policing and protective services *not* provided by public sector police, funded by taxation, and delivered free of charge to citizens. It also excludes security activities provided on a voluntary or non-commercial 'community' basis.

Distinctive Features

One of the most prominent features of private security has been its rapid growth internationally in the post Second World War period. A variety of reasons have been put forward for this phenomenon. One is the steep rise in crime experienced by many countries, especially in the 1970s and 1980s. Additional factors include improvements in security technology (especially alarms and closed circuit television), enlarged legal obligations for the protection of visitors, the growth of 'mass private property' (such as shopping malls and sporting facilities), and increased prosperity with more private property and consumer goods to protect. The industry has continued to grow despite declining or stable crime rates from the 1990s. In this context, it is likely that continuing relatively high rates of crime in many countries continue to feed demand. A more general consciousness regarding the need for 'self protection' and the value of place-based applied security management has also taken over from the older reliance on police for crime prevention.

The growth of private security has been distinctive in proceeding through market mechanisms rather than large scale government policies of privatization or changes to legislation. However, the exact dimensions of growth are difficult to identify. Security work cuts across official government census and industry categories, and census figures usually only capture workers' full-time occupations. As much as 50 per cent of employment in security in many countries may be secondary and part-time. Nonetheless, some general points can be made about the size of the industry. The first is that, since about the 1960s, private security guards (along with many public sector guards) have become highly visible in everyday life. Some scholars describe guards as 'ubiquitous' – as is commercially provided security hardware – especially in areas such as shopping malls, stadiums and transport hubs. Studies that attempt to measure expenditures and staffing – especially by comparing the core groups of police and guards – have found enormous variation between countries. Some, especially many European countries, have tended to have less security guards than police; and others, such as the US, appear to have significantly more. De Waard's (1999) international study – the most comprehensive to-date – estimated the number of security personnel in Europe averaged 160 per 100,000 persons. Britain had the most, with 275 per 100,000; and Greece had the lowest, with 19. South Africa was counted as having the highest proportion internationally, with 900 security personnel per 100,000, followed by the US with 582.

Private security can be delivered in divergent forms. The largest sector is 'contract security', where an independent security firm supplies security services direct to clients. Clients can include government departments, resulting in a mixed mode of public-private delivery. Private security also includes 'in-house', or 'proprietary', security employees within larger firms, such as 'store detectives'. Some governments also have small security units that contract services to other government departments or even offer services on the open market. There are also numerous examples of limited commercialization by police departments. Prisoner escort duties have been contracted out in some jurisdictions, and some police departments encourage sponsorship of crime prevention programmes or pieces of equipment, such as rescue helicopters. Traditionally, police have also engaged in a variety of commercial activities, including hiring out officers for security at large events or for traffic control at road works. Police departments, especially in Western countries, are increasingly active in providing a range of services on a commercial basis to police departments in developing nations – including training, forensic services and even general policing. Overall, however, these activities remain largely at the margins of state-controlled police work.

The contemporary prominence of private security is not entirely unique. The period of the apparent dominance of public police – from the early 1800s to the 1970s – may be a transient historical aberration – as argued by Johnston (1992). Modern policing was preceded by growth in private security associated with the mercantile period of expanding global trade. It also overlapped the industrial revolution and colonial period, which saw significant growth in private recovery agents, private prosecution societies and 'company police'. One major difference is that where the first wave of private security was focused on detection and recovery, the second wave has been focused on protection. At the same time, detection and recovery have been features of the post-1980s corporate response to problems of computer hacking, insurance fraud, and copyright and patent violations. Massive growth in personal credit in this period has also contributed to the growth of private debt recovery services.

Evaluation

Is the growth of private security, and its almost ubiquitous presence, good or bad? Responses to this question have been dogged by ideological agendas and conflicting evidence, much like the wider debate about privatization. The rapid growth in private security and its infiltration into all areas of life have been accompanied by alarm over insidious forms of social control, loss of privacy and compounded divisions in society. A social justice critique of private security argues it entails a shift away from an egalitarian public policing system to a 'user pays' system in which fundamental democratic rights of safety and security depend on capacity to pay. Critics also allege that security in various forms, including gated communities, tends to exclude minority groups and displace crime to poorer areas. There have also been concerns about 'private justice' processes where suspects may be expelled from premises or have their employment terminated without due process. One counter argument to these critiques is that private protection by wealthy persons frees police to provide a better service to the general public. Public sector policing, it is also argued, remains locked into a largely reactive system of rapid response to crime calls by patrol officers and follow up investigations by detectives. There is little capacity in the public system for more effective on-site tailor-made preventive measures of the type provided by security services.

The growth of private security has been accompanied by numerous scandals and recurring problems of misconduct by security personnel, including violence, insider crime, fraud and incompetence. These problems have obliged governments that may be wedded ideologically to deregulation to enlarge controls on the industry. Conduct issues have meant that in this case privatization has not been accompanied by deregulation on the whole. The trend internationally is towards greater control of private security by governments through licensing regimes, including mandated training, criminal history checks for disqualifying offences and complaints investigation.

Despite the critics, the future of private policing is most likely one of increasing prominence in a mixed economy of policing, both as a low cost front-line preventive presence and in specialist corporate operations. Improved government regulation should go someway to reduce misconduct in the sector, and may also improve the status and conditions of private security personnel.

Tim Prenzler

Associated Concepts: auxiliary policing, citizen's arrest, contractualism, closed circuit television, commodification of security, pluralization, privatization, responsibilization, security, security networks, third party policing

Key Readings

Dempsey, J. (2008) *Introduction to Private Security*. Belmont, CA: Thomson Wadsworth.

de Waard, J. (1999) 'The private security industry in international perspective', *European Journal on Criminal Policy and Research*, 7: 143–74.

Gill, M. and Hart, J. (1997) 'Policing as a business: the organization and structure of private investigation', *Policing and Society*, 7(2): 117–41.

Johnston, L. (1992) *The Rebirth of Private Policing*. London: Routledge.

Sarre, R. and Prenzler, T. (2005) *The Law of Private Security in Australia*. Sydney: Thomson Lawbook Company.

Wakefield, A. (2003) *Selling Security: The Private Policing of Public Space*. Cullompton, Devon: Willan Publishing.

PRIVATIZATION

Definition

Privatization is described by Saunders and Harris (1990: 58) as 'a confused concept which carries many different meanings'. Variants include 'outsourcing', 'commercialization', 'user pays' and 'deregulation'. Most simply, it refers to a process in which government-owned assets or services are wholly or partially transferred to private companies.

The concept is seen by a number of commentators as having evolved to embrace a range of actions whereby the delivery of public services is exposed to market forces. Pirie (1988) identifies 21 different types of privatization, while Saunders and Harris (1990) summarize these diverse forms in a four-fold classification. They categorize actions according to the locus of responsibility (producers or consumers) and the change in the government's role (change of ownership or change of control). Changes of ownership comprise 'denationalization': the selling of a state-owned agency to a private service provider; and 'commodification': the selling of state-owned resources to those who consume them. Changes of control consist of processes of 'liberalization', where responsibility for providing or financing a good or service is retained by the state, while non-state agencies are partially or fully responsible for its delivery; and 'marketization': the provision of allowances to consumers to purchase goods and services previously delivered by the state.

In exploring the relevance of such a movement to policing, Johnston (1992) refers to the 'privatization mentality' seen by some to have taken hold in UK government policy from the 1980s. This has been manifested in a number of policy developments, many of which have been mirrored internationally, paralleled by intensifying marketplace developments as new commercial opportunities have been realized.

Distinctive Features

According to Pirie (1988), the concept was little used before 1979. As a product of the managerialist movement that has swept through industrialized countries since the 1980s in the drive for greater efficiency in public sector management, privatization has been a key feature of political economies, spreading internationally following a rigorous privatization programme in the UK. Thus, most countries have seen government-owned institutions, such as banks, and monopoly services such as railways and electricity, sold to private companies. The justification has been that commercial competition and the profit motive provide powerful incentives for more efficient and better quality services to the public. There has also been a decisive shift to 'user pays' principles, based on the idea that competition promotes efficiency and resources can be allocated most efficiently when consumers bear the whole cost of the product, in policy areas such as education and health.

Equally subject to tightening financial accountability, such principles have been applied to police services, albeit in a more limited way. Johnston (1992) identifies three trends in policing which he terms 'privatization', although he also applies broader labels such as 'commercialization' and 'liberalization' that are arguably more suitable. The first of these is termed 'load shedding', as certain areas of policing are supplemented or replaced by commercial or voluntary provision. This is reflected primarily in the substantial growth of the commercial security sector, but Johnston also uses the term to include instances of police actively encouraging or 'responsibilizing' third party action, as in the case of neighbourhood watch schemes, as well as situations when some police functions are 'usurped' by voluntary action. An especially visible example is that of street patrol, carried out by community groups on a voluntary basis (such initiatives are particularly developed in New Zealand where they are represented by a national body, the Community Patrols of New Zealand Charitable Trust) or private security firms hired by residents' collectives.

A second category of police privatization is 'contracting out' or outsourcing, whereby police enter into contracts with third parties to purchase goods or services from them. While this has been a longstanding and uncontroversial practice in the procurement of goods such as stationery and police equipment, and ancillary services such as cleaning, catering and maintenance, other areas of police work or the police organization more generally are now increasingly subject to outsourcing. These include custodial and prisoner escort services (also extending through the criminal justice system to electronic monitoring and private prison services), opening up whole new areas of business for the private security industry; forensic services; and information technology development and delivery.

Johnston's third category concerns the levying of charges for certain police services, or 'user pays' policing, a further form of 'contractualism'. Police services can be sold to other public institutions as well as commercial interests. In Australia, the Australian Federal Police is responsible for the policing of the Australian Capital Territory (ACT), including the nation's capital Canberra. The Canadian government contracts with the Royal Canadian Mounted Police (RCMP) for policing services provided to most of the country's provinces and territories. An interesting development in the UK has been the expansion of community policing through the sale of additional patrol services (including auxiliary police known as 'police community support officers') to other public institutions such as local authorities. Such a practice sees the police effectively engaging in active competition with alternative service providers such as local authority employed wardens or private security. Also of interest in the UK is the financing of the British Transport Police, responsible for the policing of the railways and underground rail systems, provided mainly through the charges for its services made to the private franchises of the rail network. In the US it has been permissible for a long time for individual police officers to 'moonlight', supplementing their pay by providing uniformed security and sometimes equipped with firearms at special events and private establishments such as bars and nightclubs, banks, apartment complexes and retail outlets. Police forces also provide such services directly for private hire.

Evaluation

Operational policing has been largely immune from deliberate policies of privatization or commercialization, although there is some international movement towards the civilianization trends that have been so substantial in the UK. Suggestions made in the UK that certain areas of police activity would be suitable for outsourcing, first outlined by the Adam Smith Institute in 1984 and later reflected in the terms of reference of the Home Office Review of Core and Ancillary Tasks in 1993, in practice led to little in the way of 'selling off' of police facilities or police tasks. In other countries debates have not progressed this far. This is because profit making is seen as being incompatible with the ideals of impartial justice and universal service intrinsic to modern policing. Police numbers are also always a politically charged issue and perceived threats to public police are considered an electoral liability.

There has, however, been a *de facto* privatization of policing which has resulted in a revolution in how policing is being done. This has occurred largely through rapid growth in the demand for private security, resulting in phenomenal growth in the sector. Some of the demand has come from government, but there do not appear to be any clear cases where governmental 'contracting in' of private security has been associated with significant long-term cuts in police resources. Rather, privatization has been one part – albeit a very significant one – of a more general diversification and growth in law enforcement and crime prevention services worldwide. Notably, such *de facto* privatization of policing by market forces has been a major feature of societies in transition from communism to capitalism, such as China, Russia and Eastern Europe. In the disturbing case of Russia, for example, burgeoning crime has led to a corresponding demand for private security in a now crowded security marketplace, including services of protection both by and from a ubiquitous Russian Mafia.

Alison Wakefield and Tim Prenzler

Associated Concepts: auxiliary police, commodification of security, contractualism, managerialism, multi-agency policing, pluralization, private security, responsibilization, third party policing, transnational policing

Key Readings

Adam Smith Institute (1984) *The 'Omega File': Justice Policy*. London: Adam Smith Institute.

Johnston, L. (1992) *The Rebirth of Private Policing*. London: Routledge.

Pirie, M. (1988) *Privatization*. Aldershot: Wildwood House.

Prenzler, T. (2004) 'The privatization of policing', in R. Sarre and J. Tomaino (eds) *Key Issues in Criminal Justice*. Unley, SA: Australian Humanities Press.

Saunders, P. and Harris, C. (1990) 'Privatization and the consumer', *Sociology*, 24 (1): 57–75.

Wakefield, A. (2003) *Selling Security: The Private Policing of Public Space*. Cullompton, Devon: Willan Publishing.

PROBLEM-ORIENTED POLICING

Definition

Problem-oriented policing (POP) is an approach to policing within which primacy is attached to preventing the recurrence of problem behaviours which fall within the remit of the police rather than merely reacting to individual calls for service as and when they occur. POP involves an outcome-focused and strongly analytic way of working. The aim is both better to serve the public and to reduce demand on the police by developing effective tailor-made responses to systematically identified police-relevant problems of community concern.

Distinctive Features

The term 'problem-oriented policing' was first coined by Herman Goldstein, an American professor of law and former advisor to the Chicago police service. He outlined his ideas in an article published in 1979 and later developed them further in a book length discussion published in 1990. Goldstein criticized police services' preoccupations with maximizing organizational efficiency rather than with their core purpose as he saw it: that of reducing the harm caused by the very wide range of problems of concern to citizens which fall within the remit of the police. The delivery of POP is associated with systematic interrogation of police-relevant problems and critical examination of existing practice. Responses based on that analysis and insight should be developed and implemented. If appropriate, these responses should go beyond conventional police enforcement and draw in non-police agencies. There should be rigorous assessment and evaluation of the impact of the new responses to guard against one ineffective response replacing another; to ensure that a response is effective over time; and to ensure that the response does not revert back to its reactive, traditional form.

Since the early 1980s a large number of police services around the world have attempted to implement POP. There are many examples of good practice in delivering POP and a great deal of evidence to suggest that it can be effective in reducing specific problems. The winners of the annual Goldstein and Tilley Awards, in the US and the UK respectively, provide notable examples.

Two mnemonics have come to be used almost universally in efforts to undertake of POP. The first is 'SARA' and the second 'PAT'. SARA summarizes the main processes involved in the conduct of POP. 'Scanning' refers to the identification and prioritization of problems on the basis of evidence. 'Analysis' refers to the collection and interrogation of information about that problem in order to answer questions about its nature and the crucial conditions for its manifestation. 'Response' refers to the formulation and then delivery of tailor-made measures, normally including those going beyond the criminal justice system, to reduce, remove, or ameliorate the effects of the problem behaviour. 'Assessment' refers to measurement of the intended and unintended impacts of the new responses.

'PAT' refers to the Problem Analysis Triangle. PAT is commonly used as an heuristic device to help think about problems and to formulate responses to them. It highlights three features of crimes and other problems that should be considered. These are the location(s) in which the crime (or other problem behaviour) is happening, the offenders (or other individuals) whose actions are creating the problem, and the victims (or the complainants). While not identical, PAT connects conceptually most clearly to 'Routine Activities Theory' (RAT). According to RAT, three conditions have to come together in time and space for a direct contact predatory crime to take place: a motivated offender, a suitable target, and the absence of an effective intermediary. An effective intermediary could be either a 'capable guardian' (someone who might plausibly intervene on behalf of the target or victim to protect them) or an 'intimate handler' (a significant other who might lessen an individual's disposition to offend at that time and place). The implication of RAT is that any scope there might be to manipulate any one of the essential elements for crime comprises an opportunity for preventative intervention.

Evaluation

The appeal of POP is not difficult to understand. It promises simultaneously a way of better managing resources and of improving services to the community. Despite the prominence of POP in the rhetoric of policing policy and practice, studies have shown that it has been difficult to deliver on the ground. Successful attempts at police service wide implementation of the ideal are indeed rare and the delivery of most problem-oriented policing is probably best described as a series of individual projects, many of which are associated with highly motivated individuals. Commonly identified problems and obstacles to the routine delivery of problem-oriented policing include the following:

(1) *Weaknesses in the analytic capacity*: There have been limitations in the capability for and resources allocated to analysis in police services, as well as in the quality and availability of suitable data. These have restricted what can be achieved.

(2) *Inadequate involvement of partners*: The police are rarely in a position directly to implement longer-term solutions to the recurrent problems to which they are called. Engagement of third parties is therefore crucial. This has proved to be

difficult, and has affected the range of interventions which could realistically be implemented in tackling problems.

(3) *Failure to appreciate the variety of means that might be used effectively to deal with problems:* There is no organized body of knowledge about how to deal with the wide range of problems to which the police are called. The development of problem-oriented responses may be hampered by police officers' lack of expertise in methods of dealing with problems other than through conventional criminal justice avenues.

(4) *Inattention to and weaknesses in evaluation:* Evaluation is rarely well done. It is commonly omitted altogether or limited in scope where it is attempted. This is at least partly because evaluation is a specialist and time consuming task for which the police are normally ill-equipped.

(5) *The imperative for and cultural emphasis on responding to emergencies:* It has proved difficult to shift the dominant reactive police organizational culture and the pressure to respond to emergencies as they occur.

(6) *Hasty and inadequately thought through implementation:* It is common for the time that it takes to deliver problem-oriented policing to be underestimated. The project management skills required to coordinate implementation are not widely available.

(7) *Lack of relevant training and education:* Officers may find it hard to translate the concepts of problem-oriented policing into practice. There has been very limited availability of competent training in the concepts and techniques of problem-oriented policing within and across police services.

(8) *Inadequate incentive and reward:* Measurement of officer performance is traditionally based on response times, arrests and detections. This may conflict with delivering POP which calls for critical thinking and the development of wide-ranging responses.

As well as obstacles to delivering POP, there have been misunderstandings about what the term means in practice. Common misconstructions of POP include the following:

(1) *That problem-oriented policing equates to problem-solving:* That detailed and systematic analysis which is crucial to POP is not required for dealing with many of the day-to-day problems for which the police service has responsibility.

(2) *That problem-oriented policing is conducted only at local (individual and beat) levels:* POP can be applied to problems at a variety of levels, from the local to the national or even global. Though generally manifesting themselves locally many problems are widely found and may be open to analysis and intervention at a broader level.

(3) *That problem-oriented policing is synonymous with community policing:* POP normally begins with those problems identified by communities and sometimes it will involve mobilizing community resources as a means of tackling a problem but this will not always be the case.

(4) *That problem-oriented policing is the same as intelligence-led policing:* The primary concern of intelligence-led policing is the informed and targeted delivery of enforcement interventions. POP aims to tackle significant police relevant problems for which normal policing methods have failed. Law enforcement may be one means of doing so, but is not generally sufficient where efforts are being made to find and implement long-term solutions.

Karen Bullock and Nick Tilley

Associated Concepts: community policing, intelligence-led policing, multi-agency policing, performance management, policy transfer

Key Readings

Bullock, K. and Tilley, N. (eds) (2003) *Crime Reduction and Problem-oriented Policing*. Cullompton, Devon: Willan Publishing.

Bullock. K., Erol, R. and Tilley, N. (2006) *Problem-oriented Policing and Partnerships: Implementing an Evidence Based Approach to Crime Reduction*. Cullompton, Devon: Willan Publishing.

Goldstein, H. (1979) 'Improving policing: a problem-oriented approach', *Crime and Delinquency*, 25 (2): 236–58.

Goldstein, H. (1990) *Problem-Oriented Policing*. New York: McGraw Hill.

Leigh, A., Read, T. and Tilley, N. (1996) *Problem-Oriented Policing: Brit POP*. Crime Prevention and Detection, Paper 75. London: Home Office.

Read, T. and Tilley, N. (2000) *Not Rocket Science?: Problem Solving and Crime Reduction*, Crime Reduction Research Series, Paper 6. London: Home Office.

Scott, M. (2000). *Problem-Oriented Policing: Reflections on the First 20 Years*. Washington D.C.: U.S. Department of Justice, Office of Community Oriented Policing Services.

PROFESSIONALIZATION

Definition

A *professional* is a member of a group which has attained the status of a profession and *professionalism* is an ideology subscribed to by individuals aspiring to professional status within either an occupation or a recognized profession. Historically and contemporaneously, a profession can be reduced and defined into a set core of criteria which, if fulfilled, can result in the attainment of professional status through a process of professionalization. The term *police professionalization* can therefore be used to describe the process by which policing moves to become a profession.

Distinctive Features

While numerous studies have been undertaken and a vast amount of literature has been written, there is very little concurrence upon a single definition that encapsulates the notion or defines a profession, exacerbated by confusion due to the wide and excessive use of the word. Perhaps the greatest discourse has occurred within the disciplines of psychology and sociology where an approach to defining professions that has dominated, labelled as the 'taxonomic approach', provides a checklist of particular attributes that could be utilized to distinguish professions from non-professions. Perhaps one of the best known among those who have adopted this approach is Ernest Greenwood who asserted that professions have the following attributes: a systematic body of theory, professional authority, community sanction, ethical codes and a professional culture. Other defining attributes offered include full-time occupation, commitment to a calling, identified with their peers – often in formalized organization, possession of esoteric but useful knowledge and skills – based on specialized training or education of exceptional duration and perhaps of exceptional difficulty, service orientation, and professional autonomy.

Following the lead of their US and English counterparts, in the 1990s the leaders within Australian policing announced their intention to professionalize policing, choosing the US Police Executive Research Forum's (PERF) eight characteristic 'attribute' approach to defining a profession, namely:

(1) An organized body of knowledge constantly augmented and refined;
(2) Involves a lengthy training/education period;
(3) Operates so as to serve its clients best;
(4) Operates autonomously and exercises control over members;
(5) Develops a community of practitioners through professional standards;
(6) Enforces a code of ethics and behaviour;
(7) Establishes uniform standards of practice; and
(8) Provides full professional mobility.

In March 2006, the Australian and New Zealand Police Commissioners established a working group to review the professionalization of Australasian policing. As a result of a comprehensive literature review and study of numerous professions from around the world, the working group identified six key objectives integral to the attainment of full professional status for policing, namely to:

(1) Develop a definition of the profession of policing;
(2) Implement university-based education for policing;
(3) Develop a body of knowledge;
(4) Propose ongoing professional development;
(5) Develop registration and standards for policing; and
(6) Establish a professional body for policing.

Evaluation

Over time the police role has evolved and the environment in which police are required to practice is becoming increasingly complex and demanding, with practitioners requiring the ability to exercise sound judgement and technical knowledge in a broad range of complex situations. Police have considerable discretion in the application of laws and procedure, which must be ethically applied in an increasingly vigilant and litigious society. The artisan status of police is no longer appropriate and professionalization of police is now increasingly necessary to assist in meeting the current and future sophisticated demands and expectations upon our policing practitioners from all facets but particularly the community.

While some argue that this is a natural evolutionary process, others assert that full professionalization will only really be achieved through the reorganization and radical restructuring of police organizations from the existing militaristic model to one that is more conducive to the professional police practitioner, where control is through professional freedom, individual accountability and autonomy.

Academics and authors from a number of countries around the world have for almost a century been exploring the issues surrounding the professionalization of policing and whether in fact policing is already to be regarded as a profession. While by far the majority of literature originates from the US, there still remains considerable disagreement as to the current status of policing, Dantzker being of the view that it is only a matter of time before American police attain professional status whereas Trautman considers that they are only now in the process of becoming a profession. Others argue that, while policing remains locked within a militaristic model of hierarchy, policing can never achieve professional status.

A common theme across the US, Australia and elsewhere, however, is that improved education and training is fundamental to the professionalization of any police agency and that police professionalism will only exist when policing is primarily knowledge driven rather than a function of organizational, political and economic exigencies. A distinct and constantly augmented organized body of knowledge must consist of evidenced-based empirical research through robust partnerships between academics and practitioners. Royberg, in his 2004 US based study, provides overwhelming evidence that college-educated officers are, *inter alia*, less authoritarian, have more open belief systems, greater problem solving capabilities and are more flexible and ethical in their responses. He states that while higher education is simply another tool, along with training and experience, officers who have such use force less frequently and receive fewer complaints while having lower rates of absenteeism, and perform their roles in a more satisfactory manner than their less educated peers. Despite this research however, he noted that advances in raising educational requirements for police have been slow and sporadic.

One rather shallow argument against professionalization of policing often cited is that policing is a dirty job often requiring brawn rather than brains and that by embracing higher education, the occupation will exclude 'good coppers'. While there is no doubt that policing at times involves a physical dimension, this argument however 'dumbs down' policing and fails to recognize the increasingly complex environment that police are operating within.

In 2003, Sir David Phillips as the outgoing President of the UK's Association of Chief Police Officers noted that in its visibility, the policing profession is almost unmatched, and as enforcers of the law, police must been seen to represent the highest standards in society. The police role is not static; it is complex and diverse and has been evolving over the last century and a half. There is no longer a role for the artisan practitioner who cannot satisfactorily deal with the complex problems faced on a daily basis; the professional police practitioner needs to be fully equipped to meet the increasing demands and expectations of the community, which necessitates higher order underpinning knowledge as delivered in the higher education sector. It has been said that if policing cannot deal with the more complex and intellectually demanding aspects of police work, then police may be left with only the routine and more mundane aspects of their present role; occupations that fail to lead the agenda in advancing their own professionalization may well forfeit that role to other more influential agencies; and police might be relegated to becoming the foot soldiers of the judicial system, rather than leaders in community policing.

The professionalization of policing has been an agenda of many countries and while, arguably, significant progress has been made towards advancing professionalization within many, policing remains at a crossroads. It needs to decide whether, on one hand, it should retain the status of an occupation, albeit a very honourable one, or whether it can achieve full professional status. Professionalization of policing has the potential to produce policing practitioners who are the analysts and strategists of society's policing problems. However, this may necessitate a radical rethink as to the current hierarchical militaristic structures, in which individuals lack the autonomy and accountability that is normally an inherent characteristic of a profession.

Ian Lanyon

Associated Concepts: culture, education and training, ethical policing, leadership

Key Readings

Auten, J.J. (1981) 'The paramilitary model of police and police professionalism', *Police Studies* (US and England), 4 (2): 67–77.

Carr-Saunders, A.M. and Wilson, P.A. (1934) (reprinted 1959) 'Professions', in E.R.A. Seligman, (ed.) *Encyclopaedia of the Social Sciences*. New York: Macmillan Co.

Dingwall, R. (1976) 'Accomplishing profession', *The Sociological Review*, 24 (2): 331–49.

Greenwood, E. (1957) 'Attributes of a profession', *Social Work*, 2 (July): 45–55.

Klockars, C.B. (1985) *The Idea of Police*. Beverley Hills, CA: Sage.

Vollmer, H.M. and Mills, D.L. (eds) (1966) *Professionalization*. Englewood Cliffs, NJ: Prentice-Hall.

PROPERTY CRIME

Definition

The term 'property crime' is a conceptual, as opposed to a legal term that refers in general to crimes against property, as distinct from crimes against the person, crimes against morality (such as obscenity), or crimes against the state (such as espionage, treason, or sedition). Property crime has traditionally entailed theft of or damage to property.

The distinction between these types of crime is by no means clear-cut, as some crimes entail multiple elements. For example, robbery (taking property by force or threat of force) entails elements of both crimes against the person and crimes against property. So too can extortion (demanding property under threat of harm at some time in the future), when the harm threatened involves harm to a person. Sexually explicit graffiti may violate laws against vandalism and obscenity. And some crimes against the state (those involving terrorism, sabotage, or insurrection) may entail damage to or destruction of property, public or private.

A distinctive quality of property crime today is its diverse, indeed florescent, nature. There is no universally accepted typology, but the following groupings are illustrative:

Burglary	Robbery	Theft of	Trespass	Fraud	Arson
Larceny	Extortion	intellectual		Forgery	Vandalism
Embezzlement		property		Uttering	Malicious
		Theft of		False	damage
		trade secrets		pretences	Sabotage
					Contaminating
					goods

In addition, there are a number of offences incidental to the commission of property crime. These include possession of burglars' tools, engraving plates for the printing of bank notes, receiving stolen goods, rebirthing of stolen motor vehicles, theft of credit card details, and money laundering. The latter embraces both concealing ill-gotten gains, and concealing otherwise legitimate income from taxation authorities.

Some of these basic types of property crime set out above are themselves quite varied. Consider, for example fraud, which is generally defined as obtaining something of value by deception. This includes a vast array of activity, including misrepresentation of products offered for sale, false billing, fraudulent investment solicitations, fraudulent solicitation of charitable contributions, tax fraud, fraudulently obtaining a public benefit (such as a welfare payment), share market manipulation, fraudulent diversion of shareholders' assets for personal use, credit card fraud and bankruptcy fraud.

Some jurisdictions specify in minute detail the nature of property in question. These specifications tend to arise in the aftermath of well-publicized incidents, as a reaffirmation of the seriousness of the conduct in question, or in cases where actual or perceived loopholes are apparent in the law. Legislators obviously see some virtues in redundancy.

The New South Wales Crimes Act 1900, for example, contains separate provisions relating to the theft of cattle, dogs (or skin thereof), pigeons, fish, shrubs, trees, stone, live or dead fences, aircraft, firearms, motor vehicles, vessels, goods in the process of manufacture, books in a public library, wills or codicils, court records, dead wood, plants in gardens, and plants not growing in gardens, *inter alia*. Section

106 covers breaking and entering places of Divine worship and committing serious indictable offence. Section 260 proscribes the forgery of East India bonds, exchequer bills, or debentures. Section 133 applies to 'whosoever corruptly takes any money or reward, directly or indirectly, under pretence, or upon account, of aiding any person to recover any dog which has been stolen'. Section 523 makes it an offence to offer shipwrecked goods for sale.

Distinctive Features

The evolution of human society has seen proliferation in forms of property crime, followed closely by development in the law of property crime. Originally, theft at common law entailed what was called 'asportation,' taking and carrying away physical property without the consent of the owner. Among the more prominent is the *Carrier's Case* (1473) 13 Edw. IV, f. 9, pl. 5 (Star Ch. and Exch. Ch.). This matter arose when a person who was hired to transport merchandise on behalf of another kept the goods for himself. The court held that temporary possession on behalf of another did not confer property rights, and that the carrier had engaged in theft. This type of crime is now referred to as larceny by a bailee. The advent of the industrial revolution saw the emergence of joint stock companies, credit, negotiable instruments and other accoutrements of trade. All created new opportunities for property crime. So too did the proliferation of consumer goods beginning in the twentieth century.

Technological change has also transformed some of the faces of property crime. These changes have provided new criminal opportunities that were promptly seized upon by resourceful offenders. There are fewer safecrackers today than there once were, but today the more competent thieves are able to access the assets of a bank remotely. The advent of digital technology, and the intangible property that it produces, has been accompanied by further developments in the law. Illegal copying and distribution of text, music, video, and multimedia combinations can be achieved without depriving the owner of possession. Information may be damaged or destroyed remotely. Just as the law evolved to accommodate the circumstances of the carrier's case, the law has extended to protect intangible property. In addition, it is now an offence in many jurisdictions to interfere with the lawful use of a computer, whether by means of worms and viruses or a distributed denial of service attack. The new trespass is reflected in the unauthorized access to data. The new vandalism (or in some cases, fraud) is the unauthorized modification of data. Legislatures in many jurisdictions often respond to an increase and the volume of crime with new laws, even if they may essentially duplicate laws already on the books.

As befitting a concept with such vast reach, motives for property crime are extremely varied. Most theft tends to arise from greed, which may be inherent in the offender's character or may result from financial strain. This in turn can arise from unavoidable hardship or from lifestyle choices. But there is much more to property crime than simply greed. The desire for power or control, to achieve mastery of a situation, may be a motive for fraud. Embezzlers may be seeking revenge against an employer. Some offenders, electronic and terrestrial, may be motivated by adventure. Vandalism or damage to property may be motivated by revenge or rebellion. In the case of graffiti, it may arise from misplaced artistic expression or adventure. Some arsonists may obtain sexual gratification from lighting fires. Some white collar offenders seek to sail as close to the wind as they can, when the line is blurred between what is legal and what is not (as is the case with some complex commercial transactions). Many computer criminals are motivated, at least in part, by the desire to control complex systems.

The abundance and diversity of property in all but the poorest nations of the world has been accompanied by the enormous growth of property crime since the end of the Second World War. This has been accompanied by a commensurate growth in crime prevention initiatives, including the private security industry (including the information security sector), and in technologies of crime prevention. The field of situational crime prevention, embracing everything from surveillance technologies to architectural design to product design, exists to make property crime more difficult or less lucrative.

In Western industrial societies at least, one sees the emergence of two basic police responses to property crime. The most prominent is police deference to private interests in securing the citizen's own assets. With their capacity limited by resource constraints, and more calls for service than they can handle, police in many jurisdictions will simply ignore minor property crime. This will include minor acts of theft or vandalism, fraud, and computer crime. In this sense, police are defining deviance 'upward'. Traditional police investigation will be limited to the most serious offences, and victims of minor crime will be left to manage their losses as best they can.

The second basic theme is the adoption by police of a more strategic response to property crime. This entails the identification of elements of property crime that are amenable to policy intervention, and developing partnerships with other governmental and private institutions to develop the most productive policies and practices. Decisions made in many policy domains, including health, education, housing, public transport, and local government, can impact on property crime. So too can decisions made in the private sector, from banking to retail sales. Some police services, because of their small size and/or lack of capacity, may be ill suited to engage in policy entrepreneurship. But where police do command such skills, problem diagnosis and policy development will become increasingly important.

Evaluation

One may expect the concept and the law of property crime to continue to evolve with developments in society and technology. Human motivations are unlikely to change, and offenders will continue to devise new ways to acquire things of value that do not belong to them. Owners of property will continue to devise new ways of protecting their possessions. Legislatures will continue to react to new variations on an old crime type by writing new laws. And while advances in surveillance and identification technology may assist to some extent in the investigation of property crime, the most productive investments are likely to be achieved 'upstream' by police working more closely with public and private sectors.

Peter Grabosky

Associated Concepts: crime prevention, criminal investigation, cybercrime, situational crime prevention, technology

Key Readings

Bronitt, S. and Bernadette, S. (2001) *Principles of Criminal Law*. Sydney: Law Book Company.

Clarke, R. (1997) *Situational Crime Prevention: Successful Case Studies* (2nd edn). Guilderland, N.Y: Harrow and Heston.

Hall, J. (1952) *Theft, Law and Society*. Indianapolis: Bobbs Merrill.

Wall, D. (2007) *Cybercrime*. Cambridge: Polity Press.

Weatherburn, D. and Grabosky, P. (1999) 'Strategic approaches to property crime control', *Policing and Society*, 9(1): 77–96.

Weisburd, D. and Braga, A. (2006) *Police Innovation: Contrasting Perspectives*. Cambridge: Cambridge University Press.

PUBLIC EXPECTATIONS

See Community Engagement; Community Policing; Consent; Legitimacy; Patrol; Public Reassurance

PUBLIC ORDER

Definition

The policing of public order represents special challenges for the police, operationally in terms of choice of tactics and strategies, and politically with regard to the social environment within which events take place. Such policing is highly visible, and has a potentially high impact. Failure to prevent violence through police inaction, or escalating violence through police intervention, are constant dilemmas faced by police as they respond to specific kinds of events and situations.

Public order policing as defined here does not include the more mundane types of public order offences (such as being drunk and disorderly) or the routine policing of public spaces (such as downtown areas and shopping malls). Rather, public order policing refers to the policing of protestors, campaigners and other large gatherings of people, at events that may be either planned or spontaneous in nature.

Distinctive Features

Planned events at which the police would normally provide a visible presence include, for example, the policing of football matches and other sporting events, large festivals and concerts, demonstrations, trade union pickets, and mass celebrations including national days, royal coronations or marriages, or large student gatherings such as 'spring break' (US) or 'schoolies week' (Australia). It is crucial to the policing of these events that there is prior knowledge of the event in order to construct police tactics and strategies appropriate to the gathering.

Spontaneous events can present more of a challenge for public order policing. These can include gatecrashed parties (which can involve hundreds of people, spilling out into public thoroughfares such as walkways and streets), riots, illegal raves and flash mobs (involving large groups of anonymous individuals who gather suddenly in specific locations and for no apparent reason, to do something 'silly').

Planned events may also involve some degree of unpredictability, as when crowd behaviour – for whatever reason – morphs into disorderly mob behaviour. Similarly, although public order policing within and around event venues may achieve a modicum of peace (for example, within the sports stadium), violence and fighting may well be displaced to places outside the sporting venue itself (such as surrounding streets and plazas). Some degree of prior planning by police is still possible for many of these events, for example the production and distribution of Party Safe Information Kits by police in Australia.

Evaluation

Evaluating public order policing is partly a technical matter and partly an issue of philosophical orientation. Much depends upon what the mission and objectives of the policing are, and the social and political context within which it takes place. A lot always depends upon the relationship between the police and the policed. Consider for instance the following examples that range from riots to political demonstrations.

Australian experience with riots indicates that police action can sometimes be the spark that leads to rioting among members of a particular community. This was the case, for example, both in Redfern, Sydney and Palm Island, Queensland in 2004, whereby each riot was precipitated by the alleged killing of an indigenous person by the police. The role of the police in precipitating riots thus is an important area of analysis and strategic thinking.

Police activities in dealing with riotous behaviour can be analyzed in terms of the dynamic interaction between the police and members of the public, an interaction which is seen to pre-empt and de-escalate potential disorder, or to lead to increased conflict. Here the key issue is how the policing methods themselves shape general outcomes within the context of a 'riot curve' (or 'disorder model') understanding of conflict (King and Waddington, 2004). Recent work in the UK and Europe demonstrate this. Reicher et al. (2004), for example, argue that a badly managed riot can destroy the relationship between

police and an entire community, but if a riot is managed properly, it can achieve good outcomes for both. King and Waddington (2004) examined rioting in Burnley in 2001 and through close examination of policing practices illustrate the gap between the more managerial strategic policy-making level (with its emphasis on informed community analysis and communication, based on understanding the relationships between different groups of people) and practical public order policing on the ground (with its reliance on a 'criminal' frame of reference, based on viewing people mainly as actual or potential offenders).

Police assumptions about those being policed, the techniques and style of intervention, and the operational strategies employed in dealing with riots all impact upon the course and consequences of riots. They are central to the management of public order events, and reflect the fact that policing has moved well beyond simply reacting to social conflict.

Such factors are also relevant in regards to the policing of sporting events, and the public order challenges presented by, for example, the 'hooligan'. As with related forms of potentially unruly situations (such as gate-crashed parties), it would seem that 'low profile' policing and good respectful practice is generally more effective than a coercive paramilitary style of policing (Stott et al., 2007). Reaching for the 'big stick' may in fact antagonize protagonists and generate the kinds of violence that good policing is meant to minimize. Again, police stereotypes and attitudes towards hooligans have been shown to influence how police contribute to the conflict, including the escalation of conflict (Reicher et al., 2004). This research has shown that the classical view that all members of a crowd are inherently rational and suggestible is wrong and, if adopted by police, may lead to negative outcomes in crowd control.

The use of highly coercive crowd control tactics by police has been criticized in relation to the policing of industrial relations conflicts as well. A New Zealand study of an industrial dispute which saw the death of a picketer argued that public order maintenance does not have to be aggressive or confrontational. Rather, as per police instructions, the 'preservation of peace' via negotiation and monitoring is, and ought to be, the paramount objective of policing public and industrial order (Baker, 2003). While specific 'flashpoints' (such as court decisions) have been identified as the spark for pitched battles on the picket lines, it is essential to bear in mind the ways in which rapport between police and unionists is influential in avoiding violence and maintaining reasonable order over long periods of time.

The policing of demonstrations in recent years has been accompanied by critical examination of policing practices, including police violence and over-reaction, whether this be Melbourne, Seattle or Genoa. Three main inter-related strategic areas for protest control have been identified: coercive strategies (such as use of weapons and physical force), persuasive strategies (such as discussion between police and protestors), and information strategies (such as widespread information gathering before, during and after a protest) (Della Porta and Reiter, 2006). Years of experience with demonstrations, across many different national contexts, have been consolidated into forward planning and preventative work that draws upon all of these strategies. Simultaneously, protest movements have learned from experience how to maximize their political impact, even if this, at times, leads to conflict with police.

Further issues of public order policing relate to matters such as the influence of the wider political environment on specific event policing, the tensions between paramilitary styles and peacekeeping modes of operation, and the precipitation and amplification of violence due to the policing approach adopted. Good practice in public order policing is hard to separate from political pressures to operate in particular ways. Whether it be policing of hooligans, anti-globalization protests, environmental activists or rioters, the method of intervention has practical as well as symbolic purchase.

Where policing of public order has involved the military as the key agents of control, as with Tiananmen Square in 1989 and Bloody Sunday in 1972 in Northern Ireland, extensive loss of life has occurred. By comparison, even though some deaths at police hands have

occurred (as with Genoa, Italy in 2001), fewer casualties occur with police crowd management compared with military intervention. It has been argued, however, that the paramilitarization of police, particularly in regards to public order policing, is redefining the police role by switching it from protection and peacekeeping to active aggression (McCulloch, 2001). When combined with political pressures to adopt certain policing styles, this could well be a recipe for repressive rather than enlightened policing methods.

For example, a comparison of public order policing in Canada and Bolivia around anti-globalization demonstrations provides evidence of the politicization of policing to the detriment of good policing practice. It is observed that police tactics are increasingly being influenced by transnational political agendas, which are about avoiding embarrassment, instead of the use of the most appropriate, effective and non-violent methods (Sheptycki, 2005). In contrast to the 'negotiated management' policing that is adopted in many other public order situations, in the specific case of anti-globalization events, the emphasis tends to now be on escalated use of force and extensive coercion. This, in turn, has major implications for public order policing generally, including the relationship between the police and the policed in planned and spontaneous events.

Rob White

Associated Concepts: anti-social behaviour, force, order maintenance, paramilitary policing, peacekeeping, police property

Key Readings

Baker, D. (2003) 'Policing industrial disputation: lessons from the Lyttleton picket line tragedy', *New Zealand Journal of Industrial Relations*, 28 (3): 258–69.

Della Porta, D. and Reiter, H. (2006) 'The policing of global protest: the G8 at Genoa and its aftermath', in D. Della Porta, A. Peterson and H. Reiter (eds) *The Policing of Transnational Protest*. London: Ashgate Publishing.

King, M. and Waddington, D. (2004) 'Coping with disorder? the changing relationship between police public order strategy and practice – a critical analysis of the Burnley riot', *Policing and Society*, 14 (2): 118–37.

McCulloch, J. (2001) *Blue Army: Paramilitary Policing in Australia*. Melbourne: Melbourne University Press.

Reicher, S., Stott, C., Cronin, P. and Adang, O. (2004) 'An integrated approach to crowd psychology and public order policing', *Policing: An International Journal of Police Strategies and Management*, 27 (4): 558–72.

Sheptycki, J. (2005) 'Policing political protest when politics go global: comparing public order policing in Canada and Bolivia', *Policing and Society*, 15 (3): 327–52.

Stott, C., Adang, O., Livingstone, A. and Schreiber, M. (2007) 'Variability in the collective behaviour of England fans at Euro2004: "hooliganism", public order policing and social change', *European Journal of Social Psychology*, 37(1): 75–100.

PUBLIC REASSURANCE

Definition

Public reassurance is the intended outcome of action(s) taken to increase public confidence in and user satisfaction with the police, and to improve perceptions of safety and reduce fear of victimization. Dictionary definitions suggest 'restoring confidence' is the prime function of reassurance. Thus public reassurance in relation to policing can be seen to relate to perceptions of police 'effectiveness'. This is reflected in the types of questions used in performance surveys in many countries, such as 'how satisfied are you with your local police?' Analysis of terminologies used in literature on public reassurance (Dalgleish and Myhill, 2004) suggests the concept can also be seen to relate to another set of policing issues – those around 'fear of crime' and increasing feelings of safety.

'Reassurance' as a term has appeared in literature relating to policing for a number of years. The earliest mention of the term was in an article by Charles Bahn in 1974. Writing about foot patrol in the US, Bahn defined reassurance as 'the feelings of safety and security that a citizen experiences when he sees a police officer or police patrol car nearby', emphasizing police 'visibility' and 'accessibility' as key mechanisms for effecting it.

In 2001, Her Majesty's Inspectorate of Constabulary (the UK's body responsible for improving the efficiency of the police in England and Wales) conducted a thematic inspection on the police role in public reassurance (titled *Open All Hours*). They defined reassurance as 'the extent to which individuals perceive that order and security exist within their local environment'. They also added the concept of 'familiarity' between police officers and local communities to the delivery mechanisms of visibility and accessibility.

However, effecting public reassurance has been recognized as being more complex than simply providing a visible, familiar, and accessible police presence. Ditton and Innes (2005) argue that a certain degree of 'fear' in a community is healthy as 'under the right conditions, fear of crime is a key stimulus that encourages people to join together', thereby fostering informal social control. Also, a uniformed police presence may not necessarily be reassuring, depending on an individual's personal experiences and neighbourhood context. That said, visible foot patrol has generally been popular with the public internationally as a means of making people feel safer.

Distinctive Features

In terms of practice, a public reassurance role requires of the police a range of tactics and approaches. Perceptions of police effectiveness and feelings of public safety may be impacted by mechanisms such as high visibility foot patrol. Many models of community policing attempt to match named officers to specific areas, or 'beats', for periods of time sufficient to promote familiarity between local police and communities. However, Ditton and Innes (2005) suggest that successful policing programmes usually have in addition some degree of targeted problem-solving at the local neighbourhood level. Thus, effective 'fear management' or 'perceptual' interventions should focus as far as possible on issues and problems that are seen as most important by the specific local communities involved. Community engagement, comprising a range of activity from information provision through consultation to partnership and community empowerment, can be viewed as the delivery mechanism for much of the operational policing activity associated with reassuring the public.

Though the ways in which it is measured have been criticized, fear of crime has come to be seen as a problem in itself in many countries. The International Crime Victimization Survey suggests that nearly a quarter of people feel unsafe when walking alone after dark. This proportion varies by country, and is not consistently related to actual risks of victimization. The term 'public reassurance' became prominent in the UK in the new millennium, in part due to a disparity between falling crime levels and public perceptions of crime. Although fear of crime, as measured by the British Crime Survey, decreased in the decade from 1995 to 2005, in line with declining rates of victimization, public perceptions of the level of crime remained relatively high. This disparity between actual and perceived crime became known as the 'reassurance gap'.

As a result of public perceptions of rising crime and declining confidence in the police, public reassurance became a primary strategic objective in an ongoing agenda of police reform in the UK. The UK government also funded the National Reassurance Policing Programme (NRPP), a major intervention that formalized the concept of reassurance policing, which had developed out of joint work between a UK police force (Surrey) and a nearby university. Reassurance policing had at its heart the 'signal crimes perspective' – the idea that certain events have a disproportionate impact on levels of fear (see Innes, 2004).

Though the range of operational approaches and tactics associated with public reassurance are common to many countries in the world, use of the term itself has been slightly less widespread. In the US the term is not often used, and reassurance activity comes under the general rubric of community policing. Other countries, notably Australia and New Zealand, have adopted some of the terminology associated with *Open All Hours* and the NRPP. The New Zealand police *Statement of Intent 2006/2007* talks of providing 'further community reassurance' and 'making policing more visible, accessible, and familiar to the public'.

Evaluation

Dalgleish and Myhill (2004) undertook a review of international literature on policing interventions and public reassurance. Included studies were drawn principally from the US, UK, and Australia. Interventions were included if they focused on perceived police effectiveness, containing measures of satisfaction and public confidence, or if they focused on feelings and perceptions of safety. Several major evaluations of community policing programmes focused on both elements. Within this dichotomy, interventions were presented according to the principal mechanism(s) used. Key mechanisms were: patrol-based strategies, both random and targeted foot patrol intended to increase levels of contact between the police and citizens; accessibility strategies, such as beat policing and community police stations; environmental change, such as improved residential security, street lighting, or closed circuit television; and community-based strategies, where the police and the public work in partnership, as with Neighbourhood Watch.

The review used the Maryland Scientific Methods Scale (MSMS) to appraise experimental and quasi-experimental outcome studies on public reassurance. The MSMS classifies interventions as 'what works', 'what doesn't work', 'what is promising', and 'what is unknown'. The review found interventions based on improving police visibility and familiarity to work in relation to improving perceptions of police effectiveness. Community policing interventions that utilized foot patrol and other forms of community engagement were found to be promising. In relation to increasing feelings and perceptions of safety, the review found interventions utilizing increased and targeted foot patrol to work. Community policing interventions to increase police visibility, accessibility, and familiarity, and interventions to increase residential security, were found to be promising.

Since the 2004 review of interventions, the NRPP has been subject to both a process and a quasi-experimental outcome evaluation (Tuffin et al., 2006). Of the original 16 neighbourhood-level sites that took part in the trial, six were pair matched with controls who undertook not to implement any aspect of reassurance policing.

The NRPP had three key mechanisms: the presence of visible, accessible and familiar police officers; community engagement to identify local policing priorities; and targeted problem-solving to address these priorities. Impact on a range of indicators over a 12 month period in each site was assessed using a panel survey of local residents. The evaluation showed a programme effect on several key indicators, including self-reported victimization, perceptions of anti-social behaviour, public confidence in the police, and feelings of safety after dark. The process evaluation revealed that the greatest impact was seen in sites that implemented most successfully the key programme mechanisms – particularly visible patrol and targeted problem-solving. The NRPP piloted some of the mechanisms later adopted in a wider national programme of 'neighbourhood policing' – community policing focused on defined geographical areas – launched in England and Wales in 2004.

It is likely that public reassurance will remain a key goal of police agencies as long as community policing models are dominant. In the UK, where the concept has arguably been most prominent, a programme of neighbourhood policing has subsumed much of the policing activity associated with reassuring the public.

Andy Myhill

Associated Concepts: closed circuit television, community policing, community engagement, fear of crime, neighbourhood watch, patrol, victim

Key Readings

Bahn, C. (1974) 'The reassurance factor in foot patrol', *Criminology*, 12 (3): 338–45.

Dalgleish, D. and Myhill, A. (2004) *Reassuring the Public – A Review of International Policing Interventions*. London: Home Office.

Ditton, J. and Innes, M. (2005) The role of perceptual intervention in the management of fear of crime, in N. Tilley, (ed.) *Handbook of Crime Prevention and Community Safety*. Cullompton, Devon: Willan Publishing.

Innes, M. (ed.) (2006) Reassurance and the 'New' Community Policing. *Policing and Society*, Special Issue, 16 (2).

Tuffin, R., Morris, J. and Poole, A. (2006) *An Evaluation of the Impact of the National Reassurance Policing Programme*. London: Home Office.

PUBLIC VALUE

Definition

Public value is a theory of public sector leadership and management that privileges knowledge based practice over academic analysis. Public value can be instituted as an organizing principle in a public sector organization, providing a focus in which individual employees are free to pursue and propose new ideas about how to improve the working of the organization, in terms of services or efficiency.

Distinctive Features

In recent years, public value has been the subject of much study. Recently, academics across the UK and US have begun to apply the concept of public value to policing. While this entry draws on some of the work compiled in the UK by the think tank Demos it should be noted that the public value of policing has also become a subject area of research in numerous European and Asian countries.

The UK spends £10.8bn of public money a year on its policing. In the past few decades the police have had to respond to innovations in crime as well as dramatic changes in society. However the relationship between the police and the public remains inadequate, lacking a shared account of the value that policing creates for the public who pay for it.

A wave of thinking in the 1980s under the banner of New Public Management (NPM) approached this challenge by borrowing from efficiency techniques imported wholesale from the private sector. Emphasizing cost-effectiveness for the 'consumers' of public services – taxpayers – these approaches challenged traditional approaches to public management in which the priorities of professionals and public service institutions dominated. In this approach what was measured was what mattered to public servants in local and national government. This led to a narrowed emphasis on measurable inputs and outputs, which did not take sufficient account of other things that citizens cared about and which were not so easy to measure. For example, service quality and experience, trust, fairness, and input into how decisions were made.

Public value developed as a way of remedying some of these defects. Some have argued that it has improved on earlier theories of public administration by drawing attention to a wider range of ways in which public services such as the police create value for the public in what they do, how they do it, and the relationships they build with citizens in the process. In particular, it draws attention to the role of public service leaders in actively seeking new forms of direct engagement, dialogue and deliberation with their communities and with politicians about what they should be doing, rather than relying on the channels of formal politics to define their goals and confer legitimacy on their actions.

Public value takes as its starting point the idea that leaders in the police and other public services cannot take the underlying purpose of their institution, its legitimacy, or the value it creates for citizens to be self-evident, simply because they are public institutions whose mandate has been supplied by democratically elected governments. Instead public institutions need to be more proactive and flexible in three key respects:

- In searching for valued purposes for their organization (through activities that meet the changing needs of citizens);
- In providing opportunities for citizens and other stakeholders to authorize these purposes (through processes of local accountability and deliberation), and
- By doing more to identify and represent the value their work creates (through evaluating and communicating their performance more effectively).

This multifaceted approach gives rise to Mark Moore's concept of the 'strategic triangle' (see Figure 1) as a way of describing the full range of ways by which public service leaders can create value for citizens.

For example, in the authorizing environment, police leaders create public value by building more open and transparent ways for citizens to influence what the police do and affirm what they think is valuable about their work. In the operating environment, police leaders create public value by searching for things their organization can do to meet people's needs, responding to changing circumstances and looking for new, more efficient and effective ways to bring the resources at their disposal to bear on solving citizens' problems. In the envisioning environment, police leaders create public value by working to identify and capture the value their institution creates.

Evaluation

The first place we can look for evidence of the public value the police create is in their relationship with the public, from which such publicly valued outcomes as trust and accountability emerge. Trust in policing as measured by survey responses has been steady for the last two decades, although it is below that of some other public service professionals (doctors and teachers) and other parts of the

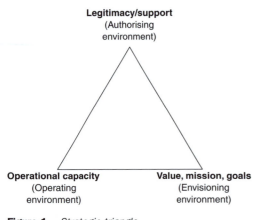

Legitimacy/support
(Authorising
environment)

Operational capacity   Value, mission, goals
(Operating   (Envisioning
environment)   environment)

Figure 1   *Strategic triangle*
Source: Moore (1995)

criminal justice system (judges). Others, however, have argued that an 'accountability gap' has opened up between the police and the public, citing as evidence the growing numbers of victims [who] fail to report crimes, in the belief that the police are either unwilling or unable to do anything about them.

The second area in which we need to look for evidence about the public value being created by the police is the operating environment: how good have police forces been at creating organizations that meet public needs? The obvious place to start is with levels of crime, which for many people remains the key test of policing effectiveness. According to the British Crime Survey (BCS), levels of crime in the UK peaked in 1995 and have been falling steadily since then.

We can also look at evidence about the public's experience of interacting with the police as an organization. While some academics have suggested that public value has failed to make an impact on citizens because of rigid management structures in organizations (see Stoker, 2005 and Rhodes and Wanna, 2007), policing in the UK is hampered by strong societal pressures. In contrast to other public services, for instance, where 'familiarity breeds favourability', personal interaction with the police has a negative impact on citizens' perceptions of it. The police were more likely to be rated as doing a good job by people who had had no

contact with them over the previous year (77 per cent) than by those who had been in contact with them over the previous year (72 per cent). According to figures from Her Majesty's Chief Inspector of Constabulary, the number of victims very or fairly satisfied with the police response to their experience fell from 68 per cent in 1994 to 58 per cent in 2003/04.

In the case of the US, public trust and confidence in the police is generally low, with minority group members especially mistrustful of the police. As one study demonstrated, 'trust is most strongly influenced by public judgements about the fairness of the procedures that the police follow when exercising their authority'. Further, it is stated, 'These process-based judgements are more influential than are either assessments of the effectiveness of police crime-control activities or judgements about the fairness of the police distribution of services' (Tyler, 2005: 322).

In some countries, for example Australia, rolling monthly telephone surveys measure community satisfaction levels with police services across states and territories. The levels of satisfaction are relatively constant and most organizations can boast 70 per cent or more satisfaction levels. These results are published annually by the federal government. These surveys stand on their own and of course are not comparable with victim surveys, which may reveal differing sentiments.

Using Moore's strategic triangle, the third place we can look at the public value the police create is in the envisioning environment. How good have police forces been at representing and communicating the value of their work to the public?

Here the BCS shows that there is a great deal of work to be done, because the public's fear of crime has been slow to respond to falling levels of actual crime. Although for some specific issues it is beginning to shift, around two-thirds of people still believe that overall the national crime rate over the last two years has risen a 'lot' or 'a little more'. In a pattern that is reflected in other public services, people tend to have a more positive view of the situation locally than of the national picture. Only half believe crime in their area has risen 'a lot' or 'a little more'. The stubbornness of fear of crime helps to explain the political emphasis being placed on the 'reassurance agenda' in policing. However, 'reassurance policing' will only be successful if it is part of a broader and long-term community policing strategy that seeks to respond to neighbourhood priorities and is assisted by the media and other institutions in communicating positive messages.

The modern world presents a series of new challenges to policing, and responding to these will put neighbourhood forces to the test. Due to the increasing interconnections of our globe, these new challenges are pertinent virtually anywhere, from the impact of globalized criminal networks to the threat of terrorism. Public value has become a recognized lens through which a discussion about the future of policing and of public service reform can be viewed. However while much work on public value and the concept's relevance to policing has been discussed from local and national perspectives, the public value of policing has to become a recognized framework for international discussion and debate.

When Sir Robert Peel set out his nine principles of policing, he affirmed the requirement 'to maintain at all times a relationship with the public that gives reality to the historic tradition that the police are the public and that the public are the police, the police being only members of the public who are paid to give full time attention to duties which are incumbent on every citizen in the interests of community welfare and existence'.

That historic idea remains a powerful and animating ideal today. It makes it incumbent on the police to break down barriers between its institutions and the public they serve. It makes it incumbent on the police to give the public a stronger voice in assessing and directing its performance. And it makes it incumbent on the police to make the creation of public value, in all the multifaceted ways that can be achieved, the central goal of a renewed, activist policing profession over the next decade and beyond.

Charlie Edwards and Silvia Guglielmi

Associated Concepts: accountability, community engagement, managerialism, reassurance policing

Key Readings

O'Connor, D. (2005) *Closing the Gap: A Review of the 'Fitness For Purpose' of the Current Structure of Policing in England and Wales*. London: Her Majesty's Inspectorate of Constabulary. http://www.crimereduction.homeoffice.gov.uk/policing16.htm.

Kelly, G., Mulgan, G. and Muers, S. (2002) *Creating Public Value*. London: Cabinet Office Strategy Unit.

Hills, D. and Sullivan, F. (2006) *Measuring Public Value 2: Practical Approaches*. London: The Work Foundation, http://www.theworkfoundation.com/products/publications.

McHugh, D. (2004) 'Serious but not yet terminal: the disconnection between people and politics', *Politics Journal*, 5, http://www.politicsjournal.org/journals/pdf/5/2004/mchugh.pdf.

Moore, M. (1995) *Creating Public Value Strategic Management in Government*. Boston: Harvard University Press.

Rhodes, R. A. W. and Wanna, J. (2007) 'The limits to public value, or rescuing responsible government from the platonic guardians', *Australian Journal of Public Administration*, 66 (4): 406–21.

Stoker, G. (2005) 'Public value management: a new narrative for networked governance?', *American Review of Public Administration*, 36 (1), 41–57.

Tyler, T. R. (2005) 'Policing in black and white: ethnic group differences in trust and confidence in the police', *Police Quarterly*, 8 (3): 322–42.

Q

QUALITY OF LIFE POLICING

See Anti-Social Behaviour; Broken Windows Theory; Compstat; Order Maintenance; Zero Tolerance Policing

R

RACIAL PROFILING

Definition

Racial profiling refers to the use by the police of generalizations based on race, ethnicity, religion or national origin, rather than individual behaviour, specific suspect descriptions or accumulated intelligence, as the basis for suspicion in directing discretionary law enforcement actions such as stops, identity checks, questioning or searches among other tactics. Racial or ethnic profiling is distinct from 'criminal profiling', which relies on forms of statistical categorization of groups of people according to identifiable characteristics believed to correlate with certain behaviours. Profiles of serial killers, hijackers and drug couriers have been developed over time. However, racial or ethnic profiling differs from criminal profiling in its use of race, ethnicity, religion or national origin rather than behaviour as the basis for differential treatment. Racial/ethnic profiling thus departs from the principle of equal treatment under the law and is a form of racial discrimination that is illegal under international and regional standards and the national laws in many countries.

Distinctive Features

The current understanding of racial profiling developed out of the 'drug courier profile' that was created in the mid-1980s by the US Drug Enforcement Agency (DEA) in an effort to combat interstate drug trafficking under the rubric of the 'war on drugs'. The DEA trained local law enforcement officials to look for 'indicators' based on a drug courier profile that included race as well as behavioural clues such as nervousness, use of rental vehicles and indications that drugs may be concealed in the vehicle despite the fact that many studies have shown that African-Americans and Latino/as are no more likely to use or transport drugs than their white counterparts. DEA training materials described and pictured predominately minority faces. The targeting of minorities for traffic stops became so ubiquitous that it earned its own nickname: 'driving while black or brown' or 'DWB' – a twist on the crime of driving while intoxicated or DWI. After the attacks of September 11, 2001, the 'war on terror' extended the practice of racial profiling to include Muslims and those perceived to be of Arab or Middle Eastern descent. Racial or religious profiling has been identified as occurring through car stops, aggressive enforcement of immigration laws and alien registration, intrusive security screening in airports and removal from planes. Since then, 'flying while Arab' has also entered the lexicon of profiling.

Specific definitions of racial or ethnic profiling vary along a continuum ranging from the use of race alone as the reason for the stop to those using race along with other factors as the reason for the stop. Using a narrow definition, racial profiling occurs when a police officer stops, questions, arrests and/or searches someone *solely* on the basis of a person's race or ethnicity. A narrow definition is also to exclude activities that are legally supportable in terms of reasonable suspicion or probable cause, but are nonetheless racially biased, such as the use of pretext stops or youth loitering laws. A broader definition acknowledges that race may be used as one of several factors involved in an officer's decision to stop someone. A stop is likely to be made on the confluence of several factors such as race or ethnicity along with age, dress (hooded sweatshirts, baggy trousers, perceived gang dress, etc.), time of the day, geography (looking 'out of place' in a neighbourhood or being in a designated 'high-crime area'). This definition reflects the fact that racial profiling may be caused by the purposefully racist behaviour of individual officers, or the cumulative effect of the unconscious use of racist stereotypes, but may also result from institutional factors, such as the use of enforcement techniques and deployment patterns, which impact on ethnic groups unequally. The paradigmatic context is drug interdiction on American highways, yet racial/ethnic profiling is apparent in a wide range of present and historical contacts between minority communities and the police. Profiling can take place in other stops or contacts with the public by any type of law enforcement officer or other authorities such as traffic stops in cities as well as highways, stopping and questioning of pedestrians in public places in urban areas, sweeps of trains and buses, immigration status checks by immigration officials, and airport security and customs checks or searches. Patterns of profiling can also be seen in discriminatory treatment after a stop has taken place, such as black motorists being given traffic citations while white motorists are let off with a warning, or Latino/a youth, but not white youth, being cited for noise violations.

Although racial profiling is widely recognized in the US and UK, it is only recently gaining recognition in Europe. While evidence suggests that profiling is a longstanding practice across Europe, the issue has garnered greater attention in the context of post 9/11 terrorism threats and growing anti-immigrant feeling. In Europe, racial profiling has been identified as occurring in a range of different methods and contexts, including mass controls in public places, stop and search and identity checks, data mining and raids on places of worship, businesses and organizations.

The UK remains one of the few countries systematically collecting data on race and the criminal justice system. The statistics show black and Asian people are overwhelmingly more likely to be stopped and searched by the police than their white counterparts. Disproportionality is greater under powers that do not require reasonable suspicion, such as those for terrorism and suspicion of violent crime, indicating that where levels of police discretion are highest, generalizations and negative stereotypes play an even greater role. Individual studies have identified racial profiling as prolific in other parts of Europe. A study conducted on the Moscow Metro found that non-Slavs are on average 21.8 times more likely to be stopped by the police than Slavs although they make up only 4.6 per cent of the riders in the Metro system (Adjami 2006). A 2006 study in Bulgaria, Hungary and Spain found that Roma and immigrants in Spain are more likely to be stopped on the street for the purpose of identity and immigration checks and once stopped are more likely to be treated disrespectfully by police officers (Miller 2007). In Germany, racial profiling has been used in the context of the post September, 11 terrorism threats. Between 2001 and 2003, German police undertook a massive data mining or *Rasterfahndung* operation to identify potential terrorist sleeper cells. The police collected the personal data of approximately 8.3 million people and 'trawled' the data using an ethnic profile that included the Muslim religion and nationality or country of birth from a list of 26 states with predominantly Muslim populations. The 'hits' generated by the database as potential terrorists were then singled out for further investigation (Moeckli, 2005).

Evaluation

In the 1990s, allegations of racial profiling in the US drew political and media discourse and public concern. Many law enforcement agencies were able to deny the existence of racial profiling using the narrow definition, which utilizes race as the sole factor in developing suspicion. Other proponents argue that it is just 'good policing' and that such information can increase the productivity of searches as minority groups are more likely to commit certain types of crime. Yet landmark court cases statistically proved the existence of racial profiling and challenged the notion that racial profiling is an effective law enforcement tool. Racial profiling can only be justified based on the assumption that the race or ethnicity of the person being profiled is knowable and that there is a consistent and statistically significant relationship between race or ethnicity and propensity to commit crime. In fact, neither of these is consistently true. Racial profiles are over-inclusive and under-inclusive – over-inclusive in the sense that many, indeed most, of the people who fit into the category are entirely innocent, and under-inclusive in the sense that many other types of criminals or terrorists who do not fit the profile will thereby escape police attention. Racial profiling also faces the problems of predictability and evasion; the more predictable police profiles become, the easier it is for perpetrators to adapt to circumvent the profile.

Court decisions and consent decrees have mandated data collection as a means of identifying and addressing racial profiling; more than 700 US law enforcement agencies and 14 states have passed legislation mandating racial profiling policies. Although there are significant methodological differences in the collection of stop data, the salient feature of the data that has been collected across the US and in the UK is its consistency in demonstrating similar 'hit' or arrest rates across racial groups. In several studies ethnic minorities are statistically significantly less likely to have contraband or other 'seizable' evidence found following a search. This evidence refutes the proposition that minorities are more likely to be involved in crime and highlights that racial profiling is an ineffective use of police resources, by

engaging in stopping and searching practices that are likely to be unproductive. Indeed, despite the collection and trawling of the data of 8.3 million people, the *Rasterfahndung* operation in Germany failed to identify a single terrorist (Moeckli, 2005). In 1998, the US Customs Service responded to allegations of racial and gender profiling and low hit rates across all ethnic groups. In 1998, 43 per cent of searches that Customs performed were on African-Americans and Latino/as. US Customs changed its stop and search procedures removing race from the factors considered when stops were made and introduced observational techniques focusing on behaviours such as nervousness and inconsistencies in passenger explanations; intelligence improved the supervision of stop and search decisions. By 2000, the racial disparities in Customs searches had nearly disappeared. Customs conducted 75 per cent fewer searches and their hit rate improved from under 5 per cent to over 13 per cent; the hit rate for all ethnic groups had become almost even (Harris, 2002). Using intelligence-based, race-neutral criteria allowed Customs to improve its effectiveness while stopping fewer innocent people, the vast majority of whom were people of colour. Other attempts to address profiling have included improving internal supervision, training and the development of early warning systems to identify officers who are potentially racially profiling.

Critics have noted that racial/ethnic profiling exacts a high price on individuals, groups, and communities that are singled out for disproportionate attention. For the individual stopped and detained the experience, sometimes of frequent repeat encounters with the police, can be frightening and humiliating. Racial/ethnic profiling serves to stigmatize whole groups, contributing to the over-representation of ethnic minorities in other parts of the criminal justice system, legitimizing racism and scapegoating and fostering mistrust between communities and the police. This in turn destroys the trust of those communities in the police and reduces their willingness to cooperate in criminal or terrorism investigations and turn to the police to control crime in their neighbourhoods.

Rebekah Delsol

Associated Concepts: criminal investigation, drugs, legitimacy, police property, terrorism

Key Readings

Adjami, M. (2006) *Ethnic Profiling in the Moscow Metro*. New York: Open Society Justice Initiative.

American Civil Liberties Union (2007) *Race and Ethnicity in America*. New York: ACLU.

Delsol, R. and Shiner, M. (2006) 'Regulating stop and search: a challenge for police and community relations in England and Wales', *Critical Criminology*, 14 (3): 241–63.

Harris, D. A. (2002). *Profiles in Injustice – Why Racial Profiling Cannot Work*. New York: The New Press.

Miller, J. (2007) *'I Can Stop and Search Whoever I Want' – Police Stops of Ethnic Minorities in Bulgarian, Hungary and Spain*. New York: Open Society Justice Initiative.

Moeckli, D. (2005) 'Discrimination profiles: law enforcement after 9/11 and 7/7', *European Human Rights Law Review*, 10 (5), 517–32.

Quinton, P., Bland, N. and Miller, J. (2000). *Police Stops, Decision-making and Practice*. London: Home Office.

REFORM

Definition

In recent decades, established ideas about who provides policing services, how policing is conceived and performed, and what ends it is designed to achieve, have been radically reconsidered. Reform of the public police has been shaped by a plethora of opportunities, drivers and challenges in terms of internalities (conditions within institutions that provide policing) and externalities (conditions within the external environments within which such institutions operate) that are conducive or otherwise to police and policing reform.

Distinctive Features

The last decades of the twentieth century witnessed something of a 'watershed' in policing, involving in particular a 'multilateralization' of policing provision (Bayley and Shearing, 1996). A shift has occurred from a near state monopoly (or at least a claimed monopoly) over policing policy and provision to a situation of plural or 'nodal' governance. Reform of the public police has been fundamental to this 'quiet revolution' in security governance.

The latter years of the twentieth century, and the early years of the twenty-first century have been a period of great geo-political upheavals around the world. With the collapse of communist regimes, particularly in Eastern Europe and Asia, and the fall of totalitarian regimes in many other countries in the world, there has been a veritable host of countries 'in transition' (usually towards more democratic institutions of governance, and from centrally controlled to more 'open' market economies) that are in various stages of radically transforming or reinventing their policing provision. These 'externalities' have given rise to an international policing reform 'industry', in which technology transfer and assistance has become a foreign policy instrument of donor countries, often under the auspices of the United Nations.

Hand-in-hand with this geo-political repositioning has been an ideological refocusing that emphasizes the need for policing not only to be 'culturally appropriate' but also 'democratic' and respectful of fundamental human rights. This has forced a reconsideration not just about the technologies of policing, but also of the acceptability of orders that providers of policing are being asked to police. Acceptable policing, it is argued, is not just policing that efficiently and effectively polices a prescribed order, but policing that conforms with internationally accepted norms of civility, dignity and human rights. This has led to a growing trend towards international 'harmonization' of policing standards and practices.

Alongside these international upheavals and transformations, major transformations have been occurring within established democracies, which are driving policing reform. Among these have been transformations in the character and uses of property, increasing population migration (transforming domestic populations into increasingly multi-cultural societies), and demographic trends leading towards increasingly older populations while at the same time producing booms and 'echo booms' in the 'crime-prone' age group. Add to these trends the exponential development of new technologies that simultaneously generate new policing problems and 'solutions', and it is no surprise that policing providers have found themselves under growing pressures to enhance, upgrade and 'reinvent' themselves.

Alongside these broader social and international trends, policing providers are being expected to adapt to changing approaches towards the content and delivery of 'justice' to which their efforts are expected to contribute. The traditional relationships between policing and formal criminal justice systems and institutions are being called into question, and alternative responses are being advocated and tried. Diversion from criminal justice processing and conceptions of 'restorative' rather than retributive justice are the most prominent manifestations of such.

Under pressure from governments to be more efficient, cost-effective and accountable, police services have transformed themselves internally. Traditional 'command and control' approaches to management have given way to approaches prevalent in the private sector. Public police organizations were encouraged to see themselves as service organizations providing a service for their 'client' governments and 'communities'. In many jurisdictions they found themselves competing with other potential policing providers, both in the public and private sectors, for the resources and 'contracts', and were required to enter into 'purchase agreements' with their government sponsors. Police chiefs and commissioners became parties to limited-term contracts and 'performance agreements' that were strictly audited by their employers. Their performance was subjected to a growing array of accountability mechanisms.

Alongside these organizational demands for change, the 1980s and 1990s saw a radical rethinking of what public policing involved. 'Community policing' became the prevailing mantra for police services around the world, requiring them to develop completely different relationships with the 'communities' they policed. In time this led to other ideas about how policing can best be accomplished, variously labelled 'intelligence-led', 'evidence-based' and recently 'reassurance' policing.

All these developments generated the need for enhanced resources, both technological and human, for policing, and a police labour force with new skills and mindsets. Police officers required enhanced communication skills, enhanced technological, managerial and leadership competencies, and enhanced political skills.

Another significant driver of reform during the last thirty years or so has undoubtedly been the competition that the resurgence of private and other non-state policing has engendered. The private sector in particular has generated new models, approaches and tools for policing that have forced the public sector to 'raise its game'. In turn, the need to achieve legitimacy and respect has forced private sector policing organizations (the 'private security industry') to raise its standards of professionalism, integrity and commitment to 'the common good' rather than just to profit. And for both the public and private sector, the development of viable and productive partnerships has become an inescapable imperative.

Finally, scandals – of which the Rodney King affair in the US, the Fitzgerald and Wood inquiries in Australia and the Stephen Lawrence saga in the UK are perhaps the best known recent examples – have played an important role as drivers of reform.

Evaluation

Even with the best will in the world, those who seek to reform policing frequently face substantial challenges and obstacles. In many countries of the world still, these take the form of an enduring culture and history of corruption, of dominance by partisan interests, and of other reform priorities that understandably are given precedence over reform of policing. Reforming policing is neither inexpensive nor easy and, absent of the necessary political will and commitment from politicians and indeed the police themselves, will rarely be successfully accomplished.

In many countries, corruption and its common progeny, poverty, continue to render reform of policing, and removal of obstacles to it, unachievable. Police officers who are not paid enough to look after themselves and their families, and are not provided with essential resources (like vehicles and/or petrol, for instance) for effective policing, inevitably resort to corruption and other assorted forms of deviance, including brutality and extra-judicial 'justice', to supplement their incomes and satisfy the demands of their superiors and political masters. Improving the quality of policing in such circumstances can be a very difficult task, for obvious reasons.

Countries 'in transition' that have only recently emerged from major conflict, civil wars or authoritarian regimes are often poorly placed to achieve effective reform of policing without a lot of outside assistance and support. Even when this is available, legacies of enmity and mistrust can easily derail even the most genuine reform efforts. Proponents of reform are often no more trusted than the police they seek to reform. Even in countries that do not face such obstacles, achievement of significant reform of policing is often hindered by a lack of understanding or acceptance, by politicians and the public more generally, of any need for it. Old ideas die hard, and without public support, reform initiatives often cannot get off the ground. In this respect the media, from whom both politicians and the general public derive so much of their understanding of policing issues, can often inhibit as much as encourage reform efforts.

Simply keeping up with new forms of crime, such as cybercrime, often poses huge challenges for reforming policing, and in this respect it is no surprise that public police institutions as often as not find themselves following the lead of the private sector, rather than leading themselves. The more substantial resources of non-state sponsors of policing, for instance, typically allow them to invest in new forensic technologies more quickly and more substantially than their government counterparts.

Despite the demographic changes that have occurred within many police services, many are still led by senior officers of the 'old school', who joined the service in the 1960s and early 1970s when attitudes to police work and police leadership were very different than they are today. Within many police organizations, therefore, there remains considerable resistance to change, which is not infrequently echoed by conservative leaders of police associations and unions. In particular, the view that public police officers are the only people who can and should be entrusted with the job of policing, and that any innovations in policing must be with the agreement, and under the direction, of the public police, is still prevalent. The extent to which police employee organizations can obstruct change differs across countries.

Many public police officers still regard private security organizations as both inferior and inherently suspect because of the risk of infiltration by criminal elements. Such attitudes, which persist despite the fact that many, if not still most, of the leaders of private security organizations are themselves former members of public police services, inevitably hinder the building and maintenance of effective public-private policing partnerships. Such partnerships thus commonly flourish informally while not being publicly acknowledged or approved, and police associations and unions in particular, and perhaps quite understandably, resist and decry privatization of functions and services that have, for the last hundred and fifty years or so, been regarded as the more or less exclusive preserve of public police. Even within the public sector, 'turf wars' over policing functions between different organizations are not uncommon.

The notion of 'police independence', according to which any political direction of the public police is presumptively suspect and undesirable, continues in many countries to underpin police resistance to politically directed reform initiatives that do not command police support. Despite a theoretical division of authority between 'policy' (regarded as a legitimate sphere for political direction) and 'operations' (within the exclusive authority of the police themselves), the 'operational' sphere is still interpreted very broadly by many police leaders, leaving the police budget (and even then only in the most general terms) the only legitimate subject for political determination.

From this very brief review, it will be evident that the drivers, motives for, and commitment to reform of public policing institutions, and the balance of opportunities and challenges for such reform, vary greatly from one context to another. It will also be obvious that when it comes to reform of policing, timing is usually of great significance. When (and why) the right conditions for reform will arise in any jurisdiction has been difficult to understand or predict.

What has been reasonably clear for sometime, however, is that the beginning of the twenty-first century appears to offer unprecedented opportunities for such reforms. In fact the opportunities for reform of public policing institutions around the world may be greater now than they have been since the radical reforms of such institutions in the early 1900s. The challenges for reform, however, must not be underestimated. What is evident from the literature on policing and police reform is the fundamental importance of the particular historical and contemporary context in which it takes place. One of the features that shapes context and makes it so important is that reform is always a contested terrain with differing visions of reform and a variety of sources of resistance to any particular reform vision. One cannot understand reform simply through a focus on mentalities that shape governance – no matter how important they might be. Reform is shaped by context because people and circumstances matter.

Clifford D. Shearing and Philip C. Stenning

Associated Concepts: accountability, community policing, culture, democratic policing, globalization, human rights policing, managerialism, performance management, pluralization, privatization, professionalization, technology

Key Readings

Amir, M. and Einstein, S. (eds) (2001) *Policing, Security and Democracy: Theory and Practice.* Huntsville, TX: Office of International Criminal Justice.

Bailey, J. and Dammert, L. (2006) *Public Security and Police Reform in the Americas.* Pittsburgh, PA: University of Pittsburgh Press.

Bayley, D. (2006) *Changing the Guard: Developing Democratic Police Abroad.* Cambridge: Cambridge University Press.

Bayley, D. and Shearing, C. (1996) 'The future of policing', *Law and Society Review,* 30 (3): 585–606.

Shearing, C. and Stenning, P. (eds) (2005) 'Reforming police: opportunities, drivers and challenges', in Special Issue on 'Reforming Police: An International Perspective', *Australian and New Zealand Journal of Criminology,* 38 (2): 167–80.

RESEARCH

The development of police studies in terms of the trajectory of research is observed by Skogan and Frydl, who note how, 'police research has become a substantial industry in 35 years, with a dedicated core of scholars, a large body of published work, several specialized journals, many accessible data sets, and regular professional meetings' (2004: 22). For example, the authors report how one of America's largest library collections of police texts held 2,934 such books at the time of writing. The development of social scientific interest in policing from the 1950s onwards says much about the political developments that have placed institutions of government – with the police serving as the most visible expression of state authority – under increasing scrutiny, and established law and order as one of the most prominent themes of public debate. Skogan and Frydl identify an emerging social concern associated with police fairness, particularly discrimination against black Americans, as having been a major driver of research interest in the US.

An annual feature of the journal *Police Practice and Research: An International Journal* assesses the main trends in policing research by means of a yearly quantitative review of the international literature. The latest findings by Variale et al. (2007) analyzed research published in 2004, dividing the literature into six topics which were found to have weightings as follows: measurement (that is, development of models for measuring policing effectiveness): 2 per cent; citizen satisfaction: 3.9 per cent; attitudes and behaviour: 12.3 per cent; accountability and misconduct: 17.4 per cent; organization of police: 19 per cent and, in the majority, police strategies: 44.5 per cent. Of the police strategies, the greatest emphasis was on community policing, the focus of nearly a third of such studies at 30 per cent. In terms of methodology, 'correlate research' (based on survey or secondary data analysis) was found to exceed all other methodologies (38.6 per cent), followed by 'thought research' (theoretical work) at 30.5 per cent, 'outcome research' (empirical evaluations) at 16.25 per cent and 'descriptive research' (describing implementations or processes) at 14.7 per cent.

Policing research comes from a range of sources, with the majority generated in universities until relatively recently. Government bodies and police organizations themselves are now major contributors, as significant governmental investment in research to improve the organizational and operational effectiveness of the police has nurtured the expansion of an evidence-based, policy research tradition that is especially evident in the US, the UK and Australia. Other important contributors to the policing body of knowledge include independent research organizations, think tanks and private consultants.

Bradley et al. (2006) separate policing research into two major paradigms: the critical and policy traditions. A critical tradition in early police scholarship was shaped by normative concerns and political values. Early ethnographic studies of the police brought to light the problematic aspects of police discretion in what was shown to be a closed and hidden occupational culture, providing latitude for discrimination, violence and corruption. As Bradley et al. observe, the critical tradition remains strong in the university sector, free from the sorts of constraints that apply to 'official' research in its various forms, and therefore valuable in its capacity to inform policing reform agendas. Such research, however, is often not addressed directly to practitioners and policy makers and for such audiences may be difficult to engage with, whether in terms of agenda, language or simply where it is disseminated. It is also possible that they may, for a number of reasons, be unwilling to acknowledge specific research findings.

A policy research tradition associated with the managerialist movement of the early 1980s onwards has brought researchers and practitioners/policy makers much closer together. Some researchers based in universities bestride both traditions, and others are employed directly by central government agencies, police forces and other public bodies. However, Bradley et al. note various obstacles that are limiting the impact of such research on policing practice, arguing that relationships need to improve between key stakeholders – government policy makers, police managers and university scholars, and that in the research process this needs to extend to 'a sustained interface between researchers and practitioners throughout all the phases of knowledge generation, validation, diffusion and adoption' (2006: 190).

Our intention in this entry is to demystify some aspects of the research process and body of research literature. Policy makers and practitioners can benefit from understanding how research is conducted, how to interpret specific findings and how a research project and its findings might apply in a specific environment. Those working in the criminal justice environment will often have to review reports and statistical tabulations. Knowing how to identify research methods and whether or not they have been appropriately applied is an important skill. Police practitioners are increasingly being asked to justify their expenditure and practice with reference to evidence-based practice. It is important therefore that they are in a position to recognize quality research. In social science research, researchers measure aspects of reality and then draw conclusions. How they measure that reality and how the conclusions are arrived at are determined largely by the research question and the method they identify as being most appropriate to address the issue.

The following section provides some broad (and brief) explanations of the main research methods used in criminal justice research. In a brief discussion, some of the ethical issues associated with empirical research are also discussed. There are hundreds of books devoted to the various research methods and this discussion cannot effectively cover the range of characteristics and techniques associated with each one. The aim is to identify those methods that are most closely associated with police research and encourage readers to look further afield for more information.

Qualitative Research

Most simply put, qualitative research is data that is not based on numerical data. All research begins as qualitative research – it is the researcher who will decide whether or not to convert initial observations into quantitative data. The reasons why a researcher might do this are discussed below. Qualitative research has developed out of a range of social science disciplines and intellectual traditions. Although closely associated with the interpretivist sociological and anthropological traditions, other disciplines that have long been associated with quantitative research methods and 'scientific' analysis (for example, psychologists) are now more likely to engage in qualitative research, either as a method on its own or as a way of adding

a greater depth of meaning to their quantitative data. Qualitative research is interpretive because it is concerned with how the social world is interpreted, understood or experienced. Data is produced in a specific context and this context is taken into account when qualitative data is analyzed. Qualitative data is generally rich in description and detailed. Focus group research, participant observation and semi-structured interviews are examples of qualitative research.

The qualitative researcher is very much part of the process. Thus, it is frequently said that a qualitative researcher cannot stand outside their subject in an objective manner and take a neutral stance in the face of the knowledge and data they are generating. It is true that as a participant observer (who is purposefully engaged with the activities of their subjects), for example, the researcher must be aware of his/her role in the research process. The notion of reflexivity, that is, the continuing analysis of one's role in the research process and one's relative position to the subject is crucial to ensuring that the research process is constructed out of situated and contextual decisions and actions. Qualitative research is often perceived by 'research users' as the lesser or softer methodology. This is largely because qualitative researchers do not work with specific 'road maps' but rather allow hypotheses to suggest themselves through inductive or deductive reasoning. Such a 'loose' approach to understanding and creating meaning is often marginalized by those who prefer the solidity of hard numbers. While many researchers and indeed practitioners appreciate the usefulness of qualitative research, it does not generally enjoy the same approval ratings as the more (seemingly) substantial traditions of quantitative research. Those commissioning research are often more interested in a quantitative approach that will give them statistics and numerical data they can use easily and often without qualification. With the increasing interest in criminal justice knowledge and data, researchers acknowledge that both qualitative and quantitative research methods are legitimate.

Topics and context will often determine the more useful research approach and in some cases one approach may prove to complement aspects of the other.

Ethnography

Ethnography is a qualitative research method that uses fieldwork to provide a descriptive study of an organization or society. There is a long tradition of ethnography in social science generally. This is particularly true amongst those influenced by social anthropology. Hence the term 'ethnography' to describe the research strategies that emphasize observational methods. Policing researchers have long acknowledged the importance of ethnography in policing studies and significant works have, in varying degrees, supplied scholars with Geertz's (1973) 'thickly descriptive' accounts of policing activity, wholly 'interpretive and evocative of being there'. Early policing studies were built on a set of ethnographies from the sixties and seventies. These works emanating primarily from the US focused largely on patrol work in the rough areas of large cities. For the most part these studies were not welcomed by police administrators revealing as they did some of the harsh realities of police work and the difficulties police encountered in combating crime. More recently, ethnographic studies have looked at police and policing with new conceptual lenses. Policing ethnographers are recording police in transitional societies such as South Africa and tracing the activities of senior police officers in a variety of contexts. They are observing police actively patrolling violence in public spaces and they are scrutinizing police in regional cities and specialized units. They are looking at private security operators who are engaged in traditional police roles as controllers and guardians of specified space.

There are many ways of talking about ethnographic research. Some researchers distinguish between the complete participant (whose researcher status is concealed from those who are being observed); the participant observer (someone who actively participates with the group under study but is also

'known' as a researcher); the observer as participant (one who identifies themselves as a researcher but makes no attempt to participate in activities) and the complete observer (who remains completely detached and observes only from a distance). Whatever the level of participation, the task of the ethnographer is to set down the perceived meanings that particular actions have for those they are observing and then suggest what these 'thick descriptions' tell us about the organization in which they are found.

In practice the definitional boundaries of ethnography are unclear and it is for this reason that ethnography is often seen as unscientific. Critics suggest that ethnographers tend to privilege research over theory. This is probably true. Most ethnographers use the inductive approach and build their theory from the bottom up from their understanding of specific social situations rather than formally testing hypotheses. Others see this as a strength of the method, because it does not determine the focus before the research begins, enabling categories of interpretation and explanation to be employed which have not been considered in advance of the research (although most acknowledge that interpretations and explanations are in the end largely bound by what the research has been able to formally observe). Others argue (but not necessarily as a critique) that ethnographic research is open to many interpretations and can therefore never be conclusive. In response, committed ethnographers argue that all research methods are open to multiple interpretations.

Despite the slow but steady trickle of ethnographic accounts of police work there is some suggestion among researchers that police organizations are thinking very differently about what research they are prepared to allow to proceed. There is an argument that policy-oriented methodologies that are more likely to provide evidence-based research findings that will inform policy and practice are being favoured over qualitative in depth research projects that are rarely conclusive and difficult to use as a comparative management tool. Whether or not this is the case, ethnography with all its limitations remains an important research method in police studies. Its strength lies in its ability to explore the complexities of cultural meanings and normative bonds – a method rarely found in other forms of police research.

Quantitative Research

Quantitative research is numerical research. Those who engage in this type of research argue that quantification makes an observation explicit, data is easier to summarize and aggregate and the numerical form allows statistical analysis that can range from simple 'descriptors' and basic averages to complex formulas and mathematical modelling exercises. Quantitative research, like its qualitative counterpart, focuses on specific variables and specifies meaning. However, as quantitative researchers are obliged to specifically identify what they will include in any measurement, they will often exclude other possible explanations. As a result the quantitative data is going to be more superficial than the more detailed qualitative description.

In qualitative research the researcher collects the data. In quantitative research the data is collected via surveys or other instruments to collect numerical data. The central aim is to classify features, count them, and construct statistical models in an attempt to explain what is observed. The objective is to collect precise measurement and analysis of target concepts, for example, through surveys or questionnaires. Criminal justice researchers rely heavily on such data and official statistics are considered an important resource and an important tool for researchers.

In quantitative research the aim is to determine the relationship between one thing (an independent variable) and another (a dependent or outcome variable) in any given sample. Quantitative research designs are either descriptive (subjects are usually measured once) or experimental (subjects are measured before and after an intervention). A descriptive study establishes associations

between variables. An experimental study establishes causality.

For an accurate estimate of the relationship between variables, a descriptive study usually requires a sample of hundreds or in some cases thousands of subjects; an experiment may need only tens of subjects. The relationship is less likely to be biased if you have a high participation rate in a sample selected randomly from a given population. In experiments, bias is less likely if subjects are randomly assigned to interventions, and if subjects and researchers are blind to the intervention.

As suggested above it may be a mistake to think about these two methods in opposition – that is, 'qualitative *versus* quantitative'. Many criminal justice researchers see merit in using both methods to interpret data. So for example, quantitative research on a community's expectations of its police service may find that they correlate with age and gender. A qualitative approach may put some flesh on the bones of this research and help to explain why these people hold these expectations and why they vary according to age and gender.

The mixed method approach is one that has much support among researchers. What should be avoided however is the immediate assumption that one method can automatically validate the other and that if you measure the same topic from a variety of angles or methods you will get a more accurate measurement. That would suggest that there is one 'knowable social reality' and that all researchers have to do is to establish the right connections between a variety of research methods in order to establish the 'truth'. It is unlikely that a researcher will be able to use different methods to corroborate each other. Some research situations and contexts may be more suited to the 'softer' qualitative approach while others would benefit from quantification. Many projects may require a mixed method approach in order to fully interpret a topic. Patton (1993) cited in Maxfield and Babbie (2001: 24) optimistically observes, 'Research, like diplomacy is the art of the possible'.

273

Action Research

Action research is a reflective process of progressive problem-solving led by individuals working with others in groups to improve the way they identify issues and solve problems. It can be undertaken by larger organizations or institutions, assisted or guided by professional researchers, with the aim of improving strategies, practices, and knowledge of the environments within which they practice. In recent years police organizations have sought to access research opportunities with tertiary institutions and consultants. Much of this research has been information gathering and in many instances this has meant that the researcher/consultant has worked alone with little involvement with police themselves. As a result, for many police organizations such research has been difficult to disseminate or perhaps more specifically, to legitimate to police officers. As well, where research has recommended an evidence-based practice it has often been difficult to implement.

Increasingly, police organizations interested in pursuing research that will inform practice are becoming an intrinsic part of action research projects in conjunction with tertiary institutions. With the emphasis on mutual collaboration, trust and reciprocity, this research method is referred to as participatory action research (PAR) – a method that seeks to bridge the traditional gap between research and practice.

PAR originated in less developed countries in the 1960s and was traditionally utilized as a way in which disenfranchised communities might more readily be involved in state-building with a view to creating democratic societies. This inclusive and collaborative approach is seen by many as a suitable method for police research whereby police and researchers develop specific goals and objectives and work towards them together. This empowering of police in the process of generating knowledge contributes significantly to the validation and dissemination of the research. Police participants (in conjunction with researchers) identify a problem/focus, collect and analyse data, reflect on and share their findings, plan for further activity, carry it out, check their results, and plan again for further action.

Working with police organizations is not without its challenges. Police organizations are not organized around research imperatives nor do they have the funds and resources to engage with research as part of their everyday duties. Management are concerned with quick wins and short-term solutions to what are usually well developed problems. PAR is not suited to such requirements. Individual officers are rarely required to demonstrate their research capabilities and if management does not value such skills they are unlikely to develop them in their own time. As well, academic researchers (as opposed for example to private consultants) have research and publication obligations and other accountability measures that are quite different from the obligations and accountability imperatives of police organizations.

However, despite these challenges, action research generally and PAR specifically is becoming a method of choice amongst academics and police practitioners as it can be designed in ways that meet the needs of both academics and practitioners.

Research Ethics

Any discussion of research methods must make mention of research ethics. Ethics is generally understood as being associated with morality – appreciating the difference between right and wrong. In the context of research, being ethical is about conforming to specific standards usually set by a given profession or institution. Adhering and conforming to a set of ethical principles is particularly important in the context of police research because such research is by definition sensitive and transgressive. Police are powerful and largely insular organizations that are concerned with potential transgressions and unhelpful publicity. Such research invariably focuses on people: vulnerable people who are often victims or offenders; people who may have committed illegal acts that they wish to remain confidential.

In almost all cases ethical guidelines are established and agreed upon prior to the research beginning. This is true in the context of the researcher *vis-à-vis* the university and the researcher *vis-à-vis* the police organization itself. When this is established, informed consent will need to be granted by voluntary participants. In some instances voluntary participation may not be wholly established. Police focus groups for example may be arranged by senior officers who 'invite' junior officers to participate. There is often little opportunity to refuse! The researcher may have no influence over this but must be even more meticulous in ensuring that other ethical principles are upheld.

Information should be provided by the researcher about the terms of reference, methods and potential outcomes of the project and what part the participant will play in the research. It is important that the researcher is scrupulously honest in providing these details. Confidentiality if relevant will be established at this stage. This will be particularly important if participants are required to reveal personal and private information about themselves. It may be that the researcher uses identifying numbers rather than names to protect confidentiality. Researchers will of course be expected to minimize risk or harm to participants. So for example, interviews with rape victims may cause distress to the participants. Researchers would be expected to ensure that counsellors or other relevant practitioners would be available if such a situation were to arise.

Ethical concerns have been a feature of police research for many years. Universities and other organizations have established organizational research ethics committees that endeavour to promote compliance and ensure that certain ethical principles are adhered to. They are also useful in identifying potential problems with analysis and reporting and also clarifying the parameters of legal liability. Police organizations as well are increasingly setting up 'ethical standard units' or other divisions to monitor research and obtain certain promises and commitments from researchers in the context of what they will do with their research and what vetting rights (if any) the organization will have in relation to publications. Most countries will have national organizations that assist in promoting compliance with ethical principles. Codes of conduct are common among certain professions. The British Society of Criminology, the Australian and New Zealand Society of Criminology and the American Sociological Association have specific research codes for their members. So for example in the US, institutional review boards (IRBs) assess the risks of such research in the context of the expected benefits. They are particularly concerned with the ethical principle of voluntary participation. Federal legislation governs the activities of the IRBs. In Australia, the National Health and Medical Research Council provide guidelines for various types of research including indigenous people's research, animal research and research involving human subjects. Researchers often complain that such organizations are not designed for social scientists and that their deliberations are based on a limited understanding of criminal justice issues. Such complaints have to date gone unheeded.

Jenny Fleming and Alison Wakefield

Associated Concepts: education and training, evidence-based policing, managerialism, professionalization, reform

Key Readings

Bradley, D., Nixon, C. and Marks, M. (2006) 'What works, what doesn't work and what looks promising in police research networks', in J. Fleming and J. Wood (eds) *Fighting Crime Together: The Challenges of Policing and Security Networks.* Sydney: University of New South Wales Press.

Geertz, C. (1973) *The Interpretation of Culture.* New York: Basic Books.

King, R. D and Wincup, E. (eds) (2000) *Doing Research on Crime and Justice.* Oxford: Oxford University Press.

Mason, J. (1996) *Qualitative Research.* London: Sage Publications.

Maxfield, M. G. and Babbie, E. (2001) *Research Methods for Criminal Justice and Criminology* (3rd edn). Belmont, CA: Wadsworth.

Neyroud, P. and Beckley, A. (2001) *Policing, Ethics and Human Rights*. Cullompton, Devon: Willan Publishing.

Skogan, W. and Frydl, K. (eds) (2004) *Fairness and Effectiveness in Policing: The Evidence*. Washington, DC: The National Academies Press.

Varriale, J. A., Gibbs, J. C., Ahlin, E. M., Gugino, M. R. and Na, C. (2007) 'Trends in police research: a cross-sectional analysis of the 2004 literature', *Police Practice and Research: An International Journal*, 8 (5): 461–85.

RESPONSIBILIZATION

Definition

'Responsibilization' is a term developed in the governmentality literature to refer to the process whereby subjects are rendered individually responsible for a task which previously would have been the duty of another – usually a state agency – or would not have been recognized as a responsibility at all. The process is strongly associated with neo-liberal political discourses, where it takes on the implication that the subject being responsibilized has avoided this duty or the responsibility has been taken away from them in the welfare state era and managed by an expert or government agency.

Distinctive Features

The term 'responsibilization' first appears in the governmentality literature in the mid-1990s where it refers to a neo-liberal strategy associated with the assumption that under the governance of the welfare state, liberal subjects had sloughed off or been divested of the responsibility for governing themselves or assisting others reliant on them. In particular, responsibilization is understood as being a process in which government 'passed back' these responsibilities to individuals and communities. In general terms, it is illustrated by such slogans as 'no rights without obligations', and in the change of government terminology away from discourses of social security 'benefits', towards more 'contractual' imageries. In the latter, recipients of pensions or services are regarded as responsible for earning payments (for example, earning unemployment assistance by performing all the tasks associated with being 'job ready') rather than attracting them by right.

In the field of crime control and criminal justice, responsibilization has been identified in several major senses. First, government agencies, police and politicians have promoted the idea that the police had taken on a great array of duties that were not originally assigned to them and that rightfully should be performed by others. In particular, people and companies should recognize that police cannot provide blanket protection, and thus all subjects should regard themselves as potential crime victims. As such they have been made responsible for taking 'sensible' precautions against becoming victims, such as avoiding high-risk settings, and reducing the opportunities for offenders to rob or burgle possessions. Linked with this development, police, government departments, neighbourhood watch programmes and the insurance industry have 'empowered' citizens by providing them with relevant information and skills to assist them in taking on these duties. This has included publishing information about the distribution of crime risks over time and place, about basic techniques for rendering the home or the office less vulnerable through installing security hardware, and about how to change one's actions and routines in order to minimize exposure to crime. By implication, those who become crime victims take on some degree of responsibility for their victimization.

Second, these subjects are expected to take on responsibility for identifying and reporting to police any crime risks in their locality. Especially through such schemes as neighbourhood watch (or rural watch, farm watch, etc.), citizens are made responsible for sur-veillance of their neighbourhoods and partic-ularly of their neighbours' properties. By extension, whole communities have been made responsible for a form of crime preven-tion policing, with the corresponding assump-tion being that those communities taking seriously their responsibilities would benefit from reduced crime rates. More than this, the closer interaction that would emerge between police and citizens implied that communities receive the policing they deserved. Through such techniques as police-community consul-tation committees and public audits, citizens have been expected to become active on their own behalf – responsible customers of police services who should not passively accept what was provided, but should make the effort to demand 'world class' service. Where police services are poor, again the implication is that this is at least in part the responsibility of citizens.

Third, seemingly outside the domain of policing and crime prevention, offenders have been rendered responsible for their actions. Responsibilization here was assumed to reflect the fact that the welfare state had made excuses for criminals by blaming social conditions rather than recognizing that offenders make choices. Its corollary has been that in the new order offenders will receive their just deserts. In practice this has fed back into the policing and crime preven-tion domains by stressing that because crimi-nals are rational choice actors, crimes are 'caused' by opportunities. In such examples, it becomes clear that responsibilization is linked both to neo-liberal axioms, but also to the increasing prominence of risk as a way of governing. Responsibilization has as one of its key components taking on responsibility for the management of risks, while at the same time a renewed emphasis on personal respon-sibility has shaped the ways in which risk is used to govern problems.

Evaluation

As a practice of government, responsibilization has been extensively critiqued. In particular it has been argued that it tends towards blaming the victim. Feminist critics, in particular, have pointed out that government programmes individualize responsibility for problems that have more systematic origins. Thus, advice to women to avoid high-risk settings has often highlighted risks associated with women being alone in public places, with the impli-cation that it is not the responsibility of police or government to render these settings safe, and that women should restrict their lives in ways men may not have to. As noted, blaming the victim is a frequently noted problem asso-ciated with responsibilization, for the corol-lary is that those who become victims have been irresponsible or remiss in some way. By implication, this provides a technical and objective gloss that removes responsibility from police, and more generally, it is argued that responsibilization almost invariably devolves government downward. Few main-stream criminologists appear to take seriously the idea that responsibilization does more than relieve government and police sectors from some measure of work and exposure to criticism.

As a theoretical tool, it is perhaps too read-ily assumed that responsibilization is some-thing foisted on the unwilling and that it invariably represents a cynical or calculated exercise in relieving government of its responsibilities. This overlooks the fact that many features of neo-liberalism were fought for by both the political left and right. One constant criticism of the welfare state, by feminists, Marxists and others, was precisely that people were subject to technocratic interference. Responsibilization owes at least some of its nature and impetus to politically Left demands to take back control from the state and expertise – even if the result has not always been that intended. Similarly, citizen responsibilization in the policing field was partly a response to minority, feminist and working class complaints about the insensi-tivity of police to local conditions and demands.

It should also be noted that there is an ever-present danger in assuming that respon-sibilization is a new process, rather than a reinvented one. That is, as with many other techniques of neo-liberal government such as the use of 'markets' as a way of governing many problems, responsibilization has taken tools associated with nineteenth century government and used them in new ways. Individual responsibility, in particular, has never been far from the surfaces of government in the past 200 years, and it cannot be assumed that all examples where individuals and communities are held responsible are examples of neo-liberal responsibilization.

Pat O'Malley

Associated Concepts: community engagement, crime prevention, governmentality, neighbourhood watch, third party policing, victim

Key Readings

Garland, D. (1996) 'The limits of the sovereign state: strategies of crime control in contemporary society', *British Journal of Criminology*, 36 (4): 445–71.
O'Malley, P. (1992), 'Risk, power and crime prevention', *Economy and Society*, 21 (3): 252–75.
O'Malley, P. and Palmer, D. (1996) 'Post Keynesian policing', *Economy and Society*, 25 (2): 137–55.
Osborne, D. and Gaebler, T. (1993) *Reinventing Government.* New York: Plume Books.
Rose, N. (1999) *The Powers of Freedom.* Cambridge: Cambridge University Press.

RESTORATIVE POLICING

Definition

Restorative policing is a problem-oriented, community style of policing that aims to resolve conflict in civil society more amicably and sensitively without always resorting to strict law enforcement. It calls on police officers to exercise their judgement and use negotiation and persuasion to resolve problems. It is in many ways a return to Sir Robert Peel's vision of police as 'only members of the public who are paid to give full time attention to duties which are incumbent on every citizen in the interests of the community welfare' (cited in Weitekamp et al., 2003). It is part of a shift from the paradigm of traditional reactive policing with its focus on keeping order, making arrests and providing rapid response, towards a more proactive approach which calls for recognition that incidents are often only symptoms of more entrenched community problems. The emphasis is on community safety and crime prevention and on enhanced cooperation between police and citizens. Restorative policing sees coercive force as a last resort in addressing criminal behaviour; it is more concerned with the underlying cause of such behaviour and resolving it.

Distinctive Features

The objective in restorative policing is for police to adopt a different attitude in their dealings with the public, including victims and offenders, so that they behave 'restoratively'. This implies less confrontation and more attention to problem-solving. It usually also implies close relationships with community groups through multi-agency partnerships and aims to bridge the gap between the criminal justice system and community-based agencies. Some advocates make more radical claims for it, suggesting that it can be taken further with greater use of the civil courts for minor offences, less harsh dealing with minor street offending and greater attention to problems of net-widening with young offenders. They also foresee its use in schools, in the resolution of workplace disputes and in police complaints procedures.

Restorative policing can be operationalized at a number of levels. At the level of street policing it entails the resolution of disputes informally wherever possible: for example, an argument over a parking space that threatens to escalate into violence could be dealt with through a 'there and then' face-to-face discussion between the disputants facilitated by the beat officer. Nuisance and disorder offences which take up so much police time can be addressed through restorative cautioning, a modification of the cautioning system used in countries with British-style policing. In contrast to traditional cautions, which usually consist of a ten minute 'telling off', restorative cautions follow a structured dialogue in which the offender participates actively and which may last 40 to 60 minutes. The aim is to encourage offenders to take responsibility for their actions and for repairing the harm caused to the victim, the offender's family and the wider community.

A higher level restorative policing intervention entails a restorative conference, attended by the victim of the offence as well as the offender and his/her supporters, together with any other members of the community affected by the crime. Participants discuss the offence and its consequences in the presence of a trained facilitator and then decide what should be done to repair the harm and ensure that it does not happen again.

This pyramid of escalating restorative interventions was taken up in a mainstream way in the mid-1990s by the Thames Valley Police in the UK. They have been adopted by other police forces in the UK and in Canada (where they are known as Community Justice Forums), though rarely on such a committed basis. Restorative policing is an attractive concept to senior police in many jurisdictions but difficulties are often encountered in bringing about the changes in police culture entailed in fully operationalizing it and in funding the more intensive staffing it may require.

Evaluation

Although there has been no rigorous evaluation of 'street' restorative policing, there are some programmes that have explored its value in addressing low level social conflict. For example, in one London borough a large number of police officers and police community support officers have been given training in dealing in a restorative manner with incidents they encounter on the street and several other British police commands are piloting similar programmes.

Research on *restorative cautioning* carried out on the Thames Valley Police programme (Wilcox et al., 2004) suggest that there is a great deal of support, especially among victims and other members of the general public, for the police to use restorative strategies in their response to crime. There is also some evidence that it improves relations between the police and the public. The reconviction study was equivocal, however, and could not establish definitively whether there was any impact on the rate or type of future offending.

Police-led *restorative conferences* have been tried in many settings around the world, including Canada, Australia, the US and the UK. They have been the subject of intensive evaluation in Thames Valley itself (Wilcox et al., 2004), and of rigorous controlled trials comparing cases randomly assigned to restorative conferences or to normal criminal justice processing in Australia (Strang et al., 1999; Sherman et al., 2000; Sherman and Strang, 2007), in the US (McCold and Wachtel, 1998, McGarrell et al., 2000) and in the UK (Shapland et al., 2006).

Reoffending studies show variable results. It is evident that restorative conferencing works differently on different kinds of people, though rigorous tests have found substantial reductions in repeat offending for both violent and property crime. Other tests have failed to find such effects, but with different populations, interventions or comparisons. In one instance, involving Aboriginal offenders in Australia, conferencing appeared to backfire with much higher rates of repeat offending compared with court. But in general, conferencing appears to reduce crime more effectively with more, rather than less, serious crimes. It seems to work better with crimes involving personal victims than for crimes without them; it also seems to work with violent crimes more consistently than with property crimes.

However, the great majority of victims of crime appeared to benefit from the experience of participating in a conference compared with victims whose cases were dealt with in court in the usual way. When asked they say that they are less fearful, less anxious and less angry after the opportunity to meet their offenders and more often feel a sense of closure about the incident. There is also preliminary evidence that when victims take part in a conference they obtain short-term benefits for their mental health by reducing post-traumatic stress symptoms.

Aside from these research studies, in one pilot currently taking place in London police officers have been given intensive training in facilitating restorative conferences with both adults and juveniles who are identified as 'Prolific Priority Offenders' and who are therefore eligible for more intensive monitoring and support when they are released from custody. These conferences are also attended by the victims of these offenders, together with supporters of both parties who discuss the offence and its consequences and what should be done to repair the harm caused. Reoffending is monitored after one month, six months and twelve months and compared with offending in the preceding two years, but no results are yet available.

Restorative policing is based on restorative justice principles that include deliberative dialogue between all parties affected by an offence and, ideally, the transaction of apology and forgiveness between a restored victim and a remorseful offender. However, it must operate in a wider world of police culture and criminal justice procedures where this new tool may be at odds with prevailing practices. It remains to be seen whether policing is ready for the cultural change necessary if a restorative approach is to fulfil its potential to give equal regard in an inclusive

and reintegrative style to all parties involved in the disputes and conflicts that are the everyday events of police work.

Heather Strang

Associated Concepts: community policing, multi-agency policing, problem-oriented policing, victim, youth

Key Readings

Shapland, J., Atkinson, A., Atkinson, H., Chapman, B., Colledge, E., Dignan, J., Howes, M., Johnstone, J., Robinson, G. and Sorsby, A. (2006) *Restorative Justice in Practice: The Second Report from the Evaluation of Three Schemes*. Sheffield, Centre for Criminological Research: University of Sheffield.

Sherman, L. W., Strang, H. and Woods, D. (2000) *Recidivism Patterns in the Canberra Reintegrative Shaming Experiments (RISE)*. Canberra: Centre for Restorative Justice, Australian National University.

Sherman, L. W. and Strang, H. (2007) *Restorative Justice: The Evidence*. London: The Smith Institute.

Weitekamp, E., Kerner, H-J. and Meier, U. (2003) 'Community and problem-oriented policing in the context of restorative justice', in E. Weitekamp and H-J. Kerner (eds) *Restorative Justice in Context: International Practice and Directions*. Cullompton, Devon: Willan Publishing.

Wilcox, A., Young, R. and Hoyle, C. (2004) *Two-Year Resanctioning Study: A Comparison of Restorative and Traditional Cautions*. London: Home Office.

S

SEARCH

Definition

Searching by the police involves the intrusive examination of persons, property or terrain in order to obtain evidence of wrongdoing that is likely to be concealed. Searching people, property and terrain exemplifies how police are set apart from other citizens by the actions they perform. In all jurisdictions police have the power to search and thus breach the barrier between the public and private domain. However much it might be hedged around with qualifications, police are duty-bound to search for evidence of wrongdoing that may be concealed about one's person, or property, or hidden (e.g., buried).

Parents often turn to the police to search for missing children, not only because police have officers and equipment (e.g., aircraft) that can readily be mobilized to survey the terrain in which the child has disappeared, but also because the police can look where others cannot. House-to-house inquiries may be conducted routinely, but few other citizens would feel entitled to ask perfect strangers whether they have seen a missing child. Police can venture onto private property and look in outhouses and other places where a child might hide. They may survey the terrain from the sky using aircraft and thus scrutinize what is normally kept from view by walls and fences. Even if this is done with the agreement of those who are questioned and onto whose property the police

venture, it is an intrusion into privacy that is socially exceptional.

When a serious crime has been committed the police will often search the entire 'crime scene'. This may involve collecting items of potentially evidential value (e.g., microscopic remnants of fabric). While most popular portrayals of this process focus upon the remarkable skills of forensic scientists, what is often neglected is that in order to 'eliminate' potential suspects from the inquiry their privacy must be intruded upon. For instance, mobile phone records might be searched to reveal who phoned whom and from where, all of which a person may wish to have remained private.

The more actively the police intrude into privacy the more heavily the police rely upon their legal powers. Depending upon the legal provisions in particular jurisdictions, if the police have more or less firm grounds for suspecting that a citizen is carrying contraband (e.g., illicit property or an illegal weapon) they invariably have the power to search that person. It is important to note that the degree of certainty required for acting upon such a suspicion usually falls far short of that required for an arrest. Once a person is arrested then searching is almost routine, partly to find evidence to support the arrest, but also for the health and safety of the public, the police officer, and the suspect themselves. Items that might be used to cause injury are normally removed, which routinely extends to belts and neckties. All the clothing of an arrested person may be removed for forensic examination in some cases. Such searching can become extremely intrusive, including the examination of body cavities.

Another aspect of searching is the identification of the person who has been under arrest. Fingerprints and DNA samples are routinely taken to reveal whether or not the arrested person is concealing their identity and/or other important personal characteristics, such as previous convictions and outstanding warrants for arrest.

Depending upon the law in the respective jurisdiction, the property of an arrested person may be searched routinely for evidence ancillary to the arrest. Most commonly this extends to vehicles in the possession of a person at the time of arrest and their dwelling.

Dwellings and other real estate may be searched prior to arrest, but normally after a judicial warrant has been formally issued. Obtaining a warrant usually requires that the police give their reasons for believing that evidence of wrongdoing may be found in the premises. Entry into premises under a warrant may vary in the amount of force used. Often, the police present themselves at the entrance, show the warrant to the occupier and enter more or less consensually. If the police have sufficient reason to believe either that they might face resistance and/or that occupiers will seek to destroy evidence, they may employ the methods of what in the US is called a 'no knock' search. Using various battering rams, from sledgehammers to converted armoured military vehicles, the police literally break into the premises, overpowering resistance and securing all the rooms. Inevitably, these methods entail the arrest of the occupants of such premises, but this is ancillary to the main purpose of the forced entry.

Distinctive Features

Generally, the more liberal a state, the higher the threshold for suspicion sufficient to warrant a search. Extending powers of search are usually controversial and must be warranted, at least initially, on the grounds that exceptional measures are justified. Thus, the terrorist emergency that has afflicted the Western world since the infamous '9/11' attacks, have been widely accompanied by extended powers to search, especially to stop and search in public.

Stopping people in a public place and searching them *in situ* is a particular *cause célèbre* in many jurisdictions because it is believed that visible minorities are treated selectively. In Britain it has been referred to as 'disproportionality'; elsewhere in the Anglo–Saxon world it is more commonly known as 'racial profiling' or colloquially as 'walking/driving while black'. However, such complaints are not restricted to *searching*. It is as much an issue of police stopping and *questioning* fellow citizens that indicates how suspicion alights more easily upon some sections of the population than others. Controversy has been stirred by the assumption that if some sections of the population are stopped and searched more than others, then this is a manifestation of police prejudice and stereotyping. Others have suggested that it may equally be due to differences between sections of the population in their use of public space. However, what is undoubtedly true in most, if not all, jurisdictions is that those stopped and searched are disproportionately young men.

The misuse of the power to stop and search is not restricted to disproportionality in the stopping and searching of visible minorities. A concern raised during the enactment of legislation in Britain to codify police powers (the Police and Criminal Evidence Act 1984) was that searches of property under warrant might be used to search for anything incriminating – so called 'fishing expeditions'. Attempts were made to require the police to specify in the warrant application exactly what they were searching for, but the police seem to have had little problem in bringing cases to court that rely on the fortuitous discovery of contraband uncovered during a search for something else.

Another persistent issue is that of searching with the consent of the person or the occupier of premises being searched. This is a classic example of police operating within the 'shadow of the law', for a person who refuses to be searched consensually draws suspicion upon themselves. What have they to hide? Moreover, police breach the barrier between the private and the public in other ways too. For instance, those who complain of burglary may need to prove lawful ownership of goods that were stolen.

The searching of citizens and their property relies upon them having unfettered rights to be free from such intrusions, but that freedom is not as all encompassing as may be supposed. For instance, police have extensive powers to stop motor vehicles on the public highway, because driving is not a right, but an activity *permitted* or *licensed* by the state under certain conditions. Police can stop and search a vehicle to establish the *bona fides* of the driver, take samples of breath, and search the vehicle to ensure roadworthiness.

Police may also permanently or temporarily cordon off areas of otherwise public space and restrict access to those who consent to be searched. For instance, on security grounds, those wishing to view royal ceremonials in London from close quarters are only allowed to stand on the highway in close proximity to where VIPs will pass if they pass through electronic 'search arches' and have hand baggage physically searched.

Such locations demonstrate the ambiguity that surrounds the apparent dichotomy of the public and private domains. What is otherwise public may, for the duration of a specific event, be transformed into something more akin to private space. During the Provisional Irish Republican Army terrorist bombing campaign in Britain in the late 1980s and early 1990s this extended so far as to demarcate the financial district of London (the *City* of London) as effectively a private space into which vehicles were permitted only if they could be searched – the so-called 'ring of steel'.

Of course, those entering entirely private spaces do so not as citizens, but as parties to a private contract that may include provision for searches to be conducted by the owner of the premises of his or her agents. It is also worth noting that in most jurisdictions much greater powers of search and seizure are granted to customs and immigration officials at ports of entry.

Evaluation

Searching after a specific crime has been committed occasions little controversy for the need to collect evidence and detect offenders is clear. Controversy tends to focus on the crime prevention purpose of searches conducted at lower levels of suspicion, most notably stop and search. The rate at which offences are revealed by these searches is frequently modest, but Sherman's (1997) appraisal of 'what works' in policing generally found that stop and search was one of the few policing tactics that bore fruit. Objections to stop and search often concern not the tactic itself, but the manner in which police officers conduct searches, for example, their willingness or otherwise to give a credible reason for the search.

P.A.J. Waddington

Associated Concepts: arrest, crime prevention, criminal investigation, institutional racism, racial profiling, police property

Key Readings

Bowling, B. and Phillips, C. (2001) *Racism, Crime and Criminal Justice*. Essex: Longman.
Miller, J., Quinton, P. and Bland, N. (2000) *Police Stops and Searches: Lessons from a Programme of Research*. London: Home Office.
Sanders, A. and Young, R. (2003) 'Police powers', in T. Newburn. (ed.) *Handbook of Policing*. Cullompton, Devon: Willan.
Sherman, L. W., Gottfredson, D., MacKenzie, J., Eck, J., Reuter, P. and Bushway S. (1997) *Preventing Crime: What Works, What Doesn't, What's Promising*. Washington, DC: Office of Justice Programmes, US Department of Justice.

SECURITY

Definition

Security has a broad and complex set of meanings spanning the pursuit of national, military, or community safety; the end goal of objective safety from threat; the subjective condition of feeling safe; and the assurance or guarantee thereof. In these different guises it also carries a normative meaning as a public good that must be defended by the state. Yet increasingly security is used also to denote a commodity, produced by private security firms, traded commercially, and enjoyed as a 'club good' by those with access to it. Security thus refers to both the public and private security industries and their respective outputs. Its antonym 'insecurity' drives crime control, policing, anti-terrorism policies and corporate security production and in the UK is substantially responsible for the rise of 'reassurance policing' and community safety programmes, as well as the proliferation of security hardware and technologies. Finally, its derivative 'securitization' denotes the adverse ethical and analytical consequences of framing diverse policy debates in terms of security.

Distinctive Features

Security was once primarily the domain of international relations, political science, and military studies where it was used to denote the sanctity of the sovereign state against external threat. The power and rhetorical appeal of security has since seen it attached to a long line of neologisms (global security, international security, cooperative security, and human security) that deliberately use the term to mobilize political support and economic resources. It has also become an important plank of domestic crime control and policing policy, partly because of a growing concern with individual and communal safety, and partly as a consequence of a shift away from traditional reactive measures and towards preventive measures that seek to maximize security proactively. Important also

to its rise to prominence is the massive growth of the private security industry whose largest firms employ several hundred thousand personnel, such that private security personnel now outnumber state police in many states. More recently, the proliferation of terrorist threat has served to break down the distinctions between external and internal security, between terrorist threat and serious and organized crime, between anti-terrorist measures and crime prevention, and between security services and the police. Whereas the rise of the private security industry challenges the dominion of the state, the effect of terrorism is rather to enlarge state power through anti-terrorist legislation, the proliferation of security measures, and increases in security personnel.

Several factors are said to drive demand for security. They include rising crime, economic restructuring, fiscal restraint, changes in informal patterns of social control, and growing sources of insecurity that together feed consumer demand. Security also has an important spatial aspect. A key driver of private security provision is said to be the proliferation of 'mass private property' (such as shopping malls, airports, university campuses, and leisure facilities). These large enclosures are privately owned and policed by private agents able to restrict access, notwithstanding their quasi-public status and usage. Distribution of security varies according to the private provision of protection, access to insurance, to safe housing areas, and to private transport. Security scholars seeking to describe the new distributions of security employ numerous metaphors including security 'assemblages', 'patchworks', 'quilts', 'webs', 'bubbles', 'networks' and 'nodes'. Network analysis has been particularly important in seeking to establish the relations and links among different security providers. More recently, 'nodal governance' has focused attention upon the providers of security, in particular communal nodes capable of communal self-rule or 'local capacity governance'.

Private security production has generated advances in technological hardware such as surveillance systems, closed circuit television and satellite-tracking devices, as well as more amorphous forensic and actuarial tools, security computer software, and security management systems. In turn new security technologies alter practices of policing and police culture. Changes in the distribution and production of security thus have important implications for the relationship between security and governance. Where once security was a central justification for state power, its diffusion into the market place has created competitive new security providers and a new role for the state as collaborator and regulator. Regulatory mechanisms for the security industry vary throughout the world, and in the UK include the industry's own 'British Security Industry Association' and the recently established state 'Security Industry Authority' responsible for setting standards and ensuring accountability in private security provision.

Evaluation

Although it is commonly presented as an unconditional good, security is not without costs and paradoxical consequences that inhere in its very nature. Security pursues risk reduction but presumes the persistence of crime; the prominence of security has enlarged not diminished the penal state; security promises reassurance but in practice tends to increase anxiety; security is posited as a universal good but presumes those who threaten; and security promises freedom but its pursuit tends to erode civil liberties (Zedner, 2003). These largely inescapable costs have generated a lively debate about the governance of security, the need to develop new normative structures, new regulatory mechanisms, and in the UK even an overarching 'security authority'. A growing academic literature on the governance of security (for example, Johnston and Shearing, 2003) seeks to develop new principles and values fit for a 'security society'. Less positively, attention has also been drawn to the ways in which social life is increasingly governed 'through security'.

The growing provision of security by a mixed economy of public and private actors challenges the very nature of security as a public good. Diversification and privatization of security disputes the role of the state as provider and guarantor of security and diminishes its role. The 'marketization' of security results in private security clubs or contractual communities (such as gated communities), and virtual communities of credit and insurance. It results in uneven distributions that create 'security differentials' leaving some cocooned in security bubbles and others largely outside protection. Some welcome changing patterns of security distribution as permitting local communities to develop their own capacity for self-governance and meet their own security needs. Others resist it, defending security as an inalienably public good that only the state can properly guarantee (Loader and Walker, 2007). They reject the commodification of security, its provision and trading on the market as inimical to a fully social conception of security that resides in collective provision and mutual guarantee.

Security is a slippery and contested concept whose lack of definitional clarity permits expansive interpretation and wide application. Notwithstanding its inherent imprecision, or perhaps because of it, security has gained considerable prominence not only in contemporary crime control and policing but also across adjacent policy fields. Yet the progressive 'securitization' of socio-economic and political issues has a worrisome tendency to demote other concerns, foreclose debate, and to legitimize emergency powers all in the name of security. The danger is that competing interests, not least civil liberties, tend to be sacrificed to the more pressing claims of security. The metaphor of balance has proven a powerful tool for those arguing that increases in security threats (be they crime or terrorist attacks) licence a rebalancing away from liberty and in favour of security and greater state power. Such demands lead some security scholars to declare themselves 'against security' or to suggest that we can have 'too much security' (Zedner, 2003). Others go further to argue that since security is a relational concept dependent on threats as yet unknown we would do better to abandon the pursuit of the unobtainable. Instead they explore the possibility that risk has a positive aspect or 'uncertain promise' that unfettered pursuit of security fails to acknowledge.

Lucia Zedner

Associated Concepts: commodification of security, community safety, crime prevention, homeland security, human security, private security, privatization, public reassurance, security networks, terrorism

Key Readings

Johnston, L. and Shearing, C. (2003) *Governing Security: Explorations in Policing and Justice.* London: Routledge.
Loader, I. and Walker, N. (2007) *Civilizing Security.* Cambridge: Cambridge University Press.
Crawford, A. (2005) 'Policing and security as 'club goods': the new enclosures?' in J. Wood, and B. Dupont, (eds) *Democracy, Society and the Governance of Security.* Cambridge: Cambridge University Press.
Wakefield, A. (2003) *Selling Security: The Private Policing of Public Space.* Cullompton, Devon: Willan Publishing.
Zedner, L. (2003) 'Too much security?' *International Journal of the Sociology of Law,* 31 (3): 155–84.

SECURITY GOVERNANCE

See Pluralization; Security; Vigilantism

SECURITY NETWORKS

Definition

A security network is a set of institutional, organizational, communal, or individual agents or nodes that are directly or indirectly connected in order to authorize and/or provide security for the benefit of internal or external stakeholders. A node is an organization or an individual that belongs to a network, and is linked to other organizations and individuals within this network by a set of relations that facilitate collaborative behaviours. The security network concept derives from the realization that the complexity of crime problems exceeds the sole capacity of police organizations. Although police organizations play a central role in many security networks, they are only a node among many others. Security networks are particularly well suited to crime prevention objectives, but they can also be mobilized to combat terrorism or high-tech crime. This normative perspective of security networks needs to be complemented by a more empirical one, which emphasizes the proliferation of ties between nodes to fulfil a variety of needs (share information, exchange personnel, plan joint operations, assess the reliability of other partners, monitor best practices), and therefore the difficulty of these nodes to fully appreciate the complexity of the overall network to which they belong and their position within it.

We can distinguish four types of overlapping security networks:

- Local security networks harness public and private resources available in local communities in order to resolve common crime problems such as vandalism, social disorder and retail theft. They commonly involve a range of actors derived from the community and the public and private sectors.
- Institutional security networks predominantly involve police organizations seeking to rationalize their resources through flexible arrangements that allow them to share costs for expensive services such as forensic labs, specialized training programmes, or public order units.
- International security networks emerge to respond to transnational criminal and terrorist networks and as such, question the notion of state sovereignty over internal or homeland security affairs. The globalization of exchanges – and the private flow of

goods and services it creates – will enhance the need for international security networks that combine public and private nodes.

- Informational security networks include the technical arrangements that allow the controlled flow of information between security nodes. The proliferation of policing (public and private) databases and communication systems play an important role in the connectedness of physical security networks.

These four categories do not capture the diversity and uniqueness of security networks, which are strongly influenced by, among other things, spatial, temporal, functional and personal contingencies.

Distinctive Features

Security networks have a long history. The Police Union of German States represents an early security network formed in the mid 1850s in order to exchange information across international borders on political revolutionary movements. This precursor to Interpol was a police initiative, but at the same period, across the Atlantic, the Pinkerton Detective Agency was also busy casting a web of linkages with police organizations from the US and beyond. What distinguishes these early security networks from current ones is the current proliferation of potential nodes (public, private and hybrid) with a stake in the production of security, and the development of information and communication technologies that allow networks of a different scale to develop.

The membership of a security network is by definition plural and open. The pluralism implies that even if police organizations occupy a central and prominent position within most security networks, other nodes such as private (or contract) security companies, in-house (or proprietary) security services, technology vendors, professional associations, workers' unions, regulatory authorities, non-governmental organizations, community groups and even in certain contexts, organized crime, can be significantly involved in the collective delivery of security. The openness of security networks reflects the importance of trust as a binding factor between their members. As a result, informal ties based on reputation and reciprocity are more efficient as regulatory tools of the network's membership than centralized bureaucratic procedures. In the case of public security networks, the need to keep up with innovations introduced by other members, both organizational (e.g., intelligence-led policing) and technological (e.g., less than lethal weapons), will also constitute a powerful incentive fuelled by the need to maintain one's standing, which can hardly be matched by bureaucratic directives.

Security networks are attractive to their members for a number of reasons: they are flatter than hierarchies and it is fairly easy for each member of the network to access information held by other members. Networks are more open to innovation than hierarchies. They are also more flexible (less procedures and more trust), a clear benefit in the context of high risk and unpredictability which characterizes the security field. The flat and distributed structure of networks means that in adverse situations, they can easily overcome the loss of some of their members by quickly shifting their responsibilities to remaining nodes, under the same principles that make the Internet so resistant to localized attacks. This property is called resilience.

Security networks are gaining currency as a policy tool in several countries. In the UK community safety partnerships and the 'extended police family' approach represent concerted efforts to increase the networking capacity of public agencies. In Australia, the Victoria Police Service is running its experimental Nexus Policing Project in order to build a network of key service providers and community groups to address issues related to indigenous, multicultural and youth affairs, sex offending or public transport safety. While engaged in the process of drafting a new legislative framework to replace the 1958 Police Act, the New Zealand police convened a conference on networked policing in 2006, whose findings were integrated in the proposed changes to the legislation. The same year, in the Netherlands, the Board of Chief Commissioners produced a policy document titled *The Police in Evolution*, where a 'nodal orientation' is prescribed to better control the flows of people, goods, money and information.

The study of security networks is confronted with a boundary specification problem. How a network's membership is determined has important implications for the subsequent analysis of its structure and dynamics. In the field of security, some nodes can be considered as networks in their own rights. The Department of Homeland Security, which was created in the aftermath of the 9/11 terrorist attacks in the US, received for example the mandate to integrate various organizations into a single agency, but it can also be conceptualized as a network of competing interests responsible for the coordination of more than 87,000 different governmental jurisdictions that have security responsibilities at various levels of government. Furthermore, the interdependence of security issues with other policy domains such as health, housing and public transport, calls for problem-solving partnerships that overlap strict sectoral boundaries. This blending of policy and organizational networks further complicates the task of identifying what nodes should be included as full members of a given security network, in contrast with more peripheral actors. In this context, it is important to realize that while some networks are the results of well-planned and coordinated initiatives, others emerge organically through everyday practices that address very specific problems or needs.

Evaluation

Security networks are notoriously hard to coordinate and their accountability is limited because of the distribution of responsibilities and informality of exchanges. Few deliberate attempts to assess security networks as such have been made so far, but indirect data can nevertheless be found. The 9/11 Commission report makes for example multiple mentions of dysfunctional information sharing practices among the network of US intelligence and

policing agencies prior to the terrorist attacks. Indeed, one of its main recommendations has been to remove the bureaucratic hurdles that were seen in the report as the cause of the network's ineffectiveness. This report, and the policy orientations it provoked, vividly illustrates how security networks must coexist with bureaucratic structures and market rationales that often undermine each other. Mazerolle and Ransley (2005) offer a more positive assessment in their research on third party policing, where they show that a range of incentives can be mobilized to assist security networks in achieving desirable outcomes in their efforts to control drug and crime problems. Their systematic review was focused on legal levers as the main incentive, but less coercive strategies are also frequently found (Cherney, O'Reilly and Grabosky, 2006).

When assessing security networks, it is important to remember that they do not operate in a vacuum, and that the ultimate indicator of their performance is their ability to engage and control 'dark' networks operated by organized crime, terrorists, armed militias or even street gangs (Raab and Milward, 2003).

Future evaluations of security networks will need to measure their effectiveness, as well as their legitimacy in the eyes of stakeholders and citizens. But their procedural efficiency is also of interest. How much information flows between members? How relevant is this information to the members? At what speed does this information travel? How does the network arrive at its decisions and enforce its norms? Who are the most influential and powerful actors? Do patterns of exchange facilitate clandestine or backchannel arrangements in order to elude traditional accountability systems? These are all questions that should be answered if we want to better understand the complex and messy reality of security networks. Social network analysts in other fields, such as sociology or management studies, have already designed some of the indicators that could be used for such assessments (Wasserman and Faust, 1994), but security-focused methodologies will also need to be invented to ensure that what is measured is what matters.

Benoît Dupont

Associated Concepts: community safety, crime prevention, intelligence-led policing, pluralization, multi-agency policing, security, technology, third party policing, transnational policing

Key Readings

Cherney, A., O'Reilly, J. and Grabosky, P. (2006), 'Networks and meta-regulation: strategies aimed at governing illicit synthetic drugs', *Policing and Society*, 16 (4): 370–85.

Dupont, B. (2004) 'Security in the age of networks', *Policing and Society*, 14 (1): 76–91.

Dupont, B. (2006) 'Delivering security through networks: surveying the relational landscape of security managers in an urban setting', *Crime, Law and Social Change*, 45 (3): 165–84.

Fleming, J. and Wood, J. (eds) (2006) *Fighting Crime Together: The Challenges of Policing and Security Networks*. Sydney: UNSW Press.

Mazerolle, L. and Ransley, J. (2005) *Third Party Policing*. Cambridge: Cambridge University Press.

Raab, J. and Milward, H.B. (2003) 'Dark networks as problems', *Journal of Public Administration Research and Theory*, 13 (4): 413–39.

Wasserman, S. and Faust, K. (1994), *Social Network Analysis: Methods and Applications*. Cambridge: Cambridge University Press.

SEXUAL ASSAULT

Definition

The term sexual assault refers to a broad category of behaviours which have been differentially defined in international legislation. The range of behaviours covered includes rape, indecent assault, and various forms of unwanted or coercive touching of a sexual nature or in circumstances of indecency. The offence recognized in law as the most serious is the crime of rape, which typically carries maximum penalties placing it as the second most serious offence on the statute books.

The question of determining which behaviours constitute rape has provoked considerable international debate, and definitions are still variable. The issues include consideration of the extent to which rape should be limited to acts involving penile penetration of the vagina, or in some countries simply the female genitalia, or extended to include other forms of coercive sexual behaviour. Traditional definitions of rape recognized only the possibility of men as perpetrators and women as victims. While there is no international consensus on this matter, many countries have moved towards greater gender-neutrality in law and introduced provisions allowing for the recognition of male victims of sexual assault as well as female perpetrators.

A further definitional issue pertains to the extent to which rape in marriage has been criminalized. Even in contexts where laws exist specifying penalties or precluding defences for marital rape (for example, England and Wales, New Zealand, Australia), rates of under-reporting are particularly high, police responses variable, and convictions rare. This reflects societal views of 'real rape' constituting attacks perpetrated by strangers, and a continuing reluctance to acknowledge the sexual violence component of domestic violence.

Distinctive Features

The distinction between rape and non-rape is sometimes hard to clarify, since aspects of violence or coercion are present in many women's sexual encounters. Seduction narratives obscure the ways in which traditional male expectations of sexual entitlement operate to secure submission and portray it as consent. Many women struggle to define their experiences of coercive sex as rape, and there is widespread consensus that the overwhelming majority of rapes and sexual assaults are never reported to the police. Other factors affecting reporting include fear of the perpetrator, self-blame and guilt, fear of the reactions of friends and family, apprehension over the police response, and apprehension regarding going to court and being cross-examined. Rape trials are so arduous for the victim that they are commonly experienced and referred to as a 'second rape'.

Crimes of rape and sexual assault pose investigative challenges for the police. Stranger assaults are difficult because the offender has to be identified and located, necessitating a complex process of evidence gathering and analysis. This can be particularly taxing in cases involving serial sex offenders, where considerable media and community pressure can be placed on the police to find the perpetrator.

Most rapes, however, are not committed by serial attackers. Prevalence studies internationally have shown that the overwhelming majority of sexual assaults committed involve perpetrators known to the victim, typically acquaintances, partners, family, friends and others such as colleagues and persons consulted professionally (including doctors, therapists, and police officers). Police investigators have to combat the lack of evidence, since such assaults typically leave little to corroborate the use of physical force and the question comes down to the matter of consent, often his word versus her word. At this point issues of credibility are considered, with the impact of common societal rape myths continuing to affect investigative decision-making (Hazelwood and Burgess, 2001). The tendency for many in society to see victims as 'asking for it' removes responsibility from the perpetrators and results in high levels of victim-blaming. Victims are often likely to internalize such attitudes and hold themselves accountable for what happened.

The effects and consequences of sexual assault victimization are complex and varied. Victims may experience long-lasting impacts on their levels of fear and safety, lose trust in others and in themselves, display out of character and/or risk taking behaviour, develop food or alcohol disorders, and display a range of physical and psychological health symptoms. The application of the term 'post-traumatic stress disorder' to sexual assault survivors arose from recognition of the parallels exhibited with survivors of war and other major traumas. Once a person has been sexually assaulted, they may be at risk of subsequent sexual victimization or offending unless they receive validation and positive interventions. Victims of child sexual abuse, for instance, may be at increased risk of sexual assault in adulthood. International victimization studies reveal a small group of victims are vulnerable to experiencing repeat victimization, often within the context of violent intimate relationships.

Growing recognition is being given to the ways in which victims resist and survive sexual assault. Discourses of 'victimhood' have overlooked the many ways in which victims avoid rape or, even if a rape is completed, the ways in which they physically and mentally survive such attacks. Greater victim participation in the criminal justice system is also being explored, considering the possibilities of various alternatives to the rigours of existing trial formats.

Evaluation

The history of policing reflects the growth and development of a hierarchical, conservative, male-dominated institution. The personnel who comprise our police services are drawn from the wider society and may typically adhere to the popular beliefs and myths about rape that continue to be socially prevalent. A major challenge for criminal justice systems internationally is to improve responses to victims and increase the chances of perpetrators being held accountable. Recent research indicates that, despite the rhetoric of improvements in the system, the attrition rate for rape is actually increasing – it is harder to secure a conviction for rape now than it was twenty years ago (Kelly et al., 2005).

The police play a pivotal role through their positioning as gatekeepers to the justice system. Police actions and responses to complaints of sexual assault largely determine the likelihood of complaints being fully investigated and charges brought against the alleged offenders. The factors associated with the greater likelihood of prosecution and conviction include attacks perpetrated by strangers and the presence of visible, physical injuries. The reality for most victims of rape and sexual assault, however, is that they will be raped by those already known to them, with fear and threats securing their compliance without the need for other forms of violence.

Police investigative decision-making may often be influenced by their anticipation of case outcomes. Of growing concern is the extent to which police sexual assault investigations may be prematurely halted as a result of judgements made regarding the complainant's credibility. Concern has been widely voiced regarding the 'culture of scepticism' surrounding sexual assault allegations, manifest also in inflated beliefs regarding the frequency of false rape complaints (Jordan, 2004).

Recent international trends in law enforcement around sexual violence reveal similarities in approach, and recognition of the importance of preventing secondary victimization. There has been greater recognition of the extent to which victims of rape and sexual assault should have a support person present while they are medically examined, interviewed by police, and cross-examined in court. Victims should be offered the option of support from a trained crisis worker – family members or partners may be struggling to accept the situation and may themselves need support. Increasing recognition is being given to the advantages of police participation in multi-agency partnerships based upon a tripartite response comprising police, medical/forensic, and crisis support agencies (Her Majesty's Inspectorate of Constabulary, 2007). Such partnerships do not, however, absolve police services of responsibilities for victim care and support.

Victims of rape and sexual assault may present displaying extensive trauma effects and an ambivalency about entrusting the process to police. Growing recognition of such factors has led to an increased awareness of the investigative specialization required. Investigating officers need to be specifically trained and experienced, and selected on the basis of their empathy, sensitivity, professionalism, and attitudes. Individual victims' wishes to give their statement to an officer of a particular gender should ideally be met,

given the importance to the victim of having a degree of control after the disempowering nature of rape, as well as the importance to police of obtaining the most complete statement possible.

As well as the role they play in law enforcement, police agencies are increasingly recognizing their potential impact in crime prevention. Traditionally, crime prevention advice promoted the perpetrator of sexual violence as a stranger, encouraging potential victims (particularly women) to be vigilant in public places, and to avoid dark alleyways. Such advice fails to acknowledge that most sexual assaults are committed by known acquaintances in private and often domestic settings. It also shifts the focus away from the actions of those responsible for the offending and onto the victim, reinforcing victim-blaming attitudes. More relevant crime prevention advice addresses specific locations and scenarios and forewarns potential victims about the range of tactics which motivated or opportunistic sexual offenders may employ, including the use of alcohol and drugs and the targeting of specific and vulnerable victims such as the young, elderly or mentally impaired.

Assessment of how sensitively and professionally police officers respond to sexual assault allegations can function as a barometer of the extent to which police organizations have moved away from their traditional masculinist ethos to embrace and reflect gender equality.

Jan Jordan

Associated Concepts: criminal investigation, culture, domestic violence, investigative interviewing, policing, victim

Key Readings

Gregory, J. and Lees, S. (1999) *Policing Sexual Assault*. London: Routledge.

Hazelwood, R.R. and Burgess, A.W. (eds) (2001) *Practical Aspects of Rape Investigation: A Multidisciplinary Approach* (3rd edn). Boca Raton: CRC Press.

Her Majesty's Inspectorate of Constabulary (2007) *Without Consent: A Report on the Joint Review of the Investigation and Prosecution of Rape Offences*. London: Her Majesty's Inspectorate of Constabulary HMCPSI and HMIC Thematic Report.

Jordan, J. (2004) *The Word of a Woman? Police, Rape and Belief*. Basingstoke: Palgrave Macmillan.

Kelly, L., Lovett, J. and Regan, L. (2005) *A Gap or a Chasm? Attrition in Reported Rape Cases*. London: Home Office.

SITUATIONAL CRIME PREVENTION

Definition

Situational crime prevention (SCP) is a way of thinking about prevention that was introduced into criminology by Ron Clarke when he was Director of the UK's Home Office Research Unit in the 1970s. The critical feature of the situational approach is that the emphasis is entirely on the environment, not on modifying the criminal or violent dispositions of offenders, the preoccupation of much traditional criminology. SCP's emphasis on very specific aspects of the physical or social environments, such as unlocked doors or informal workplace 'codes' that legitimize sexual harassment, makes it attractive to governments and managers sceptical about the prospects of engineering improved human beings.

Distinctive Features

In the last quarter century several schools of situational thought have developed, with the result that it is not possible to present a summary of the situational perspective that would meet with universal agreement. There is disagreement in particular about how much the perceived rather than the objective physical environment should be emphasized, whether techniques designed to induce a sense of guilt or shame in potential offenders should be classified as situational, and about the extent to which offenders engage in a process of conscious target selection and decision making as opposed to their actions being directly precipitated by provocations or other kinds of immediate environmental contingencies.

Most commonly, situational prevention has been understood as focusing on the *opportunities* for crime present in specific settings or environments (following the old adage that 'opportunity makes the thief'). This version of SCP is based on the assumption that human beings generally act in a purposive way to maximize benefits to themselves or to those they care about, and that their behaviours involve some degree of rational calculation and careful decision making to achieve these goals. Under certain circumstances, it is argued, a very wide range of people can be tempted to act in illegal or anti-social ways, even those who under 'normal' circumstances would never engage in crime. For example, a cashier who has lost her weekly wages at the horse track may be tempted to raid petty cash at work, meaning to 'pay the loan back' when she is next paid. Generalizing this thinking, proponents of situational approaches argue that prevention should comprise:

> ... opportunity reducing measures that (1) are directed at highly specific forms of crime, (2) involve the management, design or manipulation of the immediate environment in as systematic and permanent way as possible, (3) make crime more difficult and risky, or less rewarding and excusable as judged by a wide range of offenders.
> (Clarke, 1997: 4)

Examples of specific techniques include steering column locks on cars (that *increase the effort* required to steal a car, an example of target hardening); improved street lighting (improving natural surveillance, an example of *increasing the risks* involved in committing crime); rapid removal of graffiti (a form of *reducing the rewards* of crime by denying the graffiti artist the satisfaction of seeing her work displayed); and sexual harassment codes (that set or clarify rules, *removing the excuses* that someone might use to justify their actions).

An important development of SCP theory was the concept of 'situational precipitators' introduced by Richard Wortley. He distinguished *situational precipitators* and *situational regulators* in a two-stage model:

> In the first stage of the model, a range of psychological processes are proposed that may actively induce individuals to engage in conduct that they may not otherwise have performed. The behaviour may be avoided entirely if relevant precipitators are adequately controlled. In the event that behaviour is initiated, then, in the second stage of the model, performance of that behaviour is subject to consideration of the consequences that are likely to follow. The absence of appropriate disincentives or constraints will permit or encourage behaviour while appropriate disincentives or constraints will prevent or discourage behaviour. (Wortley, 2002: 56)

Situational precipitators include:

(1) environmental cues that *prompt* the individual to behave anti-socially, which can be controlled by such means as setting positive expectations (for example, gentrifying licensed premises so that they appear clean, well ordered and safe);

(2) environmental cues that exert *pressure* to misbehave, which can be controlled by such means as reducing inappropriate conformity (for example, dispersing troublemakers);

(3) environmental cues that reduce self-control and *permit* individuals to engage in behaviour they would otherwise self-censure (for example, videos or music encouraging violence against women) which can be controlled by rule setting, or clarifying responsibility; and

(4) environmental cues that can produce emotional arousal that *provokes* a violent reaction, which can be controlled by such means as reducing frustration (for example, prison inmate control of comfort settings).

In light of these developments, the situational perspective is properly understood as an *interactionist perspective*, since it attempts to explain behaviour in terms of an interaction between an actor and the features of the setting within which an act is performed. The immediate environment plays a fundamental role in initiating and shaping action; it is not just a passive backdrop against which action is played out.

Police are increasingly using SCP thinking, particularly as part of the *problem-oriented policing* (POP) movement. POP proponents argue that instead of just responding to crime incidents as isolated phenomena, police should attend to the underlying conditions that give rise to recurring incidents. This might mean, for example, recognizing that many incidents involve the same people as repeat victims, and devising ways of reducing their risks through SCP techniques such as marking property to deter theft or installing security.

Much SCP and POP thinking in police services around the world is being introduced through the training of crime analysts, a new breed of employees who are replacing intelligence officers (who traditionally have simply assisted individual crime investigations). Crime analysts search for and analyze patterns in crime and other relevant data, often using mapping and statistical techniques as well as criminological theories such as SCP to devise preventative solutions. For example, a concentration of assaults in and around a small number of drinking establishments in a downtown entertainment area might call for police visits to these premises to meet with owners and to require the implementation of a code of practice that leads to both opportunity reduction and to violence precipitation control strategies. Opportunity reduction might involve entry screening for weapons (increasing the perceived risks of offending), and precipitation control might involve training security staff to use respectful and face-saving techniques in handling disputes with patrons (thus reducing provocations).

Evaluation

Situational prevention is not popular with many criminologists. At a general level, many critics question the ethical and social vision of SCP, arguing that it promotes an exclusionary society (e.g., gated communities) and a narrow, managerial approach to prevention. One recurring criticism is that SCP ignores the 'root causes' of crime, namely social disadvantage and the associated risk factors such as child maltreatment, chaotic home environments, and delinquent peers. Situationalists argue in response that they are not social reformers but just want to reduce crime (which disproportionately affects the poor), and that in any case there is no conflict between the two perspectives, since they deal with different points in the causal chain. For example, an adolescent may be at risk of offending as a result of his family upbringing, but the actual decision to commit a specific offence is dependent on opportunities and provocations in the immediate situation that can become the focus of situational methods. A related criticism is that SCP simply *displaces crime* to another place or time because determined criminals will offend anyway, but the empirical evidence on the whole does not support this argument. In fact research suggests that often there is considerable *diffusion of benefits* of SCP – for example, successfully preventing burglary in repeatedly burgled houses in a housing estate can reduce burglary even in houses that were not targeted for preventive measures.

Most critics concede that SCP is useful for certain problems. Certainly its highly pragmatic approach and capacity to be easily taken up by police, the security industry, city planners and many others mean that its influence is likely to grow. Moreover, the situational perspective has contributed to criminological theory by extending knowledge about specific types of crime and their geneses in opportunities or provocations arising in specific types of social and physical settings. Reflecting this, some of the major new developments in the use of SCP are for 'non-traditional' types of crime such as animal smuggling, terrorism, and e-crime, and for crime prevention in developing countries.

Ross Homel

Associated Concepts: crime prevention, displacement, diffusion of benefits, problem-oriented policing

Key Readings

Clarke, R.V. (ed.) (1997) *Situational Crime Prevention: Successful Case Studies*. Guilderland, NY: Harrow and Heston
Clarke, R.V. (2005) 'Seven misconceptions of situational crime prevention', in N. Tilley (ed.), *Handbook of Crime Prevention and Community Safety*. Cullompton, Devon: Willan Publishing.
Crime Prevention Studies: a series of volumes published by Criminal Justice Press.
Graham, K. and Homel, R. (In press) *Raising the Bar: Understanding and Preventing Violence in Bars, Clubs and Pubs*. Cullompton, Devon: Willan Publishing.
Von Hirsch, A., Garland, D. and Wakefield, A. (eds) (2000) *Ethical and Social Perspectives on Situational Crime Prevention*. Portland, Oregon: Hart Publishing
Wortley, R. (2002) *Situational Prison Control: Crime Prevention in Correctional Institutions*. Cambridge: Cambridge University Press.

SOCIALIZATION

Definition

Socialization generally refers to a process whereby the individual learns to conform to the moral standards, codes of conduct and role expectations in any specific society or organization. In entering into an organization or society, new members negotiate their sense of self-identity through interacting with others. As Simmel (1908) puts it, socialization is the process of recognizing what is 'I' and what is 'Not-I'. The 'I' does not disappear, rather survival in any new environment (particularly within occupational organizations such as the police) is heavily dependent on the individual coming to share collective principles, working rules and practices. This may mean shedding parts of the 'I', adapting the 'I' to fit in with shared ideas and practices or finding ways of accommodating the 'I' within a new environment.

Distinctive Features

It is widely thought that the police occupation defines not just what you do but who you are. In the police officer's view, policing is not just an economic activity, it is a vocation. McNamara, in his study of the New York Police Department in the 1960s came upon a handout given to new recruits at the academy. The handout, given out as part of the induction process, states that the police officer 'may not achieve the material rewards of other professions, but he has the greatest opportunities for spiritual satisfaction' (McNamara, 1967: 216). Joining the police, then, presupposes a complete reinvention of the self and for a greater good.

Drawing on the work of Van Maanen, Janet Chan (2003: 13) suggests that police socialization begins even before the new recruit enters the police. In the 'anticipatory socialization' phase, those intending to join the police begin to orient their values, attitudes, skills and knowledge towards those that they view as required by police organizations. More than most other occupations, the socialization of new police recruits is institutionalized. Police socialization is 'collective, formal, sequential and fixed' and aims at producing conformity. Formal socialization begins with training where new recruits attain organizational knowledge. The more informal socialization takes place through social assimilation in the field where 'real' policing takes place.

Any understanding of police socialization must be linked to a discussion on police culture. At the most basic level, police culture refers to a system of shared values, assumptions and craft rules that inform ways of thinking and acting and are passed down from one generation of police to the next. It is now pretty well accepted that there are variations in the expression of police. However, even those most critical of the idea of 'a police culture' accept some broad generalizations about its existence. Manning, for example, argues that police 'act in such a way in situations that their decision-making balances the rational legal bureaucracy and its public face with the paternalistic day-to-day work that is policing'

(Manning, 2008). Occupational culture is shaped largely by police responses to their organizational environment which is often experienced as uncertain by the police. The institutionalized police socialization creates an atmosphere of solidarity, secrecy and brotherhood in the face of an organizational environment that is uncertain.

Evaluation

The formal socialization process begins with police training and then more informally through ongoing interactions with other police officers, particularly when in the field or on the streets. Yet completely shared ways of thinking and making sense does not necessarily underpin all police responses. The responses of individual police officers are often situationally determined. There are a range of possible ways of responding to a particular event or problem that depend on a range of factors including, for example, the organizational resources available to police, the established relationships and even the social contract that exists between police and communities in a particular area, and the kinds of supervision and command during a particular event. Pockets of subcultures and individualized solutions may emerge on the ground to deal with uncertain events or situations (Manning, 2008).

These situational matrices put 'common sense' police responses to the test. But it is not these matrices alone that create the space for contestable police practice. While early socialization no doubt encourages organizational affiliation, individual police officers may differ in their interpretation of their policing experiences, including their socialization within the police organization.

Individuals enter the police with their own sets of experiences and webs of meanings. They do not blindly follow the rules of acting or even the tricks of the trade that are displayed by more seasoned police officers. Rather, even on the part of new recruits, there is a continuum of responses to socialization ranging from rebellion to compliance (Chan, 2003). As Nigel Fielding puts it,

... one must not forget that entry to the police is not automatically entry to the culture, that some police officers will not and never will wish to fit into that culture, that there is more than one police culture, and that individual decisions are always an expression of the individual's perspective at the time as he or she uniquely makes sense of all perceived influences.

(Fielding, 1998: 54)

People do not enter the police organization as cultural blank slates. Rather, they are more or less imbued with values and norms embedded in their own social environments.

The point that Fielding makes is not simply about the process of socialization and its success. More broadly, he and others caution, it is important to bear in mind that police occupational culture 'cannot be reduced to a minimal set of norms, values, or attitudes' (Manning, 2008). The assumption that there is something called 'police culture' is at best naïve, and results in crude generalizations in the quest for common characteristics so as to make the results virtually meaningless. Not only do police agencies differ from one another in terms of their milieu, within individual police agencies, departments and rank groupings also display different cultural responses. The public order specialist, the rural policeman, the traffic cop and the detective all experience police work in different ways. While there will always be a dominant police culture within any particular police organization, subcultures (sometimes even counter-cultures) do exist within police organizations. How subcultures and individualized solutions are received is in large part determined by the extent to which a particular police organization values innovation and difference.

Hobbs correctly points out that individual police institutions 'are not concrete monochrome entities, but merely segmented spheres of activity that occasionally brush each other at information pick-up points and are bonded by a skeleton of concentric hierarchies' (Hobbs, 1991: 606). Familiarizing new recruits with this skeleton and instilling a commitment to its basic logic is at the core of formal police socialization. But the way that individual police officers ultimately think and act and their commitment to the police organization itself is shaped by their varied personal situated realities, their location within the police organization (in terms of rank and function) and even their affiliation to identity-based organizations or representative organizations. Instead of looking for the unifying impact of police socialization across departments, cities, regions and countries, it may be wiser to tease out the variable outcomes of formal and informal socialization processes.

Monique Marks

Associated Concepts: culture, education and training, identity, unions

Key Readings

Chan, J. (with Devery, C. and Doran, S.) (2003) *Fair Cop: Learning the Art of Policing.* Toronto: University of Toronto Press.

Fielding, N. (1998) *Joining Forces: Police Training, Socialization and Occupational Competence.* London: Routledge.

Hobbs, D. (1991) 'A piece of business: the moral economy of detective work in the East-End of London', *The British Journal of Sociology*, 42 (4): 597–608.

Manning, P. (2008) 'A dialectic of organizational and occupational culture', in M. O'Neill, M. Marks and A. Singh (eds) *Police Occupational Culture: New Debates and Directions.* Chicago: Elsevier.

McNamara, J. (1967) 'Uncertainties in police work: the relevance of police recruits' backgrounds and training', in D. Bodua, (ed.) *The Police: Six Sociological Essays.* London: John Wiley and Sons.

Simmel, G. (1908) 'Exkurs über den Fremden', *Sociologie.* Leipzig: Duncker and Humblot.

SURVEILLANCE

See Closed Circuit Television; Criminal Investigation; Cross-Border Policing; High Policing; Intelligence Agency; Technology

TECHNOLOGY

Definition

'Technology', defined by *Webster's Collegiate Dictionary* (9th edn) as 'a particular means for achieving ends', is a denotative definition, but it is hinged on the notion that 'ends' can be unequivocally defined, formalized and assessed. Technology includes what is seen and visible – the material, logical and social facets of technology – as well as the cognitive and imaginative work that is required to understand, fix, maintain and use such technology. As technologies become increasingly computer and information based, the fact that they both produce and process information confounds easy definition of technological means, ends and processes. The term 'police technology' generally refers to those mechanisms that local police employees use virtually every day in the course of their work.

Distinctive Features

Information systems form a major part of the policing infrastructure at local, state, national and international levels, supported by growing inter-agency cooperation. Nations are seeking to develop linkages and exploring mutual data access and exchange, and international communication and intelligence systems, most notably Interpol's I-24/7 system, the European Computer System provided by Europol, and the European Schengen Information System, are providing a platform for such collaboration including access to other countries' national databases.

The UK's national police infrastructure includes the Police National Computer, holding details of persons, vehicles, crimes and property, and with links to other central databases including the National DNA Database and the National Automated Fingerprint Identification System. In the US, parallel databases and surveillance capacities are found in the National Security Agency, which gathers information internationally via many satellite listening and imaging systems including, for example, the ECHELON network of Anglo-Saxon countries; and the Federal Bureau of Investigation (FBI). The FBI maintains the National Crime Information Center (a database storing information on wanted and missing persons, stolen vehicles, firearms and property), the National Instant Criminal Background Check System (for identifying those disqualified from owning firearms), the Automatic Fingerprint Identification System, the Uniform Crime Reporting Program and National Incident Based Reporting System for recording crimes, and a National DNA Index System. Individual states maintain files of criminal records.

Six types of police technology are currently in use by local police. These police technologies are slotted into current strategies and tactics and have had modest, if any, discernible impact on management or administration. Mobility technologies increase rapid and flexible means of response and patrol. The role of material technology providing mobility has changed little since the 1930s except for increases in the speed, number, and types of available vehicles. The vehicle is the core material technology: a mobile office, an insulated compartment, a retreat and a work setting, a place in which patrol officers may spend from eight to twelve hours, a focus of conditions of work and union contracts.

Training technologies are systematic means to modify people, their attitudes and behaviour (of officers themselves as well as the public). They vary, but tend to be brief, and combine in-class lecture learning with field training by field training officers (FTOs). Little is known systematically about the content and learning impact of formal police training. Field training tends to be diverse in content and focus, a function of the skills and interests of the FTO, and to produce highly variable skills in young officers.

Transformative technologies extend human senses and present technical evidence in scientific form. Most of the advances in this domain are processes for refining, enhancing and reviewing criminal evidence. Forensic scientists, once restricted to fingerprint evidence and blood typing, are now able to identify individuals by their DNA, or place them at the scenes of crimes using a variety of trace evidence (e.g., hair, fibre). The FBI and some states are also creating a DNA bank of known felons convicted of certain crimes, and the FBI is sponsoring the use of computerized fingerprint files for online checks of criminal records. Some police cars are equipped with video cameras, giving them the capacity to monitor in video and audio their interactions with citizens.

Analytic technologies are designed to aggregate, model, and simulate police data to facilitate crime analysis, crime mapping, and crime prevention. Police are better able, given large mainframes and servers, to acquire, store, and aggregate raw data. In the US, Department of Justice figures show that most municipal police forces staffed by 100 or more officers now use mobile computers or terminals in the field. The access to such data in the field has been shown in a few select studies to increase productivity, but these are studies of the speed of records retrieval.

Communicative technologies are used to diffuse information to the public. The external network of communications centred at the police department has been radically expanded and made more sensitive in the form of the Internet, the World Wide Web, and changes in the screening and allocation of calls to the police using 311 and 911 calls. Technological advances have allowed, if not for greater direct contact with the public, greater sharing of information and feedback to citizens. E-mails are not favoured within police departments because of concerns for secrecy and the uncertainty of insuring that the directive has been received, understood, and acted upon. The FBI is ambivalent about computer based communications inside and outside the office because of concerns for security and data theft or the compromise of data.

A full range of weapons – fatal and non-fatal, the final sort of technology, are now used in all police departments. The larger the department, the more varied and powerful their weapons up to and including automatic weapons, armoured vehicles, helicopters, and heavily armed dynamic entry or paramilitary units. Some data indicate that their use is increasingly widespread and that they are subject to 'mission creep,' an ever widening use for more diverse incidents (Kraska and Kappeler, 1997). It should be noted that the incidence of violence is very low in American departments, estimated at less than 5 per cent of incidents. While the range of non-fatal tools is astounding, few other than everyday tools are used: pepper spray, cars, fists, feet, flashlights and nightsticks.

Evaluation

Police technologies are inward-looking in many respects. The information gathered is screened, coded and decoded in terms of police categories and classification systems which crudely reflect legal categories of offences or disorder. Classification systems are relatively impervious to recent changes in law, social conventions, or local knowledge. In spite of the growth in surveillance technologies such as closed circuit television, cell phone/cameras, fixed cameras to record car plates on turnpikes and toll roadways, facial image databases and satellite systems that can be used with global position systems to locate calls and callers' movements, traditional state policing typically remains reactive and crime focused. Local police departments are little capable of focusing on surveillance and preventive actions, for example, anti-terrorism and homeland security, because they have no training or experience in such policing. With growth in reflexive communication and surveillance by citizens of police (use of mobile phones/cameras to record police violence, crimes in progress, or suspicious activities, and lightweight cameras used by media connected worldwide via satellite feeds), police activities are more transparent. As a result of the use of computers and other devices linked to the Internet that in turn leave traces and data-trails that can be tracked, policing will soon be forced to reckon with the sources and kinds of data it should gather and that which is linked directly to its historical, common-law responsive mandate. At present they are overwhelmed with facts, images, and data without a capacity to convert these facts into information, which makes a difference in making future resource allocation decisions.

It is fair to say that at present no police department has refined a systematically integrated collection of technologies to facilitate problem-solving, crime prevention, policy analysis, or community interfaces. The police have focused publicly in their rhetoric, their crime-based capacities, their online network of databases and immediate short-term applications rather than developing their capacities:

(1) analytical: the ability to integrate, reflect upon, change and refine databases;
(2) interoperability capacity; the ability to talk to, merge, and integrate analytically databases and software;
(3) 'housekeeping': the ability to clean and eliminate faulty or misleading data rather than simply gathering more;
(4) data sharing: with other agencies, integrating and distributing it, and mutually defining data uses, protection, security and other constraints on use;

(5) developing records management systems: the ability to integrate past and present records.

While the police have argued that they are a scientifically based profession for over ninety years, the fundamental fact is that their core technology is verbal, and their other technologies are acquired casually. This accretion strategy produces an ill-fitting *ad hoc* clustering, a technological midden heap. Police are increasingly an 'information-dependent' organization. This grows from their increasingly myopic focus, visible since the professionalization movement, on 'crime' defined as that which they can eradicate by scientific means. This focus has increased their technological dependency, distanced them from their publics, and had dubious impact on crime. Ironically, this distance is a result of their becoming far more competent and sophisticated in gathering, recording, and storing data bearing on human failings. While police technologies have become more diverse, complex and sensitive to nuance in the last twenty years, their impact on practices is still being explored. The impact is clearly related to what is seen as useful amongst patrol officers; as they discover its value, it comes to be utilized.

Peter K. Manning

Associated Concepts: cross-border policing, calls for service, closed circuit television, Compstat, criminal investigation, firearms, homeland security, Europol, intelligence agency, Interpol, professionalization, terrorism, transnational policing

Key Readings

Chan, J., Brereton, D., Legosz, M. and Doran, S. (2001) *e-Policing: The Impact of Information on Police Practices*. Brisbane: Criminal Justice Commission.
Chan, J. (2003) 'Police and new technologies', in T. Newburn (ed.) *The Handbook of Policing*. Cullompton, Devon: Willan Publishing.

Dunworth, T. (2000) 'Criminal justice and the information technology revolution', in J. Horney (ed.) *Criminal Justice,* Vol. 3. Washington', D.C.: NIJ/Office of Justice Programs.

Kraska P.B. and Kappeler V.E. (1997) 'Militarizing American police: The rise and normalization of paramilitary units', *Social Problems,* 44 (1): 1–18.

Manning, P.K. (1992) 'The police and information technology', in N. Morris and M. Tonry (eds) *Crime and Justice.* Chicago, IL: University of Chicago Press.

Manning, P.K. (2008) *The Technology of Policing: Crime Mapping, Information Technology, and the Rationality of Crime Control.* New York: New York University Press.

TERRORISM

Definition

The policing of terrorism, sometimes called anti- or counter-terrorism, refers to a complex of multi-agency activities by mainly public bodies, such as the police, directed at those who support, threaten or use violence in pursuit of a political agenda. That is to say it relates to the policing of criminal activities for political purposes as opposed to crimes committed for economic or personal gain. Depending on the criminal justice system, the use of violence by extremists, such as animal rights groups, who seek only very limited policy changes can also come within the scope of the policing of terrorism. It is not a function that is exclusive to police forces as, depending on the resources available to the police in particular states, the services of security and intelligence agencies and the military are often required. It encompasses actions to prevent, pre-empt and manage terrorist activities with an increasing emphasis on the prevention and pre-emption aspects as modern societies become more risk averse. An initial appreciation of its scope and content in a particular state may often be found by reference to the details of specific legislation, for example, the UK's Terrorism Acts and the US Patriot Act, by reference to national counter-terrorism policies such as the UK's 'Contest' strategy and the French 'Vigipirate' plan, or to organizational structures like the US Department of Homeland Security (DHS).

Distinctive Features

The discharge of this function is a highly location and problem specific activity. Its parameters will vary according to whether the terrorism is largely internal to a particular state, as with ETA in Spain, or is more international in character as with some forms of Islamist terrorism. The specifics of a terrorist threat and the political perception of the threat can determine whether the problem is treated as just an aspect of law enforcement, as in the UK and the Netherlands currently, or as a 'war on terror' matter, involving more of a military response as is evident in the current US response and as has characterized Russia's response to the situation in Chechnya. In this latter case and in others, such as the Malayan Emergency (1948–1960) and Northern Ireland (1968–1998), the terrorist activities were on the scale of an insurgency which is normally tackled under emergency legislation with suspensions of civil liberties and high profile roles for both ordinary and special military forces (SAS, Delta Force, etc.).

The multi-agency nature of the policing of terrorism is partly historical, reflecting different national organizational structures and, more contemporarily, it reflects responses to what has been termed, post September, 11, 'new terrorism' under which mass-destruction or mass-effect may be sought by terrorists without any clearly articulated political goal linkage and where the response clearly requires international cooperation between police and other agencies. Thus, in respect of primacy in the domestic gathering of intelligence on terrorists, in the US it is the task of a federal law enforcement agency, the FBI and in France that of the Direction de la Surveillance du

Territoire which is part of the *Police Nationale*. By contrast, in the UK the task is assigned to a non-police agency, the Security Service (MI5) as is also the case in the Netherlands where it is the task of the General Intelligence and Security Service (AIVD). Border control forms an important aspect of the prevention of terrorism and this may involve police (a UK example is the Special Branch Ports Units), customs and immigration services. In the US the largest category of personnel numbers in the DHS, 96,266 as of 2004, were to be found in its Transportation Security Administration.

Even if intelligence gathering on terrorists is primarily the responsibility of a non-police body, all aspects of the policing of terrorism for police forces are still likely to be seen as requiring a number of distinct specializations within police work. For example, police intelligence liaison with a civilian intelligence agency may be assigned to a specialist police intelligence body, for example, the Special Branches in UK police forces and, clearly, tackling explosive devices with or without a CBRN (i.e., Chemical, Biological, Radiological, Nuclear) element will require specialist skills. In the UK, in 2006 the police had 7,000 CBRN response trained and equipped police officers representing about 5 per cent of the total police operational strength. Another common specialization relates to that branch of policing terrorism which focuses on the financing of terrorism. The example of this specialization also serves to draw attention to the fact that key aspects of the policing of terrorism necessitate the involvement of the private sector, in this case those private bodies, like banks, which may have a statutory duty to report suspicious financial transactions. However, it must be noted that while terrorist acts may not require large amounts of money (the 2004 Madrid bombings were estimated to have cost around £5,000), the financial trails can be important investigative tools.

A particularly distinctive feature of the policing of terrorism, in democracies, is the degree to which its legislative framework may contain special provisions that amend or suspend normal civil liberties. These provisions may include extensive surveillance powers and detention without trial, which was known as internment in Northern Ireland or even, as the US has done via extraordinary rendition and Guantanamo detention, taking powers to completely remove some terrorist suspects from the normal due processes of law. Signatory states to the European Convention on Human Rights need to derogate, in part, from that Convention in order to legislate for various forms of detention without trial which is a controversial action, as the UK government has found in respect of the Anti-Terrorism, Crime and Security Act 2001 and the Terrorism Acts 2005 and 2006.

Evaluation

A number of common issues arise irrespective of whether the policing of terrorism is carried out under a 'law enforcement' (police primacy) or a 'war on terror' mixed military/police mode. First, the policing of terrorism must always encompass some form of political attention to causal factors. Second, terrorist investigations, whether for the purposes of disruption or apprehension of suspects are likely to be long-lasting and resource intensive and raise considerations of opportunity costs in terms of the potential for diverting scarce police resources from more commonly encountered crime problems. Third, performance indicators are more problematic in this area of policing because the overriding objective is early disruption and therefore traditional performance measures, such as arrest statistics and conviction rates, are of less significance than low rates of terrorist incidents.

The following recent UK examples of the policing of terrorism illustrate some of the general points raised above. The post 9/11 demands on the Metropolitan Police anti-terrorist specialists were described by former Commissioner, Sir John Stevens, as involving a workload which was two to three times that required for the IRA bombing campaigns of the 1970s to 1990s and which necessitated a three-fold expansion of the Anti-Terrorist Branch. Following the 2005 London bombings, Assistant Commissioner Hayman provided details of the scale of those police operations and referred to the storing of 38,000 exhibits, 1,400 fingerprints, over 160 crime scenes and the investigation of 54 murders and other crimes. The 2006 UK operation in connection with suspected plots to bomb transatlantic passenger aircraft has already shown similarities of scale to the response to the July 2005 London bombings. The police anti-terrorist operation has involved 69 site specific searches, including houses, the seizure of 400 computers, the examination of 200 mobile phones and the seizure of 8,000 removable storage devices such as memory sticks for further examination. In total, 6,000 gigabytes of data have had to be accessed and assessed for evidential value.

It is important that the understandable response to 9/11, within police work, should be balanced by due recognition of the continuance of other more familiar forms of terrorism. The European Union's 2007 report on terrorism in the EU area (TE-SAT, 2007) identifies terrorist threats as arising from Islamist terrorism, ethno-nationalist terrorism (in the Basque region of Spain and Corsica in particular), left-wing and anarchist terrorism and right-wing terrorism. Of 498 incidents related to terrorism recorded in the EU in 2006, 424 were linked to ethno-nationalist groups and only three to Islamist groups. Nonetheless, the clear political emphasis being given to the importance of the police countering what is seen as the relatively greater threat from Islamist terrorism is shown by the 2006 terrorism related arrest statistics in the EU, which record that 70 per cent of the reported arrests were of those suspected of involvement in Islamist terrorism.

Frank Gregory

Associated Concepts: criminal investigation, cross-border policing, high policing, homeland security, intelligence agency, security networks, transnational policing

Key Readings

Akerboom, E.S.M. (2007) *Counter-terrorism in the Netherlands*. The Hague. AIVD, http//:www.english.nctb.nl/publications/reports/avid/.

Clutterbuck, L. (2004) 'Law enforcement', in A.K. Cronin, and J.M. Ludes, (eds) *Attacking Terrorism – Elements of a Grand Strategy*. Washington DC: Georgetown University Press.

Europol (2007) *EU Terrorism Situation and Trends Report 2007*. The Hague: Europol, http://www.europol.europa.eu/publications/TESAT/TESAT2007.pdf.

Friedrichs, J. (2007) *Fighting Terrorism and Drugs, Europe and International Police Cooperation*. London: Taylor and Francis.

Gregory, F. (2007) 'Police and counter-terrorism in the UK', in P. Wilkinson, (ed) *Homeland Security in the UK*. London: Routledge.

THIRD PARTY POLICING

Definition

Until recently, public police dominated the delivery of modern crime control. But trends in governance and the regulation of society have led to the pluralization and privatization of policing efforts, and the growth in administrative and regulatory agencies with crime control and prevention functions (Ericson, 2007). Additionally, a trend to responsibilization has meant that communities and individuals are expected to contribute to their own regulation, security and safety (Crawford, 2006). Contemporary policing services are increasingly provided by networks of public, private and welfare organizations, with public police as one node of the network.

Against this background, third party policing (TPP) has emerged as a way in which public police can steer crime control networks, by mobilizing other parties and making use of their resources. TPP occurs when police engage with other organizations or individuals and use a range of civil, regulatory and administrative laws to create or enhance crime control and prevention networks. In TPP, the focus shifts from sole police responsibility for preventing and responding to criminal and anti-social behaviour to networks, using a wide range of legal options. Public police form one node of these networks, with private police or security firms, other government and regulatory agencies, communities, business owners, schools and parents as other nodes. TPP networks focus on risk identification, surveillance and prevention, rather than on traditional, reactive police strategies. Networks may be developed by the police or by third parties, or they may be mandated by governments to deal with entrenched problems where traditional policing practice is seen as having failed. Some of the legal measures used in TPP include property forfeiture, licence restrictions, evictions and injunctions.

Distinctive Features

The key distinctive feature of TPP is that police use it to harness networks and partners and with them a broad range of legal measures to enhance crime control or prevention efforts. Common legal measures used include local, state and federal statutes, ordinances and by-laws, health and safety codes, building standards, child welfare and drug nuisance abatement laws, and liquor licensing. The legal basis does not necessarily need to be directly related to crime prevention or crime control. Indeed, most TPP practices use laws that were not designed with crime control or prevention in mind. Civil sanctions and remedies available under TPP schemes vary greatly, but include court-ordered repairs of properties, fines, forfeiture of property or forced sales to meet fines and penalties, eviction, padlocking or temporary closure of a rented residential or commercial property, licence restrictions and/or suspensions, movement restrictions, lost income from restricted hours and ultimately arrest and incarceration. Often, several civil remedies and sanctions may be initiated simultaneously to solve one problem.

For example, shop owners may be encouraged by police to install better lighting or employ private security patrols to deter people loitering outside the premises selling drugs, and local schools may be encouraged to boost anti-truancy efforts. Police might join with liquor licensing authorities to encourage bar and nightclub operators to adopt better policies on serving alcohol to intoxicated and underage patrons to deal with a night-time disorder problem in nearby streets. Frequent calls for service from a particular property could prompt police to cooperate with building inspectors or rental agents to target the source of the problem. By forcing a physical upgrading of the property, or the eviction of problem tenants, a source of neighbourhood crime may be diminished. Police may encourage local governments to pursue civil injunctions to disrupt gang membership, and child welfare agencies may be involved to help close clandestine drug laboratories.

Each of these examples is a form of TPP, with common features being that police form networks with third parties to take advantage of legal powers and levers not otherwise available to them (such as engaging private security, licensing laws, building codes, tenancy agreements, civil injunctions or child protection laws). Someone with power to act on the crime problem is given an incentive to do so, either voluntarily (for example, to improve shop custom) or with the expressed or implied threat of coercion (for example, licensing or building penalties, contract termination or removal of children). For police, their tools and strategies are extended beyond the usual criminal justice responses (criminal prosecutions, cautions, etc.) to include a range of civil penalties and pressures that do not attract the protections afforded to criminal justice actions, such as the need to identify particular offenders, or to amass sufficient evidence to satisfy a criminal standard of proof.

Recent transformations in governance and regulation have created these new crime control opportunities; in the past, many regulator and local government powers were weak or underused and there was little incentive for police to partner with them to reduce crime. Now, as the scope of civil regulation has increased, it is convenient and mutually beneficial for both parties to come together to solve a problem.

Police provide around the clock service, and have powers of arrest not usually available to non-police agents. Non-police third parties have powers available to them (such as confiscation, licence revocation or closure of premises) that are more easily enforced, with lower burdens of proof than required under criminal law.

There are many different ways that police implement TPP practices including when partnerships are mandated by law (for example the UK's Crime and Disorder Act 1998) or in response to an external inquiry or task force (such as on child safety). It may arise within the context of problem-oriented policing or situational crime prevention programmes, or through the *ad hoc* utilization of third party principles initiated in an unconscious manner by patrol officers who are simply trying to find a way to solve a problem. For these police there is no script to follow, no policy that they are working within, and generally very little accountability for their actions. Because of the different ways that it arises, and because much of it occurs through informal practice rather than public strategy, it is difficult to say precisely how much TPP occurs. While there is much consensus that pluralized policing and contract-based governance is now prevalent in crime control in North America, the UK and Australia (see Ericson, 2007; Crawford, 2006; Mazerolle and Ransley, 2005), as discussed below further research is needed about the role and extent of TPP in this environment.

Evaluation

Because TPP has arisen in a largely episodic and unplanned way, its implementation and management are under-researched and evaluated. Mazerolle and Ransley (2006) conducted a search of the international literature to uncover evaluations of police tactics involving TPP. They identified 77 studies that included an evaluation component and also involved a TPP tactic. The review of these studies suggested that using third parties and legal levers (many of which were not intended for crime control purposes) seems to be an effective tactic to expand the responsibility for crime control, sometimes even among unwilling third parties. The evidence surrounding the use of third parties for violence and drug control was the most reliable. However, evaluation evidence is limited and of variable quality, and very little systematic effort (until recently) has been expended to document, collate and consolidate it.

Other issues requiring further study are the potential side effects of TPP, and how accountability for its outcomes can be ensured. Possible negative side effects fall into three main groups: adverse social consequences arising from police co-opting other organizations and individuals to deal with crime, the possibility that TPP displaces crime into other areas or times, and the impact on legal rights, civil liberties and laws. Many traditional assumptions about the role and nature of police accountability are threatened or weakened by developments such as TPP. The monopoly on police use of force is being broken, as coercive powers are extended to other agencies and officials. Legal and institutional mechanisms directed at controlling and making accountable police uses of power do not necessarily affect other providers of policing functions, particularly those that are not state agencies. Similarly, while TPP holds promise of improved efficiency and effectiveness, how are managers to be held accountable for individual projects and their expenditure and outcomes, particularly when some of the resources are actually co-opted from other agencies and individuals? Where agencies are mandated, or choose, to work together towards crime prevention and control, who bears ultimate responsibility for the success or failure of their decisions? More research and evaluation is needed to answer these questions.

Janet Ransley and Lorraine Mazerolle

Associated Concepts: auxiliary policing, citizen's arrest, contractualism, multi-agency policing, pluralization, private security, privatization, responsibilization, security networks

Key Readings

Crawford, A. (2006) 'Networked governance and the post-regulatory state? Steering, rowing and anchoring the provision of policing and security', *Theoretical Criminology*, 10 (4): 449–79.

Ericson, R.V. (2007) 'Rules in policing: five perspectives', *Theoretical Criminology*, 11 (3): 367–401.

Maguire, E.R. and King, W.R. (2004) 'Trends in the policing industry', *Annals of the American Academy of Political and Social Science*, 593 (1): 15–41.

Mazerolle, L. and Ransley, J. (2005) *Third Party Policing*. Cambridge: Cambridge University Press.

Mazerolle, L., Roehl, J. and Kadleck, C. (1998) 'Controlling social disorder using civil remedies: results from a randomized field experiment in Oakland', in L. Mazerolle and J. Roehl (eds) *Civil Remedies and Crime Prevention, Crime Prevention Studies Vol. 9*. Monsey, N.Y.: Criminal Justice Press.

TRAINING

See Education and Training; Professionalization; Socialization

---

TRANSITIONAL POLICING

Definition

The term refers to those forms of policing that occur in conjunction with political transitions. The concept of transition indicates a distinct break between two successive sets of political arrangements, rather than a gradual evolution within what can be viewed as an essentially seamless and peaceful set of circumstances. The term is distinguishable from *post-conflict policing*, another term sometimes encountered, as some transitions do not emerge from violent conflict (e.g., Hungary, Czechoslovakia, former East Germany). The objective of transitional policing is, on an interim basis, to stabilize matters sufficiently within societies undergoing transition, so as to permit other processes of governance reform and economic development to take place. As its name suggests, transitional policing is not intended to last indefinitely. It is policing that occurs after regime change or state failure pending the establishment of more permanent policing under new political arrangements. Most commonly, the policing in question is state policing, rather than private or community-controlled policing.

Another term of related interest is *transitional justice*. This phrase has a broader connotation, referring not just to the activities of policing agencies in transitional settings, but also to such matters as truth and reconciliation commissions, dealing with past crimes (tackling impunity), and the broader range of justice needs of societies emerging from profound political and social upheaval (courts, prosecutions, prisons, etc.).

Distinctive Features

Policing associated with or following political transitions can take a range of forms, and can occur for different reasons. While many transitions follow protracted periods of internal conflict (for example, Northern Ireland) or external intervention (such as Iraq), others may occur less dramatically (for example, South Africa). Political transitions involve a regime change or some other kind of profound political rupture that signifies the end of a previous set of political arrangements and the beginning of another. Most political transitions are anything but smooth, and are often accompanied by high levels of violence, property crime and other forms of disorder. Political transitions leading to changed policing arrangements can result from internal and external pressures for change. Internal pressures for change may arise from a desire among the elite for change, from political compromise between different political groups, or from the overthrow or defeat of the ruling elite by opposition groups. External pressures for change often emerge from powerful nation states with strategic interests in the country in question, or from multilateral organizations such as the United Nations (UN) on humanitarian, security, or other grounds. Often transitional policing will emerge from a combination of the two. In the case of the Solomon Islands in 2003, the largely paralyzed government of that country invited Australia and other Pacific neighbours to intervene in the country's political and social crisis by sending police and military personnel to restore order.

In many transitions, police reform is a fundamental requirement of the broader transition process. Police have previously been a source of insecurity, rather than security, for ordinary people. The police have protected the specific interests of the political elites, rather than the general safety of the population at large. Often this has meant that police have acted repressively and even brutally, resorting to extra-judicial punishments including murder, rape, torture, and 'disappearances'. For many people in these countries, the police have historically been distrusted, even feared. Policing reform, in these circumstances, becomes a kind of litmus test for wider political change. If police carry on under the new arrangements in similar ways to the old police, then many will be inclined to judge the wider political transition process a failure. In order to render the new police more accountable and responsive to the community at large, there has often been a strong demand for democratic policing as part of a wider process of democratization, and for the police to be subject to the rule of law.

Transitional policing arrangements are often put in place by outside interveners (e.g., the UN) immediately following a political transition in order to contain disorder, provide basic public safety services, and deal with those committing criminal offences. A primary form of transitional policing is police *peacekeeping*. Police peacekeepers have typically helped to monitor ceasefires ending internal conflicts and provided basic law and order services while other transitional processes can occur. This form of transitional policing has become much more common

since the late 1990s, especially under the UN flag. The UN Department of Peacekeeping Operations (DPKO) has played a major role in the last decade in organizing and directing police peacekeeping missions in places such as Haiti, Timor-Leste, Congo, Kosovo, Burundi, and Sudan. These peacekeeping missions have typically been composed of policing personnel from a large number of nations who have been authorized under a UN Security Council resolution to provide policing services for a fixed period in a particular country. Current indications suggest that the need for more police peacekeeping will grow rather than diminish in the coming years.

A second form of transitional policing has emerged out of the peacekeeping role. In recognition of the need to reestablish effective institutions as well as maintain the peace in many violence-stricken countries, the mandates of recent UN police peacekeeping missions has been expanded in several instances (e.g., Timor-Leste) to include *capacity building*. Capacity building by police forms part of broader state-building and nation-building exercises in countries such as Iraq and Timor-Leste. It can take a variety of forms, but it is broadly focused upon constructing or reconstructing local police forces in these countries that will be capable of operating effectively as police once the formal transition process has ended. Thus, for example, police capacity building will often focus upon strategic planning and resource management, the establishment of police training academies, implementation of community policing programmes, and the strengthening of criminal investigation skills. An important part of police capacity building is mentoring local police personnel as they learn new skills and develop their abilities as police in order to take over from the international police at some point.

Evaluation

As political transitions vary in nature, so does transitional policing. The transitions evident in the South African case were arguably less extreme, for example, than what has occurred in the case of Timor-Leste. In the latter case, there had been no indigenous police force prior to the UN intervention in 1999 as the country had been policed by the Indonesian police for the previous 24 years. As a result, the UN needed to build a police force from scratch, while undertaking executive policing during the transitional phase. In South Africa, by contrast, there was considerable continuity between the apartheid-era police force, and the recast South African Police Service in the post-apartheid phase, even though the political transition was propelling a significant reform process within the police. In short, it is difficult to generalize about transitional policing, as the political settings in which it occurs will influence what occurs.

Transitional policing, especially of the externally driven kind, in keeping with other state-building exercises, too often ignores the characteristics of the local settings in which it operates. A lack of familiarity with the local environment is often compounded by a preoccupation with a foreign-imposed policing agenda. The result is often to alienate local people, and to engender often stiff resistance from those threatened by the proposed changes to policing. It is a mistake to think that transitional policing will necessarily be widely accepted or supported. Inevitably policing is political in terms of how it is perceived and its material consequences because it impacts upon established interests and individual life chances in ways that seem to, or actually, create 'winners' and 'losers'. In countries emerging from political conflict, with past histories of abusive or negligent policing, the perceived lack of impartiality of police is widely and deeply held. This has been true in Northern Ireland in respect of attempts to reform the Royal Ulster Constabulary, as it has been true in many other instances of transitional policing. Moreover, the kinds of reforms promoted by transitional policing will sometimes be viewed as Western-centric and not appropriate to local circumstances.

A range of practical issues also make transitional policing difficult. The entrenched nature of the political conflicts that has led to the transitional phase is often such that a sustained period of reform is required. This means that the transitional policing arrangements may be required in some form for five years, ten years or even longer. Finding parties willing to support policing transitions over this time can be difficult given the associated costs and often fickle support for such ventures among voters in the donor countries. Another practical difficulty concerns the multilateral nature of many transitional policing arrangements. Relying upon policing personnel from a large number of countries, as the UN tends to do, creates a variety of logistical, planning and service delivery issues. In particular, foreign police will often vary in terms of their philosophies, levels of training, levels of equipment and willingness to work cooperatively with police from other countries. These differences can create problems of consistency and appropriate standards that affect both peacekeeping and capacity building.

Lastly, transitional policing can sometimes take place, or look as if it is taking place, separately from other governance and development agendas. While getting effective policing arrangements into place is essential to encouraging people to start resuming normal lives after periods of conflict and major transition, there are other important human security needs (e.g., education, shelter, food) that must also be addressed simultaneously within political transitions if overall security and well-being is to be improved.

Andrew Goldsmith

Associated Concepts: human security, Pacific policing, peacekeeping, security, transnational policing

Key Readings

Bayley, D. (2006) *Changing the Guard: Developing Democratic Police Abroad.* New York: Oxford University Press.

Chesterman, S. (2004) *'You, the People': The United Nations, Transitional Administration and State-building.* New York: Oxford UP.

Goldsmith, A.J. and Sheptycki, J.W.M. (2007) *Crafting Transnational Policing: Police Capacity-building and Global Policing Reform*. Oxford: Hart Publishing.

Marks, M. (2005) *Transforming the Robocops: Changing Police in South Africa*. Durban: University of KwaZulu-Natal.

Oakley, R. Goldberg, E.M. and Dziedzic, M.J. (2002) *Policing the New World Disorder: Peace Operations and Public Security*. Honolulu: University Press of the Pacific.

O'Rawe, M. (2002–2003) 'Transitional policing arrangements in Northern Ireland: the can't and the won't of the change dialectic', *Fordham International Law Journal*, 26 (4): 1015–73.

TRANSNATIONAL POLICING

Definition

The benefits of globalization, associated with open trade and the free flow of goods, services, capital and people around the world, allied with new communication technologies, bring with them costs that extend beyond national borders in their impact and in terms of their control. Such costs include the globalization of crime threats, such as the 'new terrorism', and the international expansion and development of illicit market opportunities in goods, people and services. National policing agencies are adapting their practices, broadening their expertise and establishing partnerships in order to move beyond their countries' borders to address these 'global village' challenges.

Transnational policing is premised on the international cooperation that allows national policing agencies to operate beyond their own jurisdictions and work with those of other nations. Given the sovereignty of nation states, the authority of international law is contingent on states' voluntary observance and enforcement of its conventions, treaties and standards. The term 'transnational' therefore more suitably describes the bulk of conventional cross-border policing activities

taking place than others that might imply a more collaborative mission or operational intervention, such as 'international', 'global', 'multi-national' or 'supranational'. This is the case despite the increasingly vital role of international policing organizations in transnational policing (most notably Interpol and Europol) and the United Nation's multi-national peacekeeping missions.

Distinctive Features

An important, if under acknowledged, aspect of early transnational policing was the transport of policing models across the world, through the British and French empires. France's centralized policing structure was transported to other continental European countries as well as its imperial outposts. The 'New Police' model established by Sir Robert Peel in London in 1829 was transferred to American cities. Mawby (1999) suggests the British government may have deliberately created a distinctive, militaristic type of policing for its empire – one that was seen to be better suited to controlling colonial populations – first employed in Ireland, in the form of the Royal Irish Constabulary, where the police could not rely on public consent. These historic policing models, and others that have evolved internationally, give a sense of the different policing cultures and organizations that come together in the intergovernmental structures of transnational policing, helping us understand structural similarities between national police forces, the respective challenges they face, and the tensions in collaborative relationships.

International cooperation against crime is not a new phenomenon. It was at an International Police Congress held in Monaco in 1914 that the idea of establishing an international support agency to help combat crime across the globe first came about – an idea that was to lead to the establishment of Interpol. The concerns of that meeting, Higdon informs us, were 'to discuss possibilities for simplifying and accelerating the international search for wanted suspects, improving methods of identification, harmonizing extradition procedures and centralizing information concerning international criminals' (Higdon, 2001: 29). He observes that these imperatives remain valid and continue to underpin the role of Interpol, the international non-governmental police organization, which now has 186 member countries.

International organizations such as Interpol, Europol and the United Nations Office on Drugs and Crime operate to support states' responses to the globalization of crime. As well as providing operational assistance, they contribute to a vast transnational information technology infrastructure which allows data sharing between states' police, security and intelligence agencies, other governmental institutions such as customs and immigration departments, and private interests. The development of such technologies is one illustration of the way in which policing is becoming more intelligence-led, emphasizing information gathering and analysis, although such an approach has always been an inherent characteristic of the 'high policing' of intelligence agencies and their established transnational networks, including the signals intelligence network established in 1947 between the UK, US, Canada, Australia and New Zealand. Signals intelligence, such as the ECHELON system operated by this Anglo-Saxon alliance, includes the routine mass screening of telephone and Internet traffic in the interests of national security, and is a disquietening and secretive element of transnational policing.

Another significant but under researched aspect of transnational policing is the emergence of an elite group of officers who are managing cross border police work. The intriguing question is the role they are playing in various projects to standardize technical and operational procedures and practices. Their role is, for example, likely to be critical in the next stages of attempts to harmonize policing discourses and mentalities and operational methodologies across the expanding Eurostate. The task for the next generation of 'Eurocops' remains the overcoming of:

- Inadequate national conceptualization of transnational policing activities;

- Insufficient cooperation amongst member states; and
- An under-developed European Union legal framework.

At the same time, we need to be attentive to the attempts by the US to 'Americanize' those Latin American police forces that fall within its sphere of influence. In its most benign incarnation, this is being realized through the policy transfer of the community-oriented, intelligence-led and democratic policing paradigms. However, this 'state capacity building' is co-joined with the transmission of paramilitary policing and counter insurgency expertise and paraphernalia (Andreas and Nadelman, 2006).

The most distinctive feature of transnational policing is the absence of any defining organizational structure and, as Loader argues, what we see is in fact 'a field composed of dispersed, though overlapping sites of power and authority' (2002: 297), while Walker describes 'a complex matrix of competition and cooperation' (2003: 131). The nodes of the matrix are the infinite diversity of public, commercial and voluntary bodies operating at international, regional, national and local levels. These bodies undertake policing tasks that require them to operate across borders, whether as a matter of course or on an occasional basis. Such policing practices are inevitably routinized within a global society of strategic nodes.

Evaluation

The costs and limitations of transnational policing include the accountability issues it raises, and the imbalances in its attentions. The insecurities generated by the 9/11 and subsequent terrorist attacks, and the geographical reach of the 'war on terror', have challenged established ideas as to where an acceptable balance is to be found between human rights and security. The military action and policing and national security practices of the US, the UK and their allies have also reemphasized the limits of the value and authority of international law. The 'extraordinary rendition' programme operated by the

US's Criminal Intelligence Agency (CIA) is an extreme example from the suite of extra-legal practices routinely adopted by intelligence agencies and involving serious infringements of human rights, reigniting such debates as whether torture can ever be justified.

Other aspects of transnational policing practice that raise accountability questions relate to the fact that it is of low public visibility: much of it is about information sharing; it is typically distant from the immediate concerns of most citizens, whether in terms of geographic disassociation or complexity (e.g., financial or cyber crime); and public knowledge is steered by the 'global crime panics' of news media reporting (see Loader, 2002). This limits political pressures to extend the limited and piecemeal structures of oversight that govern the cross-border activities of police agencies, and address the still greater accountability gaps where the activities of national security and intelligence and commercial organizations are concerned.

The shape of transnational policing is determined as much by the gaps in its attentions as its core activities, and also by the effective 'division of labour'. Crimes on the margins of international or national criminal law, such as corporate environmental crime, or those committed by states themselves, often challenge the structure and scope of transnational policing, although Interpol pronounces an active commitment to the policing of corruption as one of its six primary areas of intervention. This links to points made by Loader in relation to European policing: that there is present 'a deep *asymmetry* in the social distribution of its benefits and burdens'. Reminding us that policing burdens in general fall overwhelmingly on the most disadvantaged groups and individuals, Loader observes that 'the policing of transnational crime is an activity directed largely at *Others* (migrants, organized criminals, drugs-traffickers etc.) on behalf of *us* – Europe's citizens' (2002: 298).

Further imbalances are evidenced in the areas of transnational policing activity that have been subject to *de facto* privatization, as global corporate interests resort to self-policing where states' policing cannot meet their security needs. Emerging crime threats for global corporations represent new opportunities for the commercial security sector, quick to offer specialist services where security gaps exist, and often better placed than state policing agencies to develop the necessary skills and resources. All kinds of specialist commercial security services are now tailored to corporate and governmental customers. These services address specific threats as varied and challenging as maritime piracy, pharmaceuticals fraud and the plundering of antiquities, as well as general security needs through threat assessment and protection of people, premises, commodities and information.

Alison Wakefield and Eugene McLaughlin

Associated Concepts: cross-border policing, Europol, high policing, Interpol, intelligence agency, peacekeeping, pluralization, postmodern policing, transitional policing

Key Readings

Andreas, P. and Nadelman, E. (2006) *Policing the Globe: Criminalization and Crime Control in International Relations*. New York: Oxford University Press.

Hall, B. and Bierstaker, T.J. (eds) (2002) *The Emergence of Private Authority in Global Governance*. Cambridge: Cambridge University Press.

Goldsmith, A. and Sheptycki, J. (2007) *Crafting Transnational Policing: Police Capacity-Building and Global Policing Reform*. Oxford: Hart Publishing.

Higdon, P. (2001) 'Interpol's role in international police co-operation', in D.K. Das and D. Koenig (eds) *International Police Co-operation: A World Perspective*. Lanham, MD: Lexington Books.

Loader, I. (2002) 'Governing European policing: some problems and prospects', in *Policing and Society*, 12 (4): 291–305.

Mawby, R.I. (1999) *Policing Across the World: Issues for the Twenty-First Century*. London: Routledge.

Walker, N. (2003) 'The pattern of transnational policing', in T. Newburn (ed.) *The Handbook of Policing*. Cullompton, Devon: Willan Publishing.

U

UNIONS

Definition

Police employee organizations, also referred to as associations or federations or lodges. Organizations that seek to protect the rights, interests and welfare of their members.

Distinctive Features

Police unions have become an increasingly prominent feature of the modern police organization although most were formed in the early twentieth century. Despite initial resistance to the unionization of police, even in Western liberal democracies, police unions have been remarkably successful in achieving benefits for their members. Although the aims of police unions are largely stated as improving the wages and working conditions of their members, the legal service many of them provide to members accused of misconduct or other infringements is an important aspect of membership. Some research suggests that this service alone ensures almost 100 per cent membership in many police unions.

The police union acts as the body representing police employees. Most police unions only represent sworn police officers, sometimes organized around the various ranks (as in the UK and some parts of Australia and the US) or otherwise including all members from recruits to the Chief Police Officer. In the UK the Police Federation of England and Wales (PFEW) represents all ranks to Chief Inspector. Superintendents have their own Association. Chief Police Officers belong to the increasingly powerful Association of Chief Police Officers. In the US and Canada police chiefs meet separately and enjoy significant influence in determining the priorities for their departments.

In the US and the UK, associations of police officers are often established as autonomous bodies with a view to representing a specific demographic within the organization and to address issues they perceive as being specific to their group. For example, in the UK there are now Black Police Officers' Associations in many of the 43 English and Welsh constabularies. The Muslim Association, the Asian Association, the British Association of Women Police and the Christian Police Association are other examples of such minority groups. Similarly in the US, in addition to the numerous police associations throughout the country, a number of groups such as Lesbian and Gay Police Associations and Black Police Associations are well established.

Some police unions include non-sworn members in their membership and/or have an Associate membership provision. The Australian Federal Police Association for example provides a full membership to all employees of the Australian Federal Police, and an Associate membership for previous members and any employee of the Commonwealth engaged in a law enforcement role.

Police unions derive their resources from membership fees and/or levies on all members. These resources are often enhanced by the arrangement with the police organization itself whereby Presidents or Secretaries of the police union are allowed to undertake union business on full or part-time secondment arrangements. Most police unions have their own newsletter/journal published on a regular basis and distributed not only to members but to the wider political community. As well as their own internal 'executive' meetings, police unions hold regular conferences. These conferences provide an opportunity for delegates to discuss and debate police issues. While criminal justice reform, legislation and policy are on the agenda, much of the time spent at these conferences concerns union business. Delegates discuss 'union business' in terms of mandate, duty of 'fair representation' and their role as bargaining agent. Union 'business' also includes the management of the union – a thriving business in many ways and fiduciary responsibility, election of officers, standing committee reports (such as legal assistance), budgets, planning and general day-to-day operations consume much of the conference time. These forums invite police union representatives from other jurisdictions to contribute to debate.

Almost universally, police unions are organizations without full union status (as defined by broad labour relations legislation) or independence and are legally prohibited from taking strike action. The reality is though that police unions have generally been reluctant to strike, preferring instead to engage in public campaigning or alternative industrial action when it has been deemed appropriate. Such strategies include 'blue flu' whereby police officers call in sick *en masse*. A variant of this occurs when police officers collectively turn in their vehicles for service on any given day. Letter drops, marches on parliament, media comment, work-to-rule campaigns, picketing activity and advertising campaigns are other examples. Many organizations have their own research units which are used to inform police union comment. Others use professional consultants to provide evidence for their cause. Legislation providing stricter controls on when and how unions may legally engage in industrial action (in Australia for example) has not proven to

be effective against police union industrial activity.

In the UK, US, Canada, New Zealand and Australia police unions have circumvented the constraints around industrial activity in other ways. The political lobbying strategy has been widely used in the UK by the PFEW. Activities include issue-based lobbying of parliamentarians, one-on-one lobbying with individual members of parliament, Federation funded 'parliamentary advisers' and working with other organizations to achieve political objectives (networking). In Australia, the Police Federation of Australia plays a pivotal coordination role in bringing together the resources of eight police union organizations and provides a peak lobbying service for the Australian police union movement. In recent years it has been involved in police tax campaigns, police superannuation legislation and more recently national retirement provisions for Australia's 52,000 police officers. In the US where police are very much part of the political canvas, the numerous police unions have proven adept at utilizing the political environment to advance members' interests. In all these cases it is not an exaggeration to suggest that police, through their unions, have become pivotal 'insiders' in the criminal justice network influencing policy, administration and legislation.

In recent years police unions have begun to broaden their areas of interest with many organizations looking beyond the wages and better working conditions remit and assessing their place in the future of policing practice. Private security, tertiary education for officers, professionalism and family/work balances are now an additional part of the unions' continuing agenda. Additionally, while police unions have always been involved in police networks with a view to consolidating and extending their reach at the national level, police union groups are now expanding their networks both regionally and internationally.

Evaluation

Despite the relatively long history of police union rights and the institutionalization of police unions in many Western liberal countries, not all countries enjoy the freedom to unionize. While there are a number of jurisdictions around the world who with government support have gained the right to bargain collectively and/or administer a collective agreement, it is not the case for all. There is now a considerable amount of activity within 'non-Western' countries where police officers are now demanding that their right to organize and to bargain collectively should be recognized. This agitation for labour and social rights for police is currently underway, for example, in Swaziland (Southern Africa), and in Bucharest (Eastern Europe).

According to the International Labour Organization (ILO), freedom of association and the right to organize and bargain collectively are fundamental human rights. However these ILO 'guaranteed' rights do not apply automatically to police and the armed services. In 2003 for example, Argentinean police offices approached the ILO when their government refused to allow them to unionize. The ILO concluded its deliberations in favour of the Argentinean government, citing national laws and regulations as taking precedence in the case of police and armed forces. Similarly in Swaziland, industrial relations legislation prohibits police or the security forces more generally from forming a union. Indeed the only police union in Africa is the Police and Civil Rights Union in South Africa. In Mauritius while police officers have collective representation rights they have no real collective bargaining rights. The Mauritius Police Association is currently seeking broader labour rights concessions and has looked towards more established police unions for assistance in securing these rights.

International networking for police unions began formally in 1996 when the International Law Enforcement Council was formed in Canada. Early members were Canada, England and Wales, Scotland, Northern Ireland and the US. Australia, New Zealand and Denmark joined in 1998. In 2006 the network was expanded and now includes representatives from South Africa, and organizations from the South Pacific. The network is now called the International Council of Police Representative Associations (ICPRA) and meets bi-annually. The European Confederation of Police (EUROCOP) is the European umbrella organization of 33 police unions and staff organizations covering 28 countries. EUROCOP is committed to supporting countries like Spain and Portugal in their quest for police workers' rights. ICPRA has been helping those organizations such as the Swaziland Police with strategic direction, legal advice and financial aid with a view to assisting them in their quest for the right to unionize. It has also been giving support to the *Guardia Civil* in Spain whose rights have been limited by the Spanish government.

In most Western democratic countries police unionism is accepted by governments. However, the relationship between police unions and their employers (government) and managers is not always harmonious. Given their potential to seriously disrupt 'peace and order' and their capacity to fundamentally challenge managerial prerogative, they are generally regarded as disruptive entities. Equally important, they are viewed as bodies that resist reform, acting defensively rather than contemplating the 'real' governance changes that have impacted on the provision of policing services.

The continued scepticism about police unions' capacity to build the policing enterprise is perhaps not a response to their mere existence. It is more likely due to the reality that police unions have hastened the breakdown of militaristic aspects of police organizational culture and have become a pivotal node in police decision-making processes. Police managers and employers alike are cautious of the consequences of making decisions or creating plans without the 'buy-in' of the unions. The unions' high profile 'insider' status and subsequent influence have become an important factor in law and order debates. Significantly police unions invariably enjoy strong levels of support from their communities. This has made it difficult for politicians to dismiss their claims and public discourse as irrelevant.

Jenny Fleming and Monique Marks

Associated Concepts: democratic policing, identity, law and order politics, socialization

Key Readings

Burgess, M. (2006) 'Police unions as network participants', in J. Fleming, and J. Wood, (eds) (2006) *Fighting Crime Together: The Challenges of Policing and Security Networks.* Sydney: University of New South Wales Press.

Finnane, M. (2002). *When Police Unionise: The Politics of Law and Order in Australia.* Sydney: Institute of Criminology, University of Sydney.

Fleming, J. and Marks, M. (2004) 'Reformers or resisters? The state of police unionism in Australia', *Employment Relations Record,* 4 (1): 1–14.

Holdaway, S. and O'Neill, M. (2004) 'The development of black police associations: changing articulations of Race within the Police', *British Journal of Criminology,* 44 (6): 854–65.

Marks, M. and Fleming, J. (2006) 'The right to unionise, the right to bargain and the right to democratic policing', *The Annals of the American Academy of Political and Social Science,* Special Issue, 605 (1): May, 178–99.

Marks, M. and Fleming, J. (2007) 'Police as workers: police labour rights in Southern Africa and beyond', *SA Crime Quarterly,* 19, March: 13–18.

Reiner, R. (1978) *The Blue Coated Worker: A Sociological Study of Police Unionism.* London: Cambridge University Press.

V

VICTIM

Definition

The word 'victim' is generally used to refer to someone who has suffered some kind of harm or misfortune, however, in the context of policing it is normally used to refer to the complainant of a crime.

Distinctive Features

Historically police work has been generated by, and has relied upon the victim (the complainant) for much of its workload despite popular and police cultural presumptions that the prime concern of police work is catching criminals. The importance of the victim to police work lies both in relation to their willingness to report a criminal event and in their willingness to act as a witness following the instigation of court proceedings. Arguably, as crime rates have risen in different international contexts, policing has become much more focused on the quality of its relationship with the victim. As Mawby (2007) reports, public and victim ratings of police performance appear to have worsened in many international jurisdictions. In particular, dissatisfaction is expressed in relation to the problems of no arrests having been made and/or no goods being recovered. Police performance seems to be especially problematic for victims of acquaintance violence, an issue that we shall return to below.

Superficially identifying the victim (complainant) of a crime appears to be straightforward. However, as Christie (1986) argued some time ago, some victims acquire the victim status much more readily than others. This happens as a result of the powerful effect of what he termed the 'ideal victim'. For Christie (1986) the 'ideal victim' is the victim of the Little Red Riding Hood fairy tale: a young, innocent female out doing good deeds who is attacked by an unknown stranger. This ideal stereotype results in some people being viewed as deserving victims, that is, acquiring the victim label very readily and easily, while others are labelled undeserving victims and as a result may never acquire the victim label. Conceptualizations of the 'ideal victim' also contribute to the assumption that victims are good and offenders are bad.

This effect has prompted Carrabine et al., (2004: 117) to talk of a 'hierarchy of victimization'. At the bottom of this hierarchy would be the homeless, the street prostitute, the drug addict, the drunk – indeed all those categories of people for whom it is presumed expose themselves to victimization thus making a claim to the label 'victim' for them very difficult. Moreover, historically these are exactly the kinds of people that many police officers routinely have contact with. They constitute what Lee (1981) called 'police property': the kinds of people who need to be kept off the streets, sometimes for their own safety (as in the case of the drunk), or who are seen to be a threat to public safety and social order (as in the case of the drug addict or the street prostitute). Consequently, these groups of people are much more likely to be identified by police officers as offenders rather than victims, though in reality they might be both. So despite the importance of the victim (complainant) to the work of policing, not all complainants are necessarily accorded victim status. While police officers in many jurisdictions use their discretion in deciding whether or not an incident that has been reported to them constitutes a crime or not and is therefore recorded as such, the use of discretion is particularly powerful in circumstances in which there might be evidential dispute over what has taken place. This can be particularly problematic when the victim and the offender are known to each other. These are also the kinds of circumstances in which, in addition to noting the importance of the hierarchy of victimization discussed above, achieving the status of victim in the eyes of a police officer can also be problematic. This returns us to the issue of acquaintance violence mentioned above.

The police response to victims of sexual and physical violence has been the subject of particular criticism and victim dissatisfaction. While much of that criticism has been focused around how women as victims are treated by the police, it should be noted that policing perceptions of legitimate victim status apply in other circumstances in which a complaint of a crime has occurred, as for example, a fight in the street between two men. However, feminists have been particularly vocal in their criticism of the police handling of victims of sexual violence and domestic violence, particularly with respect to the perceived unwillingness on the part of police officers to take such complaints seriously. These criticisms have led police services in many different jurisdictions to engage in specialist training to enable officers to respond more appropriately to these kinds of complaints as well as developing specialized units to help and support victims (complainants) to participate in criminal proceedings. These specific concerns have prompted a more generalized response to supporting the victim of crime especially in the UK. There are now Witness Care Units run jointly by the police and the Crown Prosecution Service whose purpose is to facilitate victims' participation in the criminal justice system.

As the victim of crime has become an increasingly important motif in the political and policy response to crime especially in the Anglo-speaking world, so the victim has also become a much more central feature of the daily routine of police paper work. This is perhaps epitomized by the introduction of different models of victim statement schemes in different jurisdictions in which police officers are expected to take a statement from the victim that documents the impact that a crime has had on them. Such statements form part of the documents that are presented at court and while they are taken at different points in the different kinds of schemes that exist internationally, the police, as the first point of contact for all victims in all jurisdictions, are contemporarily increasingly involved in gathering this kind of information. In addition, the work of police officers has been increasingly reoriented towards working with victims and offenders as initiatives under the umbrella of restorative justice have been embraced, again primarily within the Anglo-speaking world. These developments, alongside the requirements made of policing in relation to various codes of practice and victims' charters, reflect the efforts being made to ensure that the central importance of the victim (complainant) to the work of the police is put to the forefront of the policing task.

Evaluation

In the last fifty years it has become clear that the victim of crime can no longer be said to be the forgotten party of the criminal justice system. The police as the first point of contact with the victim, and often the only point of contact, are central to the victim's experience of, and levels of satisfaction with, the criminal justice system. Maintaining levels of satisfaction of victims and the general public with policing is of crucial importance in ensuring continued support for the task of policing and the legitimacy of the police to engage in that task. Much effort has been made over the last 25 years to recognize the role of the victim in this respect and especially to recognize the need on the part of the police to respond more appropriately to women as victims. These developments, along with increasing police involvement with victims in taking impact statements, supporting them as witnesses, and working with them in the context of restorative justice, may lead to an erosion of the impact that notions of the 'ideal victim' have, and by implication may also lead to more subtle conceptualizations of 'offenders', thus blurring the boundaries between images of the two. It is clear, however, that the police use of discretion plays an important part in who is responded to, how, and under what kind of circumstances. Their use of discretion, mediated as it is by organizational values and culture (often referred to as 'cop culture') always needs to be taken into account in order to understand how and why victims may or may not be responded to in particular circumstances. The police use of discretion notwithstanding, all that victims of crime frequently want is to be treated with dignity and respect. The police have an essential role to play in ensuring that, despite the difficulties in reorienting the work of policing from the priority of catching criminals to responding to the victim, the victim's experience of their contact with them reflects these qualities.

Sandra Walklate

Associated Concepts: calls for service, discretion, diversity, domestic violence, police property, restorative policing, sexual assault

Key Readings

Carrabine, E., Iganski, P., Lee, M., Plummer, K., and South, N. (2004) *Criminology: A Sociological Introduction*. London: Routledge.
Christie, N. (1986) 'The ideal victim', in E.A. Fattah (ed.) *From Crime Policy to Victim Policy*. London: Macmillan.
Hoyle, C. and Young, R. (2003) 'Restorative justice, victims and the police', in T. Newburn (ed.) *Handbook of Policing*. Cullompton, Devon: Willan Publishing.
Lee, J.A. (1981) 'Some structural aspects of police deviance in relations with minority groups', in C. Shearing (ed.) *Organizational Police Deviance*. Toronto: Butterworth.
Mawby, R. (2007) 'Public sector services and the victim of crime', in S. Walklate (ed.) *Handbook of Victims and Victimology,*. Cullompton, Devon: Willan Publishing.

VIGILANTISM

Definition

The term *vigilante*, meaning 'watchman' or 'guard', is of Spanish origin, its derivation having the Latin root *vigil* ('watchful'). Organized vigilante activity is a recurring theme in the history of policing and social control in the US. The first American vigilante movement appeared in 1767 and, from then until about 1900, vigilantism was a constant feature of American life. It is estimated that organized vigilante groups executed more than 700 people between 1767 and 1910, though if the activities of lynch mobs and Ku Klux Klansmen are added the total probably exceeds 6,000. In the UK, by contrast, organized vigilantism – as opposed to informal self-policing within communities – has been rather less prevalent. Nevertheless, activities described as 'vigilantist' are commonplace in most societies. Writing on the topic in the early 1990s, for example, Johnston (1992) described examples of recently reported vigilante activity in various countries including the UK, Haiti, the Philippines, Brazil, China, Denmark and France.

However, vigilantism is a contested concept. Popular definitions tend to focus on those circumstances in which citizens 'take the law into their own hands' in order to deter criminality and punish wrongdoing. Yet both historical and contemporary evidence suggests that this view is inadequate. In nineteenth century America, Missouri's 'Bald Knobbers' not only punished criminal wrongdoings but, like members of the 'White Cap' movement, also undertook 'moral' vigilantism against wife beaters, adulterers and women considered to be lewd or lascivious. Similarly, in more recent times, the Republican and Loyalist 'punishment squads' once prevalent in Northern Ireland, not only regulated burglary and joyriding against local teenagers but also disciplined members who contravened the rules of paramilitary organizations.

There is considerable dispute among writers on vigilantism as to its precise character: whether or not it is inherently violent, conservative, extra-legal, organized and directed only towards criminal acts; whether it can be undertaken by agents acting on behalf of the state (such as the police) as well as by private citizens; and whether it is a genuine social movement or a mere social reaction to events. Whereas some writers caution against stretching the concept to encompass a wide range of activities (from membership of the Ku Klux Klan to participation in anti-criminal street patrols) others describe a wide range of apparently heterogeneous behaviours as being vigilantist. The most extreme example of the latter is Rosenbaum and Sedeberg's (1976) depiction of vigilantism as 'establishment violence' – any form of violent behaviour undertaken in defence of establishment values.

Distinctive Features

The problem with such generic definitions is that they preclude the analysis of specific behaviours; or, to put it another way, by explaining everything they explain nothing. In the light of this, Johnston (1996) outlines six characteristic features of vigilantism with the aim of constructing a criminological definition: that it is planned, premeditated and organized to at least a minimal degree; that it is undertaken by private voluntary agents rather than by state agents; that, being undertaken by private voluntary agents, it constitutes a form of 'autonomous citizenship' (that is, one lacking state authority or support); that it involves the use or threatened use of force; that it is a reaction to crime and social deviance; and that it constitutes a social movement the aim of which is to facilitate personal and/or collective security.

This definition differs in two respects from previous ones. First, it makes no assumption that vigilante action is necessarily extra-legal, an issue that has caused confusion among commentators. This may be seen in Brown's (1975) authoritative analysis of vigilantism in the US which contains two quite different definitions. The first – 'organized extra-legal movements the members of which take the law into their own hands' (1975: 95–6) describes the American

historical vigilante tradition. By contrast, a second broader definition – 'associations in which citizens have joined together for self-protection under conditions of disorder' (1975: 130) is meant to incorporate the many citizen patrol groups to have emerged in the US and elsewhere since the 1960s: groups which Brown regards as a valid component of that same vigilante tradition. Second, the definition makes no reference to punishment. Though punishment is a common feature of vigilantism, it is by no means universal, even in circumstances where violence is inflicted on a victim. This can be illustrated by two British examples. The 'Norfolk Two' case involved the seizure, by two men, of a 16 year old youth suspected of having committed several burglaries and thefts; his interrogation for 20 minutes; threats being made to cut him with a knife or douse him in petrol if he refused to provide the information demanded; and his eventual dumping by a roadside. Here, though violence was clearly inflicted on the victim, there was no evidence of his subjection to punishment. By contrast, the 'informal justice' inflicted by punishment squads in Northern Ireland constituted a classic form of punishment: ritualized, systematic and having, like the formal justice it mimicked, 'tariffs' according to the 'seriousness' of the offences committed.

Evaluation

Research on the efficacy of vigilantism is limited, though there have been two empirical studies of the Guardian Angels (summarized in Johnston, 1992: 169–73). One examined the impact of the group's activities on crime and fear of crime on the New York subway, concluding that the number of crimes and incivilities occurring in the project areas was so small as to make meaningful conclusions about preventive impact impossible; that most people (54 per cent) reported 'seldom' or 'never' seeing a patrol, despite the group's claim to have more than 1,000 members; and that, whether present or absent, patrols had little impact on people's overall and long-term levels of fear of crime. In another study, 60 per cent of respondents in San Diego claimed to feel safer as a result of Guardian Angel activity, with women and older people being particularly positive. However, the same study found that patrols had no impact on recorded levels of violent crime and only limited short-term effect on recorded levels of property crime, thus suggesting that random citizen patrol, like random police patrol, may be effective at reducing fear of crime but have minimal impact on recorded crime levels.

As for the implications of vigilantism, three issues are worthy of brief note. First, anthropological work on vigilantism has important implications for our understanding of governance in developing societies. Studies undertaken in Uganda (see Johnston, 1992: 161 for a summary of Heald's (1986) study) and in Tanzania (see Abrahams, 1998: chapter 2; Heald, 2002) are particularly noteworthy. In the case of Tanzania's *Sungusungu* movement, Heald (2002) describes a form of vigilantism that has, to a degree, 'domesticated' the state. Initially, as Abraham's (1988) earlier work showed, *Sungusungu* constituted a vote of 'no confidence' in the state. Later, the movement carved out a particular place for itself, 'co-opting government and, in turn, [being] co-opted by it' (Heald, 2002: 23). Under these arrangements communities took back power, developing their own policing capacity and in so doing, both reformed and reclaimed the state.

Second, defining vigilantism as a form of autonomous citizenship (that is, one lacking state support or legitimacy) involves both rejecting the concept of 'state vigilantism' (c.f. Rosenbaum and Sedeberg, 1976) and drawing a distinction between vigilante acts and similar violent or threatening acts committed by commercial security agents. One reason for making those discriminations is to draw attention to the 'nodalized' character of contemporary security governance: the fact that security governance is parcelled out among a plethora of relatively discrete commercial, state and citizen-based nodes. Relations between these nodes are invariably complex. In the case of vigilantism, for example, the police's stance is sometimes inconsistent: both critical of autonomous initiatives, yet willing to 'trade' with them when circumstances demand it. In the Norfolk case described above, it was alleged – though Norfolk Police denied it vehemently – that the information on which the vigilantes acted had been supplied to them by a community constable, frustrated by his inability to accumulate sufficient evidence for prosecution against a 'known' offender.

Third, Brown (1975) draws a useful distinction between 'classic vigilantism' (directed against horse thieves, outlaws and the rural lower classes up to 1900) and 'neo-vigilantism' (directed at urban Catholics, Jews, Negroes, radicals and labour leaders in the twentieth century). This slippage between 'crime control' and 'social control' is a recurrent theme of vigilante movements, 'moral panics' about crime sometimes being manufactured to justify violent actions against minority groups.

Les Johnston

Associated Concepts: responsibilization, patrol, pluralization, privatization, third party policing

Key Readings

Abrahams, R. (1998) *Vigilant Citizens: Vigilantism and the State*. Cambridge: Polity Press.

Brown, R.M. (1975) *Strain of Violence*. New York: Oxford University Press.

Heald, S. (2002) 'Domesticating Leviathan: Sungusungu groups in Tanzania', *Crisis States Programme, Working Paper No. 1*. London School of Economics: Development Research Centre.

Johnston, L. (1992) *The Rebirth of Private Policing*. London: Routledge.

Johnston, L. (1996) 'What is vigilantism?', *British Journal of Criminology*, 36 (2): 220–36.

Rosenbaum, H.J. and Sedeberg, P.C. (eds) (1976) *Vigilante Politics*. Pennsylvania: University of Pennsylvania Press.

W

WOMEN IN POLICING

See Culture; Leadership; Diversity

Y

YOUTH

Definition

The identification and targeting of children and young people (typically those under the age of 18) for proactive policing and variously justified in the name of child welfare, crime prevention and public protection.

Distinctive Features

The presence of young people on the street has always attracted the concern and the ire of adults – whether directed at the 'street Arabs' of the early nineteenth century, the 'hooligan gangs' of the late nineteenth century or the 'joy riders', 'hoodies', or 'happy slappers' of the early twenty-first century. Indeed the original identification of juvenile delinquency in England in the early nineteenth century was only made possible through changes in policing practices, together with the creation of new criminal offences. Descriptions of the rookeries in the East End of London, for example, may have catalogued the activities of young 'precocious' traders and 'loutish' vagabonds, but youth independence and streetwise lifestyles were anathema to a growing number of middle class commentators. The issue was viewed as having as much a moral as a criminal character. Accordingly the remit given to the Metropolitan Police in 1829 included apprehension of 'all loose, idle and disorderly persons not giving good account of themselves'. This made many more 'street children' and street sellers subject to criminalization.

That said, up until the mid twentieth century a majority of police interventions with young people in most Western jurisdictions were made on an informal basis, involving warnings, citations, 'moving on' and on-the-spot admonishment. Given the then localized nature of policing this might also involve acting with or on behalf of parents to informally punish the child with the proverbial 'cuff around the ear' (UK) or 'at the end of a nightstick' (US). There were also a growing number of child specific offences such as truancy clauses in education acts or neglected children statutes that increased the grounds for police intervention. These 'status offences' (as they were known in the US) provided the police with extensive (and often ambiguous) mandates for monitoring the conditions of family life. Such 'welfare policing' eventually was to become more formalized in attempts to prevent or divert delinquency by the establishment of police-citizens boys' clubs (Australia), police athletic leagues (US) and the use of informal and formal cautioning programmes in place of prosecution (UK). By the mid twentieth century specialized juvenile units and liaison bureaus could be found in most Western jurisdictions – sometimes explicitly trained in social work methods (as in Belgium).

Today police led diversion programmes typically take the form of police/school partnerships with dedicated officers advising students on the consequences of crime and drug use. One particular program, DARE (Drug Abuse Resistance Education), was widespread throughout the US during the 1990s.

The past decade has, however, also witnessed a significant resort to proactive policing whether through stop and search, dispersal orders, juvenile curfews and the targeting of low level street offences (usually justified by the ethos of 'nipping crime in the bud').

Evaluation

Crucial elements of the relationship between police and young people have been (and continue to be) forged on the street. Much of this centres on the age-old disputes over the ownership and use of public space. Local places and spaces – the street corner, the city centre, the shopping centre, the precinct – hold a special significance for young people, arousing emotional attachments, cementing a sense of territory and identity and providing one of the main arenas for leisure as a consequence of age-based exclusions from private spaces and other cultural resources. Yet it is in these places where young people are at their most visible and liable to police and public scrutiny. Such visibility has almost certainly been compounded by the contraction of spaces deemed to be 'public'. Young people for example, using shopping centres as a meeting place are, quite literally, rendered 'out of place'. From the point of view of 'consumption', unemployed and dispossessed youth are 'virtually worthless' and need to be moved on (White, 1994).

Despite this perpetual concern, detailed qualitative studies of youth-police encounters are (somewhat surprisingly) relatively rare. However some of the statistical evidence is revealing. A report to the US Department of Justice in 2007 found that those in the 18 to 24 age group had the highest percentage of contact with police (29.3 per cent) compared to those aged 65 or older who had the lowest (8.3 per cent). American research on police-juvenile interactions conducted in the 1960s and 1970s reported that the majority of encounters resulted from a complainant's request for police assistance. However 20 years later further research based on a study of police patrols in Indiana and Florida suggested that the police themselves were now initiating about a half of their encounters with juveniles

as a result of giving greater attention to less serious quality of life ('broken windows') offences (Worden and Myers, 1999). In a study in Edinburgh, Scotland in the early 1990s, 44 per cent of a sample of over 1,000 11–15 year olds had been 'moved on or told off', 13 per cent had been stopped and searched and 10 per cent had been arrested or detained in a police station in the previous nine months.

Police/youth relations also appear to be highly racialized and gendered. Afro-Caribbean youth appear especially vulnerable to 'proactive' policing. Currently in the UK, black young people are up to six times as likely, and Asian youth twice as likely, to be stopped and searched than white youth. Further, when black young people come into contact with the police, whether as victims or witnesses, their perceptions and experiences of the police tend to be worse than for white young people (Webster, 2006). It is also a highly gendered relation. In one of a very few ethnographic studies, research in St Louis, US found that while African American young men routinely describe being subject to aggressive policing and being treated as a suspect regardless of their involvement in delinquency, young women typically describe being stopped for curfew violations and being sexually harassed (Brunson and Miller, 2006). In the UK, Loader's (1996) interviews with police officers in Edinburgh revealed that one of their most prominent and consistent views is that young people hanging about in groups will be either directly or indirectly involved in criminal behaviour.

The evolution of police cautioning programmes in the UK provides a telling example of recent shifts towards more proactive and interventionist forms of policing young people. From the early 1970s until the mid 1990s the delivery of a caution was one of the major means the police used to deal with young offenders. Inspired by a 'protective' and 'treatment' logic that young people's behaviour should be challenged but that formal proceedings were more likely to do harm than good, cautioning (in the form of a verbal admonishment usually with parents and a social worker present) was promoted as a key means of ensuring pre-court diversion. In 1970, 35 per cent of under 17 year olds arrested were cautioned; increasing to 50 per cent by 1979. Home Office circular 14/1985, furthered the process by encouraging the police to use 'no further action' or 'informal warnings'. By the 1990s about 60 per cent of young offenders were being dealt with informally although there were wide and fluctuating regional variations.

There is little doubt that the police discretion to informally caution made a significant impact on reducing court appearances and protecting young people from the stigma of a criminal record (as well as reducing police paperwork). However this policy was to prove short-lived. Some critiqued the process because of its potential to administer a punishment without any judicial hearing; others argued that it simply widened the net by targeting the minor 'pre-delinquent' (Pratt, 1986). But the most influential governmental critique of cautioning was eventually to emerge in the white paper *No More Excuses* which preceded the 1998 Crime and Disorder Act. It claimed that police cautioning (whether informal or formal) was applied too readily, inconsistently and haphazardly. Moreover it was argued that there was often little or no follow up so that youth were allowed to 'flout the law with impunity'. The interventionist (rather than diversionary) principles of the 1998 Act saw the replacement of cautions by reprimands (on first offence) and final warnings (on second offence). The latter drew in particular from the experience of 'caution plus' approaches and placed the police under a statutory duty to refer the young person to a youth offending team (YOT) for assessment and with the expectation of some eventual 'programme of intervention'. In 2005 the Youth Justice Board for England and Wales set a target for all YOTs to include intervention in at least 80 per cent of final warnings. This removed large parts of police discretion and effectively abolished informal action. The result, however, has not been a decline, but a rise in the number of prosecutions. In 2004 the Audit Commission reported that too many minor youth offences were being brought to court, taking up time and expense. The current evidence suggests that the formalization of early intervention, particularly through final warnings, has indeed led to a net-widening where more children and young people are being prosecuted for trivial offences and with a subsequent related impact on the rate of custodial sentencing.

Such a 'push-in' effect is also notable in the recent use of anti-social behaviour (ASB) orders, where the UK (especially England) can legitimately claim to be the world leader. ASB has become almost synonymous with police perceptions of youth disorder particularly in 'high crime/sink estates'. Youth has once more come to be understood as some pre-delinquent 'menace', requiring pre-emptive intervention designed to act on 'known risks' such as teenage pregnancies, irresponsible parenting, truancy and 'hanging about'. Almost 50 per cent of all ASBOs are given to those under the age of 18. The Anti-Social Behaviour Act 2003 introduced a further range of enforcement led interventions including parenting contracts, fixed penalty notices and dispersal orders. The police were granted powers of 'dispersal' to remove under 16 year olds from public places if they 'believed' that a member of the public might be 'intimidated, harassed, alarmed or distressed'. Some of the more bizarre applications of this legislation have been bans on 'hoodies' (to allow closed circuit television identification) and preventing ownership of stereos (to prevent noise nuisance).

John Muncie

Associated Concepts: anti-social behaviour, broken windows, crime prevention, discretion, diversity, order maintenance, police property

Key Readings

Brunson, R. and Miller, J. (2006) 'Gender, race and urban policing: the experience of African American youths', *Gender and Society*, 20 (4): 531–52.

Loader, I. (1996) *Youth, Policing and Democracy*. London: Macmillan.

Pratt, J. (1986) 'Diversion from the juvenile court', *British Journal of Criminology*, 26 (3): 212–33.

Webster, C. (2006) 'Race', youth crime and justice', in B. Goldson, and J. Muncie, (eds) *Youth Crime and Justice*. London: Sage.

White, R. (1994) 'Street life: police practices and youth behaviour', in R. White, and C. Alder, (eds) *The Police and Young People in Australia*. Cambridge: Cambridge University Press.

Worden, R. and Myers, S. (1999) *Police Encounters with Juvenile Suspects*. Report to the National Research Council's Panel on Juvenile Crime: Prevention, Treatment and Control. Washington, DC: US Government Printing Office.

Z

ZERO TOLERANCE POLICING

Definition

Zero tolerance was launched in the early 1990s as a new style of policing, aimed at substantial crime reduction, based on rigorous enforcement of the law, particularly for street crimes and 'quality of life' offences, allowing low discretion for patrol officers and ostensibly no clemency for offenders.

Distinctive Features

Zero tolerance attracted considerable attention in policing and became associated with New York, with Mayor Giuliani and with Police Commissioner Bratton (although Bratton abandoned the term as smacking of 'over-zealousness'). In New York and elsewhere, it was based on four main elements: assertive and visible policing of the streets with robust law enforcement, swift analysis of crime data translated into pressure on district chiefs to perform, the 'broken windows' concept for multi-agency initiatives to tackle community problems (Kelling and Coles, 1996) and a new *élan* for policing with strong leadership, political backing, enhanced resources and rhetoric of success (Sampson et al., 1997).

The call for assertive policing drew partly on environmental criminologists who believed a strong anti-crime orientation in a neighbourhood could channel efforts into removing the visible signs of disorder that impact on the quality of everyday life. This would reduce overall crime through a shared sense of neighbourliness and renewed trust. This 'collective efficacy' (Sampson et al., 1997) could be engendered through police taking the lead in 'cleaning up the streets' by removing petty offenders who were held to form the vanguard of more serious crime. The zero tolerance approach overruled the conventional discretion of officers to permit 'street people' to remain unmolested in certain public places. The aim was that by arresting and prosecuting them a less disorganized and threatening environment could be created which, in turn, assisted community recovery (the 'broken windows' approach).

The top-down pressure on quality of life enforcement was widened to other crime control strategies that tackled drugs, youth crime, firearms, auto theft, domestic violence and traffic violations. This was augmented by focusing on performance and holding police managers to account for the crime rates in their precincts. This 'war on crime' was guided by twice-weekly 'Compstat' meetings where commanders had to demonstrate how they solved crime problems and were held to account for failures. The new emphasis was on technology and digital mapping to identify crime trends and 'hot spots': this directed limited policing resources in an 'intelligence-led' approach. The press and outside agencies were invited to these meetings. This aggressive if not intimidating style supported the institutional message of being 'tough on crime'. Bratton motivated his officers by high profile announcements that zero tolerance policing was working and that being tough on the streets had brought down crime levels.

The early political backing, with a substantial increase in personnel, played a significant role in establishing a concerted policing effort. Crime had risen to alarming heights throughout the 1980s in America and there was widespread fear of crime plus substantial economic costs. Giuliani, Bratton and the New York City Police Department (NYPD) were symptomatic of a new resolve to bring down crime. There was a political thirst for successful crime control headlines and this was matched by the public's willingness to tolerate what critics saw as an assault on the poor and inadequate (or 'broken heads'). But the resulting crackdown in American cities had considerable impact on policing strategies elsewhere throughout the 1990s.

Evaluation

The New York model elicited global attention. After decades of relentlessly rising crime, the police claimed they had reversed that rise, and this 'miracle' attracted foreign criminal justice pilgrims. But this raised the key questions: had zero tolerance reduced crime and how did it transfer to other cultures?

Academic opinion maintains that crime was dropping anyway, in other cities and countries, and it fell in US cities without zero tolerance policies (Bowling, 1999). A large increase in patrol personnel focused on specific offences undoubtedly reduced some categories of crime (but with likely dispersion), but this did not explain the fall in violent crime. Furthermore, critics argued that the assertive enforcement was disproportionately geared towards the vulnerable and disenfranchised while there was a rise in complaints and some excesses (e.g., the abuse of Louima and the shooting of Diallo).

Those officials and politicians who flocked to the US seemed to imbibe but one message: police can reduce crime. Some returned determined to implement zero tolerance policies. But in several countries, notably the UK and the Netherlands, initial interest rapidly waned (Punch, 2007). Indeed, its impact may have been exaggerated given that assertive patrol was in vogue anyway (with growing public concern with safety), there already was a wider move to intelligence-led policing, and 'broken windows' was a revamping of problem-oriented policing from the 1970s. One explanation for

its instantaneous popularity was that politicians, and police chiefs, could employ it to promise crime reduction while conveying tough leadership, usually to electoral advantage. In Britain, New Labour observed President Clinton's popular swing to the right on law and order and, by embracing zero tolerance, outflanked the Conservatives on crime control. In France politicians, originally skeptical of an American concept, became enthusiastic with Sarkozy (then Minister of the Interior and the French President since 2007) building his tough reputation on espousing it.

Perhaps it was less a coherent and consistent policy and more a rhetorical device. It ushered in an age of rebranding policing as a commodity to be marketed with one-inliners, promises of instant success and as an export article. This marketing of simple success formulas in criminal justice also fits the analyses of critics who see this as part of America's wish to have global outreach (Brogden, 2005). And a container concept like zero tolerance can be misappropriated for the wrong reasons, as in American cities with crude sweeping operations against street people, while totalitarian regimes are nothing less than blunt exercises in 'zero tolerance'.

On implementation there was often a discrepancy between politicians and practitioners. In the UK the hype surrounding it was seized by New Labour politicians, with an ear to the populist media, who used it for their new punitive stance on crime. The view of senior police officers was far less enthusiastic. In a way the police elite had become 'Scarmanized' (following the Scarman Report of 1981): less obsessed with crime control than their political masters and liberal in response to an increasingly diverse society. As professionals they saw zero tolerance as a catchphrase rather than a coherent strategy of policing. Indeed, it even threatened the movement towards a more rights-regarding and consultative policing system by reintroducing the more aggressive style that had been discredited by the Scarman Report. A significant exception was Ray Mallon of Cleveland Police who championed the use of zero tolerance policing in Hartlepool in the mid-1990s. His strategy was seen by chief officers as a useful operational tactic, to be employed selectively against crime and disorder, but not as a long-term policy choice. It was also held to lean towards repression and Mallon became discredited; this did not prevent him being elected Mayor of Middlesborough, however, and his popularity indicates a measure of polarization between hard and soft-liners. But zero tolerance as a serious strategy for policing never gained any credibility with British cops (Pollard, 1997; Hayes, 1998).

Yet the dichotomy persists. The Association of Chief Police Officers of England and Wales, for instance, are committed to a 'neighbourhood policing style'. This is characterized by consultation, partnership, public consent and adopting a problem-solving attitude to crime and disorder. Zero tolerance is simply not in that vocabulary. Yet, in contrast, some UK politicians are still advocating an updated equivalent: the current politically correct term is 'robust policing of seemingly trivial crimes' with political pressure for the 'reduced tolerance' of low level disorder.

In the Netherlands zero tolerance, which was once popular in Dutch police circles with droves of officers visiting New York, is now dead. Some officers were disdainful of the abrasive 'Compstat' meetings in New York and called it 'management by fear'. For this top-down, 'in your face' style, with public humiliation of senior officers, did not always travel well to other cultures where police management is less confrontational. Dutch society is based more on consensus and compromise and Dutch policing is geared to community oriented policing within a relatively 'tolerant' paradigm. The term is occasionally used by populist, right-wing politicians but plays no role in policing although the broken windows notion proved popular because it fitted closely to existing Dutch policies.

In short, the components of zero tolerance policing as emanating from North America were not particularly original, but the concept drew considerable attention and found some enthusiastic followers. In a number of countries its transfer foundered on feelings that it leaned towards repression, fostered exclusion and demonization of 'out' groups and fed a bloated 'prison-industrial complex'. It will probably be periodically reinvented in response to popular feelings during a moral panic about lax enforcement of a particular offence. And it will doubtless prove popular in transient societies with burgeoning crime rates, as in Eastern Europe. But full enforcement can never be maintained and eventually proves counterproductive.

Stan Gilmour and Maurice Punch

Associated Concepts: broken windows theory, Compstat, crime analysis, hot spots, intelligence-led policing, law and order politics, misconduct, patrol, policy transfer, police property, problem-oriented policing

Key Readings

Bowling, B. (1999) The rise and fall of New York murder: zero tolerance or crack's decline? *British Journal of Criminology*, 39 (4): 531–54.

Brogden, M. (2005) '"Horses for courses" and "thin blue lines": community policing in transitional society', *Police Quarterly*, 8 (1): 64–98.

Hayes, B. (1998) 'Applying Bratton to Britain: the need for sensible compromise', in M. Weatheritt (ed.) *Zero Tolerance Policing: What Does it Mean and is it Right for Policing in Britain?* London: Police Foundation.

Kelling, G. and Coles, C. M. (1996) *Fixing Broken Windows: Restoring Order and Reducing Crime in Our Communities*. New York: Free Press.

Bratton, W. J. and Knoblach, P. (1998) *Turnaround: How America's Top Cop Reversed the Crime Epidemic*. New York: Random Books.

Pollard, C. (1997) 'Zero-tolerance: short term fix, long-term liability', in N. Dennis (ed.) *Zero Tolerance: Policing a Free Society*. London: Institute for Economic Affairs.

Punch, M. (2007) *Zero Tolerance Policing*. Bristol: The Policy Press.

Sampson, R. J., Raudenbush, S. W., and Earls, F. (1997) 'Neighborhoods and violent crime: A multilevel study of collective efficacy', *Science*, 277: 918–924.

Name Index

NAME INDEX

Subject Index

A

Aboriginal communities
  community safety, 47–48
  deaths in custody, 78, 90
  destruction of, 142–43
  policing of, 173
  restorative policing, 279
accountability, 1–4
  accountability gap, 260
  auxiliary police, 11
  bureaucratization, 15
  civilian oversight, 23–25
  community engagement, 35–36
  Compstat, 50–51
  contractualism, 56
  effect of technology on, 299
  independence of the constable, 169–70
  performance management, 224–26
  private security, 285
  surveillance, 29–30, 70, 79
  third party policing, 304
  transnational policing, 309–10
  see also democratic policing; governmentality;
    legitimacy; misconduct; public value
action research, 274
adversarial justice systems, 65–66
Africa, police history in, 141–42
agents provocateurs *see* entrapment
Americanization of policing *see*
  policy transfer
Anti-Discrimination Act 1977 (New South Wales,
  Australia), 134
Anti-Social Behaviour Act 2003 (UK), 5
anti-social behaviour (ASB), 4–6
  anti-social behaviour order (ASBO), 5–6, 323
  communitarianism, 34
  community safety, 48
  imitation firearms, 129
  interventions, 323
  reporting, 19
  see also broken windows theory; law and order
    politics; order maintenance; public order
    policing; youth
Anti-Terrorism, Crime and Security Act 2001
  (UK), 301

arrest, 6–8, 93, 281–82
  see also citizen's arrest; discretion; search
ASB *see* anti-social behaviour (ASB)
auditors, 97, 99
Australia
  community policing in, 38–39
  police history in, 142–43
auxiliary police, 8–11, 45–46
  citizen's arrest, 20, 21
  patrol, 26–27, 220, 244
  see also civilianization; pluralization; private
    security; privatization; security networks

B

biometric evidence, 67
broken windows theory, 5, 12–14, 50, 325
  see also anti-social behaviour (ASB); order
    maintenance; youth; zero tolerance policing
brutality *see* misconduct
bureaucratization, 14–16
  see also accountability; discretion; independence
    of the constable; leadership; managerialism

C

calls for service, 17–20, 219
  see also community engagement; hate crime;
    order maintenance; technology
camera surveillance systems *see* closed circuit
  television (CCTV)
Canada, community policing in, 39–40
cautions, 279, 322–23
CCTV *see* closed circuit television (CCTV)
Chicago Alternative Policing Strategy (CAPS),
  36–37, 220
Chicago School, 39
children *see* youth
China
  community policing in, 40–41
  police history in, 143–44
citizen involvement *see* civilian oversight;
  community engagement
citizen's arrest, 7, 20–23
  see also arrest; auxiliary police; private security
civil liberties *see* human rights and civil liberties